D1594929

Film, Broadcast and Electronic Media Coaching

and other contemporary issues in professional voice and speech training

presented by the Voice and Speech Review

The official Journal of the Voice and Speech Trainers Association

Cover photo: Tom Wilkinson and Jessica Lange, from the Home Box Office film, *Normal*. Photo by Melissa Moseley.

Citation Information
Title: Film, Broadcast and e-Media Coaching and other contemporary issues in professional voice and speech training presented by the Voice and Speech Review
Editor: Dal Vera, Rocco
Date: 2003
ISBN: 1-55783-522-5
Publisher: Voice and Speech Trainers Association, Incorporated, Cincinnati, OH
Distributor: Applause Books/Hal Leonard Corporation, Item Number: HL00314640, UPC: 0-73999-57718-1, EAN: 9781557835222
Description: The official journal of the Voice and Speech Trainers Association containing 67 articles on a wide variety of issues in professional voice and speech use and training, many centered on the topic of coaching actors for performances for the camera and microphone. 334 pages, 8.5" x 11", 100+ b&w photos, paperback.

Correspondence
U.S. Mail:
Rocco Dal Vera, editor
University of Cincinnati—CCM
P.O. Box 210003
Cincinnati, OH 45221

FedEx and UPS:
Rocco Dal Vera, editor
OMDA-Drama
Room 3713, Corbett Drive
College-Conservatory of Music
University of Cincinnati
Cincinnati, OH 45221-0003

Telephone:
(513) 556-1981, ms
(513) 556-3399, fax

Email:
Rocco.DalVera@uc.edu

The Voice and Speech Review is an official publication of the Voice and Speech Trainers Association (VASTA), Inc.

VASTA is a non-profit organization and also a focus group of the Association for Theatre in Higher Education (ATHE).

Editorial *by Rocco Dal Vera*

Soon, the title of this issue will be démodé. We are nearing two hundred cable channels in most markets and it will be five hundred in a few years. The line between internet and broadcast is being steadily blurred. Increasingly, all entertainment will be on-demand. In the near future, the term multi-media will apply to nearly all communication, entertainment and exchange of information. Most corporations have an on-line presence and that will soon involve animation, voice-over and streaming video as a staple of the typical website. Sales personnel are handing out multi-media business cards that are CD ROMS with video clips. Toys come loaded with sophisticated sound and video chips. Advertising will be more ubiquitous and personalized (the advertising technology shown in the film *Minority Report* exists today). More products will ship with communicative technology—voices that tell you how to operate the equipment and remind you to do things. GPS systems will be standard in cars so that not only will a voice be giving you driving directions, but will also fill you in on the interesting historical facts of the Civil War battlefields you are driving past, while the screens embedded in the back of your seats show passengers reenacted scenes from the battle.

If you want to nudge your thinking into the future, consider this developing product from Xerox: Smart Paper, a material that looks and feels very much like thick, glossy paper, but is actually a controllable display surface. It combines the advantages of paper and screen, and has countless applications. Its resolution is like that of a modern high-quality art book, and it can change so quickly that it can be used to display video images in perfect quality. Smart paper requires only minute amounts of energy, and all this comes from a tiny solar cell in one of the corners of a page. It can maintain its content without energy. All Smart Paper items can be mistaken for normal paper. Smart Books have no moving parts, no great energy requirements, and can be read safely in the bathtub, survive sandstorms with ease and can go for years without service.

Even HDTV—just now beginning to find its place—is understood to be a transitional technology: a precursor to the introduction of holographic projectors that render a performance in lifelike three-dimensions.

The future of technology is pretty cool, but why am I going on about it, here? Because even though most of us are excited about the changes technology will bring, we tend to overlook their effect on the acting profession.

Acting programs usually focus on training for the stage. There are lots of good reasons for this. If an actor can be believable and interesting to a large theatre, it isn't too difficult to translate those skills to the camera and microphone. The opposite isn't true. So, it makes good sense to attack the fundamentals of acting from a stage-oriented perspective.

However, we might be doing our students a disservice if we fail to pay attention to what's happening in the e-media world and what will be the driving economic forces shaping an actor's career.

In my town (Cincinnati), there are three well-established Equity theatres and a few others that do guest artist contracts. Interestingly, an actor can put in a full week of performances here and still not make what s/he could doing a one-hour job voicing an industrial video. A busy career as a working stage actor will barely feed one person, much less their cat.

The truth about acting careers is that most of an actor's earnings will come from media work, not the stage.

Shouldn't we be incorporating more training for this field? Remember all those emerging technologies? They will require content. Someone will have to be on-camera and on mike to supply it. Our students will be the ones to take those jobs.

I recently had a lovely discussion with my students on the differences in style among the Jacobean, Restoration, and Georgian periods. Throughout, I kept wondering if we shouldn't instead be discussing the style differences in daytime drama, sitcom, episodic drama, feature film, animated, industrial, etc. Those are all equally demanding, distinct and valid styles—and ones in which they are more likely to earn their livings.

What applies for actors will also be true for coaches.

Are we ready to teach and coach within this emerging new technological environment? Certainly, some of our skills will translate. But we may need to do some fast upgrading, or we risk being dressage instructors in the age of Henry Ford.

In this book you will read articles from both novice media coaches and veterans. All have important things to say to us about how we can translate our skills from the stage to the camera. I hope they will inspire you.

Film, Broacast and e-Media Coaching

Contents

Letters to the Editor

Pedagogy and Coaching

Pronunciation, Phonetics, Dialect/Accent Studies

Private Studio Practice

Singing

Ethics, Standards and Practices

Film, Broacast and e-Media Coaching

Cover Articles

From the President

Kate Ufema, Voice and Speech Specialist—
Professional Actor Training Program, Department of
Theatre, University of Minnesota Duluth; an Equity
actress, singer, professional director, musical director, vocal/dialect/text coach, and professional voice
consultant and trainer. Trains and coaches voices in
all performance media; contracts with CNN, CBS,
NBC, ABC, National Public Radio and American
Public Radio. Acted, directed, and coached in theatres across the country, presented workshops and
adjudicated theatre competitions and festivals from
Colorado to the East Coast and abroad. Charter
member of VASTA, and currently its President. BA,
MA, and MFA degrees from Penn State University.

This is VASTA's third issue of the Voice & Speech Review, and a very important issue it is. As technology is rapidly becoming man's largest and most complex appendage, every profession and individual must make peace with this appendage or fall behind.

I remember when e-mail came into being. And BettyAnn Leeseberg Lange (then VASTA's president) literally forced Board members kicking and screaming to each get ourselves computers so we could communicate electronically. Then Dudley Knight created VASTAVOX, followed by Eric Armstrong's VASTA website.

Now, the majority of VASTA's business is routinely conducted electronically, and many of our service publications appear on our website in one form or another. And beyond, as voice and speech professionals, we must all consider the fact that film, television, radio, and the electronic performance media are ever-increasing markets for our ever-increasing vocal knowledge and abilities. The broadcast, voice-over, and looping industries, alone, provide a wealth of opportunities for our expertise, not to mention film and television dialogue and accent coaching.

This current issue of the Voice & Speech Review addresses these expanding opportunities. And for those who have an interest and are yet to approach this part of our profession, you shall gain knowledge of what currently exists, and glimpses of what lies in our ever-changing futures.

Once again, through the Voice & Speech Review, VASTA seeks to serve its membership, and beyond, with information, ideas, and opportunities for growth and new directions. May this volume serve you in all these ways, and continue VASTA's publication tradition.

VASTA Mission Statement

VASTA is poised to become an exciting international organization and is actively planting seeds for global networking, other cultural involvement and resource-sharing.
Our mission is to:

Practice and encourage the highest standards of voice and speech use and artistry in all professional arenas.

Serve the needs of voice and speech teachers and students in training and practice.

Promote the concept that the art of the voice and speech specialist is integral to the successful teaching of acting and to the development of all professional voice users.

Encourage and facilitate opportunities for ongoing education and the exchanging of knowledge and information among professionals in the field.

VASTA is all about:

Vision
Artistry
Standards of conduct
Training enhancement and
Advocacy for our profession.

vasta.org - The VASTA Website

Visit *www.vasta.org*, the **VASTA** website. The site includes: News & Updates, Resources, Communication and Publications, Professional Index, and Website Details. Any **VASTA** member may list contact information, resume, and teaching philosophy in the Professional Index. The site also includes information on conferences and workshops, links to voice and speech related websites, the Mentoring Program, the Newsletter Archive, and organization Bylaws.

VASTA Publications

Available Online at *www.vasta.org*:
• *Guidelines for the Preparation of Voice and Speech Teachers*
• Promotion, Tenure and Hiring Resources
— *Typical Job Responsibilities*
— *Evaluation Guidelines*
— *Recommended Models for Evaluating Teaching, Creative and Service Activities*
— *Are You On the Promotion and Tenure Track?*
— *Documentation*
— *Suggestions on the Creation of a Teaching Dossier*
— *Some Questions to Consider Before Accepting a Tenure Track Position*
• VASTA Professional Index
• *How to Use a Vocal Coach*
• Online Newsletter Archive
• *VASTA Bylaws*
• Internet Resources for Voice and Speech Profesionals
• Conference Information

Available via US Mail
The Combined VASTA Bibliography
is made up of 3 segments. All segments are available together.
Member price $10.00
Non-Member price $15.00
For those who have part but not all of the bibliography:
1993 version only
Members: $6.00
Non-Members: $8.00
1995 supplement only
Members: $2.00
Non-Members: $4.00
1998 supplement only
Members: $4.00
Non-Members: $7.00

VASTA Newsletter,
published semi-annually.
Members — free
Individual Subscription $10.00
Institutional Subscription $20.00

Voice and Speech Review,
published bi-annually
Members — free
Individual Subscription $35.00
Institutional Subscription $35.00

To order any of the above materials consult the VASTA website at:www.vasta.org

We are grateful to the following experts for their close careful reviews of material submitted to the Journal:

Kathleen Campbell
David Carey
Tom Casciero
Louis Colaianni
Rena Cook
Jim Correll
Kevin Crawford
Kate de Vore
Kate Foy
Emily Groenewald
John Gronbeck-Tedesco
Marian Hampton
Jack Horton
Jeanne Klein
Nancy Krebs
Karina Lemmer
Paul Meier
Dorothy Runk Mennen
Kathy Maes
Betty Moulton
Allan Munro
Marth Munro
Bonnie Raphael
Mandy Rees
Ronald C. Scherer
Joseph Stempel
Lesley-Ann Timlick
Phil Thompson
William Weiss

The *Voice and Speech Review* accepts several types of submissions. While one of our primary missions is to publish peer-reviewed scholarship, we are also interested in presenting letters to the editor, opinion pieces, essays, interviews, reviews, poetry and other forms of writing.
Material may be submitted to:
Rocco Dal Vera, editor
University of Cincinnati
CCM, OMDA
PO Box 210003
Cincinnati, OH 45221-0003
Rocco.DalVera@uc.edu

The Ungoing Debate

The title of Dudley Knight's article "Standard Speech: The Ongoing Debate" reprinted in the inaugural edition of the *Voice and Speech Review*, suggests a kind of discourse on this very important topic that would be extremely valuable. It's not at all unusual in academic journals for respected thinkers in a field to articulate divergent viewpoints. What is unusual—and is frankly embarrassing—is that the authors of articles responding to Knight's article have seen fit to waste their time in lamentation and wounded defense of an attack on Ms. Skinner's character that is entirely in their own imaginations.

David Hammond, Sanford Robbins and Ralph Zito essentially accuse Knight of *ad hominem* attacks against Edith Skinner. These claims are not supportable. In fact, the authors don't really bother to support their accusations. Rather, they turn the tables and resort to *argumentum ad verecundiam* or "appealing to authority." They spend their energies largely on the argument that Edith Skinner was an admirable person; and to suggest ideas contrary to hers is reprehensible. As David Hammond puts it, "Her legacy and her work still merit respect and have much to teach us. Shame on those who would begrudge her that."

To suggest that Knight begrudges Skinner her legacy is preposterous. To imply, as Hammond does in his response, that Knight bashes Skinner as a cynical ploy to advance his own career is, frankly, libelous.

Now, in the interest of disclosing any potential biases or conflicts of interest, I should say that I studied with Dudley Knight and that I now teach with him at the University of California, Irvine. That experience has given me anecdotes aplenty to mount a counteroffensive on the character of my own venerated teacher. Fortunately, that experience has also taught me to distinguish what's appropriate in a discussion of this sort. Professor Knight's character can do quite nicely on its own. More importantly, his character, as much as Edith Skinner's character or William Tilly's character, is not an appropriate topic for an academic debate.

What is appropriate, and what is left largely untouched by the article's respondents, is the substance of the debate. Knight presents a tremendous amount of

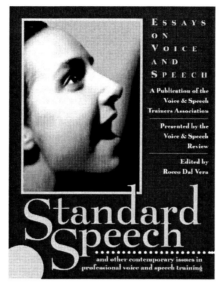

information in his two essays "Standard Speech: The Ongoing Debate" and "Standards" and so little of it has been discussed. We have yet to see a response to "Standards" and so much of the response to "The Ongoing Debate" is absorbed in irrelevance. I fear that the core ideas of the debate are potentially lost in the exchange between Knight and his detractors

Those core ideas, the ideas that are meant to have an impact on the future of theatre speech training, are stated in the seven guidelines proposed by Knight at the end of "The Ongoing Debate" and developed in "Standards." In the interests of clarifying and perhaps incrementally advancing that debate, I would like to address what I consider to be the two most important of the seven recommendations proposed in Knight's article as well as some of the counter arguments made by Zito.[1] I will then move on to address some points raised by Knight in his second article, "Standards."

The seven guidelines are:

Guideline One: *The ability to physically experience and isolate sound change in speech must precede learning any prescriptive pattern.*

Guideline Two: *Phonetic training should be descriptive before it is prescriptive.*

Guideline Three: *Phonetic training should include all sounds of the world's languages, not just the ones used in a single form of American English.*

Guideline Four: *Actors should learn Narrow Phonetic Transcription.*

Guideline Five: *Actors should learn phonetic printing, not phonetic script.*

Guideline Six: *The Detail Model.*

Guideline Seven: *Rejoining the world.*

To me, the most important guideline is the recommendation that we train actors to physically experience and isolate sound change in speech before teaching any prescriptive pattern. On its surface, that may appear to be nothing more than a statement of preference about the organization of speech curricula.

It is, in fact, a radical assertion. By "radical" I don't mean to imply that it represents an extreme political view, rather I mean to say that it represents a change "at the root" of our assumptions about speech training.

Ralph Zito, responding to this recommendation, uses Knight's term "detail model" and claims that it is not the same as a "prescriptive imperative." Zito says that Knight has omitted the possibility that the Skinner pattern can be used sensitively to teach the skills Knight mentions. In his response to Zito, Knight makes it clear that hasn't simply neglected the possibility: he rejects it as impractical. He sees a teacher working in this way as "essentially swimming upstream against the current of what a prescriptive pattern actually forces upon the student."

When Zito says that a detail model is "different from the introduction of a prescriptive imperative." He appears to be missing the point. Knight doesn't suggest that speech teachers should never prescribe a pattern of sounds. Knight allows for the introduction of prescription but only within the context of a classroom already prepared with the awareness and skill to fully interrogate the prescriptive model.

There are two key arguments in favor of this point of view. The first is simply a matter of ethics. It's dishonest to claim that your goal is the liberation of your student's articulation when you clearly have a list of "correct" answers in your back pocket. The second reason for keeping a prescriptive pattern out of the process of learning phonetic awareness is that it is inefficient. If you hand students a list of "ask" words and tell them that these words are pronounced "ask," you've posed a problem of circular reasoning. Reference to an underlying system of phonemic categorization limits nuanced perception of sound difference. The way to learn fine phonetic discrimination skills is to refer the learner to physical and auditory feedback. Reference to phonemic category actually suppresses perception of phonetic difference.[2]

Once you've accepted the proposition that phonetic skill (*the ability to physically experience and isolate sound change in speech*) must be taught without reference to a specific pattern of "correct speech" then many of the other guidelines become inevitable. Training of this type is entirely descriptive because the task is no longer to simply replace one pattern with another but to expand the student's range of potential sounds. As the students work to distinguish one sound from another, both in perception and in performance, they are working to describe the full potential of the phonetic landscape. As they work for greater specificity they must work through all the potential sounds of human speech. They must also be able to describe these sounds in the narrowest detail. They are best

served in interpreting that level of detail by using the most current conventions of description of the International Phonetic Association.

The second major piece of what I would call the core ideas of "The Ongoing Debate" is the notion of the Detail Model. This is a complicated notion but it is a crucial counterpart to Knight's insistence of perceptual training without prescription of a rigid dialect pattern. It is necessary in Knight's view to provide a "possible formulation of an American accent for use in speaking situations where listener comprehension…is more demanding than in normal conversation." He differs here from Louis Colaianni, saying that release of tension alone cannot be counted on to produce intelligible speech. He warns against the assumption hidden in that idea that those who speak in a particularly intelligible way are simply vocally freer and thinking more precisely. Colaianni objects in his editorial column in VSR II (*The Voice in Violence*) but he maintains his view that guiding actors toward release alone will lead to a "more easily heard version of their own idiolect [sic]." He refers us to the evidence of his own students' voices but he doesn't suggest any positive mechanism at work that makes them more easily heard.

What Knight is proposing is that there may be specific patterns of articulatory actions that could improve intelligibility. Knight amplifies this point of view in "Standards," but he refrains from dictating those patterns. He does say, however, that the only *standard* that can be appropriately applied to theatre speech training is intelligibility. With intelligibility, Knight proposes a sort of Occam's razor—a way of cutting away the baggage of oppressive models that Lippi-Green and others condemn while preserving a valuable standard of judgment.

It's important, though, to interrogate any proposed model for intelligible speech (inclusive of the Detail Model) because the claim of intelligibility has been made by stage dialects of the past in the absence of any evidence to support that assertion. So, what's to keep *The Detail Model* from becoming the *Good American Speech* of the next generation, oppressing future actors with a rigid pattern formulated back in the twentieth century?

The answer lies in the constant renegotiation of the details to be included for maximum intelligibility. Knight argues that, "Intelligibility is inextricably linked to the amount of linguistic detail transmitted through the through the phonatory process" but the term "linguistic detail" is inherently flexible. Knight does not follow the proposition that more detail is necessarily more intelligible. Otherwise Pig Latin would be the pinnacle of intelligibility. What he asks for, from actors, from speech trainers, and even from audiences is that we continually question our assumptions.

My hope, in restating these points is that the assumptions made by Professor Knight can be questioned. One might ask, for example, precisely what linguistic details improve intelligibility. It is possible, too, to question Knight's claim that intelligibility is the only valid standard to be applied to stage speech. An argument could be made for the value of uniformity or for the way in which a stage dialect carries information about class. But these arguments need to be clearly posed and developed in an atmosphere of civility or we lose the vital opportunity to advance our knowledge.

Phil Thompson
Associate Professor
University of California, Irvine

Notes:
1. Zito takes the brunt of the blows here because he has been brave enough to actually articulate an opposing argument. In the end I disagree with his conclusions but I admire his honesty.
2. Since Lisker and Abramson's experiments in categorical perception in 1970, evidence has been mounting that our perceptual mechanism of phonemic categorization actually suppresses our awareness of some sound differences. This leads to an effect called phonetic interference, which means simply that the phonology of our particular language interferes with our ability to hear the distinctions of other languages. The esteemed dialectician JC Wells has written a paper on this subject called "Overcoming Phonetic Interference." Published in *English Phonetics*, Journal of the English Phonetic Society of Japan, 3.9-21 (2000).

❦

Dear Editors,
In your last two publishings we were all challenged to engage in a discussion regarding methodologies in voice and speech training. Particularly with regard to the validity of "Standard American," "General American" or any derivation thereof, signifying some kind of neutral national broadcast-type speaking.

I, and several of my colleagues, have been reluctant to respond, as the "discussions" ultimately turn to self-serving arguments. No one training method must be made wrong, in order for another to be right. If there were one "right" way to teach voice and speech, everyone would be using it. In the end, it's all about the students, and what will meet their ultimate professional skill requirements, according to their goals and learning styles. Although the means remain flexible, the ends remain constant.

I have spent several years as a voice and speech coach for leading classical companies. I thought it might be valuable to let your readers know what is currently expected by professional theatres across the country. I know nothing about film and

television—but perhaps some other reader could respond with that information.

- Actors should have strong vibrant voices that carry with-out shouting.

- Voices should be as free of tension and glottal attacks as possible, and actors should be facile with a variety of breathing techniques to accommodate different acoustical environments. Otherwise, they won't last through eight performances a week for a four to twelve week run of a production.

- Actors should have some sense of ownership of their voice and speech, in all its forms. Organic ownership of one's communication tactic is expected, as is versatility. If the actor only has ownership of the voice and speech tactics they grew up using, they are only able to organically speak as themselves, ignoring the needs of the character they're playing and/or the production they're supporting.

- Actors should have a strong, comfortable, and specific facility with some kind of "neutral" dialect, (call it what you will—I think it's the semantics that cause the problem here), as well as the articulation principles that will allow them to change that dialect for different time periods and/or social status. Good storytelling demands that Caesar is probably not from Indiana, and doesn't have the communication tactic of a plumber. No disrespect to plumbers or Hoosiers intended. It's also practical to expect actors from different regions to be able to come together and have some common way of speaking, thereby being able to play family members or inhabitants of the same community, without having to learn a new dialect for every production.

- Actors need some knowledge of grammatical structures and stress representing different periods of writing. If they come in without any experience of spoken syntax and idiom from other periods, (as these things change with each new generation), they will be imposing contemporary emphasis on old fashioned phrasing, which will mar the rhythm of the text, causing it to lay in-organically.

- Actors should have some kind of specific process for learning a dialect. As time is often a consideration, it is probably more useful if they have mastered one or two commonly used dialects than generally exploring twenty or thirty. British RP, cockney, and Irish are among the most commonly requested dialects, regardless of race, due to color-blind casting. If they haven't any experience of organically mastering one or two dialects in an acoustically stage-worthy way, they will be hard pressed to achieve anything consistent over the course of a normal rehearsal period.

- Actors who wish to do Shakespeare should have some general principles of scansion—the less fancy the better as complex strategies tend to muddy an actors' decision making process—and the pronunciation knowledge necessary for antique words. To young actors, many words seem modern, but took a different emphasis four hundred years ago. The ability to pronounce them comfortably with the correctly stressed syllables proves to be some of the best verse assistance you can give them.

- Actors should have phonetic technology, and research tools for looking up name and word pronunciations from a variety of sources. Artistic Directors prefer actors who can look up answers themselves, rather than rely on "overpaid" Voice & Speech coaches or Dramaturges.

In the end, methodology doesn't matter, comprehensive teaching does. Over the years I have had occasion to coach groups of actors from many of the major actor training programs under professional conditions. Although most programs sporadically put forth good students with a variety of strengths, in my experience three MFA programs consistently turn out actors with "chops": Penn. State University, the University of California-Irvine, and the University of Delaware-Newark.

This is primarily due to the expertise, dedication, and consistency of the trainers who have served these programs for many years. Perhaps the departments as a whole deserve some of the credit for the value they assign to voice and speech work, but in the end it's the tireless commitment of those teachers that make the grade.

Were we to put the voice and speech trainers responsible for these verbally gifted actors in the same room, they might well have a fist fight. The verbal/vocal teaching strategies of these three schools are distinctive and diverse, yet ultimately put forth the same excellent product: Actors with such strong voice and speech facility, they can easily oblige any requests made of them by directors and coaches. Therefore these actors are able to turn their rehearsal attention to more interesting fodder, and ultimately get re-hired, season after season.

Your students' ability to get a job simply means they audition well, which may or may not reflect your verbal training success. Their frequency of re-hiring is the proof in the proverbial pudding. Actors who must spend all of their rehearsal time simply trying to be heard and understood, or learning a dialect—neutral or otherwise—are unlikely to achieve any sort of artistry in their overall performance. They are also unlikely

to be asked back by that theatre. In short, their voice and speech teachers have let them down.

Actors shouldn't have to use the word "choice" as an excuse for habit. If they can't change it—with consistency and comfort—it's not a choice. They need practical skills, able to support them under a variety of production and acoustical circumstances. They need real choices, based on real research, that match a variety of genres. They need supported understanding and practice of those skills beyond the classroom, in the university theatre.

They need "chops".

Large companies that can afford professional coaches can tweak an actor's training to fit the production, but the best of conductors can't make the music if the musicians aren't skilled. Being a competitive professional actor is hard enough without having to acquire basic skills per production. I challenge all of you to abandon argument and embrace a more inclusive sharing of ideas. Debate can be useful, but it is most useful when it is about learning and sharing, rather than winning and being "right". Send the future of the American theatre forth with practical verbal and vocal technique, and use whatever paths you can beg, borrow or steal to get there. In this way, you honor your students, as well as your teachers, and in the end—you can all be "right".

Huzzah!

Tyne Turner
Free-lance Voice & Speech Coach
Utah Shakespearean Festival, Seattle Repertory Theatre, Dallas Theatre Center, Alabama Shakespeare Festival, The Guthrie Milwaukee Repertory Theatre, (etcetera)

A Response to Natalie Stewart's Essay "Some Breathing Physiology Basics and Voice Training"

A Letter From an Alexander Technique Teacher to Voice Professionals: *The Trouble with Teaching Breath with Metaphors*

I write this response knowing that for some voice, speech, and singing teachers I am posing a difficult teaching question. When I have talked to various voice professionals informally about teaching the anatomically accurate version of breathing rather than using metaphor, I have been greeted with both interest and anger. Yet, I do think you want to know what many students in Alexander classes have discovered: they have believed the metaphors to be true, and have created roadblocks in their coordination, their breathing, and consequently in their voices, in an effort to embody the metaphor.

Natalie Stewart, in the 2000 edition of *Standard Speech*, says that students "also sometimes have misconceptions about the basics of breathing anatomy and physiology." She finds that "it is helpful, therefore, to take the time to explain some of the basic concepts of the anatomy and physiology of breathing, including the role that the recoil force of the lungs, rib cage, diaphragm, and abdomen play in breathing for singing and speaking." (Stewart, 239) I heartily support Stewart's assertion and want to provide some observations from my work to illustrate the need for anatomical accuracy. My observations come from my experience of working with hundreds of voice, speech and singing students and performers for over 20 years. These students have had their training in many places, and in many techniques so my examples are not representative of one institution, or one style of training.

As I began writing this article, a student in a beginning Alexander Class was having trouble with some voice work. I helped her create the coordination in herself that she needed to do the voice work and she was shocked to discover that breathing did not work the way she had been taught in her voice classes. "Why do they lie to us?" she exclaimed. I have frequently encountered this question in many different forms. I believe that Natalie Stewart's approach, giving clear, accurate anatomical information, would have saved many students months or years of less than optimal voice practice.

Kelly's Story

In my experience, many misconceptions about breath and sound begin with anatomically inaccurate metaphors. With another student's permission, I am going to tell a story about his work to illustrate what often happens with metaphors about breathing. This story is by no means unique. I could tell many similar stories.

The situation: Kelly is in a production and is losing his voice. The Voice teacher and I, his Alexander teacher, offer to meet with him to see if we can figure out what is happening. Kelly walks into the room and says:

"I am so glad both of you are here. Cathy, you tell me that my lungs are up here (touching his rib cage) and to the voice teacher he says, "you say I should breath down here (touching his belly slightly below the ribcage.)"

"Oh, Kelly, that is a metaphor!" is what the Voice teacher replied.

In that moment, we both realized that the habitual pattern of Kelly's movement (a depressed ribcage and a pelvis that swung forward limiting the action of breathing as well as limiting the

motion at the hip joint) was probably, at least in part, the result of this misconception about breathing.

In the next few minutes, I helped Kelly with the Alexander Technique to use the real anatomy/movement of breathing to restore his coordination. As he allowed his ribcage to move as the air went in and out, his whole torso came into a more healthy alignment and he got more and deeper movement in his abdominal area with each breath. This change in coordination and conception of breathing allowed Kelly to use his voice in the way his voice teacher was helping him to do.

What had happened was that Kelly had been acting on the metaphor he learned in Voice class as if the metaphor were anatomically true. He was doing this even though his voice teacher, when she taught the idea, was very clear that she was using a metaphor. (And I will note here to be truthful to Kelly's perception, that he said that he never heard it was a metaphor. My guess is that when metaphors are used in teaching, even if there is an initial explanation, only the metaphor is repeated on a daily basis. The once-heard explanation disappears in the daily repetition of the anatomically inaccurate metaphor.) Students whose teachers have not clearly identified the metaphor they are using as a metaphor can be even more surprised when they find out that the metaphor is not the truth of breathing. I have often wished that I had a camera to record the looks on students' faces when they feel they have been "duped" by a metaphor that they have taken literally.

I can and do explain to the students that the metaphors are intended to be helpful. Since I myself learned voice, speech, and singing using many of these metaphors, and then had to "undo" the non-anatomical aspects of them myself, I can put the metaphors in context for the students. My question in this letter is: wouldn't it be possible to teach breath accurately rather than metaphorically?

Why don't we trust our students with the truth of breathing? As an Alexander Technique teacher who is trying to get students to carry out the instructions of voice and speech teachers effectively, it is my experience that the truth would be a good idea. If voice and speech teachers could be in the classroom when I am teaching the students some simple anatomy, they might be surprised by some of the conversations. I ask students to draw a skeleton and draw the lungs on the skeleton-- many draw their lungs in their stomach area, and some extend the ribcage all the way to the pelvis because they know they are supposed to breathe into their belly and the lungs are in the ribcage. The exclamations of surprise, anger, and hurt as the students realize that their lungs are not in their bellies has taught me a lot about being clear in my teaching

The diaphragm isn't below the ribcage? No.

There is a bit of lung above the 1ˢᵗ rib? Yes.

Are you sure? Yes....

Then why do they tell us not to move the ribcage? Why do they tell us to breathe low? Why do they...? Why do they...?

Again, I remind the students that their teachers are using metaphors hoping to help. Unfortunately, the anatomical inaccuracy of the metaphor often works against the voice/speech/singing teacher's intention. What I so appreciate in reading Natalie Stewart's descriptions of breathing is their accuracy!

Psychophysical Unity
Each day that I teach the Alexander Technique I appreciate more and more that we are a psychophysical unity and that what we think manifests exactly as we think it in the body. One of the reasons that we seek metaphors in teaching is to take advantage of the power of mind-body unity. If we can find a metaphor that opens up a new range of thinking, a new possibility of movement for our students, it can help "unfix" a fixed pattern. Yet, it is the very power of psychophysical unity that makes an inappropriate metaphor powerfully unhelpful. What we think, what we ask our bodies to do, our whole self will attempt to do, even if it is "against the design."

A non-theatre student was using a metaphor in a way that clearly illustrates the power of psychophysical unity. She had taken a workshop in some kind of healing technique in which they had told her to breath into the left side of her brain and out the right side of her brain. As this student gave herself the instructions for this breath, her whole system attempted to carry out what she was asking for. As she inhaled, she tilted her head to the right and tightened the right side of her face. She also squeezed her whole body together, probably in an effort to get the air to her brain instead of her lungs. As she exhaled, she tilted the other way and continued to squeeze her torso tightly together. In the momentary suspension between breaths, her torso got a bit of release from all the tightening. *Although the breath instruction she was given was clearly impossible to do anatomically, her system tried to carry out exactly what she was asking.* I have never heard a voice, speech, or singing teacher use such an extremely inaccurate metaphor for breathing, but I chose this one deliberately to illustrate that people will think what you ask them to and their systems will attempt to do exactly what they are telling themselves to do.

**The Myth of "Low Breathing," "Belly Breathing,"
"Diaphragmatic Breathing, etc.**
In breathing, air goes to the lungs.

The whole torso moves in all directions as the air goes into the lungs.

There is no air in the belly.

There is movement in all directions in the torso as we breathe. Even the spine moves as we breathe.

If the ribs do not move, we are not getting our most useful inhale or exhale.

We see the belly move the most because there are no bones close to the surface of the body in the abdomen, and we move in every direction as we breathe.

Yet, often when I help students to free their ribcages to move, they tell me that they are doing something wrong; their voice teacher said that they should breathe low. Or, when I encourage students not to push down on themselves in a way that pushes their bellies forward, they say their voice teacher said they needed to make their belly move out when they breathe in. When you tell students that you want them to breathe low, you may not mean that you want them to tighten their ribs, and you may not mean that they are supposed to push into their bellies, and you probably don't even mean that you want the air to go to the belly. (I say probably because, unfortunately, a few voice teachers I have taught realized that they had been thinking that air went to the belly.)

It is in this area, that I have one concern about Natalie Stewart's descriptions. In describing the movement of the diaphragm for inhalation she says that "when the diaphragm contracts for inhalation, it tends to flatten and pushes against the abdominal wall which moves partially in an outward direction." (Stewart 240) She then goes on to describe how putting your hand on the abdomen can help you know that you have contracted your diaphragm. While this is accurate, Stewart's emphasis on the forward outward direction de-emphasizes the "partially" in her anatomical description. Many students end up thinking that the diaphragm directly pushes the belly forward which gives them a skewed notion of their anatomy. Emphasizing that the downward movement of the diaphragm moves the viscera downward and indirectly outward gives a more complete picture.

It is true that not all students are affected by inappropriate anatomical images. Some of the ones I talk to say that they never listen to metaphors like that because they just don't learn well from them. And some say that they know the real anatomy and they understand what the metaphor is heading for so they know to use the metaphor as an idea not a reality. My message to voice teachers is that many of your students do treat metaphors as reality. They might not know that is what they have done because they don't have the accurate information they need to analyze what is happening. All they know is that something isn't working. Because we are a psychophysical unity, the very metaphors that you intend as helpful are teaching them to do something ultimately unhelpful.

Metaphors Can be Wonderful

The voice professionals that I have talked to that have been most upset about my concern with metaphors are those who think that I advocate using no metaphors in teachings. That is not true! What I am questioning are metaphors that misrepresent physical processes. Imagining a sound has a color, for instance, is not a metaphor that can be confused anatomically. A "blue" sound has no physical correspondent, whereas "sending breath to your belly" can be misconstrued anatomically.

Possible Solutions

Giving the students the true picture of the process works well when I have done it in the context of an Alexander lesson. Most people have very little idea of how we breathe, so the real picture can be just as surprising as a metaphor might be. I think that Natalie Stewart's description of the recoil force is excellent. You do not, however, need to start with that level of detail if you are new to anatomical descriptions. Incorporating accurate anatomy can be as simple as having an anatomy book or chart available for both you and your students. The "draw your own skeleton" exercise that I mentioned earlier is a great self-teacher. Everyone simply draws a picture of their own skeleton (it is important to mention that it is their own skeleton) and compares it afterwards to the real thing. I often ask my theatre students to put a dotted line to indicate where the lungs are.

Verbally, the direct replacement for things like "breathing low" could simply be to say, "let the belly move as you breathe." Although that, for me, is incomplete because it implies that there is only a forward movement in the belly—after years of experimenting, I have finally come to saying to myself that "everything can move that wants to when I breathe." This particular phrasing appeared as I got a more and more clear anatomical perspective.

Simply changing breathe into your belly, breathe into your back, breathe into your ribs, etc. with "let your belly move as you breathe," "let your back move as you breathe", let your ribs move as you breathe" or "notice how there is movement in every direction in your torso as you breathe" would solve a lot of the misconceptions that I encounter as I help students with their coordination.

Other contributing factors

This discussion would be incomplete if I didn't

acknowledge some other factors that contribute to the difficulties in using metaphors in teaching breathing. For that, I will continue with Kelly's story from the beginning of the letter.

*The voice teacher and I cleared up Kelly's confusion about the breathing process. And then, Kelly said "Can this help me do really long phrases, because I can't breathe during my lines?" Again, the voice teacher and I were "what? Of course you can breathe! In fact, with as much running around as you do in this play (*Noises Off*), it is absolutely necessary."*

Kelly said, "No, the Director told me to breathe through my lines." At this point, there was a funny quick look between teachers because we didn't know what the director could have meant. But in the next few moments of questions, what mattered was that Kelly had decided that the director meant that he couldn't breathe during a line.

"Kelly, we don't know what he meant, but we do know that he didn't mean 'don't breathe' during the line."

It took some convincing, but we both knew that whatever the Director meant, he had enough awareness of physiological needs that he would never have meant for Kelly to try and say all his lines on one breath.

In this instance, breath was used as a metaphor for some desired result in performance. And while this metaphor came from a director to a student rather than a voice teacher to a student, it is illustrative of a kind of use of breath as metaphor for a non-breathing process that I believe further complicates any anatomical misconceptions that the student might have. Other examples of this use of breath as a metaphor for a non-breath process include relaxation work that asks people to breathe into their arms, legs, feet, etc. Some students have misconceptions about breathing that come from Yoga instructions, martial arts classes, or from playing wind instruments.

I have even worked with someone who was doing meditation and asked me to watch what he was doing. As soon as he started to watch his breath consciously, he started doing some very bizarre movement. On the inhale he sucked in his belly excessively and puffed out his chest. On the exhale he collapsed his chest and expanded his belly excessively. After some investigation, he realized that he had copied the breathing of what had been his favorite Saturday morning cartoon character!

Our students often arrive in voice and speech class with so many inaccurate ideas about breathing, that learning the real process is the idea that "unfixes" the misconceptions. Because there are so many misconceptions about breathing to begin with, it becomes more vital to "clean the slate" with a view of what is really going on. And, in fact, it can be a very simple solution. Returning to Kelly's story:

The story had a happy outcome. Two days later, I went back to see the show. I had never heard so much volume and resonance from this actor in performance. Several days later when I worked with him in a movement-based class, he was moving more efficiently than he had ever been able to. And he is continuing to improve.

Criteria for Useful Metaphors

Teaching voice/speech/singing is an art as all of you know more than I. I do not want to suggest that metaphors are never appropriate as teaching tools. I do suggest that metaphors are not useful if they are misleading anatomically. Some criteria for choosing metaphors that are more likely to be helpful to your students are:

1. When teaching a physiological process, the actual accurate anatomy is probably the most helpful choice. Trust your student with the truth of how they work. **This is my primary recommendation.** It is a powerful choice, and it does work. Again quoting Stewart: "Explaining the anatomy and physiology of the breathing mechanism to students may also empower them to analyze exercises and to choose appropriate exercises for themselves." (Stewart, 251)

   I will also note that Stewart, in the exercises she chose as examples for breath and voice exercises, did not use metaphors. She used clear anatomical descriptions.

2. If you do feel that you need to use a metaphor to teach a physiological process, choose a metaphor that is parallel to the actual anatomy, and teach the anatomy too. And mention the actual anatomy each time you use the metaphor.

3. Metaphors that present accurate moving pictures of whatever process you are teaching are more effective and accurate than static images.

4. Choose metaphors that are about the process (what you are asking them to do) rather than the product (how it should feel or sound). Aiming for a specific kinesthetic experience can cause difficulties because the kinesthetic sense is a relative rather than an accurate measure.

5. Remember that the metaphor will probably live beyond the moment that you use it—don't sacrifice a long-term learning for a short-term success.

Cathy Madden
Assistant Professor
University of Washington

Works Cited
Stewart, Natalie. "Some Breathing Physiology Basics and Voice Training." *Standard Speech and other contemporary issues in professional voice and speech training.* Edited by Rocco Dal Vera. New York: Applause Books, 2000, pp. 239-251.

The *Voice and Speech Review* welcomes comment from our readers. Letters may be edited for clarity or space considerations. Please send your responses to:
Rocco Dal Vera, editor
University of Cincinnati—CCM
PO Box 210003
Cincinnati, OH 45221-0003
<Rocco.DalVera@uc.edu>

Pedagogy and Coaching *Paul Meier, Associate Editor*

Editorial Column *by Paul Meier, Associate Editor*

It has been my pleasure to work with the ten fine authors whose work graces this section of the journal. Aptly for this issue, which foregrounds the work of film, broadcast and electronic media coaches, the following successful specialists in our field are spotlighted: Eric Armstrong, Cynthia Blaise, Linda Brennan, Gillian Lane-Plescia, Carla Meyer, David Smukler, and David Alan Stern. As a media coach myself, it is particularly rewarding to bring you my conversations with three of these in interview form. We welcome back Robert Barton and Katherine Maes whose recurring columns have enriched the journal's first two editions. I know you will also find provocative, Bonnie Raphael's fine peer-reviewed essay, *Carryover: Bringing Skills Acquisition from Studio to Life*.

Paul Meier is Head of Voice and a Professor in the Theatre and Film Department at the University of Kansas. He is Founder and Director of IDEA (International Dialects of English Archive), on the web at http://www.ukans.edu/~idea. He is the author of *Accents and Dialects for Stage and Screen*, and *Dialects of the British Isles, Volume 1*, used as textbooks in many theatre departments. Both are available, along with his dialect booklets and CDs, from Paul Meier Dialect Services, on the web at www.paulmeier.com. His "show-specific" dialect CDs are leased world-wide by theatre companies, while he has coached a dozen feature films in the last five years, including Ang Lee's *Ride With The Devil*, and Paul Cox's *Molokai: The Story of Father Damien*.

Essay *by Linda Brennan*

"T"s and Sympathy: Adventures in the Hollywood Dialect Trade

Linda Brennan is Head of the Voice and Speech Department at the American Academy of Dramatic Arts, Head of the Voice and Speech Department of South Coast Repertory's Professional Conservatory, and is on the faculty of the Shakespeare Intensive Conservatory at Will Geer's Theatricum Botanicum. She has taught at the Stella Adler Conservatory, Lee Strasberg Theatre Institute, Long Beach Civic Light Opera, Opera Pacific, etc., and is an associate of David Alan Stern's Dialect Accent Specialists. She has coached productions at South Coast Rep, Pasadena Playhouse, El Portal Center for the Arts, etc. Linda has coached numerous film and TV productions, including, *American Pie, The Hughleys* (UPN), *That's Life* (CBS), *We the People* (Lifetime) and *Sonny* directed by Nicholas Cage. Linda has an MFA in Acting from Brandeis University, and an MA in Clinical Psychology from Antioch University. As well as being a voice, speech, and dialects teacher, Linda is a licensed psychotherapist. She specializes in trauma resolution and creativity and performance enhancement.

As a conservatory voice, speech, and dialects practitioner in Los Angeles, I am often called upon to coach professional actors for roles in film and TV. In the more predictable world of theatre coaching there is often time for research, consultation, feedback, and for the process to consolidate artistically. However, in the fast-paced, unpredictable arena of TV and film production, time is a luxury. Being a professional coach has many challenges, and I have learned to expect the unexpected.

Be prepared, be flexible. And listen to your mother's relatives.

A young star of a hit TV series needed accent coaching. A late night call came from a producer who explained that there had been a string of eleventh hour rewrites for that week's episode. It was decided that she needed a Swedish accent because her character had to disguise her identity in a key scene. Could I coach a Swedish accent? Could I describe how I would do it? It was crucial that the accent be authentic so could I demonstrate how it would sound? Could I just speak in a Swedish accent? On the speaker phone? To the team of producers and writers? Now?

By imitating my mother's cousin, Ulla Britt, I landed the job which was to take place the next day. A script arrived on my doorstep at dawn. I reviewed the text, organized my phonetic notes, filled out my sound inventory, and ran off a sample tape of exercises which the actress could use in her dressing room before shooting.

I arrived at the studio, and was taken to the actress. With the producer, director, and head writer looking on, I began the lesson. But the actress sweetly interrupted, "Can you make it Polish? That would be so fun! I just saw Meryl Streep in *Sophie's Choice* on video and that would be way cool." She was the star of the series, so they indulged her and agreed this was a wonderful choice. This meant on the spot I was to change Swedish to Polish! Drawing from another relative, I quickly revised my notes. The actress applied them and soon the job was done. Cool. Whew!

There are times to let go. And there is often a safety net.

I was contacted by a major studio inquiring if I could teach an Arabic accent circa 3000 BC. Hmmm…where I could find a sample of that? After a phone consultation with the producer and director, I was hired to coach the co-starring actor in a "general sort of Arabic accent", as well as to be on set to do spot-coaching for some of the supporting roles and one-liners. We met several times a week, applied the accent to his lines, and kept up as he received new pages. The producer consulted with me regarding the actor's progress. So far so good. I was enjoying the luxury of time.

After completing these scheduled one-on-one sessions, I was called to the location, which was amazing. An ancient Middle-Eastern city had been recreated down to the smallest detail. There were hundreds of extras dressed as harem girls, beggars, lepers, soldiers, and merchants. There were buildings and huts, palm trees and roads, with live camels, horses, monkeys, parrots, goats and snakes and their wranglers. And there was the director and the 1st AD (assistant director), straining to move things along.

The star did his accent well. But in this maelstrom of activity, I noticed that other actors were using a variety of accents and dialects including Arabic, General American, British, etc. Between takes I was to work quickly with some of them right before shooting.

The first actress looked at my phonetic chart and immediately understood the phoneme changes that were to be made. She easily and gratefully applied my notes regarding pronunciation, resonance and pitch changes. The take went smoothly, and the director had time to try various approaches. Everyone seemed pleased. The 1st AD shouted, "New deal!" The crew sprang to life and began to set up for the next scene, and I relaxed and waited with the cast. That had gone well.

Then a call was relayed from walkie-talkie to walkie-talkie: "Get the dialect coach on the set please, NOW!" I was driven to another part of the "city", past a herd of goats to a group of harem girls. They were almost ready to shoot. I was brought to one of the actresses who had a line, and I was asked to help her get a "flavor" of the accent. This encounter would not be as easy.

She rehearsed her line. The director and I listened. The "harem girl" had quite a lot of nasality, retroflexed "r"s, and an upward inflection typical of Southern California. He pulled me aside to ask how she sounded. I told him the truth: our harem girl sounded like a "Valley Girl". The 1st AD shouted, "Nice and quiet please!" Hundreds of extras, actors, and crew were hushed to silence.

We returned to her. I asked her to drop her larynx, and to lift her soft palate to move the resonance back. But as soon as the word "larynx" popped out of my mouth, I realized she didn't know what I was talking about. She was annoyed. The 1st AD looked impatient. The set was silent.

Trying a different approach, I asked her to imitate a breathy quality I was making, and to apply it to the line, but her attempt sounded more like a cat choking on a hairball than a sexy seductress. The director gently persuaded her to keep trying, but time was ticking. People were waiting. The 1st AD shouted, "Quiet! Keep your positions!"

This time, I tried a pronunciation note. I showed her how to "tap" her "r"s, which I described as a "soft 'd'". I demonstrated the line slowly, with breathiness, inserting soft "d"s for the "r"s, and encouraged her to imitate. She looked at me with

daggers. After a beat she whined, "I can't." The dungeon door had fallen. The other harem girls rolled their eyes. The crew shuffled. The 1st AD was ready and nodded to the director. Time to shoot. "Absolute quiet on the set!" We moved away. The director called, "Action!"

The harem girl adjusted her veil and struck a sultry pose for the camera. But she delivered her line like a "Valley Girl". She even added an alveolar click! "Cut!" the director yelled. "New deal!" said the 1st AD.

As the crew moved the equipment, the director asked how I thought she sounded. I admitted there was not much improvement. He said, "Don't worry, we'll fix it in post." In post-production they would *loop* the line, meaning they would dub in another voice to replace hers. With so much money involved, he couldn't slow down the production schedule for one line reading.

I had to let this one go. There's a saying in the film business: "There's good, there's fast, and there's cheap, and you can only have two." I realized I had fallen into the world of "good enough." But *in post*, there's a safety net!

Professional help can come in disguise.

A Puerto Rican accent was needed for the lead actress of a network pilot. I arrived on the set with my *dialect bag*, which contains sound inventories, a tape recorder, tapes, highlighters, pens, headphones, dictionaries, handouts, etc. I had researched the accent, had a phonetic chart on my clipboard, sample sentences and exercises on separate pages, and a tape of some native speakers in case she wanted to listen. I was armed and dangerous.

I was to work with her while she was in hair and makeup. In a General American dialect, she greeted me warmly. She told me that she was from Puerto Rico and could do that accent easily. But she was troubled. She felt the accent was integral to the character, but one of the network execs was not sure about her using it. She wondered aloud if he thought it wasn't authentic because I had been hired to ensure she was doing it correctly. I listened to her. She sounded great! My support seemed to bolster her confidence to stand firm in her choice. Beyond that, there was little to do.

I set up camp at the *video village* which is an area off-set where video monitors are grouped so the director, script supervisor, and producers can watch scenes being shot. As I waited, and waited, I took out a blank sound inventory, and started doodling in phonetics. The AD noticed, and said, "Hey, what's that?" I described briefly what the IPA is, and he said, "Wait right here!"

Moments later I was rushed off-set to a meeting room. The show was being filmed in front of a live audience in less than an hour, but a heated discussion was in progress. The actress and director wanted her to use the Puerto Rican accent. The producer and executive producer disagreed. This was a creative stalemate. Both sides were adamant, and appealed to the VP in charge of network programming who listened to both sides. It looked like she was about to give her final word when she said, "I'd like to hear what the dialect coach thinks." One by one, each person in the room turned towards me. "Yes, Linda, what do you think?" It was up to me to break the tie.

I looked at the actress. She looked anxious. I informed them that "her voiced and unvoiced alveolar plosives are properly dentalized, she is unvoicing her medial and terminal consonants appropriately, and her 'r' taps are lovely, especially those in-between vowels." There was a beat. Eyes were darting. "Yes, I agree," the VP said. Argument over. The actress looked at me gratefully and was allowed to use her Puerto Rican accent. As it turned out, although she didn't need my pronunciation help, she needed help of a different kind: a stamp of approval.

Time is a luxury, but laughter is a well-spent indulgence.

Los Angeles is a diverse city with a wide selection of dialect and accent resources. I have collected information and samples from waiters, neighbors, rabbis—yes, and even my mother's relatives.

I was hired to coach an internationally-known Oscar-winning film star who was doing a recording of a best-selling book which had international characters. This actor, a known perfectionist, was upfront in his demand that the pronunciations be absolutely authentic, as he would be performing all of the roles. This job had a daunting feel. I needed to research pronunciations in Norwegian, Gaelic, German, Russian and Italian. There were a few phrases in Italian that were from a specific locale, and I wanted to get the correct pronunciation and lilt. And translation.

As usual, time was an issue, so I took advantage of the fact that I lived near the Italian Consulate. I called and described my situation, and was given an appointment to meet with someone from the Cultural Affairs office. I arrived with my script, tape recorder, and notes. I met with a regal lady who was beautifully coiffed, and I sensed that she did not quite know what to make of my request that she read lines from a script, although she seemed delighted to provide pronunciations for a famous actor. As she spoke little English, her intern from the UCLA linguistics department was on hand to translate

our conversation. As she spoke, I recorded and took notes. The first few lines went smoothly.

But halfway through the recording her face turned red! She glared at me, stood up, turned on her heel and was out the door. I looked at the intern and asked what had happened. She looked at the script. She gulped. The words were vulgar, scatological, profane! I had no idea! I was stunned and apologized. She was amused and promised that she would explain this to her boss, and generously provided the rest of the information.

At the recording studio, I met with the client, who peered at me from above his horn-rimmed glasses, ready to review the script. We were to start with the Italian. Brusquely, he asked for the translation of the lines to prepare his motivation. As I hesitated, I could sense he thought I was unprepared. I described what had happened. And provided the translation. Exactly. Expressionless, he looked down at the words, then up at me, then burst into laughter. This really broke the ice! We spent the rest of the day laughing over this. I hope the regal lady eventually did too.

Who me, scared?

My first professional coaching job came by surprise. I had been studying with Rocco Dal Vera, and he had landed a gig coaching a TV superstar. At the last moment, she decided she wanted a female coach, so Rocco asked if I were willing to work on the project. I had never coached anyone before, but I was being asked to step up to the plate. I couldn't say no! Rocco assured me that we would design the dialect and structure the sessions, but I would be the female vocal model she insisted on.

I met with the client in her home. As I spied her acting awards in the case, I feared I had gotten myself in deep water. We began the repetitive drilling required. Later, I met with Rocco, reviewed the tape of that day's session and planned for the next day. This became our pattern for weeks. My strategy was to stick to the material that Rocco and I prepared, and to say little beyond what was necessary to coach the accent.

I knew she had never attempted a dialect before. She didn't know I had never attempted to coach anyone before, so I tried to maintain my air of authority. She must have interpreted my restraint as expertise or efficiency, because one day she wistfully stated how fortunate I was to have trained professionally. She explained that her fame had come quickly, without time for formal training. She then tearfully revealed how intimidated she was by this process, and how she feared exposure and failure. I wanted to say, "That makes two of us!"

So this star, who intimidated me, was intimidated by me! Along with pronunciation notes, my role was to instill confidence in her by behaving confidently myself, by acting "as if". In the end, she did beautifully, was critically acclaimed and awarded for the work. But this was an early lesson in how fame and fortune do not always bring ease or confidence. And even icons are scared.

Boundaries help.

An actress contacted me to help develop a different voice to distance a new character from her well-known TV character. We met at my office. I sensed she had to negotiate other people's reactions to her celebrity status, so I kept a businesslike focus, enabling her to settle into the work and to feel free to experiment without having to live up to her TV "persona". We worked together productively. After that first project, she asked if I would conduct future lessons in her home. I agreed.

Initially that was pleasant. However, there were long interruptions by assistants requiring to speak to her "for just a minute," the doorbell ringing, and always important phone calls every few minutes. It was impossible to maintain any continuity in the lessons and sometimes no work would get done. All of my refocusing techniques were failing. I felt uncomfortable taking money for doing no work, but I reminded myself that I was getting paid for my time no matter how she chose to use it, and maintained this rationale for a few more lessons.

The tornado of activity escalated. There were wardrobe fittings, personal training, even a request to coach during a bath! She had hired me to be her voice and speech teacher, but in the end this arrangement was letting her down. She had already referred other clients to me, and I knew this was an important professional relationship. She was also very used to having people accommodate her. Nevertheless, I gathered the courage to set some limits.

I said, "I respect you tremendously and love working with you, but this isn't productive. I feel like part of the household staff, and we aren't getting much done. If you want to work with me, you have to make the time, come to my office, and work on my terms. And don't cancel."

Her jaw dropped. She paused. I thought, "What have you just done? She is a major star and you have blown it! You'll never work again!" We held eye contact. I waited. I imagined working in a shoe store.

"Okay, call my assistant," she said. I didn't say anything. "No, wait," she added with a nod and a smile, "I'll have my assistant call you."

It worked. After that our work together was very productive, and continued to be. But this was an early lesson in boundaries. It is easy to get caught up in the whirlwind of the business, the last minute nature of it all, and to feel that someone's fame can dictate the direction of the work. Often it can, and sometimes it does, but boundaries help.

Expect the unexpected!

Perhaps the most unnerving job involved a legendary R&B voodoo-inspired singer who made a second career as a movie actor. I was to coach him in a French Haitian accent. The director suggested that I make him feel comfortable, as he was nervous about having a dialect coach. I told him I would do what I could. I arrived at his hotel, and was given a look by the clerk at the front desk when I asked for the client's room. I knocked on the client's door.

His smoky room was filled with voodoo paraphernalia: mummies, skulls, small animals in jars, shrunken heads, dried chicken's feet, and a stuffed alligator. And I was to make him feel comfortable?! As I got my bearings, the client eagerly showed off his menagerie. I knew he needed to trust me, so I admired the petrified rat as if it were a kitten. He appreciated my "interest", which helped me ease him into the work. After the lesson, I was even invited to stay for lunch! Too bad, I had another appointment! Bye!

It's all acting.

Many Los Angeles casting directors and agents seem to want "the character" to walk in the door at an audition, and are less patient with the transformative process that actors go through. Over and over I have heard from actors that they must speak in the speech of the targeted role during the interview/audition process. I have had many clients who want to learn Standard American (as well as an emerging, particular brand of LA speech) not just for roles or specific auditions, but also for daily conversations with agents, casting directors, producers and directors.

One Australian client, who had a successful TV career in her country, had a not uncommon situation. She could speak with an American accent perfectly when she had time to work with the text. But when she met with casting directors, producers, directors, they would ask, "Where are you from?" In an interview with an agent, she slipped and was asked, again, "Where are you from?" When she answered, she was told, "You need to lose that accent before I can send you out." So, like many of my clients, she became determined to pass as an American, which meant speaking in the US dialect 24 hours a day. She would call the agent weekly so he could hear her over the phone, but if he heard one sound that he thought wasn't American, she would not be sent out that week.

Beyond the routine pronunciation, resonance, pitch work, etc., our work included altering the minute facial, physical, and even attitudinal patterns needed to pass as an American. As she practiced she would tearfully complain that she didn't feel like herself. "God, I just want to act!" she would moan. "Why do I have to sound like someone I'm not just to be seen? Give me a chance to study a role, and I can do it!" Finally, when her American accent was perfect, she changed her "biography" to further mask her country of origin. Her voice and speech work became the key to "getting in the door" and ultimately her livelihood.

Another actress, an American, was up for a part in a mini-series. We had studied a British dialect for her acting class, but the character she was up for was French. We worked on the script and she was able to pronounce the lines beautifully. However, her agent told her the producers decided they were looking for a French actress. At the audition, she gambled by telling them she had grown up in France! It worked. She was called back by the head of casting, then producers, executive producers, network, and finally the advertisers. But at the last audition, the Executive Producer told her, "We've decided to go in a different direction. We want the character to be English!" Calmly my client did an about face, and chatted in the British dialect about how even though she was "part French", she had an English mother, and had spent years in England. Her story legitimized her speech work to the producers. She won the role.

Old tricks, new tricks: sometimes the twain can meet.

A character actress was annoyed that the producers of her TV show wanted her to get dialect coaching. At our first meeting she looked at my phonetic material, narrowed her eyes and asked, "Weh did you stuhdy?" I told her. Coldly, she replied, "AHy studied with EEdith Skinnah at CAHnugie." I let her know that I did not work with that system. She let me know that she was not open to any other way. I was a little irritated, and could feel her resistance, and a downward spiral. I tried to combat it with reason. Gently, I explained that I would have loved to have studied with Edith, but by the time I received professional training, she unfortunately had died. But logic didn't work here. Instead, I was pitied for missing the boat!

To get us on the same page, I could see that I needed to speak her language.

I began to ask her a series of questions about what it was like to study with Edith Skinner. Each one softened her, and she began to sweetly reminiscence. She told me the famous "YOUah FAAthah DAHied!" story, and my genuine interest in her brought her defenses down. I asked her to show me the Skinnerian script she remembered, and we began to pass the notepad pad back and forth, writing words in script. She wrote with a flourish, a twinkle in her eye.

Slowly, but surely, the ice melted. She needed to be appreciated, and I needed to be flexible and to join with her. I even persuaded her to try a few exercises that I had developed. She now seemed interested in my material, in new developments. At the end of our lesson, she said, "Well, you're quite good." Old meets new. Victory!

About two months later, she phoned. She was starring in a play, and needed help with a Cockney dialect. I felt validated. I had won her over. She was calling back.

"Linda dear, would you please transcribe the role into phonetics for me? Entirely in EEdith's script?" Aaaagh!

But that's another story.

Essay *by Cynthia Blaise*

Dialect Coaching for the Camera

Introduction

Like more and more of my fellow VASTA members, I have found opportunities to coach dialects for film and television. While the vast majority of my experience has been in the theatre, I have also worked on ten films in the last eight years, beginning in 1994 with a TNT production called *Tecumseh*. *Tecumseh* came my way through a colleague, who received another film project three days before work on *Tecumseh* was to begin. This colleague had a mere three hours notice for this second project, while I, on the other hand, enjoyed the benefit of a few days preparation. Nonetheless, I was at something of a loss. I knew how to ready the dialect work—theatre coaches know the process of research, analysis, application and support—but I had no idea how to work on a movie set.

You may be wondering, as I did, why there should be such last-minute drama in a medium where production preparation can take half a year or more. An important actuality to understand is that most productions are in dialect denial. They may have cast a New Zealand teenager to play a Long Beach mob moll but until the moment that teenager opens her mouth at the read-through everyone will want to pretend that that casting choice is not going to cost any money. Hence, there follows the last minute drama and the subsequent frantic phone call. This scenario explains the hurried nature of so much dialect work in film. One must learn to go with the flow. For my first project, *Tecumseh*, I was able to refer to some basic guidelines my aforementioned colleague faxed me on her way out of town. Now, with considerably more experience, I can pass on what I have learned and help other coaches feel more prepared. This article will not address how to teach dialects for film, but rather to make your valuable contribution productively and confidently.

Practical matters

Many particulars of your employment may be negotiable, such as the class of travel, your accommodations, reimbursements, etc. If you have representation, an agent will handle these aspects of your contact. Agents are worth their weight in gold, but they are usually acquired by invitation only. If you procure an agent, you will pay ten percent of your gross every time you yourself are paid. S/he will insure that you have time to rest after a long flight or insist that you are provided with satisfactory lodgings. The agent knows the business and will see to it that you are treated well. Until that time, you will have to negotiate a contract on your own. Make inquiries and determine what others at your level of expertise are earning. If you accept a job and are not compensated according to an accepted rate of pay, you will be doing a disservice to all coaches. Be sure your understanding of the agreement is in writing.

Once you have been hired, the production office will contact you. Ask them to send you a script as soon as possible. Unless you drive yourself, they will make arrangements for your transportation. If you fly, you will probably receive an itinerary by fax or email and your tickets will be waiting for you at the airport. It is customary for a driver to pick you up from your home and take you to the airport. Otherwise you should arrange to be reimbursed for this expense. When you arrive at your destination someone from transportation, holding a sign that bears your name, will be waiting to take you to your

Cynthia Blaise is an Associate Professor at University of Illinois at Chicago. She is an actor and director as well as a voice and dialect coach, having coached over a hundred plays in regional theatre and the actor training programs at Temple and Wayne State University. Cynthia is a certified Associate Fitzmaurice voice instructor, an associate editor for IDEA, and she conducts voice workshops for performers at Second City. In film and television, some of her clients include: Hilary Swank, Frances O'Connor, Julia Ormond, Jeremy Northam, Lena Olin, Gabriel Byrne, Ellen Burstyn, Simon Baker, Adrian Brody, Mekhi Phifer, and David Morse.

hotel. Depending on the size of the city and the budget of the production, your accommodations can vary wildly. Generally, you should be where the other department heads are staying.

When you arrive at the hotel, check to see if there are any messages waiting for you. Be prepared to give the hotel a credit card that will guarantee your payment of *incidentals*, including phone, laundry, room service, mini-bar, etc., for which you are responsible. Production should pay for your room and tax on the room. If Production gives you a rental car you should arrange for them to pay for parking, if applicable.

Your first order of business is to call the Production Office. Determine its location and go there as soon as possible. If it's not reasonable for you to walk, speak with the production coordinator and s/he will make arrangements for your transportation. The production office is where all of the business of the film takes place. There are offices for the director, producers, payroll, assistant directors (AD) and more. Introduce yourself and ask for copies of updated script rewrites, the cast list, contact sheet, the *one-line* or production schedule and a call sheet for that day and the next.

Next, make arrangements with the director's assistant. This is a different person than the assistant director. Ask to speak with the director so that you will be clear about what s/he wants you to work on with the actors. Ordinarily some of this information will be conveyed during a phone conversation before you arrive. An additional meeting is not at all unusual. Often the dialect coach is reminded to, "Keep the dialects light." The director's desires are paramount. S/he is the final word.

It is important to follow the lines of succession. Find the 1ˢᵗ AD[1], introduce yourself and let him or her know that you are available to work with actors and would like to make arrangements to do so. S/he will tell you to deal with the 2ⁿᵈ AD whom you ask for appointments to meet the actors you will be coaching. Also, request that your name be put on the distribution list for department heads so that you will receive memos about changes in the schedule, meetings, etc. You are your own department. Many films do not have a dialect coach so it's easy to be overlooked.

Go to the Accounting Office. Have your driver's license and Social Security card or your passport with you to be copied for immigration forms. Ask them for a *Start Package* and fill out all required paperwork including tax forms and payroll information. You may be required to fill out a weekly time card. Also, at this time you should receive your per diem. It will range between $35 and $100 a day depending on the location. It will be in cash and should be one week's worth, in advance. In another week you'll receive per diem again, distributed on the set with your paycheck. Unless you negotiate otherwise, meal deductions will be taken from that amount in advance for meals you will have on set. Ask about these amounts, and have Accounting explain any paperwork that is unclear. Finally, be sure that you understand the overtime policy.

When your business with the Production Office is complete, go back to your hotel room and study the one-line. Know the schedule for the week,

1. At the top is the 1ˢᵗ AD, followed by the 2ⁿᵈ AD, followed by the 2ⁿᵈ 2ⁿᵈ, followed by the PAs.

especially for the next day. Study the call sheet. It contains the time of sunrise and sunset, the expected weather, which actors are working and which scenes will be shot, usually in the order listed, and whether they are interior or exterior. If you are working days you will probably be working from sunrise to sunset. If you are working exterior nights, you may be called at 2 PM and work till dawn the next day. Dress for the weather! Familiarize yourself with names and departments, especially the ADs, the Production Assistants (PAs) and the Sound Team. Study the next day's dialogue and make sure you are eminently comfortable with that material. I try to memorize all of the lines. Set the alarm the hotel gives you and assume it won't work. Place a wake-up call order and assume they won't call. Then set the alarm you brought from home and try to get a good night's sleep.

Coaching

If you have been brought into the film before shooting has begun, you will have the relatively rare opportunity to rehearse. During the preparation period all days will be scheduled tightly and will routinely include work like costume, hair and makeup preparation and camera tests. Usually, a dialect coach is not required to attend these calls. However, if the actor anticipates down time during a long test day, s/he may ask you to come to the soundstage. Test day schedules are usually optimistic and might, for example, say something like 8-10, Camera Test and 10:15-12:15, Dialect Coaching. In this case your actor will probably be late or possibly not even make the appointment because s/he has been sent out for highlights or eyebrow waxing. Check in with the ADs and go with the flow.

When the actors are called for rehearsal with the director, you may be asked to attend, depending on the preference of the director. If you are invited to rehearsal your function is to observe only. You may take notes but do so discretely. This is a "safe" space for the actors and director and no one will want to feel performance pressures such as the demands of using a dialect. The read-through or table read is important for the dialect coach. Make sure you let the ADs know you will want to be included. Occasionally, you will be asked to read stage directions or even a small role, often not cast until days before a scene is shot.

Dialect rehearsals are your time to teach the actors how they will be expected to speak. With luck, you may have a couple of hours a day with each of your actors. Once shooting begins, it will be rare to have this kind of opportunity again so use this time wisely. I always have a copy of *Speak with Distinction*,[2] which enables me to drill sound changes without using the script. By the time I arrive, I have determined where all dialect changes occur. Do not count on the actors to do this work. I also prepare word lists including every word that changes, categorized by those changes. Don't expect the actors to know, appreciate or be interested in IPA, but some actors will pleasantly surprise you. Using basic symbols may be necessary, if you use them at all.

Sometimes actors are interested in warm-ups. Ask whether they care to warm-up or whether you can prepare a warm-up that they can do on their own. Once in a great while an actor is interested in receiving a vocal production note, but this is rare. Most of my notes are speech-related, either dialect or clarity concerns. Occasionally, I'll give a note regarding syntax, inflection or

2. Timothy Monich and Lilene Mansell, *Speak with Distinction* (NY: Applause, 1990).

stress, but this gets dangerously close to encroaching on acting choices. However, such issues are better addressed in rehearsal than during shooting.

Now is the time to discuss with the actor how they will want to work on set. Questions such as: "May I give you notes between takes? Do you like to rehearse the lines before going to set or would you prefer to review the words that have changes? What would be the most comfortable way for you to work?" are appropriate. Keep in mind that many film actors are young and inexperienced with this kind of technical work, and often your guidance will be welcome.

Principal photography

Your call time will be listed on the call sheet. Make sure to ascertain whether it is a *pick-up* call,[3] or a *set* call.[4] Call sheets are distributed on the set at the end of the day. If your actors finish before the workday is complete you may not be on set to receive this information. Call the 2nd AD when you're fairly certain the workday is over, or *wrapped*, to find out when your actors are expected to arrive on the set the following day. This determines your call time.

If you arrive on set in the morning before *Crew Call*, you can have breakfast at the catering truck. Otherwise, drop off your belongings in the space you will have negotiated for yourself, usually one of a dozen closet-sized rooms in a long trailer called a *honey wagon*. Ask a PA for the *sides*[5] for the day. Shooting plans frequently change, such as the order of the scenes, the dialogue, and so on. Check to see if your actors have arrived. Go to the set for a preliminary rehearsal, if one is called. If your actors are in the *works*[6], you can poke your head in and say hello, but don't attempt to work there unless the actor makes the request. Sometimes hair and makeup people will object. Let the actor know that you are available when they're finished.

Now, the waiting begins and it will be useful to know how to wait. Let a PA know you will be in your trailer and that you would like to be notified as soon as your actor is available. Have some coffee and go over the text being covered. If you can get a radio, you can listen for your actor's location. If you don't have a trailer or a designated space, set up camp somewhere so that you can keep apprised of the actor's status. In inclement weather, the lunch tent can serve as a place to wait. Make sure a PA knows where you can be found. Ideally, there will be time to work with your actors before they go to the set. At that point you may warm-up (if desired) and run-through the text a time or two. Some actors may prefer not to spend much time in this manner. Whatever the case, make sure the actor knows that you are happy to be helpful and supportive.

You need not be on set if there is no dialogue. Technically, you don't need to be there if your client is not working, but many coaches will be there to listen anyway, making note of anything you would like to bring to the editor's attention.[7] Still, your priority is with your client and if staying at base camp, close to the actors, presents you with an opportunity to work on some text, take advantage of it.

3. This is the time that a van will pick you up at your hotel.

4. This is the time that you are expected on the set.

5. This is a reduced copy of the scenes that are going to be shot, usually but not necessarily in the correct order.

6. Hair and makeup

7. Record notes for each take. For example, Scene 99, take 1- actor lost necessary r-coloration in... /give specific line. Sc. 99, take 2—fine, and so on. The next shot would be Sc. 99A followed by Sc. 99B, and so on. When the setup is complete, check with the script supervisor to find out which takes the director decided to print. You only have to report notes to the editor on those takes. I record my notes on my laptop nightly. At the end of each week, send your notes to the editor at the Production Office.

When the crew is ready, the actor(s) will be called on to the set. The hair and makeup artists, a member of the costume crew and the dialect coach will follow and remain fairly close to the actors. The 1ˢᵗ AD calls a rehearsal. The director may or may not like to have people around at this time. If you are asked to step out, do so quickly. After private rehearsals, they will call for *Keys*, department heads and assorted others, including you. Step in at this point and watch what will essentially be a blocking rehearsal. Then the 1ˢᵗ AD will call in *Second Team*, (which means stand-ins), and at that point, the grips, electricians and set dressers will light and ready the set for shooting. There is no telling how long this can take. The actors may relax somewhere nearby or return to their trailers. This is often an ideal time to work with actors who are finished in the works. This is how rehearsal will work for each scene throughout the day.

When the cameras are ready the 1ˢᵗ AD will call for the *First Team*, including the actors, the director, hair, makeup and camera people. You should go in with the first team. There will be another rehearsal, sometimes more. Take and give notes but be aware of staying out of the way. This rehearsal time is mainly for the camera, the director and the actors. When the 1ˢᵗ AD calls for *Final Touches*, hair spray, powder, distribution of weapons and other last minute adjustments are made. Make your dialect adjustments and then head back to your chair.

Generally, your time to work with the actors is before they come on set. Once on set, limit yourself to clear, quick adjustments. Depending on the sensitivity of the actor, you might be able to give notes to the actors while they are being touched up. Otherwise, it may be necessary to wait until hair and makeup is finished and then quietly pull the actor aside. Get in there, do your job and move out. Once the camera is ready they need to roll.

Always remain close enough to literally dash in when necessary, only giving notes between takes or between *set-ups*[8]. There may be two takes or eighty, depending on the director and the complexity of the shot. Be attentive to the location of the director. If s/he or the Director of Photography (DP) is giving notes, back away. If you are on the set when the 1ˢᵗ AD says, "clear the set" or, "give it to the director" or, "rolling" step out immediately. If the 1ˢᵗ AD instructs not to "break it up" after they've cut on a take, this means, no adjustments. No one steps in but the director.

8. Each different camera shot is a set-up.

Make friends with the sound designer immediately. The mixer is the boss. The boom operator is often responsible for distributing Comteks, (a remote receiver) and headphones, through which you will listen to the actors. Introduce yourself and explain that you will need a Comtek. The mixer actually owns all of the sound equipment and he rents it to the production. Unplug the headset from the battery pack during long waiting periods. If you start to loose volume or get static, take it to a member of the sound team and tell them that you may need a new battery. They expect to replace batteries. I wear mine all day and return them when we wrap. Don't wear it home! Also, Comteks are magnetized: *never* place your Comtek on top of the mixer's tape recorder, the Nagra.

9. See 'Set Etiquette' for a definition of Video Village.

Unfortunately, no one is going to approach you and say, "Now we are going to do thus and such." Stay close to Video Village[9] and listen. Essentially, this is how your day will proceed, over and over and over again. When the day is over, or sometimes during lunch, the editors will screen dailies (called *rushes* overseas) to watch the prior day's work. Dailies are usually open to department heads and you should go whenever you can, as it a good opportunity, not only to listen to your own work in a more objective setting, but also to learn what others are looking for in their work. The days sound long and they are. In movies patience is not so much a virtue as a survival skill.

Actors

Find ways to help an actor embrace your note. "If we can hear the final consonant it would support your interpretation of that line." Once again, be careful of giving a note that could be misconstrued as an acting note.[10] Know that movie directors can be a territorial breed, and sometimes touchy about your giving notes to actors on the set. Use your best judgment and proceed with caution. On an independent film called *Second Chance*, I was hired to coach two actors who were cast to play John F. and Bobby Kennedy. One actor appreciated my support and advice while the other actor resisted the work. The director was aware of the situation and was not terribly concerned. As a result, one brother used a dialect and one did not. Without the support of the director and the producer there is no way to reconcile this sort of situation. Make it clear to your actor that you are working with them at the director's request.

Occasionally, you will encounter an actor who avoids you like the plague. While shooting *Tecumseh*, an actor told me that he "…didn't work with dialect coaches." And he didn't. Be prepared to work differently with different actors. One might want to run the scene with you before going to the set, and then receive no notes during shooting. Another actor will never want to run the scene before hand, but wants notes on the set. Some actors will become annoyed if you give them too many notes while another will be concerned if you are not giving them enough feed back. Again, determine how the actor likes to work. You needn't correct an actor when they are speaking off-camera or when the camera is on their back only. The only exception would be to keep the actor from getting severely off-track for the rest of the day.

Sooner or later, you will work with an actor who is accustomed to working with his or her own coach. The actor may have asked for their regular coach and when s/he was unavailable (or too expensive), wound up with you instead. I would suggest that you sympathize with the actor's frustration. It is understandable that an actor may become accustomed, comfortable and even dependent upon an existing actor-coach relationship. You might reassure the actor that you understand their anxiety and hope that you can find a way to be helpful. They will be reassured of your good intentions and willingness to accommodate their needs. Respect existing actor-coach relationships. Try not to question another coach's work, even when you strongly disagree with their choices. If you think it would be helpful, contact the other coach. The support and guidance of more experienced coaches can be invaluable. Try to remember that these actors are under a great deal of pressure and often the stakes are fairly high. As is the case with a professional athlete, these actors are being paid a substantial amount of money and are expected to perform.

10. While on the set of *Tecumseh*, I coached a Hispanic actor to 'lift' his voice. Although we had discussed the concept of placement before, the actor applied my note to his acting, which contradicted the way the director asked him to say the line. The director was furious. Fortunately when I explained myself to a producer, he smoothed things over with the director. Apparently I came close to being thrown off of the set. The director teased me about this during the entire shoot and every time he brought it up I reassured him that I wouldn't dream of challenging or contradicting his direction.

Those dialect changes that cannot be adjusted on the set may (or may not) be fixable in Post-Production. This is the film and sound editing work that begins when principal photography ends. If an actor is not taking a note and appears to be struggling with the acting, it may be that the most productive contribution you will be able to make is to inform the editor via your notes rather than pushing the issue with the actor. (You send notes to the editor for his/her use in determining which takes were better for dialect and why.) You may need to back off and allow actors to work through their difficulties. This is also a judgment call. Later, you may be asked to work with the actors during these post-production sessions. I suggest reading Rocco Dal Vera's essay on Audio Digital Recording (ADR), published in the last VASTA Journal,[11] to provide you with some insight regarding how this work is executed. However, some films do not have extensive budgets for ADR. That which can be fixed on the set saves the film money in the studio.

11. Rocco Dal Vera, "Looping: Voice of Violence on Film," *The Voice in Violence and other contemporary issues in professional voice and speech training* presented by Voice and Speech Review (2001): 113-117.

If I have no notes for an actor, I try to catch their eye and reassure them that the dialect is going well. This can be accomplished from a distance with a comforting nod and does not have to occur after every take. If the actor is on a roll, it is better not to interfere, but some actors need to know that you are listening.

An alarming number of actors don't learn their lines. Perhaps they want to keep their performance fresh or maybe they expect the lines to change. Still, this unfortunate fact can make coaching difficult. Scripted lines are inclined to change, so endeavor to keep apprised of these changes. The script supervisor will be keeping track as well, in case you require verification. Stay positive and, once again, go with the flow.

Set Etiquette

Video Village is where the director, script supervisor, producers and actors sit. The monitors are set up here so that the director can watch the shot. The writer may be there, as well as friends of the director or the cast, media folks, etc. Try to find a place to set up your *camp* (including your stool or chair, equipment, backpack) close to Video Village. You may have to relocate often, since setting up a new shot often includes moving Video Village. If your contract guarantees you a chair, it will be moved for you. If Video Village is too crowded and you can't get close enough to see the monitors, set up near the sound team or the hair and makeup people. Always sit in your own chair!

You may be asked to be on book. This is usually the script supervisor's responsibility but it may be necessary for you to do so. I have also read the lines of an actor who was not present to read with an actor being filmed. This is not part of your job, however, if I am asked, I always say yes. In general, I try to draw as little attention to myself as possible and quietly do my work. Make sure your cell phone is off when you are on set and wear nothing that jingles.

Quarters are close. You will be surrounded by people either standing around waiting or working very hard and very fast. They may be carrying heavy equipment in what seems to be a definite urgency. Get out of their way! Be extremely careful of leaning or sitting on set pieces or scenery. Never touch anything labeled, "Hot Set". Watch your step and be sure not to stand on cables. Always stand behind the camera. If you can see the lens, it can see you. Remember that once the director (or the 1st AD) says, "action," be perfectly silent and absolutely still. One final note, don't ever have a bad day on the set. Actors and directors will have bad days, as needed. No one else is afforded this luxury!

Directors

Remember that although you are there to serve the director's concept of the film, you should not expect to have much contact with the director. Indeed, s/he may not seem to know who you are. They know. Your work with an actor will probably be decided before shooting the film. Don't be offended if the director is not involving you, but know that he or she might turn around at any moment and ask you a question. Some directors have a more vociferous manner than others. This summer I had the pleasure of working with Richard Donner who directs with a measure of drama, while being a lovely person.[12] Don't allow yourself to become unsettled by this kind of behavior. If you hear something in the film that concerns you that might be crucial to the film's integrity, I suggest asking the script supervisor whether the discrepancy should be addressed.[13]

What to Pack

Bring a small chair with you, such as a collapsible hunting or camping stool, ideally with pockets. You will have to transport your belongings and should be prepared for plenty of walking or hiking. Carry with you only what you need, such as the script, writing implements, a dictionary/thesaurus, and possibly gloves and a flashlight for night shoots. Much of what you may require should be provided on set, such as first aid, caffeine, snacks and water.

Unlike most theatre production, movie-making can include a hefty portion of nature's chaos. Be ready for whatever the day throws your way. Know your location and its hazards: poison ivy, pollen, ticks and mosquitoes. You may encounter vast quantities of dust, dirt, sand, mud, rain, cold, heat and snow. Equip yourself with a hat, insecticide, sun block, mouthwash, antihistamine, lip balm, and cleansing wipes.

Bring a machine for making cassettes and an ample supply of empty tapes of various lengths. Leave this in your honey wagon or hotel room. See that you are reimbursed for the tapes you prepare for actors. Have extra batteries with you, as you may not have access to a store. I have collected quite a few dialects on movie sets. The drivers and crew can be a good source as well as local individuals hired as extras. If you come prepared, you will probably have ample time to supplement your (and IDEA's)[14] dialect collection.

Final Thoughts

It seems that more and more non-American actors are being cast to play American characters in film and TV today. As an actor, I have some difficulty with this fact. As a coach, this means more work! You may be teaching an Irishman a Texas dialect and an Australian to sound like she comes from Brooklyn. This can also make our work more complicated. You may be there to coach one person or several, one dialect or many.[15] If

12. Director of *Timeline*, (to be released in April of 2003) as well as *Superman*, *Goonies*, the *Lethal Weapon* series, *Maverick*, etc.

13. For example, in a rewritten scene the actor says, "My Lord," and you know (or suspect) that during said period, the character would be more likely to say, "My liege." Being a director myself, I would definitely want to hear this information. If the film has a medieval language consultant on set, let that person do his job.

14. "International Dialects of English Archive" Online. Internet. Available:http://www.ukans.edu/~idea.

15. I took over *Polish Wedding* so that dialect coach, Susan Haggerty, could go off to coach 53 actors for *Titanic*

you should take over a film for another coach, ask to see the dailies so that you'll know exactly how the actors sound. You're there to insure consistency. Similarly, when I prepare someone for a film I will (probably) be contacted by the coach hired to work on the film set. S/he will instruct me to prepare the actor in a precise manner.[16]

Coaching work comes in various forms: I have prepped actors for auditions and for films without working on the film. I have not been hired for post-production work for a film that I did not coach, but there are other coaches who have. While on a film set, actors have approached me and asked for help in preparing for an audition, or in reducing their dialect outside of the film. I always try to make myself available.

Dialect coaching is an incredibly interesting line of work. Traveling and working with actors you respect can be rewarding. I have a friend whose first job lasted for nine months. She traveled from Norway to the Caribbean. This is not the norm but it gives you an idea of what is possible. I've been to Europe and to Canada several times. I almost went to Istanbul and Australia but many offers don't come to fruition. Nonetheless, there is also a down side. Working away from home and family, living in hotels, long hours, significant boredom and challenging actors can make the work difficult, but hopefully these guidelines and suggestions will make this challenging job more manageable.

16. I did this for a very successful coach. She was happy with my work and later recommended me for re-shoots on the same film, *The Affair of the Necklace.*

Works Cited

Tecumseh. Dir. Larry Elikann. Turner Pictures, 1995

Titanic. Dir. James Cameron. Paramount and 20th Century Fox, 1997

Polish Wedding. Dir. Theresa Connelly. Lake Shore Entertainment Cooperation, 1998

The Affair of the Necklace. Dir. Charles Shyer. Warner Brothers, 2001

Second Chance. Dir. Robert Dyke. Destination Earth LLC, 2002

Timeline. Dir. Richard Donner. Paramount, 2003

Iron-Jawed Angels. Katja Von Garnier. HBO, 2003

Rocco Dal Vera. "Looping: The Voice of Violence on Film." *The Voice in Violence and other contemporary issues in professional voice and speech training presented by the Voice and Speech Review,* Distributed by Applause. (Cincinnati: Voice and Speech Trainers Association, Incorporated, 2001) Pp. 113-117

Essay *by Eric Armstrong*

This is *Normal?*: A Theatre Coach Works in Film

Eric Armstrong taught Voice, Speech, Dialects and Shakespeare Text at Roosevelt University in Chicago and has just recently joined the faculty at York University in Toronto. He is a Dialect and Voice Coach for theatre (and film on occasion!). Recent coaching projects include *I Just Stopped By to See the Man*, at Steppenwolf Theatre Company, *Phaedre*, directed by JoAnne Akalaitis at The Court Theatre, and *Mad Forest* at Piven Theatre Workshop. Eric's interview with Andrew Wade of the Royal Shakespeare Company was published in *The Voice in Violence*... and he had an exercise published in Janet Rodgers' *The Complete Voice and Speech Workout: Book & CD*. He was the Associate Editor for Illinois with the International Dialects of English Archive (IDEA). Eric Armstrong is a VASTA Board Member, was Director of Conferences 2001-2002 and continues as VASTA's Director of Technology/Internet Services.

1. Sometimes called a "dialogue coach."

2. Tom Wilkinson was nominated for an Academy Award™ for his role in *In the Bedroom*. Most people know him as the older man in *The Full Monty*. An excellent biography can be found at http://www.hollywood.com/celebs/bio/celeb/1677495.

3. I shared the coaching with my classmate Diane Pitblado.

4. I would learn to regret this, as I soon was traveling to set far more than anticipated.

The role of the film dialect coach[1] is one of the most richly rewarded job opportunities for those in the Voice and Speech training field. To compete in this arena, one must have a thorough knowledge of dialect coaching and an expertise appropriate to working with the world's most successful film actors. However, to apply the experience of theatre dialect coaching to the medium, one must emphasize the benefits of the working environment and work around its idiosyncrasies.

I have been working at Roosevelt University since 1999, and last year began to actively pursue coaching work in Chicago. After a year of theatre coaching in a variety of venues, I received a call at the end of the semester from the producer of *Normal*, an HBO film being produced in and around Chicago. Starring Tom Wilkinson[2] and Jessica Lange, the film follows the story of a Midwest tractor inspector who reveals after his twenty-fifth wedding anniversary that he wants to have a sex-change operation. The coaching gig, as originally pitched, was to work with Tom Wilkinson for a few hours in the rehearsal week while they were based in Chicago, and then to monitor his dialect on set, an hour and a half west of the city, for the first day or two of shooting.

I arranged to have a meeting with the producer, Lydia Pilcher of Red Tractor productions. I outlined my experience, where I coached and taught. One small feather in my cap was a film-coaching gig that I had done in Canada. In 1994, David Smukler, my mentor at York University, had arranged for me to assist him[3] on a film. That, and a few small acting roles in TV and film when I was based in Vancouver was all I knew of the film industry and its practices. In my interview, I emphasized my theatre and teaching experience. Then, the time came to discuss remuneration, to arrange "my deal." The Producer felt that, since Tom was so successful with his accent, he wasn't likely to need much coaching on the film. Based on what I thought the job would be, I asked for a healthy hourly rate (twice my private coaching rate) and a daily rate, for any day where I was on set for five hours or more. The crew was being housed in a hotel an hour and a half away from Chicago during the week, and they were being shuttled to the set half an hour beyond that. Since I was expecting to be on set only one or two days I didn't negotiate travel time.[4] The producer told me that I should hear something early the next week.

Late the next week I hadn't heard a thing, which seemed typical of the film business. I assumed the worst and that I was destined to a quiet summer of holding my new baby. Friday I got a call from the producer's assistant: could I come to the read-through on Monday and meet the director and actor? Seems I was the one after all.

So I had the job, and only the weekend to prepare! I quickly got on the computer and did some research. The International Movie Database, <imdb.com>, proved helpful with information on the actors, director and producer. It made me feel more confident, knowing that I wouldn't stick my foot in my mouth by asking about films that Tom wasn't in. I hadn't managed to see *In the Bedroom* when it was in general release, but it wasn't in the video stores yet, either. I felt I had to see it before I met the man. In a small theatre in the far western suburbs of Chicago I sat listening desperately, trying to assess the accent as best I could, while trying not to get lost in the story.

What I Prepared

I developed a series of work sheets for Tom, which outlined a dialect based on a sample of a rural northern Illinois dialect that I had collected from the Dictionary of American Regional English (DARE) at the University of Wisconsin at Madison. They were designed to use what I had heard Tom doing in his other North American films.[5] Each lexical set key word[6] was described in terms of the sound changes that were familiar to Tom, followed by a long list of practice words that he could use to drill the sound changes. I planned to provide him with a tape or CD, of primary source material from DARE and my demonstrations of the sound changes, once I had a better idea of his needs. Ultimately he didn't want that, so I managed to avoid it.

Vowel Sound Changes:

I started with the changes I thought would be easiest, and then proceeded to the more challenging ones, that contrasted the most with GenAm patterns or what I had heard Tom doing in other films. I used a narrative form to describe the sound changes of the Northern Illinois (rural) dialect, rather than attempting any kind of phonetic transcription. What follows is a highly edited[7] version of what I gave Tom.

1. HAPP<u>Y</u>: In this dialect, final "y"-endings are more closed (or "tense"), and so they are the same as FLEECE.[8]

2. Where L follows a vowel, it is very dark[9], and so tends to affect the vowel too—especially in FLEECE *(feel)*, STRUT *(gull)*, FOOT *(full)*, GOOSE *(fool)*, FACE *(fail)*, PRICE *(file)* and CHOICE *(foil)* word-groups. In some instances these can even go so far as to be broken into two syllables "fee-yul,"[10] especially when the words are heavily stressed in a sentence.

3. DRESS: a bit more relaxed than in Received Pronunciation[11] (or RP).[12]

4. FOOT: a bit more relaxed than in RP.[13]

5. TRAP/BATH: TRAP words are ones that RP speakers say roughly the same as American speakers, while BATH words are usually different (though this is changing). In most of North America (except perhaps some parts of New England), TRAP and BATH are pronounced the same. N.B. "arrow, carriage, guarantee, Larry, carry, marriage, etc." ("ARR" words) *are not part of this group!* They are part of the SQUARE group.

6. PRICE: Not like *Ride with the Devil*, like *In the Bedroom*[14] a closing diphthong. N.B. –ile endings are *not* PRICE words in North American dialects, where the sound is reduce to *schwa* [ə]. Missile is *not* like "miss" + "isle," it's like "missuhl."

7. CHOICE: close your mouth a *little* bit more[15] than in RP (more like "o", less like "aw")

8. STRUT: This sound is further back in the mouth, darker sounding.[16] Not quite as dark as in *Ride with the Devil*, but close. N.B. "Dull, pulse, bulge, etc." are essentially FOOT words,[17] the L affects them so strongly.

9. COMM<u>A</u>: This sound, which is normally the unstressed vowel *schwa* [ə] in most dialects, becomes the same vowel as STRUT when it ends a phrase, or if the word stands alone.[18] When spoken at speed, in flowing speech, the sound remains an unstressed *schwa* [ə]. It should never have R coloring when linking to another vowel, e.g. "Irma‿and Roy."

5. At that point, these films were *In the Bedroom, Ride with the Devil* and *Molokai: The Story of Father Damien*, though I never managed to see the latter. VASTA member and IDEA founder Paul Meier coached the last two films.

6. Lexical Sets were defined by J.C. Wells in *Accents of English*; Cambridge University Press; May 1982; ISBN: 0521297192;

7. I also included two sounds, for the lexical sets FACE and GOAT, which were accurate for the dialect, but in the end we chose not to do, as they were too extreme, and didn't match what others were doing.

8. [i]→[i]

9. [l]→[ɫ]

10. ['fi.jəɫ]

11. [ɛ]→[ɛ̞]

12. Received Pronunciation, or Standard British Speech. Tom and I used this as a reference point.

13. [ʊ]→[ʊ̞]

14. *Ride with the Devil*: [a]→ *In the Bedroom*: [aɪ]

15. [ɔɪ]→[oɪ]

16. [ʌ]→[ʌ̱]

17. [dʌl]→[dʊl]

18. [ə]→[ʌ]

19. [ɝ]→[ɹ̩] (this is really hard to represent with IPA!)

20. Essentially, I'm saying [ɝ]=[ɚ] and that the only difference is one of stress.

21. [aʊ̆]→[aʊ̆]

22. [aʊ̆ɚ]→[aɚ]

23. I used the British spelling conventions for words like "color" in my notes for Tom as a courtesy.

24. [ɪɚ]→[iɹ̩]

25. [ɪɹ]→[iɹ̩]

26. [ɛ̞ɚ]→[ɛɹ̩]

27. [aɚ]→[aɹ̩]

28. [ʊɚ]→[ɔɹ̩]

29. [ʊɚ]→[ɹ̩]

30. [ɒɹ]→[ɔɹ̩] (this is similar to footnote 21 above)

31. [ɒ, ɔ]→[a]

10. NURSE/SURE: As mentioned earlier, this vowel-R sound is very strong, much like the sounds used in *Ride with the Devil*. To make it, pull the tongue tip back (either up to the roof of the mouth, or so it points toward the uvula). The tongue root should tense and pull down toward your larynx.[19]

11. LETTER: Final, unstressed "er, ar, or, etc." endings are unstressed versions of the NURSE vowel.[20]

12. MOUTH: This diphthong sound starts bright and forward in the mouth (not quite the sound in TRAP—think of the Southern US pronunciation of PRICE). It heads toward the FOOT vowel sound, but the lips stay completely relaxed.[21] Similar to *Ride with the Devil*. N.B. "flour, sour, hour, etc." essentially do not slide back toward the FOOT sound before the R.[22] However, they are one syllable, compared to words like "flower, tower, cower," which are two.

13. NEAR: This R-colored[23] diphthong starts like FLEECE, then slides into the strong R-quality of the NURSE words.[24] Similar to *Ride with the Devil*. N.B. words with KIT in RP and NEAR in GenAm: "mirror, spirit, myriad, Syria, delirious."[25]

14. SQUARE: This R-colored diphthong starts like DRESS, then slides into the strong R-quality of the NURSE words.[26] Similar to *Ride with the Devil*.

15. START: This R-colored diphthong starts like FATHER (see below), then slides into the strong R-quality of the NURSE words.[27] Similar to *Ride with the Devil*.

16. NORTH/POOR: These word-groups, normally distinct in other dialects, are joined together in this dialect.[28] Most POOR words become NURSE words (like "sure")[29]—we've seen them already. N.B. the following words are LOT words in RP—they become NORTH words in the Midwest[30]: "Laurence/Lawrence, laurel, laureate, quarrel, quarry, warrant, warren, warrior, Warwick, Norwich"

17. FATHER/LOT/THOUGHT: These word-groups, distinct in most British-variants, are all joined together in this dialect.[31] This (particularly the THOUGHT group change) is different from *In the Bedroom*.

I figured that, once I got to talk with the director and Tom, I would need to adapt the dialect. What I had in mind was to go somewhere between this accurate regional dialect, and GenAm.

The Read-Through

The first read-through coincided with my last day of work for the semester. Immediately upon arrival I was introduced to Mr. Wilkinson, and we began to discuss what he had done in the past. I knew that Tom was very good at dialects and that he needed just a little guidance, thanks to a call to Paul Meier who had worked with him before. We discussed other films requiring a dialect that he had worked on, most notably *In the Bedroom*. He shared that his preferred method of rehearsal was to rehearse the scenes with the coach present, and then get feedback on what he was doing. They had worked in this manner on *In the Bedroom*, apparently. This would mean that I would be in rehearsal for four half days before filming began. So I had a quick chat with the producer, who thought that that would be fine: I would attend all the rehearsals and give Tom his feedback there.

Next, I met with the director, Jane Anderson[32], who had written *Leaving Normal* as a stage play, which had premiered at LA's Geffen Playhouse, starring Laurie Metcalf and Beau Bridges. It became clear that she wasn't looking for a specific Midwest dialect, but more of a general Midwest quality. So my detailed analysis evaporated in smoke as I ditched some of the more unusual sound changes and opted on the spot for a more typical General American, Inland Northern speech. She did say that she wanted strong Rs and a flatter intonation pattern (which were both part of what I had prepared).

The read-through was similar to any theatre read-through I had ever been to. Not being an actor, it seemed wrong for me to sit around the table with them. The production team's table was too far away to hear properly. I set my chair up as near to the actors as possible, trying to see Tom Wilkinson's mouth. Tom's dialect, for the most part was excellent—there seemed to be little need for a lot of coaching, though certain pronunciations popped out as inappropriate.

Through the read-through, I listened to Jessica Lange's reading[33] with the thought that, after 25 years of marriage, perhaps he might pick up some of her speech qualities. However, since her speech seemed atypical of the kind of speech I had been hired to coach, frequently lacking rhoticity, I abandoned that idea. As I listened to the local Midwest actors, I got a sense of what Jane had in mind. Randy Arney[34] who played the couple's pastor in the film, is from Southern Illinois originally, and had "the perfect sound" as I heard Jane say once. Joe Sikora, a talented young actor from Chicago who had recently made the plunge to relocate to LA, was the exception. Back in his native environment, Joe was slipping into a strong North-side Chicago accent. After the read-through, I spoke with Jane about this, and she suggested that I work with Joe a little as well, to help him drop the Chicago quality that made him stand out from his onscreen family.[35]

Having worked in film as a bit-part actor only, I had never had the luxury of being in on rehearsals for a film. It became clear that a large part of the rehearsal process was to review the script, and from the actors' point of view, cut it in parts where it remained too stagy. Both Jessica Lange and Tom Wilkinson were very good at this. Generally, their comments were of the "I can *act* that, I don' t need to say it" variety. What struck me about the process was that they never wanted to rehearse much—establish the bare bones of the scene and then leave it—so that the scene stayed "fresh" for them. I'm more familiar with a theatre model, where one is expected to emotionally connect with the material in rehearsal. It really was "it'll be there on the day." That's fine for the acting... but what of the dialect? If the actors never really *do* it, then how does one know what they're really going to do? This is one of those dilemmas that evolved through the rehearsal process.

One thing was clear: the idea that I was a dialect expert was a given. Tom, an actor with 25 years of experience in theatre and film, spoke outside of his acting in a mid-Atlantic accent (as in, somewhere in the middle of the Atlantic, with some features of British speech and some of General American), a combination of his American dialect and the realities of communicating. On one break, Tom and I headed out to the parking lot while he had a smoke. As we spoke, he suggested that he might "just talk" and I could correct him on

32. Anderson has won an Emmy for her writing of *The Positively True Adventures of the Alleged Texas Cheerleader-Murdering Mom* (1993), and was nominated for writing and directing *The Baby Dance* (1998), and for writing *If These Walls Could Talk 2* (2000).

33. I had been told that Ms. Lange would use her own speech pattern, having grown up in the Midwest. It has never seemed to me that her speech sounded particularly Midwestern, but I wasn't about to say so.

34. Arney, who is a member of Steppenwolf and its former Artistic Director, commissioned *Leaving Normal* for Geffen Playhouse, where he is the current Artistic Director. Arney subsequently hired me to coach his production of *I Just Stopped By to See the Man* at Steppenwolf in November 2002.

35. Jane told him to stop hanging out with the Teamsters, who, to a man, spoke with the best Chicago dialects I have heard.

anything that was wrong. I may be good, but I couldn't do that. Either
we could have a conversation, *or* I could listen to his speech and comment. The subtlety of his "mistakes" required my full attention. I am not
sure whether this is something all dialect coaches encounter, but it was a
form of multi-tasking that was beyond my capabilities.

So, as the days went on, the work would go something like this: the
actors would rehearse, and I would listen and take notes. At the end of a
run-through of the scene, a brief discussion would ensue between actors
and director/writer, and then just before another stab at the scene, I
would sidle up to Tom and point out things that needed some work.
Gradually, I could begin to predict where Tom would make mistakes,
and generally I would be right. He confided to me that, until he knew
what he was doing, he would continue to make these mistakes, so I
shouldn't be too stressed if he couldn't nail it before we got to set.

One hazard of the rehearsal space, a vast soundstage with dull work light,
was the sound-deadening acoustics. Designed to soak up sound so that
the microphones would catch only sound coming out of the speaker's
mouth, this was the worst theatrical space on earth. On top of that, these
actors liked to play very intimately, at the level appropriate for a close-up,
and it made hearing the dialect almost impossible at times. The concentrated listening required was unlike anything I have ever had to do in
theatre, where actors are at very least *trying* to fill the space. I wanted to
get closer, but the vast space of the stage made moving in seem
inappropriate.

By the end of the rehearsal week, I felt that I had armed Tom with a
wealth of notes to prepare for each scene, and written them out for him

37

Tom Wilkinson and Jessica Lange
in a scene from *Normal*

so that he could refer to them each night as he prepared for the following day's shooting. On occasion I could supplement these notes with the materials that I had prepared the previous weekend, so that wasn't a complete waste.

I also had an opportunity to do a little coaching with Joe Sikora, who played Tom's son, and it became clear that his dialect genius was enhanced by living in the UK for a year, where he had been exposed to a multitude of dialects. At lunch one day, he entertained us with a dialect tour of the British Isles that was a virtuoso display of dialect skills. However, playing a dialect that was very close to his mother tongue was much more challenging for him. He excelled with dialects that were very different and struggled to make a subtler shift.

On Location

Filming began with one of the longest scenes in the script. Arriving the first morning, we prepared for an on-set rehearsal, or *blocking*. As the *first team*[36] entered, the First Assistant Director[37] shooed me out of the room. This was a change! After a week of free access to rehearsals, this onset rehearsal was a different beast. He wanted me to be there only when the *department heads*[38] entered. Granted the location was *tiny* and so fitting into the room was very difficult with so many people. When I finally got into the room with the rest of the gang, I was so far away from the actors and they were speaking so quietly, that it was an exercise in futility. Over the course of the shoot, rehearsal became more and more frustrating. It became clear that, once the blocking had been established in the first rehearsal, the actors would only mark their way through the scene. Tom would stop doing the dialect! The 1st AD never really got the point, and always did his best to protect the intimacy of his set for the actors, making it very hard to do my job.

At this point the actors were sent back to *base-camp* where Tom would go into hair and makeup. Tom likes to run his lines while wandering around the

36. First team refers to the actors, while Second team refers to the stand-ins who replace them and serve as reflective surfaces for the DOP, or Director of Photography, and Gaffer, or head lighting technician, to bounce their lights off.

37. 1st ADs are the film equivalent of Stage Managers, who with their team of 2nd AD, 2nd 2nd AD and PAs (Production Assistants), juggle the minute-to-minute organization and logistics of creating a film.

38. Which includes representatives from Props, Lighting, Sound, Continuity, Production, the studio, etc. etc.

parking lot, smoking a cigarette. This was a particularly cold May morning, and so I walked beside him, trying to cue him from the sides, shivering madly. As we wrapped up our run of his lines, he suggested that we go into hair and makeup together. Though this is mostly a time where Tom would just sit and be "done up", later in the day I was asked by the ADS not to enter the hair and makeup trailer, because it would slow down that department. I was never sure whether hair and makeup had complained or whether it was just the ADS trying to be efficient, but it made matters rather difficult for Tom and me. For the next few days, as he would finish with the blocking, they would race him through hair and makeup, and then race him back to set to shoot. This left no time for me to coach Tom for the day's shooting, and since he had elected to do it on the day, he would arrive on set prepared yet unpolished for the dialect demands at hand. Only after some time of great frustration did I put my foot down and say, I must have time with Tom before you can begin final rehearsal and prepare to shoot.

Finally, with a set of headphones and a Comtek cordless receiver from the sound mixer[39], I could hear what the actors were saying! Most of the production team would huddle around the monitor so that they could watch the filming. I soon realized that this was not the best choice for me. Back in theatre school, Patrick Tucker (of First Folio fame) taught me Acting for Film and TV. One suggestion he had for learning about film acting was to watch the performers with the sound off. This kept you from being swallowed whole by the story, and allowed you to focus on just what the actors were doing. I have found that, as a dialect coach, the corollary appears to be true—turn off the visual and you can hear what they are doing much better. So I would huddle myself in a corner with the script or sides in one hand, pen in the other, circling words and noting scene, setup and take numbers[40] in the margins. As soon as the take was finished I would do my best to squeeze onto the set in order to give Tom some feedback. Often that would be one or two words, and over the course of the day's shooting, I would need to do this less. At first, though, it was very difficult getting past the crew and insisting on the time to coach Tom between takes. The actors, particularly Jessica Lange, were eager not to have much time between takes, and wanted to get on with the business of acting. So the AD again tried to keep me from getting to the actors.

In a frantic email, I wrote to Rocco Dal Vera[41] for advice. He suggested that I carry a pad of paper and write with a large marker the offending words that needed adjustment. Thinking this a brilliant idea, I armed myself with 4 different colors of Sharpies and a pad. The next morning, I stepped onto the edge of the set and held up my sign, only to have Tom tell me that he was terribly shortsighted and that he couldn't see a word! Back to the drawing board. Ultimately, I learned to insist that I must have time to do my job, and slid onto set with the hair and makeup people who were doing "final touches" before the next take.

I made a point of working on the idea of preceding good news with bad, always encouraging Tom with his dialect successes before reminding him of the glitches. I have found that if one is only the bearer of bad news,

39. The *Sound Mixer* is probably the most important person on the film crew and developing a healthy relationship with him/her and his cable puller and boom operator is essential. I was blessed with the wise professionalism of David "Obi" Obermeyer, who patiently answered my dumb questions, and chatted with me during the endless hours of waiting. It has been pointed out by other film coaches that a direct connection (with wired headphones) to the mixer's sound board gets better fidelity in hearing exactly what is being recorded than a wireless Comtek.

40. These numbers are written on the clapperboard for each take, and spoken aloud by the sound mixer - so if you pay attention, he/she will tell you what to write down for each take.

41. Rocco Dal Vera, editor of The Voice and Speech Review has served as a dialect coach on countless productions. His advice was just what I needed.

actors begin to dislike your appearance on set. At one point, during a scene shot with just Jessica and Tom, Jessica remarked to Tom as I approached, "Oh no, you're in trouble now!" as a joke. Though Tom didn't really get the joke at the time, the effect on me was quite powerful. It was as if she was saying that my job was to chastise Tom for his mistakes rather than guide him toward greater success. Granted, I was a little oversensitive, but it made me wary of Ms. Lange, and I made a conscious effort to support Tom's work by encouraging as much as possible.

I made it a goal for myself that, taken as a whole, each set-up would have all the words spoken correctly on at least one take. Recording the glitches in a manner that would be helpful in the editing process was also a process of trial and error. At first I would speak with the Continuity person[42] after each setup to describe what mistakes had been made and at which point. But soon it became apparent that a page of notes could be passed on to the editor at the end of the day. I observed that the sound mixer also handed in a daily report that covered the recording process. He had a stock of forms printed for the film with columns for Date, Scene, Setup and Take numbers, and Comments. The forms were done with carbonless copies so that he could keep a copy for himself. This was a very wise idea, one that I regret not copying on this production. I handed in my notes at the end of the day, and I no longer have any notes on those takes aside from what I wrote in my script. In the future, I plan to make forms like this so that I too can keep a record for myself. Preparing for post-production, I was very glad to have my notes in my script.

One of my worst moments was the day that I realized on the last take of the day that I had missed a sound change through every setup of the day. There are some sound changes that Tom would make that aren't GenAm, yet which sound naturally "right" to me because I'm Canadian, as these British features are part of "General Canadian."[43] In this case, Tom was saying "to*mor*row morning" and making the vowel in the second syllable of the first word match the first syllable in second word. "tuh-More-oh,"[44] which is wrong for this part of the Midwest. As the last take of the day was not on Tom, I knew that there was no point in trying to fix it at that point. I prayed that we'd be able to fix it in post!

The other Canadian thing that got me into trouble is the word "been". In British and Canadian speech, this word is pronounced to rhyme with "bean"[45] when it's in a stressed position. This word stands out like a sore thumb to all Americans, particularly directors and producers of films. Though Tom could be perfect with every other sound in a scene, if this word popped up incorrectly pronounced, the producer and director would come to me and say "He's sounding too Britishy." Naturally, I would ask "what part of his speech is catching your ear?" Invariably it was the word "been". So, after a few days of this, I learned to search out the offending word in every instance. "Too Britishy" was a vague term that kept coming back to me, often as a result of acting issues that were beyond my scope.

A case in point was when Tom was working on a scene later in the script, where his transformation from male to female was further along. From my point of view, the fear was that Tom would look and sound like the cast of

42. aka the Script Girl in the bad old days

43. Technically speaking, there is no such beast as "General Canadian." I grew up with an Ontario (Ottawa Valley) regionalism, with strong influences from my mother's Montreal and my father's South-Central Ontario dialects.

44. [təˈmoɹˌɹoʊ] should have been [təˈmɑˌɹoʊ]

45. [bɪn]→[bin] strong form in British and Canadian.

Monty Python in drag. His costuming and wig were mature, to say the least, as they had to make choices that worked with Tom's large frame and big head. My feeling was that Tom's model for this kind of character was a more matronly type woman, which is more of a British stereotype than a Midwestern one. He was being perceived as British because he was acting British, rather than because he was sounding British. The area where his sound probably needed work was in the area of intonation, which was definitely the most difficult aspect of the dialect to discuss. The sound-change errors he was making were ones that I knew he could fix, but they kept slipping in repeatedly. The director seemed to lack confidence in Tom in this moment, and he seemed to be struggling with the right way to make the scene work.

On the other hand, if Tom was comfortable with his acting preparation, the choices he had made, if he "knew what he was doing" as he would say, these issues would disappear, and the offending words would seem to correct themselves. On days when Tom had a particularly challenging scene, my skills were needed even more. The problem was that Tom knew when he was having difficulty, and so my appearance on set was another reminder of those challenges. On those days I worked the hardest at being supportive. On some occasions, it felt as if Tom and I were conspiring to make this character work, secretively sharing notes and encouragement, and ultimately celebrating victories together.

This transformational role, of a man who becomes a woman, was very challenging. From my vantage point, it appeared that Tom didn't really like to do too much research. For the voice of this transgendered person, Roy-becoming-Ruth, Tom chose that he would maintain his own voice up until the point when he felt he was pretty much completely changed into a woman. I was curious about how he planned to sound when he got to the stage where the script called for him to be feminine to the extent that his father, suffering with Alzheimer's disease, is fooled by his transformation. We discussed a number of possibilities for the character, based upon the ideas I worked on with a private transgendered client. Tom made it clear that he wasn't comfortable with raising his voice; after our discussion he left me with something that sounded an awful lot like "it will be there on the day." So when that day came, I was excited to hear what Tom had concocted for Ruth's voice. As we prepared for the day's dialect demands, Tom disclosed that he had chosen to go "husky, like Kathleen Turner." This was an interesting choice and certainly played into the breathier quality that often is used by transgendered male-to-female individuals. His husky voice was a *lower* pitch[46] than when he had been in the midst of the male-female shift. However, because he spoke the majority of it off his voice, in a very breathy manner, this deep sound was effectively masked. All I can say is I am extremely thankful for the sound enhancement of the Comtek wireless headset; without it I would have heard absolutely nothing on those days.

Recurring Issues

The kinds of notes that I gave soon became predictable, and most of them were small details in the difference between British casual speech and American:

46. During the course of the shoot, it had become clear that Tom's voice was a true basso profundo. In a scene shot in the first week, where Tom was needed to sing in a choir, I had been brought in to coach Tom's learning of the song, as I have been a chorister all my life. In exploring the melody of the song it became clear that Tom needed the song to be lower in his register. We re-arranged the song so that Tom could sing the higher parts of the song down the octave, and Tom tried it out. When he came to the part where the song dropped very low, even in the original arrangement, Tom easily took that down the octave, a full fifth below a low C (G_1).

- "loved you" needed to be "love-jew"
- lateral plosions of \t\ into \l\, as in "cute look," needed to be avoided
- final Rs needed more rhoticity
- words like "all, always" were too rounded (not in the PALM[47] lex-set)
- intervocalic-Ts, like "better, isn't it" were too crisp or aspirated; they needed to be more D-like
- words like "poor" needed to be pronounced the same as "pour"
- MOUTH words, like "out, now" were too open (they began with [ɑ])
- short LOT words, like "off, God," were too rounded (LOT should merge with PALM)
- GOOSE words, like "loose," featured onglides
- in trying to avoid the onglide in GOOSE, in a words like "use," he would get stuck in the middle with a Scots/Irish type vowel [ʉ]
- GOAT words, like "Oh no," weren't rounded enough [ʌʊ]
- liquid Us, like "knew," weren't dropped
- TRAP words, like "hammer," were too open [a]
- words like "marry" needed to be like "merry"
- DRESS words, like "pleasant," were too close

One word that was a huge challenge was Jessica Lange's character name, Irma. The final vowel tended to lead Tom into a pronunciation which featured a slightly intrusive R. Getting him to really open up to the STRUT vowel, particularly when he finished a phrase or sentence ending in "Irma" was an endless challenge. I found it somewhat frustrating when Tom would change "Honey" in the script to "Irma", adding yet another instance of the word!

One of the most daunting aspects of film making for me was the endless hours of waiting for the shot to be ready. Once the blocking rehearsal was over, Tom would go into Hair and Makeup and I would be left to wait. Often it would be two hours before the shot would be lit and Tom would emerge from the trailer done up like a fifty-something lady. In those two hours, I often spent my time reading or writing, or, once their set-up was done, talking with the sound mixer, boom operator or cable puller. Later in the day, once the first shot was done and the lighting was being redone, I often spent the time in conversation with Tom and other crewmembers. I'm afraid to say that I am not the world's most comfortable maker of small talk, and this is a *big deal* on the set of a film. Chat is an important aspect of the life of the crew; what was appropriate discussion material took some time to learn. As many members of the crew lived in Chicago, discussing good food and drink establishments in town was always a safe bet, though it's something I know little about. Films that members of the crew had worked on previously were topics that lent themselves to a few good anecdotes. And for the crewmember based in LA, discussion of where you live, and what your home was like, always bore fruit.

Six weeks after filming began, we wrapped. I missed the last few days of shooting due to a teaching engagement I had booked six months before I got hired for the "few days of coaching" on this film. I prepared Tom as best I could for those days by rehearsing those scenes while on set my last day. There was little else I could do. I felt quite confident because in the last week,

47. For those unfamiliar with Wells' Lexical Sets, the PALM group features the unrounded open back vowel [ɑ]. Many Midwesterners pronounce this word with a very dark L [ɫ], which causes the preceding vowel to be darkened considerably to [ɔ]. However, words like "All, always" don't get so darkened, and may have little to no L quality in some settings.

Tom's dialect had gotten to the point where I wasn't giving him many notes on set.

Post-Production

At the very end of September, I got a call from the post-production manager to find out whether I would be available to travel to LA to coach Tom during looping.[48] A week before my trip out, I was sent a copy of the rough cut so that I could review the film and make suggestions for lines to be re-done in the ADR studio. I was very pleased with the quality of the film, and made a series of suggestions that I ranked for the Director of ADR on a scale of one to three. Those lines given a "3" *had* to be redone, "2" *should* be redone, and "1" could be skipped if necessary, as the dialect issue would only be noticed by the most judgmental listener. On arrival at the looping studio, it became clear that we were only doing those marked "2" or "3." In reviewing the film, I discovered that the "tomorrow morning" line I had so agonized over had been cut, and there had been nothing to worry about! I felt validated in noting that the majority of the lines marked "3" had been filmed on the days I wasn't available.

When Tom arrived, he announced that he *hated* looping, and then proceeded to demonstrate his remarkable skill at this performing challenge. After warming up with a few lines, which took several takes, Tom became a veritable one-take-wonder, and zipped through the day. One of the reasons why my job had been fairly easy was clearly demonstrated on our looping day: Tom has a fantastic ear for dialogue. He could recreate a line with exactly the same pitch, quality and inflection after more than 3 months down time. I was glad I was there to challenge him to be more accurate, on the few instances where one or two words began to sound somewhat Irish.

I did have to make some compromises. For instance, on a line where Tom stammered his line delivery (very effectively, I must say), there was no way that he would be able to match it. I had to concede that it was a fairly minor deviation from what I perceived the dialect to be.

I feel that I was extremely lucky to work with such a talented actor for my first foray into the land of film. It was a gentle introduction to the hard world of film. Yet, I don't plan to aggressively chase film jobs, at least for the next few years. The aspect of the job that had the greatest impact on my life was the film's schedule. With a young family, it was extremely difficult for me to be away from home for a week. At the end of our looping, Tom implied that he would really like to work with me again, but he knew that I wasn't really interested in being separated from my family for months at a time. I loved my experience, but the lifestyle isn't for me at this point in my life.

48. Looping is the process whereby actors do "additional dialogue recording," or ADR, for the film in post-production (after filming has ceased). Short clips of the film are looped (played repeatedly) and the actor rerecords his lines while watching it projected on a large screen.

Essay *by David Smukler*

Dialogue Coaching for Film: One Part of My Work

Definition of a Dialogue (Dialect) Coach

The Dialogue or Dialect Coach on a film or television production is one of the craft people at the service of the directors and producers to help the performance of the talent. Each project has different requirements and needs. The primary task is to aid the actor(s) create the illusion that the human behavior and the speech and language patterns reflect a particular community or world.

The first step in creating the illusion is to create the world which shapes the particular physical patterns, the language patterns, the vocal patterns, psychological influences, cultural influences, and finally the specific speech sounds. The next point to investigate is what are the specific clues (the short hand) that will make this particular world recognizable or definable for the audience. The technical information around any dialect needs to be adjusted to fit the actor, the character and all those other elements that help to create the illusion that we are in modern Istanbul or 19th century Moscow.

How I Stumbled into Being a Dialogue Coach

My early childhood was spent in a totally Eastern European urban neighborhood where multiple languages flowed in and out of English and I was unable to distinguish one language from another. In fact, I didn't gain a sense of spoken American English language until Edith Skinner told me how I should be speaking. I did not have natural skills as a mimic. Hopelessly struggling to speak in dialect class with Edith, I put my time and effort into writing out the phonetics clearly. I became good enough to help my classmates write their assignments for them. Edith quickly figured out that I wrote out many of the dialect homework sheets even though I could not utter them effortlessly. There was obviously potential because she sent me to Teachers College at Columbia University to train to be a phonetician. Alas, I found out that no one was teaching phonetics and I focused my Masters degree on Speech Pathology and other areas of speech and drama education.

When fate (and a push from Edith) led me to Kristin Linklater and Voice Teacher Training, the amazing discoveries of finding my voice and discovering how to live and teach from an embodied psycho-somatic approach knocked any thought or interest in dialects out the window. For the next ten years, I would have nothing to do with speech training and dialects unless it was demanded of me. Yet, right from the start of my career with half the year in New York with the Open Theatre and NYU and the other half at the Stratford Ontario Shakespeare Festival, I sensed that I was living and working in two different body voices and two different languages (dialects).

When I moved to England I had to find "my voice" in the theatre RP immediately. Interestingly, most of my private coaching was with actors and singers for whom English was a second language or their dialect was not RP and they needed help to find their voices in English RP.

When the opportunity came to work in the Netherlands. I made the commitment to myself that I was going to master another language well enough so that I understood what it felt like to think, feel, teach and perform in a language that was not native to me. It was hard work, but I got to the point where I could do various Dutch dialects in Dutch and I began to actually

David Smukler, one of the senior voice teachers in the Canadian theatre, is Director of the National Voice Intensive held each May in Vancouver, is on the faculty of York University's Department of Theatre, as well as teaching professional classes at Equity Showcase Theatre. As a voice coach in Canada, England, the Netherlands, and the United States, he has worked in the entire range of theatre from classical theatre, opera, musical theatre, film, television, radio, to contemporary and experimental theatre and music with such companies as: Stratford Ontario Shakespeare Festival (nine seasons), Alberta Theatre Projects, Canadian Stage, The Royal Alex, The National Arts Centre (Canada); the Tyrone Guthrie and the Open Theatre (United States), the Royal Court and the English Opera Group (England); as well as the Apple, Centrum and Globe theatre companies in the Netherlands. He has taught at NYU's Tisch School of the Arts, Carnegie-Mellon University, LAMDA, the Toneelschool (Amsterdam), the National Theatre School, the Native Theatre School, Simon Fraser University, The University of Calgary and other actor training institutions across Canada. Mr. Smukler is in demand as a dialogue coach for film and television productions.

sound like a Frenchman or German in my limited skill in those two languages.

An important event for me occurred one day in Amsterdam. We were in the 5th or 6th week of the fall term. I was teaching a first year class who had never heard me speak English except when I asked for a translation at a meeting. I cannot remember what I was attempting to communicate, but it was probably something to do with tapping their actor sources when I realized they weren't getting it. I knew that they had heard me. My voice was coming from a clean source inside me. They probably got frightened and went into classic student role of "Something happened that I don't understand. I'm confused. I don't know what you mean." So I said to them let me explain what we have just done. I made every effort to make sure that the information was absolutely intellectually correct and as I spoke, I simultaneously read the shock on their faces and realized that my voice had shifted from the Dutch Utrecht dialect to a British RP in the Dutch language. Excited by this discovery I then said, let me give you an emotional example; breathed down and out of me came my voice in a mid-western American voice in Dutch. I now knew that I was finally in possession of a road map down and that this road map was not only the one for language English words and feelings, but it was the road map for living and acting in different languages and dialects.

The next big step came eight years later after a Sunday afternoon run-through of *Death of a Salesman* at the 1983 Stratford Festival. After the run-through the director and I talked through some vocal problems but nothing was said about dialects. Prior to rehearsals we had agreed that dialects were not necessary. Then I drove back to Toronto for my day off. When I arrived home in Toronto, there was a message on the answering machine from Stage Management asking me to coach all the Canadian actors in New York dialects on Tuesday morning. The Willie Loman was so heavily Brooklyn that he was throwing everyone out of balance. When I recovered from my panic, I got on the telephone and telephoned friends in New York City. On Tuesday morning, I coached New York dialects.

One year later, on a Thursday afternoon, I received a phone call from a film production company asking if I could coach Scottish Dialect on Monday. I had the wisdom to ask which Scottish dialect. When they got back to me on Saturday, I had already begun preparation. Every time they put back the first day of shooting I got to practice more. By the time I met with the cast on Friday afternoon, I was comfortable with the "Ayrshire". Monday on set, there were so many problems getting a pair of oxen across a wooden bridge that I got to coach

only one line while the three producers (Scots, Canadian and American) fought over how heavy or how light the dialect should be. I was very flattered when the Scot kept complimenting me on what I had done.

Twenty years later I face the same problems on almost every film and television coaching job:
1. They call in the coach at the last possible minute.
2. They often request the wrong dialect.
3. There rarely is adequate prep time for either actor or coach.
4. Often the director and the producer or producers fight to claim authority over the coach.
5. There can be everything from a minor discussion to an acrimonious confrontation around the degree or texture of the dialect.
6. The script will call for a particular dialect but it is neither written nor phrased for that dialect.
7. We spend hours waiting for technical problems to be solved. The oxen are more important than the acting.
8. The production companies are chronically late in paying me for prep work, even with a union contract. Will I have to wait six weeks or six months for my check? Thank God for the agent.

Getting the Coaching Job
Originally, the calls came from the casting directors. Now it is usually the local production manager who contacts the agent or me. For ten years I have helped to build a team of eight of us who do dialect coaching through one agent. We cover dialogue coaching, acting coaching, movement coaching and there is one child specialist. There are probably three or four additional coaches serving the Toronto industry. Most of us do it around our teaching schedules. In winter, I do mostly prep work and go on set in the summer and on weekends.

The Call
A regular feature of a Friday is the late afternoon telephone call from a production company or my agent. I have never understood why, when they have known for two weeks that they needed a coach, they haven't given us any warning. Sixty percent of the time, the request is for a dialect or language that I do not know. I am to coach the actor, the "star" in their hotel room on Sunday evening and they go to set on Monday morning. Within an hour the script is at the door. I read the script and do a breakdown. I then spend Saturday hunting down a native speaker of the dialect or rummaging through my tapes and reference materials. Somehow, I arrive at Mr. or Ms. X's hotel room at 7 PM on Sunday evening and I coach.

Preparing the Script
No matter whether I have a lot of time to prepare the script or

a short time, I mark my script. For the first reading, I go for story, mood, atmosphere, location, style, and who the characters are. The second step is to look at the character's journey through the script. I try to be sensitive to anything that might impact upon the dialect and how the character might use the dialect to achieve their character goals. I look for their world (social, economic, political and cultural clues). I look for possible physical and language clues for the character and dialect. I look for how the writing supports the dialect or may complicate it. Then I start researching the cultural background of the character or characters that I will be working with. If the Production Company has any research materials, like videos, I request copies.

Then I will focus on the actual dialect. I will then mark my script in IPA or other appropriate notations. I note voice placement, rhythms, intonation patterns, stress, tone, etc. The other notations may be other sources or influences including painters, music, writers, geography, political, social and historical events that impact upon these people as wess as any other clues. I need as much ammunition as possible to be ready to improvise with the actor.

Materials

One of the most important things for me to come out of the investigation of dialects is an understanding of style. I scour the Sunday New York Times, National Geographic and other journals for clues about changing styles and cultures and how they are manifested in the walk and talk of a particular society. I obsessively collect books on languages and cultures. I have file drawers of clippings.

I try to keep my eyes and ears open to the social, economic, geographic, cultural and linguistic elements of cultures for insights to a particular dialect. It is as important for me to evolve a physical sense of the world of these people as to know why they make the sound changes or rhythms that are theirs. I now read fiction to hear the character's voices.

I collect videos of all kinds of movies in order to build a library of insights. I don't care about the acting work but will it give me insights into Trinidadian, Iranian or Mexican society? Will it give me behavioral clues? Will it give me social-economic information and how that affects the voices of the characters? I keep files on each of the dialects I collect.

I listen to the radio and the television to try to catch clues about the speaker and what they represent. I attempt to imitate the voices I hear on the radio.

Working With the Actor

The very first step with the actor is that I need to know their

vocabulary. I need to know how to talk with them so that I am giving them the most efficient clues possible. At our first meeting I try to get them to talk about their background, their training, the important elements of the particular character and script and to hear how they talk. Sometimes I have to spell it out for them. Have they done dialects before, how do they like to be coached, what are their concerns. Sometimes, it feels that I have to set up stupid questions, and do silly chatter as I search for the way into the work. All of this needs to be done in about ten minutes. I want to know how I should most effectively work with them.

Typical Problems Prior to Going on Set

1. The actor has never acted with a dialect before in their career.

This can be complicated when the actor has modified their original language or dialect. I seem to be making a specialty of aiding British actors in their first experience with a North American dialect. One successful British actor had only worked in his own regional dialect. At our first session he was almost white with fear and trepidation. Slowly and gently we talked about how he worked. Over a two-day period we actually were able to reduce his dialect of origin, but then a strange pattern began to appear. He began to slide into a lispy campy pattern and I broke out into a cold sweat. Had I unleashed something that this man didn't know about? Then I realized that this other thing I was beginning to hear was actually another dialect. I asked him to talk about where he lived in London. He offered that when he and his wife moved to London, the locals could not understand his dialect of origin, so he had layered on local patterns. I was relieved. I told him what my experience had been over the past minutes and we had a good laugh and he was then able to quickly cut through his double dialect layer and begin to actually identify the sensations of the desired North American pattern. The three co-stars were an American, a Canadian and this Brit. The first day of dialogue on set, I just sat with the three of them and helped them find a common pattern for them to work with. I just listen for clues and to make sure that they were having fun sorting out their common dialect. Later that afternoon in an interior close up the director kept the Brit on camera asking for dozens of different ad-libs while the poor guy sweated. But, he stayed in North American no matter what and I was proud of the work we had done.

2. The actor does not have much of a technique and doesn't have a clue how to work with a dialect or work with a coach.

One of the most difficult tasks was working with two actors who were playing brothers. One was a highly disciplined graduate of an acting program, the other had no formal training and been picked up as a natural. In his first year and a half in the film industry he had done four or five films but had no sense of craft. He would demand help but couldn't retain it. When he had trouble on set with anything, I became the scapegoat. It was my fault that he was having trouble.

3. They have forty pages of text and we have two hours.
A recent job was complicated because I needed two different French dialects. Not only was I to prepare a dialect of Haitian in the English language, I needed to find translators for both Parisian French and Haitian French. The two Haitian characters spoke Creole to each other and Creole dialect English to others. The actor speaking the Parisian did not need coaching. The dialects covered two episodes of a series. I was put on standby on a Tuesday. I received the scripts Wednesday night. Thursday afternoon, I tracked down translators and typed out copies of the specific lines for the translations. Saturday, I was able to tape the Haitian. Sunday night, I received two additional pages of text to be translated. On Tuesday evening I was scheduled to coach the two actors in the Haitian. I had exactly two hours per actor to coach both the actual Haitian Creole as well as accented English. Just before I was to start coaching, the production office faxed me more text to be translated and coached. Fortunately, both of these actors were bi-lingual, but one of these two actors spoke French with a Quebecois accent and the other with Franco-Ontarian accent. The two lovers met for the first time in my living room as one arrived for coaching and the other was leaving. My heart went out to them; they were scheduled to shoot all the big emotional scenes the following morning. I was not going to be on set. All I could do was hope and pray that I had given them enough clues and that their tape recorders would be working with their tapes of the translator's voice and of their coaching sessions.

4. They were hired the previous day and they have not yet figured out who the character is and they go on set the next morning.
This is a regular pattern in the industry. About two years ago, the call on Friday afternoon was to coach an "Irish" dialect. The actor would arrive from Australia that evening. They sent over the script. Everything indicated Northern Ireland. At midnight I got the go ahead for Northern Ireland. I met the actor on Saturday afternoon after he had a music rehearsal. I sat with the actor and the producer, who was actually very helpful and we plotted the character and the dialect in two hours. The actor had Sunday to get over his jet lag, learn the lines and do the character work and be on set Monday morning. The following week, I get a call; they would like to change the dialect from Northern Ireland to Dublin, because it was going to be too difficult for the general American audience to relate to the Belfast choice. The producers were not

concerned about continuity because there would be a week between the two episodes. Ten days later I coached his murderers. Although the script indicated the North, I coached them on Dublin.

5. They have had difficult experiences with coaches in the past.
One actor spent three quarters of our first session telling me all his horror stories about coaches. My task is to keep trying to take back the session by asking how I can help. I need to balance this item with telling you about one of the most delightful experiences. I was called in to work with one of the most beautiful women in the industry whose third language is English. All of her English film work is with an accent. She had done excellent preparation of the role with one of the New York City colleagues but as she started to improvise on the set the actress was finding problems with the script. She had obtained permission of the director and the producers to rewrite scenes and build upon what she had been developing. I spent several Saturdays in unabashed pleasure working the scenes, sorting out word and pronunciation choices. Another "star" was such a grump during our first session that I thought the whole thing was a waste of time. I was shocked the next day when I found her beaming. She had spent the day trying out my unorthodox suggestions and they had worked.

6. They actually know the dialect better than I do.
Here my task is to listen for consistency. I listen for placement, rhythmic, intonation and melodic patterns.

7. They want to use me as an acting coach or to hold their hand.
I try to be careful and focus all chatter into the framework of character and cultural information that would influence the actor choices and therefore the dialect.

8. Often, I am given a budget and told that I have to do all the coaching within the certain budget.
This is usually a situation of preparing samples of the dialect on tape for the actors and sending them out. When it is applicable or when I am unable to obtain audio material, I will write out a descriptive guide sheet giving lots of social, economic, political cultural and behavioral clues and the sound clues in a non-IPA phonetic pattern. The production companies sends out tapes and guide sheets along with scripts. Then it comes down to sitting on the telephone. When this happens, I have to keep a telephone time sheet. Five minutes with actor 'A', ten minutes with actor 'B'. The tighter the budget, the fussier the Production Company is about record keeping. When I telephone I ask if the tape or the printed material was

useful. If I get a brush-off, I try to gently point out a couple of clues that the director will be looking for. I find that a useful suggestion is that when they go on set that they are prepared to work with both a heavier and a lighter version of the dialect.

9. I find that I have to be extremely sensitive to coaching communities that are sensitive to their status in society in general.

I am a tall thin white male from Eastern European ancestry with a big voice and a non-specific dialect. Here it is important to make sure that I do not come across as an expert on their culture but I am there as their assistant.

10. Coaching films that are based on actual events creates its own problems.

One particular docu-drama required that I watched twenty-four hours of the rough footage of the news reports covering the events and tape audio samples from it. On this particular piece I had to set up tapes for each segment of society: upper-class Afro-American male, middle-class Afro-American male, working-class Afro-American male, Upper-class Afro-American female, middle-class Afro-American female, working-class Afro-American female, upper-class white male, middle-class white male, working-class white male, upper-class white female, middle-class white female, working-class white female. The director and I went through the character list and plotted out who would receive the appropriate tape.

Physical Aspects of Coaching On and Off Set

The key event on set is being there for the actor, being an external pair of ears. With each actor, everything hinges on reading them to find out when they are receptive to receive coaching. The degree of receptivity can vary from take to take.

There is never a seat for the coach. Sometimes we can use the chairs set for the actors. A year or two ago I bought my own camp chair which I can fold up and sling over my shoulder. I try to set myself up as close to the monitors as possible. The dialogue coach is a low man on the totem pole. I have worked on sets where the director and continuity welcomed me to be with them on the monitors and had other experiences where it was clearly indicated to me that I was a necessary evil and should stay as far away as possible.

There are practical things: make sure they spell my name correctly, if I leave the set early I am faxed the next day's call sheets, I have a room in a honey wagon or other private space set aside. I make sure that I have a crew list and learn the names of the people that I will primarily interact with. I get a "Day out of Days", which is the scene break down so that I know exactly when I expect to be called. Often, I have to

badger for sides (hand holdable copies of the daily call sheet with the text of that day's scenes). When I get the sides I transfer all my notes from my main script. Sometimes I have to fight for a space in a honey wagon although the contract calls for it. I collect a set of earphones each morning from sound and return them at the end of the day. I always have pencils with good erasers to make notes and script changes. On a feature film there is usually time to establish a good relationship with continuity and I try to let them know if one particular take had a better dialect than another did.

When I actually go on set, I take plenty of reading. I try to have a book that I can rest my sides on. I try to stay in contact with the continuity person, the ADS [Assistant Directors] and the sound people.

When to go in to give notes again varies from actor to actor, scene to scene, production to production. It is quite frustrating when we are unable to establish a good rhythm. One of the more pleasurable coaching jobs allowed the leading man and me to do thumbs up or thumbs down communication at the end of each take and then we didn't fuss but could do the notes when he was ready.

Where do we do the coaching? Guess? Right! We use every available space. When it is an out of town actor, most of the preparatory coaching is done in their hotel rooms. There have been situations where the bodyguard was in the room. When coaching on one series, the lead actor's character would "play characters" and he played in various dialects in order to track down the villains. Often they were shooting two or three episodes at the same location, so I would hang around the set and coach in every free corner that we could find. I loved those trips to the set at eleven o'clock at night. One particular morning, I coached him in a southern dialect and around nine in the evening the production office telephoned. They had forgotten that his co-star also needed a southern dialect for a scene the next morning. I was at hair and make up at 6 the next morning for the co-star. She arrived, said hello and I sat and listened to the gossip for almost two hours. (I was on payroll) and then at 8 AM we rode to set and we started working. The scene was in a gas station. As we arrived at location it began to rain, so we stood on the forecourt of the gas station with me holding an umbrella as we worked through a very hot sexual confrontation until they called the shot. Then I walked her up to the office and stood there while she walked in, dialect and acting work at full sexual drive and scared the pants off the actor playing the villain. At which point, she winked at me and the producers thanked me and off I went.

Last March [2002], on a pilot, there were so many helicopter scenes that I became just another static on the walkie-talkies and one scene I was coaching from a city block away. It seemed that every time I could actually get through to my actor, they told me they had the shot and were moving onto the next one. It was on that pilot that I was called in for eleven a.m. at a farm an hour's drive out of the city. We finished at 5.30 the next morning with a chase scene in the woods. At least the actor and I had a good two-hour nap on the farmhouse floor between one and three in the morning. From location, I drove right to the university and slept on my office floor for an hour and then taught four hours of big energy exercises.

One crazy experience involved going on set with a Russian actor who had scenes in both Russian and English. They wanted a coach on set to make sure that his English was understandable. I had been at rehearsals to insure that the Anglophone actors playing Russian characters were in the same dialect patterns as the Russian-speaking actors. One particularly difficult scene was in a restaurant. The scene was to be played in Russian with English subtitles. The director realized that although I am not a Russian speaker, I was the only person who was able to follow the Russian text. I became an assistant director and did all the cueing, which was fine until the Russian-speaking actors started ad-libbing and I had to hold them to the agreed text. I enjoyed hero status with the director and the ADs for about fifteen minutes.

That does not make up for the time when I sat in the honey wagon waiting for the call that never came. I checked with the AD several times and kept reminding them to call me when my actor walked to set. I then fell asleep. They forgot to call me. I missed a scene completely. I am a nuisance for the ADs. Dialogue coaches are often at the bottom of the list.

Styles of Coaching

When going in to meet the actor for the first time, there are usually only minutes to figure out what is the most useful style of coaching for that actor. If I am lucky I can prepare samples. Too often, I have been given the wrong information. One production company told me that I would be coaching a leading Italian actor in a working class Latin American dialect. All the references in the script were to working class Bolivia. I arrived at the hotel with samples of Panama, Costa Rica and Bolivia to work from. On the way to the actor's hotel room, I met with the director and he said, no, this particular character was to be from Argentina. As there was so much Italian influence in Argentina, the priorities was to help reduce the Italianisms from the body and voice. Fortunately, the actor had a tape of an Argentinean speaking in English. That led to two hours of pure improvisation on my part.

On several films, there has been an acting coach. Usually this means that the actors have an established relationship with the acting coach. My favorite experience working with an acting coach involved two stars who had worked with her for several years. At our first meeting I barreled in by asking her what her vocabulary was. I told her that as dialogue coach, I didn't want the actors to have to deal with two layers of vocabulary, so that I would try to frame my coaching in her vocabulary. This led to a pleasant working relationship. All through the shoot, she kept saying that she had never worked with a dialogue coach who cared for anything but the correct sounds.

Coaching in ADR (Audio Digital Recording-post production voice work) as with coaching on set can run the gamut of situations. Each time I have done coaching for ADR it has been a situation where I had not been on set and I was called in because the director or the producers wanted to make changes. In ADR, I have helped change dialects, adjusted vocal qualities, put in sounds for other characters and helped the actor fix problems that came up in the editing.

Why Do I Do It?

For me, in the daily practice of the voice work, the premise is to allow the breath to drop into the individual's sources, into the sensations, intuitions, emotions, feelings and thoughts which lie at the core of each of us. Each breath takes us to what is familiar and yet unknown. This also applies to my experience in languages and dialects. Each time I engage in an investigation of a culture or society's language or dialect it is frightening, challenging and strangely comforting. Dialect work forces me to redefine my voice. It is an even greater challenge to share this with a colleague. These challenges live at the very core of my search for my own sense of language and voice.

Essay *by Mel Churcher*

Sound Speed: Voice on Film

This article stresses the importance of a fully-supported voice for actors working in film, and offers advice on how they can avoid replacing too much dialogue in post-production. It examines the differences between vocal production for theatre and film, looks at the importance of unimpeded breath flow for both the visual as well as the aural aspects of filming, and explains why the actor may need more volume than she or he expects. There are some hints and tips for voice teachers working with actors on preparation of film scripts and to help with those last-minute vocal problems.

Many actors have a mistaken idea that they can whisper and mumble their way through a film. One well-known actor, who whispers her way through the shooting and knows she'll have to replace every line, has learnt not to move her mouth to make ADR easier! Now both sound and performance suffer.

ADR, or automatic dialogue replacement, enables the actor to replace lines after shooting by doing a new sound track, which will be married onto the final print. Hollywood actors, who accept it as a way of life and often prefer it, call it looping. This is because, in the old days, before digital technology, the clip of film the actor matched to went round and round on a loop.

Nowadays, technology has moved on, but ADR is still no ideal solution. All film makers prefer to be in the happy position of using the original soundtrack. The verisimilitude of the original ambience and the energy of the performance can never completely be matched. ADR has to be done months after shooting, alone in a sound studio and all lines have to be timed exactly to match the original mouth movements. The actor watches the clip of film on a screen and a white line passes across it, three beeps sound in the actor's ear, and the line must be said on the instant of the imaginary fourth beat. The actor has to find the same emotional energy, sound level (made harder as all background noise has been removed from the track) and remember the plot whilst probably already engaged on a completely different project. Without craning the neck forward and reducing the voice to a squeak, the actor has to whisper sweet nothings into the microphone's ear with no popping plosives while watching that embarrassing original footage time after time after time as he or she misses the beat.

Every sound mixer has the intention to use the original soundtrack as it will contain the natural ambience as well as the spontaneity of the acting. Sometimes this isn't possible because of outside circumstances or the problems of squeaky floorboards or clanging armour, but it can simply be due to the actor's vocal shortcoming. Many film actors have had little or no vocal training and some feel that anything above a breathy whisper is not "real." Because the visual aspects of filming are so important, directors often cast for the perfect "look." This often means a vocal coach is then required on set to help with the dialogue. It is usually much easier for a trained actor, used to theatre, to adjust the volume down to suit the circumstances than for an untrained performer to find a supported resonant sound that will carry intention, feeling and script nuances effectively.

So how can the actor avoid ADR? In film, unlike theatre, there is no audience. So the sound need only be as it would be in life. Instead of playing *to* an

Mel Churcher has worked for many years in drama schools and theatres including the Royal Shakespeare Company, Manchester Royal Exchange, The Royal Court and London's Regent's Park Open Air Theatre and is currently serving on the council of The British Voice Association. Coaching on movies includes *The Secret Garden, The Fifth Element, Joan of Arc, Madeline, The Count of Monte Cristo, Lara Croft: Tomb Raider, 102 Dalmations, The Hole, The Forsyte Saga* (TV) and, most recently, *Danny the Dog* with Jet Li. Mel's book, *Acting for Film: Truth 24 Times a Second* was published by Virgin Books in 2003.

audience, the actor is observed *by* a camera. Only the other characters need to hear the dialogue, and they will usually be standing much closer than in theatre (or even life), in order to fit into frame. Having said that though, it needs to be a whole supported voice at a natural level. No amount of technical wizardry will give emotional life and resonance to a breathy, unsupported sound. And if an actor does need to whisper—it has to be heard. One sound mixer told me a story about Peter O'Toole. He asked the actor, whether it was true that he could be heard in a whisper round the block. Peter O'Toole walked fifty yards away and whispered, "It is true"—and it was!

Sometimes an actor will be asked to give more volume than normal for a shot. There can be several reasons for this:

• Microphone booms often can't get close in wide shots as they will be seen by the camera or create shadows. Sometimes a radio mic can't be used as it makes the sound too "intimate" for the scene.

• There may be unbalanced sound levels between the actors in the scene. This is particularly true if there's a woman playing against hearty men.

• There might be a sound track to be laid underneath the scene later—like a train or rain or dance music. If the actors are too quiet, not only will it be hard for the sound department to get the level up technically, but it will also sound false. In life they would use a different quality of voice to compensate for the background noise.

This last reason is a particularly difficult one for the actors. Whilst playing the scene, they have to constantly imagine that background noise. Inevitably, after a few moments, the actors lose level—especially in an intimate scene.

Boom operators are very skilful. Wielding a long telescopic pole with the microphone attached, they balance precariously above the actor, keeping out of shot, to catch every word that is said. It's important that the actor rehearses at performance level and doesn't vary volume too much on different takes or make any surprise moves. It is also worth checking that the level isn't dropping to match another actor's performance or because the camera has come in close.

Often the actor is fitted with a radio mic. This is hidden on the clothing around the neck and the transmitter is concealed in the petticoats or is strapped to a leg. Tell them to beware silk underwear—it will rustle horribly! Also to avoid noisy jewellery, thumping the chest on "I" and "me" or poking a

partner in the microphone. When using props, dialogue should be separated from any noisy cutlery, keys or loose change. Actors should shut a door or move the drum-kit before or after the line and avoid noisy shoes.

Sometimes there will be a fixed microphone as well. You remember that famous scene in *Singin' in the Rain* where the microphone is hidden in the flowers? Every time the heroine speaks, she turns her head away and the sound fades out mid-sentence. Well, the sound department's resources have become more sophisticated since then, but the actor may still need to favour the microphone's direction and it is certainly helpful not to hit it during dialogue!

In his book on film acting, Michael Caine advises the actor to forget the sound technician as he always has a problem. Because film is so visually oriented and there is the possibility to replace dialogue later, sound *is* the Cinderella of the film industry. And yet sound makes up a great part of the final film's effect. In television particularly—where dialogue is less readily replaced in post-production—many viewers will listen as much as watch. They don't want to miss the plot as they pour a cup of tea or slip a stitch.

We know that voice is the most sensitive indicator of feeling. When a study was carried out on lying, it was discovered that radio revealed the truth more than any other medium. If the actor doesn't use a voice that resonates with the "ring of truth," no amount of visual clues will compensate. Actors need to take voice as seriously as any other aspect of communication on film. Because film deals mainly in subtext, the sound of the voice doesn't seem as important as the feelings underneath. But the two can't be separated. If the thought is strong—the voice will be. If you drive what you want either through the words or under the words, a free released voice will carry your intentions or your subtext.

And if the actor is working in a different dialect, it is important that the voice doesn't lose its full resonance or change the performance in any way that isn't intended. American actors, particularly, have a tendency to let their voices become higher, thinner and generally "nicer" when they move to an English accent. British actors often do the same when confronted with a period movie and a "period" accent.

Dialogue in film, Pinter and Mamet excepted, is not always well written. There are few long speeches and the words may be banal or prosaic. This encourages an actor to hold back the sound—to bring the false vocal folds across, use too little breath and go into "creak." Breathing work is as important in film as in any other branch of performing. This is not because the actor needs to project but because, if the stomach is held, then the voice will not respond freely. Nerves are a real problem in filming. Adrenaline is flowing, the set goes silent, the shot is called, the clapper falls and "Action" rings in the actor's ears. If the actor takes a high clavicular breath—all is lost. The scene will seem false and there will be no access to emotional feelings. If the actor stops breathing, he or she will stop listening. And listening is the most important part of acting in film.

In close-up, the camera acts like a microscope. The face may be blown up to fifty times its real size on a large screen. Every twitch of tension, raised eyebrow or trembling lip will be magnified and seem enormous. Keeping the breath flowing will work wonders to take tension off the face. I advise actors to keep a hand on the abdomen in an emotional close-up. By checking they are breathing and sending their emotional energy from this hand, the face will be relaxed, the eyes alive and the voice responsive. (It also works like magic when an actor wants an intimate confidential tone for a voice-over after shooting.)

Incidentally, when the actor is in a single close-up shot, it is important they don't overlap the dialogue with the off-camera lines. Because, on film, sound and picture are married together at a later date, overlaps make for difficult editing. Level and energy are also required from the actor speaking off-camera to help the person in shot respond in the same way that they did in the original scene.

If you are helping an actor with a film script, it is worthwhile suggesting that they make extensive notes or even write out separate cards for each scene. These notes should take account of the plot situation and relationships to the other characters as well as the character's drives and actions. Because films are shot out of sequence on such a long time-scale, actors need an aide-memoir to help them place a scene in context. Breathing places for new thoughts can also be marked if the actor has a tendency to rush scenes through nerves. As parts of scenes have to be repeated in many takes, whispering the lines slowly just before a take will refresh the original meaning and drives behind the words.

Film actors benefit from the same warm-up as any other performer and I recommend abdominal-diaphragmatic breathing work. I use a simplified version of the "Accent Method" pioneered by the Danish voice therapist, Sven Smith. If the actor has never done voice work before, then getting them to lie down and to feel the rise and fall of the abdomen during relaxed breathing is a good start. This movement can be built on gently with the breath expelled on "sh," feeling the contraction of the abdominal muscles and then their release as the

breath drops in. More energetic breathing exercises can then be introduced, where the breath is expelled on three beats (with the middle beat taking the strongest energy):
sh—sh—sh (flattening stomach gently inwards and upwards) stomach releases and breath drops in
sh—sh—sh
and so on.

Voiced sounds and then words and phrases are added until the actor can ensure that the abdomen is not contracted or held during the incoming breath—thus avoiding clavicular breathing and the "flight or fight" syndrome.

I also use many exercises for resonance and articulation such as humming and feeling vibrations on the body, clasping hands in front and shaking out a sound, hanging over and releasing sound, throwing lines, "chewing" words and singing dialogue—all the work, in fact, that I would use for theatre actors but with the emphasis on resonant, relaxed but supported voice production rather than projection. Sometimes, of course, one is working on an accent too and that will influence the choice of vocal exercises: working on oral or nasal resonance, consonant production, increasing the range of vocal qualities available to the actor or changing tune and cadence.

I add a few quick-tips for emergency help on set:

• If the actor finds the pitch rising—tipping back the head very slightly with an open mouth, and swallowing on the way back down releases tension in the larynx and the pitch will revert to its natural level. If the voice sounds creaky—breathing in and out through the open mouth and making it completely silent will open up the false vocal folds and increase breath flow (putting hands over ears makes it easier to monitor). If the voice is breathy—get a gentle adduction of the vocal folds by wiggling the finger as if telling someone off on "Uh-Uh, Uh-Uh" and take that sound into text.

• If the sound seems to be produced too far back—press the knuckle gently into the alveolar ridge and say the line, then remove the knuckle and repeat the line, imagining that it is bounced off the "buzz" on the hard palate. (This gives a very gentle "edge" or "twang.")

• After several hours on set, ask the actor to siren up and down gently on "ng" a few times—this stretches the vocal folds and then they seem to "mesh" together better giving a more supported sound. (It also helps relieve tired vocal folds.) As sets are often hot, dry places I talk about vocal health and encourage actors to drink enough water, use steam if there is vocal strain and to take the re-hydration drinks offered on hot locations.

• After the twentieth take, the brain stops working and the words lose their meaning. Taking a second to shut the eyes and whisper the words very slowly puts the actor back in touch with the original impulses and intentions.

You will have many little tricks of your own. It's lonely out there on set and the actor has to stop and start so many times that a few tips for tension and voice quality are really helpful. When I mention that an actor in a major role on a feature film works for around twelve weeks (sometimes longer) doing twelve hour days, you will see how many shots and takes there will be to shoot a film. A major movie is only looking to shoot one to two minutes of eventual screen time a day. So there is no chance to "find your voice" or experience the linear journey of the character as there is in theatre.

There is also very little dialogue on most films. To root the voice in the character, or to make the actor comfortable with their own sound, I suggest that he or she improvises some physical work or tasks that the character might do whilst improvising dialogue. For example: I had to work with a softly-spoken Welsh actor who had to play a medieval blacksmith. As part of the preparation for the role he had to learn horse riding. I suggested that he improvised lines when riding and when mucking out the stables. Out of these improvisations emerged a strong resonant sound that was both healthy and right for the role and avoided any quick decision to "take the voice down" which could have led to vocal strain.

The voice that will emerge through this work will be "organic" and grounded in the body so that it not only feels right to the actor but also has enough physical "substance" to please the sound mixer.

There are times when all this work will go for nothing. Concorde keeps going over, the waterfall is too loud or the dialogue was too steamy for the aircraft version. Then ADR will save the day. But with good voice work, the actor will ensure that most of what she or he says will be heard. Heard both in the sound mixer's cans and, because less will end up on the cutting-room floor, in the final film.

As a last thought—it's worth mentioning to actors that they will always have a secret audience on set. The director, producers, sound crew and coaches all wear headphones and all microphones stay on during shooting. There are things they might not want heard—so they should hold back that expletive! And remind them to ask the sound operator to release them from the microphone and transmitter when they need to leave set. I have to confess that on my first film, mine did reach a watery grave!

Book references:
Caine, Michael *Acting in Film* 1990 (Applause)
Kotby, M.N. *The Accent Method of Voice Therapy* Singular Press 1995
Thyme-Frokjaer, K, Frokjaer-Jenson, B *The Accent Method* Speechmark Publishing Ltd. 2001

Essay *by Barbara Houseman*

Preparation for Casting for Film and Television

There are two main difficulties involved in helping a client prepare for a film or TV casting.

First, there is the time factor: actors are rarely given more than a couple of days and sometimes less than 24 hours to prepare anything from one to three scenes. Secondly, there is no way of knowing for sure what interpretation the director is looking for: he or she often won't know themselves until they see it.

So, how do you explore the scene or scenes deeply, even though you are having to work fast, and how do you give the actor a secure enough grounding from which they can shift the character and scene/s in any direction, according to what the director or casting director asks of them?

The work described below can be done in one or two two-hour sessions— which is usually all I have with a client. I have done this work with people of all levels of experience ranging from models, who are beginning to pursue an acting career and have little or no professional training, to well-known actors, who have a raft of stage and film experience behind them, as well as a formal drama school training.

I usually start by reading through the character breakdown the actor has been given. This gives me some sense of what is being looked for at the casting. I then ask the actor to read through the scene or scenes, with myself reading the other part(s) as necessary. This gives me the chance to see where the actor has got to on their own, what is already working for them, and what areas we need to focus on.

I then look at the general scene dynamic. I ask the actor to identify the main emotion or preoccupation in the scene and then to look for what I call the "hidden opposite." For example, the obvious emotion or preoccupation might be determination and certainty, while the hidden opposite might be fear and doubt. I then ask them to imagine a line across the room and ask them to place the main emotion or preoccupation at one end and the hidden opposite at the other and to imagine that the line is a spectrum or continuum sliding from one emotion or preoccupation to the other. The actor stands at a point on the line that they feel represents where they are on the spectrum at the beginning of the scene and the actor reads the scene again, moving up and down the line as feels appropriate as the scene progresses.

The first thing I look for in this exercise is whether or not it is providing a good tension or dynamic. If it is, the actor will find that the scene is flowing and beginning to have more energy. If it isn't, the actor is likely to run out of steam and find it hard to finish the scene. If the necessary dynamic is not there, the actor and I discuss it and change one or both ends, as necessary, and then repeat the scene again moving along the continuum.

This exercise also allows me to see clearly what choices the actor is making and it is very easy to say, "Try moving to the fear/doubt rather than the deter-mined/certain end at that point" or "Make a stronger choice there, walk further along the line and quicker." This is positive for the actor because, firstly, there is no criticism of what he/she has been doing and, secondly, what is

Barbara Houseman has worked for over twenty years as a voice and text coach in theatre, television and film and as theatre director. She spent six years in the Voice Department at the Royal Shakespeare Company before going to the Young Vic in London as Associate Director. She has worked with many of Britain's leading actors and directors and has also taught worldwide. Her film and TV work includes *Gladiator, Kiss Kiss Bang Bang, The Piano, Harry Potter and the Chamber of Secrets, Jonny English* and the Swedish detective series *Dance with an Angel.* She now works as a freelance director and coach. Her first book *Finding Your Voice* was published in July 2002 (by Nick Hern Books in London and Routledge in New York). She is presently working on her next two books *The Actor's Toolkit* and *Enabling Actors.*

now being asked of him/her is clear and straight forward. It also encourages the actor to commit more, to make stronger choices and although the dynamic is very crude it does give the scene a tension very quickly.

I then build on this exercise to bring in more colours and nuances. I ask the actor to list all the possible emotions or pre-occupations in the scene, starting with the obvious ones and then moving on to ones that might offer a different flavour. For instance, if a scene seems predominantly angry, I would ask them to look for softer, lighter or happier emotions or pre-occupations that could also truthfully exist in the scene, even if only for a millisecond. I write the list down as the actor comes up with the suggestions, only adding if I feel there are obvious gaps which need to be filled.

Once the list is done I write each emotion or preoccupation on a separate piece of paper, about half A4 size, and the actor places the pieces of paper around the room in whichever order/ position feels appropriate.

I ask the actor to start by standing nearest to whichever emotion/preoccupation feels most appropriate for the start of the scene. The actor then reads the scene again, moving from piece of paper to piece of paper as feels appropriate. I encourage the actor to really take their time with this exercise, moving around the room to find the emotion or preoccupation that feels right before they say the next part and not being afraid to go back and make a different choice if the one they made didn't feel right. I also remind them that they do not need to use every piece of paper! I never stop them in the middle of the exercise but simply watch the choices they are making. If they have found more colours and the scene has shown variety of pace and temperature and they feel that they have really learnt something from the exercise I will leave it there. If it feels like there are some colours missing we may add some new emotions or preoccupations and then try it again. This time I may make some suggestions as they go through it, but I try not to disturb their flow too much since I want them to have a sense of the scene as a journey.

These two exercises very rapidly allow the actor to have a sense of the shape, tension and progression in a scene. If there is more than one scene and we are short of time, we will discuss potential spectrums and lists of emotions/ preoccupations for the other scenes so that the actor can do the actual work on these at home.

I then move on to "unit-ing" the script. We break each scene down into small units of action: each unit representing a step within the journey of the scene. As we go through I ask the

actor to give each unit a snappy title. I encourage them to find a title that describes action rather than emotion, for example: "She quickly takes control of the situation"/ "He tries to wriggle out of the argument"/ "She refuses to let him off the hook". I will help them if they are stuck, especially if they are finding it difficult to come up with active titles. However, I prefer them to come up with as much as possible because I know, given the short amount of preparation time they have, that the work will take hold better if most of the suggestions have come from them.

Once the scene is divided into units, the actor reads it through focusing on the title of each unit and committing to it as completely as possible. This helps to sharpen the journey of the scene, since it adds precision. It also helps the actor to shift energy and tack very rapidly, even though they are only in the opening stages of the work.

Having done all of this work I then return to look at character, looking at the ways the character resembles and is different from the actor. Sometimes there is little work to do here and it is just a question of a quick chat. However, if the actor is finding it difficult to get a feel for the character I would use some of the following work.

If I feel the internal energy of the character is heavier than that of the actor I ask the actor to read the scene while pressing heavily against the wall. Conversely, if I feel the character is lighter I ask the actor to read the scene whilst moving around the room as if gliding or floating. If I feel the focus of the character is more direct I will ask the actor to walk with a sharp sense of purpose and direction as they read the scene(s). Conversely, if I feel the focus of the character is less direct I will ask the actor to meander around the room as they read the scene(s).

To look at the rhythm of the character in terms of whether it is more sustained or more staccato I use an excellent exercise of Cicely Berry's. This involves the actor walking as they speak the scene and changing direction on every punctuation mark. If I am reading the scene with them I will do the same for the other character(s) so we get a sense of the differing or similar rhythms in the scene.

By working physically as I have suggested above the actor is able to have a much stronger sense of how the character might operate differently from them than if we had simply sat and talked about it and this is usually enough to set them on the right road.

If I feel that it is not the weight, focus or rhythm of the character that needs to be looked at but rather the whole motivation we will discuss how the motivation differs and try to come up with a snappy phrase such as 'I have to be in control' or 'I want to avoid conflict' which the actor repeats in their head as they play through the scene again. Obviously, such a phrase is very simplistic but I have found that working simply is the best way to access complexity. It is as if the phrase is the tip of an iceberg which carries with it hidden depths.

Having done the work on character, the actor is often ready to go away and finish learning the scenes. As they do so, the various strands of work that we have explored—and which they can continue to explore at home—start to interweave so that despite the shortage of time the scene(s) have a depth and the actor has a firm basis on which they can build, so that they can easily adapt to the demands made by the casting director or director during the casting.

If the actor is less experienced I may need to add some of the following exercises. The first is another excellent exercise of Cicely Berry's and it is very helpful where actors are not following the phrasing of the script. It helps them to find the rhythm of the thoughts and character and to understand how each phrase is built upon the one before.

For this exercise you place two chairs side by side; they need to be chairs without arms. The actor starts sitting on one chair. He/she speaks the first phrase, which is up to the first punctuation mark. Then he/she shifts across to the second chair before speaking the second phrase there. At the end of that phrase he/she shifts back to the first chair before speaking the next phrase. The actor continues throughout the scene in the same way shifting from seat to seat between each phrase. If I am reading the scene with them I will also have two chairs side by side and shift from one to the other at the end of the phrases of the character(s) I am reading. This helps them to feel the rhythm of the other character's thoughts and how their phrases build.

Another issue with less experienced actors is that they find it hard to make the script sound conversational especially when they have so little time to learn it. If this is the case I get them to talk the scene to an inanimate object in the room—maybe a plant or a lamp or a chair. I ask them to take it phrase by phrase to really make contact with the object and really talk. I will stop them at any point if I feel they have disconnected and are simply reading. I have found that practising this exercise with inanimate objects is easier for them than talking it to me. Once they have a sense of what really talking, really communicating, feels like then they find it easy enough to translate into talking to another person. I also find this exercise

useful as a way of helping more self-conscious actors to keep the focus off themselves during a casting by really focussing either on the casting director or director while doing the scene, if they are reading with them, or else to choose an object in the room, possibly even the camera to talk to.

These exercises are very simple to do and I have found that the actor enjoys the work and leaves the sessions feeling excited about the casting rather than daunted by it. Clients with whom I work regularly will prepare the spectrum and the lists before they come and may even have tried those exercises at home, so that we only go over them if they are having difficulty. They will also tend to have practised the chair and the talking exercise. We therefore can spend more time on the "unit-ing" and the character differences.

The feedback from directors and casting directors after my clients have prepared in this way has been excellent and even if the client has not been cast they have usually been called back for other castings by the same director or casting director at a later point. This has led my less experienced clients to gain a great deal of confidence and my more experienced clients to feel less exposed by the swiftness of the casting process.

Many clients return after they have been cast to work in a similar way on all their scenes so that they feel thoroughly prepared for shooting and, again, the feedback has been excellent with clients being able to achieve what the directors want in a very small number of takes.

Interviews with Three Film and Television Coaches:
Carla Meyer, Gillian Lane-Plescia,
and David Alan Stern

Paul Meier is Head of Voice and a Professor in the Theatre and Film Department at the University of Kansas. He is Founder and Director of IDEA (International Dialects of English Archive), on the web at http://www.ukans.edu/~idea. He is the author of *Accents and Dialects for Stage and Screen,* and *Dialects of the British Isles, Volume 1,* used as text-books in many theatre departments. Both are available, along with his dialect booklets and CDs, from Paul Meier Dialect Services, on the web at www.paulmeier.com. His "show-specific" dialect CDs are leased world-wide by theatre companies, while he has coached a dozen feature films in the last five years, including Ang Lee's *Ride With The Devil,* and Paul Cox's *Molokai: The Story of Father Damien.*

An Interview with Carla Meyer

Carla Meyer attended Connecticut College and Carnegie-Mellon University, where she studied with Edith Skinner and Robert Parks. She then worked as an actress for 20 years before committing herself full-time to voice, speech and dialect coaching. She has taught at The Neighborhood Playhouse, UC Irvine, and ACT Her film coaching credits include *The Crucible,* Nicole Kidman in *To Die For, The Perfect Storm,* Albert Finney in *Erin Brockovich,* Cate Blanchett and the company of *The Gift, Road To Perdition,* and Kate Winslet in the soon-to-be-released *The Life of David Gale.* At the time of the interview she was working on the Tim Burton film *Big Fish* with Albert Finney, Ewan McGregor, and Jessica Lange.

PM: Let me ask you how you trained and what was your avenue into dialect coaching for film.

CM: It was all Carnegie Tech [now Mellon] and Edith Skinner. I went to Carnegie as a drama school student and had every intention of being an actress—"Those who can, do; those who can't, teach"—so I had absolutely no interest in teaching. Edith, bless her heart, every year would pick a speech assistant and generally he or she was the person that she thought had a good ear. She chose me and my ear.

She was such an extraordinary woman and such a character. When she decided that I was good enough, she just acted on that notion. I was good at it. I didn't love it with the passion that she loved it. But I had a fairly strong liberal arts background because I'd transferred to Carnegie from Connecticut College. So I had a nice context for her work.

For me the concreteness and the order and the whimsy of Edith was very grounding as I went through the acting experience, which is harrowing in so many respects because the process of becoming an actor in many schools is the taking away all your resources, (an acting teacher will call them tricks), but *everything* you relied on before gets called into question. It can be pretty unnerving and so for me speech was quite anchoring.

As graduation was coming near there was a job that came up at The Repertory Theatre in St. Louis and the Drama School of Webster College.

PM: What year was this?

CM : The early seventies. It was a great experience to work in what was at that point a fledgling drama program working its way to being a good one, with I thought very good leadership at the time. You didn't train there did you?

PM: I trained at the Rose Bruford College of Speech and Drama in London.

CM: Well you may have bumped into the great dilemma for young actors: how do you get into Equity or how do you get into SAG? Your first two years after graduation are figuring out that issue.

PM: It's worse in England.

CM: Really? Luckily for me and thanks to Edith and speech, I sailed right through that one. I became an Equity member which meant I could become a SAG member and an AFTRA member. So I taught and worked in the Rep company there for a year. Then they disbanded the Rep company ...and I was anxious to move to New York anyhow.

So I went to New York and then my speech teaching was really secondary to my acting. I think within a year I started working in the musical, *Godspell*, which took me to Boston for a year and a half.

When I came back to New York in the mid-seventies there were four tracks that I was following. One was doing commercials to make a living, another was working as a spokeswoman, (a talking head at PBS in New York, WNET), the third was doing theatre and the fourth was teaching at the Neighborhood Playhouse and coaching people privately. I did that off and on for several years and then Edith threw me in the deep end.

Dustin Hoffman was directing a play by Murray Schisgal called *All Over Town*, which had a phenomenal cast headed by Cleavon Little, Pamela Payton-Wright and Polly Draper. Everybody had an accent! There I was at the age of 24—in way over my head—and madly scrambling to figure out how I was going to teach Greek, Swedish, French, and Southern. But I did it, and the show opened. It wasn't a booming success but not because of the accents. The accents were fine; the actors were wonderful. I had a great time doing that.

I was working with different theatre companies and with individuals, and at the Neighborhood Playhouse while I was in New York. Then I got a call in the spring of '79. I had taught the previous summer at ACT in their summer training program. A man named Robert Cohen was running the drama department at UC-Irvine. Bob had directed me in a play years ago at Connecticut College, when he was at Yale, and he saw my name on ACT and Neighborhood Playhouse brochures and that I was teaching voice and speech. He wanted me to come out to UC-Irvine and teach voice, speech and acting—which dovetailed perfectly with a restlessness I was feeling to go out to California. And that was a wonderful blessing because it was a tenure-track job, although I still wasn't committed to teaching.

It was shortly after that I started to work more in the movies. Tim [Monich] and Edith had more people than they could handle back in New York and they called and asked if I could pick up the slack. By that time I was living in Los Angeles,

Carla Meyer with Ben Chaplin on the set of *Washington Square*

working with The Ensemble Studio Theatre West, doing commercials and commuting to Irvine.

PM: Still doing a bit of this and a bit of that, right?
CM: Yes. But making my basic living as an actress. It was around that time, early eighties that—and I don't think there's a coach working that wouldn't credit Meryl Streep with having raised the bar on what people could expect in a film actor in terms of voice, speech and accent. And she was accompanied by Kevin Kline and Bill Hurt. The Yale and Juilliard, and NYU trained students were getting much more film work then they had previously. And so there was more of a demand for coaches. Because Edith had trained someone at Yale, Edith many of them called on Tim and Edith—and I started working on films.

I realized then that the actors who had even *slept* through speech class were so much better prepared to do any of this work than the film·business was asking of them.

Early on I worked with Holly Hunter who had gone to Carnegie, and she knew phonetics. She understood *hearing* sounds as opposed to taking them from the written word. If I could pinpoint one thing—that's what actors who have been through a training program take away. You don't have to have to have been a great speech student to have grasped that.

On the same film, Laura San Giacomo who also went to Carnegie came in. She was under great time pressure to get a difficult accent quickly. And she did. She got it quickly because we could talk short-hand.

There were some students in drama school who loved speech and found it fun and interesting and a nice diversion from the more emotional, psychological intensity of acting class. And there where others who gravitated toward what was going on in acting class and to them voice and speech was really a wash. They weren't interested, didn't see how it related to them, thought you were trying to make them be who they weren't. There was all kinds of resistance to the structure that speech class insists upon. It is the most like "school" of almost anything else you'll get in a drama-training program.

A lot of people who are drawn to acting are drawn to acting because it's not like school—it's an art form—and to find the space where the discipline of speech marries the creativity of an actor is what we all are aiming for. It's tricky and it's hard because it's a different style for every actor.

PM: I was fortunate enough to fall in love with my phonetics teacher, Greta Stevens.
CM: That makes all the difference—and a teacher who was wonderful for you, someone else is going to make fun of, or be bored by, or threatened by in some way shape or form. What I did when I graduated from drama school was to start looking for teachers who were comfortable with improvisation because that's what I had shied away from. Conversely, I found that I was very often teaching Carnegie grads voice and speech because they realized that as soon as you get out into the world you need it all. The more you have the better you are.

In the academy that can get lost. I think any rigor that is helping a young artist become a mature artist invites inevitably a certain amount of rebellion. That's part of the process, and I think very often in acting school you can't rebel against the acting teachers because that's your life blood—that's all you've ever wanted to be in your life—an actor. It's so important to do well and get approval, or stake your claim, that very often the discipline-driven parts of training are the focus of rebellion. Those of us who love it find it difficult to understand, but I do understand.

PM: Getting to the nuts and bolts of your approach to dialect roles in a film, what kind of techniques do you prefer to use?
CM: Well, it is the most individualized kind of program. I don't come into a meeting with an actor with a set agenda or course of study for them—because my only goal is for them to learn the accent and—equally important—for them to do it in a natural way that doesn't in any way limit their creativity because acting is too hard! Especially in movies where you have such limited rehearsal time. Very often the first time you do a scene is the day of the shoot. So if I have someone who can do an accent perfectly in my office and shows up on the set and doesn't feel comfortable with it, I haven't done my job.

PM: How do you get them there?
CM: It's different with each person because some people love the order of phonetics, and if they haven't learned phonetics then I use a sort of made-up mix of phonetics and their own markings. If they decide to mark a sound in a certain way, I'm not going to correct them and tell them to use the phonic symbol because that's not going to mean anything to them. And if we're *very* lucky we have three weeks to do it.

Others don't want to see things written down, I've worked with one actor, who's wonderful, who really wants to hear her lines read in a fairly neutral fashion in the dialect. Now, in that case, I will very often try to find a native speaker. But you're always exploring.

Meryl Streep, I understand, works by finding the person who embodies what it is she's trying to capture in the speech. In my experience, sometimes we'll find that. Again, if we're very lucky, we find the person with the right accent and the right personality that matches the character, but most often it will have to be a hybrid.

But I always consult a native speaker and often ask them to read the dialogue, if the actor wants that. Especially if it's a British accent. There are so many nuances that a native British speaker will know that I won't, and I have a nice mutual relationship with a number of coaches in England.

PM: What about primary sources?
CM: I have what I think is a fairly substantial library and never once do I have exactly the right thing especially if I'm going to design the dialect for the whole film.

PM: So are you constantly recording people?
CM: Yes. For almost every major assignment I will go to the area either ahead of the actor, or I will find somebody I can record over the telephone. I mix genders. I don't feel that women need only hear women and men need only hear men.

If something is unique, for instance the accent that we used in *The Crucible*. Everybody listened to the same man for that. In a sense we were doing with the speech what Arthur Miller did with the dialogue—which is he took a certain amount of the dialogue from the transcripts of the trial and then he added his own poetry. We had to find a way of speaking that had authenticity to it but matched his level of language. Daniel Day Lewis felt comfortable and really liked this one man's dialect, as did Nicholas Hytner, the director. So we used him as our model.

I try to give the actor as much leeway within what Edith would call "the latitude of correctness", so that they're not trying to match their characters to a dialect sample. Rather, so that they can find a dialect sample that suits them in their creation of the character. It's always on an individual basis, and I'm directing myself towards the actors' ways of learning and what they feel most comfortable with.

PM: How much do you wrestle with stereotypes and the difference between the stereotype and the reality. How much do you have to fight actors and directors to get something more real?

Pedagogy and Coaching

Interviews with Three Television and Film Coaches:
Carla Meyer, Gillian Lane-Plescia and David Alan Stern by Paul Meier (continued)

CM: I think it comes down on both sides of the coin because very often I'll find directors saying, "I just want a touch of..." And they're saying they just want a touch of Boston/Italian. And you're saying, "Uh, that's kind of a strong accent to get just a *touch* of."

PM: How much are you influenced by the resistance the audience has to hearing their favorite stars in another voice. How do you approach that difficulty?
CM: That always depends on the actor. George Clooney for *The Perfect Storm* didn't feel comfortable doing a New England accent. It wasn't going to be right for him. Now, for me it was a shame because he has a great ear. He has a wonderful ear for picking up accents, but I had to respect the fact that he was coming right off another film and didn't have a lot of prep time. The New England accent is, I think, one of the trickier American accents to teach because the audience is not used to hearing it.

There was one director I worked with who said, "If I have to choose between historical authenticity and dramatic authenticity, I will choose dramatic authenticity every time." And I thought there was some real wisdom in that for us—because if you, Paul, were going to approach the dialect in a film with your phenomenal sense of accuracy for a given accent, there would be plenty of notes, and I would give myself plenty of notes on things. But because it is so collaborative and it is this wild organic beast that you're trying to wrangle during the shooting of the film you want nothing about the accent to be distracting. I think that very often it's like a great costume. It gives the actor something to work with, it makes them look more like the character but you don't spend the movie thinking, "What great dresses. What fantastic pants."

PM: Could I get you to talk about the difference between English language dialects and foreign language accents? If we could use those terms, and what comes to mind when I make that distinction.
CM: One of the early films I worked on was a film by Larry Kasdan called *I Love You to Death*, where Tracy Ullman, who of course is British, was playing an American character whose mother was from Yugoslavia. Her mother was played by Joan Plowright—also British; her husband who was played by Kevin Klein, was an Italian-American. There's one dinner party scene where Kevin is speaking American English in an Italian accent and also speaking in Italian. Joan is speaking American English in a Yugoslavian accent and also in Croatian, and Tracy in the middle is speaking American English, and also Italian and Yugoslavian to two different actors!

I had a native Italian speaker and a native Croatian speaker with me on the set that day because I'm not a linguist, and

even with French, which I speak a bit, I would have a native speaker on the set; because if a native French speaker is listening you want all of the slang to be correct. So I want to vet my work with a native speaker if it's a big role or if they're going to improvise.

Another anecdote about that. My first movie was *Milagro Beanfield War*, and I was working with Sonia Braga. She is from Brazil, and her native language is Portuguese. We'd be reading through the dialogue and she'd leave out all the little words: *in, of, a, an.* They just weren't there. When I asked why she said, "In Portuguese we don't bother." She had done *Kiss of the Spider Woman* by rote—she really wasn't speaking English very much—so this was her first English-language film. It made me very aware of how many idiosyncratic differences there are, *and* that we can never assume!

PM: What do you think of the movies' proclivity to cast widely disparate people from all different cultures and then put them in a second culture. Australian actors, Irish actors, English actors and American actors. And they all have to sound like they're from Missouri. That's what happened to me on the Ang Lee film.
CM: Isn't it wonderful that we have such a wide network of really talented actors that the directors can choose whoever they want because they know they can hire a voice and speech professional to then help form a sound for their film. I didn't feel this way when I was acting!!!

PM: First you think it's never going to happen and then it does, doesn't it?
CM: I love it. You know, all we can do is all we can do. The question that I give to my colleagues and that I ask myself: Is the dialect better because I'm there? And the answer always has to be yes.

An Interview with Gillian Lane-Plescia

Gillian Lane-Plescia was born and educated in England, trained in the Drama Division of the Royal Academy of Music, taught in a school in the slums of the industrial Midlands for three years and then in a girls' school in Bermuda. After moving to the US in the 1960s and running a children's theatre for several years, she got her MA in Theatre from Florida State University and began teaching voice, speech and dialects. She later taught at UNC-Chapel Hill, then The University of Michigan before moving to Chicago to work as a freelance voice and dialect coach. Since then she has gradually moved almost exclusively into dialect coaching, and works in theatres all over the US. In 1989 she started producing her dialect tapes, which are now sold in the US, UK, Canada and Australia.

PM: Could you briefly describe the training that prepared you to become a voice coach?
GLP: I trained in the Drama Division of the Royal Academy of Music, now part of the University of Middlesex. We had the usual heavy concentration on Voice and Speech and my first and best Voice teacher was Iris Warren. We studied speech, vocal anatomy and phonetics with Greta Colson. I was always particularly interested in the latter and did well in the

IPA exam. I got my MA in Theatre at Florida State, where I began teaching voice. Later, I attended an extended workshop with Kristin Linklater and The Working Theatre.

PM: How long were you in academia and how did you become a freelance coach?

GLP: I taught in academia at the university level for nine years full time, then fled to Chicago, where I already had professional contacts from working as vocal coach at The American Players Theatre in Wisconsin during the summer. Though I continued to teach part time at Columbia College, I very quickly moved into the professional coaching field when I met Robert Falls and was engaged as voice coach on his production of *Hamlet* first at Wisdom Bridge, then at the Civic Theatre. I also had coached professional theatres attached both to the University of North Carolina, Chapel Hill, and the University of Michigan, so my professional contacts were pretty good and my timing was lucky. During this time I also offered private coaching and classes, the latter starting with a ready made group from Barbara Gaines Shakespeare Group.

PM: Were dialects always your specialty as a coach? Or are you equally strong in voice, diction and text?

GLP: At first I worked mainly as a voice and text coach and teacher, but little by little began to be called upon do dialect coaching. The level of dialect work in Chicago when I first got there was not great—people seemed mostly to get away with cliché and generalized accents, and few theatres hired a dialect coach for productions. By the time I left Chicago I was still teaching voice and was usually called in by The Goodman Theatre for voice and text coaching when they did Shakespeare, but most of my theatre work apart from that was as a dialect coach, and I also did a lot of individual dialect coaching. It was in Chicago that I started producing my dialect tapes. Since moving to Connecticut five years ago my work has been almost exclusively as a dialect coach.

PM: You seem to indicate that the American theatre has become more sophisticated in its appreciation of the role of dialect in production.

GLP: I think it has, though I also think that this happened on

Gillian Lane-Plescia

the East Coast sooner than it did in Chicago. When I moved east I was surprised to find actors much better prepared and much more eager to improve their accent work. I also think audiences have higher expectations due to a greater awareness of accents which they have gained through greater mobility and through modern communications. There's a downside to this, however, in that expectations of authenticity are sometimes unrealistic, leading audience members and sometimes dialect coaches, to demand a geographical specificity that effectively requires all actors to be expert dialecticians. This is a pet peeve of mine—don't get me started! But at the same time, more and more theatres are willing to employ a dialect coach, even though many of them have still not really addressed the need for an adequate budget to pay for as much dialect coaching as is needed. Have you noticed how the dialect coach in movies is usually listed after just about everyone else, including assistant hairdressers, pet handlers and so forth? But at least dialect coaches are being brought in.

PM: Coaching for film and coaching for the stage are notoriously different jobs in many ways.

GLP: I believe that's true, though I have done very little coaching for film. I think in film there must be much more of a problem with casting actors who have box office value, but who have very little ability with dialects, such as Kevin Costner as Robin Hood. But I suppose they only need to get it right once, for the soundtrack, not for every performance. On the other hand, film goes anywhere, so the dialects may come under greater scrutiny. It's interesting that theatre and film critics like to go after dialects (what, I ask, are *their* qualifications?), often in a very ignorant way. It's one of the reasons I try to discourage the directors I work with from getting too tricky with the dialects. I mean, for example, trying to make too many class or regional differences in a show. The critics, and audience members, tend to jump on that as evidence that the actors are inconsistent or bad at the accents. Have you noticed, incidentally, that most people, to some extent, consider themselves experts on accents?

PM: I have. I suppose because dialects have always functioned as tribal markers—"You speak like me. I like you. You don't so

I'm not sure."—everybody to a greater or lesser extent discriminates very small differences in dialect as part of their social radar. So they feel qualified to critique dialect and accent work in films and plays. Given this sensitivity to tiny differences in accents on the part of the general population, doesn't it sometimes seem impossible that you could coach an actor so that he or she could hope to fool a native speaker? It sometimes seems to me an almost arrogant presumption that actors could aspire to authentically inhabit a culture not their own.

GLP: I don't think we should be concerned about fooling a native speaker. I have serious issues with the search for 100% authenticity, which is *almost* always beyond the reach of actors. I think I have encountered no more than five actors, if that, who have this ability. I don't mean to imply that we should not coach authentic rather than stereotypical or cliché type accents, but I don't think we should, in general, worry about precise geographical accuracy—you know, the particular street in the Northern Quadrant of Such and Such a city, behind the Railway station; or even the exact county in Ireland. (An actor recently told me that he does 23 different Berlin accents, and I almost said "who cares?").

Even those native speakers who criticize an actor for an accent are not infallible. When Kenneth Branagh and Emma Thompson did *Dead Again*, I had two people come up to me on the same day, one raving about how wonderful their American accents were, the other deploring them.

Apropos of inhabiting a culture, this does seem to me to be important on many levels, though the dialect coach in professional shows doesn't really have much time to deal with it. Sometimes the dramaturgy does a useful job in this respect, and sometimes emphatically not. But I recently worked on an Ayckbourn play, the director of which had no idea of the kind of suburban culture essential to an understanding of the play, and therefore had not given the actors (MFA students) any guidance in this matter. I find when coaching English plays with Americans that they often mistake irony for deadly seriousness, which can definitely have an effect on, for example, intonation patterns.

PM: Something I have serious issues with—and I know you share this—which is why I started IDEA: *real-life models, primary source samples.* I found in my earlier years that actors often simply imitated other actors who had imitated such and such an actor whose dialect in this or that film or play they had liked. In other words, we didn't just have cliché dialects in the theatre; we had highly conventionalized or stylized versions which simply happened to be *wrong*! As we started to amass large numbers of samples on IDEA, of German speakers for example, I was struck by how they rarely conform to received stage German. The strength of your instructional tapes is that they are built around recordings of native speakers. I assume your coaching practice is like that too?

GLP: Yes, I'm collecting Italian at the moment, and not one single person does that old stereotypical " I like-ah dis-ah place-ah" accent.

In coaching, I use primary source material exclusively, but I also try to help people to find approximations of sounds, when they have a difficult time producing the exact sound of the original. For example, some people are quite unable to roll an R, make the uvular French R, or achieve some of the subtleties of Irish diphthongs. I do encourage actors to accept that a dialect may initially feel very strange in the mouth, may make them feel a certain way—e.g., the very guttural Afrikaans accent often makes actors feel that they sound like rotten people, German can make people feel like Nazis, Standard British makes them feel ultra affected. I stress that they have to persevere until the dialect simply becomes another way of talking, without connotations of personality or emotions. This is one of the reasons I encourage actors to practice just talking in the dialect, initially to themselves, then going shopping making routine phone calls and so forth, so that the dialect exists in language not just in the text.

PM: You say you use primary source recordings exclusively. Meaning you don't personally demonstrate the dialect? In my practice as a coach I often wonder what the right balance is between demonstrating and letting the actor soak up the dialect from primary source recordings. We coaches are often faulted for getting the perceived balance wrong between these two modes of instruction.

GLP: I'll demonstrate a Standard British Accent without hesitation, and sometimes other British accents—Cockney, Donegal Irish, Belfast, General Scots, Liverpool, French, etc., but usually only as a short cut if the dialect has to be learned in a hurry, or if this is the only way an actor seems to be able to get it. I try to avoid demonstrating anything that I am not absolutely sure I can be authentic with. The work that I do recording people and talking with them about accents has made me aware of how generalized our concept of dialects has been, and made me less secure about my ability to demonstrate accurately. I feel, for example, that if I do Scots, I am probably doing a magical mystery tour of the country, with bits of Edinburgh, Glasgow, Aberdeen, the Highlands and so forth all mixed up together. I almost always refuse to read a speech that someone is working on "in the dialect". I have no problem with demonstrating individual words in any accent I am coaching. I will read lines and so forth in Standard British, often simply to demonstrate the possible different intonation patterns that might be used.

I recently worked with a group of eight children in a production of *Peter Pan,* and for them, in collaboration with a very helpful Sound department, made each of them CD demos of all their lines. This was mainly because my time with them was limited and occasional, and I wanted them to drill the dialect every day.

This sort of flows over into the problem of line readings. I will sometimes suggest a line reading to someone, and ask them to imitate it to see if they can "feel" a different meaning when they say it this way. Often they'll be amazed at the discovery and will use it. I always preface this by remarking that I know line readings are considered absolutely forbidden by some, and explain why I'm doing it. I find this especially when I'm coaching Standard British because, as a Brit, I sometimes see things in a text that an American might not see. This is especially true with the tags "didn't we, wasn't I, isn't it" etc. Americans tend to give these an upward inflection, honoring the question mark punctuation which they usually carry. But I know that they are often an affirmation, expecting, even demanding agreement, rather than a question *needing* agreement or an answer. This can substantially change the tone of an exchange, and I like to alert them to this, so they can decide how to treat them. Do I make myself clear?

PM: You do. Another topic that interests me very much is the extent to which tonality, rhythm, and intonation patterns—as opposed to phonemic accuracy alone—are important in capturing the essence of dialect. I would love to hear you talk about the relative importance of these various aspects of dialect work.
GLP: I don't have a clear sense of what you mean by tonality but I think that if an accent that captures key aspects of the rhythm, melody, and pitch range of an accent, even if there are some imperfections with regard to the sound changes, the result will be more acceptable than an accent that is sound change perfect but has no feeling for those other aspects. I find this particularly true with Standard British. At the same times, going back to the matter of line readings, it's hard to teach melodic and rhythmic aspects of a dialect without demonstrating. When I am teaching, as distinct from coaching, I have people select a passage from primary source material, perhaps something that is close to a character monologue they are working on, and try to imitate everything: sounds, melody, rhythm. I also suggest setting up a separate recording device so they can play a phrase or sentence, then repeat it, and so on to the end of the piece. Then they can play back the resulting recording and compare what they are doing to the original. I also use the intonation exercises on my Standard British tape/CD for practice, augmented by some others I have which are along the same lines.

PM: So we have *pronunciation* (which can be captured through IPA), *melody* or *intonation pattern* (which can be notated), and *rhythm* (referring to the speaker's arrangement of stresses). But how do you refer to or deal with what I call *tonality*? By *tonality* I mean the difference in the tone of voice between different dialects—the males in Southern England, France and the American mid-West for example have signature voice tones, or perhaps you disagree. Doesn't David Stern call this the "imaginary point of resonance"—his way of approaching that topic?
GLP: I really find this approach doesn't work for me personally, so I tend not to use it in working with others. However, if

someone says to me that they feel the voice in a certain parts of the face, and they are sounding authentic, then I say, "Good, use that." A few people have told me that they find this aspect of Stern's tapes very helpful, but when I tried it with one of his American for Brits programs it didn't help me at all, simply made me feel as if I was going to swallow my tongue! I feel sure that it is an individual thing. I do tell people that for Standard British they will feel it in the jaw and the lips more than when they speak American English, but this is not a question of tonality. Very High Brit (High Spotty) does have a strong mask resonance, and I do mention that, though in general I advise people to stay away from this accent except, perhaps, in certain kinds of comedy.

PM: What about the habit of some French men to use a gruff, pharyngeal quality? Or the habit of some Londoners and Appalachians to use a lot of nasality? These require the actor to manipulate tonality, right? Dialects are not all tonally the same.
GLP: Oh yes, the nasality of some dialects is certainly something that I work on, those you mention and others like Australian, and with many foreign accents some of these considerations arise. But once again, you've got me stumped with exactly what you mean by the gruff pharyngeal quality of some French men. I *think* I know what you're referring to, but I'm not sure. And I suppose the word *placement* would be more familiar to me than *tonality*. I remember someone writing an impassioned letter to VASTA (I think) complaining about the lack of scientific clarity in the terminology used in the teaching of voice, but I think so much of our teaching is intuitive and personal that it can't be pinned down quite so definitively.

PM: How about tonal placement as the term? Yes, terminology in this area is difficult. Let me switch gears here. We now have over a century of recorded voices, so we don't have to rely on written accounts or imprecise terminology when documenting dialect evolution during the last hundred years. So we know how people spoke in 1920. Yet I see very little attempt in films and plays to capture the sounds of English in earlier eras. I see Merchant Ivory films, for example, where the younger actors use today's dialects and are clearly fifty or sixty years at least out of date. Any thoughts there?
GLP: This is a great topic and one that has long bothered me. I noticed it first in child actors on *Masterpiece Theatre*, playing supposed children of aristocratic families, and sounding quite wrong. Their governesses would have been fired if they had spoken that way. But I also noticed that my own nephews and nieces, and especially their offspring, spoke with this off accent, despite their upper class background. Since I left England in the 60s, there has been a significant shift in pronunciation of RP (Standard British), and traditional regional dialects too have become very much diluted so that it's hard to find "the real thing" in people under 70 years old. That's true

here as well as in England. I know that in England acting students have become quite radical about refusing to part with their regional accents though they are generally required to learn RP, which is not the same RP as I was taught in Drama School. For this reason, I suppose that contemporary English actors under about 50 are not even aware that when they do Wilde, or Coward, or various *Masterpiece Theatre* and feature films, their accents are not historically correct. For example I found Emma Thompson's accent in *Sense and Sensibility* very inappropriate and very modern. However, if actors did make their accents historically correct they might well be perceived as sounding unacceptably affected. It's interesting that in this country I can get away with coaching actors in the older form of RP, which to American audiences still sounds right. If an actor does the slightly off modern version, he or she may be criticized for sounding Cockney!

If you listen to old American movies you also notice how accents have changed. Listen to many women actresses from the 40s, people like Grace Kelly, who used an upper class East Coast accent close to what is called American Stage speech. You seldom hear that accent in today's movies.

When I reflect on all this, I'm not sure that it's feasible or even desirable to try and recapture the authentic accent of a period, though it continues to be distracting to me when I hear the modern accents used by people wearing period costume and riding around in carriages.

Sometimes I am asked to help out on an American historical accent, for something like *The Crucible*. Well, one can speculate, but there are no recordings, no sources, and I generally feel that it's up to the director to decide how they should sound. I know that when they did it in New York recently, Deb Hecht together with Richard Eyre, the director, came up with something that seemed appropriate to them. Again, I'm not sure that this is necessary. On the other hand, I think we have to avoid a very contemporary sound in such situations. When I recently watched students in scenes from Shaw or Wilde, where they were not using dialects, I felt that their generally limited range and their often unsatisfactory diction strongly detracted from their successful rendition of the scenes.

It's a puzzler since we don't have a universally accepted formal stage speech in America, notwithstanding those who espouse the Skinner approach. But something is needed.

PM: Here's a question I have put to other dialect coaches. And one that concerns me as a dialect coach very much. What, at root, is our place in the art of theatre? What exactly is it we dialect coaches do? Are we mere consultants on verisimilitude, having little to do with acting? Or are we working at the intersection of acting and culture, there to assist the project find a creative way to embody and support the world of the play as expressed through the voice and speech patterns of the characters? In professional terms where should the dialect person's name belong in the credits? Among the designers? Or in some place lower down—Special Thanks, for instance? I guess it comes down to how much potency theatre folks believe the human voice has to reveal cultural hierarchies and values, and the psychological states of characters. I happen to believe that dialect, in its broadest sense, embodies the values of a culture and is the sum of a character's life experience. Thus the dialect expert in a production is working right at its center—not at its margins. For example, RP, as we both know, uses fewer strong stresses than General American, and delays the strong stresses until later in the sentence. Brits often seem to preface and qualify the points they are about to make, whereas their American cousins often seem to value directness more, leading to earlier and more frequent strong stresses. The rhythmic differences between these two dialects are not, to my mind, arbitrary linguistic features attempted by actors in mere deference to verisimilitude, but are deeply revealing of the habits of mind of the characters in their world. Thus the dialect coach is there to assist actors fully inhabit another culture not their own *as expressed in the text*—hardly a marginal undertaking, and a function that one could certainly attach equally well to directors.

GLP: I think, under certain circumstances, that the dialect coach is there, as you say, "to assist the project to embody and support the world of the play", and I think that we should be given program billing among the designers when that is clearly the case. I would apply this when the play is one in which dialect concerns are dominant. Many British plays would fall into that group as would plays set in specific regions of the US—those of Tennessee Williams among the most obvious. Your example of the rhythmic difference between American and English speech is basic. and, as I mentioned before, a misunderstanding of the tag endings "didn't we," "isn't it" etc. can lead to a misreading of British texts. So we perform a function that is just as important as that of the designers, though they might not agree with us and I find some theatres do not even have to be asked to give me front page program billing, while others are amazed if I ask for it.

PM: A final issue for us to talk about before you have to dash off to coach several *Christmas Carol* productions: the inability of some casting directors to take an actor's skill in dialects into account. Why do some casting directors have to have the character walk in the door? On the other hand, a lot of casting takes place without any reference to the actor's skill in dialect—often when important dialect work is needed.

GLP: I've all too often run into the problem of working with actors who have no ear for dialect. This is particularly true when children are cast. Although children are often quite good mimics, have less inhibitions than some adults and pick up accents quite quickly, there are still some who cannot do an accent to save their lives. Bonnie Raphael once sent me her guidelines for dialect coaching in the theatre, and she included the ideal situation of the coach being present at call-backs and doing a little workshop with the actors to get an idea of their ability with accents. It involved some non-threatening games of sound imitation. She would then be able to warn directors of possible trouble if they cast certain people. I found it an excellent idea, since directors are seldom well enough versed in dialects to be able to tell if an actor is capable or not. But this idea is seldom adopted, especially where casting directors are used on Broadway and in film. There it is so often the star name that is most important. So we dialect coaches are left to struggle as best we can, and let's face it, we are the easiest people to blame if the results are bad. I don't know if we can change that. Perhaps we can if, as we discussed before, we can raise the status of the dialect coach to be as essential, if not more so, as the set and costume designers, to the truthful interpretation and staging of a play.

An Interview with David Alan Stern

After earning a BFA in acting from the University of Connecticut and a PhD. in speech from Temple, David Alan Stern taught at several universities before establishing Dialect Accent Specialists in Hollywood. Among those he coached for professional roles are Geena Davis, Olympia Dukakis, Mike Farrell, Sally Field, Julie Harris, Jack Klugman, Edward James Olmos, Liam Neeson, Lynn Redgrave, Julia Roberts, Forest Whitaker, and Michael York. He has authored over fifty instructional audio programs for voice improvement, accent modification, and dialect acting. He is now back at UConn as Professor and Associate Head of Dramatic Arts and a performance coach for Connecticut Repertory Theatre. Recently, he has also served as dialect coach for several productions at the Berkshire Theatre Festival.

PM: Tell me about the early years. What got you started?
DAS: I was transplanted from Brooklyn to southeastern Connecticut at the age of five. My father was a semiprofessional magician whose act always involved a great deal of storytelling and comic patter. Apparently I started "performing" with his expressive style almost as soon as the babbling stage ended. I stumbled upon my abilities with accents and dialects at age ten when my father was playing his Broadway cast albums of *My Fair Lady* and *Finian's Rainbow*. I began singing along with the English RP, Cockney, Irish and "Missitucky" characters almost immediately, producing pretty authentic-sounding dialects. For the next five years I became increasingly aware of my ability to parrot back almost any speech pattern I heard, but I did little with it other than telling the occasional dialect joke—often using the Brooklyn and/or Yiddish patterns that surrounded me.

I started acting in high school and majored in Theatre/Acting at the University of Connecticut (to which I returned as a professor twenty-five years after graduation). I played mostly dialect roles in school. After all, I was the one who could do the accents. After graduation, I "left theatre forever" (for the first time) and pursued a PhD. in Speech. Though I was a "communication" major, Speech & Hearing was in the same department at Temple, and the curricula overlapped

somewhat. Also, my advisor, Donald Ecroyd, was co-author of several Voice & Diction texts. So when I went to Wichita State as their "Speech Ed." person, they had me resurrect their long-abandoned Voice & Diction course. Most of the students were Public Address or Broadcasting majors—just a few actors among them.

In Wichita, I was also fortunate to study voice disorders and therapy with Dr. Kenneth Burk of their Speech Science Department. In my own department, I team-taught with our "Theatre Ed." professor, Audrey Needles, one of the most talented directors I've ever encountered. She rekindled my passion for theatre, then said the fateful words, "You perform accents so well; why don't you teach my cast how to sound English?" Though my first attempts at dialect coaching were not overwhelmingly successful, they thoroughly redirected my professional focus. My interests shifted toward studying as many accents and dialects as I could and trying to develop techniques for successfully teaching them to actors—especially those who didn't share my abilities as a dialect mimic.

PM: How long were you at Wichita? And where did your career turn next?
DAS: It seems impossible that I was there for only three years, 1974-1977. But, time goes by more slowly in the "youth" of both one's life and one's career. Two avenues of creative activity began for me during that period. Along with Howard Phillips, a Welsh actor/architect, I did a comedy review called *Piccadilly Silly: An Evening of British Humour*, consisting of material by Peter Cook & Dudley Moore and sketches from several BBC radio programs. And, of course, I started looking for better techniques for teaching dialects and accents. In mid-1976, having failed to produce acceptable stage accents by having actors imitate me or read phonetic transcriptions of lines or "sing" different melodies for different dialects, I started playing with another approach that created muscularity/resonance changes and then pitch movement *within* (not between) stressed vowels *before* creating any phoneme substitutions.

In late 1976, my cousin Ken was playing The Artful Dodger in *Oliver!* I "wrote" him a brief audio letter containing my resonance exercises for the Cockney dialect. It worked. In the spring of 1977, Audrey [Needles] asked for dialect help on her production of *The Boy Friend*. Since I wasn't available for many rehearsals, I recorded a series of lessons with my resonance, lilt and pronunciation drills for Standard British. These recordings were the seeds of what became the first *Acting With an Accent* tapes two years later.

My primary research and teaching interests were now voice, speech and dialect instruction for actors. But strangely, the

Interviews with Three Television and Film Coaches:
Carla Meyer, Gillian Lane-Plescia and David Alan Stern by Paul Meier (continued)

David Allen Stern (with pad) coaching students at the University of Connecticut

Wichita State powers still wanted me to do the things that they'd hired me to do—which had very little to do with theatre. So that same spring, I decided to start applying for theatre voice-speech-dialect jobs during the following year. Surprisingly, I didn't have to wait the year. Within days of my decision, Penn State listed such an opening. I don't know how I convinced them I was qualified; maybe they liked the early training tape I sent with my resume. But by mid-August of '77, I was officially a voice, speech and dialect trainer, coaching two main stage dialect show during the first ten-week term.

I owe a tremendous debt of gratitude to many of my former colleagues at Penn State. Though I was there, also, for only three years, directors and acting teachers embraced my work enthusiastically, permitting me to hone my skills as a voice and dialect coach and supporting my efforts to create instructional materials. I'm particularly grateful to Manuel Duque, with whom I team-taught several studio acting courses. Manuel gave me my most valuable insights into what the craft of acting really was. Perhaps as a portent of things to come, I also received invaluable support then from the late Valerie Schor, my Voice & Speech predecessor at UConn. Val was the loudest cheerleader for the creation of *Acting With an Accent,* often inviting me to come to Connecticut and experiment with her students.

PM: So why only three years at Penn State; what motivated the move to Hollywood?
DAS: At Penn State, and also at many other schools in the late seventies, assistant professors were earning between $11,000 and $17,000 annually; inflation was 12-13%, and salary increases were 2-3%. I was losing almost 10% of real income per year, working close to seventy hours a week and wondering how long it would be before I became eligible for food stamps. At the same time my dialect workshops and tapes were getting a tremendously positive reaction from teachers and actors. Since I had managed to stash enough money to live on for nine to twelve months, I decided it was a good time to try industry work without a university base. Though born in New York City, I didn't think I had the constitution to live and work there day after day. So I arrived in LA in September of 1980. I started advertising in the trades and *very slowly* began gathering some private students. But that wasn't an immediate concern. My first try at mail-order marketing the tapes produced results ten times beyond my wildest

expectations. Drama Book Shop and the Samuel French stores and catalog soon picked them up, and things really accelerated. So, having a living wage from the tapes almost immediately, I could promote my coaching skills slowly and effectively. I volunteered to lecture in acting workshops, worked for free on important Equity-waiver shows, and accepted "deferred salary" on some independent films. Through those activities, I met and worked with many influential acting coaches, directors and actors. By 1982, when the business moved from my apartment to an office suite near Paramount Studio, I was already teaching and coaching some pretty big names in the industry. Interestingly, for the entire twelve years in LA, no matter how much teaching or coaching I did, about 75% of my gross income always came from the recordings.

PM: What were some of the biggest thrills during those years?
DAS: Well, obviously, coaching some of the actors whose work I had admired for years, but also training really talented "unknowns," some of whom later hit it really big. But there were other wonderful experiences, like my first production job being on the sound stages where *Gone With The Wind* and *Citizen Kane* had been shot, or working in the Disney Animation Building where some of the great movie experiences of my youth had been created. *Some* of the travel was exciting. I spent nine weeks on location in Buenos Aires, mostly coaching actors who had never performed in English before. The work was fun and satisfying, the culture was amazing and my own Spanish improved immeasurably. The film, however, never saw the light of day (or the dark of a cinema).

PM: How do you find the attitudes of actors and directors toward voice speech, dialect and text coaches have changed and evolved in the nearly thirty years since you became one?
DAS: That would be easier to answer if I had been working consistently on similar projects with similar actors over the years. I'd say that other factors, not the passage of time, most affect actors' attitudes toward voice or dialect coaching. But even those factors change with the context and the setting.

Let's start with university training programs. There will always be a certain percentage of student actors who start out skeptical about having to change any voice-production and speech behaviors. Sure, that attitude seems less of a factor now at UConn than years ago at Penn State, but the reasons probably have more to do with me than with the students. First, my own rhetorical abilities have improved; I'm better at convincing them early in the game that vocal skill and acting skill are inseparable. Also, I now have more of what the Greeks called "initial ethos." Most new students know my name and/or have worked with my materials prior to arriving at UConn.

That factor enhances my early "window of opportunity" for winning their minds and hearts.

When I've worked on professional stage productions, performers' attitudes toward coaching often depended on how early my presence was established. If I came in at the beginning of rehearsals (or ideally, for the audition process as well), folks were usually positive and enthusiastic about the process. If, as has happened a few too many times recently, I was brought in during the second or even the third week of rehearsals, attitudes ranged from joy ("I'm so grateful someone is here to fix this!") to mild annoyance ("Now there's something else I have to think about.") to blatant hostility ("How dare they let me learn it one way and then have you come in and tell me to change what I'm doing!")

Most actors I worked with on feature films were very positive about having a dialect coach. But, for the sake of full disclosure, that's partly because my services were often engaged directly by the actors rather than by the productions. When working for the production itself—especially if I'm on the set during shooting—attitude problems are more likely to come from directors than from actors. Some directors don't want to hear about dialect errors in "takes" they really liked ("Go away, David, we'll fix it in the loop room!"). Others crave all the feedback I can give. Some directors want my actor notes limited to "correct pronunciation" only. That's very difficult for me. Since I believe that authentic-sounding performances must use a dialect's muscularity and inflections to help physicalize the actor's intentions and actions, it's almost impossible to avoid some crossover between dialect and acting notes. Some directors applaud this; others are appalled, considering it to be the greatest sin a "speech person" could commit. Eventually, I started insisting on discussing coaching philosophy with directors *before* deciding whether to accept a major coaching assignment.

But it's not just directors. Actors sometimes run screaming from sound artistic/linguistic choices. Some have said or implied, "I don't care if I'm the only one in the family who doesn't have the regionalism; I will only use my own speech pattern." *or* "I've won acting awards for doing characters with a certain type of regionalism, and I'm going to do that again even if it's wrong for this character." But happily, I had to deal with very few such situations.

PM: You bring up a good question—crossing the line into direction. Let's stay with that for a second. I wrestle with the taboo about giving "line readings." Yet choreographers demonstrate dance steps, choral directors demonstrate how they want a line of music to go, why shouldn't a dialect coach demonstrate the rhythm, intonation pattern (the lilt to use your term) of the dialect they are coaching?

Pedagogy and Coaching

Interviews with Three Television and Film Coaches:
Carla Meyer, Gillian Lane-Plescia and David Alan Stern by Paul Meier (continued)

DAS: I'm relieved to hear that you're wrestling with this concern as well. So we're both treading on the same somewhat dangerous ground. Yes, I certainly believe that a dialect coach who is a good performer (which I sure hope he or she is) should be demonstrating to some actors how to embody speech patterns into performances. How else are actors going to learn how the dialect functions within the context of a theatrical reality rather than an off-stage reality? Sure, it's great for actors to hear dialect samples of native speakers. But that's not nearly enough. Paul, if I were the director and you were the dialect coach on a show with characters from Devon or York or Cardiff, I'd want the actors to hear how Paul Meier adapts the dialect *for performance.* Yes, from you they would hear authentic sounding speech, as they would from samples of native speakers. But unlike most such samples, you would also achieve intelligibility for an American audience; you would make the moments interesting; you would be sure that the accented speech reflected changes as you moved from moment to moment. And those are my coaching goals when I'm "demonstrating." I don't give actors the "one correct *reading*" for a given line or moment. No such truth exists. But I want to show them, and I want them to explore, different options for various moments in the script. So I try to demonstrate how characters function when their specific impulses or discoveries or actions are physicalized or given voice through the muscularity, inflections and pronunciations of the target dialect. This, as opposed to their concentrating solely on the creation of the accent and hoping that an inner process will somehow remain alive. As I said earlier, I've been very fortunate in my career that most (but certainly not all) of the directors I've worked with in academic and commercial projects support and even encourage that approach to the speech or dialect coaching.

PM: So what exactly is it we dialect coaches do? Are we mere consultants on verisimilitude, having little to do with acting? Or are we working at the intersection of acting and culture, there to assist the project find a creative way to embody and support the world of the play as expressed through the voice and speech patterns of the characters? In professional terms where should the dialect person's name belong in the credits? Among the designers? Or in some place lower down—Special Thanks, for instance? I guess it comes down to how much potency theatre folks believe the human voice has to reveal cultural hierarchies and values, and the psychological states of characters. I happen to believe that dialect, in its broadest sense, embodies the values of a culture and is the sum of a character's life experience. Thus the dialect expert in a production is working right at its centre—not at its margins. For example, Standard British English, as we both know, uses fewer strong stresses than General American, and delays the strong stresses until later in the sentence. Brits often seem to preface and qualify the points they are about to make, whereas their American cousins often seem to value directness more, leading to earlier and more frequent strong stresses. The rhythmic differences between these two dialects are not, to my mind, arbitrary linguistic features attempted by actors in mere deference to verisimilitude, but are

deeply revealing of the habits of mind of the characters in their world. Thus the dialect coach is there to assist actors fully inhabit another culture not their own *as expressed in the text*— hardly a marginal undertaking, and a function that one could certainly attach equally well to directors.

DAS: Clearly, there are cultural issues that can influence the way speakers of a given accent will think, react and use language. Though I have no objection to having actors study some of those cultural/interpersonal phenomena, we must be careful not to cross into overgeneralization or stereotyping. Most importantly, I don't want actors to limit the number and kinds of options they give themselves for making choices about objectives, intentions or action verbs because they've read that people from a given country or region would not be likely to do a certain thing. Actors should be informed by those observations, but they must remember that drama is rarely about what usually or normally happens. It is often about people doing things differently on this day than they have done on all other days.

As to the question of program credit (or screen credit), I think that can and should change from project to project. At UConn's Connecticut Repertory Theatre, if the production is a major language piece or requires a fair amount of dialect coaching, I get credit up front with the designers and a bio. in the *Who's Who.* If I'm just checking in occasionally to guard against vocal abuse and sloppy diction, my name appears under "Production Staff." In films, I have sometimes exercised the option of *not* having my name appear in the screen credits, particularly when I've not been given enough instructional time before shooting or enough contact with the actors during shooting for the results to be to my liking.

PM: Having been back within a university theatre program and an EQUITY-U/RTA company for almost ten years, what would you say are the most important voice-speech-dialect goals you have for students in a professional actor-training program?
DAS: Above all my primary responsibility is teaching student actors to avoid vocal strain and injury, regardless of the degree of projection or emotional content required for a given role.

PM: How do you work toward that goal?
DAS: Once I've taught actors to coordinate breath support with relaxed phonation for a "normal" stage-projection level, I apply several techniques for creating increasingly loud phonation (first, completely devoid of emotional context) with minimal laryngeal tension. I then use other specially designed exercises to get actors to respond with this same "relaxed shouting" even when their characters are in the middle of extreme emotional outbursts. Actors whose screaming and yelling "technique" creates lots of unnecessary tension between the vocal cords and in the throat walls are kidding themselves into thinking they're producing moments of truthful emotional intensity for the audience. No, as my former colleague

Manuel Duque would say (quoting the Scottish King), they are creating "sound and fury, signifying nothing." An old directing textbook discussed the necessary theatrical balance between empathy and aesthetic distance. When actors create emotional intensity through blatant vocal strain, not only are they hurting their throats, they are hurting the performance as well. No matter how intense or emotional the moment is supposed to be, loudness *without* vocal strain or damage can be totally "believable" within the dramatic convention if it's connected to a truthful inner life. When actors begin screaming with unsupported, tense, vocally damaging sound, audiences experience the vocal discomfort *of the actors* rather than the emotional pain of the characters. That breaks aesthetic distance and creates negative empathy that pushes viewers farther away from the intended type of theatrical reality.

PM: And another important goal is...?
DAS: ...for all actors to increase drastically their skills in using vocal variety. Actors must have access to several different elements of voice variation: (a) the number of and duration of pauses during lines, (b) the duration of syllables, (c) movement within a large pitch range and (d) changes in intensity or loudness. Such vocal variety is essential for both reflecting and reinforcing many aspects of the inner, moment-to-moment acting process. Without it, actors rarely generate and audiences rarely experience the sense of first-time interaction with spontaneous discoveries of actions, images and words. Perhaps my single most important rule-of-thumb for vocal variety is to expand the pitch range and *use* that expanded range. Actors should almost always avoid monotone delivery. Monotone speech, on stage or off, is just plain boring. Monotone performances may still convey emotional intensity, albeit a general intensity often lacking in depth and specificity. To me, monotone is anathema to a self-reinforcing, moment-to-moment process. Teachers and directors often tell actors to make more and different kinds of choices about their intentions, actions or strategies as they progress through a scene. Many actors answer with claims that they are already making clear choices and changing their actions. And in some of these cases, I believe the actors *have* made internal changes, but have not (or cannot) let the voice respond in a way that gives vocal reality to that process. You can't believably discover new ideas if all of those discoveries are made on the same note—both literally and figuratively. You can't convince an audience that you're *doing* different things, if all the actions begin on the same note or repeats the same inflection/rhythm pattern. Vocal variety doesn't exist only for its own aesthetic sake; it helps create more believable moments on stage.

PM: We're right back again to the middle ground between teaching/coaching voice and teaching/coaching acting. What's the reaction of directors when they hear you telling actors to start a new moment at a different pitch or to speak at a faster or slower rate after what you've called "a new discovery"?
DAS: Some directors and acting coaches fear this kind of feedback terribly. They believe that any choices about external vocal changes are doomed to create artificial and patterned speech. Now, that fear would be warranted if the choices or directions were exclusively about the outer voice. I'm not saying that jumping to a new pitch guarantees a believable new discovery or action. It doesn't. But I am saying that a totally internal change in intention or impulse is often hidden from the audience (and from the other characters as well) if it is not carried to the listeners through vocal changes. Some directors will never buy this idea. I try hard to avoid working on their productions. Other directors, three of whom (Eric Hill, Bob McDonald, James Warwick) I work with regularly at two different theatres, give those kinds of directions themselves, and were doing so for years before they met me.

PM: Can I assume that the last of your goals is for student actors to become skillful with a range of different accents and dialects?
DAS: Not with a range of them, but with one (well, maybe two) of them—specifically, contemporary, non-regional American English and its somewhat "heightened" counterpart. I want all of my students, if they are seeking careers in this country, to achieve clarity and intelligibility with a basic American pattern that is free of any blatantly regional inflections, resonance traits or phonemes. I want them to acquire this skill even before modifying or "elevating" this basic pattern for playing more poetic or "classical" pieces.

PM: Would you care to give us your position within the ongoing "standard speech" "stage speech" "heightened speech" "good speech" debate?
DAS: Sure. I believe firmly that our students require two different levels of "standard" American speech for success in today's theatrical world. As I just said, American actors first must learn to create a colloquial, non-regional impression for contemporary American characters that don't speak with recognizable regional dialects. Second, there is an added level of speech "elevation" required to support the more poetic, more language-centric characters in Greek, Roman, Elizabethan, French Neo-Classical, or Restoration scripts, and even in many translations of the Nineteenth Century European Realists. Though I make it clear to students that *directors are perfectly within their rights to insist on a different speech aesthetic than mine*, I'll try to spell out the basic distinctions that I make.

For contemporary American characters who are not dialect speakers (by the dictates of the script or by the choice of the

69

Pedagogy and Coaching

Interviews with Three Television and Film Coaches:
Carla Meyer, Gillian Lane-Plescia and David Alan Stern by Paul Meier (continued)

director), there should be clarity of diction, but there need not be aspects of speech "elevation." For such colloquial characters, I do not ask for "pure vowels" in unstressed syllables. I don't require (or even want) pure, voiceless pronunciations of medial [t], [k], and [p] nor the elimination of post-vocalic R-coloration. Rare is the contemporary, "non-regional" American who actually speaks with these traits, and I see no reason why American actors should affect them in such roles.

But for the elevated/poetic language world of the classics, I do advocate the pure form of several phonemes. When other aspects of voice and speech are heightened to create these "worlds," then letting unstressed vowels regress [from /ɪ/] toward /ə/ or "schwa" in words like _accept, marriage, achievement, largest, occasion_ creates moments that are inconsistent with the heightened language environment. But, a caution! When using these purer vowels, actors must avoid the potential overcompensation of putting too much emphasis on these still-unstressed syllables.

Most Colloquial American speakers substitute "_almost_ fully voiced" [d], [b] and [g] for voiceless medial consonants in words like _beautiful, scatter, tempest,_ and _taken._ As I already said, I see no need for _contemporary_ American characters to substitute pure, voiceless [t], [p] and [k]. In elevated speech, however, this American near voicing of medials detracts from the classical speech style (as did the lack of vowel purity discussed above). Though these voiceless medials are also characteristic of Standard British speech, I believe they do not negate an elevated American impression when the speech act is heightened. _but,_ except for these plosives, I don't generally want other clearly British phonemes in American productions of most classics. Using the triphthong "o" in _go home,_ or totally eliminating R-coloration in _the bird soared through the air,_ or substituting the low-back vowel in _transferred to the grass_ or the "short I" in _Mary was very lively,_ not only aren't necessary for maintaining a heightened sound, they can lead American audiences to think actors are trying, unsuccessfully, to sound British. There are obvious exceptions. I fully support accurate British speech for actual English characters, whether in contemporary plays or classical works such as Restoration pieces and many of Shakespeare's histories. (I just performed the "narration" for an orchestral performance of Sir William Walton's _Henry V: A Shakespeare Scenario,_ and, by all means, both my Chorus and my King Hal were very, very English.) But North Americans need not become British or pseudo-British for all works of classical theatre.

PM: Getting back to my earlier comment, you haven't included general accent and dialect instruction among your most important voice and speech goals for actors-in-training. I imagine many within our field would find that quite strange coming from you.

DAS: Well, it's true that my name is strongly associated with accent and dialect coaching. And during my non-academic years, I certainly earned the greater portion of my income engaging in that activity. However, I was a Voice & Speech Trainer before becoming a dialect coach. And during my industry years, I never stopped teaching basic voice and speech, sometimes to my dialect students, but often to others who came strictly for non-dialect work. And now, since my return to UConn, less than a quarter of my teaching and coaching time involves dialects. In fact, it's only since Karen Ryker joined us last year that I resumed teaching an undergraduate dialect class. Five years earlier, as the sole Voice and Speech Trainer, I had to choose between teaching a yearly dialect class and offering a barely sufficient number of voice and speech classes. The decision was easy. My dialect reputation aside, I would have been shirking my primary responsibility if the price of a dialect course were inadequate basic voice speech training. Of course, I remained an active dialect coach for CRT productions. But, in the end, I'd rather hear supported, expressive voices without accents than strained, monotonous voices with them.

PM: What were the best and worst things you experienced in coaching for all those films and television shows?
DAS: The best things: most of the actors. The worst things: many of the producers. Somewhere in the middle: the directors. The first time I was about to coach a "star" whose work I admired (and who had just won an Emmy), I was very nervous. Since she was being sent in by the director and playwright to "fix" a difficult dialect only a week before a world premiere. I feared that she would object strongly to being coached at that stage. But she walked into the office, and almost cried the words, "What am I going to do?" Our work was both joyful and successful. In spite of Hollywood's reputation as the home of the lazy actor, most of my clients have been very professional and eager to acquire needed skills. I could count on my fingers the number of professional actors with whom, in retrospect, I'd rather not have worked. And of those ten or so, only three had readily recognized names—which I'd never reveal without having at least two glasses of wine poured into me first. That's not to say that every coaching _situation_ was a joy. When working for a production (not directly for an actor) there were many times when I simply was not permitted by the producer or director or production coordinator to do my job effectively, often causing major frustration for both coach and actors.

PM: What's the stupidest statement or request you've heard in your capacity as a speech or dialect coach?
DAS: It's a tie between the top two. A casting director at Paramount called in the mid-80s to ask that I prepare an actor for a screen test requiring "an Asian accent." To make a painfully long conversation short, I asked if he could be more

specific, pointing out that Indian, Arabic, Hebrew, Persian, Japanese, and Chinese were all, in fact, Asian accents. Absolutely nothing I said elicited any response other than, "It doesn't matter; it just has to be Asian." I insisted that he double check with the director and/or writer and get back to me. He never called back.

The second example involves a TV show that I will identify. One of the projects that I pursued with a passion was the mini-series of *The Thorn Birds*. I loved the novel and wanted to be a part of that production. I developed a written and recorded "dialect prospectus," detailing the linguistic challenges of New Zealand characters moving to Australia early in life with speech patterns changing as they grew—of having Irish characters going to different countries, etc. After several follow-ups, I received a letter from one of the executive producers. After thanking me for my interest and my efforts, he ended with these words—words that were repeated exactly in the official casting call several weeks later. He wrote, "However, New Zealand and Australian accents will not be needed since this production is being shot in Burbank." This was just one of the factors contributing to my eventual conclusion that twelve years in Hollywood were enough for any sane human being.

❦

Peer Reviewed Article *by Bonnie Raphael*

Carryover: Bringing Skills Acquisition from Studio to Life

The University of North Carolina at Chapel Hill has the finest women's soccer team in this country with the best win/loss record of any team in the history of US collegiate sports. In 2001, the undergraduate women on this team won 24 out of their 25 matches, losing only at the NCAA final match—by one goal. In its 21-year history, this team has won 16 national championships and played in 120 "final four" competitions. A great deal of its unprecedented and ongoing success has been attributed to Anton Dorrance, the team's remarkable coach. A good part of what he has to say about successful coaching is directly applicable to skills acquisition and carryover far beyond the world of sports:

> Getting your team to transcend ordinary effort is the challenge in every training session and every match. To get this effort, you as a coach are regularly dealing with the emotional strain of not accepting the lower standard of performance and effort.[1]

Many acting and voice and speech teachers and coaches can relate directly to the "emotional strain of not accepting the lower standard of performance and effort." It makes very good educational sense to set challenging standards, but it is no easy task, either for beginning teachers and coaches or for those of us who have been teaching and coaching for decades. Coach Dorrance observes:

> After a while, your coaching development ceases to be about finding newer ways to organize practice... you soon stop collecting drills. Your development as a coach shifts to observing how the great ones motivate, lead or drive player performances at higher and higher levels.[2]

It is one thing to get actors motivated in the first place and quite another to keep them motivated—over the course of a rehearsal period and the run of a show, or over the course of a semester, a year, the length of a training program, perhaps even longer if one is doing ongoing work with a resident acting company. In order to better understand both possibilities for sustaining motivation and techniques for facilitating carryover, it is important to identify the stages of the learning process itself.

Learning theorists tell us that in skills acquisition, there are four identifiable stages:

Stage I: *"You don't know you don't know."*—Ignorance is bliss, and many athletes or performers achieve a certain degree of success on the basis of their native ability or talent—without training of any kind and without giving any thought to their technique. But, as they continue to pursue their dreams of getting to the top of their respective fields, many of them eventually confront the realization that their abilities have limits.

Stage II: *"You know you don't know."*—An athlete will fail to qualify for the quarterfinals of a match, or a singer will get eliminated in the final stages of an important competition; something will happen to demonstrate the limits of their present capabilities. An actor may be asked to fill a large theatre without shouting or to audition in an unfamiliar dialect or to sing a piece of complicated music, and realizes that coursework or coaching or some form of assistance is needed in order to do so. So help is sought.

Bonnie N. Raphael has taught and coached professional voice users for over thirty years—at the University of North Carolina, the American Repertory Theatre and its Institute for Advanced Theatre Training at Harvard, the National Theatre Conservatory, Northwestern University, and the University of Virginia, etc. Bonnie has coached hundreds of productions, at PlayMakers Repertory Company, American Repertory Theatre, Missouri Repertory Theatre, Dallas Theater Center, Denver Center Theatre, Repertory Theatre of St. Louis, Colorado Shakespeare Festival and elsewhere, working with Garland Wright, Andrei Serban, Jerry Zaks, Robert Brustein, Michael Kahn, AnneBogart, Robert Wilson, Ron Daniels, and others. Actors she has coached include Annette Bening, Christopher Lloyd, Cherry Jones, Christopher Walken, Kathleen Widdoes and Claire Bloom.

1. Anton Dorrance, in a speech to the 1997 convention of the National Soccer coaches Association of America (NSCAA).

2. Ibid.

Stage III: *"You know you know."*—When in training, the actor finds (to his great dismay) that behavior modification brings with it a period of discomfort or struggle or awkwardness, or the feeling of being phony or unnatural. His or her ability to act may suffer temporarily; the lines that were so perfectly memorized may no longer be available; the actor's customary ease may disappear because of a distracting need to concentrate on breathing or alignment or support for the voice or pronunciation or phrasing. This stage can be very uncomfortable, and disconcerting enough to interrupt the learning process if not to end it entirely.

Stage IV: *"You don't know you know."*—If, however, the actor has the vision, the faith and the courage not to give up or is encouraged by those who believe in process, then change of another sort finally begins to happen. After a concerted period of practice, repetition, incubation and carryover, the new skills become the default position, behavior that can be relied on even when the actor's attention is elsewhere. Then—and only then—can the new skill be considered fully integrated.[3]

3. Adams, James L. *The Care and Feeding of Ideas: A Guide to Encouraging Creativity*. Reading, MA: Addison-Wesley Publishing Company, Inc., 1986.

Even after Stage IV has begun to take place, the actor cannot simply "forget" new skills and let the chips fall where they may. Any time he or she meets a particularly challenging situation (e.g. working over a respiratory infection, dealing with unexpected aural competition emanating from the audience, playing in a particularly inhospitable acoustical space), the actor will have to shift gears a bit, rearranging priorities in order to bring technique to a more conscious level rather than simply taking it for granted or simply hoping that it will work. If the developmental process has been truly integrated, then self-consciousness will have been replaced with a habitual self-awareness that will allow the actor to make a series of minor adjustments during performance, precluding the need for a noticeable, major adjustment when a given challenge becomes formidable.

We who teach and coach actors, even on the graduate or professional levels, spend a good part of our effort facilitating Stages II and III, which just happen to be the least enjoyable ones for the learner. To make matters even worse, our job, to a certain extent, consists of making actors aware of skills not yet mastered and then facilitating the gradual acquisition of these skills. How might we do so in a way that enables them to get to Stage IV in the most direct and unimpeded manner?

It may be useful to consider two separate but important hierarchies that can be helpful in finding some solutions. For example, let us suppose that an actor has a relatively inactive soft palate, so that the quality of his speaking voice is hypernasal. According to learning experts, the method according to which you get the actor to energize and control the soft palate is important, but equally important is the need for familiarizing this actor with **two hierarchies for skills acquisition:**

1) The first hierarchy relates to the **degree of difficulty**. This means that whatever behavior is to be changed is modified most easily when it is mastered in roughly the following sequence:

A) In isolation—having the student acquire the desired ability by itself, out of any particular context. For example, the actor can learn to differentiate between the raised palate position and the lowered palate position as an isolated and discrete action—by breathing in and out on a clear, crisp "k" sound, or by moving from "ng" to "ah" and back with a dropped and relaxed jaw, taking care to enjoy nasal resonance in the "ng" while not allowing it to bleed into the "ah".

B) In words—having the student avoid any hypernasality first in words containing no nasal consonants to eliminate either general or phonemic nasality, then on the vowels occurring adjacent to different nasal consonants to eliminate assimilative nasality, and then on vowels adjacent to the consonants "l" and "r" (which tend to allow some hypernasality as well because of the tongue position required for their articulation).

C) In phrases and sentences—first in those devoid of nasal consonants and then in those with increasingly challenging numbers of nasal consonants in them.

D) In cold readings—so that the actor can use the sight of an "m", an "n" or an "ng" on the page as a visual reminder to lift the palate for the vowels and non-nasal consonants in the vicinity. (Even here, it is important to make sure that the material being read is not treated as cannon fodder or exercise but rather that the student is playing actions, making sense, communicating meaning to a listening audience.)

E) In memorized materials—so that the student can incorporate an appropriate use of the soft palate in a monologue or a poem or a lawyer's address to a jury. By bringing a consideration of content and given circumstances to performance, the actor is asked to master the challenges of incorporating this new behavior while concentrating elsewhere. (It is extremely helpful, at this stage, to select material for performance that requires or is conducive to the use of balanced oral-nasal resonance—e.g. a monologue from Shakespeare would be preferable to one from a Sam Shepard play.) Most actors have a stronger desire to act better than to simply sound better. So if the sounds being used directly contribute to the effectiveness of the overall performance, then feelings of phoniness or unnatural behavior are less likely to interfere.

F) In spontaneous speech—so that the actor can take the skills cultivated and strengthened in the above five steps and use them even as he or she invents rather than reproduces language, improvises rather than remembers lines, expresses self-generated thoughts rather than transmitting those of the playwright.

2) The second hierarchy refers to the **challenges offered by different environments** in which new behaviors may be strengthened. There is certainly a "usual" or "most likely" progression of environments but this hierarchy works best when it is personalized by each individual actor and then applied to the process of behavior modification. A typical hierarchy of environmental challenges might be:

A) the voice and speech studio

B) at home or in the car or out walking alone

C) other studios—acting, movement, singing, etc.

D) rehearsals for a production or for a scene being prepared for acting class

E) performances of a play, starting about 2-3 days after opening night

F) previews and first few public performances of a play

G) use of the new behavior on a daily basis until it becomes a default position during spontaneous speech—on the telephone or in short conversations with strangers, each lunch hour, etc.

H) use of the new behavior under higher levels of pressure or stress (auditions, interviews, interactions with potentially difficult or judgmental people, etc.)

It is essential to remember that this hierarchy can be unique and personal for each learner. Some may find an initial change of behavior easiest to effect when on the telephone, for example, because nobody is looking at them and they can concentrate fully on the new habits they're acquiring. Others may find it extremely useful to practice in short conversations with strangers because these people (delivering their newspaper or checking out their groceries or mending their shoes) have no expectations or preconceived notions about how the speakers have sounded in the past. Even a highly talented and experienced actor in the process of acquiring new behavior may be doing splendidly until the artistic director of a theatre pops in unexpectedly to watch a bit of rehearsal, at which time there might well be an unanticipated regression. When the stakes are high, when stress is present, behavior will tend to revert to old habits until new ones are truly ingrained. If and when a teacher or a coach is able to help the actor to feel empowered to make a vital distinction between self-awareness and self-consciousness, between process and product, then the path may be a bit more linear and less uncomfortable. If and when the learner can adjust the mindset so as to embrace the discomfort as a sign that new and better behaviors are replacing old habits, then his or her innate preference for comfort or balance can be countered and bettered by an exhilarating sense of growth.

Anton Dorrance's remarks in a speech to the 1997 convention of the National Soccer Coaches Association of America are quite relevant:

> Your strength in coaching is having the courage to constantly deal with the athletes that unconsciously try to take things a bit easier... What is missing that makes most of us ordinary? Maybe what we start to lack is energy, or maybe it is a kind of combative courage which we are sick of soliciting to fight the human tendency to be comfortably mediocre... There is an emotional battle that is constant when we are trying to take our players to higher levels and our players are unconsciously fighting us to stay at a more comfortable level... The way the lower-level coach eventually loses the respect of his team is by not being demanding enough, not harping on a higher standard and not making the stressful passionate investment which may lead to a loss of popularity... They win the popularity contest, but sacrifice respect. The result is that the standards are lowered.[4]

4 Dorrance, Anson and Gloria Averbuch. *The Vision of a Champion: Advice and Inspiration from the World's Most Successful Women's Soccer Coach.* Chelsea, MI: Sleeping Bear Press, May 2002.

If we decide to make this "stressful passionate investment," then what steps might we take to better facilitate our actors' ability to bring their newly-acquired skills out of the studio and into the rehearsal room, onto the stage, even into their lives?

1) We can set standards of excellence and serve as models for our students by doing our best to practice what we preach.

2) We can teach the importance of both process and product, the value of not finding shortcuts or seeing what we might get away with rather than taking the time and making the commitment to discover what we can achieve.

3) We can explain the process of skills acquisition and carryover, so that the students have some guidelines to help assure them of being on a path; guidelines that can help them to embrace the temporary discomfort as a positive sign that new ground is being explored.

4) We can help our actors to both set goals and to reset them along the way, so that they realize that they are always in process; so that the best of our students don't rely on the general level of class competency to set their personal goals and so that the weakest of our students take responsibility for not remaining at the bottom of the pack. We can encourage each student we teach to compete only with him or herself and not with anybody else.

5) We can find feedback processes that are based on reward and pleasure, avoiding, as best we can, any kind of punitive relationship with those whom we train.

6) We can make sure to evaluate each of their performances in both relative and absolute terms, on the one hand rewarding baby steps rather than seeking breakthroughs and on the other hand, always keeping the needs of the profession in mind. We can reward effort and consistency and improvement rather than mere talent but we can't forget the market our students will enter at the end of their training. Only then can each student be made aware of both where he or she is in relation to where he or she started the process and in relation to where he or she needs to get in order to have a better chance to achieve any and all professional goals.

7) We can do our very best to solicit both support and reinforcement for this process:
   • from the acting and movement and singing teachers and coaches with whom our students also work;
   • from their directors, stage managers and even artistic directors if possible;
   • from other members of their class or cast, who can provide feedback to the actor in our absence and reward new behaviors when they hear or see them.

8) And last, but certainly not least, it is essential that we not only encourage our students to dream big dreams, to "go for the gold," but that we don't give up on those dreams either because of our own expectations for any student or even because of our own previous track records as teachers and coaches.

Coach Anson Dorrance has something to say about this that is perhaps surprising but also quite encouraging:

> Excellence is actually mundane. It is accomplished through deliberate actions, ordinary in themselves, performed consistently and carefully, made into habits, compounded together, added up over time.[5]

5. Ibid.

Bibliography

Adams, James L. *The Care and Feeding of Ideas: A Guide to Encouraging Creativity.* Reading, MA: Addison-Wesley Publishing Company, Inc., 1986.

Dorrance, Anson. *Training Soccer Champions.* Cary, NC: JTC Sports, March, 1996.

Dorrance, Anson and Gloria Averbuch. *The Vision of a Champion: Advice and Inspiration from the World's Most Successful Soccer Coach.* Chelsea, MI: Sleeping Bear Press, May 2002.

Column *by Kathryn Maes*

Applying Theories of Learning Styles and Modalities to the Challenges of Coaching

Kathryn Maes (ADVS, Central School of Speech and Drama-London; PhD. University of Pittsburgh) Kathy currently serves as Chair in the Department of Theatre, Film and Video Production at the University of Colorado-Denver. Professionally, Kathy has served as dialect coach for four productions for the Royal Shakespeare Company and co-dialect coach with Joan Washington on the Royal National Theatre's Olivier Award-winning production of Arthur Miller's *American Clock*. Kathy has coached such notable actors as Ralph Fiennes and Brenda Blethyn. She served as Head of Voice at the Denver Center Theatre Company for four years prior to coming to the University of Colorado-Denver in 1992.

In my first two articles on applying theories of Learning Styles and Modalities to the teaching of voice and speech, it was established that all learners absorb information to be learned in either a **sensory-intuitive-experiential** way or in an **analytical-reasoning-logical** way, and then process the information by actively using it, or reflectively observing or thinking about it. It was further asserted that the information to be processed is finally stabilized (i.e., learned) through repetition or repeated use either by doing or actively using the information in some connected way.

I also presented four basic learning styles preferred by all learners as set forth by Bernice McCarthy in her book, *The 4MAT System*. The **Innovative Learners** like to take in the information in a concrete manner and process the learning reflectively; **Analytical Learners** prefer to take in the information in a more abstract way and process the learning reflectively; **Common Sense Learners** like to take in the information more abstractly and then like to experiment with the learning; and **Dynamic Learners** prefer to take in the information in a concrete manner and then like to experiment with the learning. Additionally, learners also have a preference as to what senses they utilize the most in taking in the learning or the experience: visually, aurally, or kinesthetically. As teachers/coaches, we need to incorporate a variety of experiences in our teaching and coaching that encourages learning *across* the styles and modalities, which hopefully will provide a "hook" for all learners. The goal of such an approach is to broaden and enhance their ability to learn in a variety of challenging situations (i.e., to make them better learners).

I think we would all agree that coaching actors in a production is one of the most challenging of all learning situations. The particular challenge for the actor is the pressure they bear to master the new work (or new combination of skills) in a relatively short period of time at an extremely high level of performance. Few productions provide the luxury of maturation time. Additionally, because of all the composite skills needed by the actor for his/her performance, the actor is placed in a constant state of multi-tasking in an attempt to meld all of the required talents into a seamless, artistic performance. The coach's job is to assist the actor master or combine these skills rather quickly—but artfully!

The coach's challenge, on the other hand, is three fold: to assess where the actor is in the learning process, to determine what needs to be learned, and to establish how best to facilitate the learning in a compressed period of time. As a coach, I don't like taking on any coaching job (either large or small) unless I know I am given the time to accomplish the job to my satisfaction. This is where it becomes essential to meet with the director and discover the director's particular vision of the vocal goals and needs for the production. Are they realistic ones? Most directors know the vocal *results* they would like but lack the understanding of what it may take to achieve those results. It is the coach's responsibility to help the director understand what is a realistic expectation, what possible modifications or adaptations might need to be accommodated, and what compromises must be agreed upon in order to achieve the desired results. More often than not, this translates into giving the coach a reasonable amount of time spent working with the actor(s). It is also essential that a consensus is reached between the director and the coach regarding the "vocal vision" for the production.

Because of the compression of time, in a one-on-one session it becomes critical that the coach be able to assess the Learning Style and preferred Learning Modality of the actor rather quickly. In private coaching, the coach's focus must be on expediting the learning and mastery (i.e., a short–term goal) rather than on making the actor a better learner (i.e., a long-term goal). The coach must be able to walk out of the first session with a clear understanding of how this actor learns the best, and structure all future sessions with that insight in mind. The first session, therefore, must have two goals: to present the initial material to be learned, and to put forward the material in a way that will aid in the assessment of the actor's preferred Learning Style and Modality. In essence, the first session should cover the material by incorporating a variety of experiences, teaching across the four Learning Styles and the three Modalities as a means of testing the actor's learning preference. By using a combination of the coach's personal observations of what seemed to yield the quickest and best results and by asking the actor what s/he felt worked the best for them during the session, the coach should be able to fairly accurately assess the preferred Learning Style and Modality of the actor.

The situation becomes more complex in a group coaching session. In that instance, the coach must carefully continue to structure all sessions to teach across the Learning Styles and Modalities in an attempt to reach all actors in the group. In a private breakout session, however, it might prove helpful to ask each individual actor what particular parts and/or activities of the group session they felt worked the best for them. This may well help the coach to quickly establish the individual's preferred Learning Style and Modality. At least it will provide a reasonable starting point for the session.

Let's put this theory into practice in a hypothetical coaching situation. The following is a coaching plan for an initial session for either a single actor or a group. The plan is designed to present the sounds of the Cockney accent across the four Learning Styles and the three Modalities. Some of the planned activities may well accommodate several Learning Styles and Modalities and will be noted.

Sample Initial Session for an Individual Actor or Group Learning the Cockney Accent

Goal of the Session: To develop awareness of and facility with the phonemic changes of the Cockney accent

I. Taking in the Material: Introducing the sounds of the Cockney accent
  A. Concrete Approach (accommodates Innovative Learners and Dynamic Learners):
    1. Have the actors listen to words spoken in the accent (either live or recorded) isolating a specific sound change—**accommodates Aural Modalities**—and have the actors repeat the words—**accommodates Kinesthetic Modalities**. Do this for the remaining significant sound changes in the accent.
    2. Create a list of words isolating a specific sound change and have the actors create a new spelling of the word that (to them) represents a close approximation of the pronunciation in dialect (e.g. "rine" for the word "rain")—**accommodates Visual Modalities**—and have the actors repeat the words—**accommodates Kinesthetic Modalities**. Use this method for the remaining significant sound changes in the accent.
  B. Abstract Approach (accommodates Analytical Learners and Common Sense Learners)
    1. Because the activity of acquiring a stage accent is by its nature engaged in an active development of a skill, I would use the same listening activity found above in #1 under the Concrete Approach.
    2. Have the actors identify a phonetic symbol (or alternate phonetic symbol of their own creation) with the sounds they identified in the spoken list—e.g.:

"rain"	[reĭn] to [raĭn]	IPA
"rain"	(rAYn) to (rIn)	Berry
"rain"	(R Trombone, +Y Buzz, N Violin)	
	to (R Trombone, 6y, N Violin)	Lessac
"rain"	("r-eye-n")	Individual

    This accommodates the Visual Modality.
II. Processing the Material: Using the sounds of the Cockney accent in Connected Speech and Text
  A. Using the Material Reflectively (accommodates Innovative Learners and Analytical Learners)— Again, because the activity of acquiring a stage accent is by its nature engaged in an active development of a skill, I would use the same activities found in to the following category of "Using the Material Experimentally".
  B. Using the Material Experimentally (accommodates all Learners)
    1. Create a list of sentences that uses the words from the word lists given to the actors focusing on a specific sound change (e.g., "It rained late the same day they gave the Shakespearian play.").
    2. Create another list of sentences that mixes the words from all word lists as well as additional words with the various sound changes (e.g., "Well, you see, now I think I ain't got a lot of hope or nothing at all that

I can hang me hat on—let alone do I have a mother or father!").

3. Begin exploring the script with the actors, having them discover the sound changes as they occur in the dialogue.

All of the suggested exercises may be easily adapted to the session at hand and to the specific needs of the actors. Never negate the value of conscious-connected-sensory repetition (versus unaware tedious activity) for both physical as well as mental activities to be mastered. Changing articulation patterns requires a muscle memory that is best achieved through sensory repetition and focused perceptive practice that will ultimately stabilize the learning of the accent. This type of repetition will allow the muscles of articulation to develop "habitual awareness" (Lessac) associated with the sound, and it is this awareness of feeling that will keep the actor on the dialect path, and allow the actor's mind to focus solely on the moment-to-moment reality occurring on the stage—where it belongs! In the final analysis, artistic stage accent acquisition is centered in the body *through* the mind—making the activity a total stabilized learning experience.

Bibliography

Berry, Cicely. 1974. *Voice and the Actor*. New York, NY: Macmillian Publishing Co., Inc..

Leamnson, Robert. 1999. *Thinking About Teaching and Learning: Developing Habits of Learning with First Year College and University Students*. Sterling, VA: Stylus Publishing, LLC.

Lessac, Arthur. 1997. *The Use and Training of the Human Voice: A Bio-dynamic Approach to Vocal Life*. Mountain View, CA: Mayfield Publishing Company.

McCarthy, Bernice. 1987. *The 4MAT System: Teaching to Learning Styles with Right/Left Mode Technique*. Barrington, IL: Excel, Inc.

Column *by Robert Barton*

Many "Right" Ways: Honoring Diverse Teaching Methods and Learning Modes

Vocal Character, The Sound of Emotional Intelligence

An open secret in education is how unreliable standardized tests and grades are at predicting success. Mental intelligence is only part of it. In acting, talent is also only part of it. With an epidemic of students suffering from entitlement, disengagement and a lack of resourcefulness, emotional intelligence research has evolved to investigate what *else* it takes to succeed.* Educators have often chosen to revive the more traditional term "character" to identify those skills (self-discipline, integrity, ability to motivate self and others, capacity to defer gratification, control and channel urges) characteristic of long term success.

Research on the amygdala (our storehouse of emotional memory), norepinnephrine (the hormone secreted in heightened reactivity) and the neocortex (home for long term feelings) all show a specific kind of activity of key brain areas, entirely different between those with and without what I will alternately refer to as character or EI. Those with it have a self-aware, observing ego (very akin to Stanislavski's Creative State) which allows them to monitor their own reactions while having them. They have a specifically activated neocortex, which lets them be aware of their mood *and* of their thoughts about that mood. EI is a combination of interpersonal (understanding other people) and intrapersonal (understanding oneself) savvy. It involves knowing emotions, managing appropriate feelings, soothing oneself effectively, competence in handling relationships, attunement to subtle social signals, and setting clear goals. It is so powerful that once learned, it reprograms the mind.

The emotional brain is highly attuned to symbolic meanings and to the mode Freud called the "primary process", the messages of metaphor, story, myth, the visual arts. The emotional mind is quicker than the rational mind, often with a strong sense of certainty. The interval between emotional trigger and eruption can be virtually instantaneous. Rapid perception mode sacrifices accuracy for speed, since the emotional mind is radar for danger. It reacts to the present *as though it were the past*. Unfortunately, this fast, automatic appraisal may prevent one from realizing that what was once the case is no longer so. Those low on EI are often trapped into repeating past responses. Much instruction therefore is about retraining through new symbolic meanings.

I suggest that our acting programs begin to address character more directly. I also suggest that we consider the voice and speech characteristics of such awareness as part of our training. What are the vocal dynamics of emotional competencies and interpersonal awareness? What is the sound of its opposite—selfishness, violence, meanness of spirit or simply being "passion's slave"? What is the sound of the bland midpoint where the absence of any of the overt qualities above is reflected by innocuous vocal choices? How has this "non-voice" become so commonplace in film acting? And what can be done about it?

Character is not only about ethical resourcefulness but also complexity, interest and texture. Close your eyes and imagine the voices of Katharine Hepburn, Humphrey Bogart, Bette Davis, and Cary Grant, then replace them with those of Julia Roberts, Tom Cruise, Meg Ryan or Ben Affleck. In

Robert is head of the Acting Program at the University of Oregon and the author of the widely used texts *Acting: Onstage and Off, Style for Actors,* and (with Rocco Dal Vera) *Voice: Onstage and Off* as well as numerous articles. He is the recipient of the ATHE's Best Book Award as well ACTF's Outstanding Acting Coach award. He has acted professionally in most of the plays of Shakespeare and has directed half of them.

* A substantial amount of research on this subject has been collected by Daniel Goleman in his seminal work *Emotional Intelligence.* The subsequent effects on our lives have been analyzed sharply by Robert Hughes in *The Culture of Complaint.* The need to teach EI has been acknowledged in primary and secondary school education where the use of texts such as *Building Character in Schools* by Kevin Ryan and Karen E. Bohlin is increasing. The pioneer course in this subject, called Self Science, was first developed at Nueva Learning Center in San Francisco and other classes with titles such as Social Development, Life Skills and Personal Intelligence have emerged within health, science or social science curricula. Oddly enough, little inroad has been made in higher education, almost as if by then it has already been accomplished or is too late.

screen acting of the moment, voices often play a very small part in the impact of the performer. If we could teach vocal character, we would probably not only produce more resourceful, well-adjusted actors but far more interestingly spoken performances.

What else do we know about EI? It invariably involves laughing easily, which research has demonstrated helps people think more broadly and associate more freely. It involves self-efficacy, psychology's term for belief that one has mastery over the events of one's life and can meet challenges as they come up. Such persons easily achieve "flow" (a behavioral science term comparable to what athletes call "the zone"), a state of focused self-forgetfulness, the opposite of rumination and worry. Flow only occurs where skills are well-rehearsed, neural circuits are most efficient, and hard work can seem refreshing or replenishing rather than draining. Students who excel are often drawn to study precisely because it puts them in flow.

Those with character or EI empathize (from the Greek empatheira "feeling into") easily, intuiting another's subjective experience through acute reading of nonverbal channels. They have a tacit sense of the rhythm of relationships. Emotions are contagious, whether toxic or nourishing—we catch feelings like a social virus—but those with character are more socially adroit so that less disturbing emotional leakage will unsettle their encounters. They are good at being interested, knowing what kind of behavior is expected, how to rein in impulses to misbehave, how follow directions and how to ask for help. They possess confidence, curiosity, intentionality, relatedness,and cooperativeness and are adept at impression management. According to Goleman "In that sense, they are like skilled actors." One of the mysteries in applying this state to actor training is why then are so many performers only selectively adroit and often disastrous in interpersonal connections?

At the opposite end from EI are those who regularly experience "flooding" or susceptibility to emotional distress, who are swamped by unsettling, out-of-control feelings. These subjects often cannot match an emotion physically or vocally in others, have more self-defeating answers on ways to make friends, and when asked to role play being sad, angry, etc. give the least convincing performances. They are often socially tone deaf. They may see facial expressions and hear speech but fail to connect a name with a feeling and a feeling with facial or vocal expression. Obviously, actors are the opposite of most such research subjects, yet puzzlingly are often victims of flooding as well. Why do actors, after demonstrating considerable mastery, sometimes shift to emotional illiteracy?

If an acting program addresses character as a general survival issue and a means of creating characterizations of greater depth and interest, it is not unreasonable to assume that vocal lives of actors and their characters would also benefit. However, I believe that we can address voice and speech more specifically. Some questions to consider:

- What is the most appropriate way to move beyond technical or metaphoric terminology for vocal choices? How can a vocal EI vocabulary be developed?

- Why do the subtleties or constraints of film acting often result in editing of vocal depth and complexity? How can this be rectified?

- What happens when actors who exemplify all the qualities of character in one context, drop them completely in another? How can we find transference strategies so our students will be more resourceful in more contexts?

- If an actor masters all the basic qualities and skills of EI, what will that sound like?

Pronunciation, Phonetics, Linguistics, Dialect/Accent Coaching *Louis Colaianni, Associate Editor*

Editorial Column *by Louis Colaianni, Associate Editor*

With this our third issue, this department offers a small, yet penetrating complement of articles. Phil Timberlake's lively article informs us that the so-called "pirate accent" lives as much in our imaginations as it does in any geographic location. We are also treated to Rhonda Cundy's side bar, which enumerates pirate characters in the Opera repertoire. Our own David Carey interviews Penny Dyer, one of England's premier dialect coaches, on her approach to coaching for Film and Television. Finally, Doug Honorof's treatment of lexical sets provides illumination for anyone concerned with variable pronunciations of word groups, such as, "ask, dance, class" and "Duke, student, new." Each of these contributions proclaims a unique point of view. As always, vsr celebrates diversity in the world of voice and speech.

Louis Colaianni, associate editor, is the author of *The Joy of Phonetics and Accents* (Drama Publishers, 1994) and *Shakespeare's Names: A New Pronouncing Dictionary* (Drama Publishers, 2000). He has given workshops and lectures internationally on voice production, speech and phonetics. Colaianni is a tenured, Associate Professor of Theatre at the University of Missouri-Kansas City and a Voice and Speech Coach in the professional theatre. His biography appears in *Who's Who in the World,* (Marquis, 2000).

Peer Reviewed Article *by Phil Timberlake*

"A Voice So Cruel, and Cold, and Ugly": In Search of the Pirate Accent [ɑɚ]

Phil Timberlake recently received his MFA in Voice and Speech Pedagogy from Virginia Commonwealth University where he taught Voice, Speech, Dialects, and Acting. Phil was the 1996 Annette Kade Fulbright Fellow to France (studying voice at the Roy Hart International Arts Centre) and VASTA's 1999 Clyde Vinson Memorial Scholarship recipient. He appeared in numerous Off-Loop theatres in Chicago where he lived for 10 years. Phil was an Adjunct Professor of Voice and Speech at The Theatre School, DePaul University, and led "extended voice" workshops with Lookingglass Theatre, Roosevelt University, and Purdue University. Phil is an Associate Teacher of Fitzmaurice Voicework.

1. http://www.google.com

2. http://users.lanminds.com

3. http://cc.chronoshock.com

4. http://www.forestfaire.com/languageguide.htm

5. http://www.mmjp.or.jp/amlang.atc/di&legends/audrey/episode8.htm

Interview with a Pirate

The Pirate made his entrance in an undergraduate Stage Dialects class. The assignment was to collect a "real life dialect" for personal study, and an imaginative student, longing for an interesting dialect, suggested she would go and find a pirate to interview. The room immediately filled with swaggering, snarling students saying, "Make him walk the plank," "Aye, matey," "More rum, m'boy," and the rhotic verbal exclamation, "Arr," [ɑɚ].

Of course, it would be possible for the student to interview a pirate—somewhere in the world someone is robbing someone else at sea. But would it be *this* pirate with *this* accent? Surely not. And that made me wonder. How did everyone, including me, know how to "do" this "pirate accent?" How had a growling, spitting, [ɑɚ]-ing pirate wormed his way into our culture?

Initial Search

As a simple, non-scientific experiment to sample the presence of the supposed pirate accent in popular culture, I went to the internet. On the search engine, Google[1], I typed in the phrase, "pirate accent." The number of "hits" (entries containing the phrase "pirate accent" in websites) was 134.

Some examples: a transcription of an interview with David Hyde Pierce from the February 15, 1999 program of *Late Show with David Letterman* that describes Mr. Hyde Pierce relating an anecdote in a "pirate accent."[2] A website for the role-playing game, "Chrono Cross," lists the character named "Fargo" as speaking in a "typical pirate accent."[3] The Santa Barbara Renaissance Fair has posted an "Elizabethan Language Guide" which prompts their actors to pronounce the consonant /r/, "with all the glory of a pirate...(as in) fatherrrrr."[4] My favorite was the "Princess Diana Memorial Fiction Library" which features a fictional vacation taken by Princess Diana and Audrey Hepburn. It includes this exchange about the sailboat they'll be using:

> There she be," said Audrey in a pirate accent.... 'A sprightly-looking craft she be, too,' (said Princess) Diana match(ing) Audrey's accent.[5]

The people who posted these Web pages assumed that the average internet surfer would know what was meant by a typical pirate accent. And that we'd be able to imagine Audrey Hepburn and Princess Diana using it.

From this selection of websites, it seems that there is a typical pirate accent imbedded in contemporary popular culture. I will now raise three sets of questions regarding this phenomenon:

1) What are the qualities of a typical pirate accent? What are the sounds I was hearing in class and that the internet writers assumed we know? Is it an accent from a particular region of the world?

2) Is it accurate to call this a typical pirate accent? In other words, what is a typical pirate?

3) How did it get implanted in the popular culture? Was it through books? Films? Or something else?

What is a "typical pirate accent?"

The pirate accent I heard in the Dialects class had two main qualities: *gruffness* and *rhoticity/retroflexion*.

A gruff voice might be described as harsh, crusty, rough, bearish, growly, snarly—you get the picture. This gruffness tends to manifest itself in a relatively low pitch. I imagine the pirate accent as a Baritone or Bass voice. The placement of the voice is in the throat, chest, or abdominal cavity.

In addition to the gruff nature of the accent, I would add the quality of rhoticity/retroflexion. Nancy Elliot, in her article "A Study in the Rhoticity of American Film Actors," defines rhoticity as:

> (t)he presence or absence of a pronounced [r] in the syllable coda (i.e., an /r/ found before a consonant or at the end of a word). ...Accents of English can be categorized as *rhotic* accents in which syllable coda /r/ is categorically pronounced, or non-*rhotic* accents, in which /r/ is categorically deleted. ...There is a third category, *variably rhotic* accents, in which speakers exhibit a variable rate of rhoticity.[6]

I would maintain that the typical pirate accent is rhotic. In fact, extremely rhotic, with a retroflex /r/, [ɑɚ], as the standard pronunciation of a syllable coda /r/. I will call this quality rhoticity/retroflexion.

So is it an identifiable accent? When I mentioned my exploration of pirate accents to voice trainers Louis Colaianni and Rocco Dal Vera, they both offered the opinion that the typical pirate accent was a West Country British accent. The West Country of England is in the southwest of the country and includes the areas of Bristol, Somerset, Cornwall and Devon. These counties and towns are often noted for the rhoticity of their accents, and use of the retroflex /r/, [ɑɚ].[7]

Is it accurate to call a rhotic, gruff, West Country accent a typical pirate accent? In other words, what is a typical pirate? Is a typical pirate a native of the West Country of England?

Pirate History

To find out, let's begin with a brief history of pirates and piracy. The Oxford English Dictionary defines a pirate as "One who robs and plunders on the sea." As this broad definition indicates, piracy has occurred wherever and whenever sea travel happens. If someone got in a boat to travel from point A to point B, someone else got in another boat and tried to rob them. The Mediterranean Sea supported piracy dating back to at least 78 B.C.E., when a young Julius Caesar was kidnapped by pirates based in Cilicia (modern day Turkey).[8] The Barbary pirates in North Africa continued the Mediterranean pirate tradition from the 16th through 19th centuries.[9]

Other pirate "hot spots" included the Caribbean Sea, the Indian Ocean, and the South China Sea. The "buccaneers" (originally called *boucaniers*, French for "barbecuers") began to raid the Caribbean in the early 17th century[10]. On the west coast of India, the Angria family created a pirate dynasty that plundered sailing vessels for more than fifty years in the 18th century.[11] On the other side of the Indian Ocean, the island of Madagascar provided a haven for European-born pirates in the late 17th and early 18th centuries.[12] The South China Sea saw its share of pirates as well. As trade between Europe and China commenced in the 19th century, piracy flourished due to the weakening Manchu dynasty.[13]

6. Nancy Elliot, "A Study in the Rhoticity of American Film Actors," *The Voice and Speech Review* (2000): 103.

7. Robert Blumenfeld, *Accents: A Manual for Actors* (New York: Limelight, 1988), 58-60.

8. Jeffrey Richards, *Swordsmen of the Screen* (London and Boston: Routledge & Kegan Paul, 1977), 230.

9. Jan Rogozinski, *Pirates! Brigands, Buccaneers, and Privateers in Fact, Fiction, and Legend* (New York: Facts on File, 1995), 21-23.

10. See Nina Gerassi-Navarro, *Pirate Novels: Fictions of Nation Building in Spanish America* (Durham, NC: Duke University Press, 1999).

11. Jan Rogozinski, *Pirates! Brigands, Buccaneers, and Privateers in Fact, Fiction, and Legend* (New York: Facts on File, 1995), 11.

12. See Jan Rogozinski, *Honor Among Thieves: Captain Kidd, Henry Every, and the Pirate Democracy in the Indian Ocean* (Mechanicsburg, PA: Stackpole Books, 2000).

13. Rogozinski, *Pirates!*, 304.

14. "A significant factor to the elimination of piracy was the increasing importance (of) the slave trade... by the mid-seventeenth century...." (Gerassi-Navarro, p. 37) In other words, the economy of the slave trade was important enough to Europe and North America that the pirates needed to be hunted down.

15. I don't mean to imply that the 17th century featured the first incidence of pirate plots. Fictional piracy is as old as actual piracy. Ancient pirate tales include Homer's *Odyssey* (8th century B.C.E.), *The Ephesian Tale* by Xenophon of Ephesus (2nd century C.E.) and *An Ethiopian Romance* by Heliodorus of Emesa (3rd century C.E.).

16. Alexander Oliver Exquemelin, *Buccaneers of America*. Quoted in Rogozinski, *Pirates!*, 117.

17. Ibid.

18. This tome is widely considered to be authored by Daniel Defoe. Defoe also created the character of Robinson Crusoe, who was also a victim of piracy.

19. Ellms, *The Pirates Own Book*, p. iii.

20. Rogozinski, *Honor Among Thieves*, xviii-xix.

21. George Gordon Byron, "The Corsair", in *Lord Byron: Selected Poems*, ed. Peter J. Manning and Susan J. Wolfson, New York: Penguin Books, 1996, 256.

By the late 19th century, the "golden age" of piracy was over. The Caribbean buccaneers were weeded out in the early 18th century[14]. The Barbary Wars (1801-1815) had broken the strength of the North African pirates. The Angria pirate dynasty in the Indian Ocean was defeated by England in 1756. The pirates havening at Madagascar had either left or retired by the 1720s. The pirate fleets in the South China Sea were surrendering for pardons or being hunted down by the late 19th century. In other words, piracy as a global phenomenon was at an end.

No matter where I looked, I found no such thing as a historically typical pirate. Pirates have existed in every major sea where commerce occurred, including ancient Rome, North Africa, Europe, the Indian Ocean, the Caribbean, and the South China Sea. Their accents could have ranged from Arabic to French. They certainly wouldn't be limited to West Country British accents. So if this accent didn't arrive in my Stage Dialects classroom through history, where did it come from? If it did not arrive through fact, perhaps it came through fiction.

Pirate Fiction
So what's in pirate fiction? Is there a pattern of rhotic/retroflexed and gruff vocal qualities in the portrayals of pirates? Do fictional pirates typically hail from Britain's West Country?

In each of the 17th, 18th, and 19th centuries, a book was published that established the familiar image of the brutal pirate villain.[15] Each of these three books focused on the base cruelty of pirates in semi-factual terms. In 1678, Alexander Oliver Exquemelin wrote the autobiographical *Buccaneers of America*, in which he claims "I shall give no stories taken on hearsay, but only those to which I was eyewitness."[16] For example, he profiles his first master (as an indentured servant) who was "the most perfidious man that ever was born of woman."[17] In the 18th century, stories of pirate brutality were published in *A General History of the Robberies and Murders of the Most Notorious Pyrates* (Volume One in 1724, Volume Two in 1728) by Captain Charles Johnson.[18] Johnson's pair of books detail the bloody careers of Blackbeard and Captain Kidd, as well as the female pirates Anne Bonny and Mary Read. In 1837, Charles Ellms' *The Pirates Own Book: Authentic Narratives of the Most Celebrated Sea Robbers*, became a best-seller. And no wonder, as he promises his book is filled with the "desperate exploits, foul doings, and diabolical career of these monsters in human form."[19]

The vernacular in Ellms' quotation hints at one of our typical pirate accent qualities: gruffness. Words like "desperate," "foul," "diabolical," and "monsters" certainly call to mind rough, harsh sounds. But Ellms, like Exquemelin and Johnson before him, does not detail his pirate's vocal traits. These tales, though wildly popular, cannot be the source of our rhotic, gruff, and possibly West Country, typical pirate accent.

In contrast to these portrayals of "monsters in human form," the 19th century saw a rise in a romantic depiction of pirates. These books present pirates as characters that Jan Rogozinski calls "Noble Hero(es) ...fight(ing) for freedom ...."[20] Lord Byron's epic poem, *The Corsair*, tells the tragic tale of the romantic pirate, Conrad, whose "dark eyebrow shades a glance of fire,"[21] yet was full of "love—unchangeable—unchanged"[22] for his beloved lady, Medora—all in rhymed couplets. And it was wildly popular—*The Corsair* sold an astonishing 10,000 copies on its day of publication in 1814.[23] *The Pirate* by Sir Walter Scott followed in 1822, as well as two pirate novels by James Fenimore Cooper, *The Water Witch* (1830) and *The Sea Lions* (1849), all presenting romantic pirate leads.

As for the accents of these fictional pirates, both foul-mouthed ruffians and silver-tongued rogues hailed from all over the world, presumably speaking many different accents. More to the point, the authors neglect to mention the voices and accents of their subjects, though it is possible to imagine what they sound like. But I was looking for a clear vocal description in black and white, recorded for all time. So is there a fictional, literary basis for the typical pirate accent?

Indeed there is. The literary root of our typical pirate accent appears in 1883, in the form of Robert Louis Stevenson's *Treasure Island*. Stevenson directly addresses the *qualities* of the voices of his characters, particularly the pirates. Billy Bones' singing voice is described as a "high, old tottering voice that seemed to have been tuned and broken at the capstan bars."[24] Blind Pew first speaks to Jim Hawkins "... raising his voice in an odd sing-

Treasure Island (1934) Jackie Cooper and Wallace Beery

song...," but then grabs Jim violently, and Jim says, "I never heard a voice so cruel, and cold, and ugly as that blind man's."[25] Later, on the titular island, Jim meets Ben Gunn, who has been marooned for three years. Jim states, "his voice sounded hoarse and awkward, like a rusty lock."[26]

Aha! What does a voice "tuned and broken at the capstan bars," "so cruel, and cold, and ugly," or "hoarse and awkward, like a rusty lock" sound like to you? It could be described as creaky, raspy, squeaky, rough. In other words, it is our definition of "gruffness." So perhaps in *Treasure Island*, Stevenson has not only begotten the most enduring pirate tale to date, but also secured one element of our typical pirate accent—gruffness.

What about our other key elements of a typical pirate accent—rhoticity/retroflexion and the possible West Country roots? *Treasure Island* hints at both of these. The story begins near Bristol, and Long John Silver owns a tavern in that town. Bristol lies in the midst of the West Country of Britain. As a caveat, however, the story's initial location may not reflect the origins of the characters. The pirates in the story have spent years pillaging the Caribbean, and could have been born anywhere. They seem to be native English speakers, but Stevenson does not talk about their hometowns. Their backgrounds are not specifically discussed.[27] But the Bristol setting is a possible geographic link to the West Country rhoticity-retroflexion of our typical pirate accent.

22. Ibid., 259.

23. In a letter dated February 3, 1814, from publisher John Murray to Byron, Murray states, "I sold on the day of publication—a thing perfectly unprecedented—10,000 copies, and I suppose 30 people, who were purchasers (strangers) called to tell the people in the shop how much they had been delighted and satisfied." From Andrew Rutherford, *Byron: The Critical Heritage* (London: Routledge, 1970), 69.

24. Robert Louis Stevenson, *Treasure Island* (1883; reprint, New York: Barnes and Noble Books, 1994), 2.

25. Ibid., 24-25.

26. Ibid., 121.

27. Long John Silver owns a tavern in Bristol at the outset of the book, so perhaps that adds some weight to an argument for his being a native of the city. Then again, considering his piratical background, perhaps he wouldn't want to return to his hometown.

With *Treasure Island* we have found our first solid clue to the source of the typical pirate accent. Here we have an immensely popular book in which the author gives vocal descriptions that fit our definition of gruffness, with rusty, creaky, raspy adjectives. The tale's Bristol/West Country location hints at rhoticity-retroflexion. Now we're getting somewhere.

But we're not finished. Could a book, merely by describing the voices and implying an accent have infiltrated the culture, the internet and that Stage Dialects classroom? It seems more likely that we've really heard this accent, or perhaps heard an actor using this accent. Due to the aural nature of this investigation, perhaps we should look for evidence that postdates the advent of sound recording.

Captain Blood (1935) filming of a swordfight between Basil Rathbone and Errol Flynn

Pirate Films

One primary medium of popular culture that utilizes sound recording is, of course, film. So what's been done in film? If this typical pirate accent is imbedded in the popular culture, and if this accent originated in films, then it would logically follow that there should be a clear pattern of actors in films using this accent. Is there a typical pirate accent, typified by rhoticity/retroflexion, gruffness, and possible West Country origins for movie pirates?

The Sea Hawk (1940) Errol Flynn (center)

My expectation as I sat down with my VCR and my pile of videotapes was that, yes, there would be a long history of work containing gruff, rhotic, West Country pirates. Much to my surprise, it was quite the opposite. In fact, the actors' accent choices have been so varied, it is difficult to categorize them. Whether heroes or villains, there is a wide range of rhoticity/retroflexion, dialect origin and gruffness.

First, I will detail the non-rhotic/retroflex, non-gruff pirate heroes. Some, like the title characters in *Captain Blood* (1935) and *The Sea Hawk* (1940) (both played by Errol Flynn), are British and speak in Received Pronunciation.[28] Other films feature heroes of unclear nationality, played by American actors who don't change their vocal qualities at all. These include Bob Hope in *The Princess and the Pirate* (1944), Gene Kelly[29] in *The Pirate* (1948), and Burt Lancaster in *The Crimson Pirate* (1952). Even within the last decade we have an example of heroes without accents: 1995's *Cutthroat Island* featuring Geena Davis and Matthew Modine. Davis and Modine seem to have made no vocal adjustments for their roles and sound like they've walked off the set of the latest American sitcom.

What about when world accents are utilized? Are those accents confined to the typical pirate accent, namely West Country? On the contrary, the actors' accent choices in these films are representative of the reality of the history of pirates: these fictional pirates represent multiple nationalities.

Both Basil Rathbone, as the aristocratic La Vasseur in *Captain Blood* (1935), and Cris Campion, as Jean-Baptiste (called primarily "The Frog"), in *Pirates* (1986) use French accents. Walter Slezak is the villain, Macoco, a pirate turned politician, in *The Pirate* (1948). Slezak uses a light Spanish accent that gets thicker when his piratical past is exposed. In 1990's Cable-TNT adaptation of *Treasure Island,* Oliver Reed chose to make Billy Bones Scottish.

The Princess and the Pirate (1944) L to R: Victor McLaglen, Walter Slezak, Bob Hope

Cockney is used by both Charles Laughton in *Captain Kidd* (1945), and Walter Matthau in *Pirates* (1986) for different effects. Matthau's character, Captain Red, uses his lower-class Cockney accent to make himself appear stupid, thereby lulling his enemies into a false sense of security. Laughton's choice of a Cockney accent appears to be a strange choice considering that the historical Captain William Kidd was Scottish. A. H. Weiler in the *New York Times* noted: "Mr. Laughton… (was) as much the posturing comedian as the blood-thirsty buccaneer…."[30] Other viewers are not so kind. Historian David Cordingly states, "Charles Laughton reduced the part to a hammy caricature with a Cockney accent…."[31] I, however, found his Cockney accent to be perfectly in tune with his tongue-in-cheek performance as a ruthless pirate who desperately wants to become a gentleman.

The Princess and the Pirate (1944) Walter Brennan and Bob Hope walk the plank.

The "conspicuously inappropriate accent" award goes to actor Roy Kinnear in *Pirates* (1986). Since Kinnear plays a character named "Dutch" who is labeled a "son of a… whore from the reeking gutters of Rotterdam," one might reasonably expect him to sound like a native of the Netherlands. But, inexplicably, he speaks with a British accent.

Two movies are down right multi-cultural: *Peter Pan* (1953), and *Swashbuckler* (1976). A third, *The Island* (1980), creates an entirely new dialect. Disney's animated adaptation of *Peter Pan* features Captain Hook (Hans Conreid), tapping his /r/'s like the good public school boy he once was. But Disney also attempted to represent a variety of nationalities. It's as if the Neverland pirates have recruited their crew from all areas of the globe, including several countries underrepresented in pirate films. These broad accents include Swedish, Turkish, and German.

Pirates (1986) Walter Matthau

Swashbuckler (1976) also features numerous accents and nationalities. It seems to be an attempt at multicultural, interracial pirate society. The pirate captain, Ned Lynch (Robert Shaw) is an Irish gentleman, very much in the tradition of the Noble Hero. His first mate, Nick DeBrett (James Earl Jones), is an escaped slave with a West Indian accent. Other nationalities in the crew include the apparently Polish Polanski (Avery Schreiber), although he speaks with an American accent, and an unnamed Scottish pirate complete with kilt (in which he even climbs the rigging!).

The Island (1980) presents a community of pirates who are descended from the 18th century buccaneers and are still plundering the Caribbean. Rather than focusing on a specific accent, the author, Peter Benchley, constructs a dialect pulling from English, French, and Spanish. This makes sense in light of the mix of these cultures in buccaneer society. The result, however, garnered some harsh reviews: "…the pirates… speak a pidgin Jacobean English that sounds like fractural biblical."[32]

None of these performances utilize rhoticity/retroflexion.[33] They do not feature West Country accents. There are, however, many instances of pirate gruffness. The Princess and the Pirate (1948), features Victor McLaglen as "The Hook." The Hook speaks in a gruff bass voice, but it is non-rhotic and non-accent specific. Cutthroat Island (1995) featured Frank Langella as the evil, fratricidal, and vocally crusty "Dawg Brown." Supporting characters in pirate movies have notoriously harsh voices, including John Carradine and Sheldon Leonard in Captain Kidd (1945), Torin Thatcher in The Crimson Pirate (1952), Bob Hoskins in Hook (1991), and Lionel Barrymore, Ralph Truman, and Christopher Lee in adaptations of Treasure Island (1934, 1950, and 1990, respectively).

In reality, a serious look at accents in pirate movies reveals very little in the way of a "standard" or "typical" accent. The accent choices of these actors (and directors and producers) reflect the variety of nationalities represented by historical pirates. It would seem that the typical actor does not choose to follow the typical pirate accent that I heard in the Stage Dialects classroom. Where was the combination of rhoticity/retroflexion and gruffness? Where is the supposed West Country accent? We are adding up some clues. We have gruff voices in Stevenson's Treasure Island and in a number of movies. We also have possible rhoticity/retroflexion in Treasure Island's West Country setting. So will we ever find the true source of the typical pirate accent?

The "typical pirate accent:" Long John Silver

There is, in fact, a cinematic source for a rhotic/retroflexed, gruff, West Country-centered typical pirate accent. It's time to revisit Treasure Island and the character of Long John Silver. The book that provided our first literary glimpse of the typical pirate accent has been adapted for the screen several times, and provides the mother lode of typical pirates.

28. RP is also used, strangely enough, by Spanish characters in both *The Sea Hawk* (1940) and *Pirates* (1986), even when they were speaking to English speaking characters.

29. Kelly does use a slightly lower pitch range when his character impersonates a vicious pirate.

30. A. H. Weiler, *New York Times*, quoted in James Robert Parish, *Pirates and Seafaring Swashbucklers on the Hollywood Screen* (Jefferson, North Carolina: McFarland and Company, Inc.), 42.

31. Cordingly, David. *Under the Black Flag: The Romance and the Reality of Life Among the Pirates.* New York: Random House, 1996; Harcourt Brace & Company, Harvest Books, 1997, 176.

32. Archer Weinstein, *New York Post*, quoted in Parish, 89.

33. Oliver Reed's Scottish accent is rhotic, but trilled, not retroflexed. And Robert Shaw's Irish is very light, also rhotic but not retroflexed.

The 1934 adaptation of *Treasure Island* introduces an identifiable West Country accent. Wallace Beery, who plays Long John Silver, has taken Stevenson's setting fairly directly and given Silver a Somerset-style accent. In his book, *Accents: A Manual for Actors,* Robert Blumenfeld notes that in the Somerset accent, "Stressed syllables are usually long and spoken on a rising, then falling tone...."[34] Beery uses this rising/falling tone regularly, especially when talking to Jim Hawkins. But Beery's Silver is loveable, and eschews excess gruffness in his speech. In addition, his accent is rhotic, but not retroflexed. So Beery uses a West Country accent, but does not have the true gruffness and retroflexion in the typical pirate accent. Beery is not quite our typical pirate.

Decades later, in 1990, Charlton Heston tackled the role of Long John Silver for TNT-Cable. He was critically praised for his performance. What's more, he was critically praised for his accent:

> Heston, as Long John Silver, seems to have absorbed the accents and acting styles of such predecessors as (Wallace) Beery and Robert Newton, and his rich Cornish brogue is commendable.[35]

I agree that Heston is using a Cornwall accent. His accent is rhotic, using the retroflex /r/, and his vocal placement seems to agree with Blumenfeld's *Accents,* which recommends the actors "say *me me me him him him...* to set the correct general position,"[36] which I take to encourage a vocal placement far forward in the mouth behind the teeth. Heston utilizes a tight-jawed, teeth-baring grin in his characterization which adds to both this forward placement and the overall creepiness of the pirate. Blumenfeld also ascribes "short diphthongs"[37] to the accent (in contrast to the Somerset/Bristol accent) which Heston uses. Heston also continues the tradition of vocal gruffness. So Heston gives us a typical pirate accent. But considering the recent release date (1990), we can't really trace the typical pirate accent to this film alone.

It was the 1950 adaptation of *Treasure Island* that birthed the typical pirate. Actor Robert Newton imbued his portrayal of Long John Silver with the rhoticity/retroflexion, gruffness, and West Country flavoring in an identifiable typical pirate accent. In fact, Newton played Long John Silver twice: in Disney's 1950 adaptation of *Treasure Island,* and the 1954 sequel, *Long John Silver.*

Newton played Long John Silver with a "swarthy face, slow menacing voice, and malicious intensity."[38] (In other words, with gruffness.) Newton also revels in retroflex /r/ codas, using a very tense tongue. The director of *Treasure Island,* Byron Haskin, describes "orchestrating" the movie's cast of thirty six speaking roles:

> By the time (Robert) Newton's manners were to be considered I could do little more than let him 'rip.'[39]

And "rip" he does. In *Long John Silver* (also directed by Haskin), Newton was accused by critics as being:

> ...outrageously hammy, to the point of freakishness, with his squinting and popping of his eyeballs and growling in a bastard Irish brogue.[40]

"Bastard Irish brogue" is an apt description of his accent, and leads us to the West Country influence. His first line in *Treasure Island* is the stereotypical

34. Blumenfeld, *Accents,* 58.

35. William K. Everson, *Video Review,* quoted in Parish, 188.

Robert Newton as Long John Silver in *Treasure Island* (1950)

36. Blumenfeld, *Accents,* 59.

37. Ibid.

38. Rogozinski, *Pirates!,* 240.

39. Parish, 185-186.

40. Bosley Crowther (*New York Times*), quoted in Parish, 95.

Long John Silver (1954) Robert Newton

Irish phrase, "Top o' the morning to you gentlemen." (This phrase does not appear in Stevenson's book.) Newton utilizes musicality in his phrasing and elongation of vowels, like one might expect from an Irish "lilt."[41] But I find it hard to believe that he was striving for accuracy by including an intrusive /r/ in the word, "Amen," ([ɑɚ.mɛn]). "Bastard Irish brogue" also highlights the dialectal similarities of the West coast of England (including the West Country) and the East coast of Ireland. Newton combined the musicality of an Irish accent with the retroflexion of a West Country accent, added gruffness, and "let it rip."

Newton also introduces an additional quality to a typical pirate accent. Apparently not satisfied with merely sounding gruff, he actually growls. And here, at last, is the sound the students were speaking in Stage Dialects class. Not only does Newton growl, but he growls with a retroflex /r/ that sounds something like [ɑɚ]. This actually becomes a meaningful interjection for Newton. It can mean, "back off," "I hate you," "damn my luck," or all of the above simultaneously.

In 1952, in between these two portrayals of Long John Silver, Newton played the title role in *Blackbeard the Pirate*. Once again, Newton uses retroflexion to comic advantage. But he has eliminated the melody and lilt, paring down the Irishness of his bastard brogue, bringing it nearer to a West Country accent. The reviews for this film were similar to the ones he would receive for *Long John Silver*.

> Mr. Newton, who is the whole picture, must be seen to be believed.... (He) transmits a volume gamut of roars and even belches, (and) wallows through an outrageously flamboyant caricature of his Long John Silver part in Disney's *Treasure Island*.[42]

Newton died in 1956. We will never know what he may have done to continue or discontinue his pirate accent tradition. What is certain is that his three pirate films within four years—*Treasure Island* in 1950, *Blackbeard* in 1952, and *Long John Silver* in 1954—created a lasting impression on the public mind. Newton set the gold standard for pirate accents. Contemporary films continue his tradition of rhoticity/retroflexion and gruff accents, primarily for comic effect. Some examples include *Yellowbeard* (1983), and *Captain Ron* (1992), starring Kurt Russell as the title character with a rhotic (though still American) accent, and a gruff smokers' voice. Because of the similarities between these vocal choices and Newton's, I would say they are paying tribute to Mr. Newton's portrayal of Stevenson's pirate.

What makes Newton's accent popular and therefore "typical?"
We have now seen from where the typical pirate accent, with its rhoticity/retroflexion, West Country influence, and gruffness, came: Long John Silver and Robert Newton. We can see how it invaded the Stage Dialects

41. Blumenfeld, *Accents*, 68.

42. Howard Thompson (*New York Times*), quoted in Parish, 27.

classroom. We have also seen that this accent is by no means typical of most historical pirates, with their global backgrounds. Nor is it typical of fictional pirates, with the exception of Stevenson's intimations. Neither is it the typical choice of actors portraying pirates in films, who have used everything from Cockney, Irish, and French to West Indian and Turkish. Throughout the decades of movie pirates, the actors have chosen a variety of pirate accents that reflect the broad possibilities of historical pirates. So if we are looking to place the responsibility for the popular culture myth of the typical pirate accent, where do we place it?

I contend that the responsibility rests with the audience. Newton's track record of three broad, West County, rhotic/retroflex, gruff, and growling pirate performances within a span of four years (1950, 1952, and 1954) points to a measure of success with those performances. The audiences loved it. The critics loved it, hated it, and loved to hate it. And now not even his death can stop the audience from imitating him and spreading his influence, from the internet to my Stage Dialects classroom. Writers (albeit internet amateurs) are even ascribing his dialect to Princess Diana and Audrey Hepburn!

43. Angus Konstam, *The History of Pirates* (New York: The Lyons Press, 1999), 15.

Perhaps the typical pirate accent is irreversibly entrenched in the popular culture. As Angus Konstam says in his *History of Pirates*:

> It is now almost impossible to divide myth from reality in the context of popular perception of piracy. The damage done by novelists, playwrights, and film producers has been too extensive, and the best we can probably hope for is to enjoy the popular image of the pirate....[43]

So, what do you think? Shall we enjoy the damage that's been done? All together now, squint, pop your eyeballs, roar, and belch. And in your best typical pirate accent "let it rip":

A land-lubber I'll never be!

[ə land lʌ.bɚ̩ ʌĭɫ nɛ.vɚ̩ bŏi].

Abbot and Costello Meet Captain Kidd (1952) L to R: Lou Costello, Charles Laughton, Bud Abbot

Pirate Practice
For those of you who wish to practice your pirate accent, typical or not, I include the following phrases:

From *The Sea Hawk*
"It's cutlasses now, men!"
"Aloft there, clear your leash line!"
"Clear away your mizzen banks!"
"Heave to your halyards!"
"Take away your true line!"

From *Captain Kidd*
"Satisfied, gallows meat?"

Against All Flags (1952) Maureen O'Hara, Errol Flynn

From *Treasure Island*
"Shiver my timbers!"
"You're smart as paint, y'are."
"You can't touch pitch and not be mucked, lad."
Song:
"Fifteen men on the dead man's chest -
Yo-ho-ho, and a bottle of rum!
Drink and the devil had done for the rest -
Yo-ho-ho and a bottle of rum!"

From *The Princess and the Pirate*
"Curse you for a lily-livered wench!
"You'll dance the devil's horn-pipe at the end of the mainyard!"
(or "dance the devil's tattoo…")
"I'll cut out your gizzard!"
"You sons of unholy mothers!"

The Black Swan (1942) L to r: George Sanders, Anthony Quinn, Tyrone Power

From *Long John Silver*
"Why, you white-livered scum!"

From *Peter Pan*
"Back, you pewling spawn!"

From *The Pirate*
"Ladies go to pieces over Pieces of Eight." (Thank you, Cole Porter!)

Old Pirate Song from Ellms, *"Pirates Own"*:
"Drain, drain the bowl, each fearless soul,
Let the world wag as it will;
Let the heavens growl, let the devil howl,
Drain, drain the deep bowl and fill."

Anne of the Indies (1951) Jean Peters,
Thomas Gomez

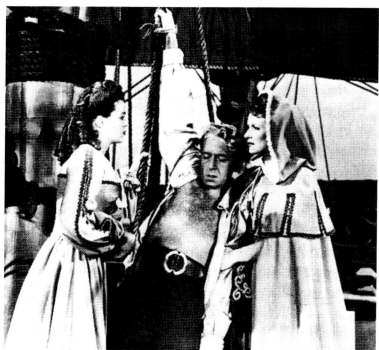

The Spanish Main (1945) Paul Henreid, leaning on Maureen O'Hara

Bibliography
Books and Articles

Baepler, Paul, ed. *White Slaves, African Masters: An Anthology of American Barbary Captivity Narratives.* Chicago: University of Chicago Press, 1999.

Barrie, J. M. *Peter Pan and other Plays.* New York: Charles Scribner's Sons, 1930.

Blumenfeld, Robert. *Accents: A Manual for Actors.* New York: Limelight Editions, 1988.

Butler, Lindley S. *Pirates, Privateers, and Rebel Raiders of the Carolina Coast.* Chapel Hill, NC: The University of North Carolina Press, 2000.

Byron, George Gordon. *The Corsair. In Lord Byron: Selected Poems,* ed. Peter J. Manning and Susan J. Wolfson. New York: Penguin Books, 1996.

Cordingly, David. *Under the Black Flag: The Romance and the Reality of Life Among the Pirates.* New York: Random House, 1996; Harcourt Brace & Company, Harvest Books, 1997.

Elliot, Nancy. "A Study in the Rhoticity of American Film Actors." *The Voice and Speech Review* (2000): 103-130.

Ellms, Charles. *The Pirates Own Book: Authentic Narratives of the Most Celebrated Sea Robbers.* Boston: Samuel Dickinson, 1837; Salem, MA: Marine Research Society, 1924; New York: Dover Publications, Inc., 1993.

Exquemelin, Alexander Oliver. *Buccaneers of America. 1678. Quoted in Rogozinski, Jan. Pirates! Brigands, Buccaneers, and Privateers in Fact, Fiction, and Legend.* New York: Facts on File, Inc., 1995.

Gerassi-Navarro, Nina. *Pirate Novels: Fictions of Nation Building in Spanish America.* Durham, NC: Duke University Press, 1999.

Konstam, Angus. *The History of Pirates.* New York: The Lyons Press, 1999.

Parish, James Robert. *Pirates and Seafaring Swashbucklers on the Hollywood Screen.* Jefferson, North Carolina: McFarland and Company, Inc., 1995.

Buckaneer's Girl (1950) Yvonne de Carlo

Richards, Jeffrey. *Swordsmen of the Screen*. London and Boston: Routledge and & Kegan Paul, 1977.

Rogozinski, Jan. *Honor Among Thieves: Captain Kidd, Henry Every, and the Pirate Democracy in the Indian Ocean*. Mechanicsburg, PA: Stackpole Books, 2000.

_____. *Pirates! Brigands, Buccaneers, and Privateers in Fact, Fiction, and Legend*. New York: Facts on File, Inc., 1995.

Rutherford, Andrew. *Byron: the Critical Heritage*. London: Routledge, 1970.

Stevenson, Robert Louis. *Treasure Island*. 1883. Reprint, New York: Barnes and Noble Books, 1994.

Films

Blackbeard, the Pirate. RKO, 1952.
Captain Blood. Warner Bros., 1935.
Captain Ron. Buena Vista, 1992.
Captain Kidd. United Artists, 1945.
The Crimson Pirate. Warner Bros., 1952.
Cutthroat Island. Artisan Entertainment, 1995.
Hook. Buena Vista, 1991.
The Island. Universal, 1980.
Long John Silver. Distributors Corp. of America, 1954.
Peter Pan. RKO, 1953.
The Pirate. Metro-Goldwyn-Mayer, 1948.
Pirates. Cannon, 1986.
The Princess and the Pirate. RKO, 1944.
The Princess Bride. Twentieth Century-Fox, 1987.
The Sea Hawk. Warner Bros., 1940.
Swashbuckler. Universal, 1976.
Swiss Family Robinson. Buena Vista, 1960.
Treasure Island. Metro-Goldwyn-Mayer, 1934.
Treasure Island. RKO, 1950.
Treasure Island. TNT-Cable, January 22, 1990.
Yellowbeard. Orion, 1983.

Photo treatment services for this article provided by Steven Klinko.

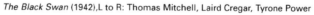

The Black Swan (1942),L to R: Thomas Mitchell, Laird Cregar, Tyrone Power

Sidebar *by Rhonda Cundy*

Singing Pirates

Avast, me hearties, there are enough singing pirates out there to shiver your timbers. Along with individual performers, amateur and professional ensembles abound. All are dedicated to singing pirate songs and sea shanties in musicals, light operas, concerts, festivals, fairs, cruises, and theme parks. Stylistically, the singing pirates' repertoire ranges from intricate Renaissance madrigals, to mellow ballads, to shanties raw as any sea dogs' rhotic *rrr's*. And there is a singing, squawking parrot pirate at the entrance to Disney World's *Pirates of the Caribbean*. He sings, "Yo ho ho, a 'parrot's' life for me."[1]

Rhonda Cundy's career as a performer and stage director in concert, music theatre, theatre, opera, and performance art, spans 30 years in the USA, France, and Germany. Teaching at Northwestern, she developed and taught their singer's diction program. She has been an Artist in Residence at Harvard, Performer in Residence at the University of Wisconsin-Madison, Director of Opera Theatre at Kent State, and taught spoken voice for actors at the University of Wisconsin-Green Bay and St. Norbert College. With Louis Colaianni, Rhonda is currently adapting his *Joy of Phonetics* work for singers and singer-actors, including additional IPA pillow symbols for Italian, Latin, French, German, and Spanish.

The Pirates of Penzance (1983) L to R: Angela Lansbury, Linda Ronstadt, George Rose, Rex Smith, Kevin Kline

At D'Oyly Carte, England's premier Gilbert and Sullivan company, a pirate accent typically reflects a production's individual ethos.[2] Accents in *The Pirates of Penzance* involve an added twist: all the pirates are "noblemen gone wrong." For a defining Gilbert and Sullivan pirate accent by an American singer-actor, listen to Pirate King Kevin Kline in Joseph Papp's 1980 movie, *The Pirates of Penzance*.

Captain Hook is another infamous singing pirate. Hook first appeared in Jerome Kern's 1924 musical, *Peter Pan*; next in Leonard Bernstein's 1950 *Peter Pan*; followed by the 1954 musical, *Peter Pan*, by Charlap and Styne (lyrics by Leigh, Comden, and Green), in which Cyril Ritchard triumphed as Hook.

The web holds a treasure trove of singing pirate booty: MIDI files, libretti, sing-along formats, production information, critical commentaries, reviews, glossaries, and discographies. The leading web site for light opera is *The Gilbert and Sullivan Archive* at www.diamond.boisestate.edu/gas/. Importantly, scoop up all of Phil Timberlake's pearls of wisdom on pirate accents, clearly relevant to singing pirates, and heave ho!

1. You can hear the Disney parrot at Disney World's Pirates of the Caribbean site.

2. Information on D'Oyly Carte pirate accents was provided for this side bar in February 2003 by Ian Martin, D'Oyly Carte General Manager.

David Carey is Principal Lecturer in Voice Studies at the Central School of Speech and Drama, London, and Course Leader for the School's MA/Postgraduate Diploma in Voice Studies. He trained in Speech and Drama at the Royal Scottish Academy of Music and Drama in Glasgow, and has been awarded degrees in English Language and Linguistics from both Edinburgh University and Reading University. A voice teacher for over 25 years, David has worked extensively at both undergraduate and postgraduate level. His work in the professional theatre includes 4 years as assistant to Cicely Berry at the Royal Shakespeare Company during the 1980s.

Dialect Coaching for Film and Television:
An Interview with Penny Dyer

Penny has worked freelance in her profession for 20 years. The educational backbone of her work was as Head Voice Tutor at The Central School of Speech and Drama and Speech/Dialect Tutor at RADA. Theatre credits include; In the West End: *The Revengers Comedies, Shadowlands, Another Time, Cyrano de Bergerac, The Queen and I, Miss Saigon, Shopping and F***ing,* Eddie Izzard in Peter Hall's *Lenny, A Long Days Journey Into Night, Cat on a Hot Tin Roof, My Fair Lady.* For the Donmar: *How I Learned to Drive, The Blue Room* with Nicole Kidman, *Suddenly Last Summer, Three Days of Rain, The Little Foxes* with Penelope Wilton. For The Royal Court: *Mojo, Other People, Fireface, Spinning into Butter, Redundant, Plasticine, The People are Friendly.* For Hampstead: *A Colliers Friday Night, Slavs, Speaking in Tongues, Buried Alive, The Dead-eye Boy, The Lucky Ones, After the Gods.* For the Almeida: *The Shape of Things* with Rachel Weisz, *Camera Obscura,* directed by Jonathan Miller. Also: *Five Kinds of Silence* at the Lyric and *The Beggars Opera,* directed by Jonathan Miller for The Wiltons Music Hall. T.V.includes: *Band of Gold, A Small Dance, The Passion, The Sleeper, The Secret World of Michael Fry, Take A Girl Like You, Anna Karenina, Plain Jane, Surrealismo, Daniel Deronda, Sparkhouse.* FILM includes: *Bhaji on the Beach, Let Him Have It, Immortal Beloved, The Englishman Who Went Up A Hill...,* Antony Hopkins in *The Mask of Zorro, Oscar and Lucinda, The Beach,* The Award-winning *Elizabeth* with Cate Blanchett, *RKO 281,* Tim Roth's *The War Zone, Felicia's Journey, Heaven,* Oliver Parker's *The Importance of Being Earnest,* and most recently The Award-winning *Dirty, Pretty Things,* directed by Stephen Frears and starring Audrey Tautou and Chewitel Ojiofar.

DC: Penny, let me introduce you for the benefit of readers of The Voice and Speech Review. You are a British voice and dialect coach who works in film, television and the theatre, and you have done now for about fifteen years?

PD: Eighteen years, but I was also teaching students up until 1995, so I was unable to actually go on location as such until, I think—summer of '94 was the first time I did location work.

DC: What I'd like to begin with is just to ask you to talk a little about how you prepare generally for work on dialect coaching, whether it be in film or theatre. What sort of considerations have you got in your mind and what sort of research might you do?

PD: If it's a dialect that I'm not familiar with, then obviously there's a lot more research that needs to be done than if it's something that I am familiar with—and that process would be the same whether it's theatre or film. So if it's something I don't know, then I'll find every which way I can to find resources from the actual people themselves speaking with the dialect to visiting the National Sound Archive, for instance, which is now at the British Library. I find what I do is, I put out feelers—often mental feelers—and it's extraordinary what comes in. You'll suddenly be in a situation, and because you're receptive to that particular accent or sound, somebody will be talking about something and you'll pick up and realise that that person may indeed know somebody who has that accent. It's extraordinary how that sort of thing comes about. I remember once I was needing to research some New England accents, and I was just standing in the supermarket and the woman next to me sounded like she came from New England—and she did! And with that I said, 'Well, can I come and meet you and tape you?' And that was the scenario.

DC: Wonderful.

PD: It's obviously a lot easier when it's a British Isles dialect, because you can actually go to the place itself—which is something I would always do—and tape a selection of voices. Even if I know the character is of a certain age, I would still want to get a broad spectrum of people on tape. Now, of course, if you're talking about a dialect that is, for instance, American, nobody is going to give you the financial resources to go across the Atlantic to find that accent. Then, as I said, another way is the National Sound Archive, or whatever I already have on tape that might be approximate but not accurate. But you ring round all the other voice coaches and dialect coaches that you know—and "got any of this?"—and so there is a lot of bargaining that goes on.

DC: Right, so they'll say yes I have got a bit of that but...
PD: ...what have you got that you could offer me in exchange. It's good, it's a very good system. And I do that regularly with the likes of Jeannette Nelson and Charmian Hoare and Julia Wilson-Dickson and William Conacher and Jill McCullough, exchanging the dialects, and that's very, very useful. What I would also do is, I would read around the dialect. So I would read around the environment that the accent is in, and I would probably study maps. I'd read a bit about the history of the area, and research the changes that have taken place in accents, which is another reason for wanting to get various different aged voices for that process. I would try to read and study as extensively as possible.

Now if I find exactly what I want, then we get down to analysing it phonetically—and by analysing it phonetically I mean that I am taking it apart for the vowels, the consonants, the tune, the rhythm, the inflection patterns, and stress patterns—and obviously that's very technical. What I would always do is make sure that I understand the process of the accent. But the most important thing for me is to make all of those technical points come to anchor points for the actor, because what I don't want to do is flood the actor with technique. Most of the time they don't want to know [about the technical points]. It's much better to get in there and start talking to the actors straight away in the accent, and my preparation would have obviously been involving a lot of speaking the accent aloud. I would do that possibly by listening to the voices I've taped or acquired, and tracking them, and then gradually taking that into my own lingo.

I would find a scenario by which I can start when I first meet the actor or actors, whether it's a theatre workshop on it or a one-to-one session. I would immediately want to start speaking in the accent. That point of course is, in some cases, when the greatest amount of nerves set in. But hopefully after about ten minutes you start realising this isn't so bad after all, it's going okay, and then you get into the swing of it. And while speaking in the accent, what I would do is talk about the environment, the people, anything that is sort of relevant to a) the area and b) the actual subject matter that we're studying.

I remember when with *The Lucky Ones* for the Hampstead Theatre in London, the director, Matthew Lloyd had said to me, 'It's Berlin, German Berlin, Jewish,' which of course

sounded very specific. And I said, 'okay'. I knew I had some Berlin on tape, and I knew I had some German Jewish, but I didn't have Berlin German Jewish. So I went out and bought the *Voices of the Holocaust* and listened through the entire four tapes. I had about six voices already on tape as well, and then of course, the great thing was that I actually met the family that the story was based on. But before I got to that point I had already realised Berlin had nothing to do with it, because we were talking about educated people. We weren't talking about a Berlin accent—which is a bit like a London Cockney accent—so that was irrelevant. And I explained that to Matthew. I said, 'You know, they are not going to have any of that. What they are going to have is traces of German Jewish, which ironically,' I said, 'merge and become similar anyway, in many respects.' And that was then influenced by the English, because these people had come to England. When the play starts they have actually been in the country for thirty years already.

What's always something that's very important to remember is that no two people ever sound the same and that's not giving you a cop out or a way out...

DC: ...it's giving the actor choice...
PD: ...it gives the actor choice and it's so important, because people change their accent or don't change their accent or move forward in certain areas in the ways they speak or indeed change the voice as opposed to the accent subconsciously, or consciously, sometimes a bit of both.

DC: Yes, we accommodate in different ways, at different times in our lives.
PD: And it depends on the work environment, as we know, and so many different factors. And in the case of these four people—that were German Jewish Berliners who had come to this country through Kinder Transport—we decided that all of them would have the same dialect reference points, which I obviously gave them, but each and every one of them would follow their own pattern with that. And we ended up with obviously one person having a stronger accent, another person having, perhaps, a slightly stronger rhythm, because, ultimately, that's what made them feel comfortable. And as long as I was there to do the usual tweaks, and make sure that we're not going too far down the route of something that makes it start to sound cod or unbelievable or unreal to the language, then that's fine and that's very important. So that's a big digression but I think an important one...

DC: ...no that's great...
PD: ...and I did want to say that in the process of preparing, I always take on board what's going on physically of course. I am a great one for believing in the muscular memory patterns.

And at the end of the day, it's all very well saying, 'This vowel becomes this vowel, and this consonant becomes this consonant, and you can hear it and you can hear me doing it.' But for the actor, if they're coming from Glasgow, not even by way of Received Pronunciation (RP), in order to get to Deep South American, they've got to start working at a very early stage to change those muscular memory patterns. And that means what I call full blown speech aerobics—you know, full blown relaxing and releasing of the jaw and speech muscles, and relating right through to the breath, so that they start to realize that the breath dynamic of the accent is going to be very different to their own, and how they can incorporate that. So for me the physical side of the work ultimately becomes the most important, as long as you've fed the imagination and they've got their technique.

And I would do—I think probably as most of us do—worksheets that will have sentences. You know, 'That black cat that sat on the mat having a nap is fat,' and that gives you your 'a' vowel. I always say to them, 'Make up your own sentences, if you want to'. And then a sheet which is just words for vowels, and then another one. I do three general sheets that can work right across the board for any accent, rather than giving specifics for dialects now. I used to do that, but I've realised that actually it works—for me anyway—it works much better just to have a pivotal point. And they can come into that and realize how, 'Oh yes, I could do that for Glaswegian. I could do that for Welsh. I could do that—Oh great!' And I say to them, 'These are the sentences I've made up, but you can always make up your own.' The important thing is, is that it's quite a good thing—just to pull you in—you're standing in the wings, you know, just before the camera rolls, 'What was that sound? Ah, yes, don't go home alone with nose tones to throw at unknown bogey men. That's the one!' Or anything silly and stupid like that, so the worksheets are very important.

The other part of the process for me is having really felt I've got on top of speaking in the dialect, which, as I say, if it's a new one will take, you know, some time or a little time, depending on how much time you've got. I will make a master tape for the production company, or indeed for the actor, and that might mean that you're making several depending if there are several accents to be dealt with. And the master tape will normally, if I can, encompass some original material—in other words, one or two speakers that I feel would be helpful to that person's character—and then me. And that may be the part that I do in the workshop. We just click the tape machine on and I say, 'I'm taping this for you. I'm going to talk to you about the accent. Please feel free to ask questions anytime.' And that then goes onto the tape that they then receive, and

Penny Dyer

that will more than likely also have me going through the vowel sounds with sentences or whatever is relevant. And again, what I'll try and do is simplify, pick out the key vowels, key consonant changes rather than all of them which is always, you know...

DC: ...a bit overwhelming...

PD: ...yes, and try and relate things to images as much as possible. That's what I try to do anyway. You know, if you're doing Northern Irish, I always say to them, 'It's like going down a ski slope. You go all the way down the ski slope and jump off the end'. And there's just that feeling of having something that's actually physical that you can think about. Yes, you find all sorts of things like that, but I think that's about making it fun, because we always have to remember that actors are doing plays. They're not working, they're playing.

DC: Can we focus specifically on work on film for a bit. I'm aware that you've recently been working on projects like *Importance of Being Earnest* with Reese Witherspoon, *Heaven* with Cate Blanchett and Steven Frear's most recent film, *Dirty Pretty Things*. And I'm just wondering, first of all, how much of what you do with those projects would you actually classify as dialect work?

PD: Yes, okay. In the case of Reese Witherspoon we're talking about bringing somebody from American to Standard English by way of Wilde—a very specific type of Standard English and use of language. So I think it's fair enough to say that if you're a well qualified, competent voice teacher, you don't have to be skilled in dialect to bring somebody from American to RP. I think to bring anyone to RP, you don't need to have, necessarily, the skills of somebody who obviously leaps around the country doing lots of strange sounds, or leaps around the globe doing lots of strange sounds. So in terms of Reese Witherspoon—when you're working in theatre, a lot of the time you work with people who have had some sort of training. It's not always the case, but the more prestigious the theatre the more likely it is that there is a training there of some sort. And of course that means that the actor is already skilled in his or her technical process to a greater or lesser degree. It's a major stepping stone in the process. Reese doesn't have a training. She's extremely hard working. She comes from Tennessee. Her physical features are very American, and the sound is very, very full-blown modern American, with the Tennessee in the background. And we had five weeks—twenty sessions in all—to bring her from that to Cecily in *The Importance of Being Earnest.*

So, what I find I do more and more in the film work—and particularly if we're coming to RP, which, let's face it, is probably the most difficult thing for anybody to move into because it is so sure and subtle—is I will start straight away by saying, 'okay, you're going to learn how to do a complete facial warm-up, a muscular warm-up.' And I talked to Reese about the fact that she has muscles that want to say the sounds this way, and I have muscles that say sounds this way. And then I would immediately start by working with completely releasing jaw, lips, tongue, soft palate and freeing up the whole voice. And on the whole, most actors find it great fun. I mean it starts off by being a bit odd, and of course there are a lot of things they can't necessarily do—particularly if they're completely new to it—but it's to get them into the discipline that you did every day with your students. And, whereas you've got two years of technical work before they start performing in most drama schools, you've got five weeks in film. So you know that you've got to keep pushing as much as you can into the actor's mind that this is something you've got to start doing twice a day. And you have to build it. And I always say to them, 'When you start going running, for instance, you don't start with an eight mile run. So I'm not going to start by saying to you do this particular exercise twenty times. It would be crazy. In fact, I would probably never say that to you, but start slowly and build it up.' It's all musculature. And I think it's fair enough to say that, by the time you get to week four in that process— particularly if you're coming from quite a long muscular journey—you'll start seeing some good results.

So what I got Reese to do, and what I would do again with other actors in this process—and it doesn't necessarily have to be with RP though—was to immediately start to make her realize how that's got to feed into her physically. That the dynamic by which she speaks RP is going to be very different to the way you speak American. So we talk about resonances, and we work with resonances and where to find them. 'Particularly with Wilde,' I said, 'all of your voice happens in front of your face almost. And that doesn't mean it detaches from you. It's a subtlety, but for you it's a good thing to think at this point.' And we put it out there. And we worked a lot outside. And I did that purposely, because, I said, 'A lot of what you're doing in this particular play is outside. You're sitting outside in that garden the whole time, and what you have to do vocally,' I said, 'is bigger and bolder than you would if you were in a more intimate relationship, a more intimate setting.' So we worked a lot outside. We worked with her walking and using and embodying the accent, and she began to realize that she had to change an awful lot. And I wouldn't automatically take on board the responsibility for physical work—we did actually have a choreographer, but she was only there a minimal amount of time. So I didn't tread on anybody's toes, but I just made sure that the voice came from the body.

DC: Yes, and you're also taking it in to social manners and general behaviour.
PD: Yes that's right, exactly. She was a very quick learner, Reese. There were a lot of muscular problems to overcome and I think, on the whole, and I hope you'll see the film David…

DC: …I'm hoping to…
PD: …she did a relatively good job. I really, on the whole, was very pleased with her. We had awful problems with wind and trees and planes. We spent the whole thing outside, and there was an awful lot that had to be ADR'd that wouldn't have had to have been ADR'd for the dialect, and that was a great, great shame.

That's how we started. She also moved into worksheets, and we also worked with text that wasn't the text she was going to work with, but similar styles. And I said, 'Everything you say has got to be aloud, straight away. It's the only way you are going to start getting into the process.' And we would work with different exercises to help her keep it in her own voice and her own pitch of the voice without changing that. Because at one point, when she did the RP, she did the classic thing and (*Penny speaks in head voice*) went up there. And I said, 'Well, that's not you.' And she said, 'No it's not.' So I said, 'Let's take it phrase by phrase. You do it first in your voice, your accent, and then let's just hear it as you move to the RP. And you'll see that you can keep a true sound behind that.'

And then what I always do on a film—and it's something I started doing with Cate Blanchett, actually. She was the one who actually gave me the idea—I don't know where she got it from. I think it might have been from an American coach. I've no idea. There's something about the process that's very, very, definite, very specific and what I like about it is that it takes the words out of context, but it means you are still using the words that you're going to actually use when you come to filming. And you literally take the script and you take as many words as you can from the script and put them into lists according to the sounds. Now they could be vowels—and obviously you pick out the sounds that you know are causing perhaps the most problems—they could be Rs, they could be Ls, whatever—and you just make lists of words. But because it makes the muscular memory change, you start to absorb the new words, but in a different way, and so that they become more like second nature. Also what I would do is take phrases—phrases from the script—and jumble them up, so that you just come across these phrases. And the good thing about that then is that you don't get stuck into a way of saying things. And I don't tend to come to the actual text till certainly no more than two weeks (if not less) before filming commences, because on the whole I find that's what actors want. When I worked with Nicole Kidman on *The Blue Room* she was very keen to drill the text, she was doing five different accents, so I sort of understand her but I said to her let's not do that, and I really tried to keep her off doing that for as long as possible.

DC: Now, you spoke about ADR just now, and I just wanted to ask you to talk a little bit about the kind of technicalities of working on film which will be peculiar to the medium, and what maybe you've had to learn in the process of doing that.
PD: I always think, when on a film set, one of the first people you make sure you make a strong bond with, if you can possibly do so, is the sound man. I always refer to myself as 'surrogate sound', and run around and make the odd cup of tea and coffee, generally suck up actually. And on the whole I've found it works. I have found that I always get on very well with the Sound Department. And ultimately it's good, because that's really where you want to be sitting or standing—by sound if it's possible. The relationship with sound is very important. I'm not a great technical buff by any means, but you realize how important it is. For instance, I remember when I first did a film the sound man said to me, 'You going to go in?' And I said, 'Why?' Because as far as I was concerned the accent was fine. 'Because there was a fluff!' And I thought, 'There was a fluff. Of course, there was a fluff.' But I was so concentrating on the accent that I missed it, so I said 'Where was the fluff?' And of course, as it so happened, he said, 'Don't worry. I'll go in because I'm used to doing that.' But sometimes you can get to a point where you have such a good

relationship with sound that you just look at sound and say, 'Do you want me to go and say something?' And they'll either agree or say, 'No, it's alright. I'll go and say something.' Because he's got something more technical to talk about or there's the ruffling of the microphone in the costume. But yes, you start realising you go in there when there's possibly a little fluffing or a little hesitation that doesn't work in the line or...

DC: ...so you're listening to more than just the accent?
PD: ...oh my goodness, the dropping of words! I remember on one film I just thought, 'My god, I'm more like a script editor really, because what we're not getting here are any of the words right.' The text is...

DC: ...the text monitor...
PD: ... the text monitor is a very good word for it, and the director is so busy thinking about everything else that he's also not necessarily hearing that. The great thing with a director like Stephen Frears on *Dirty Pretty Things* or indeed Oliver Parker on *The Importance of Being Earnest* is that I was working with directors who understood and appreciated language and what it meant to get that right. And on *Dirty Pretty Things* I had three actors who had never acted in English before. One actor had never spoken English before the film started pre-production –and we had two and a half weeks pre-production—and the other two actors who did speak English but had never acted in English before. Audrey Tatou, a wonderful actress, is French, and she was speaking English for the first time in a film but with a Turkish accent. And she did fantastically well, but she said, 'I was completely blind.' She sent me a card at the end. I was on a bicycle and she was on roller-skates behind, holding me like this. (It wasn't us, of course, but two children.) And she said, 'That's what it was like.'

DC: She played in *Amelie*, didn't she?
PD: Yes, that's right, and she's really very lovely and she's an actress, she is an actress, there's nothing starry there at all. But she didn't have any idea when it was right or not. She said, 'I had to completely rely on you.' And Stephen was extraordinary, because he was on the ball all the time about it. Yes, we had a Spanish actor who was wonderful, but who arrived going 'eh? eh?' And with us all going, 'It's lovely to meet you.' He said to me afterwards, 'I didn't understand a word anybody said from the first time I arrived.' And he had to speak copious amounts of English and understand what he was saying. So the relationship between the director and myself was a very close one—and had to be. We worked together in rehearsal and in the trailers with the actors—Stephen would be talking about the actor's journey, the character's journey and I would be adding to that—how that could be helped by the vocal

journey. So it was very much that feeding process that I am used to doing in theatre more often, but not so necessarily in film—and it's just a joy when you do.

DC: That was to do with the relationship with the director as much as the situation itself.
PD: Yes, exactly.

DC: Do you think also that the use of European actors, or non-English speaking actors, speaking in English is increasing?
PD: Yes, I do, definitely. I think it's an interesting one, I do. I think it makes for a richer diversity in a way.

DC: I was reading an article about the new wave of Spanish American or Southern American film directors, and many of them are also working in English or the films are...
PD: Extraordinary, that's right. And the new wave of Spanish and Southern American actors. I've worked recently with four Spanish and South American actors, and they're all great, and all really keen and they handle English in a way that puts us to shame, because we're absolutely hopeless at handling South American or Spanish in comparison. It's very definitely something that at the moment is the current trend—and these things do go in trends. We've had the trend of English to American, and American to English, and Australian to English—not so much English to Australian, I've noticed, but maybe that will come. But you are dealing with different things the minute you start working with English as a foreign language.

DC: You were talking just now about working with Stephen Frears on *Dirty Pretty Things*, and how that was much more like working in the theatre. Could we just move on to talk a little bit about that in terms of recent experiences you've had? You were mentioning earlier about *Camera Obscura*, a play set in New England. How did the process go on that production?
PD: I'm pleased to say that it was the second time I'd worked with the director, Jonathan Miller, so I knew Jonathan's process, and it's an idiosyncratic one. Jonathan has a wonderful mind and often chooses interesting, unusual projects. *Camera Obscura* was the true story of this reclusive gentleman living in New England. He was originally from the South—Georgia, I believe. I didn't have to work with the actor concerned—he did his own thing because he'd lived in the South. We made some good noises in the beginning, and then we left that to him. And this reclusive gentleman lived from 1930 right through to the late sixties in New England—never left his house, agoraphobic—and people would come there to 'entertain' him. He was married, but he had many ladies who came to 'entertain'. And they were all interesting eclectic people, and most with these New England accents. However, Jonathan is not at all technically minded. So when it comes to

voice and dialect work, he's not at all aware of the journey or what has to be done, but he absolutely knows what he wants as his end product. So the important thing for me was—having worked with him before—was knowing that I had in the production two young actors who were very inexperienced. Now, ironically, both of them had received trainings, but technically were not that apt. And they were very panicked by the idea that they had to find these idiosyncratic voices that belonged to these two young girls who used to visit Arthur Inman in New England. And these voices were in abundance on this CD-ROM that Jonathan had presented the actors with, and which I managed to procure. That's the other thing—you suddenly realize, of course, that they haven't actually thought that possibly the voice coach might like to hear this. And so you find yourself getting that copy by hook or by crook. And obviously what I needed to do there, was to listen to those voices and find what would work for the girls—the actual actors that I was dealing with—because one had a very strong Welsh accent, and one had quite a modern sound; and so when she went to American, it was very good but it was very modern. And the Welsh actress—wonderful actress—but she'd never ever, ever, ever, ever had to do an accent before in the profession. So we had to work with what would be right. At the same time, again because I knew Jonathan, it was easy for me to be able to go to him and say, 'Now, Jonathan, the important thing here is that that's going to be a problem for this actress to achieve because....' And if I put it in black and white terms, he would completely accept that. So we would come together and talk to the actor. But I was very aware, because Jonathan's process is so cerebral, that I would have to put this a little bit more into plain terms—translate it for these young actresses. And we got there. So there was a process where I was very much involved with the director. But it's a completely different involvement. It's not an involvement where the director is completely one hundred percent involved in the process of the language. It is a process where the director is there with all his wonderful ideas, but actually he has no connection at all to the technical process.

DC: So you do work both as a dialect coach but also as a diplomat, translator and acting coach to a certain extent.
PD: To a certain extent that happens and I'm always very loath to go too far down that road...

DC: ...of course...
PD: but recently I did some work on a production in the West End of *Sleuth* which is on in the West End at the moment and the director is somebody I've worked with a great deal before—Elijah Mojinsky, and he's a wonderful director. That was very much a process by which the two of us got together and absolutely worked side by side to find, to help the actor find what he needed vocally as well as dialect

for both his character of Milo and as the Wiltshire policeman that he takes on board. Sometimes I was aware in rehearsal that Elijah would—and he actually said it to me at one point—'I'm looking to you now to make some suggestions,' he said, 'because I don't know what else to say at this point.' And you suddenly find yourself in that position where you think, 'I can't possibly say anything like that, because that's an acting note and that's not up to me to say. And I'm not sure it's the right note to say.' So I will always, again diplomatically, put the ball back in his court, and obviously only talk about the process vocally or dialectally. I mean, obviously, there is a marriage between the two, and yes, you can say to a person, 'Isn't it extraordinary how, by using that inflection, you're starting to portray the character's real inner thoughts? Now that's something you should explore.' And that's as far as one goes. And yes, again, you've got to be deeply aware of how much the actor is happy to receive and not—and obviously each actor is very different. I think, on the whole, I've always been very lucky. I've worked with actors who are very receiving.

DC: Just to finish off—what would you say are the key distinctions between working in film and working in theatre?
PD: I think the work in film is ultimately more intense. It's unlikely on a film that you would ever get enough pre-production time to really know that you can do the work, and the work's got to that point where the technique is no longer being thought about. I think also it's more intense because a lot of the time with film actors there hasn't necessarily been a thorough technical training. So you're coming up against that, and you have to find ways of taking short cuts that work. And yes I think on the whole, the whole process of filming is more intensive. You know, it's happening, it's done. You haven't got the rehearsal process—'okay, that didn't quite work, we'll go again'—it's not like that. It's like, the director's now suddenly found what he wants and that's it, it's in the bag, it's done. The whole way of working is much, much more intensive and of course the other thing I was thinking about with film is that the voice that is explored is the inner voice. I mean, it's the inner voice of the actor. So they work and explore off the inner. When you're in theatre, it's much more to do with the outer, but the outer has to come from the inner. Now the irony is that I think that when you work in film, you need to know your technique so well—if you've got that technique it's an absolute bonus, it's a massive benefit—you need to know it so well that you can still find the subtlety by working completely for something that is very intimate.

DC: If you've got the technical muscular skills you can adapt, you can modify, you can make it subtle. You can increase the energy, or intensity.

PD: The thing that you come across so many times is actors thinking that by going into something that's sort of half whispered, sort of slightly off a half breath, it is going to do the necessary…

DC: …which you get so much in soap opera in this country…
PD: …exactly and it's like 'Why are they whispering, why is that happening?' So, you know they'll have their ideas and you hopefully can help them to overcome them and find different ways. Whereas in theatre, the freedom of the space itself—just the fact that you're in a theatre space that's free and creative at all times throughout the rehearsal process, I think, makes an enormous difference. On a film set you're surrounded by people, objects, lights, cameras, props all the time. It's a bit like being a troglodyte in a way, isn't it, even if you're in the open air…

DC: …you're still closed in…
PD: …yes, closed in. I think that makes it a very different process, and for us it becomes a lot more intensive. I think that's the best way I can put it.

DC: Thank you, many thanks, Penny.

Peer Reviewed Article *by Douglas N. Honorof*

Reference Vowels and Lexical Sets in Accent Acquisition

1.0 Introduction

It is difficult, while reading aloud, to produce a believable *unfamiliar accent* (where the term *accent* is used to refer to the pronunciation of any variety of speech, with the term *dialect* reserved for features of the grammar and vocabulary following Hughes & Trudgill, 1996). For some, it is doubly difficult to act *past* the accent once off book. Although mastering prosody (intonation, rhythm, etc.) may provide a quick means of suspending the audience's disbelief about our ownership of a character's voice, I propose that much of the awkwardness we communicate while acting 'in accent' stems from our fear that we will become confused if we allow ourselves to stop monitoring the details of our consonants and vowels so that we can focus on our actions.

Over the past few years, I have been experimenting with a fun, actor-friendly, linguistic approach to accent training intended to reduce accent anxiety. Within this approach, actors are encouraged to explore extensively the coordination of gestures within their own vocal tracts, thus training their ears in the process. Through exploration of their own instruments, actors make new and extremely useful discoveries that help extend their range and flexibility. They are also encouraged to memorize *cross-accent* sound-spelling correspondences (lexical sets), which diminishes confusion over sound-spelling mappings. The internalization of the lexical sets frees actors to focus on acting tasks more central to the performance moment. This two-pronged process— gestural exploration and lexical set familiarization—has fostered remarkably improved consistency (subjectively judged) and noticeably better performances, both in conservatory settings and in 'quick-fix' coaching contexts.

Doug Honorof has worked on-camera and off as an actor and coach (accents and dialects), serves as an Associate Editor for IDEA and has taught at the Yale School of Drama, Voice One and CAP21, the undergraduate musical theatre studio school at NYU/Tisch. He trained under theatre faculty at Yale and at several institutions in New York including the Actors Center and the Upright Citizens Brigade Theatre. Doug also holds a PhD in linguistics (phonetics and phonology) from Yale and serves as Senior Research Scientist at Haskins Laboratories in New Haven, Connecticut, where, under federal funding, he investigates imitation of speech.

Some actors are intimidated by the notion of an analytical, linguistic approach to work that ultimately must become synthetic and organic. Before describing the details of a linguistic approach to accent acquisition, I offer arguments in favor of the approach, arguments that have been inspired by the naïve objections of actors who have not experienced the work. Then I define what I mean by the term *gesture* and introduce the cardinal vowels of Daniel Jones and the lexical sets of John Wells. Finally, I walk the reader through a diagnostic narrative intended for use in developing phonologically balanced speech-sample archives.

1.1 Motivations for beginning with linguistics

While it may be wise to adjust our training approach to the learning styles of individual students and actor-clients, it is not entirely reasonable for an actor, especially an inexperienced actor, to dictate the nature of training sessions from the start. As experienced teachers and coaches, we may be able to suggest techniques to actors that may work better for them than the techniques with which they are already comfortable. Therefore, in order to enlist the actor's fullest cooperation for what may sound like an unnecessary, highbrow foray into linguistic science, a bit of salesmanship is in order at the outset. In the next four subsections I outline slightly more sophisticated versions of some of the motivational arguments I have successfully employed.

1.1.1 Analytical preparation breeds confidence for later creativity

Adult actors must be well enough prepared to speak in accent extemporaneously, ideally before they are even off book. Otherwise, they find the rational mind thrust into overdrive during a performance. The actor's overtaxed 'left brain' drowns out the character's inner voice, taking the actor entirely out of the moment. The performer loses touch with even a carefully constructed imaginary world and loses all sense of *complicité* with scene partners, hearing only the voice of an inner accent-critic. Every mangled vowel, every misplaced "r," every unintended muscular tension and every inauthentic tune will resound in the actor's consciousness, preventing him or her from committing fully to living the moment in character. Fear of failure with the accent can be battled only with the confidence that naturally arises out of success in rehearsal. Hard intellectual work fosters success in rehearsal, even, perhaps, when linguistic talent is lacking. Present success breeds future courage.

1.1.2 Accents are not created *ex nihilo*

As complex as a phonological system (accent) may seem, with training and experience, there is always enough time to learn an accent well because we are never really starting from scratch. Again and again my students and actor-clients have made a small adjustment to the placement of the voice or have adopted a new feature of a target accent, and have realized on their own that the accent suddenly sounds more authentic. Mysteriously, it would seem that we know when an accent is true, even when we have never used it before. Furthermore, many of us outsiders can identify native speakers or very talented mimics when we hear them (but see Trudgill, 1983, on the limitations of passive grammatical competence). Perhaps we all have a great deal of very specific passive knowledge of accents we have heard but in which we have never spoken. I suggest that such passive perceptual experience with a range of accents can quickly be turned into active production. By way of analogy, it has been said that we need not be dead to play dead. Perhaps we can play dead because we have seen corpses and because we can draw on our own memories of rest in life. Along these lines, I suspect that we need not have produced a familiar accent to judge its authenticity because we can draw on our memory of having perceived it in the past. It may even be that actors who hone their imitative skills can sense intuitively what they would need to do to produce an accent they hold in short or long-term memory even if they lack the rhetoric to describe what is going on in their vocal tracts when they do so.

Passive competence is far from well established in the literature. The devil's advocate might argue that we know an accent sounds false simply because it is stilted or forced, or because it relies on too a narrow a range of expressive tones and rhythms. Given passive competence, however, my working hypothesis would be that the experience of having analyzed and practiced a reasonably familiar accent in advance frees the actor to turn

passive knowledge into active expertise during a performance as he or she dares to believe against all evidence that he or she is indeed a native speaker of the target accent. Under such a view, the accent breakdown is simply be a tool we use to discover what, at some level, we already know sympathetically. If we learn to access our passive linguistic expertise, we start with a definite "leg up." Besides, we do not really have to get the accent perfect for the character to be believable even to a native speaker; real people are rarely pure exemplars of a type. We accept a character as real if the actor believes and has done at least *most* of the homework.

1.1.3 It gets easier with each new accent

As hard as it may be for some of us to really work at our new first accent several hours a day until we have it down pat, there is hope. Accent work is like riding a bicycle. Once the accent is there, it does not take much of a refresher to re-access it even after a long hiatus. Perhaps the breakdown and embodiment of that first new accent reactivates a dormant accent-learning mechanism in us. Whatever the case, subsequent accents become easier and easier to acquire. It is as though, with each new voice we possess, we gain more hooks on which to hang new sounds. This hope alone should give courage to the fainthearted; courage sufficient to conquer the fear of a *seemingly* monumental task. Many of my more experienced clients report that, with the accent device once again thrust into full gear, it eventually becomes possible to simply commit to a simple inspiration, and to produce a new voice with no preparation at all, say, for an audition.

1.1.4 Analytical and synthetic approaches are compatible

We all fear the unknown. Linguistics is unknown to most actors. The fear of being asked to master abstract linguistic concepts causes some actors to simply refuse to audition for accent parts, while others insist on approaching accent work synthetically with recordings alone but no coach. Although shadowing audio recordings is crucial, doing so helps the actor more after the accent has been properly broken down. Although those hoping to master an accent by relying on their ears alone ultimately have the right idea, even the most talented among them may miss important details when they jump past the analytical work. Furthermore, even those who get the prosody and all the consonants and vowels right may not always know which words take which sounds. The right vowel in the wrong word can be jolting to the listener. Although hit-and-miss accent work may suffice for voicing cartoons or teenage twitch games, many film, television and legitimate theatre roles call for more than what I call an *accent-shaped object* (ASO). Granted, there may be legitimate differences in learning style. There may even be unusually gifted actors who do not need but a note or two from us. (See Markham, 1997, for a survey of what is known about ranges of individual achievement at accent learning.) Still, the average actor who objects to analytic instruction may, in part, actually be objecting to something inherently confusing in the traditional sound-substitution training paradigm. With a simpler and more focused linguistic approach, the actor can get past the hard work quickly, and be freed to take risks with the synthetic work.

2.0 Overview: Gestures, reference vowels and lexical sets
I borrow the notion of the *gesture* from *articulatory phonology* (e.g., Browman & Goldstein, 1991) and from the *direct realist* theory of speech perception (e.g., Fowler, 1996), frameworks related to Gibson's work in *ecological psychology* (e.g., 1966). A gesturalist might say that we learn, produce and directly perceive dynamically *coordinated* movements within the vocal tract rather than acoustic features or static orthographic symbols that stand for segments (Fowler, 1995).

Actors are often delighted to hear that the analytical work I teach is based on coordinated movement. Movement is very tangible. I tell actors next to nothing about the technical specifications of the gesture—much less than I will describe below—but my gesturalist disposition toward articulation does lead me to teach actors a second linguistic construct: the cardinal vowels. These articulatorily defined reference vowels serve as a prerequisite to the third linguistic concept I believe actors need to know about: *lexical sets* (Wells, 1982). Each of these areas is described in more detail, below.

2.1 Definition: Gestures
My colleagues at Haskins Laboratories have spent over a decade presenting experimental data that are slowly nudging phoneticians and phonologists around the world away from a fixation on static, transcription-based (that is, alphabetic) units such as phonemes and the phonetic features of which they are comprised, toward the study of dynamic articulatory gestures which may or may not cohere into segmental units. Within the Haskins model, speech gestures are decomposed into synergies of participating articulators and further specified for such parameters as constriction degree, constriction location, aperture, protrusion, articulator orientation, etc. With these parameters in mind, speech may be viewed in terms of movement, or, more accurately, as a system of coordinated movements. This perspective on speech bears striking resemblance to the decomposition of dance into timing, direction and spatial relationships as will be familiar to students of eukinetics and Labanotation, though our definition of the gesture itself is based on a different set of principles. Fortunately, movement is something even the most non-analytical of actors can relate to, as well. The following subsection outlines some gesturalist assumptions about speech in fairly non-technical terms.

2.1.1 Coordination within a gesture
We adapt from Bernstein the notion of the functional organization of muscles into *coordinative structures* (1967). *Coordinative* is the operative word. Let us first consider coordination within the gesture that corresponds to the lip closure for a 'p'. (Note: We refer to the letter 'p'. More traditional linguists might refer instead to the phoneme /p/ or to the phone [p].) In defining a specific gesture, we look for evidence of coupling among a *synergy* of articulators and specify the geometry (closure, protrusion, etc.) targeted by the named articulators working in tandem. For 'p', the key articulators of the oral tract would be the upper lip, lower lip and jaw. The geometry aimed for would be a closure of the vocal tract at the lips, though the individual articulators might contribute in varying degrees to the closure. From a gesturalist perspective, all lip closure gestures are functionally equivalent no matter which articulator moves the greatest distance or with the greatest velocity. Perhaps accents and idiolects differ according to the favored weighting of the contributions of the individual articulators that make up the lip closure gesture, but even within a single talker, that weighting can vary with gestural context and performative circumstances. In fact, an early piece of evidence for the gesture was unearthed by experiments in which the jaw was tugged downward by a mechanical device during the production of a lip closure gesture (Kelso et al., 1984). The experiment revealed that talkers compensate almost immediately for the perturbation of the jaw (and, consequently, the perturbation of the lower lip riding on the jaw) by lowering the upper lip and raising the lower lip more than usual in order to achieve a closure of the lips at all costs. At a functional level, it is the task of closure itself that matters.

The Haskins group has devised a (computational) gestural model that allows the researcher to view the midline of a two-dimensional talking head on a computer screen, and to hear the synthetic speech it produces. To condense the technical specification into one sentence: The model relies on a differential equation that treats each gesture as a critically damped mass-spring system, the gesture having its own internal stiffness—a variable that affects the rate of movement towards a target, and therefore movement duration. (See Saltzman & Munhall, 1989.)

Intrinsic duration is one property that most strikingly distinguishes gestures from static, timeless phonemes. The math behind the model is beyond the scope of the present paper and way beyond the concerns of the actor learning an accent. Fortunately, one need not understand the math in order to benefit from a coordination-oriented way of thinking about speech. If the gesturalist is correct, the mapping between gesture and sound will be a more natural one than the mapping between a letter of the alphabet and sound, which may partially explain the difficulty so many actors experience in learning to read from transcription. It may even explain the difficulty experienced by children who have reading disabilities; the gesture corresponds to linguistic objects in the real world, while the phoneme is merely an overlaid, learned concept, and one that is easier for some to learn than others (Mattingly, 1972; Read et al., 1986). Although a number of highly regarded techniques have been devised for teaching speech through transcription (e.g., Catford, 1988; Colaianni, 1994), in production coaching where I tend to have less time with an actor than one has in a conservatory program, I begin by making the actor aware of his or her own gestures as quickly as possible, and only then touch on transcription if at all—in fact, narrow transcription at that; even in transcription, I skirt the phoneme.

2.1.2 Coordination between gestures

Clearly, words involve multiple gestures, but even to produce just the sounds spelled with the letter 'p', we must move beyond lip closure. We must specify a velic closure gesture to channel airflow through the mouth but not the nasal passages. We must also specify a laryngeal abduction (that is, glottis-opening) gesture to keep 'p' from sounding like 'b'. The degree of abduction and the relative intrinsic duration of the glottal gesture will vary with context in an accent-specific way. A word-initial 'p' heading a stressed syllable in many accents of English will have a much wider—and therefore, *ceteris paribus*, temporally lengthened—opening of the glottis than will a medial 'p' (*pot* versus *taper*); the larger opening of the glottis gives the 'p' in *pot* its aspiration. A specific temporal 'point' in the large glottal abduction gesture may be phased to a specific 'point' in the lip-closure gesture, but the glottal abduction gesture is not part of the 'p' itself. 'P' does not exist except as a crude orthographic index of what is really going on. The glottal abduction gesture is itself a potentially contrastive element of syllable onsets (Goldstein & Browman, 1986). There are at least three possibilities: the laryngeal abduction gesture is absent (implying a narrowed glottis for voicing as for the 'b' in *boy*), it is present but 'less wide' (for the 'p' in *taper*) or it is wide (for the 'p' in *pot, spot, plot, prof*). Note, when a wide glottal opening gesture in a syllable onset is followed by a stressed vowel, we hear different things depending on context: aspirated 'p' in *pot*, but unaspirated 'p' in *spot*, and unaspirated 'p' followed by voiceless 'l' or 'r' in *plot* or *prof*. The phasing of a small inventory of gestures across the oral, laryngeal and velic *tiers* expresses the aspiration rule very elegantly. It is much easier to tell an actor to blow a lot of air through the lips when the syllable onset is voiceless and the vowel is stressed than it is to tell them that 'p' is sometimes unaspirated but only between vowels or after 's' before a stressed vowel, that 'l' and 'r' are sometimes voiceless, but only in after 's' plus a plosive at the beginning of a stressed syllable, etc.

Now let us consider the gestural organization for 'p' in an old-fashioned, upper-class Southern British accent, that is, the accent often referred to as Period Received Pronunciation (RP), U-RP or Marked RP. Here, the target accent does not have a wide glottal gesture in syllable onsets, thus, we hear unaspirated plosives in *pot* and no devoicing of 'l' and 'r' in *plot* and *prof*. Again, this is more technical a definition than the actor needs. Furthermore, it may be that this feature of the accent is variable, but in simplifying the task for the actor, we need only instruct the actor to blow little air through the lips for a voiceless 'p' before a stressed vowel. In fact, because the relatively more or less wide glottal aperture gesture is a property of syllable onsets, the amount of air blown, as it were, is the same whether the initial consonant is 'p', 't' or 'k'.

In addition to the phasing across tiers (oral, velic and glottal), the *oral* gesture for an initial consonant such as 'p' is phased to the oral gesture for the following vowel, etc. Phasing is simply an instruction to the computer model specifying how far into a constriction to go before forming the next (overlapping) constriction. Thus it is important to bear in mind that two talkers of the same accent who begin with the same inventory of gestures can differ not only in how they typically form the gestures (that is, in how they coordinate their articulators in the formation of constrictions *within gestures*), but also in how they coordinate gestures *with each other*. In this way a gestural approach gives us a rhetoric for moving beyond generalized accent-study to idiolect/character 'design'.

2.1.3 Summary: Gestures

Gestures allow us to work in terms of units that are more tangible than transcriptions and features. Furthermore, gestural awareness enables the trainer to give a higher proportion of articulatory notes than auditory notes—which may be very helpful given the finding of Catford and Pisoni that purely articulatory training is more effective than auditory discrimination training alone in teaching exotic speech sounds to adults (1970). The gestural approach has been discussed above in connection with consonants, but applies equally to the teaching of vowel systems as will be seen in the next section.

2.2 Definition: Cardinal vowels

When Western linguistics became increasingly concerned with less-familiar languages and when scholarly communication across borders became more frequent in the early 20th Century, phoneticians faced a challenge. Convenient sound recording equipment was still a thing of the future. How, then, might the field worker record in print the 'exotic' sounds of far-off lands for the benefit of scholars back home? Or how, even, might French phoneticians, for example, describe in print the vowels of local accents for those abroad? Editors of traditional bilingual grammars tended to simply write, for example, that the Parisian word *tout* has a vowel like that in English 'too'. Of course, a Belfaster and a speaker of just about any variety of Plantation Southern (American) would have had wildly different pronunciations for the vowel in 'too', none of them quite like the Parisian. The situation would only be doubly complicated for the Russian or Swedish phonetician who would be accessing the Parisian pronunciation of *tout* through a form of English, already a second language. The lexicographer's difficulty in mapping one accent onto another persists to this day, as lexicographers have tended to maintain the tradition of relating unknown pronunciations to the pronunciations of familiar words from accents presumed to be more familiar to the user of the dictionary or of devising equally imprecise sight-spelling such as 'uh' for the vowel in 'cup' (See Bronstein, 1998).

Daniel Jones, a British student of William Tilly and Paul Passy, advanced an alternative to cross-system sound-mapping and sight-spelling. His alternative, based on suggestions by Ellis, Bell and Sweet, will not do for general purposes such as lexicography because some training is involved, but it is simple enough to be mastered quickly by professional users of speech. The technique he developed involves learning to recognize and produce eight primary *cardinal* vowels. Eight to ten secondary cardinal vowels were later added. The cardinals serve as reference vowels belonging to no accent at all, but pronounceable by anyone who has studied the system, and are organized in terms of tongue height.

The cardinal vowel space (see Figure 1) is anchored by the cardinal vowels occupying the four corners of an imaginary two dimensional connect-the-dots chart, so it is most reasonable to begin teaching the cardinal vowels by anchoring the four corners. Beginning with cardinal vowel 1 (cv1), the student may be asked to grin from ear to ear all the while thrusting the center of the tongue into an exceptionally high position in the palatal arch, constricting the passageway to the point of *nearly* causing the air flowing over the tongue to vibrate as for a fricative. Next the student is asked to form a widely open front vowel (cv4), a gaping open (i.e., in phonological terms, *low*) back vowel (cv5) and an extremely close (that is, *high*), back vowel with exceptional lip protrusion (cv8). Having developed a feel for the four extreme corners of the 'vowel space', it is easier to fill in the lines that connect these four corners in equal steps until eight points along the periphery of the vowel space have been explored, categorized, named (cv1 through cv8) and assigned phonetic symbols.

In order to test the hypothesis that the perceived height and relative backing of the vowel correspond to the absolute highest point of the tongue along its midline, Jones lay a ferrous

chain along the center of his tongue and had x-ray stills taken of his head while producing each of the cardinal vowels in turn. The stills showed the midline tongue shape in detail, allowing him to plot the highest point of the tongue for each vowel with a single dot on a two-dimensional chart; all are pure monophthongs. With the dots connected, the resulting plot looked something like an olive, soon evolving into the familiar vowel quadrilateral adopted by the International Phonetic Association, a simplification of the chart having been suggested by Jones himself in the interest of pedagogical ease (1940). In gramophone recordings—no longer pressed—Jones himself demonstrated these vowels on a held note so that the lack of tongue and lip movement during the vowel could be heard clearly.

When teaching these monophthongal reference vowels, I place a dot on the chart for each vowel, numbering it (e.g., 'cv3') to the left of the dot for the spread vowels and to the right for the rounded vowels. In addition, I usually write the corresponding IPA symbols under the cv number for the benefit of those who have learned a transcription system, though I am careful to point out that one need not learn the transcription system in order to benefit from the exercise.

Once my students or actor-clients have taken an honest stab at the primary cardinal vowels, I teach what Jones called the secondaries, that is, reference vowels that match the eight primaries in tongue position but have the opposite lip rounding configuration—lip spread for lip rounded and rounded for spread. I simply write cv and the number (9 through 16) on the opposite side of the dot as I move around the chart a second time from upper left-hand corner to upper right-hand corner. By convention, we plot lip-spread vowels on the left and lip-rounded vowels on the right of each dot on the vowel chart reproduced in Figure 2. Next, I make a game of asking students to switch between primary and secondary cardinal vowel for the same tongue position. Finally, I ask them to hold the lip position steady while sliding between front and back for the same degree of openness or between close and open for the same front/back position. All of these maneuvers require mastering an unfamiliar pattern of coordination, much like rubbing the belly while patting the head. For the novice, this exercise can be much harder than it might seem. The above-described progression does not originate with me, but represents my own structuring of several traditional exercises in articulatory phonetics handed down to me through distillation by several preceding generations of phoneticians, and may indeed even pre-date Jones himself.

Through playing with these articulatorily defined peripheral reference vowels, the actor is sensitized to vowel parameters such as height (that is, relative openness), backing, lip rounding, etc.—a set of sensations that does not always come immediately. Having raised consciousness about vowel dimensions in this way, we demonstrate the real beauty of the reference vowels: their usefulness as landmarks on our way to the vowels of genuine accents. When ready, I ask my actor-students to simply plot on a blank vowel chart each of the vowels of a known or new accent with reference to the cardinal positions.

Rather than plotting a dot and a phonetic symbol, they plot a word containing the vowel (in fact, a *lexical set keyword*—see below), marking rounding etc. with makeshift notation. At this point, I usually immediately find myself explaining how arrows can be plotted to show the directionality of diphthongs or triphthongs, genuine accents tending not to have many pure monophthongs. For example, I might demonstrate my low, back, long, rounded monophthong in the word *law* and suggest that we plot that vowel (with a dot or in transcription) just a bit higher and more centralized than CV13, only to have a student chime in that he or she says the word with a diphthongal vowel starting almost as high as CV 15 and ending somewhat left of CV6.

In order to reduce the clutter added by diacritics, I often find it helpful to hand out a sheet with the IPA vowel symbols marked on a chart accompanied by four blank charts, one labeled 'short vowels', one 'long vowels', one 'moving vowels' and another 'vowels before coda r'. (See Figure 3.) The idea was that one would plot vowels on the vowel charts while watching a speaker produce them, thus making lip configuration a known

Figure 1. Cardinal vowel charts after Daniel Jones (1940:36-7) representing two-dimensional coordinates of the highest point of the tongue along its midline. The head faces left in all three charts. The chart on the left is the most accurate geometrically. The chart in the center represents "a compromise between scientific accuracy and the requirements of the practical language teacher [that the chart be easy to draw]" (1940:36). The more schematic trapezoid on the right represents a further simplification intended to ease the artistic burden on the "ordinary pupil" (1940:37fn), and is closest in shape and dimensions to the chart adopted by the International Phonetic Association (see Fig. 2).

2.2.1 Limitations of the cardinal vowels

As the reader will have noticed by now, the vowel quadrilateral is not ideal. In the best of all possible worlds, intellectual history would have given us separate vowel charts for lip-spread and lip-rounded vowels (Catford, 1981). The chart also conflates short, long and half-long vowels, forcing us to resort to messy diacritics. Its two dimensions tell us only about the tongue—and only about a single point on its midline at that, and nothing about voice quality, intrinsic fundamental frequency (akin to pitch) differences among vowels, etc. Still, familiarity with these charts can increase awareness of relative vowel height and relative backing. Furthermore, (optional) familiarity with the IPA symbols may allow our students to someday take advantage of such published resources as the Longman Pronunciation Dictionary (LPD) which follows the IPA in its conventions (Wells, 2000). Whether or not our students ever learn the transcription system, and whether or not they master the cardinal vowels in one sitting (which, in all honesty, rarely happens), they will come away from the session with an awareness of

variable. The justification for separating out the vowels before 'r' becomes clear once I introduce the lexical sets. Note, in order to help students remember to keep the cardinal vowels on the extreme periphery of their possible vowel space, I stress that no vowel in any real accent ever quite touches the periphery of the chart.

VOWELS

Where symbols appear in pairs, the one to the right represents a rounded vowel.

Figure 2. The vowel chart from the International Phonetic Alphabet (Revised to 1993, Updated 1996), available at no charge from the web site of the International Phonetic Association, Department of Linguistics, University of Victoria, Victoria, British Columbia, Canada (http://www.arts.gla.ac.uk/IPA/vowels.html).

Vowel Charts for _____

short vowels

long vowels

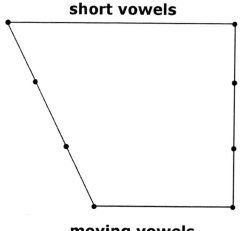

moving vowels

vowels before coda r

---

lexical set keywords after J. C. Wells (1982).
Accents of English I, Cambridge Univ. Press.

1. KIT	15. GOOSE
2. DRESS	16. PRICE
3. TRAP	17. CHOICE
4. LOT	18. MOUTH
5. STRUT	19. NEAR
6. FOOT	20. SQUARE
7. BATH	21. START
8. CLOTH	22. NORTH
9. NURSE	23. FORCE
10. FLEECE	24. CURE
11. FACE	25. happУ
12. PALM	26. letteR
13. THOUGHT	27. commA
14. GOAT	

vowels of the IPA (1996)

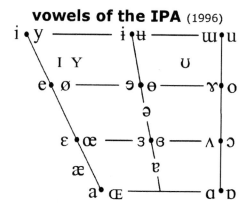

Chart courtesy International
Phonetic Association, Department
of Linguistics, University of
Victoria, Victoria, BC, Canada.

speech that they never had before. Below, I describe how students can then learn to apply their new gestural consciousness in learning to produce the vowels of an unfamiliar accent by plotting words rather than phonetic transcriptions on a vowel quadrilateral. The words I encourage them to plot are called *lexical set keywords*, and are motivated in the following section.

2.3 Lexical sets

2.3.1 Weaknesses of the sound-substitution approach

Traditionally, we trainers have presented adult actors with an inventory of sounds in a target accent and then asked them to substitute sound A for sound B or melody X for melody Y. Yet we have all had students complain of experiencing difficulty with these sound substitutions, even though they themselves may have implicitly requested instruction in these terms by asking us, "How do you pronounce 'a'?" They ask such questions, because they assume that a simple list of sound changes (or unvarying letter-sound mappings if they are especially naïve) will throw them mechanically into the new accent. My job, as I see it, is to redirect the question because the sound-substitution approach creates three areas of difficulty:

A. Speech is more than consonants and vowels. It has much to do with intonation (melody, tune), rhythm (tempo, rate), overall articulatory setting (placement), etc. This point must be obvious to our students at some level, but they may lack a rhetoric for asking about prosody and voice quality (in the broad sense of Laver, 1980). Lexical sets will not help with prosody and settings, but they do encourage a shift of focus from simple substitutions to mastery of a phonological system.

B. Our students may not be equally familiar with the assumed base accent. Suppose we are hired to teach an old-fashioned, upper-class Southern British to a mixed group of Londoners, Glaswegians and Sydneyites. If we simply teach, for example, that the 'y' in the word happy is pronounced more like the vowel in 'kit' than like the vowel in 'fleece', immediately we run into a problem. The Londoner might slightly diphthongize the 'y', the Glaswegian might produce too open a vowel, and the Sydneyite too tense a vowel—all three missing the target vowel quality. We would have to give a different note to each actor—a nuisance when we are teaching a group.

C. Even if we have already had the luxury of taking our students through a single uniform base (perhaps 'standard') system, say, in a conservatory program, there are times when the vowel system of the target accent may map in a

complex fashion onto the shared base vowel-system due to historical mergers or splits reflected in the target system. That is, sometimes a sound in the target accent does not map uniquely onto any sound in the new accent in a one-for-one substitution. We cannot simply tell our students, "A→B." The problem of complex mappings is at the focal point of the following section.

2.3.2 Complex mappings
2.3.2.1 Mergers

In Middle English, words such as *horse* and *hoarse* were pronounced with relatively more open and relatively more close vowels, respectively, throughout the English-speaking world. Hence we find the sight-spelling *hoss* for *horse* but not for *hoarse* in rendering 'Plantation Southern' to name an accent that preserves the Middle English distinction between these words. However, the vowels in these words have merged so that *horse* and *hoarse* are now pronounced with the same vowel by people in many parts of the English-speaking world. One consequence of the merger is that, when teaching 'Plantation Southern' to a Californian, for example, we cannot simply say that the vowel in the word *horse* 'goes to' a lower, more spread, shorter, more nearly monophthongal vowel than is heard in the word *hoarse*. The learner will need to be told which other words pattern with *horse*, and which with *hoarse*. Here the mapping between words in the native and target accents is one-to-two, which leads us to the problem of the *lexical incidence* of a particular vowel in a particular word.

2.3.2.2 Lexical incidence and spelling

In the case of a one-to-two mapping, our students need our help if they are to extrapolate what they have learned about *horse* and *hoarse,* for instance, onto a larger set of words. That is, they need to know which words in their script rhyme with *horse* and which rhyme with *hoarse* in the target accent. We could just tell them which words are said how, but their ownership of the accent will be more profound if they have internalized the system. Fortunately, in the case of the *horse/hoarse* sets, it is relatively easy to undo the effects of the vowel merger because, with few exceptions, the conventional *spelling* of English preserves crucial information about Middle English pronunciation, and therefore about the pronunciation of these words in contemporary accents that are conservative with respect to this part of the vowel system. We can simply ask our students to memorize the following relation: words with spellings *oar, ore,* etc. pattern with *hoarse* while those with spellings *orC* etc., pattern with *horse,* where C stands for one or more consonants. Then, to state the matter in the simplest terms, when our students graduate from one accent that has not undergone the merger (say, 'Plantation Southern') to another such accent (say, conservative Hiberno-English), they will already know which words group together. They need only learn how these vowel spellings are pronounced in the target accent. Because spelling often fossilizes vestigial information in this way, English orthography may be more helpful to us than to the average speller—a fact that I find heartening. It is perhaps a good thing for us that the spelling reforms of the 16th and 17th Centuries were not more successful. (See Dobson, 1968: 38-198.)

Sometimes lexical incidence is irregular. To pull out words that do not obey the sound-spelling rules, actors need a well-trained coach with a good ear who in turn must consult native speakers in the absence of accent-specific pronouncing dictionaries (e.g., Jones [1949 and earlier], Kenyon and Knott [1944], Wells [2000]).

2.3.2.3 Splits

Mergers as in *horse/hoarse* are not the only possible type of challenge our students must confront when one vowel system maps untidily onto another. Sometimes spelling is less helpful. In the New York City area, many strongly localizable talkers pronounce words like *man* with a mid-open vowel or diphthong so that it sounds more like *men* than it would for, say, Londoners. This is not to say that native English-speakers from London could not hear the difference between the two words as pronounced by the stereotypical New Yorker. Make no mistake, the New York vowels have not merged by any measure, it is just that the vowel in *man* is produced with a vowel that is higher (closer) than the vowel in the word *mat*, for example, while the vowel in *men* may even be lower (more open) and more central than that in *man*. That is, to simplify matters, the set of closed syllables whose vowels are spelled 'a' (*mat, man, mash*, etc.), have split over time in these speech communities. By way of contrast, for Americans in certain other parts of the country, *man* and *mat* are both said with an *identical* vowel and thus remain together as a set as they did in Middle English. The specific vowel may be different from place to place, but the entire set of words hangs together. For example, in most of the American Far West and Lower Midlands, the vowel in *both* words is fairly open (as in the New York City pronunciation of *mat*). In the cities of the Inland North (Chicago, Detroit, Buffalo, etc.), *both* words have a vowel that is relatively close, that is, high (e.g., Labov, 1991), but perhaps more diphthongal and nasal for some talkers.

Unlike the case of vowel mergers discussed above where we saw that the spelling of the vowel can help us guess correctly which words will fall together, in the case of the *man/mat* split, London actors learning New York can virtually always guess the vowel correctly only if they observe that these 'a' words always have a higher vowel when followed by 'n' in the same syllable than when followed by 't' in the same syllable. In

fact, one can list for students all the coda consonants that have the same effect on the preceding vowel as does 'n' and all the coda consonants that have the same effect on the preceding vowel as does 't'. Indeed, there really is no way to learn which word belongs with which set other than to commit to memory a list of conditioning consonants. Having to memorize how each phonetic environment conditions the split still beats having to memorize a long list of words. If we want to practice with word lists (or ask our native speaker consultants to read them for us), we can do so, but doing so need only serve as a way of assuring ourselves that the generalization about the effect of the coda consonants on the vowel is largely without exception.

Let us consider a case in point. As several Metro New Yorkers including phonetician Alice Faber have pointed out to me and as discussed on the American Dialect Society Mailing List (http://listserv.linguistlist.org/archives/ads-l.html), they can tell that Dennis Franz of ABC's *NYPD Blue* has not mastered the 'a' split, thus *backhand* has two instances of the same vowel for him (Chicago-style, if you will) rather than a lower vowel in *back* followed by a higher vowel in *hand*. His character is supposed to be from Metro New York. He has got the right social register for his character, but the wrong regional pattern. This failure on the part of Mr. Franz' speech coach is noticeable to locals, though, to be fair, it may be that the note was given and ignored.

2.3.3 How many lexical sets are there?

In order to explain why we need gestures and lexical sets, we must consider the alternative: *phonemes*. An average accent of English has perhaps a dozen distinct nuclear vowel phonemes in its inventory, depending how one counts. However, although two twelve-vowel systems, *Accent A* and *Accent B*, may both have /i/ and /e/, Accent A may use /i/ in the word *beat* where Accent B uses the vowel /e/.

Once we begin considering the entire inventory of the two twelve-vowel systems, we may discover that many regular diachronic sound changes in both accents have made our comparison of the two systems complex. We might have to draw a Venn diagram of the two systems in order to sort out which vowel-word correspondences intersect in A and B, and which do not. Doing so may give us more than twelve vowels, even though each accent on its own has only twelve. John Wells has laid out a scheme of such lexical sets and subsets of vowel-word (or, ideally, vowel-spelling) correspondences (1982). He bases his sets on a comparison of the vowel systems of one British and one American accent with which many of his readers are assumed to be familiar (many other accents being considered in the crafting of the lexical *sub*sets as we shall see).

The lexical sets rest one leg on that accent family he regards as non-localizable within the south of Britain (Wells, 1982: 117), an accent that is arguably native to 'up-market' talkers from that region and acquired by elite schooling for others. That accent has passed under various names, including the opaque *Received Pronunciation* or RP, a name adopted by Daniel Jones to indicate that the speaker of this accent would be widely understood. In examining the introduction to Jones' pronouncing dictionary (1940: x-ix), it would seem he was not advocating that social climbers learn to speak RP so that they, too, could be generally accepted, however. He was, in his own words, not a "reformer of pronunciation". He said, "I do not regard RP as intrinsically 'better' or more 'beautiful' than any other form of pronunciation." It seems RP's first and most famous codifier never intended it to be regarded as a 'standard' (1949, §61). He recorded it because he believed that this accent of the South of England was readily understood in "most parts of the English speaking world" and because it happened to be "the only type of English pronunciation about which [he was] ... in a position to obtain full and accurate information." Note that Jones regarded RP as a regional accent, associating it with "a majority of Londoners who have had a university education." Historically, it has its roots in the speech of London, so its radiation from that center of influence should not be surprising. Perhaps the spread of RP among the upper and upper-middle classes throughout the south of Britain makes it only broadly localizable. As such, RP continues to thrive. Trudgill tells us that RP is alive and well, and keeping Estuary in its place as a more narrowly local non-contender (2001).

The other accent Wells has consulted in codifying his sets is so-called *General American* or *GenAm*. Perhaps referring to GenAm as a *family* of accents here will make the term marginally less objectionable to the many linguists who have marshaled evidence that there is no single, representative, non-localizable US accent of English. Here we are not concerned with the question of linguistic relativity, that is, whether there is such a thing as an unaccented talker (Esling, 1998), but with the existence of a non-localizable US accent. Aware of the debate, Wells nevertheless says, "A recognizably local accent in the United States can only come from the east or south (1982[1]: 118)," implying that GenAm finds its home in the Midwest and Far West (though Mencken goes so far as to say that GenAm extends eastwards all the way to the Connecticut river and beyond and northwards into Canada [1936: 356-67, 371]).

My every instinct as an American speech coach tells me that Wells overstates the case, so, before explaining how Wells uses GenAm in building the lexical sets that I am advocating the

reader teach, I feel compelled to distance myself from the notion of a *general* American accent. To begin with, there are many localizable accents outside of the east and south. I have heard many Westerners report the experience of having traveled outside their hometown and unexpectedly identifying by ear a hometown stranger. Perhaps these Westerners recognize familiar speech patterns by idiom or usage, or by phonetic details pertaining to stretches of speech longer than the phoneme (intonation, rhythm, voice quality, etc.). However, I suspect that even the detailed phonetics of Far Western and Midwestern vowels can be very regionally specific. In fact, speech teachers cannot even agree about matters as simple as whether words such as *cot* and *caught* are homophones in GenAm. They cannot agree because they have different GenAm archetypes in mind—those with one low back vowel and those with two.

If local Far Western and Midwestern talkers recognize 'their own people' by voice, then, we might think of GenAm as the family of accents that *outsiders* cannot localize. Alas, even this more limited definition fails. The cartoon and comedy industries thrive on the ability of national audience members to identify specific stereotyped Western character voices ("Fargo", "Surfer Dude", etc.).

Neither can we define GenAm as a highbrow social variant. In the US, the stereotype of an educated talker is not a pretty one—it is Back Bay effete or computer nerd, perhaps. In any case, although prescriptive traditions of grammar are taught in US schools, we have no analogous, consistent, unifying tradition of pronunciation training in US schools that would produce cross-regional uniformity only in scholastic achievers.

Alternatively, one hears GenAm defined as the accent of American English that we find unremarkable on the lips of a foreigner. Unfortunately, few foreigners ever reach anything close to this standard, so this hypothesis remains virtually untestable.

One also hears that many Americans who identify themselves (or are identified by others) as descendants of West African slaves may speak a non-localizable American English, or, at least, have fewer regional distinctions in pronunciation among themselves. (See Wolfram & Schilling-Estes, 1998, for a very accessible discussion of the roots and distribution of African-American Vernacular English features.) Suppose this claim of a non-localizable 'black' accent bears some truth (and I am *not* saying it does). Why has no one has ever thought to consider a 'black' accent of American English 'general' if it is indeed the most non-localizable native accent we have in the US? Clearly,

Lexical Sets Handout

	Keywords	Typical Spellings, Simplified Subsets	Examples
1.	KIT	iC	kid
2.	DRESS	eC	bell, merry
3.	TRAP	aC—'flat A' in RP & GenAm	tap, man, hand, marry
4.	LOT	oC	God
5.	STRUT	uC	cup
6.	FOOT	uC, ooC, ouC	put, good, could
7.	BATH	(a) aff, ath (*voiceless*), ass, aft, asp, ast, ask, augh; (b) ance, ant, anch, CVCand, ample; (c) alf, alv, an't; + many unpredictable, e.g., trans-	(a) staff, path, brass, shaft, last, ask, grasp, laugh (b) dance, plant, command, example; (c) half, halve, can't
8.	CLOTH	(a), o, au + *fricative* — rhyme with THOUGHT *in GenAm and Older RP*; (b) o, — *rhyme with THOUGHT in GenAm, never in RP*; (c) or — same pattern as (b)	(a) off, soft, cross, gone, Australia; (b) moth, coffee; (c) orange, tomorrow, sorry
9.	NURSE	ur, or, ir, er, earC	fur, work, fir, fern, earn
10.	FLEECE	(a) e, ee, eCe (b) ea, oeC	(a) be, meet, these; (b) meat, phoenix
11.	FACE	(a) aCe; (b) aiC, ay, ey, eiC, aig; (c) ea	(a) cake; (b) wait, bay, obey, rein, straight; (c) great
12.	PALM	(a) native Anglo-Saxon al, a#, ah — 'broad A' in RP & GenAm; (b) a *memorize foreign words*	(a) calm, bra, blah; (b) Nevada
13.	THOUGHT	(a) auC, ough, aw, al, alk; (b) alC (other than 'k') — *in England, rhymes with* THOUGHT subset (a) *or with* LOT *depending on region and generation*	(a) caught, bought, jaw, all, talk; (b) fault, salt, also
14.	GOAT	(a) o, oCe, oa; (b) ow, ol	(a) so, rode, road; (b) bowl, roll
15.	GOOSE	(a) o, oo, oCe, ou (b) uCe, euC, ew, uiC, iew#, eaut	(a) do, too, tooth, move, group; (b) duke, feud, few, fruit, view, beauty
16.	PRICE	iCe, i, y	write, ride, hi-fi, try, type
17.	CHOICE	oy, oiC	toy, join
18.	MOUTH	ouC, ow	south, cow
19.	NEAR	(a; c) eer, ere, ier, ear; erV; (b) ierC, eirC	(a; c) beer, mere, pier, fear; serious; (b) fierce, weird
20.	SQUARE	(a; c) are#, air#, ear#, eir#, ere#; ary; (b) arC	bare, fair, bear, their, there; Mary; scarce
21.	START	(a; b) ar#; arC; (c) ar	(a; b) bar; part; (c) safari
22.	NORTH	(a) or#, ar#; (b; c) orC, uar; aur	(a) or, for, nor, Thor, war (exhaustive); (b; c) horse, order, quart; Laura
23.	FORCE	(a, bi, c) ore, oar#, oor#, our#; orC; orV; (bii) oarC, ourC	(a, bi, c) tore, roar, door, pour; fort; oral; (bii) hoarse, court
24.	CURE	(ai, b, ci) oor#, our#; ourC; oori, ouri; (aii, cii) ure, urV, eur	(ai, b, ci) poor, tour; gourd; boorish, tourism; (aii, cii) pure, plural, Europe
25.	happY	(a) y#, i#, ie#; (b) ee#, ey#, ea#	(a) city, taxi, talkie; (b) coffee, hockey, Chelsea
26.	lettER	er#, or#, o(u)r#, yr#, ure#	tiger, author, harbo(u)r, martyr, figure
27.	commA	a#, ia# — *All non-native borrowings; Middle English had no final vowel corresponding to schwa*	vodka, phobia

racist or perhaps racist-classist notions lurk within our notion of 'generality'. Any kind of specificity seems to disqualify an accent as general unless the race and class are white and middle, respectively.

Clearly I question the existence of a non-localizable form of speech native to anyone in the us. (The nativeness criterion excludes broadcast and stage speech as contenders for the title *non-localizable*.) At best we can say that a talker may, in some contexts, use so few socially or regionally marked speech features that we tend to hear past his or her regional or social identity. Even so, GenAm speakers may indeed be localizable at a level at which most people are not attending. The perception of non-localizability, within this definition, implies that the talker's voice simply manages to slip under the threshold of being remarkably distracting despite its localizable features. If there is no true non-localizable native speaker of GenAm, Wells has simply codified his own version of a cultural myth, albeit, out of descriptive rather than prescriptive motives. Nevertheless, even invented accents 'exist' at some level, so on those terms I accept Well's GenAm family of accents as a construct on an equal footing with the RP family of accents, both of which are building blocks of the lexical sets.

2.3.4 Definition: Lexical sets

Having mapped out the lexical sets by comparing RP and GenAm vowel systems, Wells selects a *keyword* to name each of 27 major sets. The keyword is always a word that belongs to the set it names and, among other considerations, is not easily confused on hearing no matter who says the word to whom, provided each party is a native speaker of some accent of English. For example, the word FLEECE is chosen over *beat* to stand for words that are pronounced [i:] in RP and [i] in GenAm. *Beat* would be unsuitable as a keyword because some talkers may pronounce *beat* more-or-less as an RP or GenAm speaker might pronounce *bait* (Wells, 1982: 123).

The list of lexical set keywords is given in Table 1, with only the most common spellings indicated—a simplification I highly recommend for teaching actors, especially as exceptional spelling-sound mappings always arise, regardless.

Table 1. Lexical set keywords, typical spellings and examples after Wells (1982). Subset names appear in parentheses, and are from Wells. Those lexical sets whose subdivision has more relevance for historical linguistics than for present day accents of English are reorganized here, e.g., CURE (ai, b, ci) versus CURE (aii, cii). Some of Wells subsets are excluded altogether. 'C' stands for one or more consonants. 'V' stands for one or more vowels. '#' stands for the end of a word (minus any grammatical endings).The last three lexical sets keywords (happY, lettER, commA) are bi-syllables. We are concerned with the second syllable in each case."

I ask my students to memorize by rote the lexical set keywords and the spellings that match each set. Where spelling is less helpful, as when two sets share a vowel spelling, I also require memorization of both sets of words along with their membership. (All sets are given in Wells, 1982, Volume 1.) For example, students familiarize themselves with the NORTH and FORCE lists if their native accents have merged the two sets. In fact, I use this example when first mentioning the lexical sets. A demonstration of the NORTH/FORCE merger in "Plantation Southern" seems to work better than a demonstration in conservative Hiberno-English for my American students. When teaching students from areas where the accents have never undergone the FOOT/STRUT split, the need for lexical sets is equally clear. As an American, I can guess with accuracy which words belong to FOOT and which to STRUT without a moment's thought; many North Country speakers, for example, would need to learn by rote which words belong to FOOT and which to STRUT in order to acquire an accent in which the two sets are distinct. Even so, there is a lot less rote work involved than in working through the Skinner materials (1990).

Although Wells has devised the lexical sets to codify linguistic reality, there is a necessary arbitrariness in the number and exact make-up of the sets. The Venn diagram of vowels one gets by settling on the union of two reference accents (in this case, RP and GenAm) produces a system that is not necessarily sufficient for every purpose. This is where the subsets come in. When I am teaching an accent that largely follows the Middle and Early Modern ("Elizabethan") English practice of keeping words with *ee* spellings, for example, distinct from those with *ea* spellings (say, conservative Hiberno-English), I simply draw my students' attention to the FLEECE(a) and FLEECE(b) subsets, respectively. Then my students can usually guess correctly whether a FLEECE word is pronounced more like *be* or *bay* in an accent with the split. However, I mention the subsets to actors as issues arise in the course of instruction. When I am asked about subsets that are not relevant to learning, say, the particular Irish accent under study, I simply say, "Don't worry about those subsets." I have yet to have an actor protest this directive. The subsets are discussed in detail in Wells, especially Volume I, Chapters 2 and 3 (1982).

Given the foregoing discussion, I believe the reader can imagine how learning the lexical sets and their subsets might help students internalize regular mappings between conventional orthography and the vowel system of any accent under study. This mapping is the consequence of the particular series of mergers and splits that have produced the target accent's vowel system over a period of centuries. Whenever teaching a new accent to students who have learned the lexical sets, the trainer

Vowel Charts for Modern RP
Impressionistic analysis © 2000-2003 Douglas N. Honorof

short vowels
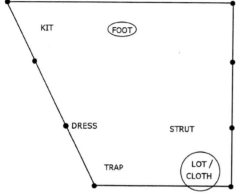

long vowels
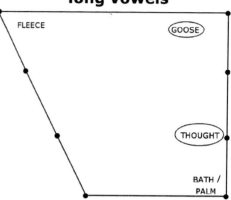

moving vowels
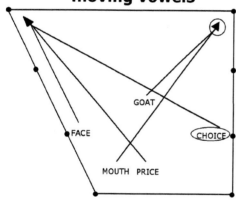

vowels before coda r
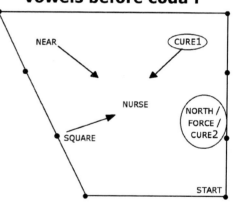

lexical set keywords after J. C. Wells (1982).
Accents of English I, Cambridge Univ. Press.

1. KIT
2. DRESS
3. TRAP
4. LOT
5. STRUT
6. FOOT
7. BATH
8. CLOTH
9. NURSE
10. FLEECE
11. FACE
12. PALM
13. THOUGHT
14. GOAT
15. GOOSE
16. PRICE
17. CHOICE
18. MOUTH
19. NEAR
20. SQUARE
21. START
22. NORTH
23. FORCE
24. CURE
25. happY
26. lettER
27. commA

vowels of the IPA (1996)

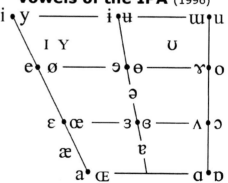

Chart courtesy International Phonetic Association, Department of Linguistics, University of Victoria, Victoria, BC, Canada.

Figure 4. The vowels of Modern Received Pronunciation. In a chronology of overtly prestigious Southern British accents, Modern RP would come between Older RP and Estuary. Lip rounding of any type is indicated with an ellipse for vowel nuclei, off-glides or entire vowels. The lexical sets happY, lettER and commA and other accent features not indicated on the charts ('smoothing', 'liquid u'/yod, consonants, rhythm, intonation, etc.) may be discussed and noted by students on the back of the sheet.

need only list the sets that are merged in the target accent, and make a note or two about specific subsets where relevant. Although the lexical sets and subsets help us remember which words rhyme with which in the target accent, the native-speaker or speech coach must still model the phonetic realization of each set in the target accent. One can imagine two accents with the same mapping of spellings and vowel categories but with different phonetic realizations. For instance, one can imagine contrasting an English accent heard in Australia with an English accent heard in New Zealand, choosing two accents, say, with essentially the same number and pattern of lexical sets and subsets, but in which the KIT set has a more close or open vowel, respectively. I state the phonetic realizations in terms of gestures, relating them to the articulatorily defined reference vowels we have already mastered. We simply plot the word KIT in different places on the two Antipodal vowel charts.

The lexical sets also help us keep track of variation among vowels that have arisen in some consonant environments but not others. For example, in RP there are many pairs of lexical sets that share a nuclear vowel, but in which one of the two sets contains words with a centring diphthong before coda 'r'. This is, in part, the reason we see 27 lexical sets for the RP/GenAm union of accents where GenAm alone has far fewer distinct vowels. In this connection, let us consider KIT versus NEAR. Wells keeps these sets distinct even though there is sometimes an 'r' following the vowel in the KIT set. *Mirror* is a KIT word, while *nearer* is a NEAR word. In RP as in many accents of English (unlike GenAm), the vowels in these words are different. The stressed syllable of *mirror* has a short monophthong in RP—roughly, [I]—where *nearer* has a centring diphthong—roughly, [I] + something like schwa (Wells, 1982[1]: 153). Similarly, in what may be the most famous potential merger of vowels before 'r', *marry* and *merry* belong to sets whose keywords have no coda 'r' (TRAP and DRESS, respectively), while only *Mary* has a centring diphthong in RP and therefore belongs to a set whose keyword has a coda 'r' (SQUARE). Such detailed information is provided here to help the speech trainer make sense of the lexical sets, though I rarely delve into such complexities with actors in the context of a production.

Through mastering the sound-spelling correspondences via the lexical sets, actors build reasonably reliable intuitions about

the history of English phonology. These intuitions are general enough to save them time and frustration whenever they approach a new accent of English down the road. The lexical sets can also be taught to foreigners learning to pronounce English, especially because the sound-spelling correspondence problem poses them especially great challenges. (See Flege, 1987, for a review of challenges largely peculiar to second-language accent work.) The spelling of English is irregular as charged, but not, as it turns out, totally unpredictable once the lexical sets have been mastered. However, foreign students benefit from memorizing all the word-set memberships, while native speakers of English need memorize only those where the mappings differ between their native accent and likely target accents. Indeed, in coaching native speaker actors for a production, I give out almost no paper. Traditional pronunciation guides may be helpful to the coach, but most actors treat them as noise and politely file them away in a drawer. Despite the slightly abstract nature of the linguistic approach I am advocating, I give each actor one sheet of paper introducing the lexical sets (see Table 1) and another containing blank vowel charts (see Figure 3) which I ask them fill in during the coaching session using whatever notation is meaningful to them. Actors are encouraged to make notes about consonants, rhythm, intonation, etc., on the back of the vowel-chart sheet. An example of a completed set of charts for a family of accents spoken in the south of Britain appears as Figure 4.

2.3.5 Limitations of the lexical sets

There are, of course, limitations to any set of words grouped by spelling. For example, there is some consonant-derived variation among vowels that the lexical sets help us address only indirectly. Thus we may need to advise actors that the consonant before the vowel dictates the use of yod ("liquid u") in the CURE and GOOSE lexical sets in virtually all accents that preserve historical 'yod'. For instance, in some American accents, we use a yod only and always after consonants that do not involve a tongue-tip gesture—a nice example of an instance in which a gestural description of speech is simpler and more intuitive than a list of consonants that happens to exclude sounds typically spelled with 't', 'd', 'n', 'l', 'r', 's', 'sh', 'z', 'ch', 'j' and the fricative consonant in such words as *measure*. However, the lexical subsets do help us sort out *which* CURE and GOOSE words never have yod after tongue-tip gestures in these accents. Specifically, most words that can start with a yod after certain accent-specific subsets of the tongue-tip consonants are spelled with *eu, eu, ui* and *uC* (CURE [aii, cii] and GOOSE [b]). Words spelled, for example, with *oo, ou* and *oCe* never had a yod historically, and so do not take yod in contemporary accents (CURE [ai, b, ci] and GOOSE [a]). Wells discusses this complex phenomenon in terms of 'yod-dropping' because he has diachronics in mind. I avoid such terms when teaching actors because I do not want my students to misinterpret such a process-oriented term as an indication that I am assuming a single base accent as the starting point for the entire group of students. I would say, instead, "whether or not we start the vowel with a 'y' sound".

The lexical sets also fail to give us any useful information whatever about irregularities. For example, we must memorize *ad hoc* whether words with the spelling *oo* belong to the GOOSE lexical set or to the FOOT lexical set. There is, unfortunately, no better solution to this problem.

In settling on RP and GenAm as the bases of the lexical sets, Wells has limited the number of lexical sets he needs to get the basic job done. Unfortunately, in working with actors, we teach many accents, including some with more conservative vowel systems than RP and GenAm. Looking at a wider sampling of accents, we find subsets that Wells discusses but does not officially list. For example, he does not distinguish between the two-to-five different spellings that encode the unmerged NURSE set in parts of Ireland and Scotland. In teaching an accent in which *fir, fern* and *fur* do not rhyme, for example (as they may not have rhymed for Shakespeare: Baugh & Cable, 1993: 229), I draw the student's attention to what could be thought of as supplemental subsets of the NURSE lexical set. These supplemental subsets are helpful because, unlike RP and GenAm, some accents have failed to obscure this older distinction through merger. This is one of the few cases in which the lexical sets do not provide us with sufficient grain, so I simply have my students plot the labels NURSE[*i*], NURSE[*e, ea*] and NURSE[*u*] as mnemonics.

Note that, in *Accents of English,* Wells gives IPA transcriptions for the vowels of the lexical sets as he discusses each accent. In fact, the use of symbols may be somewhat confusing for the non-linguist because his transcriptions are sometimes broad (that is phonemic or representative, standing for a range of variant sounds) and sometimes narrow, rendering phonetic details. When Wells uses the IPA in the Longman Pronunciation Dictionary, on the other hand, he transcribes words fairly narrowly, thankfully, except for the vowel in DRESS—Wells follows Jones in using [e]—a perpetual source of confusion that has been discussed elsewhere (Barnes, 2000: 96).

The transcription-free system I use with actors who do not know the IPA does require an additional bit of work on their part. Having plotted lexical set keywords on vowel charts in place of vowel transcriptions, the actor cannot at a glance recall whether the vowel is round or spread. Because the location of the lexical set keyword on the vowel chart indicates only the highest point of the tongue, we must indicate with a circle, color of ink or other method which vowels are produced with lip-rounding in the target accent. Information that would normally be indicated with a diacritic such as vowel duration is indicated in my four-chart system by choice of chart. The use of four charts also makes the entire system clearer and the keywords easier to read.

3.0 Comma Gets a Cure

Clearly there is more to mastering vowels than mapping spellings onto them. One needs to practice hearing and producing them in context. One could ask a native speaker to model the vowels and other features by reading aloud from Skinner's shibboleth sentences, for example, but those sentences are stage-American-specific. To address this issue, my colleagues and I have devised a passage that includes the lexical set keywords and examples of as many subsets as practical and frequently useful. The passage also contains environments for a variety of interesting consonant phenomena (linking 'r', etc.), is narrative and non-technical in content, and includes grammatical constructions intended to elicit a range of vocal expression insofar as any read passage can do. The passage has come to be called *Comma Gets a Cure.* Importantly, the *Comma* passage is available for use in accent study without special permission from the authors and has been adopted as one of the texts of the International Dialects of English Archive (www.ukans.edu/~idea). An annotated version of the passage is reproduced in an appendix to the present paper. Since the first appearance of the passage on the IDEA website, I have discovered one context that is missing, namely, the environment /tn/ potentially produced with a glottal stop in place of or accompanying the tongue-tip gesture for the /t/ and with a potentially intruded vowel rather than a syllabic nasal (*Britain, mitten*). There must surely be other oversights. However, given the number of speech samples already collected, no revisions to the passage are being proposed at the present time.

4.0 Summary and future work

I have distilled into prose aspects of a process that I have found helpful in training adult actors, focusing especially on a simple way of teaching potentially complex vowel systems. The process I have described involves kinesthetic familiarization with articulatorily defined reference vowels and the mapping of those vowels onto lexical sets, that is, onto sets of historically or potentially rhyming words. I believe that, as a consequence of the specific analytical nature of the training—not simply the fact of any training at all—I see in my adult actors improved intuitions about sound-spelling correspondences (cf. Weiss, 1992). I have argued that the process I teach is quick and general enough to be learned by actors outside of conservatory settings, but also provides an excellent way to begin teaching general speech awareness to repeat clients and to students with whom one expects to work long-term. The human ability to coordinate and perceive speech gestures has been well documented in recent years, though none of the claims made here regarding the specific approach I use in teaching accents to adult actors has been tested in any scientifically rigorous fashion. We have, however, developed a research program aimed at testing the hypothesis of passive competence that has been laid out above.

For added value, I have provided an annotation of a diagnostic passage—*Comma Gets a Cure*—a passage built around lexical sets, subsets and other accent-features. The passage has been adopted as one of two reading passages by the *International Dialects of English Archive* (IDEA) database which is searchable online at www.ukans.edu/~idea. The speech of many talkers has already been archived for IDEA using this passage, and many more samples are likely to become available. In addition to using the passage in making primary source recordings, there are no doubt many as yet unexplored ways of using the passage itself in teaching and coaching.

❧

Acknowledgements
The author received support from National Institutes of Health Grant DC-03782 to Haskins Laboratories while writing the present paper. He thanks Barbara Somerville for providing inspiration and Alice Faber for comments on an earlier draft of the paper, but assumes all responsibility for its contents. He is also grateful to Rocco Dal Vera and Louis Colaianni for their encouragement. Please address correspondence to the author at DialectDoug@yahoo.com.

References
Barnes, M. J. (2000). A critique of phonetic transcription in American actor training. *Voice & Speech Review* 1: 89-102.
Baugh, A. C. & T. Cable (1993). *A History of the English Language*, Fourth Edition. Englewood CliVs, NJ: Prentice Hall.
Bernstein, N. (1967) *The Co-ordination and Regulation of Movements*. Oxford, Pergamon Press Ltd.
Bronstein, A. J. (Ed.) (1998). *Conference Papers on Amercian English and the International Phonetic Alphabet*. Publication of the American Dialect Society 80. Tuscaloosa, AL: University of Alabama Press.
Browman, C. & L. Goldstein (1991). Gestural structures: distinctiveness, phonological processes, and historical change, in Ignatius G. Mattingly & Michael Studdert-Kennedy, Eds., *Modularity and the Motor Theory of Speech Perception* (pp. 313-338). Hillsdale, NJ: Lawrence Erlbaum Associates.
Catford, J.C. (1988). *A Practical Introduction to Phonetics*. Oxford, England: Oxford University Press.
Catford, J.C. (1981). Observations on the recent history of vowel classiWcation. In R. E. Asher & Eugénie J. A. Henderson (Eds.), *Towards a History of Phonetics* (pp. 19-31). Edinburgh: Edinburgh University Press.
Catford, J. C. & David B. Pisoni (1970). Auditory vs. articulatory training in exotic sounds. *The Modern Language Journal* LIV(7):477-481.
Colaianni, L. (1994). *The Joy of Phonetics and Accents*. New York, NY: Drama Book Publishers.
Dobson, E. J. (1968). *English Pronunciation 1500-1700*, Second Edition. Volume I, Survey of the Sources. Oxford, England: Oxford University Press.
Esling, J. H. (1998). Everyone has an accent except me. In L. Bauer & P. Trudgill (Eds.) *Language Myths* (pp. 169-75). London: Penguin.
Flege, J. E. (1987). A critical period for learning to produce foreign languages? *Applied Linguistics* 8:162-177.
Fowler, C. A. (1996). Listeners do hear sounds, not tongues. *Journal of the Acoustical Society of America* 99 (3):1730-1741.
Fowler, c. A. (1995). A realist perspective on some relations among speaking, listening and speech learning. In K. Elenius & P. Branderud (Eds.), *Proceedings of the XIIIth International congress of Phonetic Sciences*, Volume 1 (§93.2, pp. 470-477). Stockholm: Stockholm University.
Gibson, J. J. (1966). *The Senses Considered as Perceptual Systems*. Boston: Houghton Mifflin.
Goldstein, L. & C. P. Browman (1986). Representation of voicing contrasts using articulatory gestures. *Journal of Phonetics* 14, 339-342.
Hughes, A. & P. Trudgill (1996). *English Accents and Dialects: An Introduction to Social and Regional Varieties of English in the British Isles*, 3rd Edition. London: Arnold.
International Phonetic Association (1999). *Handbook of the International Phonetic Association: A Guide to the Use of the International Phonetic Alphabet*. Cambridge: Cambridge University Press.
Jones, D. (1949). *English Pronouncing Dictionary*, Eleventh Edition. (First edition published 1917). New York: E. P. Dutton & Co.
Jones, D. (1940). *An Outline of English Phonetics*, Sixth Edition. New York: E. P. Dutton & Co., Inc. Originally published by Teubner, Leipzig, 1918.
Kelso, J. A. S., B. Tuller, E. Vatikiotis-Bateson, and C. A. Fowler (1984). Functionally specific articulatory cooperations following jaw perturbations during speech: Evidence for coordinative structures. *Journal of Experimental Psychology: Human Perception and Performance* 10: 812-832.
Kenyon, J. S. & T. A. Knott (1953). *A Pronouncing Dictionary of American English*. Merriam-Webster.
Labov, W. (1991). The Three Dialects of English. In Penelope Eckert (Ed.), *New Ways of Analyzing Sound Change* (pp. 1-44). San Diego: Academic Press, Inc.
Laver, J. (1980). *The Phonetic Description of Voice Quality*. New York: Cambridge University Press.
Markham, D. (1997). *Phonetic Imitation, Accent, and the Learner*. Travaux de l'Institute de Linguistique de Lund, 33.
Mattingly, I. G. (1972). Reading, the linguistic process, and linguistic awareness. In J. F. Kavanagh & I. G. Mattingly (Eds.), *Language By Ear and by Eye: The Relationships Between Speech and Reading* (pp. 33-147). Cambridge, ma: mit Press.
Mencken, H. L. (1936, reprinted 1999). *The American Language: An Inquiry into the Development of English in the United States*, Fourth Edition. New York: Alfred A. Knopf.
Read, C., Y.-F. Zhang, H.-Y. Nie and B. Q. Ding (1986). The ability to manipulate speech sounds depends on knowing alphabetic writing. *Cognition* 24: 31-34.
Saltzman, E. L. & K. G. Munhall (1989). A dynamical approach to gestural patterning in speech production. *Ecological Psychology* 1: 333-382.
Skinner, E. (1990). *Speak with Distinction*. L. Mansell & T. Monich (Eds.). New York: Applause.
Trudgill, P. (2002). Sociolinguistic Variation and Change, Ch. 16: *The sociolinguistics of modern RP*. Washington, DC: Georgetown University Press. Viewable on-line at www.phon.ucl.ac.uk/home/estuary/trudgill.htm.
Trudgill, P. (1983). *On Dialect* (pp. 8-30). New York: New York University Press.
Weiss, W. (1992). *Perception and Production in Accent Training*. Revue de Phonétique Appliquée 102: 69-82.
Wells, J. C. (2000). *Longman Pronunciation Dictionary*, NEW Edition. Pearson Education.
Wells, J. C. (1982). *Accents of English 1: An Introduction* (pp. 117-183). Cambridge: Cambridge University Press.
Wolfram, W. & N. Schilling-Estes (1998). *American English: Dialects & Variation*. Cambridge, MA: Blackwell.

Appendix: Annotated Version of *Comma Gets a Cure*
Under the present formatting of our diagnostic passage, the first instance of each of Wells' lexical set keywords is set in small caps. The lexical sets help us classify the talker's vowels. Other vowel-related phenomena and potentially diagnostic consonant issues are underscored, though not necessarily the first time they occur and often only once. Care has been taken to include in the text the full range of consonants in all potentially interesting environments. Notes are offered sparingly on the right.

Comma Gets a Cure

by Jill McCullough and Barbara Somerville
edited by Douglas N. Honorof

Passage	Random notes on items of special interest
Well, here's a story for you: Sarah Perry was a veterinary NURSE who had been working daily at an old zoo in a deserted district of the territory, so she was very *happy* to START a new job at a superb private practice in NORTH SQUARE NEAR the Duke Street Tower. That area was much nearer for her and more to her liking. Even so, on her first morning, she felt stressed. She ate a bowl of porridge, checked herself in the mirror and washed her FACE in a hurry. Then she put on a plain yellow DRESS and a FLEECE jacket, picked up her KIT and headed for work. When she got there, there was a woman with a GOOSE waiting for her. The woman gave Sarah an official letter from the vet. The letter implied that the animal could be suffering from a rare form of FOOT and MOUTH disease, which was surprising, because normally you would only expect to see it in a dog or a GOAT. Sarah was sentimental, so this made her feel sorry for the beautiful bird.	'l' as vowel, h dropping, SQUARE/DRESS before 'r' unstressed 'been'; FACE before 'l'; GOAT before 'l' stress placement (2); cluster simplification quality of 'r', if any; yod after 'n, s' yod after 'd'; str-smoothing intrusive 'r' before C; NEARER with schwa 'l' as vowel; DRESS height before coda [st] 'l' in 'lf' KIT+'r'; aspirated plosive /_stressed V 't' as/with glottal stop locative vs. existential 'there'; unstressed 'was' linking 'r' reduction to a syllabic nasal 'w'/'wh' open vowel quality before g flapping
Before long, that itchy goose began to STRUT around the office like a lunatic, which made an unsanitary mess. The goose's owner, Mary Harrison, kept calling, "Comma, Comma," which Sarah THOUGHT was an odd CHOICE for a name. Comma was strong and huge, so it would take some FORCE to TRAP her, but Sarah had a different idea. First she tried gently stroking the goose's lower back with her PALM, then singing a tune to her. Finally, she administered ether. Her efforts were not futile. In no time, the goose began to tire, so Sarah was able to hold onto Comma and give her a relaxing BATH.	stressed demonstrative 'that' yod after 'l'; stress placement SQUARE/TRAP before 'r' vocative intonation 'ng'; 'h' before yod 'nt' with glottal stop smoothing; 'ng' before '–ing'; yod after 't' labiodental vowel in suffix; smoothing intrusive 'r' before a vowel labiodental
Once Sarah had managed to bathe the goose, she wiped her off with a CLOTH and laid her on her right side. Then Sarah confirmed the vet's diagnosis. Almost immediately, she remembered an effective treatment that required her to measure out a LOT of medicine. Sarah warned that this course of treatment might be expensive—either five or six times the cost of penicillin. I can't imagine paying so much, but Mrs. Harrison—a millionaire lawyer—thought it was a fair PRICE for a CURE.	labiodental PRICE height/_'t' PRICE height/_'d'; stress on con-; smoothing DRESS-KIT /_ nasal 'l' in 'l'+ yod

Private Studio Practice *Jack Horton, Associate Editor*

Outside the Ivy Walls

Reach Out to Media and Business to Expand Your Student/Client Base
My phone rang. A news director wanted to bend my ear about two of his broadcasters.

One had an accent problem. The other, he said, seemed so terribly "wooden"... did I think something could be done to improve the situation. I encouraged him to send them both on into my studio. The first one called to set up lessons; the second one, I am sorry to report, is still out there being wooden.

In another situation, my email had a query from a corporation department head asking if my services would include helping one of her otherwise dependable businesswomen to avoid coming across in meetings as "immature" visually and vocally. We agreed to try a series of lessons and to make a before-and-after documentation tape of the student's progress. It all worked out swimmingly.

Now wouldn't it be oh so very nice to just sit and wait for the phone or the email to unveil our new students or clients? But be assured that these situations are mostly exceptions rather than the rule.

Even if you got that dream call from a news director, the chances of the broadcaster coming in on his or her own would be slim, in my opinion. Why? So much of the time, that businessperson or that media person doesn't even know there *is* a problem. So, given that situation, where the potato is thrown back into our hands, so to speak, there still is that potential for getting into something new, interesting, and important for our own "private practice."

Want More Business? Be Open to Media and Business Clients
Yes, that's right. Look around. They are there. They need us. We just have to figure out a way to open up the lines of communication: how to market ourselves in such a way that they will come to find out that they can benefit greatly from the knowledge and experience that we as teachers and healers can give them. Also, we need to pave the way by being sensitive to their special wants and needs.

Do you have media/business clients? If you don't presently teach or treat these folks in your private teaching or healing practice, this would be a great way to expand your business.

A Media Person Who Found Her Own Way to a Vocal/Presentation Studio
We are going to be sitting at the feet of Ginny Kopf to learn how to better deal with business clients in the studio, and Erica Tobolski will hone in on coaching the broadcaster/journalist toward the magic of vocal art.

But first, let me introduce you to Stacey Spencer. Although her story is perhaps unique (she saw the light!), there are many people in her field who are simply not getting the help they need. (Just turn on your TV and look and listen.)

Entrepreneur and founder of Presenter's Studio, Jack Horton teaches cultural voice/ presentation development for Business, Media, and the Arts. Upon graduation (WVU Creative Arts Center), Jack traveled and recorded with the Robert Shaw Chorale, and toured with Goldovsky Opera, NY Sextet, and Men of Song Concert Quartet. His leading opera roles were with Lake George, Miami, Eastman Opera Theatre, The New School; as tenor soloist: Capitol Hill Society, NY Choral Society, West Point, C.W. Post, WNYC, NYU, WVU, Shreveport Symphony, St. Patrick's Cathedral and Garden City Cathedral. After 23 years of private study, teaching, performing in NYC, Horton now lives in Louisville, KY.

Stacey Spencer
A native of Louisville, KY, media personality Stacey Spencer graduated from the University of Kentucky in 1991 with a degree in telecommunications. She has had a variety of broadcast experiences, including jobs as an on-air announcer, radio news reporter, voice/talent for radio and TV commercials, producer for radio talk shows, and TV production assistant assignments. Her biggest dream came to fruition in March 1999 when she began hosting *Just Teens*, a multi-faceted production that includes teen discussions on current topics, entertainment, and computer-animated educational segments. *Just Teens*, conceived and produced locally by Ms. Spencer, has now been viewed by millions in several media markets across the country. Stacey has a long-term goal to make a difference in the lives of youth and takes on inspirational speaking engagements in addition to her media work. She enjoys fashion, is a fragrance model, an avid athlete, and teaches Braille.

So, in keeping with our media theme this issue, I thought it would inspire us to first hear the story of a hardworking broadcaster who came to know the true value of her voice in a very heartwarming way:

My Voice, My Most Valuable Professional Asset!
By Stacey Spencer

So much attention is given to the visual aspects of TV production today that I wonder if the impact of the human voice now gets too little attention.

My awakening to the importance of "voice" in media came in 1993 while seeking to support myself in the early stages of a possible broadcasting career. I had an opportunity to become a certified substitute teacher at the Kentucky School for the Blind. It turned out to be the most treasured experience of that twelve year period of my life.

I am sharing this life-changing experience also because I truly was confused about my teaching hiatus from broadcasting. While I was eager and grateful to work at the school, I thought I might never work in the broadcast industry again. Yet in retrospect, perhaps this break from a sometimes stressful industry was very necessary to prepare me professionally for what lay ahead—a career that has included many commercial voice assignments, speaking engagements, and even my own television show, *Just Teens*.

Learning the Braille code and teaching visually impaired students not only enriched my spirit, but changed my life forever! Why? My voice played a more intricate role in how this listening audience perceived me. It was not an auditorium filled with hundreds of sighted high school students or a conference room with employees and company executives. This audience was unique because they were ambitious blind students eager to learn from an encouraging voice. Because of these students, I finally took special interest in my most precious media asset—my voice!

I learned that it was an enhancement tool designed to vocally enrich the lives of others. I was forced to pay closer attention to what I was saying and how I was saying it because this audience could not see me.

I soon realized that my voice was a paintbrush given to paint stories in the minds of those students. It was an instrument to sing melodious tunes into the hearts of these young people. It was even a counseling conduit between classmates as I poured in and pulled out the appropriate emotions to resolve conflicts.

What I am absolutely sure about is this: a developed voice and delivery is golden, and an undeveloped voice and delivery is deadly.

After leaving the Kentucky School for the Blind in 1995, I headed back into the broadcast industry. I sought the professional instruction of a contralto soloist to further develop my voice as

Stacey Spencer

an announcer. In my first 30-minute session, my instructor discovered that I had a shortage of breath. I was not using my diaphragm properly to get the best air support when singing or speaking. Adjustments in my breathing habits over time caused major improvements in my voice-overs for commercials, narrations for industrials, and even speaking engagements.

But the lessons of wisdom were not over from this professional instructor. She encouraged me to make immediate lifestyle changes such as: better hydration and strategies for appropriate vocal rest when I had overworked my voice. These rules for vocal improvement ring fresh in my mind today whenever I prepare for any engagement.

Over the last three years, I have continued to use a voice/presentation development teacher for professional vocal presentation preparation and media performance projects. I feel that it is important that we—as announcers—be held accountable for our vocal impressions and growth, and the learning of new techniques. The stresses and demands of the broadcasting profession can be taxing on the voice.

However, a personal daily vocal regimen—whatever works for you—will keep your voice at its best. Remember, perfect practice will help you deliver a perfect performance, and will keep your most valuable professional asset—your voice—well tuned.

I hope you enjoy this section. Being in private practice isn't easy. Yet, it is a truly creative endeavor. Those media and business ladies and gentlemen come in out of the rain of stress into your care and teaching. There is a need for creativity, fun, learning, and the peace of mind that goes along with it... the getting caught up in the task... the zone, that very special place that makes our jobs worth while. You've seen that person look up from the checkbook and start to say something and then not know just how to put it... because there just really are not any words in the yellow pages or anywhere else that say what it is exactly that you do. And the truth is, you might do what you do even without the checkbook... yes? Keep on keeping on!

Find an easy chair and curl up and enjoy this wonderful VASTA exploration.

Yours for creative vocal expression, Jack

Essay *by Erica Tobolski*

Coaching the Television Journalist

Background

"Voice is not a luxury, it is a necessity." This quote from a television news director emphasizes the importance of vocal skills in a field where voice usage is a major determinant of success. It is surprising that members of such a group, especially those in the early stages of their careers, do not have significant voice and speech training before entering the profession, yet this is often the case. They may have taken a voice class or two, completed internships and have experience on television or radio but still have gaps in their knowledge or are unaware of how to address their limitations. Often, they are directed to enlist the assistance of one specialized in the area of voice and speech in order to retain their current position or move into a more prestigious one.

My work as a university based voice specialist for eight years and as a private vocal coach for the past four years has allowed me to differentiate the special needs and demands of the broadcaster.

Faster Results

Sequentially guiding a student through a body of knowledge is pedagogically sound and a highly desirable approach. However, the media client is a completely different story. Most often, he or she has very specific and timely goals in mind when they walk through the door: clearer speech, a "friendly" voice, a supported voice. Usually, a member of their occupation, a talent coach or a news director, has told them that they must address certain problems in order to maintain their current position or move forward in their profession. As an investment, news managers may subsidize coaching sessions, in which case the coach has two clients, the reporter and the news director. The single biggest challenge is that the client is already on the job; they don't have the luxury of time that accompanies most students. They are looking for relatively quick results, meaning weeks vs. months or years, in an area that depends on a cumulative and recurrent process. Realizing this means tailoring the training to the clients' needs and circumstances while still imparting sound and thorough instruction. It is through the given circumstance of time constraint upon which the following approach is based.

Evaluating the Client

An evaluation or diagnostic is necessary in order to assess the client's areas for improvement. It is the basis for creating the means for them to realize their vocal goals. A Voice Survey, completed by the client and returned prior to their first session speeds up the process. The survey may request basic information about the client's background: where they were born and raised, if they speak other languages, voice and health habits, and physiological conditions such as TMJ problems. It could also ask them to describe how they use their voice in regard to breath, articulation, pitch, volume, rate and vocal quality and if they feel they're communicating both the meaning and emotional content of what they're saying. To get a sense of what the client thinks about their voice, have them describe their voice and note if there are public figures whose voice they either aspire to or dislike. Wrapping up with a checklist to identify habits and potential misuse such as chronic tightness in the jaw or hoarseness is also valuable.

A survey of this type serves several purposes in assessing the client and creating a course of action. First, it provides insight into how the client thinks

Erica Tobolski currently oversees the voice component of the actor training program at the University of South Carolina. She teaches voice, speech, dialects and text to both graduate and undergraduate students and teaches acting in the undergraduate program. Erica coaches voice and presents workshops and master classes. She performs on stage and in voice-overs and conducts a private voice practice. Her exercise, "The Portrait Project," can be found in the *VASTA Voice and Speech Exercise Book*, Janet Rodgers, ed. She has an MFA from Purdue University and is a Lessac Certified Trainer.

about their voice and their use of it. Their vocabulary and how they answer the questions indicate an attitude toward their voice and the level of knowledge they have about it. It uncovers chronic conditions that may indicate a lack of knowledge or suggest a referral to a speech pathologist or laryngologist is in order. Finally, it provides an opportunity for further discussion with the client about their vocal needs and the impact of their workplace.

Another tool for assessment is watching the client on the job, either as it airs or on videotape. The client should have no trouble getting a copy of their on-air work or other taped material. It is particularly helpful to view the videotape and take notes on it before a session, then play and discuss the video with the client. This is rarely a new experience for them, but it does allow the voice coach to identify the problems while both parties are in a receptive (evaluative) rather than active (skill acquisition) mode. Of course, any assessment, whether within or outside a coaching session, should be included in the coaching fees.

If the client is specifically interested in addressing articulation and/or accent modification, using a text for phoneme testing is useful to both the voice coach and the client. Assessment tools such as *The Rainbow Passage* and *Comma Gets a Cure*[1] include phonemes and phoneme clusters present in the English language. The coach can readily diagnose missing or unformed sounds in the client's speech; the client can then use the passage for practice in order to restore or improve speech sounds.

After the evaluative session, the client is presented with an outline of issues to address based on their stated goals. It is here that the coach can identify a specific problem, e.g. hyper nasality, which will be the solution (or part of it) to the client's general goal of achieving a warmer sound. There may be other areas of potential improvement that the client is unaware of; these can be suggested as areas for future attention.

Often at this point, the client will ask, "how many sessions will I need?" There is simply no formula, and it helps for the client to understand this. Explaining that every person learns and assimilates at a different rate is an honest if not specific answer. It certainly depends on the extent of the client's goals and where they currently are at in relation to them. Clients in this field tend to be extremely motivated and verbally acute and therefore assimilate the work quickly. The very qualities that contribute to the success of the broadcast journalist— extroverted, curious, and committed—tend to carry over in their approach to voice work. One major factor conspires

against them—time for practice—and they should be encouraged to discover pockets of time (in the car, in the shower) in which to assimilate the work.

Coaching Sessions
Regular voice sessions with the media clients can be difficult, given their demanding and unpredictable schedules. They are often sent out on a moment's notice to cover a breaking story, or must tape public service announcements, or fulfill an obligation for a public appearance. Clients face limitations in time and, unless their news station is generously covering the voice coach's fees, money. Characterize the session as a stand-alone package where precision and effectiveness shorten the learning curve. Setting intermediate goals, one or two per session, gives clients a manageable workload that will lead to a higher success rate. Four key steps that target effectiveness for the client are: identifying the problem, understanding the correction, practicing the skill and assimilating new habits while performing.

Like any good teaching, it's important that the client know why they are learning a specific exercise and can re-create the steps on their own. Supplemental information, such as anatomical illustrations and seeing themselves in a mirror, helps to put the new information in a context. You may be surprised to find that a professional voice user does not have an understanding of diaphragmatic breathing, assuming that basic breath work would have been include in their training. Being able to see and feel the ribs expand outward was a simple but profound discovery for a recent client.

Sensory feedback cements the experience by expanding intellectual understanding. The use of a mirror to see a more open mouth (or to take away the fear that it "feels too big"), hearing the difference between hyper nasality and denasality, kinesthetically feeling resonance in the mask of the face, and the use of imagery to imagine space between the vertebrae of the spine recognize differing learning styles. Studies on learning styles assert that 60% of the population processes information visually. Visual tasks are often a shortcut to understanding and accomplishing the objective. With one client, the diphthong /ɔɪ/ as in *oil*, remained an insurmountable hurdle. Drilling the sound, breaking down the phonemes and then putting them back together, and using successfully pronounced words with matching diphthongs as a prompt were all attempted. As a last resort, he was asked to visualize having in his mouth a large, round jawbreaker candy that moved up on the diphthong. The image allowed the client to simultaneously increase space in the back of the oral cavity while allowing the tongue to shift into the required positions.

Another client benefited tremendously from visualization in order to raise the soft palate. She suffered from hyper nasality and a flat sound stemming from a lowered soft palate and a tight jaw. Giving her the image of the sound as a ball rolling forward and out of the mouth opened up both oral and pharyngeal cavities. An interesting note: she did a story on the growing popularity of Botox injections and as part of the story, had the injection done on her own forehead. At the next session, she reported a marked decrease in jaw tension and a greater ease in opening for the larger vowel sounds. While it would not be sound practice to recommend Botox injections as a way to greater vocal freedom, the incident demonstrates the part that muscular tension plays in voice and speech.

Getting the Work to Stick

After leading the client through an exercise, the exercise should be repeated and/or described, noting the change and how it feels, sounds, or looks like in their mind's eye. Recapping the key discoveries at the end of the session also helps to cement the new skill in order for the client to practice on their own in between sessions. In Mel Levine's recent book about learning patterns, *A Mind at a Time*[2], he explains how such repetition aids in learning by moving knowledge from short-term memory to active working memory. Using the skill repeatedly in active working memory may help to transfer it to long-term memory.

Clients may have difficulty with names, words or sounds that come up repeatedly in newscasts. Self-generated word lists keep clients practicing words or sounds that trip them up. One client experienced anxiety on camera every time she anticipated saying a foreign name that was hard for her to pronounce. By repeating the name off-camera and breathing through the anticipation, she was able to smoothly pronounce the difficult name.

Processing a new set of skills is difficult for anyone. Remind clients that it will take time to assimilate the new habit, especially while on-camera. Let them know there is a difference between understanding a concept and applying it kinesthetically, and lag time between consciously applying the new pattern and reproducing it unconsciously. For this reason, clients benefit from having a quick check list before they go on-air, such as "breathe into the back of your chair and soften the jaw," rather than think about specific details which would detract from their primary focus of reporting the news.

For the coach, it's invaluable to document the session immediately following, noting which comments, images, or descriptions worked for the client. In the heat of the moment, it is easy for both coach and client to forget the prompt and celebrate the success. Having a record is helpful, especially if a long time lapses between sessions.

Circumstances of the Media Client

The unique circumstances of the broadcast journalist or news anchor are numerous. As mentioned above, the media client has a demanding schedule with a daily deadline of the broadcast. As one client puts it, "The news rarely gets cancelled." News anchors, in addition to performing the news broadcast, are sent out to shoot, do live reports in the field, edit stories adding audio and sound bites, record voice-overs, and make public appearances. All this is in addition to the fundamental job of the journalist: to research and report stories. They work in an atmosphere of being continually judged: by the viewers, by the results of ratings, and by management. Though journalists must master an incredible number of skills, the field is highly competitive. In order to move on to the next level, these skills must be exercised consistently and performed with perfection.

Unlike radio, television is a visual media, carrying with it greater emphasis on appearance. The voice, delivery and presentation must match the visual cues in order to communicate the content. The voice must reflect the type of story being reported and the visual story needs to capture the attention of the viewer, whose focus is often not fully engaged. On television, the anchor is seen before they are heard, but the perception quickly moves to how the voice conveys information. If the voice fails to do this, the viewer is distracted and does not focus on the content. With television's multiple channel choices, a good impression must be immediate or the viewer will move on.

During a live news broadcast, many things vie for the news anchor's attention: awareness of switching cameras, relying on the TelePrompTer (which occasionally is out of sequence or at the wrong speed for reading), monitoring the rolling tape in order to narrate the picture, taking cues from the floor director, hearing direction in an ear piece, not to mention adjusting to mistakes such as the wrong or missing tape. In this stressful situation, the television anchor cannot consciously focus on fixing speech details and can greatly benefit by utilizing good breathing practices.

What is a Talent Coach?

Most often, media clients seek out specific help because of comments made by a Talent Coach. The Talent Coach is an independent contractor hired by the news station or news conglomerate to evaluate all aspects of a journalist's "package." The coach may visit a station as little as twice a year, though four to five times a year is more common. Coaches critique the overall presentation within the context of that particular market including the size of market (small, medium or large) and the style of the news station (tabloid style—fast tempo and many images vs. homegrown—camaraderie between co-anchors, a local emphasis). Holding individual sessions with the journalists, they review videotapes of previous broadcasts, looking at appearance, verbal skills, and presentation skills. The Talent Coach may be able to critique the journalist effectively and give specific feedback on strengths and weaknesses, but may not be able to address all the problems. Voice and speech deficiencies require the attention and expertise better offered by a voice and speech coach.

Conclusion

Media clients pose a particular challenge for the private vocal coach. Working within the client's time constraints, occupational stresses and necessity of incorporating new skills while on the job may seem a daunting task for both coach and client. Creativity thorough specific problem solving leads to solutions that are tailored for the broadcast journalist. Concise evaluation, setting goals and teaching with precision and efficiency are surely skills that benefit both client and coach, helping to better each in their given professions.

❦

Notes

1. Both the *Rainbow Passage* and *Comma Gets a Cure* are available online at http://www.ukans.edu/~idea/.
The Rainbow Passage can be found in Fairbanks, G. *Voice and Articulation Drillbook*. (p. 127). New York: Harper & Row, 1960.
Comma Gets a Cure: A Diagnostic Passage for Accent Study by Jill McCullough & Barbara Somerville, edited by Douglas N. Honorof, 2000.

2. Levine, Mel, M.D. *A Mind at a Time*. Simon and Schuster, 2002.

Bibliography

Barton, Robert, and Dal Vera, Rocco. *Voice: Onstage and Off*. Belmont, CA: Wadsworth Group, 2002.

Kapit, Wynn and Elson, Lawrence M. *The Anatomy Coloring Book*. New York: Harper & Row, 1977.

Kopf, Ginny. "Coaching the Business Client," *Standard Speech and Other Contemporary Issues in Professional Voice and Speech Training*. Voice and Speech Trainers Association, Inc., 2000.

Lessac, Arthur. *The Use and Training of the Human Voice, 3rd Edition*. Mountain View, CA: Mayfield Publishing Company, 1997.

Levine, Mel, M.D. *A Mind at a Time*. Simon and Schuster, 2002.

Linklater, Kristin. *Freeing the Natural Voice*. New York: Drama Book Publishers, 1976.

Rodenburg, Patsy. *The Actor Speaks*. London: Methuen Drama, 1997.

Rodenburg, Patsy. *The Right to Speak*. New York: Routledge, 1992.

Skinner, Edith. *Speak with Distinction*. New York: Applause Theatre Books, 1990.

Utterback, Ann S. *Broadcast Voice Handbook, 3rd Edition*. Chicago: Bonus Books, 2000.

Wells, Lynn K. *The Articulate Voice, 3rd Edition*. Boston: Allyn & Bacon, 1999.

Column *by Ginny Kopf*

Coaching the Business Client

Are you a vocal coach for actors and considering expanding your clientele to include Businesspersons? Coaching business clients is not as different from coaching actors as you may think. You do have to "put yourself in their shoes," however, and use a bit different kind of psychology in their training. Here are some things that should help you think in the right direction.

Consider their point of view.
The first questions business clients usually ask you before they hire you are:
- How much does your training cost? (A need to stick to a budget.)
- Where are you located? (Time is money.)
- How long will this overall training take? (They are schedule and result-oriented.)
- Do you have a practice tape or CD for use in the car or on a plane? (Their need for convenience and independence.)

Expect resistance or some denial.
Don't expect business clients to be as expressive or enthusiastic as theatre students. They take their image very seriously and often may seem cool or defensive about the speech training, at least at first. A common belief in the business world is that one must be serious to be taken seriously. Respect their need to be more reserved and introspective than you are used to with actors.

When I assess clients and point out a negative quality (as they have hired me to do) they often seem in denial. They claim that, "When I am in a real speaking situation, I don't do that." Even when we're listening/watching a video or audiotape of one of their speeches, they can't always admit they hear or see a particular fault. They may come across as defensive and proud in spite of how wonderfully I've presented the information. Since I am used to this response, I simply critique them matter-of-factly, without defensive retaliation I know that deep down they are thinking, "Gosh, she's right. I really do that, don't I?" I just ask them to think about what I've said during the week, watch themselves on video or listen to the tape again and see if they begin to hear or see what I've been talking about. They almost always come back a week or two later and admit they see it now, and they thank me for pointing it out.

Why the defensiveness? Business clients are often more cynical about their ability to change, just because they are older. Theatre students and professional actors are used to receiving specific critiques about the strengths and weaknesses of their technique. Remember, businesspersons have been out of school for years and may not have gotten a direct critique since a high school speech course. On the job they may receive some positive or negative comments about their skills, but this critique is usually saved for a more formal evaluation—unless they are the boss, and if that's the case, they may not have received feedback in years. Actors agree they will be "in training" all through their career. Businesspersons, however, though willing to learn more in order to advance, have finished their degree, and don't want to feel they are still "in training."

Also, the critique a businessperson gets on the job is usually about the end product, rarely about the process. Stage actors are used to a process of weeks of developing a role, years of developing their technique. They are used to

Ginny Kopf, author of *The Dialect Handbook* and *Accent Reduction Workshop for Professional American Speech (CD set)*, is well known throughout Florida as a Voice, Speech and Dialect trainer for public speakers, broadcasters, and actors. She coaches privately and has given hundreds of workshops locally and nationally. She has done extensive speech coaching for Disney World, and Universal Studios. Corporate clients, include United Telephone, AT&T, Florida Power, The Golf Channel, and numerous television shows. She teaches vocal courses for Valencia Community College's theatre program, and courses in voice-over and accent modification at several studios. Ms. Kopf holds an MA in Theatre and also an MFA in Voice and Speech Science.

classes that separate voice, speech, movement, dance and acting in order to hone these specific skills, and classes that integrate these into polished performance skills. Most actors enjoy the process of classes and rehearsals as much as the product (the performance).

Businesspersons, however, are oriented to the finished product, with less regard to exactly how the project gets done. They have been trained to aim at results. They want cause and effect: "You do this for this long and it results in that." They have project deadlines, based on statistics of how long similar projects may have taken. That's why you must, as a trainer, respect their schedule.

A difficult training situation is one where an individual or group is forced by their boss to get help, versus voluntarily seeking lessons. If the person has been told to get speech training, expect resistance at first. You've probably already encountered this resistance when an actor or singer is reproved and sent to you by their director for a tutorial. But your sensitive and wise approach can work through this barrier just in the first few minutes to make them feel more positive about the lesson. So too, with businesspeople. Communicate with the boss hiring you and the student, so that all understand what the training will involve.

Respect their schedule.
Voice trainers joke that their business clients want their training in pill form so they can simply pack it in their briefcase. They almost always ask if the training can be put on tape, so they can listen to it and absorb the information while commuting or flying. True, they would love for you to say that all it would take would be to read a book on it.

Their first question tends to be, "How long will it take?" This can frustrate us as theatre trainers. I used to answer this question with a long explanation: "...it depends on your motivation and aptitude, and I'll know more once I assess you, etc., etc." Now I say something that very much satisfies them (as it is more statistical sounding). Behavioral psychologists claim that if you practice something fifteen minutes a day for six weeks, it will become a new habit. Then, they say, it takes another six weeks to "set" the habit. I tell my clients they will definitely hear and see improvements in a month if they work on it every day. If they tune up their awareness and work five minutes here, five minutes there, they will grow. I tell them, "Your mouth is always with you, so you can be working on your speech wherever you are—in an elevator, in the shower, while making a sandwich, while watching TV!"

Make the training so incredibly *practical* that they can do the exercises while doing other things. I have many exercises, or at least observations, that can be done in their car, at their desk, in a stairwell. This is what they want and what they need. They probably will not sit for an hour or even a half hour to work on speech skills. Yet, if they had a tape to follow along with, yes, they might use that while driving or cleaning or exercising. So, make a practice tape for them. This is the best way to respect their schedule. Figure out exercises for them to do in the car or at their desk.

The first few weeks, I tell them I am teaching them how to teach themselves, how to monitor themselves when I am not around. This really empowers them, and proves to be very important to them. I tell them I am tuning up their awareness, making them aware of aspects of their image that is sending out a negative or confusing message. This assures them I'm not trying to tie them to me in some way as some sort of guru they are dependent upon for years.

I am actually there to shine a light on things they haven't been aware of and then to provide the tools for being able to control their speech. This involves giving initial direction for their own motivation, lending advice on how exactly to work on their technique considering their unique schedule, lifestyle, will, and degree of motivation. I promise them they will improve at a quick rate if they will take the ball I throw to them and run with it. I tell them they will actually see faster changes than if I were their personal workout trainer. (I have friends who've been told by their body trainers not to expect to see any changes in their muscles for eight months. Speech changes will happen much quicker than that.)

Respect their need to budget.
The second question business clients ask is, "How much will this cost?" They deal every day with budget restrictions and so this is important. Oddly enough, this tends to be an even bigger issue for the most well-to-do clients (because they probably got where they are by making money an important issue). So don't be put off by their concern about your fee. Struggling young actors seem to expect they must put money into their training for years and also ongoing throughout their careers. But your business clients, as I've said, are looking for the cause and effect.

I could write an entire article just on how to set prices for your training. It's a difficult issue, and there seems to be a wide range of fees speech coaches get across the globe. I think you need to charge what you think your time is worth, and must consider where you live. I know that New York and even

Atlanta coaches are getting far more than I am asking in Orlando, but our markets and cost of living are quite different. So, I try to charge what other voice coaches charge in Florida, and what my clients pay for "similar" expertise services (massages, body trainers, therapy, etc.) I have fretted about this money issue throughout my twenty-year career as a private coach. I have overbid and lost contracts, underbid and done the jobs while kicking myself that I could have easily asked for more. Yet, I am personally interested more in the process and on those private students sticking with their training than I am on the money. So now I charge what I am comfortable with, and you need to figure out a comfortable fee schedule that works for you.

Find out how they learn, and relate the training to other things they do well.

This is very important. Find out how they learn, whether it is mostly through visual, aural, or kinesthetic cues. Some clients definitely know their strongest sense. They are working in the very field that uses their strength, i.e., a graphic designer is a very visual person, a sound technician is a very aural person, etc. If they aren't sure how they have learned things in the past, interview them. Listen to and observe them.

Very visual clients will be taking copious notes or drawing illustrations of your points as you speak. They also will be watching your mouth to see how you form the sounds.

Kinesthetic learners are very interested in how it feels inside their mouth or in their diaphragm. They respond to getting up and doing it right away. They respond well to your gestural cues and how you physically illustrate things.

Aural learners will ask you for a practice tape to mimic during the week. Explain to them that you'll teach them by first approaching the speech skills using their strongest sense, but over time will incorporate *all* feedback systems so that they will truly and fully learn.

Ask what other skills they are good at, particularly sports. I feel learning about voice is like learning any sport. The training techniques and mental focus and emphasis on self-confidence have uncanny similarities. I work with pro golfers and football players, and get them to "follow through, not fading out on the idea" indicating that it's like the follow-through when hitting or throwing a ball. Every sport has discipline, a process of training and skill upkeep. So they'll realize that, as with sports, they may not see overnight changes. Doing sports also involves "isolation of tension" and a sense of economy of effort, as taught in speech. Help them see how the concept of athletic training ties in with speech training as well. Keep going back to your sports illustration. If basketball is what

makes their eyes light up because they are good at it, then they can begin to see that speech training can be approached with the same positive attitude and confidence.

If they dance or play a musical instrument, you have it made, because obviously they already understand development through drills, rehearsals, and getting critiqued.

Many clients who don't do sports or any art at all, at least work a computer keyboard. Many, many illustrations can be drawn from that skill, like crisp, exact diction, and the concept that the information or the answer is right in front of them.

If the client has any feeling of being too set in his or her ways to change, I use sports examples and they feel more like they can change their speech habits too. Someone who plays just one sport can certainly learn another one. A ballerina could learn hip-hop; a baseball player can learn basketball. It may not be easy or "comfortable" at first, but it is very possible, by using skills from one discipline and applying them to the newer skill.

Talk their talk and walk their walk.

Business people are very interested in *image*. They are interested in how they present themselves in various situations. Discuss and explore how to adjust their speech image from casual to formal situations. For example, how to present yourself at a casual lunch meeting and still be professional, and also how to adjust to all of the situations one might encounter—all the way up to more formal speaking engagements, like conventions.

Businesspeople are also interested in how to adjust their presentation skills from one-on-one to small groups to large groups. They want to know how to be friendly, without losing authority. They want to know how to inject personality and a sense of humor, without coming across as silly. Women have particular image problems, trying to balance authority and enthusiasm, so it takes a skilled coach to guide them through the confusion. Being a good example yourself is something I think is invaluable to the client. Talk their lingo. Use "buzz words" that are important to the businessperson. These are seldom the same ones actors use. Re-evaluate the way you word your explanations to your actors and consider whether or not your business client would respond to them. Here are some words that I have found business people find important: professional image, first impression, grabbing and holding an audience's attention, control, role model, reputation, authority, projection without strain, clarity, fluency. All you have to do is read a few business speech books (like *Talk to Win* by Communications Specialist Dr. Lillian Glass) to notice what wording is being used.

If you get a sense that the businessperson is impressed by your knowledge of speech science, then using anatomical words may prove effective. (With actors, the scientific words don't always help.) Your visual clients especially will respond to the photos and drawings of anatomy and physiology. It is definite and sure when it is science. I find that business professionals work best with what they can see, hear, taste, smell, and touch, rather than theories and concepts.

Respect their privacy.
Some clients want it to be confidential that they have sought help with their voice/speech, particularly powerful executives. Unlike actors and singers who are held in high esteem when they continue training with a well-known coach, the businessperson in training does not always feel they will get the same respect. They often don't want their rivals to know they are working on improving their image or sales techniques. I think the trend is growing for more business people to seek professional speech and image training, but I also think that in many circles there is still a stigma that the person should somehow have been able to correct any problems on their own. It's like admitting the need for therapy: acceptable more in acting circles than in business.

Do however, keep collecting "testimonials" from your present satisfied clients, to use in your own promotional material. But only after feeling out their need for privacy. The quote doesn't have to be a formal letter of recommendation. The business client won't have time to write one. Simply do this: When one of them praises you and your effectiveness, ask if you can include their quote on your promo sheet.

Be sensitive to their unspoken fears.
An initial resistance to vocal training is the person's fear that they'll lose their uniqueness. New actors, too, fear this, and resist technique training in their longing to be "natural". But our work as college theatre trainers convinces them that controlling technique will actually free them and give them more range in their characterizations.

Business clients will fear change. And clients with strong ethnic identification sometimes fear losing their cultural heritage. So these are things we must consider and reassure them about.

Not only will your client fear change, but their family may fear it as well. It is not uncommon for a client to say their child told them, "Mommy, you sound funny," or "Daddy, why are you talking like you're somebody else." Our closest loved ones don't necessarily like change, good or bad. So counsel your student about family support. It helps to have the child or spouse sit in on a lesson so they can see what

you're doing to their loved one! And they'll see how positive changes in the person will result in benefits that reach the entire family. It would actually be to your client's advantage to have a co-worker, friend, teenager, or spouse who will be an accountable partner—someone they can "practice on" who'll be sympathetically supportive. They can encourage them in their practice sessions through the week, even lovingly and matter-of-factly correct them. The business client doesn't have supportive acting, voice, or movement teachers and directors like actors do to help with the application of their speech training. So they need you to show them practical ways to work and practice when you, the coach, are not around. These practical methods need to take into account the businessperson's lifestyle and relationships. (We all know of actors who are straining their relationships just by the fact that they want to be actors, and are driven to continue in spite of it.) Be sensitive but extremely practical with business clients about how they can improve their speech on their own, so in the end they can have a big sense of ownership of the improvements.

Of course, your client hopes to hear and see improvements quickly and they secretly (or overtly) hope others they work with will compliment them within about a month. I can truly assure my clients that some of my students have definitely gotten compliments and reaped benefits from improved vocal image within a month, when they have really made the voice/speech work a priority. I tell them not to count on compliments however. It is not unlike a weight loss program. If you lose ten to twenty pounds over a few months and co-workers and friends see you every day, it's so gradual that you may not get an overwhelming response. However, if you lose twenty pounds and run into a colleague six months later, they probably will notice and comment. But, like weight loss, voice is such a personal thing, people may not feel comfortable saying how much better you sound, because it intimates they noticed something was "wrong" with you before. (I personally hate hearing, "Oh, you look so thin," because it means they must have thought I was overweight before!) So, a colleague may notice a change and simply be silently impressed. Or, once again, like losing weight, others may see improvement in your image, but are unable to consciously figure out what is different about you. ("New haircut? New shirt?")

Be expendable!
Businesspersons need to feel they have ultimate control, so I tell them right away that I am training them in such a way that I will become *obsolete* in their life as soon as possible! I am in fact teaching them to teach themselves what to look and listen for during their week at work, so that they then can monitor themselves and have a sense of autonomy. Empower them and they'll come back.

133

Coaching the Business Client by Ginny Kopf (continued)

Be a good—no, a great—role model.

I think it's vital that you be the very best role model for your clients as far as your own image and poise and control. I believe business clients need this even more than your actors or singers need you to be a great vocalist.

Constantly work on your own vocal and physical image. Talk about what you've personally been working on to improve and exactly how you did so, in spite of a hectic schedule. Talk about what you learned "the hard way," when you weren't your best. Demonstrate, demonstrate, demonstrate.

They really respond to seeing and hearing "bad examples" (slight exaggerations) and how much better the image is when you switch to the "good example." Clearly seeing you demonstrate "right" and "wrong" ways helps them get beyond their own denial. Not only is it a clear and powerful teaching method, but it also lightens up the session, because it's amusing to watch you "act" nervous, or nerdy, or pompous, and businesspeople need that kind of release from pressure too. As Moliere, and many other comedy writers knew so well, laughter makes us face our foibles, and then we're more likely to remember what we observed. I've found this absolutely true in my twenty years of training. As for laughter in the session, if you are more of an animated teacher, just use your sensitivity as to how serious you should present yourself. (Showing overly-serious business people the need to inject some kind of humor in all of their presentations is an entire seminar in itself!)

A (too short) note on the business WOMAN

The businesswoman has very special coaching needs of her own. It's much more difficult for a woman than a man to find the balance between being pleasant but authoritative, neither too sweet nor too intimidating and pushy. Some of my female business clients have to be encouraged to reawaken their natural, relaxed sense of humor, as they are too afraid to even smile for fear of coming across as "giddy" in the office. Your female client will most often overcompensate, ending up too wimpy or too pushy. She needs your help to find a balance of professional poise that is neither feminine nor masculine. (Read Gail Evans' book, *Play Like a Man, Win Like a Woman.*)

And finally...

No matter how much you understand this "psychology" of coaching the business client, nothing will replace experience. I've made mistakes along the way, and learned as I went along. The most vital thing you will need, as with all coaching, is something no one can really teach you—intuitiveness.

Singing *Dorothy Runk Menen, Associate Editor*

This column has the richness of diversity in presenting three artists who continue to contribute their talents in remarkable and different ways. Oren Brown has been on the forefront of the art of singing, speaking, pedagogy and vocal health. He has helped to define each of these and continues to participate in research and performance. He works actively in the various areas and encourages cooperative ventures and understanding among them.

After meeting George Hall in 1974 and observing his teaching at Central School I have a continuing admiration for his sensitivity as a trainer of actors, as well as an administrator. I chose to observe his work because he was unique, a musician, composer, actor, singer. At that time he was the only one in English theatre training who saw the training of the voice as an integrated experience (singing speaking). I soon learned that his wide experience included personal friendships and working relationships with most of the great names of theatre and music. Read *Opera News* for his reviews of the London opera scene.

Amy Stoller's interview with Marni Nixon will delight every reader. The singer's spontaneity, the variety of singing talent and the information one finds in her story is full of surprises. To music educators, the story of her growing up years is refreshing—not the usual history of a child prodigy. Her philosophy of teaching is one to be admired.

Studying "cross over" singing has intrigued me for years. Those who have done it successfully were never concerned about definitions, they just sang! Thus, Marni Nixon.

❧

Dorothy Runk Mennen, (associate editor) Professor Emerita of Theatre/Visual and Performing Arts, Purdue University, developed the original voice curriculum for their MFA; vocal director of musicals, contralto soloist, actress. Prior to university teaching, taught vocal music, theatre-speech, English in public schools in Ohio and Indiana. In 1985 was given a national award for Leadership and Performance by University and College Theatre Association, American Theatre Association. She does consulting, teaches privately; a member of NATS (served on Board of the Indiana chapter), The Voice Foundation, Founding President of VASTA. On Editorial Board, and contributor for *The Vocal Vision*, author of *The Speaking-Singing Voice, a Vocal Synthesis.*

Essay *by George Hall*

Voice Coaching with a Difference—a Memory of Edith Evans

When GEORGE HALL left the Old Vic Theatre School in 1951, Michel St Denis said, "You'll have the possibility of becoming a complete man of the theatre—you will certainly have an untidy career." The untidy part of the prediction proved to be accurate. George's first weeks in the theatre involved playing in the Tyrone Guthrie production of *Tamburlaine the Great* at the Old Vic, and then dashing to the Watergate Theatre off Villiers Street to do his first late-night revue, thus setting a pattern of alternating classical theatre and light entertainment which has characterised his career ever since.

He spent the 1950s as actor, variety comic, writer, director and composer, and by the time he went to the Central School in 1963, he had written a TV musical for the BBC, composed a couple of film scores, worked for two seasons on the Stanley Baxter/Betty Marsden TV series, *On The Bright Side*, and composed the music for the Michael Elliott/Vanessa Redgrave *As You Like It* at Stratford, as well as being resident composer and voice coach for the last Old Vic season before it turned into the National Theatre. The untidiness predicted by St Denis took him into many curious by-ways of the theatre: perhaps the most memorable of his odd jobs was giving singing lessons to Dame Edith Evans.

He went to teach at the Central School of Speech and Drama for one term which somehow turned into 24 years as Director of the Acting Course. During his time there he continued to work in the theatre as much as possible, particularly at the Royal Exchange in Manchester.

Since leaving Central in 1987, he has returned to acting and performing after a 30 year gap. In addition to running his cabaret group, The Swell Party Company, he has taught and lectured in America, Sweden and Holland, as well as working at the Royal Academy of Music, the Guildhall School of Music and Drama, RADA and the British American Drama Academy.

"Well, Georgie, have I earned my gateau?"

The speaker was Dame Edith Evans, the voice that of Millamant at her most seductive, and the occasion the end of every singing session we had in preparation for her television performance of Judith Bliss in *Hay Fever* in 1960. She was no great singer, and when she performed the role later in the National Theatre production Coward directed, he wisely cut the song he had put in for the original Judith, Dame Marie Tempest, who sang delightfully. When we started these coaching sessions, Dame Edith somehow inveigled me into promising that every time she sang well I would take her to a rather expensive patisserie round the corner and treat her to coffee and a cake. You won't be surprised to learn that the answer to the gateau question was always an enthusiastic "Yes" whether she had done well or not, and I relished every moment of our coffee conversations and indeed of every meeting I ever had with her. I always tried to find out about her early days and did my best to get her to talk about how she went about her work on a part. She professed to be unable to explain anything about her acting, ("If I analysed it, perhaps I wouldn't be able to do it any more!") but odd little gems would come out obliquely from time to time, every one of which is engraved on my memory.

I rather fear that the name Edith Evans will mean less to American readers than it does to the British, and since she died over 25 years ago it will soon mean less and less to them. But to many who saw her, she was a never-to-be-forgotten talent, and the particular nature of that talent with its enormous range of vocal colour and its ability to illumine a text must surely be of interest to all readers of this publication. Her only Broadway appearances were in *Evensong*, the Katherine Cornell-Guthrie McClintock *Romeo and Juliet* and *Daphne Laureola*, which was a huge success in London but made no great impression in New York. But her many American admirers included Zoe Caldwell, Thornton Wilder, Ruth Gordon and Cheryl Crawford. The latter wrote most movingly about a meeting with her in Sardi's. Initially disappointed by her appearance—"an aging woman with no remnants of beauty, a rather heavy, hawklike face, one eye placed lower than the other"—and puzzled at the enthusiasm Thornton Wilder had always expressed about her, Crawford asked Dame Edith to recite a speech of Millamant's. She went on to say, "I closed my eyes to see if I could comprehend what my friends meant from her voice. After a few sentences I was compelled to open them: there, close beside me sat a most entrancing woman, sexy, flirtatious, desirable. It was a miracle of transformation. As Millamant she knew she had all those qualities, and her will and imagination made them real." Sardi's seems to have been the scene of several such triumphs. Margaret Webster once turned up there with a copy of *The Importance of Being Earnest* and asked her to read Lady Bracknell. " Very pleased, she chose to bridle," says Ruth Gordon, reporting the incident. "I can't do it here, dear. You're mad! Where is it?" Ruth Gordon, who appeared with her in *The Country Wife* at the Old Vic Theatre in 1936, went on to add, "The world is full of wonderful actresses—Edith is the greatest."

Her start in the theatre was extraordinary. Working as a milliner, ("I could never make two hats alike"), she was seen in an amateur production by William Poel, the begetter of modern ways of speaking and staging Shakespeare. He immediately saw her rare talent, and so in 1912, when she was already 24, he cast her as Cressida in a production that had the 16-year-old Hermione Gingold as Cassandra. "After that I couldn't go back to my hats." Poel believed that if the plays were uncut and still able to justify the phrase "The two hour traffic of our stage," the speech had to be swift, and they only way to achieve such speed without gabble was to use an enlarged form of the inflections of everyday speech—what he referred to as "the tunes." And he certainly found someone with the vocal equipment to do justice to his theories. Although when people praised her voice she tended to be surprisingly dismissive about it—"Never cared for it much myself, but it does seem to go up and down a lot."

What I did learn was that Poel, whom she always referred to as "My old master," insisted on the actors paraphrasing the text in great detail, and she put great emphasis on understanding every word of what she said. (Pretty obvious, you may say, but you must surely see as many performances as I do in which this fundamental point is neglected.) Peggy Ashcroft remembered her praying for enlightenment over a line she was puzzled by when she played the nurse in *Romeo and Juliet*. "And when I don't know what a line means, I was always say it as though it's improper."

She claimed to have had a cockney accent as a child—hearing those aristocratic tones, it was hard to imagine. But one remark she made about her childhood seemed to me to say something profound about the nature of her love affair with language—"When I was a little girl and learned a new word, I would say it over and over again to myself all day long." She appeared in the West End from the start of her career and was grateful that she found herself working with actors who spoke beautiful English and corrected her every fault of articulation or accent. In her early years she seemed to be cast largely in what would then be called character parts, many of them quite elderly, before moving on to play what she called her "lovelies" when she was into her 30s, achieving particular success with her Millamant and her Mrs. Sullen at the Lyric

Dame Edith Evans in *The Whisperers* (1966)

Theatre Hammersmith. Then in 1924 she had a rare failure in *A Midsummer Night's Dream* at the Theatre Royal, Drury Lane, a very large house, and for the first time she was told she was vocally inadequate. She rushed off to enlist the aid of Elsie Fogerty, but made the mistake of wearing her best hat to impress the famous teacher. Fogerty thought her rather flighty—what must that hat have been like?—and declined to teach her until other friends intervened. She then worked on her voice in earnest and to the end of her life she would return to the Central School for vocal help from Fogerty's successor, Gwynneth Thurburn. She also decided that to succeed in Shakespeare she needed a spell at the Old Vic, so she joined the company and in one season of nine months she played Portia, Queen Margaret, Cleopatra, Mistress Page, Kate Hardcastle, Rosalind, the Nurse in *Romeo and Juliet*, Margery Eyre in *The Shoemaker's Holiday* and Beatrice. (She seemed surprised to find that she lost seventeen pounds during the season—can you think of a more effective way of losing weight?) Her time there is wonderfully chronicled by Herbert Farjeon, a critic of the day, in *The Shakespearean Scene*, a book long out of print, but fascinatingly informative about the changes taking place in the staging of the plays in the glory days of the Old Vic when Gielgud, Ashcroft, Olivier, Richardson, Redgrave and Guinness were making their reputations as classical actors. (I'm sure there's a public for this volume—publishers of theatre books, please note.) How gloriously Farjeon writes about Evan's Cleopatra—"there is not an actress on our stage today who could hold a candle to Miss Evans in her furies, her collapses, her recoveries, her languors, her lashings, her laments; not an actress who can strike a blow, nurse a daydream or wheedle an asp like her. How she illuminates the text revealing beauties undreamed of by the reader." And of her Queen Margaret in *Richard III* he wrote, "Miss Evans stands out above her fellow players because she works with her imagination and not with her experience. She does not assume that human nature is the same all the world over and that Portia and Margaret are therefore both Miss Evans. She plunges into blank-verse emotions inspired by the understanding that if they were the same as prose emotions, there would be no place in the English language for blank-verse. Here is an actress who can teach all our other actresses not only how to be witty, but how to curse and weep." It isn't surprising to learn that he went on to say, "If only I were Miss

Evans, I would read Shakespeare out loud to myself all day long." Her performances drew some wonderfully vivid writing from many of the other critics: St John Ervine, writing of her appearance in *The Beaux' Stratagem*, said that she moved "like a triumphant army. The dying Farquhar, creating Mrs. Sullen in his ultimate illness, must have revived had he seen Miss Evans perform the part: no man could go to his grave without a terrific struggle to live long enough to write another part for her." And there has surely never been a more memorable description of a performance than that of W.A. Darlington writing about her appearance as the Nurse: "As earthy as a potato, as slow as a carthorse, and as cunning as a badger."

I saw many of her performances, and most of them have left me with vivid memories of her reading of individual lines. I have directed *Hay Fever* twice and heartily cursed the fact that I couldn't get her inflections out of my mind. And although her second shot at Cleopatra when she was nearly sixty was reckoned a failure even by many of her greatest admirers, I can still hear her wonderful delivery of many of the lines, especially

> Sir, you and I must part—but that's not it:
> Sir, you and I have lov'd—but there's not it;
> That you know well: something it is I would—
> O, my oblivion is a very Antony,
> And I am all forgotten.

Zoe Caldwell has recently written that Dame Edith's Volumnia in *Coriolanus* was definitive: "each time she called Olivier son, my heart broke." She goes on to point out that if you look at three of her films, *Tom Jones, The Queen of Spades* and *Look Back in Anger*, you will hear her use the same voice to become three vastly different human beings. Ms Caldwell also wrote with wonderful insight and originality when she said, "She was a sensual actress because all her senses were alive to the moment, and thus whatever she encountered was conveyed to the audience. When she touched silk, an audience felt silk. If it was burlap, they felt burlap, and if it was a clammy hand, that is what her audience felt. Her handling of language was fearless." (With writing like that, what an excellent critic Ms. Caldwell could be if she chose!)

Dame Edith's speech was as vivid off-stage as on, and every utterance was so tellingly phrased and had such colour and vitality that perfectly ordinary statements sounded like brilliant epigrams. I remember the first time I met her, she was discussing the length of skirt she should wear as Judith Bliss. She was very conscious of the fact that Marie Tempest, who created the role, had wonderful legs, and when she said, "Mine aren't like Marie's, you know. They're not misshapen, thank God, but we don't what I call *show* them," the word

"show" was stretched out for some considerable time and contained nearly as many notes as her famous delivery of the phrase "A HANDBAG" in *The Importance of being Earnest*. And how I wish you could have heard her say, "I was never a beauty, but my face seemed to take the paint!"—the energy and relish of the final consonant of "paint!"

What have we to learn from such a career? The lesson all the greatest performers teach us: a superb balance between inner and outer life in the art of acting, wonderful imagination allied to mastery of means. Edith Evans would have been nothing without her inborn talent and her ability to become the characters she played, but these attributes would not have made nearly such a strong impact if she had lacked the skill to give them vocal and physical life. Her vocal resources in particular were quite extraordinary, and her enormous success over such a long period and in such a variety of parts seems to me to reinforce those words of Salvini that Stanislavsky quotes with evident agreement— "What an actor needs is voice, voice, voice." (And I think we can be sure that he didn't just mean volume and clarity.) Working with the young, I find myself growing more and more dismayed by the gap between their imaginative life and the dullness and monotony of their voices, not to mention their failure to relish language. How foggy the long sentences of classical text become when those that speak them have a range of two or three tones on a good day. But when actors can be led to a marriage of daring imagination and vocal freedom, when they start to find the true rhythm and inflection of a phrase with a wide-ranging and uninhibited instrument that reflects every nuance of thought and feeling, we can begin to hope for just a hint of the emotional colour and sensuality we find in the voices of the likes of Gielgud, Olivier, Ashcroft and Evans. Of course, Dame Edith's speech in her recordings of Millamant and Rosalind now sounds very mannered and of her time. But when I listen to her superb rendering of Lady Wishfort, which has not dated one bit, I revel in her sheer comic vitality and her ability to taste every word, and I want to rush off to work with my students, not with the slightest desire to produce a lot of pale imitations of the Dame, but to try to open the door to a way of acting and speaking that is true to our time but with all her abundant life and love of language.

So back to the question she asked me all those years ago—did she earn her gateau? For my money, a hundred times over. ❧

Essay *by Oren Brown*

Good Voice Equals Good Speaking Equals Good Singing

In a talk which I presented at the National Association of Teachers of Singing Convention in Boston, December, 1952, I made the statement that, "What is good for voice therapy is good for speech, and what is good for both voice therapy and speech is also good for singing. The only difference is the use to which we apply these basic principles."[1] I still stand by that statement.

Some years ago a young man came to me to study singing and I told him we needed first to correct his speaking habits. He replied, "I have been told that singing would affect my speaking, but no one ever told me that speaking would affect my singing." We worked for over a month on his speaking before starting singing exercises.

People speak more than they sing. If there are poor habits of phonation or articulation in speaking, it is only natural for them to be carried over into singing. Voice therapy is concerned with healthy phonation. This is at the roots of both singing and speech. This past summer, (2002), I gave a paper in Oxford, England, for the English Singing Teachers Summer Conference entitled, "Factors Which Affect the Quality of Phonation." In this I enumerated thirty-four different items which can make a difference in the sounds we make with our voices. For example, cultural norms and dialect make differences in the quality of voice but do not harm it necessarily.

Where to Start?

Given the fact that there are no two voices alike in the whole world, never have been and never will be, plus the information given to us by Lorraine Ramig at the Voice Foundation Meeting in June, 2002, that, "There are 1 10,000 neurological muscular events that take place in speech," where does this leave us in developing and caring for voices? It is my belief that we must understand how we phonate in a natural manner. We must learn what principles need to be kept in mind in developing the professional voice.

An evaluation of present speaking and/or singing habits goes without saying. Special attention needs to be given to any points of tension that might interfere with free phonation. These could have their roots in posture, breathing, pitch adjustments and/or articulation. Masters tells us that, "In the present normal course of human development, even by the end of the third year of life, coordination has become impaired in most persons."[2]

I suggest what I call *release* as one of the first things to strive for. An evaluation needs to be made of any points of tension which might in any way interfere with phonation. The intrinsic muscles of the larynx have no attachments to any bone structures. Tension in an extrinsic muscle, one end of which is attached to bone, can make it more difficult for the intrinsic muscles to adjust freely. There are a number of different relaxation methods that can be applied including the Alexander Technique, the Feldenkrais Method, Meditation, Jacobson's Progressive Relaxation, Voice Massage, and others.

Posture and Breathing

The energy needed for phonation is a flow of air. For the lungs to perform freely, one must have good body alignment. If we were on four legs, gravity would help in expanding our rib cage. Being on two legs, gravity tends to pull the rib cage down and therefore gives us less freedom to fill our lungs.

Owen Brown: Former Professor of Voice and Chairman of the Music Department at Shurtleff College and has taught voice at Principia College, Southern Illinois University, Washington University, Union Theology Seminary, Mannes College and is Voice Faculty Erneritus, The Juilliard School, where he taught for nineteen years. He has been a member of the National Association of Teachers of Singing (NATS) since 1948, serving on the Editorial Board of their Journal, their Research Committee and for six years as Chairman of their Committee on Vocal Education. He received the Distinguished Service Award from the Southern Region of NATS for contributions to the teaching profession. Lecturer in Voice Therapy at Washington University School of Medicine, Barnes Hospital, and St Louis City Hospital. Honored for his Pioneering Research and Contributions to Voice Therapy and the Teaching of Singing, by the New York Singing Teachers Association. This was the first time since the beginning of the Association in 1906 that they had ever given a citation to a singing teacher. Continues to teach and lecture internationally. Author of *Discover Your Voice*.

References
1) Brown, O.L. (1953) *NATS Bulletin*, May/June Issue. (pl6)
2) Masters, R. (1975) February 22; *Saturday Review*, (p30)
3) Gray, H. (1954) *Anatomy of the Human Body*. Philadelphia; Lea & Febeger, (p456)
4) Proctor, D.F. (1979) Breath, the power source of the voice. Transcripts of the 8th Symposium, Care of the professional voice. Party II. New York; The voice Foundation. (pl4)
5) Leanderson R. & Sundberg, J. (1988) Breathing for singing. *Journal of Voice*, 2 (1) New York: Raven Press, (p2)
6) Wyke, B. (1979) Neurological aspects of phonatory control systems in the larynx. Transcripts of the 8th Symposium, Care of the professional voice, Part II, NY, The Voice Foundation. (p42)
7) Jackson, C., & Jackson, C.L. (1937) *The Larynx and Its Diseases*. Philadelphia, Saunders. (pl7)
8) *Webster's New Collegiate Dictionary*. (1981)
9) Brown, O.L. (1996) *Discover Your Voice*. Singular Publishing Group, Inc., Thomson; Delmar Learning.
10) Hirsch, I.J. (1952) *The Measuring of Hearing*; London: McGraw-Hill. (pl26)

Gray's Anatomy tells us that the diaphragm performs its greatest excursion of a downward motion in filling the lungs when one is lying on his back.[3] Learning how our body feels when lying on our back on the floor can give us a sense of how we should feel from head to toe when standing. Two very strong muscles for breathing are attached from the under surface of the diaphragm to the inner surfaces of the lumbar spine and the femur leg bone. They are the crura and the psoas. Too great a curvature of the back elongates these muscles and prevents them from making their best contribution in the descent of the diaphragm in taking a breath. People refer to this downward physical action as "breath support." It has nothing to do with pushing the air out.

In *tidal breathing* (the way we breathe in our sleep, for example), taking a breath is an active process and the expiration of air passive. If you take a breath with the sense of being surprised and then hold it with the feeling that you are standing on ice with bare feet, there will be a firm sensation in the lower abdominal area. We have created a compression. Proctor tells us that it is easier to sing at relatively high lung volumes.[4] The lungs provide the greatest subglottal pressure when they are full. Since higher tones require greater lung pressure,[5] no pushing is needed. The thousands of alveoli in our lungs have an elastic property like a balloon. After filling them, they expel the air automatically.

The most natural and neutral phonatory sound from the larynx is the schwa, "uh." [ə] We need to get acquainted with our schwa sound by sensitizing what we do when we laugh or when we just say "uhUhh," when trying to think of what to say. The vocal folds adjust automatically just to the thought of pitch.[6] It is therefore desirable to discover what the voice feels like when starting tones lightly from above and then allowing them to slide downward. This permits the voice to make automatic pitch adjustments free of undue breath pressure.

Professional voice users are vocal athletes. In sports, we can expect world champions in their early twenties, sometimes younger. They are using arm and leg muscles that were given to them for running, pushing or pulling, etc. Speaking and singing are man-made inventions, as evidenced by different languages throughout the world and the development of music through the years. Our larynx was given to us primarily to prevent foreign matter from entering the lungs when swallowing. Of some nine functions of the larynx as noted by Jackson [7], phonation involves only two, one voluntary and the other involuntary. For example, laughing or crying are involuntary. Speaking and singing are voluntary. When engaged in strenuous activity such as lifting a heavy object or throwing a javelin, the larynx uses what is known as the "fixative action." This stabilizes the lung pressure for physical exertion. It definitely does not contribute to free phonation. Neither does coughing or clearing one's throat.

Listening to school children playing at recess time, we realize that they are capable of a wide variety of sound quality, range and intensity. When there is this kind of yelling and cheering at an athletic event, it can lead to what is known as "screamer's nodes." It involves excessive voice use over a period of time. To call to someone at a distance does not use voice for long periods of time and would not necessarily be harmful.

In singing, there is the time factor of sustaining notes or singing long phrases. There are also requirements in frequency range that speakers do not have to think; about. The singer therefore, has to develop his laryngeal muscles a bit at a time over an extended period. To become a professional classical singer, one would not be expected to reach his optimal level of performance in less than ten years of training under the best conditions. This would probably bring most singers into their late twenties or early thirties. There have been exceptions, but there are only a handful out of many millions.

Vocal Exercising

In order to exercise the voice without damage, it is desirable at first to practice for not more than perhaps twenty minutes to one half hour at a time. Then rest for about an hour before another period of practice. This could be done two to four times a day. The sessions should start with body relaxing, (paying particular attention to the extrinsic muscles of the larynx), body alignment and breathing. For the higher range, start the sounds from above and let them slide downward, like a sigh, in both singing and speech. No effort should be made to have the sounds loud. Size will come over a period of time as the tonus of the muscles grows. Everyone does not necessarily have a big voice. Carrying power and intensity are two different factors. Every student needs to find what his own voice can do and not try to imitate the voice of anyone else.

Articulation

Vowels and consonants are shapes. We can shape words silently and one who reads lips can understand what we say. On the other hand, we can phonate through wide ranges and intensities on vowels with no words being shaped and convey emotion but no other meaning. All consonants are formed forward of the vowel shapes. The vocal folds are developed through the use of vowels. This is why singers practice their scales on one vowel at a time. The technique is to allow phonation to be released through the shapes of articulation. It is as if one were performing two separate things simultaneously. Speech can also be practiced in the same way, using different ranges but no definite pitches. Always find how it feels and sounds softly from above at first. When going from a lower sound to a higher one, let it become looser and lighter.

Phoneticians state that in the *vowel triangle*, those vowels starting from "e" [1] are front vowels and those starting with "oo" [u] are back vowels. Old books on singing reverse these positions. They propose that starting with the "oo" vowel, we are forming forward, or lip vowels, even though the sensation might be felt in the back. The vowels starting on the "e" end of the triangle were considered back, or tongue vowels, since the sides of the tongue contact the upper back teeth. Certainly one should not form an "e" with a smile since it produces far too bright a quality. Trying to form the "oo" in the back of the mouth can produce a very "woofy" sound. Eventually the feeling develops that all vowels are being formed in the pharynx. This is where the fullest resonance, as well as the best overall quality and blend of the different vowels, takes place.

Proprioception

Proprioception is a most valuable guide in gaining a sense of what is happening. It is defined as, "The reception of stimuli produced within the organism."[8] It is increasingly important when performing in different auditoriums and with different costumes. Developing this sense sets one free from trying to hear what he sounds like. Before the days of recordings, teachers used to ask their students to sing where there was an echo in order to know how they sounded to others. Now we can get some idea from both recordings and video. However, gaining an inner sense of what is happening is something that can be used as a guide no matter where we are or what we think we sound like. With the help of the teacher, we learn to recognize the sensations of free phonation independent from listening.

Phonation Quality

There is a direct connection between the vocal folds and the nerve center for the emotions. For example, a cry of alarm happens without voluntarily thinking about it. This can work for us when we are performing. If we associate a situation with an experience we have had in our own lives, it is possible to release a natural sounding response. By doing this, we are therefore in control. By giving in to our feelings, we are giving up control and are the victims of our emotions. If it is a sad scene, we want to bring tears to the eyes of the audience, but not to our own eyes.

The manner in which all these exercises are practiced and their quality, in both male and female voice, is illustrated on the CD that accompanies my book, *Discover Your Voice.* [9] Although

they illustrate with singing exercises, the same general patterns can be used with inflections in speech. There is value in listening to the recordings of both singers and speakers who have had long careers. Using inflections was how many old masters of "elocution" used to train the speaking voice. With the use of microphones, a good deal of this old art has been lost by the wayside. As a result, even with a microphone, public speaking has lost much of its clarity and quality. Following these suggestions does not mean that all voice professionals will end up sounding the same. In fact, just the opposite happens. It will permit each to develop his own individuality and identity. It will also lead to a healthy voice use which can be maintained for many years.

Training Time

There is no set time schedule in developing a voice. Each comes to the task with his own physical endowments, ideas and experiences. We work from an evaluation of what is there and what is missing as a starting point. Sounds are explored within a framework of good posture and breathing. The sounds that are easiest should be used first in exploring range.

Quality of high and low notes can be compared to a church steeple, broad and full at the bottom and bright and thin at the top. This is true of all musical instruments. Consider the low notes on a violin or clarinet compared to the high ones. Also, our ears are most sensitive to the frequencies around high "C", (1088 Hz). There is a damping action within our ears which prevents us from hearing our own high sounds the way they sound to others.[10] If it were not present, those high notes would be 20 dB beyond the threshold of pain to our own ears. Don't listen to yourself!

Summary

Ask yourself where you stand with consideration to what has been said. Where are you in regard to each point that has been made? If there are statements that you do not understand, talk them over with colleagues and find out what is missing. The whole is equal to the sum of its parts. The parts go together from small, intricate details to a combination of the instrument as a whole. The development of correct technique in phonation frees the artist to interpret actions, moods, and meanings. It is better to do too little than too much. I often say, "Make haste slowly! " Establish correct responses in the first place rather than having to undo bad habits.

Marni Nixon: More Than You Know

Marni Nixon is a woman in a scurry. She has kept busy professionally since childhood—first as an instrumentalist, then as an actor and singer. Her award-winning children's television series, *Boomerang* (ABC) netted her four personal Emmys as Best Actress. She toured with Liberace and Victor Borge. She has performed with symphony orchestras from New York to Los Angeles, and many others in between (including Guadalajara, Mexico), with conductors from Leonard Bernstein to Leopold Stokowski. Her numerous recordings include *Igor Stravinsky Chamber Works 1911–1954,* conducted by the composer.

Amy Stoller is the sole proprietor of Stoller System, a dialect coaching and design business in NYC, where she frequently works with the award-winning Mint Theater Company. Other clients include Jean Cocteau Rep, Hypothetical Theatre Co., Theater Ten Ten, the Drama League, the Statue of Liberty-Ellis Island Foundation, and New York's longest-running drama, *Perfect Crime.* She also enjoys teaching individual actors How to Speak Like a Toffee-Nosed Git for Fun and Profit.™ She has performed frequently in New York and regional theatres, winning a 2000 *Off-Off-Broadway Review* Award for Excellence as dialect coach and actor in Distilled Spirits Theatre's *Northanger Abbey.* For VASTA, she edits the web page of Internet Resources for Voice and Speech Professionals.

Eventually she added "teacher" to her résumé, designing and directing the Vocal Department of the California Institute of the Arts in the early '70s. She has been Artist-in-Residence at the Cornish Institute of the Arts, University of Nevada, and Muhlenberg College, as well as teaching workshops in opera and acting. She has taught master classes all over the US and still offers them, in addition to private singing lessons.

On stage, Ms. Nixon has toured internationally with her own one-woman show and *The Man Who Mistook His Wife for a Hat,* made numerous regional and national touring appearances, and graced the Broadway stage in (among others) *James Joyce's The Dead* and *Follies.*

In a "that's show business" twist of fate, however, this multi-talented performer is still most often recognized for work she originally did anonymously: as the off-camera singing voice of Deborah Kerr in *The King and I* and *An Affair to Remember,* Natalie Wood in *West Side Story,* and Audrey Hepburn in *My Fair Lady.* Recently she didn't appear *again*—though this time fully credited—as the voice of "Grandma Fa" in *The Legend of Mulan.*

Richard Rodgers memorial (1988)

Now she's putting the finishing touches on her autobiography, tentatively scheduled for publication in summer 2003.

We caught up with this energetic artist on a warm September evening at her New York home—in an interval between one of her frequent professional engagements and a teaching session.

AS: Did you have formal training in singing, speech, and acting?
MN: The main thing is that I started very early as a musician. We had a family orchestra. This was in California. I played the violin since I was about four years old, and then we learned to read music before we learned to read books, and so we were always practicing, and we were always of course surrounded by music, which made us, I think, very ... musical! Which meant that we *listened;* we listened and imitated a lot. And when I was about eight or nine, we didn't have a lot of money. And we all played our instruments and needed money for that, so my mother started grooming us girls—there were four girls—to do shows ... and I

seemed to be talented with dramatic things, so she used to write me monologues and then I'd go to various people in Los Angeles and get some coaching on those … I then started doing extra work in the movies. I think it was just a matter of being able to take direction well, and observing, and having a lot of fun—I *loved* performing.

My Fair Lady, 1964

And then I started doing years of dramatic stock, in various companies, as a kid. They would drive me to rehearsals, I would do my homework in the car; I was a good and really smart student, and my parents really taught us all how to focus, and to really study well and quickly. So we could get through with our homework and then do these extra-curricular things. And in the meantime, I played in a training orchestra, began getting up from that orchestra and singing arias, and then people—well known people—started offering coaching lessons, and then they began giving me diction lessons in foreign languages, and—I don't remember getting any formalized speech training … I would do a lot of imitating if I had a play to do; people would tell me how to do certain things.

I remember there were certain directors that had the time to really direct; and they would give me sheets and sheets of paper: of speeches, and words, and poems and things like that, to read. And I think in those days we all had things in school, where we all had what we called elocution, so that we learned how to separate our tongues, and the articulators, and being able to make different sounds—and then I began singing, and I seemed to not have to practice as much (I thought) in singing as I did with my violin, so I gradually gave up the instrument! But then that was related more to acting and to the plays that I was doing. And it was more personal, and I just had the feeling … I kind of went along. I just had … good ears, good imitation, and because I was musical I could get the *timing* going, and then … just kind of grew on that. And so I had good coaches, I had good directors, and people, I think, that worked with me—because I was a kid they would always teach me things. And if I didn't know something, it didn't bother me that I didn't know it, and they would always come and help me, and—I think I got special attention that way, so I liked that! And so I think I was just lucky: when I was studying, I really felt like I was an alley-cat. I didn't stay with one teacher; I wasn't formally trained.

Certainly when it got to be college and university time, they would kick me out of lot of the sight-singing courses, and sight-reading, because I could read everything … so I never learned the syllables, for instance; and this has nothing to do with speech, per se, but one of my regrets is that I was not more formally trained and that I don't play the piano so well. Being a violinist, you know, that was an advantage, of course, but I wish I could play the piano better for my lessons.

I was in Hollywood … I was born in 1930, and most of my career in Hollywood was, I would suppose, starting in the late '30s, 'cause I was performing as a kid all the time, and then while I was a teenager in the '40s, I just knew everybody, and I was doing all sorts of different things. And I think the recording aspect—the jingles, the commercials—that's where you get aware of most of the technical things, 'cause you have to repeat things over and over and over again, and kind of know what you're doing and which style.

And then over the years, I have just scurried around—just gone to individual people, private people, getting incidental coaching lessons, and getting the rules down, and learning pedagogical things; but that's always after the fact, it's usually after I've *done* them.

AS: Do you have any favorite exercises, warm-ups, or learning tools for speaking and singing?
MN: I really am mostly aware of singing exercises. Now when I teach I have a certain routine that I give my students, but that's not always the same for everybody. Depending on where they come from, what their particular problems are, I know that I have to really isolate—identify, isolate and work—the tongue, the jaw spaces, the pharyngeal spaces and shapings and get everything separated. The jaw movement from the tongue … and the soft palate … the nasal passages … and then I try to give my students a picture. I've got charts over there. … I've always wanted to have a model, a *moving* model, of the anatomy of the neck and the vocal tract. I've seen them, but they're all *solid*; you want *moving parts*, I think. I think they do exist, but they're very expensive. I've never found one that I really liked. … But anyway, I like to show pictures so that the students can think in scientific terms. In their visualization process, the more you can use the actual names of things, and identify the cricothyroid and the arytenoid, for instance, and all the functionings of the voice, the better off you are.

And then, I guess I've learned *myself* from that process, trying to give my students more and more knowledge, and then I'll go scurrying around, and start working with somebody, in a brief workshop here and there, and get videos, and read books—all the time reading books and articles that, I must say, I used to go "pooh-pooh" at. Well, it's true; you can't learn to sing by just reading, you can't learn just by watching a video. You *have* to *do* it; I mean it's an experiential thing. But the knowledge "vouldn't hoit," as they say. And it really adds to that [experiential learning]; the more clearly you can define it, the faster you can get the student to really understand that.

And so, I think, I've gradually taught myself through that process: suddenly encountering a student that—you don't know *how* to fix what you *know* needs to be fixed! And the way I used to teach and the way I teach now is perhaps quite different. Sometimes I really like to take beginning students so I can see how fast I can synthesize everything and get them to "cut to the chase," as they say in Hollywood!

My Fair Lady 1964

AS: Are there differences in the way you approach Musical Theatre and Classical Song?
MN: The basic singing mechanism is … *basic*. The act of singing, what goes on, the experiencing of chest voice, falsetto, head voice, the describing the changes of register, passaggio, having them feel their voices … I think there's really no difference—*except* there's a lot of difference in, and changes in, vocal styling, coloring and choices of tones. For instance, I began a study in how to belt. That was one of the first times that I really went into pedagogical studies—and looked at fiber optics, and was having described to me, and experiencing exercises all the time, and constantly hearing scientific terms and what was going on—and *fighting* with this wonderful teacher, Jo Estill, and screaming, and going, "I can't do that, and that's not—what kind of a sound is that?" and just, you know, really, *really* a new kind of way of actually experiencing

the voice in certain registers, in certain pitches, where the actual belt lies.

In that process, I discovered that I had been getting away with murder. I had been singing, all of my life, certain kinds of roles: I was always a coloratura, I was always very high, I always had high Fs and was always dependable ... and when I started having children (I started having children when I was quite young, when I was twenty, twenty-one), I found that my voice started changing. And everybody thought that I had this fantastic technique—well, I didn't! I started scurrying around then, trying to figure out what I was doing, because my voice was getting richer, and I didn't know what to do with it. And I lost a lot of the top resonance for a while—and my larynx was too high. I think it was because I was always this gifted child; I was always singing as a child. I was always singing with my particular larynx where it was. And when it wasn't there anymore, I was still trying to sing with it high!—I think. And I got away with it, it sounded okay just because I could just sort of imagine things, and manage to survive. But according to what I found out later, I had limited myself to a lot of things that I hadn't needed to. [I found this out] because of actually trying to learn how to belt and actually *having to* belt, not just to teach it—I could *teach* it fine after a while, especially after I moved to New York. But to have to *maintain* a complete legit and musical theatre voice....

In my studio, everybody has to sing everything: I mean, they may have to stop singing "everything" after a while if they get constantly hired as a belter, then maybe they don't go any further in their training, but they do have to know how to center their voice in a legit way. And they have to know the difference between that and belting. Anyway, I guess my point is that I really discovered my voice in a different way, and I was trying to impart this knowledge then to my students, which seemed to help them a lot; and I've been able to rehabilitate a lot of voices, also. Damaged voices. Older voices. I don't have a doctoral degree—but I had such good ears and such experiential empathy, and source material readily available to study, so over time I could tell you what was going on and I could make up exercises that actually rehabilitated people. I had one student whose vocal cord—one vocal cord—was actually severed from breaking her neck, and I was able to rehabilitate that vocal cord just by the vocal behavior.

It's only in the last ten or twenty years that I've been in New York City, where I've had access to some vocal scientists, and I've served as president of NATS, and had access to all these wonderful people ... I've come to appreciate what kind of knowledge they each have; and they teach all these specialties, too. And also doctors of voice, and speech therapists. You can send students to them. They can go *see* their voices, they can go *hear* them, they can go *feel* them, and you can go along with them to a session and learn something yourself.

So in the meantime, I've been performing all along, and I've been getting more and more into—or back into—the straight acting, just because. ... I get very upset because. ... I still am doing a lot of singing, and I sing very well. You have to be careful in your choices of the things you sing. But everybody thinks that I still sound the same, but just richer. And I'm able to sustain my voice pretty well—but the roles that are offered! Well, let's see, about three years ago I did a premiere of a part that was written for me in a contemporary opera [*Ballymore*] by Richard Wargo, [at the] Skylight Opera, small chamber opera. But I haven't done any of the major roles that I used to do, for years and years and years, always thinking, "Oh well, I can always ... "—Well of course, you *can't*, I think it's too late; I could probably work some of them up, but I don't know who *needs* you at this point, all these younger people come up ...

But in music theatre, my dubbing career has become so famous that people think of me as a music theatre singer a lot, they don't realize some of the—you know, when you hear me, obviously I'm classically trained—but they don't realize sometimes, especially the younger kids, the extent of my operatic roles, nor the Grammy awards, and the years of premiere recordings of Schoenberg and Stravinsky, and New York Philharmonic and, you know, all those things. In music theatre the roles for people my age are almost always written for a non-voiced person, or a low-voiced person, just because that's what you're supposed to do when you mature, it seems: you're supposed to lose your high resonances and get gravelly. And it makes you sound older to sing lower. Things like that. So it's kind of dissatisfying musically.

So I love to act, and you can do a lot more vocally character-wise. Theatre casting tends to be more age-specific than opera, though: I could do excerpts of opera on stage with orchestra, which I do a lot, but then that's not age-specific too much, you know, I can still sing ingénue roles that I used to do, even at my age—in *concert* things. But in acting you have to throw away singer's diction. You can't [just] read things and pronounce them. You've got to be the character. You've got to eventually know how to do the dialects and the speech so well that you don't think about it, it's a part of your aesthetic sense, so one isn't distracted by the technicality of [*in stentorian tones*] "Oh, this person speaks very well ... we don't know what character it is, but it's ... " That kind of stiltedness you *don't* want.

AS: Speaking of dialects, have you ever had any formal dialect training, or worked with a dialect coach for any of your projects?

MN: For the dubbing, of course, I was taught by the actresses. They were taught by speech experts. Speech experts were all around at the same time. But I had to do what the actress did. I had to imitate them precisely. It helped me to know what they wanted. There were a lot of directors that were not necessarily dialect coaches, like we had [librettist-lyricist] Alan Jay Lerner on *My Fair Lady*, who would tell you about everything he could think of [about] how to pronounce things, but it was more like "how to be Eliza Doolittle"—and he would tell you about the words, and the syntax, but not the technical things. Then they had speech experts who would tell you that, except that half the time the actress—like Audrey [Hepburn, in the film of *My Fair Lady*] would do it the way *she spoke*—I mean there's a speech pattern, there's a conformation of their bone structure that has a certain sound, the way their lips occlude, you know, the way their lips come

The Sound of Music (20th Century Fox, 1965)

together, the way the resonances are … it's very specific. *After* I got into the dubbing, when I did *My Fair Lady* [on stage], I was coached by Anna Lee, who was one of the nuns in *Sound of Music*, and I had been coached by Julie Andrews who knew that I was going to audition for [the stage production of] *My Fair Lady* the day after *Sound of Music* stopped (I played one of the nuns in that movie). You know, I got coaching from these wonderful people, and then from the actresses doing the movies, and hearing it over and over and over, and over again. … Puerto Rican was really … well, I didn't study that at all, I only did what Natalie [Wood, in the film of *West Side Story*] did. Whether it was right or wrong, that's what she did.

I have done plays now where I've actually studied the dialect—like *Wuthering Heights*. I went to the library and

listened to some tapes, trying to do the right dialect. I came into rehearsal and I was the only one that was doing it properly. They had a dialect coach and she came to me afterwards and said "Look, we just can't have this, because nobody else is speaking like you and nobody else is going to and nobody else is paying attention to it, you're the only one that's doing it right, so just kind of take the edges off of it a little." That was rather discouraging!

And then, of course, I've done a lot of Shakespeare, and sometimes the Shakespeare is written in such a way that you really have to start developing an accent, not even knowing what the accent is, because it's kind of written in, or the flow of the dialogue kind of forces you to do it.

When I did *An Affair to Remember* for Deborah Kerr, she had an Irish song called "How Do You Get to Tomorrow-land?" and I came in and sang it for Cary Grant and Deborah Kerr, and midway they started snickering. Well, Deborah Kerr had told me at that point—I was doing the *Tennessee Ernie Ford Show* every day during that dubbing period, and we had to be on the set every single day—so she said, "Well, Marni, you know my voice"—we had done *The King and I* so many times, for so long—she said, "You know my voice, we don't have to work like we did before" (which was really a very strong working relationship, and we took from each other, but mainly I took from her: the dialect that she wanted, and she described to me the difference between British and—Mid-Atlantic, is what she called it … and then she would do it, and I would do it, an example, and finally I learned how to do it … gradually you acquire your technique and you can figure it out). I came in and she said "Here's this Irish song, and you sing it the way you think I would sing it." I thought I knew an Irish dialect. I came in there and it turned out that it was a wonderful *Scottish* dialect! I had no idea of the difference and I don't know why I thought I could do a Scottish accent, I'd never done one before. I was just a little snot, you know, and it sort of came out because of my ancestry; my father was of Scottish descent. And I've spent so much time in the British Isles—you know, you kind of think you *know*. (I hadn't done a commercial, which really makes you hone and refine that, 'cause there's a lot of authentic-speaking people who do those commercials and you've got to compete with them or not.) So that was an interesting experience! And so you learn really fast.

The most interesting dialect story that I have was maybe ten years ago ... I haven't told this story to anybody before. Carlisle Floyd

La Traviata, 1977

called me from Houston, Texas and said, "We're making a recording of my opera *Susannah*." And as you probably know, that opera is one of the few operas, maybe the only, where the dialect is actually written into the score. One is required to sing it in dialect. Of course immediately there's a red flag: "Oh, but I need to make this kind of a Round Sound"—No, it's possible to have the accent and still satisfy the singing requirements, which of course are primary. So he said he was doing this recording in France, I think ten days hence; would I go over and be dialect director and teach them Appalachian dialect? And we're talking about Cheryl Studer, and Sam Ramey, and Jerry Hadley, and—you know, wonderful people. And I was quite thrilled. Evidently I had been recommended by Boosey and Hawkes. And then the conductor, artistic director of the opera company, Kent Nagano—turns out that he's a big fan of mine (that's what he said, anyway) [called]; we made the deal on the phone, and it was to be *ten days hence*, can you imagine? Luckily I had my visa, and my husband said "Oh, good," and we canceled everything and we made a nice trip around it. ... I hung up the phone, and I'm saying to myself "What in the hell do I know about an Appalachian dialect?! I have never done an Appalachian dialect in my life!" It hadn't occurred to me—I mean everybody "knew" I could, so obviously I could (!), and I'd always said

yes to everything, so why should this be different?

So I suddenly got scared to death and I called this wonderful speech expert, Sam Chwat—he'd been recommended to me, somebody had given me his card—"Sam, can you help me, I need to do this in two days!" He's used to people doing commercials, so he said "Well, what time tonight, I'm available all night, you can come down at nine o'clock tonight and we'll work till midnight, if you need to."

And so I came down the next day with my score, with my tape recorder, with my cassette, and we planned several hours—it was quite expensive, I think; I've forgotten what it was, but it was certainly worth it to me—and he knows Appalachian, of course, like he knows everything; and he's reading the score upside down—he's reading it off, I'm saying the words, he's correcting me, we go phrase by phrase, we've got this all recorded, and then he says "repeat after me" ... we worked through the whole score this way, he then sat down and made diacritical marks, and marked up my score, and made a list, a personalized list of the rules. And he said, "There's no doubt in my mind that you can do this." I guess he was very impressed that I was used to hearing ... and I could imitate—but that I could *impart* it! Afterwards I thought, "Oh, my God! I don't want to tell him what I'm doing, because why don't they just hire *him*? Why should it be me? I don't want to reveal that I don't really know what I'm doing!" Except that he got the message immediately, and [said I'd been chosen] "because you speak Singerese, you speak Actorese, you speak Composerese, Musicianese, and you've got a good ear, and you've got the time; and I wouldn't have gone anyway, and I wouldn't have taken the way they usually treat speech experts, and I'm used to doing dialect coaching for movies, and they hardly pay attention to you, and ... " And I said, "What if it doesn't work out? Should I put my name on it?" And he said, "Are you kidding? Nobody's gonna know the difference!"

So we spent another couple of sessions, and then I decided that I would make a cassette for every character. Speak their role in the rhythm of their parts. Because there were a lot of incidental characters that had to have the same accent. Every single one of these, I made a cassette for—because I *then* found out that I was supposed to arrive on Sunday, the day of the one and only orchestra rehearsal, and they were going to start recording on Monday! There was no dramaturge, there was no production, these people were culled from all over the world, and they were coming together to make this recording, a frozen thing. Plus the chorus, who only spoke French. And so I made these cassettes—I came in, luckily, a day earlier, I got ahold of this stage manager who was from *Malta* (now you talk about *that* accent, that was very funny to me); anyway, he was very cooperative, he copied all these cassettes for me, he told me where all these people were staying, I scurried around, a lot of them were also staying in my hotel, and I was going to deliver these cassettes to them. And then I'm thinking, "Why should—I mean, who in the hell am I? They don't know 'who am I'! How do they know they're supposed to listen to me? How do I know they won't just throw me out the door and say, 'Leave me alone, I just want to sing my part'?"

Well, it so happened that every single one of them were wonderful artists, and they just fell on me with open arms, "Oh my gosh, thank you so much for helping us, when are we going to get a chance to work on this?" So the next day, every ten minutes, every half-an-hour that they had off, every lunch hour, every time before and after, they were just eating out of my hand—listening, listening (I knew they would all have Walkman cassettes), and then they would try it out.

Then we get to the recording session, and Carlisle Floyd, this *fantastic* composer, is sitting in the audience, and he says to me, "You know I'm not sure that they're going to call on me to see whether the tempos are right or not, I'm just the composer, I'm just here to give what advice I can," and Kent Nagano makes this big speech to the orchestra—they're all on stage, we're recording it on the stage of the Lyons Opera Company—there's a little raised podium on which the singers are standing with some microphones; there's a makeshift booth in a trailer in the back of the building, where all the sound is piped; and the orchestra's on stage—so Kent Nagano stands up and he says—

Oh, let's go back a minute: first of all, I have to tell you that Sam Chwat said, just before I left, "Now, Marni, you have to promise me that you will absolutely be comfortable with the fact that you are not in charge of this project. You are not going to direct this." He could see what I was headed for, whether I knew it or not! He said, "You will be the last person to be consulted. You will not be allowed to stop takes. Just take the money, do the best you can ..."

Now cut again to: All the artists are eager to have me. I did an interview with Carlisle Floyd's niece who was from North Carolina, and I said [to myself], "Okay, I'm going to talk like I'm from Appalachia for the whole interview, just to make sure I know my craft"; which I did, and *she thought that I was native*. I tell you, it was so much fun! Whoo! And then I get to this recording session and *now*, Kent Nagano stands up in front of the orchestra and he says, "And we have with us" (he's speaking in French and then translating), "an authority in Appalachian dialect; and this is a queen of diction, and perfection, and a wonderful singer, and she's going to be sitting on the podium and if anything goes wrong she's going to raise her hand and she will stop the recording, so I just want to warn you."

And then I go into the booth, and here is [producer] Martin Sauer, this fantastic engineer, who has the most fantastic ears, who speaks German and English (with a German accent), and he's hanging onto me with every take, and he says, "You have to tell me—*I* can't understand a word! You have to tell me if this is acceptable or not." And Carlisle Floyd was in the audience smiling and beaming, and I was so embarrassed, because why didn't he—you know, he could hear it too! But no, he kept saying, "Go! Go do it!" So I was able to do that. I went downstairs on my lunch hour to the chorus, and they were all having to learn English in an Appalachian dialect. We found that they knew IPA symbols. So everything I said, they had this magic symbol-writer who wrote it down and everybody else did and compared notes, and by golly, they were saying "ridimpshin" instead of "redemption"—and they were doing it consistently, per direction, *and* they were singing with beautiful tones! And Kent Nagano came screaming down because he didn't have the time but he was going to try to coach them, and suddenly he hears that they're all [doing this] and he starts laughing, and he said, "I've spent five years with these French people trying to get them to sing the King's English and now in *one hour* you're getting them to sing in a perfect Appalachian dialect"—

Anyway, it was so much fun, I just absolutely had a ball. And I was able to deal with some of the note problems, and pitch problems, and really be helpful. Cheryl Studer didn't come to the recording session; she was going to overdub her solos months later. So I was able to get her cassette to her and talk to her on the cassette, and said, "Cheryl, you are Jerry Hadley's brother in this opera, and Jerry's already recorded this and he's got this wonderful dialect; and unfortunately you really have to make an effort, if you would, to be as close to his dialect ..." She was absolutely wonderful. And Sam Ramey was wonderful. And it was just the most wonderful experience. So that's my Story of a Dialect Coach. We actually won the Grammy Award. I was a part of that whole thing. It was just so *satisfying*, it was so wonderful; and the *singing* was wonderful, and that wonderful score, it was just exciting.

AS: How do you feel about on-stage miking?
MN: Well, the problem is that one gets used to not using your own resonance. You can get used to getting away with that. And sometimes it's almost necessary to do that, to use your sound, maybe, in a different way than you would ordinarily. Music theatre is much more vernacular than opera, where everything is much more noble and much more extended; and of course in some foreign languages, that can be another problem—in opera the voice has to be completely open and responsive for other reasons than projecting on stage in speaking. When you speak you don't have that formant, the singer's formant, which lifts the voice to help the sound carry easily.

So in music theatre, using the mike can be very helpful, especially when you're speaking; and it is almost necessary now, because of the orchestrations containing electronic instruments, which have no acoustical decay. I think this acoustical problem *may* be beginning to be perceived by the producers and writers. The human voice cannot compete with bad orchestrations and voices are being wrecked. Sometimes singers are still forced to shout. But it may be changing. And I think the equipment—and the people who are running it, which is the key—are getting much more sophisticated and helpful, so that actually nowadays … when I did *James Joyce's The Dead* and *Follies*, at the same theatre (the Belasco), I think John the sound man said that they had something like sixty-four mikes in the auditorium in various places—the rafters, the walls, the ceiling, the floors, the balconies, on stage—all to bounce, enhance, reduce, augment, in order to create a certain sound and a certain ambience. And we all had body mikes (which are now placed on the face through the wigs or behind the ears), and he was able to balance all that so actually you didn't think that it was miked at all. Of course you knew that it was, but it's really fantastic what they can do. When you do a show night after night after night you can get so you need that, and so of course you need *them*. You don't want the sound man to be the star, you want to have your *own* voice, but you want him to be able to perceive what the best thing about your voice is, and also to have the dimension and the wherewithal to receive your voice in all its nuance, in multi-dimensional terms, and not overload things … and so that art, the art of doing the sound, I think has really grown up in the theatre today.

As far as opera is concerned, if I were singing at the Met … well, I don't think I would sing at the Met! I was the second place winner in the Metropolitan Auditions of the Air in 1954,

but never came back to re-audition, which they asked me to do. I think I thought my voice was too small for that auditorium … it may have been. My voice did carry in some large auditoriums, and I've sung with San Francisco Opera (I think that was the most difficult acoustically), and Seattle Opera, and humongous auditoriums like the Shrine Auditorium in LA, when I was singing in the lighter fach. I've sung Puccini, Verdi's *La Traviata*, Norina in *Don Pasquale*, Zerbinetta in *Ariadne auf Naxos* … but heavier than that I don't think I would be able to carry. So you kind of wish that maybe the mikes would be there, but you don't want it to sound like it's miked. It's kind of a double-edged sword. I hope that the mikes *per se* stay out of opera. I hope that they just gradually create smaller auditoriums, so the singers don't have to … You don't just want to hear singers who just have big, huge voices; you want to hear real singing, you want to hear music. And you want to see the acting. And you want to understand the words, if possible; you don't want to have to read them. If you buy a "good" seat, you have to look up every time [to read the super-titles]; the better thing is to buy a "bad" seat so you can see the titles as you're looking at the stage.

AS: How important is bodywork to you? Do you subscribe to any particular physical disciplines or have any particular routines?
MN: Your voice is a part of your body, and the way you breathe and the way you activate and energize the necessary muscles is all a part of the bowing (like an instrument) of the air that comes through you. You have to have full cooperation of everything you could possibly have, including tennis shoes! I mean the body is very important, and the fluidity and the energy that it takes, and the sustaining power—I think it's vital, bodywork. And that doesn't mean just lifting weights; no, anything that uses the air: tai chi, qui gong, Alexander Technique, Pilates, Feldenkrais, swimming—anything where you are guiding the energy through you, keeping you buoyant and fluid. Ballet of course is interesting; it's very good but the discipline itself sometimes forces the ballet dancers to breathe too high to be really aware of the same muscles that are needed from a lower support level. But it certainly strengthens muscles and gives grace to the body. And it helps with rhythm, which is primary. Any alignment exercise is very good.

AS: Do you have any tips aside from the ones you've already mentioned for maintaining vocal health?
MN: I like to make sure that singers know the difference between deadening and relaxing. That they know the reason for relaxing—so that there is response, muscle response—and usage of muscles and stretches. I think the singer has to be aware of their own physical makeup and chemical makeup: eating and smoking and drinking and hydrating and allergies and asthma and all of that; one has to be so aware of that.

Reflux can absolutely destroy you. And a lot of problems can be corrected if addressed (and then maintained) properly. I think exercise, physical exercise, is very important—centering yourself, doing your abs, maybe even running, swimming—very important. And, I think, your mental health: somehow, in the stream of all the craziness you have to be mentally ready to be able to open yourself up at the right time to let everything possible read, like an actress does; but [also] to have the core of yourself there so you don't use the "principal." Use the "interest" rather than the "principal," so that you can sustain it. And so mentally you have to be calm, you have to be centered, you have to be available to be responsive to what you're singing, and you have to know *technically* what you're doing. I think you really have to acquire good technique. And you have to be willing to be directed, but also to also know when something goes against your grain, and not just take anything.

I Do, I Do!, 1977

AS: Where do you teach? How does someone get to take a class with Marni Nixon?
MN: I teach in my home. Usually I don't have to worry about getting students; a lot of people call me from different walks of life. I would like to have more classical students. I get bored with the repertoire of music theatre only. And yet that varies. But the problem that I have at this point is that I'm still doing so much performing that I'm in and out of town a lot. So I have to make sure that I take students who can work in a condensed way, sometimes in consistent spurts of time, and then feed off of that while I'm out of town. I don't want to be not-there when they need me in the middle of an avalanche of new sensations or an audition season or something. So I have to deal with that.

AS: What do you enjoy most about teaching?
MN: Usually the challenge of trying to think out what that student is all about. And getting into their head and then seeing how I can get them to turn on.

AS: Any pet peeves?
MN: I hate it when somebody comes to me and says "Oh, you've been recommended to me by so-and-so and I would love to come and study with you," and usually I will lay out the parameters, and I will tell them what my schedule is, and that we should have at least a diagnostic time—we should come together and have a session and see if we get along; and then after you've had this time, which has consisted mostly of them singing excerpts from various repertoire, then doing a little vocalizing, with you all the time assessing, telling them what you think you can do for them, asking pertinent questions—and then they say, "Oh, well you know I have a list of other teachers that I've come into town to see, and so *I'll* call *you*." And I feel like, wait a minute—I was auditioning? Should I have spent my time telling her what I've done, to impress her? Should I have told her she was absolutely wonderful, and that of course I could solve all her problems and get her jobs, to keep this student? It doesn't make me feel good. I know they think they are being practical, but that's not a lesson that I gave. How can they know how you teach from that? They can see if they "like" you", I suppose. You can't possibly spend all that time auditioning for the students nor do they perceive—if I *did* give them all my credits, half the time they don't even know what that *means* in terms of how I can guide them in their vocal and career pursuits. The thing that I think that is bad is that they will only respond to, "I have this degree from this place; I have a doctorate; I have taught so-and-so, and I alone know what to do, stick with me," and I just can't abide that—can't abide thinking that I'm going to be joining souls with this person and that they will not understand the vulnerability of both of our positions—their being a student and me sharing with them what I know for the purpose of their whole "voice".

And I don't like students who then take up your time and make lessons and then start canceling. I mean you have certain policies about sickness, that's fine, or auditions; but when it's

151

too frequent then finally—usually I don't have to say it in [a harsh way], sometimes it's a mutual thing: "What's going on here; can you plan your time; is this a primary time for you; do you realize that other people want this time and I put this aside and I have a pianist coming—and even if I don't have a pianist coming, there's other people …" When there is resistance, we can usually identify it and proceed, but when they are not in the right place to work *together*, as a *team* … I understand the attrition of sickness and work, for heaven's sakes, but there are certain people that don't really understand and respect what they're hearing enough to make me want to—sometimes I can't; I get catatonic, I don't know what to say, I can't teach. I try, but it kind of stifles me.

AS: What is a question no interviewer has ever asked you that you wish they had? And what's the answer?
MN: Oh, my goodness! I find it so moving that people think they know who you are. They just perceive you and they won't ask you *why did you do this? Why are you doing it? What prompted you to go into this field? Why*—well, some people have asked me *why I didn't stay with opera*—anyway, they don't ask you; they sort of accept you as this thing that's in front of them.

I really don't know why! I don't have inductive reasoning, I can't tell you the broad picture of what something is; I can start a project and it's very focused, but it's all sorts of different things; all the details and I can be very creative about it, and in the end I don't know what the category is; what is it that I've done. And somebody who has inductive reasoning will come along and say, "Oh, you've been doing so-and-so and so-and-so. Oh, this is what you were doing," and I'm going, "Oh, *that's* it!" And it's very helpful to know that; but I'm not sure that knowing that, I could have filled in all the details like I did. So I just have to trust that I've been doing it sort of backwards all my life.

I'll do a role like that, too: I'll prepare an acting project. I can't tell you why; I will just intuitively go for something, latch onto a dialect—once [I was] on the subway reading the sides of this thing I was auditioning for and it says, "A forty-one year old Latino woman of a certain size," and I'm thinking, "Why did my agent send me out on this?" I mean, [*twinkling*] I'm at least ninety years old, and there's no way I could be a Latino woman with my red hair and blue eyes and freckles, so I just said, "I don't really care," and I just went in and I made up a person. I gave her an accent. I've forgotten what it was; I think I thought she was from the middle west—and I got the part! They just changed it to what I did. And what prompted me to do that I have no idea.

I think they've stopped asking, if they ever did, *why did you do this* or *why did you do that*. I think in the end, what I'd like to *have done* is to have used all of my talents, been able to make the best of what's been offered me, have a whale of a time doing it. But it's a challenge—it's always a challenge, I think—to try to do things better, and to satisfy yourself; to make it sound good and to make it musical, whether it be speech or music. There's a rhythm, there's a flow, and as such there's a connection. And I think that the process of teaching helps me learn, keeps me connected to what's current, keeps me scurrying around trying to learn what I think I know and to be able to impart it in better and better ways—it keeps evolving. And then, I suppose educating is like the highest form of art. And when you're performing, you're really like a missionary. You don't have to feel like you're "better than thou," but it's like you have a responsibility to be as close to yourself—that's all you have to satisfy, in the end—and then you want to try to find the means to share that in ever more efficient ways. And that's why I want *never* to leave New York. I love New York. There are experts around all the time. If you can't find them you know that they will be there soon, you just have to put out your hand and you can find them. It's a great school, it's a great place for students; you can send them to ballet classes and acting classes and coaches and performances and whatever—if they can afford it!

Anyway, nobody asks that; maybe they ask me what do I want to do when I grow up! First of all, do I ever *want* to "grow up"? What does that mean? There are a lot of things that I still want to do. I want someone to write me a show and I want to do more recordings and more film and TV straight acting roles. Another thing I want to do is to write a book, which I'm working on right now; maybe this conversation will help me clarify my ideas. This interview came along I think just at the right time to help me write my book. That's what I think; it sort of comes backwards like that.

Ethics, Standards and Practices *Marian Hampton, Associate Editor*

First Do No Harm

"I'm not interested in changing the way I talk. I like the way I talk," the UT-Knoxville student said in his broad east-Tennessee accent. Imagine my surprise when, only a few weeks later and on another assignment, he brought into class examples of various voices, characterizing the southern speech of one public figure as sounding "stupid." A few years later, in 1986, while teaching at The University of Texas in Austin, I began work with a private client who needed to adjust a mild southern accent because her boss said she sounded stupid. My first task was to convince her that she in no way sounded stupid, and then we began to work on her vowels. She still has a gentle accent to this day, has moved on to a better company and become extremely successful, served as my real estate agent on two occasions, and has become a lifelong friend.

I have known for a long time how the way we speak is connected with our sense of self, as I remember how I struggled to open up my hard mid-western "Rs" in graduate school at Yale, at a time when I strongly felt that anyone who softened their "Rs" was phony and couldn't be trusted! A panel on Standard Speech at the Association for Theatre in Higher Education (ATHE) Conference in Seattle some twelve or thirteen years ago, in which a young African-American woman accused her former teacher, Edith Skinner, of robbing her of her identity, pretty much clinched the deal for me that it was not only no longer possible to even suggest altering one's speech toward some unattainable, non-existent standard, but that this was positively destructive to the student's self-image. If we are in the position of teachers of students, surely we have the obligation, as does the medical profession, to "First, do no harm."

Of course, we still have the challenge of teaching accents and dialects to our acting students. Where do we even start? And, in a day when we have become aware also that there is no standard British speech, or standard Irish speech, or standard African speech, just as there is no standard American, how do we teach acting students that important aspect of characterization which has to do with the nationality or ethnicity of their character's voice? I found myself, upon beginning a sequence on accents and dialects, reassuring students that they needed to keep their own speech intact so that they could always play a character from their own region, but that they also needed to attune their ears to the intricacies of the ways in which others speak in order to transform their own speech to play different characters. I told them that this would involve careful listening, learning a phonetic alphabet and trying many different configurations of articulation.

While I still taught two or three generalized accents, the mainstay of my dialect courses became a *lifestudy* exercise, which I had learned in the 1950s from my teacher, Constance Welch, at Yale, as an acting exercise. However, I had added a requirement that the subject for the study possess an accent different from the student's own, preferably of some international difference, and that the student not only interview the subject on tape, creating a monologue from the interview material, but also study the physicality and gestural language of the subject, constructing a chart of phonemic and other (rhythmic, inflection) differences from how the student speaks, transcribing one double-spaced page of the monologue into phonetics. It has become a daunting but truly transforming exercise which I do every year with all of my

Marian Hampton: professional actor singer, director, voice coach, has performed and directed in San Francisco, New York, Chicago and Canada; MFA in Acting from Yale University School of Drama, BFA in Drama from Illinois Wesleyan University. Doctoral dissertation: *Teaching Actors to Sing*. Member of AEA, SAG, AFTRA; served as President of VASTA and on the Governing Council of ATHE. Published a number of articles, initiated and co-edited *The Vocal Vision*, associate editor and contributor to *Voice and Speech Review*. Taught: Allegheny College, San Francisco State, U. of Tennessee at Knoxville, U. of Texas at Austin. Currently teaches graduate and undergraduate voice and speech in the School of Theatre at Illinois State, and serves on the Academic Senate.

voice students, both graduate and undergraduate. In the process, mannerisms seem to melt away and students develop the ability to minutely observe their fellow human beings, a skill which is all too often absent from the acting curriculum.

A bonus of the lifestudy has been the development of an in-depth character which has proved useful for several students in auditions, not the least of which earned a former undergraduate student from Texas a role in New York. Acting teacher colleagues have asked me why our students' roles cannot be as fully developed as the lifestudy characters—I simply reply that they can, if the students would put as much work into their characters in plays as they do into their lifestudies.

In 1993, I presented at the ATHE Conference a paper entitled "Voices from Life: The Dialect Life Study," which was followed by a paper by Kathleen Juhl, a colleague from a nearby institution, Southwestern University in Georgetown, Texas. Her paper, entitled "Everyday Life Performance," detailed her work with students in speech classes studying videotapes of small domestic scenes, developing a way of codifying their speech and behavior, and performing the scenes as exactly as possible. Subsequently, in 2001, my paper was published by Peter Lang, in a volume of essays entitled *Perspectives On Teaching Theatre*, edited by Raynette Smith, Bruce McConachie and Rhonda Blair. (Though Kathleen Juhl's title had been kept under the rubric of "Voices from Life," her paper was somehow not included.)

In this article, I observed that the lifestudy exercise coordinates well with Stanislavski's theory of the line of physical actions; that it fully engages all of the senses, which may account for the success of the resulting portrayals; and that it develops an appreciation of the uniqueness of each subject, putting to rest the notion that there is only one way to speak. I consider this exercise to be my best tool for teaching dialects and accents, stressing as it does the particularity of region and experience in shaping one's speech.

This semester, I plunged into a project which required teaching nine languages and eleven accents to a cast mainly composed of undergraduates. During six hectic weeks of rehearsal, I recorded international sources (Russian, Bulgarian, Arabic, Turkish, Sinhalese, Polish, Azeri and German languages and accents, as well as "popular London" and Cockney accents), found among faculty and students at Illinois State University and Illinois Wesleyan University. Meanwhile, I gave my six graduate students a crash course in teaching accents as well as the languages spoken (without translation!) in the text, so that they could help coach the large cast. A major problem in my coaching was to get

students speaking other languages—to do so not only accurately but also in a fully embodied way—which meant knowing the meaning of every word and phrase and then pursuing the objective and action inherent in the words. Students could be seen everywhere with their Walkmans, working on their languages and accents. It was a madhouse for a while, but the resulting performance of *Pentecost*, by David Edgar, was hugely successful as well as a timely anti-war message, that through communication we can overcome violence in our world.

Since much violence occurs through lack of respect for or fear of others' differences, I feel certain that respecting our students is a positive step toward spreading that idea in society. Teaching them to respect and treasure differences in others is also part of that initiative. Be sure to read the articles by Judith Shahn, Clark Stevens and Beth McGee for more ideas on handling these issues. This truly is a war worth winning!

Also have a look at Brennan Murphy's article on ways to stand up for yourself as a member of the production team. As always, we are interested in investigating all aspects of the ethics, standards and practices of our complex profession. ❦

Essay *by Judith Shahn*

A New Dialect Curriculum:
The search for cross cultural training using "Interview Texts"

Over the last four years, I have been re-developing a curriculum for teaching dialects and accents to the graduate students in the MFA acting program at the University of Washington. As the student population changed to include more people of diverse backgrounds, I no longer wanted to limit my curriculum to mostly British and European stage dialects. The dialect choices needed to include the non-majority students. In addition, as time went on, I wanted to challenge myself and my white students to explore across cultural, national and racial boundaries. After all, the non-majority students had been asked to do this for years. Finally, through this re-development, we discovered the use of what I call "interview texts." The impact of using an interview with a person who speaks with a dialect or accent, as a *performing text*, rather than using the interview merely as a source to learn to acquire a dialect, yielded some profound results. I would like to share the background, the process and the new awareness that brought us to these results.

I am using the word *accent* to mean: the pronunciation of a language spoken by those for whom that language is not their native one; and *dialect* to mean: the sounds, vocabulary and syntax spoken by a particular group of people in a region of a country where that language is their native tongue. For example, English spoken by those born in England, Scotland, the United States and Australia, would be considered dialects of English, whereas the English spoken by those born in France, Italy and Germany, for example, would be considered accents[1]. As the linguists I consulted all concurred, the use of the word accent is subjective since we all speak in an accent. They use both terms with more specificity[2] than I do. In this paper, as a shortcut, I will occasionally use *dialect*, intending to encompass both the terms, *dialect* and *accent*.

In 1999, at The University of Washington, I began to experiment with changing the curriculum for the graduate actors, as well as changing *how* that curriculum was taught. I had always used taped interviews as a learning tool along with the International Phonetic Alphabet as a structure for learning dialects and accents. By listening to and studying the sound changes, one can apply those sounds to the words in a script. This method has been taught for decades. Over thirty years ago, Evangeline Machlin[3] and Jerry Blunt[4] included tapes in their work on accents and dialects. Although some samples were from actors performing text, other samples were stories told by actual persons with their specific way of speaking. Today, there are numerous tape sources, web sites, and videos available for use in training students as well as coaching productions. In the last ten years, these sources have become more and more detailed in terms of the subject's location and education.

Although this method worked well in my own training, it has not always been successful in training every student. Something was missing. For some actors, studying dialects was extremely freeing and it enabled them to explore character and deepen their work. For others, it brought on a kind of paralysis. I've seen this manifested in a whispered voice, a tight jaw, and a held breath. I began to be interested in what might best reach this kind of actor. My search began.

How could we make the leap from merely acquiring the dialect or accent to speaking as a fully integrated person, just as actors strive for in playing a character? In my own experience as an actor, I've found that speaking in a dialect

Judith Shahn has been head of voice and speech at The University of Washington's professional actor training program since 1990. She trained with Kristin Linklater and became a designated teacher in 1992. At the UW, she directs as well as coaches. Previously, she taught at Cornish College of the Arts. Professionally, Judith is one of the leading vocal and dialect coaches in the Northwest and credits include dozens of productions at The Seattle Repertory Theatre (under Dan Sullivan and Sharon Ott), the Intiman theatre (including the original *Kentucky Cycle*) and numerous productions at ACT, Seattle. Passionate about Shakespeare, Judith has coached for the Oregon Shakespeare Festival, Utah Shakespearean Festival and Shakespeare & Company. She'll be directing *Othello* in the fall. She is married to Jay Lurie and has a six year old daughter, Ella.

1. Edith Skinner writes in *Speak with Distinction*: "**Dialect**: the way in which a family, social or economic class or group of inhabitants of a particular city or region of a country speaks its native language. **Accent**: The way someone speaks a foreign language, a second language or any language that is not their native tongue." Edith Skinner and Timothy Monich were my teachers at Carnegie-Mellon University, 1973-1977.

2. I posed the question of the distinction between dialect and accent to the Ask-a-linguist website (www.linguistlist.org/~ask-ling) and received a half a dozen answers. Most agreed that *dialect* means grammar, vocabulary, syntax and lexicon, whereas *accent* generally refers to pronunciation alone. All of the linguists pointed out that everyone speaks with an accent. *Geoffrey Sampson*, Professor of natural Language Computing in Brighton said, "...so for instance, it makes sense to talk about English pronounced with a French accent, whereas there isn't a 'French dialect' of English. But equally, someone's English may have a Somerset accent, and may or may not use elements of Somerset dialect." *Joseph F. Foster*, PhD, Associate Professor of Anthropology at The University of Cincinnati writes, "...my native dialect is Southern Ozark-Ouachita

American English. People here in Ohio notice my 'hillbilly' accent. So the terms overlap. But dialect generally refers to an entire package of phonology, morphology, syntax and lexicon (I put my victuals in a sack whereas these Yankees put their groceries in a bag. Accent generally refers to pronunciation alone. So if I suddenly start putting my groceries in a bag, I will have shifted into Midwestern Yankee dialect, but will still speak it with a Southern accent."

3. Machlin, Evangeline, 1975, *Dialects for the Stage: a manual and two cassettes*, New York: Theatre Arts Books

4. Blunt, Jerry, 1967, *Stage Dialects*; San Francisco, Chandler Publishing Co.

5. Joyce, James, 1934, *Ulysses*; New York, The Modern Library

6. Deavere Smith, Anna, 1993; *Fires in the Mirror: Crown Heights, Brooklyn, and Other Identities*; New York: Anchor Books/Doubleday

7. Deavere Smith, Anna, 1992; *Twilight, Los Angeles: On the Road: a Search for American Character*; New York: Anchor Books

8. Deavere Smith, Anna, 2000; *Talk to Me: Listening Between the Lines*; New York: Random House

9. Synge, John Millington, playwright, 1871-1909

10. O'Casey, Sean, playwright, 1880-1964

11. Friel, Brian, playwright, 1929-

or an accent is a pathway to finding character. I could not embody the character of Molly Bloom in my one-woman show, (adapted from the last chapter of Joyce's *Ulysses*) until I had found her Dublin accent, tinged by her childhood spent in Gibraltar. To alter the sounds of one's speech is as profound as changing one's body. To find new rhythms and inflections must influence one's thinking and breathing. Another benefit to dialect training is the effect of traveling around the world and inhabiting other cultures, just as viewing documentaries from other countries can make you feel as if you've truly been there. When an accent is truly integrated into the human being, so that the audience is no longer cognizant of the change, this can be a remarkable element in the theatre.

In the last two years, the class and I have chosen to seek out people from different cultures and nationalities and interview them about their lives. We then used that edited interview as a performing text. I was very influenced by Anna Deavere Smith and her own performance work in *Fires in the Mirror*[6] and *Twilight, Los Angeles, 1992.*[7] When I saw her in a performance of *Twilight, Los Angeles*, she went far beyond being an actor with good dialect skills. The air in the theatre was charged. The performance was controversial, political, funny, and at times, even dangerous.

Her recent book, *Talk to Me, Listening Between the Lines*[8] served as the impetus to begin this project I call: "Interview Texts." This search has completely altered how I approach training, how I view the process of acting and how it translates to contemporary theatre. Of course, using the interview as a performance piece is not a solution in the long run. In the theatre, we do have to find a way of transferring the speech to another text. However, the process of working in this way held countless benefits.

Along the way, I had to face my personal paralysis about teaching the dialects and accents of non-white cultures, and my misconception that I had no right to enter this territory. I would like to describe the process as well as the revelations that have led my students to a new level of work. My colleagues and I have been inspired by this new approach in curriculum and training at the University of Washington's Professional Actor Training Program.

From 1990 to 1998, the Dialect curriculum was taught in a way similar to the way I had been trained. We began with Standard British or Received Pronunciation, followed by Cockney or a more modified working-class London dialect. Next came the Irish of J.M. Synge[9], Sean O'Casey[10] and Brian Friel.[11]

As a teacher, I felt passionately connected to the Irish plays. I would tell my students, "I am an Eastern European Jew (by background) with the soul of an Irishman!" Why was this world so comfortable and compelling for me to embody? Why was it so difficult for some of my students?

Along the way, there were several key moments that stand out as stepping-stones on my path to diversifying the dialect curriculum. In 1990, I had an African American student (one of two non-white students at the time) who resisted learning Irish on the basis that he believed he'd never in a million years be cast as Irish. I could see his point. I told him that learning any dialect was useful even though he may never use it in his career and that the process itself would be beneficial. Although I knew that what I was telling him had some truth in it, I also knew on some level that I was taking the easy way out. Ironically, the next year, he was cast in a professional production of *The Hostage*[12] by Brendan Behan. Both he and I were surprised to find that the Irish dialect training had paid off.

After Irish, came a taste of European accents such as French, Italian, German and Russian. We discussed the differences when playing someone for whom English is a second language. For instance, depending on the amount of time that speaker has spent in an English-speaking country, his/her education, as well as British or American influences are some of the factors to consider when working on an accent. We'd consider the material itself; is it comic, dramatic, realistic or non-realistic? We finally ended with American Southern and a "New York" accent. Of course, in reality, there are many Southern dialects (differing in region, period, class and race) and one could easily say the same about the New York area. Your dialect will vary not only from borough to borough, but will also be influenced by which ethnic group you're from.

My experience as a vocal coach has influenced my teaching greatly. The productions I've coached in the last ten years have demanded a greater level of specificity as to location. I believe more contemporary playwrights have encouraged such specificity.

For example, in 1994, after I coached *The Kentucky Cycle* by Robert Schenkkan[13] at The Intiman Theatre in Seattle, I began to include Appalachian dialect in the curriculum. Other plays were also emerging about this region, so the Southern dialect used for Tennessee Williams' plays, for example, was no longer enough. In *The Kentucky Cycle*, I had one of my most memorable dialect interviews. I had to find a Cherokee person whose first language was Cherokee. We were looking for not only the language, but also the accent from that language as it might've been spoken in the eighteenth century! After multiple calls across the country, I finally found a Cherokee medicine man in North Carolina, who told me his story over the phone. We based the character's dialect on this interview.

Similarly, the end of the dialect training always ended with a project in which students would choose a dialect or accent of their choice, interview and record someone with that dialect or accent for source material, research other sources, and then teach it to their peers. Finally, they had to find a text for that dialect/accent and perform it.

All my ideas were altered by the fact that the nature of our student body was changing. In 1990, there were two African American actors out of 36. It was too easy for me to placate the occasional queries by one or two students to incorporate Black dialects into the curriculum. However, by 1997, one third of the actors were of non-majority races and cultures. This was due to the concerted efforts of our program head, Steven Pearson, who has been determined to diversify our program. The professional theatre was also changing.

12. Behan, Brendan, 1958; *The Hostage*; London: Methuen

13. Schenkkan, Robert, 1993; *The Kentucky Cycle*; New York: Plume

Multicultural casting was becoming more widespread by the mid 1990s, and our casting policy at The School of Drama seemed to be ahead of the profession.

In 1996, Daniel, an African American student, asked me, "Why can't we study some Black dialects?" My answer was 1)"You can choose to research that for your dialect project" and 2)"I'm not expert at those dialects and don't feel qualified to teach them."

The latter was my honest assessment, but it was also, in the long run, letting myself off the hook. My presumption, at the time, was that only someone Black could teach Black dialects with integrity and only someone Asian could teach Asian accents. Yet I could so passionately teach Irish, when I'm not Irish, or Appalachian when I've barely even visited that area. Yet when it came to crossing racial lines, I was frozen in fear.

The very notion of acting is using one's imagination to become a character. Of course, we use our life experience, but imagination must be the leading ingredient. It must've been that my imagination was limited. I knew that crossing racial lines was done by my African American students all the time. They would often speak about their struggle to speak in a "white voice." The expectation was to have an impeccable British dialect, whether or not they felt connected to the material.

14. Stoppard, Tom, 1993; *Arcadia*; Faber & Faber, London

I can remember coaching a production of Tom Stoppard's *Arcadia*,[14] where there was one Asian American actor in the cast. The pressure was on for this actor to have a British dialect equivalent with the white cast. The theatre wanted to be able to justify its non-traditional casting choice by proving that the Asian American actor could be as convincing as the white actors were as British.

15. *Prime Suspect*, 1982 directed by Noel Black; Screenplay by Jeffrey Bloom

In 1999, another challenge came from a student, named Matt. He asked whether I thought that as an African American actor, he'd ever have the opportunity to use British dialect in his career. I said I didn't really know. My observation was that more and more theatres were casting non-white actors in British plays. After all, *Prime Suspect*[15] was on British television and we were seeing British Black actors in those stories. However, the history of excluding actors of color from the theatre, film and television could not be denied. We could think of relatively few productions of British plays with Black actors in them. He further asked me, "If we African American actors have to learn British, why can't the white actors learn some Black dialects?"

16. Fugard, Athol, playwright, 1932-

17. *A Dry White Season*, 1987; directed by Euzhan Palcy; screenplay by Colin Welland

18. *A World Apart*, 1988; directed by Chris Menges; screenplay by Shawn Slovo

19. *The Power of One*, 1992; directed by John G. Avildsen; screenplay by Robert Mark Kamen

This was a pivotal moment for me as a teacher. I believed this question was genuine and not a mere challenge. I knew that I needed not only to answer his question, but also to act on it. That year, instead of teaching Irish dialects, we learned South African instead, through the rich texts of Athol Fugard.[16] To prepare for these plays dealing with the Apartheid era in South Africa, I showed some clips from feature films such as *A Dry White Season*,[17] *A World Apart*,[18] and *The Power of One*.[19] I assumed that my students were familiar with the intense violence in South Africa and I neglected to fully prepare them for the nature of these film clips, except to say, "This is very rough stuff."

159

The next day tumultuous discussion arose. Many of the students felt completely unraveled by what they had witnessed. Some of the black students did not want to be in the room with white students, while viewing white violence against blacks. From this talk, we understood that as black and white people in the room, we could witness the same event, but experience it completely differently. I made a point to my students that as a white person, I felt it was my obligation to witness the atrocities committed by whites towards blacks. If Black South Africans had lived through violence or died because of it, then the least I could do was to view it. I told them it had meant a lot to me when a non-Jewish friend had sat with me to view the ten-hour documentary, *Shoah*.[20] The film contained interviews with people who had lived through every aspect of the Holocaust. My friend had been willing to witness.

20. *Shoah*, 1986; directed by Claude Lanzman

The very differences that Fugard was portraying in *Master Harold and the Boys*,[21] and *My children! My Africa!*[22] were apparent in our own classroom. Fugard's text gave form to our communication about these issues. He not only gave voice to the complexity of apartheid in South Africa, but also allowed us to voice our views on our own version of apartheid in America. Yet, this was meant to be a dialect class. Some of the students asked why it was necessary to view these films. It seemed inadequate to teach merely the sounds of South Africa, without understanding the context of the country.

21. Fugard, Athol, 1984; *Master Harold and the Boys*, Penguin Books, New York

22. Fugard, Athol, 1990; *My Children! My Africa!*

During that same year, my esteemed colleague, Valerie Curtis-Newton and I had a discussion about what the missing link for African American actors might be in training for dialects. As an example, she had just directed *Joe Turner's Come and Gone*[23] by August Wilson. The play takes place around the turn of the century and has characters who are former slaves. Her experience was that some of the African American actors had a difficult time giving themselves permission to speak in the voice with the sounds that those people would have spoken. She talked about how educated African Americans (the sound of a university professor speaking in standard English) had taken precedence over Black English (the sound of one's grandmother, for example) and that for many African Americans, the knowledge of the origin of that speech was lost. Valerie found her own process to get the actors to overcome that difficulty in rehearsal and to connect with the language of that period. She suggested to me that studying Gullah might provide that missing link.

23. Wilson, August, 1988; *Joe Turner's Come and Gone*, Samuel French, New York

Gullah, for any of you that may be unfamiliar with the term, is defined as Plantation Creole which black slaves spoke during slavery and post-slavery. It is the term for both the language and the people. As people moved out of the plantations, post slavery, and onto the Sea Islands off the coast of Georgia and South Carolina, the dialect and language survived. The words were a blend of West African languages and English. The sounds came from a melding of West African, Caribbean Islands and the British derivative of the plantation owners. Gullah is still spoken today on some of these Sea Islands and has remained, relatively unchanged through generations of Gullah people. Although there are different schools of thought as to the derivation of Black English, one school of thought is that Gullah is one of its influences and that certain elements of Gullah vocabulary and sounds have survived in today's Black English. David Crystal in *The Cambridge Encyclopedia of English*[24] cites, "…the alternative view argues that the origins of 'Black English Vernacular' lie in the use of a creole English by the first blacks in America. This language,

24. Crystal, David, 1987; *Cambridge Encyclopedia of Language*; Cambridge University Press

25. *The Story of English*, 1986; directed by William Cran

26. Mixson Geraty, Virginia, 1997; *Gulluh Fuh Oonuh (Gullah For You)*; Sandlapper Press, Orangeburg, South Carolina

27. *Daughters of the Dust*, 1991, directed by Julie Dash; screenplay by Julie Dash

originally very different from English as a result of its African linguistic background, has been progressively influenced by white English so that it now retains only a few creole features."

In order to teach Gullah, I began my research looking for source material. I found a wonderful segment from the PBS documentary entitled, *The Story of English*.[25] I discovered a book called *Gulluh Fuh Oonuh (Gullah for You)* by Virginia Mixson Geraty,[26] whose grandmother spoke Gullah. There was also the feature film, *Daughters of the Dust*,[27] directed and written by Julie Dash, which Valerie Curtis-Newton had recommended. We used the film script as a text, in addition to other texts by African American writers dealing with slavery and post-slavery issues.

Valerie Curtis-Newton had also directed a production of Anna Deavere Smith's *Twilight, Los Angeles*, in our 1998 season, using 6 female actors of different races to play all the roles. In her production, the actors had to do what Anna had done as a solo-performer; speak the words and the speech of African Americans, White Americans, Korean Americans, and Hispanic Americans. The transformations were very successful because the race of the actor became secondary to the voice and race of the character. The production was very well received and inspired me to go further in my own work.

Still, I had to face my own paralysis. How could I, a white teacher, take on the speech of African slaves and teach it with integrity to my African American students? I did not believe myself when I tried it. I was walking into a wall of white guilt and I was stuck. Here I was, the same color of those who were the oppressors. How dare I think I might understand the experience that black slaves went through? I wanted to be able to take that leap, but I couldn't as of yet, give myself *permission* to do it.

I called my mother, a former elementary school teacher, who had traveled the world over and had spent a lot of time in East Africa. When I was seventeen, I spent six weeks with my mother in Kenya. It was my first experience of being in the racial minority—a racial minority that had all the privilege, however. I told her of my plight. She told me, "You've got to do it. You've coached countless dialects. You're asking your students to do it. You're an actor. You've simply got to practice and practice it until it's yours!"

That is exactly what I did. After giving myself permission and then doing the work, I shared my struggle with my students and asked them if they would join me on this journey. We did a wonderful segment on Gullah. Now, for the first time, all the white actors were now the ones taking the leap of crossing racial lines and speaking in a very different voice. I remember taking the class to an uncrowded outdoor café, where they all spoke their Gullah text. The class cheered each other on.

In 2000, I read Anna Deavere Smith's book *Talk to Me: Listening Between the Lines*, which I mentioned earlier. She talked about her process with interviewing people in communities in crisis. Anna interviewed everyone she could find with as many viewpoints as possible and she recorded them. She listened to them over and over until she found these people inside of her. *Talk to Me* became a kind of guide for our dialect projects. In her book, she talks about what changes when someone is speaking in an "authentic voice." She talked about the fact that when the content is so compelling, one's very rhythm changes. After interviewing people in the midst of explosive riots, she became interested in the political world in Washington, DC. What would it be like to talk to people about what they couldn't say in public? In her interviews with President Clinton and others in Washington politics, she writes out the interview as she heard it spoken; in phrases, with breaths—more like a poem. I asked my graduate students if they were interested in working in this way. So, instead of interviewing someone and *applying* their dialect to a theatre text, now the interview itself became the text. It occurred to me that using "interview texts" would give the actor more of a sense of permission to cross *any* lines (gender, racial, cultural, and social) because the desire to serve the integrity of the truth of the text was even greater than with a scripted, fictional text. This proved to be the case, just as Anna Deavere Smith had demonstrated in her performances, and Valerie Curtis-Newton had done in her innovative production of *Twilight: Los Angeles*.

The new element here was asking questions that would allow someone to reveal something about themselves—not in an exploitative way, but like a documentary.

I have been fascinated by interviews for years. American culture seems to thrive on interviews, judging by their popularity in magazines, television and radio. Documentary films, which rely heavily on the interview have actually changed my viewpoint and have educated me. When I was a young actor auditioning in New York, I used pieces from Studs Terkel's *Working*[28] for auditions because I new they probably would not have been heard in this way. Oral Histories have emerged over and over in an attempt to preserve historical significance, as in Steven Spielberg's project of interviews with Holocaust survivors,[29] and The Ellis Island Oral History Project,[30] in the library at The Ellis Island Immigration Museum, where over 1,500 have told their stories of immigrating to America from their homelands.

Here's how we went about structuring the project. I decided that in order for me to understand how the process worked for my students, I needed to do my own project as well. There were no requirements for choosing, only interest in a country or culture. We looked for people with that specific dialect or accent in mind. Sometimes students had friends or family members; sometimes we found waiters or restaurant owners, teachers or other students. We combed the community for our interviews. We decided that there were no boundaries that should limit us as regards to race, culture, nationality, gender, or age. I chose a Japanese man from the School of Business, whom I had taught voice to earlier that year. Again, having coached Japanese accents, but never really doing it myself, presented a hurdle that I had to jump.

It seemed crucial to do a live interview as opposed to a phone interview because seeing the person as well as listening was essential if we were to know their expressions and gestures, and whether or not they had direct eye contact with people, for example. Unlike Anna Deavere Smith, we didn't have a

28. Terkel, Studs, 1974; *Working: people talk about what they do all day and how they feel about what they do*; New York: Pantheon Books

29. A Holocaust szemei, directed by Steven Spielberg

30. The Ellis Island Oral History Project: recordings and transcripts in the library of The Ellis Island Museum of Immigration, New York.

specific theme. The idea was to ask the person to talk about their native country (if this was an accent) and their cultural background. Each student could conduct their interview the way they chose, but we asked questions such as:

- What brought you to this country?
- What are the customs and traditions of your family?
- What do you like or dislike about the US?
- Are there any stories that stand out from your life experience?

These were very broad questions, yet sometimes they led to unexpected and amazing stories. Some of the stories were comical, some related moments of fear and pain, but all of them seemed to reveal something about identity. For example, one student, Catherine, interviewed a family friend from Hungary. She spoke of her experience during the Hungarian revolution against the Russians in the early 1950s, in which she escaped Budapest and went into the woods, disguised as a peasant. She bribed Hungarian soldiers to get them to the Austrian border and barely escaped with her life. Another interview was with a Moroccan restaurant owner who had been the chef on Christina Onassis' yacht. He was very involved with her family and was there when she died. Glenn's interview with a Scottish man wrought a bawdy pub story, complete with the details about vomiting up the pub food!

We had students representing people from all over Europe, Africa, Asia, Australia, and America. After taping the interview, and listening diligently to our tapes, we identified the major sound shifts and wrote them phonetically. We began with the structure of sounds. We then compared them with other sources we could find with this dialect.

The next task was to edit the interview from its original length to a five-minute piece. We did it by editing the tape first, and then transcribing it onto paper so that we'd actually have a written text to use as a script. As Anna Deavere Smith had done, we wrote the words in the phrasing in which they were spoken, so they often took the shape of poetic verse rather than prose.

We paid attention to every *um* and *er*, to breaths, rhythm, inflection, stress patterns, and vocal quality. We studied and practiced. Students walked around with headphones on, absorbing and repeating the words. In class, we explored how to find the body of our interviewee, now that we had found the voice.

Something occurred that was different than working on the other dialects. For instance, during the period we spent studying Gullah, the fear of mimicry, of being disrespectful was a real issue for some of the white students. In learning any dialect, it is possible to settle on a general result, therefore invoking a kind of stereotype, which loses its validity.

In the quest to be faithful to their interviewees, the students seemed to focus on being specific and accurate. Something deeper was able to come through. Actors can spend weeks in rehearsals trying to layer their work in order to find a real human being. In these classroom projects, the real human already existed, and the students' task was to find their way to this person.

Actors' familiar habits began disappearing as they told these stories because they weren't useful anymore. The need to project or embellish disappeared as well. This kind of specificity and clarity was the kind of work the faculty was seeking in other aspects of the actor training. The "Interview Texts" were so compelling, we repeated the project last year in spring of 2002. In addition, we expanded the work on South Africa and Fugard so that the acting faculty and the Alexander teacher were all collaborating on the scene work. The scene work is still essential, because actors need the tool of applying dialects and accents to theatre and film scripts. The "Interview Texts" became a tool to achieve a seamless transformation between the actor and the text.

I am continuing the search to balance the dialect training. I still want to teach Irish dialect. As a matter of fact, this year, the current class chose to work on Irish dialects and West Indies dialects (their connections as well as their differences). The Asian American actors chose to work on a scene for Japanese accent. All the students are learning each dialect and working on text in all three. There is no doubt that learning European accents are useful in actor training. As teachers, we need to teach our students what will best serve them in their careers. I want the work we do to serve the educational needs of all the students, even as that student population keeps changing. More than anything, I want to continue to explore what it means to give permission to oneself to go beyond one's comfort zone. How can we grapple with our students' paralysis until we've had a good wrestle with our own?

The theatre has come a long way. It does more than hold the mirror up to life. It has the capacity to shock, reveal, unravel, deconstruct, question and answer. If we are to achieve a theatre where cultural, racial and gender lines continue to be crossed, then we as educators need to provide opportunities for our students to experience this. Perhaps "multicultural" will cease to mean allowing people of color to participate in the white world. Perhaps, it also will mean that we, as white artists, have to step out of our comfort zone and dare to speak in a voice of another color, a darker color, and take on all the implications it presents.

❧

Acknowledgements and thanks:
1. Sarah Bryant Bertail, Associate Professor, University of Washington
2. Catherine Madden, Assistant Professor, University of Washington
3. Valerie Curtis-Newton, Assistant Professor, University of Washington
4. Steven Pearson, Professor, Head of PATP, University of Washington
5. Mark Jenkins, Robyn Hunt, Associate Professors, University of Washington—for their support and encouragement
6. Jon Jory, Professor, University of Washington—for his support and encouragement

Essay *by Clark Stevens*
Justifying Stage Standard Speech at the Historically Black College/University: Raising the Bar, Bridging the Gap or Downgrading Diversity?

Clark Stevens is currently the voice, speech and movement specialist for the Department of Music and Drama at Prairie View A & M University of Texas. During the summer months he enjoys acting for Shakespeare festivals and professional repertory companies throughout the country. Recent credits include: Leontes (*The Winter's Tale*)—Shakespeare Festival of Dallas, Launce (*The Two Gentlemen of Verona*), Duke of York (*Richard II*)—Texas Shakespeare Festival. In addition to acting, Stevens has served as a director and vocal coach for several colleges and universities in Texas. This summer he will play the lead in Moliere's *The Hypochondriac* at the Texas Shakespeare Festival (2003).

As a professor of voice and articulation at a Historically Black University, I can tell you that I am not always well received when I inform students that we will be studying and using Stage Standard speech for all of our class work and most of our performances. This is usually met with some resistance and inevitably the question arises, "Why should I have to try and sound *white*? That's not me! That's not my *natural* voice!" At this point, I really look like a hypocrite since I just presented an introductory mini-lecture on the need for using the natural voice. Other students contend that to be devoid of black dialect, and to use Stage Standard, is not necessarily an attempt to sound white, but gray rather. Many of my students think of standard speech as an unjustified amalgamation of Caucasian vocal habits, all averaged into one undesirable dialect. Why should this group of proud, young, African-American actors-in-training adopt a massive change and retrofit their speech to a standard that is largely perceived as the "white" sound of middle America? A particularly outspoken student then adds, "Why should I unnaturally alter my individuality?"

There I am, in front of the classroom, like an albino deer in the paved road at night, blinded by the cultural interrogation headlight; the beacon of diversity is now on high-beam and I find myself having to think on my feet faster than ever before. Suddenly I realize what it feels like to be completely alone as the outsider, the single member of a minority. Imagine this feeling layered with an overwhelming sense of intrusion. The students are verbally resisting the subject and focus of the course on the first day (in the first half hour). Briefly I feel trapped in an awkward, frozen moment. As a teacher, I want to be honest and certainly the last thing I want is to introduce the course, the content and myself with fear. As an actor, I do not want my new audience to know that I am briefly stumped and grasping for my next line. Questions blast through my mind: Will this group ever accept me and will they see any importance in what I am trying to offer?

So you can see the problem I am faced with in the classroom. Before you attempt to solve this problem by imagining yourself in the same given circumstances or a similar situation, you must allow me to first illustrate some of the external problems (outside the classroom). I promise we will return to the classroom in a moment.

Exactly one week later, I am called in to a meeting with my dean. With all of the new faculty present, he explains the there is a situation at hand, one that we must be aware of. He explains that there is a very strong movement on campus to remove all "non African-American" professors from the faculty. Evidently there was a loud demonstration on campus with enraged community leaders (using bullhorns), shouting to the far ends of the campus: "We want an all black university! These new teachers are ruining our 'identity'!"

This movement is reinforced and possibly fueled by older, senior faculty members who have been here since the day when there was not a single "non-African-American" on campus. At our faculty conference, an officer of the faculty senate described one of their issues: "Will we all be replaced by white teachers?" I stop and think, what would this man think of my voice and stage diction course and the application of Stage Standard? Maybe this is bad idea? Maybe I should just stick to breath work and texts by black playwrights?

Ethics, Standards and Practices

Justifying Stage Standard Speech at the Historically Black College/University:
Raising the Bar, Bridging the Gap or Downgrading Diversity? by Clark Stevens (continued)

Maybe I should let these students use their habitual voices and breath patterns and I should just move back home. After a brief, contemplative, moment, I am resolved: "No way. I came to teach. I came for the students. I will not allow these talented students, these gifted actors-in-training to be victims of reverse racism. This is the age of change and it starts right here right now—in the moment."

Just when you think you have turned your ship back on course, along comes another tempest. The next week, my program coordinator/supervisor comes into my office and verbally assaults me—in a rage. He insists that I "don't know how to teach black students," and that I am "not doing my job!" He loudly and sternly states that I am not "drilling the students hard enough with the Skinner… it's two weeks into the semester and they still talkin' in that ghetto slang!" This made me realize that the administration really wanted me to modify the student's speech. My supervisor, an older black gentleman, made an immediate priority of reducing the black dialect with the students. It is important to understand that my department supervisor speaks with a thick, lilting Louisiana accent, coalesced with AAVE (African-American Vernacular English). On a good day, I understand about half of what he is saying. He also insisted that I needed to be "more of an authority figure in the classroom." On top of that he added: "You spend too much time teachin' those kids how to breathe when you should be drillin' those consonants. You don't know these students. They only *respond* to authority figures and speech drills!" I tried to explain the importance of establishing a safe environment (to explore the voice). I tried to justify my plan—but to no avail. Passionately I tried to explain that deeply engrained speech habits could not possibly be changed until the body was free of tension. Scrambling I spouted that drilling students this early would only create more tension. I argued that, "I have to hear the students speak. Their first speech is a diagnostic speech. This gives me the opportunity to hear their habitual speech problems (individually). After that I would work on breath and then Stage Standard." In the quiet calm, long after the stormy dialogue, I realized that it was going to be *his* way or the Interstate Highway.

So now that the problems are clear and the environment is understood, let's go back to the classroom. We left our lone Caucasian vocal coach in the blinding white light of student interrogation. Remember the albino deer facing the high beams? The beams of light now assume the form of pointed questions by extremely talented, articulate, and streetwise students—the majority of which have never been soft spoken. My students are direct and to the point. So, back to the pointed the question: "Why should I unnaturally alter my individuality?" I have to quickly back pedal and state clearly that "the objective here is not to abandon your natural dialect, but it is

to learn Stage Standard for the following reasons: 1. To support the vocal conventions of the play as they relate to region, or lack of region and geographical setting. 2. To promote uniformity and in some cases, clarity on the stage. 3. To increase your linguistic and communication abilities in order to further your careers. I remind students that this is a skill. It is a tool that you may choose to use—when you feel you need it. This is a speech skill that you might use in the business world, but certainly it will be useful for your career on the stage. When the character or the situation requires a natural—or even exaggerated—black dialect, by all means, you will use it and chances are you can already do that quite well. Sooner or later in the wonderful world of theatre, you are required to perform in a dialect that may not be your own. So we will study this standard and you are welcome to use the key words and think of it as a dialect that you may choose to use in the situations that you deem appropriate—for both the theatre and beyond. Really you may think of it as the jumping off place for the study of all accents and dialects."

I present the case that: "You may find that you prefer to speak in Stage Standard—if it improves the way that people perceive and receive you. The study may improve your clarity and improve the production of certain sounds that were previously distorted and habitually co-articulated." Many young, African-American actors substitute [ks] for [sk] and say "ax" instead of "ask." Another common problem lies in the phonation of the short diphthong of "R"—which Skinner transcribes as [ɑɚ] (with r-coloring). The plural form of "car" is often pronounced "cawz." I explain to my students the following, "You may discover that you prefer saying 'ask' instead of 'ax'." All of my students replace the short [ɪ] with [i] and thus "pill" becomes "peeow" without any [ɫ] consonant. Others substitute [f] for [θ] and thus words like booth are pronounced "boof". We modify the pronunciations by drilling on key words that rhyme with the problem sounds and then substitute the standard sounds and drill them repeatedly. I always drill the class together first and then call on individuals. This semester, I made what I believe to be a wise return to the popular *Fundamentals of Voice and Articulation*[i] text by my first college speech teacher, Lyle V. Mayer. The book is now in its twelfth edition and I value the tongue placement drawings now more than ever. The exercises are well structured and fun. At this point in the journey, I offer the fact that "Oprah Winfrey uses very clear General American speech but occasionally, she turns on her dialect for emphasis in an effective manner. The choice is yours in life. However, students, the choice is generally never yours in regard to a professional stage production. The director and the vocal director make all dialect decisions. With this in view, it will only be a benefit for you to know Stage Standard as a working, professional actor."

I suggest to the students that, in the theatre, we should all strive to be colorblind, so that the rest of the world will catch on. Some of the most engaging casts I have ever seen resemble a rainbow on stage. It is a pleasure to watch a Shakespeare play with a cast that is multi-cultural and dedicated to diversity. Yet the key to a successful delivery of the text, especially a heightened text, lies in the integration of Stage Standard (ss). Why? I explain to the young vocal scholars that, when we watch this diverse and ideal cast, we want to hear and view a clear story. We do not want the audience member to disengage from the world of the play even for a moment to ask internal questions like, "What is that accent? Is that actor from Boston? Is that a Texan? or is that a Jamaican?"

Shakespeare provides us with many scenic settings that require a vocal standard. If all the characters are from Illyria, for example, they should not sound like a smear of broadly different sounding inhabitants. We use ss for the benefit of the play—*not to change who you are*. We use it to propel the convention that we are all from the same country and in this case it is a fantastical land that does not really even exist. I suggest to the students that: "If it helps you to embrace and justify the implementation of a dialect, try to think of this as a fictitious standard for a fictitious country (Illyria). Use this tool, this speech, in concert with the natural sound of your voice and see if it empowers your overall marketability as a professional actor. It is always my intention to make you more employable and to further your careers. In being open minded and willing to work with dialects and/or speech modification, you give yourself permission to take risks and open creative channels of expression. This then enables you to create a wider range of characters from a potentially wider range of dramatic genres."

Overall it is important for the students to understand that everyone in any given society makes constant, cultural-dialect choices in every moment of life. We speak in one way with our parents, we speak in another way with our peers and in a third way when speaking in the professional world. In every cultural situation we select words, pronunciations and inflections as choices that relate directly to the group we are with. To a large degree, we are all vocal chameleons. Some of us are quicker than others at shifting from shade to shade. The chameleon does not stop to think about what color he may be. He only checks to make sure he does not stick out after making an adjustment.

Even after the Oprah Winfrey example, the chameleon and Shakespeare, there is still a student who thinks I am way out of line. He is a rebellious, energetic, young actor that knows *everything*—because he won best actor at the high school play contest. This actor shows visible tension across his furled

eyebrows. I know why. He feels that his greatest dramatic strength lies in releasing strong and loud emotions with an over-affected and exaggerated black dialect. After all, he won best actor in a play by Lorraine Hansberry. He still sees the work in terms of black and white. Again, I am feeling uncomfortable. He is feeling really uncomfortable and then, a clarifying example dawns on me. I turn to a role model. After taking a deep, cleansing and empowering breath, I offer the following: "While he may not be everyone's hero in the theatre, he has recently been nationally recognized as one of our best film actors. Let's take a look at Denzel Washington. Does his vocal work in a film like *Training Day* sound the same as his character in *Much Ado About Nothing?* No." After a split second of contemplation, there is a vocal release of understanding in the room. There is laughter. The uncomfortable vibration in the room instantly dissipates into a welcome, safe feeling. I reinforce this moment with a familiar notion: "Class, I am not a black man, I am not a white man, I am a human being." There is a warming sense of agreement in the room with ripples and echoes of "right on," heads nodding with sincere support. In the theatre, color lines should not exist. We all agree and I realize that our world has more hope now than it ever did before. It goes so much further than the Stage Standard issue. These students fill me with inspiration. The young people in the classroom today are the future of the American theatre and I am surrounded by creative, positive energy. They want to learn Stage Standard now. We made a pact, and all of the students agree to use ss in the theatre building and at home. Later in the week, the students are asked to share with the class some feelings about their own voices. Many of the honest actors discuss desirable changes. Some say that they want to sound less "country," some less "slang" and two of the young ladies state that they want to sound less "ghetto." Almost all of the actors have a desire to improve their articulation skills. Now the stage is set for a semester of study, with an honest need for change. Most of my HBCU students have now embraced and adopted a standard that may have initially been perceived as an intrusion/infusion of *unnecessary*—**white**—speech curriculum. With each class the actors in this program grow more and more attentive and enthusiastic. We respect each other and the classes are fun. There is nothing like the warm feeling you receive when students clap at the end of your classes. I feel blessed and receive spiritual coins of appreciation from the students on a daily basis. In this appointment as a vocal coach, I know that I have learned as much from the students as they do from me.

Voice and articulation class now resembles a vocal boot-camp in the drilling of key words and exercises. The initial thought of drilling speech prior to establishing a safe place to learn the

Ethics, Standards and Practices
Justifying Stage Standard Speech at the Historically Black College/University:
Raising the Bar, Bridging the Gap or Downgrading Diversity? by Clark Stevens (continued)

voice and breath seemed backwards at the time, but now it is indeed the appropriate, albeit unorthodox method. I now believe that in this kind of environment, you must disarm the students **first**. Provide the drill work and exercises. Show them that they *do* have speech problems that really do need fixing. Enforce Stage Standard pronunciations. Then when they clearly see the need to change, I launch into Linklater breath and sound work. The students are required to practice a regimen of custom-designed vocal drills for a minimum of forty minutes a day. I check their individual progress after the group warm-up. This is working for them and me.

One of my students has the most amazing gospel singing voice. Yet when she speaks she slips into a small, trapped and quiet voice. I require this student to sing her text while gesturing, and then *speak* it with the same freedom and gestures using ss. The breath pattern is instantly transformed to deep-central breath. Her voice is engaging, resonant and powerful. She learned Linklater concepts in church and did not even know it. Her gospel breath is very deep, it is strongly connected to the spirit, and when she feels the connection, she releases vibrations up to the heavens. Now her speaking voice is starting to connect with core support in the same way, and the process of change inspires all of the students to release a bigger, richer sound. This progress provides me with a higher form of compensation, and a spiritual reward. The positive vocal change, the progress with students, it all reinforces my decision to stay in a place where I might not always be welcome. My students support my curricular choices and understand the need for everything on my syllabus. My students smile and let me know that I am welcome. They want to learn what I have to offer and every time I encounter a look of disdain from an old-guard faculty member, I smile and think to myself, "I am not alone," my students are right here with me—even in the long walk across campus where I am looked at like an out-of-place alien.

When I think back to the enraged community leaders and the senior faculty members staging a passionate demonstration concerning cultural identity on campus it still disturbs me. Some non-African American speech educators encountering this article may think of this as an *unusual* situation. But racism affects curriculum and administration at every university, in every discipline. Prior to my interview for this appointment, I was largely unaware of the existence of HBCUs in our country. It seems so strange to consider that there are many schools that we may associate as *Historically White Universities* or *Colleges*, yet in an age of "diversity" it is ironic, though only appropriate, that the black institutions encourage everyone to label the distinction. Why? It would be an outrage if the historically white campus existed with a sub-title behind the name of the school. Yet both institutions receive the same state

money and now we see that racism works both ways. I think it is definitely time to change on both sides. **There is a fine line between sustaining cultural identity and supporting reverse racism.** There are still those who hide behind a mask of diversity, when they are really obsessed with sustaining cultural identity—which is actually a desire for insular segregation. This is hard even to imagine in a new century! In the end, it only hurts the students. Imagine what the black professor feels like at the predominantly white university. He/she is in the same double bind. We want our academic freedom, but we have to consider what is safe to teach. Let us hope that, during this century, we will open our hearts to the abandonment of cultural identification. In times of war and peace there will always exist those who want to stay in their safety bubble. Is it fair to suggest that students graduating from an HBCU will go out into the real world and work in an all black work place—not unlike the campus with a sustained identity? Will their desired insulation actually exist anywhere in this country? What type of positive examples are the old-guard teachers and protesting community leaders providing in this quest? Surely in this age we can now realize that we all learn from each other. I learn from my students on a daily basis. I am now engrossed in the study of African-American drama and I wonder why I only had a glimpse of it in graduate school. I am elated to broaden my horizons now, just as the students are in my class.

Too much energy and money is spent on identifying the minority on every college campus, when it should be spent on teaching. So yes, if students can identify with the need for Stage Standard in the theatre, they can also relate to the fact that we are all Americans, not black, not white, not brown, not yellow, not red, but human—sharing a nation and an educational system that **can** work together. The biggest pill to swallow for everyone involved is in the acceptance of standards. Whether we like it or not, this is the age of accountability and testing for minimum skill levels. Students all have to pass at least one standardized test in order to attend most colleges today. Let us not forget that in order to attend most graduate schools you have to make an impressive score on the Graduate Records Examination (GRE). Beyond that, the implementation of an *exit* exam is gaining forward momentum in some states. The oral defense of a thesis could one day include a standardized examination that evaluates minimum skill levels in graduate actor training.

Some standards strengthen systems and some destroy systems like a cancer. Perhaps it is time to identify clearly the standards that have a negative impact and those that ensure educational advancement. I do not like the idea of standardized testing in the fine arts—and yet the writing is on the wall already—especially for the large introductory classes. It seems that as educators in the fine arts, we all fall into one of two categories. You are either bridging the gap or downgrading diversity. If we use standards in education, and that is a given, can we not use them in a humane way? As humane voice and speech trainers in an age of global tension, it is important to stress that there is not one dialect that is better than another. Each dialect and accent on this planet is a celebration of culture, individuality and expression. Actors that are well trained should be confident and competent in their ability to integrate any dialect that is appropriate for the given character. Stage Standard is just another tool. In a callback audition for a repertory company, I was once asked to do the same monologue with three different accents—so the Stage Standard tool served me well in the first of two, preliminary audition rounds. Musicians are asked to do this all the time in auditions. A competent pianist might hear a music director say, "that was good, now play the same song with a Cha-Cha feel, then a Jazz-Swing and finally a Reggae groove." The auditioning musician never has his or her cultural sensitivities offended by this type of coaching. Actors should understand that when they use a dialect (other than their own), they are not abandoning their culture or their race. As educators we have a responsibility. We must encourage students to retain pride in their own cultural identities while exploring and learning about others.

❧

1 Lyle V. Mayer, *Fundamentals of Voice and Diction*—12th edition (Boston: McGraw-Hill, 1999).

Essay *by Beth McGee*

Towards a 21st Century Pedagogy: Voice & Diversity

> "Emotion without action is abdication of your personal power."
> Nobel laureate Jody Williams

As voice teachers we are on the front line in the education of young people and future professionals. US census statistics project that by the year 2030 (a year in which the average student in his or her first year of college in 2003 will be the age of 45), 40% of the US population will be composed of what we now call "minority" groups—African Americans, Hispanics, Native Americans, and Asian/Pacific Islanders.[1] Looking to these statistics, we need to consider how we educate our students for participation in a society that is rapidly changing in its demographics, with the foreknowledge that they will need the tools to participate in a diverse American culture. Those of us whose profession is guiding young people and professionals towards healthy voice production know that "voice" has a multi-layered function within our society; it serves not just as a useful tool for vocal presentation, but also as a metaphor for who we are, what power we have, and how easily we are understood. But "being understood" is a complicated matter, especially for those not raised in the majority culture. The majority culture's prejudice against minority groups in our society is reflected in the amount of "voice" such groups are allowed to have and the power they have to change their status. Those of us within the majority culture may abhor racism, sexism, homophobia, or prejudice against people with disabilities, but the discrimination that results from these "isms" is woven into the "majority" cultural fabric. It withholds "the right to speak" from large numbers of people in our nation. We can choose to help unravel the threads of our cultural fabric and embrace diversity, but we have to be willing to do some work to educate ourselves in the actions of diversity.

It's easiest to make changes within a small culture over which we have some control—our classroom or studio environment. One way to begin is by considering the language we use. Theoretically, words are "alive" in that they are symbols that stand for real objects or ideas—objects or ideas that have specific cultural and contextual meanings for every listener. If we become sensitive to the effect our language may have on those we teach, we may realize that phrases and words that we consider "standard usage" may create an oppressive environment for others. In the United States, we of course have the legal right to say whatever we please in our classroom or studio—but it's our choice what kind of environment we wish to cultivate for our students and what kind of education-by-example we wish to impart. One option is to consciously adopt gender and culture inclusive language. I am a white woman working in a majority white male environment, and frequently find it offensive when my colleagues speak of professors with words whose connotations refer only to men, because their words tell me how little they regard women's contributions to academia and in what esteem they hold the work of women as part of the university's research agenda. At the 2002 VASTA conference, a discussion during the "things that work" session revealed that the word "master," when used in a phrase such as "master-teacher" is offensive to some African Americans, as it brings up connotations of the master-slave relationship. I am by no means arguing that we should sanitize our language in fear of offending everyone. The argument is that we should be mindful of our language so that we say what we mean and can be clearly understood. As we embody mindful language usage, our students may learn to do so themselves through our example.

Beth McGee has a wide variety of interests pertaining to diversity, ethics and the human voice. At Case Western Reserve University she serves in Administration as the Faculty Diversity Officer, and is a CWRU Ethics Fellow and an Associate Professor of voice in the Department of Theater and Dance. Outside of the university she is a member of Actors' Equity, a voice and dialect coach for academic and professional theaters, and consults professionally in areas of voice empowerment skills. Professor McGee's interdisciplinary interests have led her to apply the knowledge from her profession as a voice coach to other studies, including communication skills, teaching skills, ethics, and feminist issues. Professor McGee has a BS in Theater/Communication Education from Appalachian State University and an MFA in Acting from the University of Georgia. Recently she served as dialect coach for the film *Welcome to Collinwood*, produced by George Clooney and Stephen Soderbergh. She recorded an album of Folk songs, *Love is Teasing*, for Folkways records in 1980, which now permanently resides with all other Folkways recordings in the Smithsonian Institution's Archival catalogue.

1. Bowen, William G. and Derek Bok. *The Shape of the River*. Princeton, N.J.: Princeton University Press. 1998. pp. 11-12.

While speaking, we can choose to use both gender and race inclusive examples in our teaching. For those of us raised in the white majority, we can inadvertently make a comment from a white majority perspective, mistaking it to be the perspective of all. For example, I'm embarrassed to admit that during past class discussions of the majority American culture's reluctance to participate in group singing for pleasure or as a work relieving accompaniment, I mistakenly surmised that "all American culture" seemed adverse to group singing, completely forgetting that many African American, Hispanic American and Native American peoples continue to engage in group singing, and many regional US cultures (such as the Appalachian) and recent immigrants to our country still practice group singing in work and at play. It wasn't that I was ignorant of this fact—it was that in the midst of teaching, I inadvertently assumed my experience was the experience of all. Another caveat in changing how we use examples while teaching is to be careful of hidden cultural prejudices that may reveal themselves in the use of "positive" examples that indicate white males, and "negative" or pejorative examples that indicate women or minorities. One obvious example might be in explaining the skill of picking strong acting objectives for a man as "a man stealing money to feed his starving family," but for a woman as "a woman trying to get a man to buy her dinner."

We can choose to discuss diversity issues with our students, either outright, or through the use of plays, readings, and resources from a diverse array of authors and cultures. We can vary scenes given to minority students to include both minority-specific casting and non-traditional casting with the goal of teaching them as many characterization skills as possible. We can explore gender myths through a discussion of characterization choices when casting scenes across genders. We can be more imaginative and resourceful in the plays and scenes we choose for class, and become more familiar with contemporary plays with minority, women, disabled, and Gay/Lesbian/Bi/Transgendered (GLBT) characters for use in scenes, readings, dialect work, or discussion. We can investigate feminist and queer academic theory in our classes, or use it as it pertains to theater production and "voice."

If we're teaching at a majority-white institution with few minority students, we can become more educated concerning their experience. We cannot assume that one minority student's experience can speak for all minorities, nor should we single out the few minorities in our classroom to "speak to the point of view" of their minority affiliation, or to educate us on their particular minority group. We can, however, educate ourselves and encourage respectful dialogue with all of our students, taking care that all people who wish to speak are

171

given an opportunity to do so, within appropriate confines of the syllabus. Rather than fearing to offend, we can rely on our compassion to ask students how they wish to be affiliated: to what minority-term do they feel affiliated—Latina or Hispanic? Black or African American? Something else? We can be mindful that Asians and Pacific Islanders have a diverse array of cultures and not assume that all Asian cultures are similar. If we grew up white within the American middle-class, we need to remember that the experience of our minority students may be very different from ours. Our minority students may have a world-view colored by dealing with discrimination on a daily basis—something that white teachers may not adequately understand. Depending on where they grew up, our minority students may have led a life very different from the one we have led, and encountered schooling vastly different from the schooling we have had. When I was teaching African American inner-city performing arts high school students, I was offered a window into a world I had never seen before—a world where receiving an education with skills strong enough to land admittance to a good university was severely hindered due to the consequences of poverty: city school funding issues and lack of facilities, absenteeism, bad nutrition, health problems, and lack of parental support.

As voice teachers with minority students in our classrooms or studios, we may also be stymied by the "standard speech" debate. Does teaching minority students and students with strong regional accents American Standard Speech somehow indoctrinate them for assimilation into the white majority culture? Does it continue to propagate the myth that "educated white" speech is the only "good" speech? Do we want to be on the forefront of the movement that believes that all dialects enhance the vivacity and humanity of our common language, and are more reflective of our culture? How does this relate to preparing students for the profession of acting and speech training? Or to promoting actions for diversity?

I believe that as a culture, Americans are in a transitional period regarding how we view regionalisms and accents as "good" or "bad" speech. In my lifetime we have had six Presidents with distinct regional accents (Presidents Kennedy, Johnson, Ford, Carter, Clinton, and George Bush Jr.), and the last Presidential election gave us the opportunity to watch the two major candidates debate using two different southern American dialects. When I was a theater student in the 1980s, all broadcasters in our country spoke American Standard. Now the television offers us a plethora of vocal variety as we watch the news, listen to commercials, and tune in to our favorite programs. On National Public Radio, the formally austere, vocally "correct" BBC now provides us with newscasters speaking dialects from all over the world.

Those of us who received voice and speech training before the 1990s remember a vocal discipline that required a dialect that "made all actors sound as if they were from the same region," or hoped to create a mood in a "classic" play that did not distract the audience from its world with a jangling regional dialect. Some of us may remember a time when this dialect was taught as "correct" speech. Some of us may continue to teach it as "correct."

I prefer to frame the argument with the question as to how we wish to speak, be understood, and be part of the theater profession. As a teacher, I make the case that we should all be able to reveal our own personalities and cultural heritage through our regional accents, but to also remember that the most important speech goal is communication. Does my accent prohibit people outside of my own region or culture from understanding me clearly? We know that some dialects bring out the prejudices of others in their impressions of the speaker's intelligence or education. Is this an issue I wish to address with my own dialect? If I wish to be part of the theater profession, am I confident that my regional accent will serve me in a vast array of characterizations? Or do I wish to learn Standard American dialect in order to allow myself a broader range of casting possibilities? As voice and speech teachers, we decide what our standards are, and whether our students need to learn Standard American dialect to enlarge their marketability in the profession. We've all had students that were amenable to this, and students who were not. For my part, I believe that we have to be honest with students about the difficulties of "being marketable" in the profession and teach them as many skills as possible, but we must be honest with ourselves that in the long run, the usage of "Standard American" is ultimately our students' choice. Although I believe we should direct them down a road of the least professional limitations, students ultimately choose what kind of actor they want to become. We can all name famous actors who have done very well in the profession capitalizing on their regionalisms. Their availability to be cast in a multitude of roles may have been limited, but for some actors, their regionalisms are part of their appeal, an appeal that they take all the way to the bank. Can anyone imagine Jimmy Stewart without that *voice?*

When advocating Standard American, I advocate using it as a dialect, useful for some productions of classic plays, as a "neutral zone" for dialect research, as a way of showing casting agents that your personal regionalisms don't necessarily spill over into your acting, or as a tool when directors ask the actors in their casts to use Standard speech. Within that context I teach about "code-switching," the art of using different kinds of speech for different situations. One method of celebrating diverse regionalisms in your class is to have your students "swap" one another's dialects; as they become proficient

in the skills of IPA and dialect research, they have the fun of learning how to speak like someone else in the class without mimicking or ridiculing them. And no one is left out of the loop because his or her speech is "incorrect."

When we consider diversity issues in our classroom climate, we also have to consider how the climate outside our classroom affects our students' lives. For those of us who work in theater departments in universities, we may wish to advocate for diversity activity within our department, as well. We can begin by advocating for the diversification of both our student body and our faculty. It's very well to successfully recruit minority students, but they must have a campus culture in which they can thrive. In a theater department's case, that means a department that includes minority professors, classes that include diverse subject matter, and a production season that includes plays by female and minority authors with female and minority characters. If you have few minority students in your department, consider placing a play by a minority author in your production season and recruit non-department students as actors and backstage personnel. Call on your University's Office of Multi-Cultural Affairs for help.

In recruiting students, consider programming workshops for area minority high school students, or use the concept of "service learning" within your curriculum, and have your students provide workshops to area schools as part of their class requirements. In recruiting faculty, volunteer to learn diversity strategies from your university Affirmative Action/Equal Opportunity office, or advocate for a faculty exchange with a Historically Black or Hispanic College or University. Your department can lobby its Dean to find funding for minority guest-artists, as well.

Affirmative Action is under attack in many areas of the United States, and public opinion regarding affirmative action and diversity initiatives is fueled both by the cultural history of our nation and myths regarding fairness in application procedures for universities. Diversity initiatives are often negatively labeled as "quotas," rather than the legal right of a university community to define its educational agenda and include the value of "cultural diversity" as part of that definition. Derek Bok and William G. Bowen's book *The Shape of the River* (Princeton University Press, 1998) catalogues research of 28 academically selective colleges and universities in regard to admissions practices, and how minority matriculants admitted under Affirmative Action policies in 1976 and 1989 fared academically, in the marketplace, and in their lives outside the world of work. It also includes data of students' impressions of the educational experience with "diversity." The authors' extensive research makes a stunning case for the viability of affirmative action policies, debunking myths of "preference" given to under-achieving minorities, and highlighting that Black matriculants of selective universities have gone on to be influential leaders in their professions and within their communities. It also makes a firm case that a diverse student body positively affects all students and creates an educational atmosphere that is important to the lives of students, furthering development of their potential as leaders and professionals.[3]

There are still "pipeline" problems concerning numbers of women and minorities in specific fields, but in my experience, the "pipeline" defense is often used within less problematic fields as an excuse not to use creative and active recruitment techniques. If we want to diversify our student population and our faculty, we will not do so using techniques that are "business as usual"—those practices have led us to where we are. There are many high-achieving women and minority students and faculty who will be recruited by institutions that choose the actions of diversity. The fields where the "pipeline" is "empty" might be well advised to look to the hostility of their work climate towards women and minorities as a reason for the "pipeline problem" in the first place.

As voice professionals, the skills we teach are inter-linked with the classroom or studio atmosphere we create. It is our choice whether we create an atmosphere that reflects our nation's demographics, and teach our students skills for life in a diverse culture. It is certain to take some work on our part, and we are bound to make mistakes, but an inclusive and diverse classroom environment yields great rewards for the study of voice, and the prospect of a national culture where everyone has "the right to speak."

2. This is current law, based on the deciding vote and legal opinion of Justice Lewis F. Powell, Jr. in the Supreme Court case of the Regents of University of California v. Bakke, in 1978. As of this writing, the Supreme Court has heard the case of Grutter v. Bollinger of the University of Michigan Law School and may rule on the Bakke decision in the near future.

3 Bowen, William G. and Derek Bok. *The Shape of the River*. Princeton, NJ: Princeton University Press. 1998

Resources on the Subject of Diversity & Campus Climate
Books:

Belenky, Mary Field, Blythe McViker Clinchy, Nancy Rule Goldberger, and Jill Mattuck Tarule. *Women's Ways of Knowing—The Development of Self, Voice, and Mind*, New York: Basic Books, Inc. 1986.

Bergmann, Barbara R. *In Defense of Affirmative Action.* New York: Basic Books, Inc. 1996.

Bowen, William G. and Derek Bok. *The Shape of the River—Long Term Consequences of Considering Race in College And University Admissions.* Princeton, NJ: Princeton University Press. 1998.

Cooper, Joanne E. and Dannelle D Stevens. *Tenure in the Sacred Grove Issues and Strategies for Women and Minority Faculty.* Albany, NY: State University of New York Press. 2002.

Light, Richard J. *Making the Most of College—Students Speak Their Minds.* Cambridge: Harvard University Press. 2001.

Paludi, Michele A. ed. *Sexual Harassment on College Campuses—Abusing the Ivory Power.* Albany, NY: State University of New York Press. 1996.

Sandler, Bernice, Lisa A. Silverberg, and Roberta M. Hall. *The Chilly Classroom Climate: A Guide to Improve The Education of Women.* Washington, DC: National Assoc. for Women in Education. 1996.

Schwartz, Bernard. Behind Bakke: *Affirmative Action and the Supreme Court.* New York: New York University Press. 1988.

Turner, Caroline Sotello Viernes. *Diversifying the Faculty—A Guidebook for Search Committees.* Washington, DC: Association of American Colleges and Universities. 2002.

West, Cornel. *Race Matters.* New York: Vintage Books. 1994.

Articles:

Sandler, Bernice R. "Subtle Ways in Which Men and Women May be Treated Differently." *About Women on Campus* Vol. 8, Number 3, Summer 1999.

Sandler, Bernice Resnick. "Women Faculty at Work in the Classroom, or, Why it Still Hurts to Be a Woman in Labor." Center for Women Policy Studies Washington, DC 1993.

Spangler, Mary S. and Cathleen Wixon. "Strategies to Achieve a Diverse Faculty and Staff." *American Association of Higher Education Bulletin* June 2000.

Wilson, Robin. "Stacking the Deck for Minority Candidates?" *The Chronicle of Higher Education* 12 July, 2002.

Essay *by Brennan Murphy*

40 Angry Women in a Room

The details now are a bit unfocused, but the emotional and visual memories of that meeting of voice tutors and coaches from London and nearby surrounding areas are imprinted deeply in my mind. That year, my Voice Studies class at the Central School of Speech and Drama had decided to do some preliminary work on starting an organization of voice professionals much like VASTA here in the United States. Once the meeting was underway, many of the participants did not want to discuss forming an association. They merely wanted to let off steam! Anger and frustration seemed to permeate the room. Many present described a profession that stuck them at the lower end in a collaborative process. Those who taught described teaching appointments that were both underpaid and under appreciated. It was an amazing moment for William Conacher, the other male in the room, and me. We both felt the sad and angry energy. The year was to be the beginning of my journey to become a voice specialist, and I didn't want to believe that my situation could end up bearing any resemblance to what I was hearing and seeing with this group. The meeting ended and I left, but the memories remain vivid. Five years later, I look back on those two hours and can relate to both the anger and the helplessness of those teachers…for I, too, have been there, done that.

My twenty years of prior professional work in New York City were filled with wonderful experiences and a unique sense of the importance of successful collaboration. I formed many important and lasting friendships, including a professional support system of directors, choreographers, actors, and teachers who work in all media: theatre, film and television. My years at the Yale School of Drama were the groundwork for honing my skills insofar as the collaborative process was concerned. I rely daily on the knowledge and skills I acquired there, and those years of training remain among some of my most satisfying memories. My production work over the course of twenty years has run the gamut—from acting and dancing on Broadway to covering myself with mud and performing for subway tokens in a Tribeca warehouse. This was long before the area below Canal Street had become fashionable. Sharing what I learned from those experiences with aspiring actors has been one of the prime goals of my teaching career. These experiences did not prepare me for the next few years!

After four years of teaching in two University theatre departments, I have now experienced something quite different. With a few exceptions, I have learned first-hand what it feels like to be on your own—professionally speaking. Our mission is to train actors for professional theatre, but my years of *doing* professional theatre did not seem to interest my colleagues. Often, they lacked professional courtesy and the ability to recognize the potential of voice and speech work both in training and production. I have always felt that voice work is acting work. Some of the best actor training I have received over the years has been from voice teachers, and I have been lucky enough to have worked with some of the best. A "let's break 'em down" mentality was strongly in use by some faculty in these institutions, and unfortunately it was also directed into the treatment of faculty with new ideas.

The fall of 2000 I was starting up my second year as the only teacher of voice and speech in a BFA/MFA program. That year my assignments were considerable: teaching eight courses while trying to accommodate other responsibilities including advising, coaching, and production work.

Brennan Murphy is the Head of Acting at California State University Sacramento. He received his MFA in Acting from the Yale School of Drama and a Postgraduate Degree in Voice Studies from London's Central School of Speech and Drama. Mr. Murphy has performed in dozens of stage productions ranging from Broadway venues to regional Shakespeare productions. National commercials, soaps, and numerous workshops of new plays and musicals have rounded out his acting career. Previous to this, Brennan was a professional dancer performing as a soloist with NYC's Joffrey II Dancers and the New York City Opera Ballet.

The e-mail arrived on the second day of class—the start of rehearsal for the department's first production. It was from the director and Chair of Acting telling me what accents he wanted the actors to use for their roles for his production. There followed a long list of various accents from New York/ Brooklyn to fourteenth century Northern English. As I sat in my office staring at the screen, I actually said aloud, "He never asked me to coach this production!" Surely, he had known he was directing this play for nine months, and I was furious that he was showing no consideration in dealing with me, both as a professional and colleague. The sad truth was that the thought of asking me to be the accent and voice coach on his production was, most likely, never an issue for him. It seems he had not thought of that, or of the fact that my research might be considerable and time-consuming.

This was perhaps the most thoughtless example of my treatment by fellow faculty and colleagues, but time was to show that it wouldn't be the only one. In four short years of teaching voice and speech at the university level, I have experienced a myriad of slights by directors and faculty. I have put in hours of coaching work without even the smallest "thank you" while the choreographer spent a mere two hours teaching a few steps for 16 bars of music. His contribution was rewarded by having his name on the production page of the program just under the director's name.

There were several productions where I logged in hours of work with problem students to get them to use their voices in a safe and healthy manner. As I observed them over time, I realized my efforts had been in vain as they destroyed their fragile instruments screaming in rehearsals at the director's encouragement. On one production, a professional Chicago guest director, blissfully ignorant, assumed I could make her cast, many not my students, speak in Standard American (Good American Speech) in a few hours. And, of course, there were the faculty directors that fancied themselves voice teachers; and, in a very non-collaborative fashion, repudiated everything I was teaching in class having to do with relaxation, alignment, and breath. I thought if I heard one more male acting teacher or director tell a female actor to lower her voice (without any idea of how to accomplish it in a healthy manner) I would go running from the building straight to the looney bin!

Yes, there were meetings (often in hallways) with teachers and directors as they gave me their list of the actor's voice problems, telling me to get the student actor on track, with little or no idea of what was required to achieve the result. They simply did not understand.

After four years I had become one of the angry, one of the disillusioned—and a kindred spirit with those 40 women. As the memory of that meeting in London exercised my mind, I decided to seek answers from the people I was training my students to work for, and with: professional directors, professional voice coaches, and professional actors. I wanted to know what "professionals" think of voice support in production. When did they use voice support? How did they work with directors? How easy or difficult was it for them to implement what they had learned about voice training while they were working as actors? I needed to go beyond the liberal arts teachers and talk directly to the professionals to see how the training was being implemented in rehearsals. I hoped that with this knowledge I could create a practical system that would work in both the classroom and production. Through the years, I have taught my actors to go for their objective and to get their focus on their partner. Perhaps this wasn't such a bad idea for me, as well.

Anne Bogart is a direct, friendly, no-nonsense woman. While having dinner with her and a group of friends one evening, I was struck with her ability to put people at ease. She was interesting because she was so interested in every other person at that table. She asked questions that created lively and dynamic conversation. That evening Anne was the guest of honor and yet she made all attending feel honored. Perhaps it was this experience that made her name come to mind immediately when I commenced my project.

"It's the first thing you don't get" was her immediate response to voice support in production. "For me it's a luxury that comes at the end of a long list." She described a typical situation where budget constraints have made her not consider a voice coach in order to employ a sound designer on most of her productions. She did mention a very good working relationship with Bonnie Raphael and talked about the benefits of having voice staff at some of the theatre companies where she has directed.

As our conversation concluded, Anne said something that has remained with me, "The best coach is the room." It made me think of Patsy Rodenburg as she worked with a group of international voice teachers, of which I was one, on the stages of the Old Vic and the National Theatre's Olivier Theatre. As we stood on those stages, Patsy talked about "breathing the space." Ms. Bogart's comment seemed to live in that same world. Even if a voice coach is not part of her collaborative process, the comment makes me wonder what type of creative spirit she would want in her rehearsal.

Daniel Sullivan, the Tony Award-winning director, discussed when he felt voice support was not necessary to his process. "I would not use it at, let's say, the Mitzi Newhouse if I was working on a contemporary piece and the actors working have a similarity of vocal prowess." He quickly continued, "But I think it is always necessary when doing Shakespeare so that the instruments are at an equal level of skill—where breath control and vocal energy are expected." His views struck me as very practical. "Usually when directing Shakespeare I find I have a mix of experienced actors and kids who don't have the same instruments. I need the voice coach to get the less skilled up to the level of the actors with more experience." As he developed that thought, he finished by saying that he feels this way about any classic play. He was soon going into rehearsals for *Major Barbara* in New York City and mentioned that he would certainly have voice support on that production.

As he described his process, I began to get excited. "Working with voice people is the same as working with designers and actors—for me the process is the same. At the table reading you get a sense of who knows how to move through the verse. So the two of us meet and we discuss who needs help and what kind of vocal exercises for the whole company and what specific work is needed with individuals. I will then talk with the actor and tell him I think he needs a specific kind of work and the voice person will take it from there." His words had a profound effect on me and I wondered why I had not had this kind of conversation with any director in an academic situation before.

I thought it especially heartening to hear his views on scansion and prosody. My teaching experience had been in situations in which the acting faculty didn't spend more than a class period, if that, discussing the structure of Shakespeare's poetry. Mr. Sullivan believes that too many young actors come out of training programs and don't know the art of even simple scansion. "Basically, scansion is the structure of the music and, yes, it is interpretive, but I feel that unless you know it in all its permutations, you really can't do Shakespeare. I want the scansion from actors when we sit down. Rehearsal here in this country is too short to have to teach it."

He ended our lengthy conversation with: "I will be as clear as I possibly can be, you be too and then—just go out and do what you do." I was beginning to feel that maybe, just maybe, I had finally found both clarity and collaboration.

Moving ahead, I was eager to learn how voice specialists' experiences would compare to the directors I had interviewed. Among the latter group, there were many whose work I admired, and Barbara Somerville was one of those. She had been my coach for several productions and I had first-hand

knowledge of her methods. Her work credentials in voice and speech, both professional and academic, are exemplary. The list of directors and actors she has worked with is a "Who's Who" of current American theatre. I remembered how articulate and precise she was and hoped she'd bring that same insightfulness to my questions. I was not disappointed.

"My best experience? Well, I've had so many" was the first thing she said. "Let me talk in general terms. It's always best when a director knows my capabilities and respects me, and gives me the time to do the work…and a good stage manager, who communicates every day and works coaching into the production schedule, is essential." She mentioned several directors with whom she has had a great working relationship. Barbara talked about her experience working with Lloyd Richards on several of August Wilson's plays. "He always set goals," she said. "He was clear about what he needed from the actor and he was open to my work and how I would get the actor there. He trusted me."

"Stan Wodjewodski, Jr, is another director who collaborates particularly generously with accent and text coaches, and shows appreciation for how coaches can enhance a production. Arvin Brown, John Tillinger, David Chambers, Walter Dallas, Seret Scott, Richard Hamburger, Oleg Yefremov, Jose Quintero, Liz Diamond, Ralph Lemon—these and many more directors I've worked with have treated me as a peer. Directors who work well with coaches have confidence in their own effectiveness. They tend to work with coaches they know well, and have worked with before. All of these factors seem to eliminate any fear that the coach may affect the actor adversely."

Barbara revealed that professional experiences that were not golden usually resulted when she was not given sufficient time to prepare and/or time to work with the actors. Although in reminiscing, she didn't play up the negative, she did mention a common experience—one where a director wants perfect accents but is unwilling to apportion the time for her to coach or give notes.

Towards the end of the interview she made the comment: "You know, the good directors I've worked with consider skill and talent when they cast. They cast actors that have the ability to do the work." (At this point, I remembered my interview with Daniel Sullivan.) "Some theatre people are unaware that voice and speech work in production is a design process. You need time to collect your resources and do your work." She laughed when she detailed an incident where the director needed her to teach an actor twelve different accents for a particular speech." He wanted that accomplished "Tomorrow! With half an hour scheduled to do it in! These people are in the minority," she admitted. "But have you ever heard a director tell a designer to have a costume ready tomorrow with no fabric or measurements; or that the shop will only be allowed half an hour to build it? It comes down to respect…that kind of analogy is shocking, but I know it happens with this work all the time."

When I asked her what a teacher/coach in an academic production should expect, Barbara got down to "nuts and bolts." "As a minimum? That's simple," she responded. "They must be provided with the script early, and they should be consulted by the director long before the first rehearsal. The director has to give you a sense of what he needs and time for you to get your work done. This is common sense and courtesy. Academic directors as well as professional directors need to consider the actor's training and skills. If an actor hasn't studied accents or Shakespeare yet, avoid casting them in roles that require those skills if at all possible. Both the student and the director can become very frustrated if they try to cram a year's worth of learning into four to six weeks."

Finally, Barbara added, "Work to get the voice and speech coach's name credited on the production page of the program. At Yale Rep, Stan Wojewodski, Jr. insisted to management that this was 'only equitable', and I entirely agree with him."

Barbara, who no longer teaches at the Yale School of Drama, admits that it takes time to develop and train a faculty to provide these essential resources. I do know that she was able to get the Yale Repertory Theatre to consider budget for voice and speech in their production costs. Through her guidance, the company began to factor her time and costs into their production schedule and budget. It was great to know that Stan Wojewodski, Jr., Artistic Director, and Victoria Nolan, Managing Director, backed her in this project.

My next source of inspiration was Christine Adaire, a professional voice coach with whom I've worked closely over the last several years. Since my experiences working with her were so positive, I knew she could help me with my research. Christine is a highly respected teacher, professional actress, and a current member of Shakespeare and Company, heading up the voice area of their summer training program. When we spoke, she had just finished directing *King John* for Shakespeare and Company at their Lenox home.

As she talked about directing *King John,* Christine became very animated as she related just how exciting the experience was. "When I'm directing I am very language based, and with this production I had Margaret Janson as the voice coach…we were both 'on the same page' and we had young actors who

needed lots of work. It was a very clear and strong production reinforced by critics and audience alike. All that voice work really paid off."

I was impressed with her comment that she had never had a negative experience in her voice coaching work. She did mention, though: "I will say that the work is less satisfying when I am brought in to be the voice and speech police. Some directors want that…final consonants, clarity…just being an ear. I remember one experience when the director thought I was giving acting notes. If I were to work successfully with that director, I knew I had to find a way of putting the acting notes in voice terms. Let's face it…some directors are threatened by voice coaches."

My personal experience has been that the vocal clarity comes through clear and specific acting choices; and, Christine seemed to concur. "If I can't hear someone…yes, it's often about clarity…but the actor is probably not clear about what they are doing or saying at that moment."

When I asked her what coaching experiences topped her list, without skipping a beat, she replied: "Joanne Akalaitis! It was her *Iphigenia Cycle.* That production played both in Chicago and New York in the late nineties." What she described was a wonderful collaboration of the sort that usually seems to come only after years of working together. "She made me feel like I was part of the creative process. It was Greek…really big emotion…and with a chorus. This was set to music with a composer, and together we created their particular sound. It was very musical and rhythmic."

What my research has shown me is that coaches are in agreement about what works, and Christine was eager to share her views. "Joanne always gave me respect and authority in rehearsal. She always rallied the cast, reinforcing the importance of voice work in the production. Each rehearsal began with Joanne leading a physical warm-up and I would be the leader of the voice work."

Christine described an academic situation where cooperation helped her attain her vocal goals for the production. "I have always had the authority and respect of the actors because I have trained them and we share the same language. In a training situation, I am concerned much more with process…so I will give notes to a student actor that I might not stress as much with professional actors that I will only spend a few weeks with." After having worked with Christine for a month in June of 2001 at the Shakespeare Intensive, I can vouch for her enthusiasm and leadership in working with young actors.

I wondered what type of actor I should talk with concerning my research, and my indecisiveness became a dilemma. My criteria centered around my need to talk with a professional who had a career mainly on stage with a focus on literate language plays. I called Michael Cumpsty and he agreed to talk with me about his career and experience with voice support in production.

Michael has established a solid career as a New York actor. In his short time there, he has performed in seven Shakespeare plays at the New York Shakespeare Festival, including the title character in *Timon of Athens*. He has appeared in nine Broadway productions; and, in plays by David Hare, Brian Friel, and Tom Stoppard, to name a few. At the time this article was written, Michael was starring in the revival of *42nd Street* after a lengthy run in the Tony Award-winning *Copenhagen*. In addition, he has appeared frequently on television and film, and he often lends his voice to recording books on tape.

"Recently I have not worked much with voice coaches in any production unless the show is heavy with accents" was his first response. "They rarely seem to bring in voice support in commercial theatre. At least, in the productions I've worked on."

"However at the Public Theatre they certainly use voice coaching in terms of verse speaking and text work." He went on to describe a situation similar to the one described by Daniel Sullivan—a company of many different abilities and the necessity of getting everyone on the same page in regard to voice and text work. "At the Public, the head dramaturg will often do the text work on a production."

The conversation eventually headed towards the subject of his past experiences working with voice coaches during rehearsal. "My history is that I often felt they were giving me their preferred acting choice or line reading." As I questioned him about this comment, he said that he felt it was intrusive and that he was not far enough along in his own acting process to take on these suggestions. "Perhaps if it had happened later in the rehearsal process I might have been more responsive."

"I certainly am not against this kind of work. There are times directors are hired because they are talented and creative…the latest thing…but they aren't always deeply knowledgeable about text. When this is the case, it is imperative that there is someone to guide the actor into the text. So a voice coach that is familiar with the text, that has clarity of the text and who knows his/her function is essential. I have worked with some great ones."

Michael was equally candid in talking about his training: "It's rather checkered" was his comment. "Both enriching and

unsatisfying—Cicely Berry would come every year for a month (University of North Carolina at Chapel Hill) which was thrilling. But she would leave and we would not get a regular arduous practice that would allow a healthy process to assimilate over a long time. I had a good idea of how to do things correctly but not a good mechanism. Singing has really helped me understand the mechanism."

As our conversation wound down, Michael stated simply: "I've learned a lot on the job. It really is simple, isn't it…but the assimilation can take years."

Patsy Rodenburg often talks about the value of apprenticeship. True apprenticeship is sorely lacking in the training of theatre teachers today. Over the last several years, since I started teaching, I've tried to create for myself an apprenticeship through consulting with, and being mentored by, experienced and respected teachers. In these last months, and in the course of writing this article, I've attempted to follow a similar apprenticeship in my voice coaching. As I ruminated over the many talks I had had, in order to acquire material, I realized that my interviewees all spoke the same language and stressed the basics…respect, time, collaboration, clarity, authority, and specificity. What rings clear is our common goal, i.e., a professional situation where we can work effectively and creatively on a production while honoring the director's vision at the same time.

It seems clear that our job as coach and teacher begins with our articulation of what *we* need and what *we* expect to accomplish. We must accept the fact that we will not always be working with people who understand what we do, or who know how to effectively incorporate coaching into the production process.

I've never participated in a discussion (even at Central School) where a group of voice coaches identified what they would wish for, or need, in order to work more effectively. Last year I attempted to begin a discussion on VastaVox that pertained to pre-production and voice support. Although I did get a few wonderful responses, for the most part, it seemed to fizzle quite early on. I'd like to suggest a list of basic guidelines that coaches may suggest (or require) when working in a production situation.

• The director must ask for voice/text/accent support on the production. The coach shouldn't assume s/he is coaching for a production unless directly asked to do so by the director. This pertains more to voice teachers in training programs that have a production season.

• Coaches must be provided with a script at least one month before the production begins rehearsal. If accent coaching is required, a script must be provided six weeks before rehearsals begin.

- A meeting should be scheduled with the director several weeks before the first rehearsal in order to discuss his vocal, text, and accent ideas for the show. The director should consider human sound as s/he would any other design aspect. The coach and director should also discuss the exact accent requirements, and the social, economic, regional, and educational differences of the characters. This is also a wonderful opportunity for the voice coach to inform the director of the importance and benefit of text coaching. Some directors may not realize the voice coach's expertise in this area. The job of voice coach will not be to interfere with the director's work but will, in fact, enhance it. Text coaching should be an essential part of production in training programs, whenever possible.

- If there are accent requirements, the director should be encouraged to consider actors' voices and flexibility with accents when casting. The coach might volunteer to listen to people or lead exercises as part of the callback process. The director should feel comfortable asking the coach if an actor being considered for a role will be capable of fulfilling the voice or accent demands.

- At the first rehearsal, along with the other designers, the voice/text and/or accent coach must be allotted time to introduce the voice concept/design to the actors. The director and stage manager must make it clear at first rehearsal that all voice, text, and accent sessions are rehearsal calls. Actors must not miss appointments or be late. This is also the time for the coach to explain how s/he will work with actors on text.

- After the first read-through, the director and coach should meet again to discuss the actors' individual voice, text, and accent needs. Coach and director should continue to communicate frequently throughout the rehearsal process. Both the director and the coach may tell the stage manager which of the actors need coaching time and set priorities. The coach should give the stage manager a schedule of his or her available time a few days to a week in advance of regular production scheduling. The stage manager then sets up appointments for the designated actors within the time frames given by the coach. The stage manager is responsible for reserving a room for coaching which is clean, quiet, and as near as possible to the rehearsal space. The stage manager and the coach need to communicate often—preferably on a daily basis.

- Stage management is responsible for all photocopying and dubbing of tapes. These expenses should be included in the production budget.

- Actors who will be required to work on accents must own a small cassette player/recorder with earphones that accepts standard sized cassettes. (Student actors should generally be required to own or purchase a tape player and recorder. This comes under the heading of "supplies" in academic programs where student actors are required to own or purchase textbooks, supplies, rehearsal shoes, rehearsal skirts and jackets, and stage makeup.)

- Once the play is cast, the accent coach should supply tapes and sheets and start working on the accents with actors before the first rehearsal. Most professional actors like to work this way so they are comfortable with the accent before the first rehearsal.

The preceding list may seem laughably obvious to some of you, yet how many of you have been in a situation where these needs were not made clear? I am always after my student actors to be specific in their work; and, in retrospect, I now see that I have been particularly *non-specific* in my work as a voice coach. Looking back, it seems that I have directed most of my energy trying to fit the needs of the director while subjugating what I needed to do the job well. I can only partly blame the dysfunction on the various departments I worked in. I needed to be guided and mentored; unfortunately, there was not the time or the means for that to happen.

Nancy Houfek with assistance from Lynn Watson and Linda de Vries have prepared a wonderful and detailed document for the VASTA web-site entitled, *How to Use a Vocal Coach: A Practical Guide for Directors*. I discovered this, with the help of Rocco Dal Vera, a few years after my personal journey began. It is a terrific guide, detailed and insightful. My list represents the "growing pains" involved in my personal education—the one that laid the foundation of my standards, learned first-hand from several falls and stumbles.

I often wonder where those forty women are today. Perhaps some have traveled the same road as I, learning from their mistakes and acquiring the skills to create a better working environment for themselves. By turning anger and frustration into action, I found inspiration, and my teaching and coaching have improved dramatically. By giving voice to my feelings and finding a clear direction I have been able to articulate my needs without anger or fear. It feels great!

Heightened Text, Verse and Scansion *David Carey and Rena Cook, Associate Editors*

Heightened Text, Verse and Scansion *David Carey and Rena Cook*
Associate Editors

David Carey is Principal Lecturer in Voice Studies at the Central School of Speech and Drama, London, and Course Leader for the School's MA/Postgraduate Diploma in Voice Studies. He trained in Speech and Drama at the Royal Scottish Academy of Music and Drama in Glasgow, and has been awarded degrees in English Language and Linguistics from both Edinburgh University and Reading University. A voice teacher for over 25 years, David has worked extensively at both undergraduate and postgraduate level. His work in the professional theatre includes 4 years as assistant to Cicely Berry at the Royal Shakespeare Company during the 1980s.

Rena Cook is on the faculty at University of Oklahoma where she teaches Voice and Acting. She has served as vocal coach for the Illinois Shakespeare Festival on *The Merry Wives of Windsor, Richard III*, and *Wild Oats*. She has directed *Dancing at Lughnasa, The Prime of Miss Jean Brodie* and *Medea*. Rena holds an MA in Voice Studies from the Central School of Speech and Drama. Her theatrical reviews have appeared in *The Journal of Dramatic Theory and Criticism* and *Theatre Journal*.

Welcome to the Heightened Text, Verse and Scansion section of the Review! You will find here a rich *pot-pourri* of academic scholarship, practical research and informed wisdom about the vitality of poetic language and classical text. When so much of our language is reduced to the functionality of platitudes and "e-speak", or is inflated to the empty rhetoric of politics, it is invigorating to be reminded of the real depth and power of our linguistic potential. Many of the authors represented in this section write about Shakespeare, perhaps because, as Cicely Berry says in her interview, "Shakespeare catches people's inner need to speak." Or, as Patsy Rodenburg suggests in hers, "Shakespeare asks us to go beyond ourselves, to be better." I hope you will find much inspiration in these articles—inspiration to speak, to teach, and to go beyond yourself.

My thanks and appreciation to my editorial colleague, Rena Cook, for her guidance and encouragement—both to our authors and to her co-editor!

David Carey

Rhetoric Revisited

Dr. Jacqueline Martin is Head of Theatre and Teaching Studies at the Academy of the Arts, Queensland University of Technology. She is author of *Voice in Modern Theatre* (1991) and *Understanding Theatre: Performance Analysis in Theory and Practice* (1995). Her professional and academic career includes, Voice teacher at the National Institute of Dramatic Art, Australia and Associate Professor of Theatre Studies, Stockholm University. She has conducted master classes in Voice Pedagogy and Multidisciplinary approaches to Actor Training for the European League of Institutes of the Arts in Amsterdam and Berlin. She is an elected executive member of the Federation for International Theatre Research, where she is co-working on a forthcoming book about the Theatrical Event.

In this column I want to address the very delicate matter of female vocality. What is it that has contributed to the feminine ideal in our contemporary society and how does this influence the "ideal" to which our young actors and speakers aspire? I will be examining the myths surrounding femininity both past and present as well as the influence which the media has had and continues to exert on notions of femininity particularly where the voice is concerned.

We cannot deny the influence of our traditions and our cultural heritage. Cultural memory is, however, long and insidious. Many of the images of "the female" in today's society—the bitch, the witch, the vamp, the virgin, the diva, the divine, to name but a few—have their origins in classical mythology. It is worth asking to what end our cultural memory of Medusa, the Gorgons, or the Sirens have grounded the myths surrounding contemporary images of women? What is perhaps not always so obvious is that they have become linked with culturally encoded voice types which are signified by the moaning, the groaning, the wailing and lamentation of these classical figures.

The female actor's voice is anchored in the female body, which Josette Feral has reminded us about in a keynote speech at the XIV Federation for International Theatre Research World Congress in Amsterdam, on the theme of Theatre and Cultural Memory: The Event between Past and Future, (30 June-July 6, 2002) "Theatre is memory: the memory of text, of place, of actions…the memory of the body." We reflect back on the past and project the images on to the present. This is encoded in our reflections on female vocality usually associated with great female characters from the classics, whether it be an outraged Clytemnestra, welcoming Agamemnon back from the wars, a Medea upbraiding Jason for his infidelity, or a Lady Macbeth lamenting the cowardliness of her husband as he hesitates before killing Duncan. We have come to associate certain voice types with certain people, certain actions and certain emotions. Whether these myths are real or imaginary makes little difference to the impact which has been part of our cultural heritage.

From the discipline of rhetoric we learn of the importance of *ethos* (the speaker's bearing) and *pathos* (strong or rising feelings), of *imitatio* (imitation of suitable ideals or models) and *pronuntiatio* (a suitable delivery with maximum intended effect). There is no doubt that during the twentieth century the role of women in society has changed dramatically, particularly since World War II when women were needed in the workforce while the men were away at the front. This was encaptured in the popular media at the time—in particular on radio and film, but also in advertising, where all the rhetorical devices mentioned above were affected by women's new role in society. Since the 1950s women were seen to hang up their aprons and as the introduction of the pill allowed more sexual liberation the "feminine vocal ideal" became that of the woman of the world, manifested by an accompanying lower vocal pitch.

There followed an equation that the deeper the voice the more liberated young women were, the pursuit of which has often had damaging effects on their voices. How do young female actors in training deal with these vocal demands? Particularly the ones with "small" voices? It has often been problematic in my experience, working with young female actors, that as voice training methods endeavour to "root the voice in the body" and there is a continuous imperative to deepen the voice, that this practice can often result in "forced" tones which belie the personal identity of the speaker. In addition the vocal range of the voice becomes restricted together with the emotional range. The result is often that of an unfeeling, psychologically limited character as the symbiosis between inner and outer is not allowed to happen. As a result images of contemporary women on the Western stage are in most cases rather dull.

The size of the open-air theatres of the past demanded a training which opened up both body and voice, with the result that the vocal delivery was also extended. This has been admirably treated in the previous edition of *The Voice and Speech Review. The Voice in Violence* in an article "Vocal Clarity in the Outdoor Theatre" by Kate Foy and Paul Meier (pp.210-222). However, training the voice for psychological realism on stage, as well as for television and film, does not open up the voice in the same way, and contemporary theatre, compared with the classical, prioritizes the visual over the aural. We no longer can uphold Quintillian's observation that:

> Delivery, known as *actio,* derives from voice and gesture, one appeals to the ear and the other to the eye, through which impressions find their way to the mind, but the mind must obey the voice, and gesture conform to it (*The Institutio Oratoria*, Book IV, pp249ff).

Edith Clever's Clytemnestra in Peter Stein's famous production of *The Oresteia* in Berlin (1980) certainly had no problems coping with the size of the Schaubuhne. Hers was a classic example of a voice trained for performing on stage. However, it was extremely low-pitched. As I recorded in *Voice in Modern Theatre* (1991:117)

> …she seemed to dredge her voice up from the depths of her soul—yet it throbbed with fire and the words were spat out with a diction as clear as the image which she created on her first entrance, standing dwarfed within the framework of a gigantic door, a diminutive figure of a waiting wife, who was also a force to be reckoned with. This was confirmed later in the production as she took her revenge by mutilating the bodies of Agamemnon and Cassandra.

A similar case was recorded from a masterclass in multidisciplinary approaches to acting I co-ordinated for the European League of Institutes of the Arts (ELIA) in Amsterdam and Berlin (1994) with a group of twelve young actors from a range of drama schools in the European Union. The text we worked on was Heiner Muller's *Mediamaterial.* With voice

specialists such as Kristin Linklater and Cicely Berry conducting classes and an East German director, Angelika Waller, together with movement specialists from the Berliner Ensemble, the stage was set for some exciting exploration of voice, body and action. The young German student actor from the Ernst Busch school had the same approach to vocal delivery in the role of Medea as Edith Clever did. The voice was extremely low-pitched and forced. This was very pronounced by comparison with the pitch ranges of the young student actors from Central School of Speech and Drama (London) and from Estonia who also performed the role of Medea. What was interesting was of course the approach to acting from the German school, which followed a Brechtian dialectic, as opposed to a more psychological Stanislavskian approach adapted by the English and Estonian Medeas. This said such a lot about the role of women in society in these different countries and their inherent cultural heritage. (See ELIA publication, 1994 Masterclass on Theatre: Towards a Multidisciplinary Approach to Acting, Amsterdam).

More of a middle way was evident in the vocal delivery of Viveka Seldahl as Lady Macbeth in a production of *Macbeth* at the Stockholm City Theatre (1992), where she combined a sensuousness not often seen in this role, both physically as well as vocally. This character was very much a woman of our times nagging her husband. The voice was never forced into a "histrionic" register, neither was it too light and internal for good stage delivery and emotional range.

As we see in all these examples at the theatre we appraise the character from the voice type and as audience subconsciously place them in a role which their use of *ethos, pathos, imitatio,* and *pronuntiatio* creates. The vocal ideal seems to be a culturally-dependent one.

So I return to my question regarding female vocality and the feminine ideal in our contemporary society, and conclude that what influences our young actors and speakers today is constructed from what the media presents to society at large. The media dictates the ideals, the types, the myths, which our young actors aspire to, and the media is as insidious as our cultural memory. Still the training of voices seems focussed on naturalism and performing for television and film. The difficulty then for the contemporary female actor to exercise *persuasio* in dealing with heightened language and verse, and convince the contemporary audience, is one of trying to marry the norms of contemporary behaviour with a memory of the figures from classical mythology, as well as a memory of their own culture, without the technical skills to do so, which often results in an ill-fit—particularly where effective vocality is concerned.

Speaking Shakespeare's Last Plays

Rebecca Clark Carey is a voice and text director and resident actor/teacher at the Oregon Shakespeare Festival. She has an MA with distinction in voice studies from The Central School of Speech and Drama, an MFA in acting from UC Irvine, and a BA in history and literature from Harvard University. As an actress she has worked with the California Shakespeare Festival, Shakespeare Santa Cruz, South Coast Repertory, San Jose Stage Company, and Cornerstone Theater Company.

Introduction

The inspiration for this investigation into Shakespeare's late works came from attending three of his earliest plays, the *Henry VIs*, performed by the Royal Shakespeare Company at the Young Vic in London, over the course of a week. One of the most exciting aspects of this experience was watching and hearing the young Shakespeare grow in his ability to manipulate language to maximize its expressiveness. It made quite vivid to me the fact that Shakespeare continued to make significant stylistic advancements throughout his career; no aspect of his playwriting remained static. This development is widely analyzed by literary scholars but not much discussed in the practitioner literature. I thus became interested in exploring what implications Shakespeare's evolution might have for actors of his plays and for the voice and text coach who works with them.

In deference to the demands of practicality, however, I have not taken on the entirety of Shakespeare's career, but rather will focus on his late plays, which represent both the culmination of his work and some of the most technically complex language he ever penned. In his introduction to the Arden edition of *The Winter's Tale*, J.H.P. Pafford (1978) quotes A.C. Bradley (1904) as saying of Shakespeare's last plays:

> [T]he style, in the more emotional passages, is heightened. It becomes grander, sometimes wilder, sometimes more swelling, even tumid. It is also more concentrated, rapid, varied, and, in construction, less regular, not seldom twisted or elliptical. It is, therefore, not so easy and lucid, and in the more ordinary dialogue, it is sometimes involved and obscure (Bradley: 88-9).

Such language would seem to present very particular difficulties to the actor who speaks it. In response, I formulated my central question: how can the voice and text coach help actors to meet the challenges posed by the language of Shakespeare's late plays? Specifically, I studied the Romances: *Cymbeline, The Winter's Tale* and *The Tempest*. I did not bring *Pericles* into consideration because the authorship of much of the text is debated.

In her book, *Vocal Direction for the Theatre* (1993), Nan Withers-Wilson writes, "The work of the vocal director begins with text analysis; first to study the language of the play and, secondly, to determine the major voice and speech challenges that the play's language will present in production" (29). Taking this as my mandate, I first identified elements of these plays that are characteristic of this period of Shakespeare's writing, and then determined which ones might make more difficult the actor's job of clear and powerful communication. The three on which I will focus in this article are: enjambment (when thoughts do not end with the verse line), irregular metre (which certainly appears in the earlier plays, but is more prevalent in the later), and dense images and convoluted syntax. Each of these distinguishing elements was selected for study because it poses a practical challenge that calls specifically upon the skills of the voice and text coach. I then collected from the writings of leading teachers and directors thoughts and exercises that might be applicable to these issues. This research informed the design of a series of workshops on the late plays I conducted with student actors at The Central School of Speech and Drama in the summer term of 2001. To further investigate the question of how to help actors meet the challenges of Shakespeare's late plays, I conducted interviews with professional voice and text coaches. In this article, I will describe my research methodology, present a brief review of the relevant literature, and summarise my findings from the workshops and interviews.

Methodology and Methods

This project was designed as a piece of qualitative research in the "reflective practitioner" model (Schon 1993). I used three means of gathering data. I took notes during my workshops both on what I saw happening and on the students' comments. At the end of each workshop, I also asked the students to complete feedback forms. The interviews with professional coaches provided additional insight into the question of how to help actors approach Shakespeare's late plays.

In discussing the case study, R. Yin (1994) writes, "...the investigator's goal is to expand and generalize theories (analytic generalization) and not to enumerate frequencies (statistical generalization)" (10). In analyzing the data I have collected, I have adopted this goal. I do not presume that another teacher or coach using the same exercises with another group would duplicate my results. Instead, I aim to offer informed reflections on what kinds of work on the language of the Romance plays can yield fruitful results for the coach and actor.

There are, of course, important differences between the work I did teaching workshops to students and the work of coaching professional actors. In conclusion, however, I will show that in both instances, work which explores very specifically the structure of the language in Shakespeare's late plays can be important in helping the actor fulfill his charge to use that language effectively to pursue and communicate the intentions of his character.

Review of the Literature

My investigation into the language of Shakespeare's late plays involves the study of two genres of literature. The first is academic: works that analyze the language, plots, and themes of the plays. The second is practical: books and articles by teachers, voice specialists, and directors on speaking Shakespeare. The academic literature is useful in identifying distinguishing characteristics of the Romance plays; the practical is helpful in preparing to explore them with actors or students.

In the analytic literature surrounding the language of Shakespeare's last plays, there are several characteristics that are mentioned quite frequently. In my survey, I found the

foremost to be high instances of enjambment, irregular meter, and very dense language. Each is of interest not only to students, but also to speakers of Shakespeare.

In dating the plays, scholars look at, among other external and internal evidence, Shakespeare's "metrical development" (Evans 1974:47). An important trend in his writing is the move away from end-stopped lines to thoughts that run past the ends of the verse lines. In the early plays, fourteen percent of lines are enjambed, whereas in the late plays, the percentage is forty-one (Levin 1974:12). Run-on-lines are cited in the introduction to the Arden edition of *Cymbeline* as being a marked characteristic of Shakespeare's late style (Nosworthy 1991:lxii), and Frank Kermode (2000) writes of finding a "refusal of end-stopped lines" in *The Tempest* (288). This significant shift in the relationship between content and form will inevitably have an effect on the actor who speaks those lines.

Another aspect of metrical development that is examined in dating the plays is Shakespeare's use of iambic pentameter. One distinguishing feature of the Romances is a high instance of feminine endings. Thirty-five percent of the lines in the latest plays end with this eleventh syllable, as opposed to five percent in the earliest (Levin 1974:12). Furthermore, the verse in the late plays is marked by what Kermode (2000) calls "a rougher handling of the pentameter" (17). The heartbeat, as it were, is not nearly as regular. Kermode (1983) uses the phrase "artificially natural" to describe Shakespeare's use of irregular meter to capture the idiosyncratic rhythms of real speech (lxxix). Meter, of course, actually exists only in spoken language, and so these developments are ultimately manifest, more or less successfully, when the plays are performed.

Less quantifiable than metrical development, but also a remarkable aspect of Shakespeare's evolution, is the increasing density and complexity of his language. R.A. Foakes (1971) writes of the last plays, "...the speed of the action as well as the rapidity of thought and the vehemence of passion combine to produce imagery of extraordinary compression and of a surprising blend of elements" (224). This compression takes the form of sentence fragments, confusing syntax, word omissions, convoluted images, and undeveloped metaphors. These devices can make the language very difficult to follow. Indeed, Kermode (2000) writes, "Sometimes it seems that Shakespeare, in these latter years, is simply defying his audience, not caring to have them as fellows in understanding" (312). Occasionally in modern editions of the late plays, editors will note that they are unable to make totally clear the meaning of certain lines. The actor, however, must find a way to make some kind of sense of this compact and sometimes bewildering language.

Turning to the practice-oriented writings of leading coaches and directors, we find there is relatively little discussion of how plays from different periods of Shakespeare's career might present different kinds of challenges to the actor. For the most part, those practitioners writing about Shakespeare from a practical point of view treat his plays as a body of work rather than discussing the particular characteristics of different genres or periods. When they do address the late plays specifically, it is usually to point out the expressive power of the "metrical development" we have seen described by the academics. For example, Kristin Linklater (1992) remarks of one of Leontes' speeches, "By the time *The Winter's Tale* was written, Shakespeare was as likely to communicate emotional content in erratic rhythms of verse as in imagery and passionate language" (136). In examining such aspects of the language, the practitioners are usually concerned with how the actor can harness their expressive power.

Of the three characteristics of the late plays that I have chosen to investigate, the one that receives the most attention in the practitioner literature is enjambment. There is a general agreement that when speaking a run-on line, neither the line ending nor the arc of the thought can be ignored. There is, however, a slight difference of emphasis. Among directors, John Barton (1984) argues that natural speech is full of ungrammatical pauses and run-ons, which Shakespeare has captured in the verse structure of the late plays, and so the actor should generally phrase with the verse line (35). Dakin Matthews (1995), on the other hand, feels that Shakespeare liberated "line bound" dramatic poetry, and by the end of his career the "linguistic integrity" of the line was much less important than the syncopation of "grammatical or rhetorical counterpointing" (103). His fellow American, Robert Cohen, believes that there should be no more than a "split second" holding of the last syllable of an enjambed line, leading quickly into "a liaison from it into the first syllable of the next line" (152).

Among voice teachers, Linklater (1992) strongly agrees with Barton that particular care must be taken at the end of the line (160), while Cicely Berry gives more attention to the necessity of preserving the force and clarity of the run-on thought (1992:85) and finding the "organic drive of the verse" (2001:158). Neither, however, is absolute or dogmatic. Linklater (1992) captures the prevailing ethos in her suggestion that when Shakespeare uses this device we should always question: "*Why* does the emotion switch suddenly in the middle of a line and then apparently run on for three more lines without punctuation? *Why* is that little weak word at the end of a line? What do these patterns reveal about the character's inner state?" (155).

In discussing meter, there is a similar consensus among many practitioners that irregularities call for a close examination of the text. Barton (1984) speaks of changes in the iambic pentameter as "hidden direction" that give clues about the character's state of mind and intention (28). Matthews (1995) calls irregularity "rhythmic turbulence" and proposes that it may point to "the emotional center" of any passage in which it appears (33). Cohen (1991) instructs the actor, particularly when working on a late play, to scan the verse and look for the "dynamic tension" between the poetic stress and the rhetorical emphasis (165). Of the voice specialists, Berry (2001) is particularly eloquent about attending to the rhythm of Shakespeare's language (13 & 184). She, Linklater, and Patsy Rodenburg (1993) all emphasize the importance of learning to feel the regular beat of iambic pentameter in order to be sensitive to disruptions which may indicate "something irregular in the thought or feeling of the character" (Linklater 1992:132).

The dense and difficult language of the late plays is most directly treated by Berry in *Text in Action* (2001) in her discussion of the scene between Leontes and Camillo in the first act of *The Winter's Tale*. She comments, "In this particular text the movement of the thoughts is extremely complex, tortuous even, for each thought is made up of several different parts which have to be held together within the one whole. This is technically difficult..." (144). She then offers exercises to help the actor find the specificity that is necessary to communicate such language clearly. Matthews (1995) also stresses that when Shakespeare's language becomes convoluted, it usually serves a rhetorical or poetic purpose and is worthy of close examination (61). Such insights from those who have the practical experience of speaking, directing, coaching, and teaching Shakespeare's works provided the inspiration for my own practical investigation into the language of his late plays.

Practical Investigation

To explore the question of how the voice and text coach can help students meet the challenges posed by the language of Shakespeare's late plays, I conducted a series of workshops with actors in The Central School's MA Advanced Theatre Practice program. Each of my workshops focused on one of the characterizing aspects of the language of the Romance plays. I used both exercises I had devised specifically for these texts and exercises drawn or adapted from the works of Cicely Berry, Kristin Linklater, and Patsy Rodenburg, as well as the instruction of David Carey, course leader of the MA Voice Studies program at The Central School of Speech and Drama. In this section, I include a description of my approach to each textual challenge and samples of both those exercises that were successful in helping the students to use the language effectively and those that were less so.

The first workshop addressed the issue of enjambment. As noted, there is a fair amount of discussion in the practitioner literature about how to approach enjambed lines. In my workshop, I focused on making sense of the long and complex thoughts and exploring the value of the line-endings. The text I used was Hermione from *The Winter's Tale* III ii 22-54 ("Since what I am to say must be but that / Which contradicts my accusation...").

When we initially read the monologue from verse line to verse line, the students had a very difficult time understanding what they were reading. I felt it would be useless to focus on the line-endings before they had a basic comprehension of the text, so the first half of the workshop was spent tracing the intellectual and emotional arcs of the speech. Reading from punctuation mark to punctuation mark (Berry 1992:149), walking and changing direction at each punctuation mark (Berry 1992:179), and echoing antithetical words (Rodenburg 1993:130-31) all helped the students gain a sense of Hermione's meaning, intentions, and state of mind.

To help the students further grasp the structure of Hermione's argument, I divided them into pairs and had one read all the nouns and the other read all the corresponding verbs (Rodenburg 1993:126-27). As I was explaining the exercise and the students began doing it, I had the impression that it was far too static and intellectual, and indeed, some of the students were unclear on what constitutes a noun or verb, while others were frustrated because not all the nouns and verbs come in readily recognizable pairs. I adjusted by having them find what they thought were the three most important noun/verb pairings. They continued to struggle a bit, but their final choices were very astute, and five of the seven participants named it on their feedback forms as one of the exercises that most helped them to understand the speech. Often the most important words in a speech come at the ends of thoughts. In end-stopped lines, those words are given strong metrical emphasis as well as visual prominence because of the layout of the verse on the page. I feel that this exercise was important because enjambed lines do not signal key words and ideas as clearly. Frequently they are embedded in the middle of the line and must be sought out. In the future, however, I would pursue more physically active and imaginative ways to identify the central subjects and actions in a speech.

To begin work on the line-endings, I used Berry's exercise of kicking on the last word of every line (1992:179). This led to some significant discoveries. The students agreed that when normally weak words such as "and," "me," and "fore" appeared at the ends of the lines, they felt vulnerable and unsure of themselves. When they were kicking on thematically important words, such as "divine" and "tyranny," they felt that they

were in a position of strength. This gave them a very clear sense of Hermione's emotional journey through the speech. All of the participants responded in the affirmative on their feedback forms to the question, "Did marking the last words of the verse lines lead you to any discoveries about the speech?," and one student wrote, "...they helped to identify important words for pauses/intentions/stresses other than the ones associated directly to punctuation marks." I felt that this exercise was key in helping them come to terms with the complex way Shakespeare uses verse structure in this speech.

When we tried kicking on the last word of each sentence (Berry 1992:180), however, I found that even though the students understood the long thoughts, they still were not able to carry the energy through to the end. To address this, I instructed them to line up and, one at a time, read to a period or colon while literally carrying a chair, balanced on one hand above their heads, and then pass the chair off to the next student. As they read this way, I found that the text made much more sense than it had up to this point in the workshop, indicating that it can be helpful to get a visceral feeling of sustaining the run-on thoughts.

I had planned next to have the students rise on their toes on the last word of every line to keep a sense of marking the verse. In the moment, however, I asked them to also squat at the end of each sentence to keep the sense of honoring the weight of the thought. When reading the text, the form of the verse on the page emphasizes the ends of the lines, but I found that the sense of the thoughts can be more difficult to trace. Exploring the stops at the ends of lines yielded some valuable insights, but with these students, running on rather than breathing after each line was important for them to continue the thrust of the argument and make the text understandable. When they spoke the text to each other in partners at the end of the workshop, they did retain a good feeling for the line endings and were able to use the form of the verse to forge a connection to the character's emotional state without sacrificing the coherence of the thoughts.

The second workshop investigated irregular meter. I came to this workshop with the assumption that disruptions in the meter can reveal and express a character's state of mind, intentions, and thought processes. My goal was to help the students develop an acute sensitivity to the rhythms and use the meter to support discoveries and intentions. For my texts, I chose Miranda from *The Tempest* Iii 1-13 ("If by your art, my dearest father, you have / Put the wild waters in this roar, allay them...") and Leontes from *The Winter's Tale* Iii 284-296 ("Is whispering nothing? / Is leaning cheek to cheek? etc.").

Because the caesura can play an important role in the scansion of a difficult line, very early in the workshop I tried to have the students read through the text a half line at a time, looking for the breaks (Berry 1992:151). This exercise came far too soon for them. They did not yet have a strong enough sense of the movement of the thoughts to be able to identify when there was a turning point in the line. Furthermore, when they could identify the caesuras, they did not mean anything to them. I realized that, particularly with actors who do not have a great deal of experience with verse, it is important to get a sense of the meaning and the basic rhythm of a speech before proceeding to more sophisticated analysis.

To that end, we tapped out the scansion of the last four lines of Miranda's speech, which are very regular. The students then galloped around the room to the beat of the meter while speaking the text, which was very good for getting the rhythm in their bodies. We then repeated the sequence with the more irregular first nine lines of the speech. Doing so immediately gave them a sense of the emotional violence that breaks through in Miranda's argument. The galloping also gave them a particularly good feel for the attentiveness necessary to "ride" the rough rhythms.

With Leontes' speech, I wanted to work even more systematically to investigate the relationship between the meter and the preoccupations of the character. As preparation, we scanned the text, identifying and circling all the words that are irregularly stressed. In partners, the students then grasped hands and pulled back and forth on the strong stresses. I instructed them to pull quite strongly on strong stresses that came at the wrong place in the meter (e.g. "blind" in line 291). This worked very well to give them a sense of how those words literally pull the character off balance. One student spoke of feeling like she was tumbling through the speech. Another discovered that Leontes seems to want to make a logical argument, but it "gets away from him." On the feedback form, a student wrote, "Tug of war exercise (pulling on stress) identified the confusion and disjointed nature of speech and, therefore, state of mind (heavy stress)."

To further investigate the value of the irregularly stressed words, I had the students speak only them aloud, whispering the rest of the text. The students remarked that this took them right to the heart of what is most bothering Leontes, and one wrote, "Everything stems from the words which don't fit." Finally, I had them read the text and physically mark with a stomp or gesture the irregular stresses, which brought great energy to their readings. When they performed the speech for partners, I observed that they were able to retain that animation and the connection to Leontes' emotional state that they had found by exploring the irregular meter.

The third workshop addressed dense language. Shakespeare's late plays are marked by a stylistic economy that can make it quite difficult for an actor to make sense of the language for himself, much less for an audience. In this workshop, my goals were to help the actors make the images as specific and vivid as possible and find how the sounds of the words could help to carry the meaning. I used Imogen, lines 1-9 of *Cymbeline* IVii ("A father cruel, and a step-dame false...") and Iachimo, lines 99-112 of the same scene ("Had I this cheek / To bathe my lips upon...").

After I explained the context of the first speech, we all whispered and then intoned it together as a way of sensitizing ourselves to how the sounds of the language support the meaning of the words. The students found the intoning in particular to be very helpful. One remarked that it made the expressive power of the vowels stand out. Another wrote on the feedback form: "Atonal expression *really* aided concentration on text itself."

To work on the images of the speech, the students pretended to be cameramen filming the scene described by the text as they were speaking it (Carey). I observed that this exercise helped them find greater specificity, so that, for example, when they said "two brothers," they were making a concrete rather than a general reference. Working further in this vein, I had them create a series of tableaux to go with the speech. For each image, they worked together to create a frozen illustration of the text. This forced them to examine the language even more closely. As one student commented, "There were things I thought I understood, but I didn't," e.g. "most miserable is the desire that's glorious." Developing a visual representation required that she delve further into the language, taking it off the page and into her imagination. Another student commented that sentence fragments such as, "Had I been thief stolen, as my two brothers, happy," which had confused her before, made more sense as pictures. All the participants mentioned this exercise on their feedback forms as being helpful for understanding or communicating the text.

As an introduction to the images in the Iachimo speech, I asked one student to read it while the others echoed all the words that could have a sexual meaning (Berry 1992:163; Rodenburg 1993:129). This gave them insight into the intentions and tactics behind such potentially strained images as "stairs that mount the Capitol." They quickly realized that, although Iachimo is not being very direct in his language, he is finding ways to communicate his meaning. One wrote, "Echoing words with sexual overtones really clarified nature and impetus of text." When we then repeated the "filming" exercise with this passage, I was impressed by the nuance they were able to capture.

I next asked the students to become the "soundtrack design-ers" and use their voices and the sounds of the words to "score" the scene as they spoke the text. They could use changes of volume, pitch, tempo, tone and emphasis of speech sounds to create the mood they felt was appropriate to the language. One participant backed away from committing to sound and almost whispered the text very quickly. The others were more involved, but I could sense a degree of self-consciousness in their work as well. I think this can be a very intimidating exercise for students, and perhaps also for profes-sional actors who are unused to working in this way. Were I to use it again, I would take the exercise in steps, playing togeth-er with the sounds of a few vowels before moving on to words and eventually lines of the text. Nonetheless, the class did find some very powerful qualities in Iachimo's language, such as the heavy breathing of "hands made hard with hourly labor" and the slobbering of "slaver with lips." Once they had clarified the complex images of the text for themselves, they were able to make effective use of their voices to communicate them to their imagined scene partners and the audience. I found that to do so fully, the students needed to engage their visual and aural imaginations as well as their intellects.

Each of the workshops I taught concentrated on one particu-lar challenge presented by the Romance plays so that I could focus my observations. Examining any aspect of Shakespeare's language in isolation, however, is inherently artificial and lim-iting. Nonetheless, I found that specific, technical work in any one area strengthened the students' connection to the text in general. As they developed the skills to negotiate each of these structural challenges, they also developed their ability to make sense of each speech as a whole, which is an important step in speaking any of Shakespeare's language.

Interviews

Because I was limited in my practical study to workshops with students, I also conducted interviews with voice and text coaches who have experience working on professional produc-tions of Shakespeare's Romances. Andrew Wade and Cicely Berry of the Royal Shakespeare Company, Stewart Pearce of Shakespeare's Globe, and Scott Kaiser and Ursula Meyer of the Oregon Shakespeare Festival shared with me their thoughts on these plays and on the issues in them that I had been investi-gating. Their remarks offered me a broader perspective on how a voice and text coach can help actors meet the challenges of the late plays. Unfortunately, the recording equipment did not work effectively in the interview with Andrew Wade, so I will be drawing more heavily from the other four.

Wade did make the very valuable point that when working on a production of one of Shakespeare's plays, his attention is not on the characterizing aspects of the language, but simply on

making the language work. Ultimately, it is the needs of the individual actor and not the period of the play that will dic-tate his approach. In the course of coaching a late play, for example, he might never address the issue of enjambment if the actors are making the run-on lines work. Berry agrees that becoming too analytical or academic about the language can be a distraction, "because in the end, it is literally the spoken language that matters, isn't it? And how people enter that language."

Pearce feels that, in general, work on the Romances is different from earlier plays, "because of the way that the actor has to open his or her voice to the lyric temperament that is within these plays, which is vastly different from the epic dimension of the Histories or earlier plays." Meyer calls the late plays "more sophisticated," comparing them to modern art in their complexity and spirit of experimentation. She postulates that that sophistication is "magnified and echoed in language." Berry describes that language as having a "wonderful anarchy," which she says is what excites us about Shakespeare's last works. She encourages, "...allow that anarchy to come through." Kaiser has found, however, that sometimes directors are not trusting of the language's intricacy and will try to regu-larize syntax and rhythms that are unusual or challenging. Meyer maintains, though, that precisely because the late plays are "harder - harder to direct, to follow," they are more inter-esting and more rewarding to "crack," like a good crossword puzzle.

As in the practitioner literature, my interview subjects take a variety of approaches to working with enjambed lines. Pearce finds that, in general, the actors who come to work at Shakespeare's Globe are "very reverential about the verse struc-ture," and comments that part of his job is to "liberate" them, restore to them a sense of spontaneity in speaking the verse. Citing Berry as an inspiration, he uses exercises, "where the breath becomes the dynamic and often cascades through the enjambment, so that the suspensory pause becomes hardly even present at the end of the line."

Berry herself is mindful that in pursuit of the free flow of breath and ideas, the ends of the lines still must somehow be observed to preserve the rhythm of the verse. She also com-ments that the caesura does not have to be a full stop; pressing on to the end of the line, she says, can "make a huge difference" in preserving the dynamic of the language. One of the reasons she believes honoring the verse structure is impor-tant is that a listener can only hear so many words before needing, not necessarily a pause, but a "poise" to take in the thought. She finds that actors sometimes have trouble trusting this. "They want to keep entertaining," she says, so the coach must help them use the form of the poetry to draw people in, rather than ever pressing on.

Kaiser is acutely aware that, particularly in the Oregon Shakespeare Festival's 1,200 seat outdoor theater, the audience can only take in a certain amount of text before needing a respite. He approaches the problem by analyzing the language in terms of acting units rather than verse units, using the Stanislavskian concepts "units of sense," "personal images," and "logical pauses." Giving Imogen's speech over Cloten's headless body as an example, he explains that although a line may run on, within it there may be several actions or "moments." He continues, "What matters is how are you going to handle the individual pieces.... Who cares how long the line is, essentially. So, in a lot of ways, that's why the rhythms are funky in *Cymbeline*, because the units of sense are irregular." He notes that this technique is particularly well suited to American actors trained in the Stanislavki tradition.

Meyer uses several different methods in her coaching. She mentions working with the Linklater approach of breathing at the end of each line and with the Berry approach of marking the ends of lines but breathing to the ends of thoughts. Her recommendation is to try both to see what they reveal about the text and the character's mental, emotional and physical state. She says there is something to be learned from the "old school" technique of pausing at the end of every line. To keep the thought moving, however, she also uses the exercise of lifting one's hand all the way to the end of the sentence, regardless of breathing or line ending. In the end, a balance must be struck that serves the actor, the text, and the audience. Some actors may need help finding the momentum of the thoughts when lines are enjambed, while others may need encouragement not to rush the verse. In both instances, the language must be used to support strong acting choices.

It is interesting to note that, in a couple of instances, meter is seen as an issue more particular to text than voice work. At Shakespeare's Globe (where there is also a Master of Text) Pearce, as Master of Voice, is not often called upon to analyze meter. At the Oregon Shakespeare Festival, where he is director of voice and text, much of Kaiser's work with meter happens before the actors walk in the room. He is part of the team involved in putting together the production script, which includes notation of contractions and expansions. Once rehearsals begin, however, the actors are welcome to question decisions and offer input. In the late plays, he notes, "those irregularities always breed collaborative debate." His overriding concern in rehearsal is not to defend decisions made in the early script meetings, but to find, often through trial and error, the scansion that will serve the strongest acting choice.

At the Royal Shakespeare Company, Berry reports, the actors would be expected to come into rehearsal having looked at the scansion of their lines, although she has discovered that young actors are sometimes ill prepared to do so. She finds that simply beating out the meter with the actors can be very valuable: "It's so important for them to feel that. It tells us so much, where the meter and the sense stress don't go together. It tells us so much, again, about the state of the character and what is happening." Meyer also believes that discoveries about irregular meter can lead to discoveries about character. When a piece of text is very metrically complex and hard to "make work," she says, "that struggle is part of the character's struggle at that time." Berry thinks that in addition to being very revealing, erratic rhythms can actually be less difficult to speak than very regular ones. "The more formal ones," she claims, "are harder...because they don't quite mirror the roughness of human speech in the same way." Although challenging, specific work on the irregular meter can lead to valuable discoveries about the characters of the late plays.

When I asked Berry how she helps actors to "unpack and own" the very dense language of the late plays, she replied, "Well, you just have to go through it. There really is no easy way with those." She does point out that much of Shakespeare's difficult language, "we understand as long as each image is there and not, sort of, affected by the last one. Each is separate." She uses, among other things, an exercise of switching chairs with each new thought to achieve that specificity.

Kaiser relates that, partly because of time constraints, American directors will often cut or try to regularize difficult syntax in a script before starting rehearsals. Speaking of a recent production of *The Tempest*, he mentions that further changes were made in the rehearsal hall, "but, again, a lot of the complexities were either regularized, simplified or cut altogether." His experience is that this is a process which the actors, who feel the need to be understood, rarely resist. When confronting language that might be confusing, Meyer finds that it is important to have not just a voice coach, but also someone who is "really brilliant dramaturgically" on the production team to explain difficult language and point out how obscure images may recur in a text, making important thematic contributions.

At the same time, Berry emphasizes that not everything in the late plays can be understood literally. As in some of the sonnets, the text can be so complex that it may seem clear one week, then be cryptic again the next. Although actors (and perhaps directors) may be frustrated by this, she affirms that, "if you get them moving around and getting that language into their bodies, they begin to relax on it and begin to feel—

'yes.'" Pearce also maintains that physical work can be the key to unlocking dense language. He uses exercises in which the actor "lives the thought totally—totally embodies the thought." He describes the process used in rehearsing *Cymbeline*: "There has been a lot of clear thought... but not sitting around conceptualizing. It's been about living it. Pure living it. So you see, they've found... ways of allowing those words just to knock around inside them." Taking the time to explore the language not just intellectually, but also physically and imaginatively seems to be vital in working on the late plays.

Despite, or perhaps because of the difficulties presented by the late plays, I found that they inspired great respect and enthusiasm in my interview subjects. They spoke passionately about the richness and complexity of the language of the Romances. As Meyer commented, "I think it's very exciting to have a struggle."

Conclusions

The voice and text coach's mandate when working on any of Shakespeare's plays includes helping the actors to make sense of the language, to find a sense of connection and commitment to it, and to speak it with a strong and responsive voice. The central questions I posed in this inquiry were: what elements of the late plays might make those goals more difficult to achieve, and how can the coach meet those challenges specifically?

In *Shakespeare Spoken Here* (1995), Dakin Matthews makes the case that it is important for actors to make a very thorough study of the structure and devices of Shakespeare's language. He summarizes:

> The marks are there, the speaker must hit them; and to do that demands three things: the recognition of and respect for the specific demands of the speech (aim), the technique to do so accurately and gracefully (skill), and the creation of an inner life that makes the action of hitting them natural and human (truth) (135).

In Shakespeare's late plays, the "specific demands of the speech" can be very complex and call on quite sophisticated technique. The actor must contend with a great deal of enjambment, metrical irregularity, and dense, confusing language. I agree with Matthews that it is important for the actor to have a clear sense of these challenges and the tools to meet them with not only skill, but also truth. I believe the voice and text coach can be of great assistance in this by helping the actor achieve an intellectual and experiential understanding of how these devices work to support the human impulses the language is expressing. In the case of enjambment, this means finding both the momentum of the long thoughts and rhythm

of the line endings. When it is investigated closely, particularly through kinesthetic exercises, irregular meter can yield discoveries that feed the actor's connection to his or her character's state of mind and objectives. Working with images, sounds, and movement can help the actor come to a deeper understanding of dense language.

Over the course of his career, Shakespeare grew in his ability to manipulate each of these devices for dramatic effect. It is important that the coach help the actor likewise grow in his ability to use them to communicate with clarity and potency. Peter Brook (1998) has said, "Each line in Shakespeare is an atom. The energy that can be released is infinite—if we can split it open"(34). I feel that this is particularly true of Shakespeare's last plays. Their language requires patience and diligence on the part of actor and coach, but it unleashes great dramatic power when carefully attended to.

❧

Bibliography

Barton, J. *Playing Shakespeare*, London, Methuen 1984

Berry, C. *Text in Action: A Definitive Guide to Exploring Text in Rehearsal for Actors and Directors*, London, Virgin Publishing Ltd. 2001

Berry, C. *The Actor and the Text*, New York, Applause Books 1992

Brook, P. *Evoking Shakespeare*, London, Nick Hern Books 1998

Cohen, R. *Acting in Shakespeare*, Mountain View, Mayfield Publishing Company 1991

Evans, G.B., 'Chronology and Sources', in *The Riverside Shakespeare*, Boston, Houghton Mifflin Company 1974

Foakes, R.A. *The Dark Comedies to the Last Plays: from satire to celebration*, London Routledge and Kegan Paul 1971

Kermode, F. *Shakespeare's Language*, London, Penguin Books 2000

Levin, H., 'General Introduction', in *The Riverside Shakespeare*, Boston, Houghton Mifflin Company, 1974

Linklater, K. *Freeing Shakespeare's Voice*, New York, Theatre Communications Group 1992

Mathews, D. *Shakespeare Spoken Here: An American Handbook for Students, Actors, & Lovers*, Los Angeles, Andak Theatrical Services 1995

Rodenburg, P. *The Need for Words: Voice and the Text*, London, Methuen Drama 1993

Schon, D. *The Reflective Practitioner: How Professionals Think in Action*, Aldershot, Ashgate 1991

Shakespeare, W. *Cymbeline*, London, Routledge 1991 The Arden Edition (Ed.) Nosworthy, J.M.

Shakespeare, W. *The Tempest*, London, Methuen 1983 The Arden Edition (Ed.) Kermode, F.

Shakespeare, W. *The Winter's Tale*, London, Methuen 1978 The Arden Edition (Ed.) Pafford, J.H.P.

Withers-Wilson, N. *Vocal Direction for the Theatre: From Script Analysis to Opening Night*, New York, Drama Book Publishers 1993

Yin, R. *Case Study Research: Designs and Methods*, Thousand Oaks, SAGE Publications 1994

Interviews

Berry, C. June 28, 2001, Royal Shakespeare Company, Stratford-upon-Avon

Kaiser, S. August 3, 2001, Oregon Shakespeare Festival, Ashland, OR

Meyer, U. August 7, 2001, Lithia Park, Ashland, OR

Pearce, S. June 12, 2001, The Central School of Speech and Drama, London

Sandra Lindberg, Associate Professor of Theatre Arts, an actor/director and teacher, has taught voice, speech, and acting at Illinois Wesleyan since 1996. She also serves as a voice and/or speech coach for university and Illinois the-atre productions. Prior to coming to Illinois, she super-vised the acting program at the University of North Dakota for four years, and served as production director for a touring company called Suitcase Shakespeare that toured to schools in North Dakota, Minnesota, and South Dakota. Her acting work includes roles with Illinois and Michigan theatres as well as Shakespeare festivals in Chicago, North Dakota, Virginia, and California. Directing credits include both contemporary and Shakespeare plays such as T*welfth Night, The Winter's Tale, O Pioneers!, Hair, After Easter*, and *Fen*. Sandra is Associate Editor of the East-Central Region for the Voice and Speech Trainers Association (VASTA) Newsletter. She has presented papers on voice, text work, and/or acting at the Mid-America Theatre Conference (MATC), Rocky Mountain Modern Language Association (RMMLA), Association for Theatre in Higher Education (ATHE), and the 14th World Congress of the International Federation for Theatre Research, where an early draft of this paper was present-ed. Her MFA is from the Old Globe Professional Actor Training Program in San Diego. Bachelor's and Master's degrees are from Illinois State University. She has been a participant at the Shakespeare and Co. January Voice Intensive and has been both a participant and Associate Teacher at the Canadian Voice Intensive under David Smukler's direction.

Archetypal Image Work in Shakespearean Performance Training

The Design of this Investigation:

For more than eighty years the writings of analyst C. G. Jung have influenced approaches in both literary and performance worlds. This paper explores how Jung's influence remains strong in Shakespearean per-formance training. In particular, the paper explores the connection between what Jung called the archetypal image and the actor's explo-ration of text and character. I do not intend to suggest that archetypal image work is only suitable for Shakespeare's plays. My decision to limit the scope of the paper in this way stems from my own introduction to these approaches at the Canadian Voice Intensive (CVI). Experiences with Shakespeare's texts at CVI set me off on a journey of exploration which has brought me into contact with a significant number of theatre practi-tioners who have found that archetypal image work on Shakespeare's plays and characters enriches performance. Actors who work in this way can escape the narrow boundaries of the personal unconscious and approach the realm of the collective unconscious—an infinitely faceted jewel for which each of us, and our creative work, are but twinkling faces on its blazing surface. Because archetypal image work is not limited to work on Shakespeare's plays, future studies need to be done describing connections between this work and contemporary texts, for instance. For now, I will focus on the aspect of archetypal image work that is most known to me.

To clarify why I undertook this research a bit more, I have to go back to my first experiences with archetypal image work at the Canadian Voice Intensive. It is not that anything I was told there was so entirely different than concepts or approaches I had encountered at Shakespeare and Co.'s January Voice Intensive in the 1980s, or in graduate voice, movement, and acting classes at the Old Globe's Professional Actor Training Program, where I earned my MFA. Perhaps I was simply ready in Vancouver for "the text to do you, instead of you do the text," as I remember Kristin Linklater saying in Lennox. The folks at the Canadian Voice Intensive always acknowledge David Smukler's studies with Linklater. However, what was different in Vancouver was CVI's clear identification of Jungian ideas about the psyche, specifically CVI's acknowledgment that there is a third layer of human consciousness for the actor to explore—an aspect of the psyche Jung called the collective unconscious. Perhaps I was finally ready at CVI to understand that the conscious mind, or ego, is tempered not only by the personal uncon-scious, but is also affected by impulses from archetypes in the collective unconscious. Experiencing how this awareness could be brought into act-ing work was a little like looking around with new eyes and realizing that I was not working in a large space with walls created by my individual sense of identity; instead, I found myself working in a space where my sense of self had opened out to include a vast, timeless, and incredibly rich continuum of human experience that I could in part perceive through my connections to archetypal images. This way of working seemed to connect with mythic stories and universal aspects of human experience. And what was perhaps most enlivening was the sense I had that all actors, whether they are aware of it or not, have identities informed by this collective unconscious.

Though our contemporary culture insists that we focus on what our five senses tell us, and that we approach learning best when we employ a scientific method to that exploration, what I will do my best to discuss in the following pages is a way of thinking about the psyche and its connection to acting that simply cannot be discussed using only the rational, scientific, linear, logical, and/or analytical way of thinking that has come to dominate contemporary thought. To find words for what I have studied, I will sometimes use an image: a picture or representation in the imagination or memory. At other times I may talk about symbols: those emblems that through custom or convention come to represent something else. I may also describe metaphors: literary figures of speech in which something is said to be that which it resembles. Symbol, image, and metaphor are all terms Jung uses to describe various kinds of archetypal images. My use of these terms will also be determined by the sources I quote, and the way participants in this study use these words. There will also be times when I tell a story in order to convey that aspect of the work I hope the reader to grasp. However, I freely admit here that all my words will never be enough; only practicing archetypal image work will allow the actor to perceive the potential of this approach. This article is simply an attempt to convey a beginning sense of what the work can engender.

The Voice and Speech Trainers Association (VASTA), the Association for Theatre in Higher Education (ATHE), and the faculty of the Canadian Voice Intensive (CVI) have provided me with connections to theatre practitioners who work with Shakespeare's plays and Jung's ideas. My queries, sent to VASTA, ATHE, and CVI faculty, introduced me to many who are committed to finding the mythic and universal in their theatre work. I received responses from twenty-three theatre practitioners, as well as support and guidance from Donna Marie Flanagan, the analyst in charge of training at the Chicago Jungian Institute.[1]

The responses I received from theatre practitioners fall into three categories:
• The first group consists of practitioners clearly steeped in Jungian or Jungian-inspired knowledge who have carefully and deliberately been fostering archetypal image awareness in their work as theatre facilitators or coaches. These respondents all work with Shakespeare's plays in the classroom and in production, and they have been exploring in this way for many years. Responding to an initial set of research questions, they provided detailed accounts of their theory and practice. A summary of the initial survey questions is included in the endnotes for this paper.[2] The respondents also provided answers, via email or phone interviews, to follow-up questions I asked them.
• A second group may disavow "any scholarly knowledge of [Jung's] work" as Marya Lowry so aptly put it,[3] even as they describe the myriad places in which Jung and theatre practice have come together in research, classes, or performances. These respondents shared how they are using archetypal image work in their theatre pursuits and often generously passed along the titles of books or names of teachers who had inspired their own approaches.
• The third group is made up of those who feel they do archetypal image work but not with Shakespeare's plays. As the topic relates to their own work, these respondents offered to be readers for the paper, or have expressed a desire to read it once published. Though I have not included interview materials from the third group, their numbers suggest that further research in this

1. My thanks to the principal respondents to the survey questions: Donna Marie Flanagan, Dale Genge, Marya Lowry, Katherine Perrault, Judith Koltai, Barbara Sellers-Young, Bill Smith, David Smukler, Nathan Thomas, and Greg Ungar.

2. Theatre practitioners who expressed a willingness to participate in this investigation received the following survey questions:

Below are the questions I would like you to consider. Realizing how busy we all are, I want to emphasize that ANY response you have time to share will be valued greatly. If you want to respond with a phrase, that's great. If you feel compelled to respond with something longer, I will welcome that as well.

A) Do you use the concept of archetypes in your work as a performer, teacher, and/or director? If the answer is yes, please describe how this concept connects to your work.

B) Do you keep a dream journal for use with your artistic, teaching, or scholarly work? If you do, how has it proved useful to do this?

C) Are there other concepts or theories from Carl G. Jung's writings that you find useful in your work as a theatre practitioner? For example, is the concept of active imagination part of your process? Describe the Jungian theories or practices and how you put them to use.

D) Do you actively teach ideas about archetypes to your students or to the actors you work with? If you do, can you describe at least one instance when this happened, and how you asked the participants to connect the concept with their work?

E) Why do you feel it is important to include an archetypal awareness in your work? How has it contributed to your development as a theatre practitioner?

F) Are there challenges or dangers connected with archetypal work? What do you know or imagine they are? Have you had to contend with such challenges or dangers? If so, can you describe at least one instance when this happened and how you coped with the situation?

G) Have you ever consulted with a trained Jungian therapist about the archetypal aspect of your work? If you have, how did such consultation(s) occur and how did they affect your process?

3. Marya Lowry. Email to Sandra Lindberg. 2 October 2001.

area, designed to include theatre practitioners who work with texts other than Shakespeare's, would provide additional information about archetypal image work.

Contributors from all three groups have made this investigation possible. Perhaps the ensuing descriptions of their work will move some readers to seek out individuals mentioned here and/or the sources that inspired them. Before I discuss these individuals, I would like to provide a little background about Jung and his work.

Jung's Thoughts on Archetypal Images

Jung was a Swiss psychiatrist (1875-1961) who worked with the personal unconscious and proposed the existence of what he called the collective unconscious to account for the recurring symbols he saw in myths, fairytales, literature, and his patients' dreams. During the many decades in which he practiced and wrote, Jung published explorations on creativity and the artist, as well as detailed accounts of his approach to analysis. His writings in turn inspired literary critics and artists, including those in theatre, who were searching for a way to explore images and characters that fostered an understanding of their universal qualities. Some of these artists had begun to chafe within the boundaries of the very personal psychological perspective psychoanalyst Sigmund Freud seemed to offer.

Carol S. Pearson, a contemporary interpreter of Jung's work writes that what a man first knows as himself is his Ego, "...the seat of consciousness, the recognition that there is an 'I' separate from the mother and the rest of the world, an 'I' that can affect that world."[4] Jung theorized that the ego is affected by the other major aspects of the psyche: the personal unconscious and the collective unconscious. Jung explains,

> While the personal unconscious is made up essentially of contents which have at one time been conscious but which have disappeared from consciousness through having been forgotten or repressed, the contents of the collective unconscious have never been in consciousness, and therefore have never been individually acquired, but owe their existence exclusively to heredity.[5]

Jung reasoned that the collective unconscious exists for every person, being the source of our instincts and a part of us made up of what Jung called "archetypes,... [which are] primordial types [and] universal images that have existed since the remotest times."[6] Studying the religions, myths, fairytales, and dreams from cultures all over our planet, Jung observed patterns in the archetypal images he found there. He felt these similarities could only be explained through an understanding of the collective unconscious, the repository of our species' knowledge and experience. Jung theorized that this universal aspect of the psyche makes itself partially known to the conscious mind through archetypal images, including those that find their way into Shakespeare's plays. As Jung writes, "Everywhere we find ourselves confronted with the history of language, with images and motifs that lead straight back to a primitive wonder-world."[7]

Archetypal psychologists are careful to distinguish between the term *archetype*, and a related term, *archetypal image*. An archetype resides in

4. Carol S. Pearson. *Awakening the Heroes Within*. (New York: HarperCollins, 1991), 30.

5. Carl G. Jung. *The Archetypes and the Collective Unconscious*. (Princeton: Princeton University, 1969), 42.

6. Jung, *Archetypes*, 5.

7. Jung, *Archetypes*, 3.

the collective unconscious and is a repository of images so vast that no single consciousness could convey its scope and power. Instead, individuals perceive aspects of an archetype through the archetypal images that they encounter in dreams, myths, or works of art. Nor do the archetypal images associated with an archetype remain the same over the course of a person's life. The images are constantly transforming as the person's self-explorations bring changing awareness.[8] For the sake of conceptual clarity, this paper is careful to use the term *archetypal image* when discussing what the following theatre practitioners explore during an exercise. This paper, as Jung did, will refer to archetypal images using the term *image* or *metaphor*. Occasionally, quoted material will describe an archetypal image using the word, *symbol*. Though contemporary scholars may have different ways of using these words, all of the terms are used by Jung and other depth psychologists to describe an archetypal image. Regardless of the term used, and no matter how profound an archetypal image may be in rehearsal or performance, the single image can only partially reflect an archetype's complexity.

Partnerships between Depth Psychology and Theatre Practitioners

What I will describe can hardly be called a recent revolution in performance training. Depth psychology, a term that refers to any school of psychology focused on the unconscious, has influenced many theatre practitioners. Depth psychology may include Freudian or Jungian approaches as well as more recent interpretations of each.[9] Artists have been linked to Jungian theory in many ways. As Marya Lowry, an artist in residence at Brandeis University, observes, "[As Jung's concepts are] pervasive in our current cultural language, I find that many use his terminology as part of the everyday vernacular." While contemporary speakers may not know how Jung defined the terms, they may speak of their persona, psyche, feminine or masculine side, or their unconscious, all concepts Jung used again and again. Lowry further notes that the "Alfred Wolfson/Roy Hart work is deeply influenced by Jung," a reference to a vocal approach that goes back to the 1920s.[10] Other well known theatre practitioners who belong in this company include Michael Chekhov with his use of psychological gesture[11] as well as Peter Brook whose connection to Joseph Campbell's description of the Hero's Journey demonstrates its own Jungian roots.[12] Even more recently Pantheatre in Paris has developed a close working relationship with the archetypal psychologist James Hillman, whose work grows out of Jungian theory.[13]

Perhaps most famously connected to theories of depth psychology is Konstantin Stanislavsky's approach to acting, later interpreted in the United States by Stella Adler, Lee Strasberg, Sanford Meisner, and Bobby Lewis.[14] While Stanislavsky seems to have been aware of Jung's work, as well as Freud's, Americans teaching the Stanislavsky approach often refer to Freud's ideas about the human psyche. For example, in *Sanford Meisner on Acting*, the esteemed acting teacher refers repeatedly to Freud and psychoanalysts when justifying his theories about acting. He also argues that character results from

> two barrels inside us… one that contains all of the juices which are exuded by our troubles. That's the neurotic barrel. But right next to it stands the second barrel, and by a process of seepage like osmosis, some of the troubles in the first barrel get into the second and… those juices have been transformed into the ability to paint, to compose, to write, to play music, and the ability to act.[15]

8. Joseph L. Henderson. "The Artist's Relation to the Unconscious." *Jungian Literary Criticism*. Ed. Richard P. Sugg (Evanston, IL: Northwestern University Press, 1992), 61-62.

9. Donna Marie Flanagan. Email to Sandra Lindberg. 14 February 2002.

10. Marya Lowry. Email to Sandra Lindberg. 4 December 2001.

11. Deirdre Hurst Du Prey, ed. *Michael Chekhov: Lessons for the Professional Actor*. (New York: Performing Arts Journal Publications, 1985), 107-119.

12. Joseph Campbell. *The Hero with a Thousand Faces*. (Princeton: Princeton University Press, 1949).

13. *Pantheatre Site*. Paris and International. <http://pantheatre.free.fr/index.htm>.

14. See Joseph Roach's interesting chapter, "Second Nature," for a discussion of how Stanislavsky was influenced not only by Freud but by Diderot's *Paradoxe sur le comedien*. Roach argues Diderot posed these questions: "Is the actor's bodily instrument to be interpreted as a spontaneously vital organism whose innate powers of feeling must somehow naturally predominate? Or is it best understood as a biological machine, structured by and reducible to so many physical and chemical processes, whose receptivity to reflex conditioning determines its behavior?" According to Roach, Stanislavsky and later acting teachers "follow Diderot in mediating between the two camps, wary of both, yet borrowing from each in turn." Joseph Roach. *The Player's Passion: Studies in the Science of Acting*. (Ann Arbor: University of Michigan Press, 1993), 161.

15. Sanford Meisner. *Sanford Meisner on Acting*. (New York: Vintage, 1987), 190.

Another highly respected acting teacher, Uta Hagen writes

> To become aware of usually *subconscious and intuitive* [italic added by this author], spontaneous behavior in order to make use of it for creating a character in a play will not make you self-consciously affected or unreal. Nor will it, as I have been asked, block intuitive or spontaneous behavior in our daily experiences. I am not a scientist, a psychologist, or a behaviorist, but I *know* this is true.[16]

For both Meisner and Hagen, a working knowledge of Freud's ideas about the conscious and subconscious mind informs what they have written. But current theatre practitioners, including those in this study, often discover when approaching non-realistic texts that Stanislavsky's approach and its emphasis on the personal unconscious of the character can fail to offer an imaginative way into texts where characters have mythic proportions.

This limitation in the Stanislavsky system is the same criticism voiced by practitioners working with Shakespeare's plays, in which the scope or depth of the characters can seem diminished when character analysis is based on a Freudian view of behavior. For example, director Robert Brustein in *Making Scenes: A Personal History of the Turbulent Years at Yale 1966-1979* makes multiple references to the limitations of purely Stanislavsky-based training for actors working on classical plays. In discussing his formation of the Yale training program, Brustein recounts,

> The Master teachers claimed I was meddling in an area that was not my province, the implication being that I didn't know very much about acting training. They were right, if 'acting training' meant only the teaching of circumstances, objectives, actions, intentions. But if I didn't know much about these mysteries, I knew what I didn't like— and that was the incompetence that Studio-trained American actors typically displayed when they untypically acted the classics.[17]

Brustein is not the only one to describe the limits of the Stanislavsky approach. Uta Hagen in *Challenge for the Actor* makes a similar observation when she contends, "Stanislavsky's discoveries were based on his understanding of how the great realistic actors applied the psychology of human strengths and drives.... Sticking slavishly to his doctrines is an injustice to Stanislavsky himself."[18] Hagen's statement implies that actor training must change as our understanding of human behavior evolves.

What seems to be happening among those questioned for this paper are reexaminations of Jungian-based theory and the application of Jungian concepts to actor training. The crucial concept dividing Jung from Freud, and the one that makes the first analyst's theory useful for Shakespeare practitioners while Freud may hamper them, is Jung's vision of the collective unconscious and its archetypal images. Freud's theory stops with his description of a personal unconscious. Jung says the individual's psyche is much larger.

Acting work that stops its explorations with insights gleaned from the personal unconscious parallels what tends to happen in contemporary lives. It is the rare person who is drawn to explore past the confines of the individual psyche. Jung wrote extensively of the difficulties involved in attempting to bring to consciousness aspects of the collective

16. Uta Hagen. *Respect for Acting*. (New York: Macmillan, 1973), 32.

17. Robert Brustein. *Making Scenes: A Personal History of the Turbulent Years at Yale 1966-1979*. (New York: Limelight Editions, 1984.)

18. Uta Hagen. *A Challenge for the Actor*. (New York: Charles Scribner's Sons, 1991), 46.

unconscious, that universal entity that lurks even deeper than the personal unconscious. However, he also argues that to ignore the collective unconscious is even more dangerous. In writing about two central archetypes, the *anima* and *animus*, Jung says,

> Both of them are unconscious powers, 'gods' in fact…. To call them by this name is to give them that central position in the scale of psychological values which has always been theirs whether consciously acknowledged or not; for their power grows in proportion to the degree that they remain unconscious. Those who do not see them are in their hands, just as a typhus epidemic flourishes best when its source is undiscovered.[19]

19. C. G. Jung. *Aspects of the Feminine.* (Princeton: Princeton University Press, 1982), 178.

Jung theorized that all human beings are influenced by the powerful forces of the collective unconscious. To compare acting that focuses on the personal unconscious to work that seeks to be informed by the collective unconscious is then not an entirely accurate description. If Jung has theorized accurately, both ways of working are affected by archetypes from the collective unconscious. The difference in the work comes from the practitioner's awareness of, and willingness to wrestle with, the archetypal images that reflect an individual connection to a vast unknown. It can be argued that the collective unconscious is every actor's inheritance, though few attempt to claim it. Current theatre practitioners who strive for this connection to "primordial types,"[20] as Jung once termed the archetypes, seem able to embody universal qualities of human experience in their work, giving their performances depth and power.

20. Carl G. Jung. *Archetypes,* 42.

Four Practitioners with Extensive Experience in Archetypal Image Work

The next four sections are devoted to the work of Barbara Sellers-Young, David Smukler, Judith Koltai, and Dale Genge. These four practitioners have drawn upon ideas from C. J. Jung's writings, as well as the work of related authors, as they develop ways to combine archetypal image awareness and actor, voice, or movement training.

Barbara Sellers-Young's Approach to Movement Training

Readers of this article may know Barbara Sellers-Young as the chair of the theatre department at UC-Davis, a gifted movement and acting teacher there, as well as author of the recent text, *Breathing Movement Exploration* published by Applause Books in 2001. Her book has a section called "Archetypal Masks" that provides introductory material on Jung, Joseph Campbell, and archetypes. The section also discusses active imagination, a waking exercise developed by Jung that can be described as "a sequence of fantasies produced by deliberate concentration."[21] In her book, Sellers-Young describes "Explorations," imaging exercises that are then connected to the development of a physical score. She delineated some key concepts informing her approach, "When I was performing regularly, I used the archetypes as a means of physically exploring character. As a teacher/director, I use them in helping the actor do the same." She is a big proponent of active imagination and feels this technique helps "actors begin to create a more lively sensory imagination by asking them to activate all their senses in the process of the [character's] journey."[22] Sellers-Young's Exploration called "Activating the Imagination" instructs the actor to take a journey through an imaginary environment and to note the effect of the journey's stages on the body. From this imagining the actor is asked to physicalize the journey by creating a physical score, or sequence of physical actions, that will express what has been

21. Andrew Samuels, Bani Shorter, and Fred Plaut. "Archetype, Myth, *Numinosum*" in *Jungian Literary Criticism*, ed. Richard P. Sugg (Evanston, Illinois: Northwestern University, 1992), 49.

22. Barbara Sellers-Young. Email to Sandra Lindberg. 31 October 2001.

23. George Lakoff and Mark Johnson. *Philosophy of the Flesh*. (New York: Basic Books, 1999).

24. Sellers-Young, Email/Lindberg, 31 October 2001.

25. Barbara Sellers-Young. *Breathing Movement Exploration*. (New York: Applause, 2001), 201.

26. Sellers-Young, Email/Lindberg, 31 October 2001.

27. Joseph Campbell theorized the existence of a mono-myth he called the Hero's Journey. He believed, "The hero . . . is the man or woman who has been able to battle past his personal and local historical limitations to the general-ly valid, normally human forms." The Hero's "battle" pro-gresses through stages Campbell identified as departure, initiation, and return. Campbell contends that the person who chooses to undertake such a journey may one day return home with priceless knowledge and gifts for his or her people. Joseph Campbell. *The Hero with a Thousand Faces*. (Princeton: Princeton University Press, 1949), 20.

imagined. The exercise is designed to allow the conscious and uncon-scious mind to inform each other, creating a space in which creativity flows from a larger awareness of who they are. In an email to me, her identification of the work of linguist Lakoff and philosopher Johnson is key here, too. She points out that these authors, "have indicated in *Philosophy of the Flesh*[23] that we are creatures who think and move based on sensory images that we combine in a state of metaphor." She describes how one young woman's childhood hero was Bugs Bunny and "that she [the actor] moved in quick, darting movements." Sellers-Young saw how this actor's sense of identity and range of physical expression remained limited to a "quick, darting" quality until she became conscious of the archetypal image with which she had identified and that was defining how she moved.[24] In *Breathing Movement Exploration* Sellers-Young points out that all personal Explorations can also be done for characters, allowing these techniques to be applied directly to text.[25] She has found that "working with archetypes and associated imagery helps actors define both themselves as people in the world and as artists. This knowledge allows them to develop beyond what otherwise would be self-imposed, unconscious limitations."[26]

Archetypal Image Work at the Canadian Voice Intensive

Eight hundred miles north of Sellers-Young's California campus lies the University of British Columbia, the site of the Canadian Voice Intensive (CVI). There have been sixteen CVI workshops held for five weeks every May and June in Vancouver, British Columbia. The core faculty includes David Smukler, Judith Koltai, Dale Genge, Ian Raffel, Gary Logan, Dawn Mari McCaugherty, Eric Armstrong, and Gerry Trentham. They are sometimes joined by visiting artist teachers such as Neil Freeman from the University of British Columbia, or Claire Buckland, a Jungian analyst in Vancouver. Native storytellers such as Grey Wolf and Len George, both from British Columbia, have also participated in the Intensive. Four to six associate faculty are chosen each year to assist the core faculty and to work on the development of their own teaching approaches. CVI accepts only forty-eight participants from the many applications they receive. All of the voice, movement, acting, and text work they do is focused on Shakespeare's plays, perhaps due to David Smukler's many years of work on these texts.

As a participant in 1993 and an associate faculty member in 2001, I twice have had the opportunity to experience the "Introduction to Story," "Hero's Journey" and "Archetype" evenings that happen during the Intensive. CVI has held these evening introductions to Jung and Campbell's work for twelve of its sixteen years. The "Introduction to Story" evening happens in the first week of the Intensive and is designed to set up basic parameters for the plays and to introduce participants to the power of stories. It is from these evenings that the Hero's Journey and archetypal image work will emerge at later points in the Intensive. In 2001, the "Hero's Journey" session began in the middle of the second week of the Intensive with facilitator/teachers and participants listening as Judith Koltai described the stages in the Hero's Journey, as Joseph Campbell identified them[27]. She then invited her listeners to remember what it was like to hear a story when they were children. Koltai asked listeners to remember key aspects of that story. As she gently encouraged her listeners to remember who told the story, where they were, and how it affected them, the room grew hushed. Each person became absorbed in the memories of this most human of activities. No one in the room seemed at a loss when asked to remember such an event. This is Koltai's way of reminding her listeners how story can transform them. She describes her reasons for introducing the material in this way, "[The Heroic Journey] is the story behind the story, so to speak, since it has, as Joseph Campbell says, informed the human psyche throughout the annals of human culture, by way of ritual, mythology, and story."[28] Her presentation was followed by one David Smukler gave that focused on the historical background for the three plays to be explored at the Intensive that spring.

28. Judith Koltai. Email to Sandra Lindberg. 19 December 2001.

A week later Smukler and Dale Genge began their contribution to the "Archetypes" evening when they each told an archetypal image story. Both tales explore how psychic wounding contributes to identity development. "The Fisher King," Smukler's story, focuses on a male central character. "The Handless Maiden," Genge's tale, focuses on a woman's experience of wounding. The stories can be found in Robert A. Johnson's *The Fisher King and the Handless Maiden*[29]. Though it may seem to participants that Smukler's story is meant for the men and Genge's for the women, both stories are intended to appeal to all participants. Their choice to have a man and a woman share in the presentation of this material is quite deliberate; they hope to recognize the masculine and feminine energies in the room by building that recognition into the presentation itself. What participants may not realize is that Smukler and Genge's presentation design is intended to recognize the male and female energies also alive within each participant. Jung's writings include descriptions of two archetypes: the anima and the animus. Within a man there exists a female energy Jung called the anima. In women, there exists a male energy Jung called the animus. The beginning of a person's self-knowledge, the initial stage of what Jung called the individuation process, involves a realization that both male and female energies are alive within each person.[30]

29. Robert A. Johnson. *The Fisher King and the Handless Maiden: Understanding the Wounded Feeling Function in Masculine and Feminine Psychology.* (San Francisco: Harper San Francisco, 1995).

30. Jung, *Aspects of the Feminine*, 171.

Smukler and Genge's presentations are designed to subtly awaken participants to the possibility of honoring both male and female voices within them. The ability to balance these male and female sides of the psyche signals the early part of the process of individuation. If the individual becomes conscious of the anima or animus within and learns to balance these energies, future development of the personality will involve meetings with other archetypal figures: shadow aspects of the psyche, a father figure, a mother figure, a child archetype, and others that will contribute to the individual's psychological development.[31] By bringing anima and animus archetypal images to the attention of the participants, Smukler and Genge foster a process of introspection the actors will need to understand themselves and the characters they are asked to play.

Following the fairytales, Smukler and Genge share in describing a long list of archetypal characters, both male and female manifestations, and their shadow forms. Afterward, participants and facilitators discuss how the characters in the three Shakespeare plays chosen for the Intensive that year resemble the archetypal characters. During this part of the evening, respondents are asked to imagine how the archetypal characters could be connected, not only to the

31. Depth psychologist James Hillman describes the process of introspection involving ego with archetypal images in this way, "Know Thyself in Jung's manner means to become familiar with, to open oneself to and listen, to, that is, to know and discern, daimons. Entering one's interior story takes a courage similar to starting a novel. We have to engage with persons [archetypes] whose autonomy may radically alter, even dominate, our thoughts and feelings, neither ordering these persons about nor yielding to them full sway. Fictional and factual, they and we are drawn together like threads into a *mythos*, a plot, until death do us part. It is a rare courage that submits to this middle region of psychic reality when the supposed surety of fact and the illusion of fiction exchange their clothes." James Hillman. "Healing Fiction," in *Jungian Literary Criticism*, ed. Richard P. Sugg (Evanston, Illinois: Northwestern University, 1992), 131.

actors, but to the dramatic characters they are about to develop at the Intensive.

The discussion linking archetype to character must be handled so as not to arrive at any hard and fast decisions about these resemblances. Often, the discussion reveals that while one participant may see Marina in *Pericles* as a maiden, others see a priestess archetype at work in her, or a healer. The facilitators understand that this disagreement or multiple envisioning of the character is the truest way to understand the complexity of both character and archetype. Jung had powerful words of his own to describe this necessary multiplicity,

> An archetypal content expresses itself, first and foremost, in metaphors. If such a content should speak of the sun and identify with it the lion, the king, the hoard of gold guarded by the dragon, or the power that makes for life and health of a man, it is neither the one thing nor the other, but the unknown third thing that finds more or less adequate expression in all these similes, yet—to the perpetual vexation of the intellect—remains unknown and not to be fitted into a formula.[32]

32. Jung, *Archetypes*, 157.

The goal at cvi is to make the actor aware of all aspects of the psyche: intellect/ego as well as aspects of the archetypal structure of the collective unconscious. The "Archetypes" and "Hero's Journey" evenings offer an initial frame for this work. cvi's facilitators then have other approaches to offer that continue to foster the work in later sessions. Classes will develop non-verbal links to the ideas covered in the key evening sessions. The work actors do on their feet will teach them how to apply the ideas introduced at introductory sessions to their acting, vocal, and physical work. For example, Gerry Trentham teaches movement classes focused on "Rhythm" and "The Elements" which find body-based ways of awakening a sense of psychic journey in participants and to link archetypal images of earth, air, water, and fire to their physical explorations of character. The archetypal image work, as David Smukler describes it, "leaps us into the next layer of personalizing the text and voice work."[33]

33. David Smukler. Telephone interview. 13 February 2002.

Further Details of David Smukler's Archetypal Image Work

cvi is directed by its originator, David Smukler, professor of voice at York University in Toronto. His life and the work that has grown out of it repeatedly find connections to C. G. Jung's ideas and to those who have been deeply affected by them. His work in this area includes collaborations with the Jungian analyst and author Marion Woodman, whose workshops have included Smukler's voice exploration sessions. He writes, "Two events that proved to be strong influences drove me toward investigating the Jungian world. Both were productions directed by John Hirsch." Early in his years as an actor at the Stratford Festival in Ontario, Smukler credits Hirsch's production (1968) of *A Midsummer Night's Dream* with introducing him to archetypes, complexes, and shadow. He further observes, "[Hirsch's] 1982 production of *The Tempest* was a further step into splintering the psyche...." Smukler goes on to describe the reasons why Jung and acting inform each other so well with words that explain why he would make this work an integral part of cvi:

> If a prime goal of the Jungian work is to find meaning and under standing rather than happiness, then the Jungian work is an artist's

tool. One of the artist's primary roles is to bring to consciousness, or illuminate, the unconscious to the beholder. The actor is certainly working on manifesting the unconscious into something that is readable, observable and will effect the observer. The unconscious is the actor's palate.[34]

After the introductory "Hero's Journey" and "Archetype" evenings, Smukler's knowledge of Jungian ideas continues to influence his approach to voice and acting classes. As he has experienced how Jungian work nurtures the actor/artist's "palette," he continually looks for ways to bring participants into clearer relationship with their bodies and their inner lives.[35]

Voice classes with Smukler refer repeatedly to "the swamp", the place in the lower torso where actors can imagine all impulses and sounds are born. This swamp is an archetypal image all its own designed to invoke an awareness of the collective unconscious. David fleshes out his use of the term in this way, "I work from the SWAMP.... A swamp can be clear, murky, deep, shallow, stagnant or flowing. My pelvis is a swamp. It is an ever changing array of intuitions, impulses, sensations, feelings, emotions, and thoughts."[36] He further illuminates his use of this word by observing that the Cree word for 'swamp' is the same as their word for 'healing', as medicinal herbs come from this fecund place. The use of this word contrasts with Kristin Linklater's description for this place in the actor's torso, a "pool of vibrations."[37] Smukler also notes that a senior voice teacher once told him she chooses to work with an image of a clear lake or ocean "because she is looking for clarity." Upon hearing this teacher's reasons for her image, Smukler understood something about his own choice, "I realized that my search for clarity is never pure, it is always clarity of image or essence but that one element is always quickly being pushed aside or replaced by a very different symbol or event."[38]

In choosing to work with the image of a swamp, Smukler has found a metaphor plastic enough to evoke the many qualities of water, as well as the wide spectrum of flora and fauna that may appear to the actor as he works on any given day on any given role using this image of a swamp. His choice of metaphor reflects his goals for voice training, "If we hope to obtain an authentic voice, [it] has to be such that it is the voice of all the elements of us, not an ideal voice but one that has the potential to reflect all the elements of the psyche."[39] Smukler's use of the word "authentic" is key here. For him, the voice is not a quality or skill that the actor strives to perfect. Instead, the actor works best when an authentic voice allows him/her to make human experience transparent to an observer. Ideally, an actor will be able to convey with nuanced sound all that the performer is bringing to a character, from both the conscious and unconscious aspects of the psyche.

In addition to his voice work at CVI, Smukler describes how his work at York University has incorporated archetypal work into actor training. Each fall for the past eight to ten years, students have begun their studies with a project called "Origins." He writes, "The graduate directing students are given a specific region of the world from which they are to select a legend. They have a month to prepare the work and at the autumn orientation day, they are assigned a cast of second-year, third-year, fourth-year, and graduate actors and they have about twenty-five hours to create a fifteen-minute, collective collaboration. Not only does this give them an icebreaker, but also it gives

34. David Smukler. Email to Sandra Lindberg. 2 January 2002.

35. Smukler. Telephone interview. 13 February 2002.

36. Smukler, Email/Lindberg, 2 January 2002.

37. Kristin Linklater. *Freeing the Natural Voice*. (New York: Drama Publishers, 1976), 36.

38. Smukler, Email/Lindberg, 2 January 2002.

39. Smukler, Email/Lindberg, 2 January 2002.

them an experience creating ritual and working in primal archetypes as a balance to the main thrust of the curriculum which is focused on contemporary acting and realism. Dawn Mari [McCaugherty] and I also have established that the final project for each year's BFA voice class is a process which leads up to an Archetypal project in the fourth year." Exercises like this one clearly have contributed to the design of CVI's "Hero's Journey" and "Archetype" evenings and its continued effect on later classes.[40]

As for Smukler's personal exploration of archetypal work, he describes several practices connected to this awareness. Since 1985 he has been keeping a daily dream journal in which dreams are described and analyzed, "especially in terms of activities of the day." To this practice, he has added exercises as suggested by *The Artist's Way*.[41] As for his own actor and/or teacher process, Smukler believes that the use of active imagination is at the core of his process. For all of his Jungian work, Smukler refuses to enshrine it, or to hold it up as the only or best way to work—attitudes that could quickly calcify his process and end its effectiveness. He explains, "The danger is in perceiving that the archetypal work or any technique should be the complete, perfect or ideal way of working. Each technique is just another part of the artist's vocabulary. The Jungian work is a series of tools, a series of clues. The archetypal work helps to ground the artist in his or her own process." Smukler also believes that to set up a Jungian approach as the primary way for an actor to work would freeze it within a narrow set of attitudes, an act which would contradict every hope Jung ever had for inspiring an ever-changing awareness within us of what the universal unconscious holds. "For me," Smukler writes, "the Jungian work is neither static nor formalistic. I am constantly re-reading my earlier investigations and I am constantly examining other writers and their experience as analysts and artists. I hesitate to formally frame my understanding because my understanding is fluid, I can honestly say that I work from ignorance and seek knowledge again and again."[42]

Judith Koltai's Archetypal Image Work

Judith Koltai, who teaches Authentic Movement[43] at CVI, makes an important clarification about the nature of archetypal work: its focus is on the creative work of the actor rather than on personal or therapeutic investigation. Because Judith has practices in both physical therapy and actor/dancer movement training, she is clearly aware of the distinctions she must make between the two kinds of work. Regarding archetypal image work with performers, she notes that the actor must be both willing and able to enter "the deepest centre of themselves where the personal and universal meet." If the focus is the emotional response of the actor, this meeting fails to occur, and Judith observes, "the unity with the universal (archetype) is missed, [and] you have personal therapy, (a catharsis, or worse, 'emotional release')... which does not have the transforming potential for the consciousness of the actor or the audience." Koltai has experienced how highly emotional, cathartic responses in an acting or movement class can signal that the actor is working from a limited, personal level of consciousness. While such events might be viewed by other teachers as demonstrating a personal breakthrough for the performer, Koltai has noticed that the events rarely bring lasting change. Subsequent

40. Smukler, Email/Lindberg, 2 January 2002.

41. Julia Cameron. *The Artist's Way*. (J. P. Tarcher, 2002).

42. Smukler, Email/Lindberg, 2 January 2002.

43. Authentic Movement first began with the work of dance therapist Mary Starks Whitehouse, with important developments to the therapeutic practice coming from Janet Adler and Joan Chodorow. In more recent years Authentic Movement techniques have been embraced by artists searching for a powerful way to inform their work with connection to the collective unconscious. All of these practitioners acknowledge the influence of C. G. Jung on their work. Whitehouse has called the movement that emerges from Authentic Movement sessions "the flow of the unconscious material coming out in physical form." Mary Starks Whitehouse, Janet Adler, and Joan Chodorow. *Authentic Movement*. Ed. Patrizia Pallaro. (London and Philadelphia: Jessica Kingsley Publishers, 1999), 20.

classes or rehearsals may demonstrate no connection to the powerful work evinced in the cathartic session. In fact, Koltai has noted that some performers will feel the need to have repeated cathartic experiences, as if they keep revisiting the same troubled ground. For Koltai, this can be a signal that the performer is using class or rehearsal to work out personal psychological issues. The cathartic events cannot reliably be applied to development of a performance because these moments are really focused on the performer, rather than the art. Using theatrical work to explore personal issues may have its place and time, but it can also keep the actor from connecting with the truly transformative energy of archetypal and collective consciousness.[44]

44. Koltai, Email/Lindberg, 29 December 2001.

Koltai's distinctions bring to mind observations offered by Bill Smith from The Actors Studio in Denver. His exploration of archetypal imagery is based on approaches he developed after studying actor/teacher Michael Chekhov's use of the psychological gesture (PG).[45] "I began to explore a possible use of Jungian archetypes to access Chekhov's PG work. A couple of decades later, I offer once every two years or so, a 4 month block [of classes] that explores PG; and built into my text (handouts), I employ specific Jungian archetypes as 'models' for acting exploration." However, Smith goes on to point out the dangers that can surface when teachers link acting approaches to psychological theory. In an email full of reminders about the sometimes ill-conceived partnerships that sprang up in the 1970s between therapeutic practices and approaches taken within acting studios, Smith mentions Eric Berne's work with transactional analysis, Art Wagner's translation of psychological theory into acting approaches, and the influence of the Esalen Institute on many theatre practitioners, himself included. He sums up his feelings this way, "Jung has an effect on me... And I've read his works, but I will not include his works in my acting bibliography. It's my job as coach and director to translate... resources [for the actors]."[46] After much experience, Smith seems to have arrived at conclusions about what constitutes valid acting work that seem related to Koltai's wisdom. Regarding acting based on the Stanislavsky system, Smith writes, "I do not allow an actor to indulge in the re-creation of some incident from x number years ago, while s/he is playing the role. Think about it... Is the actor being in the moment, or is s/he playing out an unsolved fantasy from the past?"[47] Or to use this paper's vernacular, the actor Smith describes seems mired in a personal unconscious, and shows no signs of having transcended that to reach the richer archetypes of the collective unconscious.

45. Michael Chekhov. *On the Technique of Acting.* (New York: Harper Collins, 1991), 58-94.

46. Bill Smith, Email to Sandra Lindberg. 25 November 2001.

47. Smith, Email/Lindberg, 25 November 2001.

Koltai believes that the theatre's contribution to society's development lies in theatre's ability to elicit empathy in people. Jung also writes about how the artist can be instrumental in the furtherance of an entire society's development by creating works of art that help people to see how the ego can share life with those archetypes that seek to work through us.[48] Actors participate in this process when their work emerges from both the transformative potential found in connection with archetypal images and the grounding provided by a healthy ego. Koltai writes, "I have learned that people [actors] will naturally move in that direction [i.e. work in which ego and collective unconscious inform each other] if they are allowed their own way through the journey, rather than manipulated into 'release' or their experience 'interpreted' by themselves or the instructor." Koltai clarified that an actor's healthy ego meeting up with imagery of a transpersonal nature facilitates a going beyond

48. Jung is quite specific in his suggestion that the archetypes seem to operate as though they had a will quite separate from an individual's will. He writes, "Meaningful coincidences—which are to be distinguished from meaningless chance groupings—therefore seem to rest on an archetypal foundation." One way to observe this connection is to note a recurring series of archetypal images in the environment that serendipitously appear from widely different sources. The conscious person will note the cluster of related images and will let reflections on their meaning influence his understanding, as in this story of Jung's interaction with a patient:
    A young woman I was treating had, at a critical moment, a dream in which she was given a golden scarab. While she was telling me this dream I sat with my back to the closed window. Suddenly I heard a noise behind me, like a gentle tapping. I turned round and saw a flying insect knocking against the window-pane from outside. I opened the window and caught the creature in the air as it flew in. It was the nearest analogy to a golden scarab that one finds in our latitudes, a scarabaeid beetle, the common rose-chafer (*Cetonia Aurata*), which contrary to its usual habits had evidently felt an urge to get into a dark room at this particular moment. I must admit that nothing like it ever happened to me before or since, and that the dream of the patient has remained unique in my experience.
(C. G. Jung. *Synchronicity: An Acausal Connecting Principle.* (Princeton: Princeton University Press, 1960), 24 and 22.)

49. Peter Brook. "Reaching for the Trapeze." *Parabola* (15, no. 1, 1990), 104-109.

the bounds of the stereotypical aspects of consciousness. She also connects her understanding of this way of working to theatre director Peter Brook's insistence that the actor resist intellectually superimposing on his/her persona an intellectual understanding of character. Brook argues that such layering will produce a blur rather than a unique image.[49] To imagine what such a blurred image might look like, one could think of an actor working on Hamlet who might begin by doing a thorough textual analysis of his role. Meanwhile, he might dream at night that Hamlet appears to him dressed like a fool or court jester. The actor interprets the dream image to mean that he should always dance and caper as a way of physicalizing this archetypal image he now sees in the character. Though it is to his credit that he has paid attention to his dream, his ego has taken over and tried to enforce a linear connection between the dream's image and the actor's work on the role. Insisting to the costumer that he must wear motley and finding the clownish aspect of Hamlet in all of his scenes could limit the actor's experience of the Fool as archetypal image. Such an approach also would distort, or obliterate, many of the subtleties his acting analysis had uncovered in the role. Contrast that poor attempt to work with both ego and collective unconscious with a working moment Koltai describes from an Authentic Movement session:

> One of the moving and delightful instances I will never forget where this blending has happened was with a very talented actress [in her 60s at the time]. She was playing the Fool in *Lear*. In her personal life, and at a fairly late stage of life I might add, she was also learning and completely enthusiastic about tap dancing. In the Authentic Movement explorations of one of her monologues, she suddenly began to tapdance. But it was not her (the person) tapdancing; it was the Fool and it was the rhythm and the subtext of the monologue. She was astounded but thought tapdancing was not congruent with the play or character even though it felt 'absolutely right' to her. I suggested she do it in the next rehearsal without saying anything ahead of time. She got a standing ovation from cast and director… it was 'kept' and it was a show stopper every night and I was complemented on my movement coaching and 'clever choreography….'[50]

50. Koltai, Email/Lindberg, 29 December 2001.

This actress seems to have resisted the desire to let her ego control the impulse to tap dance in one of the Fool's scenes. Instead, she performed the choice though still unable to explain why it felt "right." This willingness to trust in something inside her, though her conscious mind could not explain it, can be said to demonstrate her ability to allow a working relationship between her ego and the archetypal image from the unconscious that she had found.

It goes beyond the scope of this paper to discuss in detail the practice of Authentic Movement. Koltai and others have published their own descriptions of this work. Of great interest is her article in *Contact Quarterly*'s spring 2002 issue. That volume of the journal is entirely devoted to articles on Authentic Movement.[51] This practice provides a way to integrate ego and collective consciousness through voice and movement. Koltai teaches the beginning level of this practice at CVI when appropriate and congruent within the Intensive's context.

51. *Contact Quarterly* 27 (2002).

Dale Genge's Work with "Cracking Eggs"

Dale Genge, Head of Voice at Studio 58, the Theatre Arts program at Vancouver's Langara College, in part credits the development of the experiential text approach she teaches at CVI, which she calls "Cracking Eggs," to the archetypal hero's journey frame CVI encouraged her to explore. She also acknowledges her work is inspired by the "Dropping-In"[52] text exercise she first learned at Shakespeare and Co. in the 1980s as well as Jungian analyst Russell Lockhart's *Words as Eggs*. He writes, "Words have everywhere become suspect and we turn away from the word to seek other sources of nourishment. We are likely to find that these other things do not satisfy soul's deepest hunger, because that is satisfied only when soul is given voice, only when soul hears and is heard."[53] Genge's work allows actors to explore words, the associative images they evoke, and those images' connections to sound and movement. She cites the Sufi poet Ibn-Al-Arabi's writings[54] about the imaginal world as inspiration for her work. Arabi describes the imaginal world as one providing a bridge between the physical world and the world of spirit. Genge observes that every person's body provides such a bridge. She also works from the understanding that actors and theatre performances happen most effectively when they come from the imaginal world.[55] Genge explains,

> The body is so often assumed to be unconscious, but with attention the body reveals images that are a forgotten part of the personal experience. The attentiveness to the body's sensations (including breath) and associations with words (for example, Shakespeare's) awakens the unconscious in profound ways. The personal unconscious and the archetypal universe are revealed through the images, sensations, sounds, tastes, and smells, as well.[56]

Genge, like Koltai, talks about the need to keep actor training from becoming therapy. She emphasizes that she must keep her teaching process separate from any personal psychological work she may be doing. She describes this process as "holding an empty space inside myself," what could be described as a state of creative "I-don't-know," that will allow students to work without fear of Genge using this process to benefit the demands of her own ego. She also holds this "empty space" to assure actors she will not interpret their work in ways that could limit the work's creative potential. Koltai referred to the necessity for teacher self-discipline, too. In a phone conversation with me, she observed how tempted a teacher can be to urge a student toward emotional release; the teacher can experience a sense of power as s/he watches a student crying or screaming as the result of side-coaching s/he has been given.[57] Both Genge and Koltai describe how facilitators must stay ever vigilant about this temptation, an awareness that must be a conscious and constant practice for them. Resisting the urge to pin down, interpret, or name what the actor does in an exercise also is part of teacher discipline for them both. As Koltai puts it, "the facilitator knows what an archetype looks like in literature, but does not know the student's personal expression of that archetype." For example, in working with an actor, Judith will ask herself and the actor, "What does *your* witch look like?"[58] Bringing this disciplined shape to the work allows both Dale and Judith to facilitate the actor's unique expression of an archetype, rather than imposing their own archetypal vision onto the student's work. Because Genge operates cleanly from this place, her student's work can become what she calls "the juice of life" in acting and in a larger existence, as well.[59]

52. Kristin Linklater, *Freeing Shakespeare's Voice.* (New York: Theatre Communications Group, 1992), 36-44.

53. Russell A. Lockhart. *Words as Eggs: Psyche in Language and Clinic.* (Dallas: Spring Publications, 1983), 89.

54. Ibn-Al-Arabi. *Ibn-Al-Arabi: The Bezels of Wisdom.* Ed. R. W. J. Austin, (Paulist Press, 1980).

55. Dale Genge, telephone interview by author, Bloomington IL to Vancouver B.C., 21 December 2001.

56. Dale Genge, Email to Sandra Lindberg. 20 February 2002.

57. Judith Koltai, telephone interview by author, Bloomington IL to Victoria, B.C., 20 December 2001.

58. Koltai, telephone interview, 20 December 2001.

59. Genge, telephone interview, 21 December 2001.

60. Lowry, Email/Lindberg, 2 October 2001.

61. Nathan Thomas. Email to Sandra Lindberg. 19 December 2001.

62. Perrault, Katherine. "Astronomy, Alchemy, Archetypes: An Integrated View of Shakespeare's A Midsummer Night's Dream." (Diss. Texas Tech University, 2001).

63. Katherine Perrault. Email to Sandra Lindberg. 20 December 2001.

64. Jung, *Archetypes*, 157.

65. Katherine Perrault. Email to Sandra Lindberg. 3 December 2001.

Four Respondents Who Connect Jung's Work with Theatre Training

The discussion of respondents ends with those who, in spite of exciting approaches of their own, claim the least amount of expertise about Jungian theory or its application to performance approaches. Here I will draw on material provided by Marya Lowry, an artist-in-residence at Brandeis University, Nathan Thomas at Centenary College of Louisiana, Katherine Perrault, Assistant Professor at McPherson College, and Greg Ungar, Lecturer at the University of California-Irvine. All seem to share similar goals with regard to this work. Lowry talks about how "archetypal work allows [the actor] to leave his self-image and its conditioning behind. He is free to play another role… carrying no preconceived idea of right or wrong (roles from dramatic literature can seem to have a 'right' way for the young actor and this, too, stops them in their freedom to explore)."[60] Thomas expresses a similar idea, suggesting that archetypal awareness "helps [actors] to realize that not all characters in all plays necessarily benefit from looking at them through the perspective of individualized psychology that has been a norm in 'Western theatre' for the larger part of the 20th Century."[61] Thomas' criticism of "individualized psychology" resembles the critiques of Brustein and Hagen regarding the limitations of acting based on the personal unconscious.

Though a relatively young practitioner of theatre, Katherine Perrault's responses regarding the usefulness of an archetypal image awareness reveal the extensive study she has devoted to this area. Her dissertation "Astronomy, Alchemy, Archetypes: An Integrated View of Shakespeare's *A Midsummer Night's Dream*"[62] introduces complex Jungian concepts such as alchemy and *coniunctio*. Her responses to this investigation's survey questions make it clear that she, too, feels this work is important. She explains, "…an archetypal reading of classical (and contemporary) theatrical texts leads to a more relevant 'equivalency' in the production of the text in today's vernacular, especially in the conceptualization of the text for a contemporary audience."[63] Her observation that archetypal image work can bridge distances between disparate cultures reflects Jung's thinking in this regard. He writes that we can no more ignore the collective unconscious than we can cut our existence off from our bodies, and goes on to argue,

> We are confronted at every new stage in the differentiation of consciousness to which civilization attains, with the task of finding a new *interpretation* appropriate to this stage, in order to connect life of the past that still exists in us with the life of the present which threatens to slip away from it.[64]

In other words, every age draws upon a collective unconscious that contains its own experiences as well as those of distant cultures. How Elizabethans produced Shakespeare and how our age does so will both draw upon the primordial types or archetypes that have existed as long as humanity has, but each age will generate unique archetypal images to reflect its understanding of the universal. As Perrault writes, archetypal awareness can provide a "basic unity" to a production. She further argues, "for theatre to be vibrant today, I believe we must find ways for text in performance to resonate with [an] increasingly culturally and generationally diverse audience."[65]

As an example of how archetypal awareness is brought to a Shakespearean role, Marya Lowry's description clarifies the process. She describes an actor working on Othello who "is having a difficult time engaging the body and the voice fully to find the authority of Othello." Lowry observes the actor pushing for volume and "forcing emotions, mistaking this for size and intention." Lowry coaches him to explore the Warrior archetype, as they have already explored it in a voice class. As the actor moves into this exploration, the change in his physicality is marked, "His body expands. His voice responds by deepening and taking up more space." She then takes the archetypal image work further by exploring what she calls "the roar of the Bear", also an image the actor has explored in a voice class. Lowry sees, "His body, voice, and imagination enlarge; bound energy is freed and released; his face opens up and eyes open and clear; the actors around him give way." Lowry then coaches him to take this voice and body back into the scene on text.[66]

66. Marya Lowry. Email to Sandra Lindberg. 4 December 2001.

When Lowry chooses to guide the actor through an archetypal image of her choice, her work resembles Thomas' at Centenary College, as he encourages an actor who is "too soft" as Edmund in *King Lear* "to be the evil villain." The direction, Thomas writes, allows the actor to find "an element of 'coolness' or 'steely-ness' that gave him, actually, more sex appeal that made much more sense when Reagan and Goneril start working to seduce him."[67] Though Thomas notes his approach has been influenced by Vladimir Propp's *Morphology of Folk Tales*,[68] his coaching in this case seems to encourage an exploration of images connected to a shadow archetype, the character in the psyche that holds the human qualities we try to suppress or deny. The qualities are different for each person. For this actor, "steely-ness" was not a human quality he seemed willing to explore until he was given encouragement to embody what "evil" meant to him. Another actor encouraged to explore evil, or the shadow archetype, might associate entirely different qualities with it. Jung suggests that such differences reflect how each individual's conception of an archetype is only a partial understanding of it. The archetype itself is so complex as to encompass, with ease, all individual visions because, Jung writes, "In the last resort, [it is] inexhaustible."[69]

67. Thomas, Email/Lindberg, 19 December 2001.

68. Vladimir Propp. *Morphology of the Folk Tale*. (Austin: University of Texas Press, 1968).

69. Samuels "*Numinosum*," 50.

Images of archetypes appear in dreams as well as literary texts. Sometimes a practitioner's dreams become helpful to the creative process. Many in this last group admit that their dreams play a part in creative work. Perrault keeps "records of dreams that seem significant if I am working on a project for an extended period."[70] Lowry keeps a dream journal, revealing "that when I am working on a role, or working with the Roy Hart Theatre doing a lot of voice/singing work in France or at home or sometimes when I'm teaching acting, my dream life seems particularly active."[71] Greg Ungar describes a rehearsal process for *Dionysus 2001* at UC-Irvine in which "the cast met before rehearsal for 20 minutes and discussed any dreams that people wanted to share."[72] In a follow-up email to me Ungar remembers that "relationships and connections among characters were often made as a result of discussions about dreams. For example, Ajax had sexual dreams about one of the messengers. This was discussed between the two characters and the possibilities (in terms of action-choices) were tossed about."[73] The practitioners discussed in this section are working with the archetypal images present in these dreams, a technique the more experienced practitioners I have discussed also employ.

70. Perrault, Email/Lindberg, 19 December 2001.

71. Lowry, Email/Lindberg, 4 December 2001.

72. Greg Ungar, Email to Sandra Lindberg. 2 December 2001.

73. Greg Ungar, Email to Sandra Lindberg. 29 December 2001.

Concluding Observations

The practitioners discussed in this paper would probably agree that the "juice," as Genge terms it, created when archetypal image work goes well cannot be distilled from the words on these pages. In the end, this article can only scratch at the outside of archetypal image work. Real understanding of what this perspective has to offer can only come through doing the work—and, in so doing, opening oneself to the possibility that glimmers from the collective unconscious will shine in a performance. But in that respect, the work is no different than the most technical of theatrical training. An actor who can analyze in detail the steps necessary for an effective stage combat will never wield a sword in performance until s/he practices again and again every thrust, cut, parry, and block needed for such a fight. The practice of archetypal image work is not esoteric. It grows out of the life of the body, voice, and psyche of the performer.

Early in the process of gathering responses, I began to receive replies from the Voice and Speech Trainers Association (VASTA) and the Association for Theatre in Higher Education (ATHE) listservs, as well as emails from teachers at the Canadian Voice Intensive, all strongly encouraging me to pursue this study. As I began to search for theatre practitioners interested in an investigation like this one, I was amazed at the strongly encouraging feelings respondents expressed about this work. Bill Smith, writing from Denver, urged me to promote a discussion of this topic on the VASTA listserv, "I respect this listserver's (sic) focus on the mechanics of voice/speech, but might we also discuss meaning and interpretation,… message and myth?"[74] Marya Lowry, at Brandeis University, agreed with Smith, observing, "Some things minister to the mind and some to the soul and some provoke our established ideas and push our comfort zones. This sounds like possible soul talk. Maybe even the Mother Tongue…."[75] Both of these theatre practitioners, and the many others who offered encouragement, seem to follow a path for exploring human experience that Jung believed needed our attention. Jung writes, "… in describing the living processes of the psyche, I deliberately and consciously give preference to a dramatic, mythological way of thinking and speaking, because this is not only more expressive but also more exact than an abstract scientific terminology."[76]

Jung prized creativity and the artistic expression that comes from the imagination. As the Jungian scholar Mario Jacoby explains, "The unconscious is creative, and this makes its irrational picture-language extremely valuable. All his life, Jung defended its importance against the one-sided overvaluation of rational thinking. The unconscious regulators, the archetypes, make the human imagination possible."[77] The practitioners who have contributed to this study have learned through their work that there is merit in Jung's perspective. In a world that is largely content to ignore the collective unconscious while making a god of Ego's rational and scientific thought, the artists who bring an archetypal awareness to their performances can bring moments of healing to an age cut off from its deepest sense of self. Judith Koltai Peavy knows that her work evokes "the

74. Bill Smith. Email to Sandra Lindberg. 2 October 2001.

75. Lowry, Email/Lindberg, 2 October 2001.

76. Jung, C. G. *Aspects of the Feminine*. Trans. R. F. C. Hull, (Princeton: Princeton University Press, 1982), 170.

77. Mario Jacoby, "The Analytical Psychology of C.G. Jung and the Problem of Literary Evaluation," in *Jungian Literary Criticism*, ed. Richard P. Sugg, (Evanston, Illinois: Northwestern University, 1992), 64.

story behind the story." For David Smukler work that is open to the collective unconscious constitutes, "the actor's palette." Perhaps Dale Genge's phrase says it most simply; to work this way brings a taste of "the juice of life."

Works Consulted

Brockett, Oscar G. *History of the Theatre*, 6th ed. Boston: Allyn & Bacon, 1991.

Du Prey, Deirdre Hurst. *Michael Chekhov: Lessons for the Professional Actor*. New York: Performing Arts Journal Publications, 1985.

Donna Marie Flanagan. 14 February 2002. "Archetypal Image Work in Shakespearean Performance Training." Personal e-mail 14 February 2002.

Genge, Dale. Telephone interview. 21 December 2001.

Jacoby, Mario. "The Analytical Psychology of C. G. Jung and the Problem of Literary Evaluation." *Jungian Literary Criticism*. Ed. Richard P. Sugg. Evanston, Illinois: Northwestern University Press, 1992.

Jung, C. G. *The Archetypes and the Collective Unconscious*, trans. R.F.C. Hull. Princeton: Princeton University Press, 1969.

Koltai-Peavy, Judith. 18 December 2001. "New Research Questions." Personal e-mail 18 December 2001.

Koltai-Peavy, Judith. Telephone interview. 20 December 2001.

Lakoff, George, and Mark Johnson. *Metaphors We Live By*. Chicago: University of Chicago Press, 1980.

Lockhart, Russell A. *Words as Eggs: Psyche in Language and Clinic*. Dallas: Spring Publications, 1983.

Lowry, Marya. "Research Project." 2 October 2001. Personal e-mail 2 October 2001.

Lowry, Marya. "Jung/Shakespeare Study." 4 December 2001. Personal e-mail 4 December 2001.

Pearson, Carol S. *Awakening the Heroes Within*. New York: HarperCollins Publishers, 1991.

Perrault, Katherine. "Astronomy, Alchemy, Archetypes: An Integrated View of Shakespeare's *A Midsummer Night's Dream*." Diss. Texas Tech University, 2001.

Perrault, Katherine. 3 December 2001. "Jung/Shakespeare Study." Personal e-mail 3 December 2001.

Perrault, Katherine. 20 December 2001. "Jung/Shakespeare Study Follow-Up Questions." Personal e-mail 20 December 2001.

Roach, Joseph R. *The Player's Passion: Studies in the Science of Acting*. Ann Arbor: University of Michigan Press, 1993.

Samuels, Andrew, Bani Shorter, and Fred Plaut. "Archetype, Myth, *Numinosum*." *Jungian Literary Criticism*. Ed. Richard P. Sugg. Evanston, Illinois: Northwestern University Press, 1992.

Sellers-Young, Barbara. *Breathing Movement Exploration*. New York: Applause, 2001.

Sellers-Young, Barbara. 31 October 2001. "International Federation of Theatre Research Conference." Personal e-mail 31 October 2001.

Smith, Bill. Bill491. 25 November 2001. "Accessing Acting Pro?" Personal e-mail 25 November 2001.

Smukler, David. 2 January 2002. "Jung/Shakespeare Study." Personal e-mail 2 January 2002.

Smukler, David. Telephone interview. 13 February 2002.

Thomas, Nathan. 29 December 2001. "Jung/Shakespeare Study." Personal e-mail 29 December 2001.

Ungar, Greg. 3 December 2001. "Jung/Shakespeare Study." Personal e-mail 3 December 2001.

Ungar, Greg. 29 December 2001. "Jung/Shakespeare Study Follow-Up Questions." Personal e-mail 29 December 2001.

Peer Reviewed Article *by Dan Kern*

Truth and Language

Dan Kern has a twenty-five year career as an actor and director on the stage as well as in film and TV. In Philadelphia he's appeared in *Magic Fire* at the Wilma Theater, *The Drawer Boy* at Act II and *God's Man in Texas* at the InterAct Theater. Nationally, he's appeared as Leontes in *A Winter's Tale* (Los Angeles Drama Critics Circle Award for "Outstanding Performance") and Volpone in *Volpone* at A Noise Within. At the Mark Taper Forum as Zhorzh in *The Wood Demon*, at South Coast Repertory as Salieri in *Amadeus* and The American Conservatory Theatre as Eben in *Desire Under the Elms*. Notable directing credits include his LADCC award winning production of *Juno and the Paycock* and BackStage West/Drama-Logue Award winning versions of *Twelfth Night* and *Old Times*. Dan is a member of the theater faculty at Temple University. Recent film and TV appearances include, *Frasier, Profiler, The President's Man, C-16, Star Trek: Voyager* and *Melrose Place*.

Whatever happened to the dream of an "American Voice" for the classics? Why do the names of British actors like Dench, Jacobi, Branagh, McKellen, Mirren and Redgrave spring to mind when we think of the classics but major film and theatrical producers are unable to find a comparable list of American actors? If you are one of those who is dedicated to training students for work in "heightened language," then you probably share my concern that today's American actors are not living up to their potential. Over the last several years, I've been developing a technique in this vital area of training that integrates voice, speech, movement and vocal dynamics with the intuitive and objective-based actor training employed in the Stanislavsky method. By reinvestigating the function and purpose of poetic dramatic text, the student is able to incorporate sophisticated rhetorical technique into the performance using organic, "method" based actor training. The goal is to instill both appreciation and facility for the tools needed to elevate heightened text to its proper place and value while retaining the truth and spontaneity that is the hallmark of our fine American acting tradition.

Shakespeare may be the most frequently performed playwright in America today. But how few of our actors understand how to really make his language soar to the heights where it possesses the meaning and power intended by the writer! In fact, any kind of writing that attempts to capture emotion and feeling in a way that isn't bound by some conventional notion of truth presents challenges for American actors. The following list focuses on the three basic reasons why young actors in America today have difficulty bridging the "styles" gap between "Contemporary Realism" and the heightened mode of expression found in classical and modern poetical drama:

1. **Ineffective Analysis of Text**
   a. This leads to inappropriate choice of objective
   b. Because the actors are only vaguely sure of what they're saying, they can't use the language to connect with the other actors or the audience
   c. It often causes the actors to lose the thread of meaning in more complex passages
   d. It keeps the actor from realizing the power and scope of the writing
2. **Physical Tension**
   a. Inevitably restricts the actors breathing
   b. It prevents the actor from properly supporting the voice
   c. It impedes the articulators to the point where the actor cannot be understood
   d. Manifests itself in random movement and repetitive gestures which draw focus from what the actor is trying to say
3. **Lack of Rhetorical Skill**
   a. Limits pitch range which results in lack of color
   b. Limits variety in the rate of speech and volume which results in repetitive cadences and a lack of vocal dynamics
   c. Results in the over use of the downward inflection preventing successful use of rhetorical architecture to sustain complex patterns and images

The puzzling fact is that virtually all MFA and professional actor training programs have classes and techniques in place that are designed to deal with these issues. Every worthwhile program has classes in speech, voice, movement and styles as well as text analysis. But that training isn't having the kind of impact on casting that's needed to place American versions of Shakespeare and the classics on a par with the British. Virtually every major film, TV or theatrical production of the classics features British actors. Are they better actors? Is our training all wrong? The answer to both of these questions is "NO!" With a few fundamental adjustments, I believe we have the ability to help students become more effective, more compelling, more powerful actors. The following three areas outline some solutions to the areas of concern just mentioned:

1. Young actors need to make choices of action that actually require them to use extraordinary language to obtain their objective. Students are generally led to believe that "acting is doing." While this is true, it tends to encourage choices that take place on a physical or experiential plane rather than a cerebral or abstract plane. But the language of the great classical writers is poetry. It is a more cerebral expression of passion and emotion and for students to master its use, it requires teachers who are effective in helping students understand how to select beats and objectives that are realized through language as well as action.

2. The young actor must understand that the physicalization of emotion is essential to believability, *but only to a point.* The overwhelming tendency among students is to manifest or show how they feel rather than trusting the language to help them. The consequence is excessive tension and its accompanying limitations. This problem is magnified when dealing with characters and situations where the emotional state of the character is at a very high level. At these times the physical tension in the actor can literally paralyze them to the point where they cannot even be understood. We need instructors in the classroom who appreciate the value of physical relaxation and are willing to make it a part of the instructional program when teaching the classics.

3. Our young actors must develop skills in Vocal Dynamics. Until now the training in pitch, rate, volume, inflection and rhetorical architecture has either been neglected, or delegated to the Speech and/or Voice Instructor. The limitation in this arrangement is that there is little enough class time as it is to meet the demands of a rigorous Speech/Voice program. Add to that the fact that very often the teacher either isn't qualified as an acting instructor or is prevented from infringing on the domain of the "acting class." As a result, these skills never become fully integrated into the acting work. In fact, if the actor tries to use these techniques in the acting class, the acting instructor quite often becomes impatient with the lengthy and sometimes awkward learning curve associated with mastering these skills and pressures the actor to abandon technique in favor of more "intuitive" acting styles. Vocal Dynamics needs to be organically integrated into the acting classes that deal with heightened language.

Background

In the early seventies when I was an acting student at the American Conservatory Theater (ACT) in San Francisco, I had the good fortune to be in a class of students in whom William Ball, the founder and General Director of ACT, took a particular interest. Bill recognized there was a dearth of American actors with the skills to play the classics. ACT was based on the European model of a true performing arts conservatory and Bill wanted American actors to possess the same skills found in Britain and on the Continent. He created a class called "Heroics" which was designed to develop the rhetorical skills needed to deal with the giant arias found in classical literature. Bill believed that the size of the emotion needed to support a monolog such as *Henry V*'s "St. Crispin's Day" or Paulina's attack on Leontes following the trial scene in *A Winter's Tale* is so large that the actors find themselves bound up in physical tension to the point where they are incapable of making the meaning of the monolog decipherable. His solution was to turn those great monologs and others like them into rhetorical exercises. He was literally forcing the actors to divorce all meaning from the text and to convert the words into architectural devices of pitch, rate, volume and inflection. Bill was trying to prove to us that vocal dynamics in themselves have the power to make an audience listen. Recognizing that it takes years to master the subtle and effective use of rhetorical technique, he believed it was better to learn those skills by rote, devoid of meaning, than to struggle with the associated physical tension inevitably brought on by the content of these great pieces of writing.

It was a noble endeavor that didn't really work! He tried it for a couple of years but gave up when word got around that ACT actors were doing this "Heroics" thing and they all sounded loud and phony. Since then the value of training in rhetorical technique has diminished in most actor training programs. In short, the American theater has deemed such training to be outdated and ineffectual. In a larger sense, this is probably a good thing. Stentorian acting is a bore and technique is the last thing we want to be made aware of when we're watching a play. At the same time there is no denying that actors with the skill to knit together complex images and ideas into a unified whole have the ability to make great writing move us in a way that no amount of "organic honesty" can ever achieve. There has to be a middle ground!

Heightened Language

The devices employed in poetical dramatic writing—meter, rhyme, alliteration, personification, antitheses, metaphor, oxymoron and stichomythia, are *language based* tools for elevating the passion and power of a character's emotional state. Much of this writing involves repeating images or ideas that have a cumulative effect. When it works well, they blossom or cascade in a pattern that can have a devastating emotional impact actually enhancing literal meaning. The challenge for the actor is manifold—not the least of which is to sustain the listener's focus through these poetic components to the ultimate conclusion. If the actor spends too much time and effort shaping each individual element, the listener becomes obligated to ponder the importance of each phrase. The result is that as the audience member struggles to hang on to the thread or point of all of these images, they are actually pulled out of the "dramatic moment," rather than vaulted forward to the final resolution. **The idea is not to get the audience to *think* about each and every nugget and gem, but rather to *feel* along with the character the passion that inspires him to speak such profound words. To accomplish this the actor must be able to combine effective and dynamic choice of *objective*, physical *relaxation* and sophisticated rhetorical *technique*.** The fact is that today's students are not sufficiently motivated to overcome the three problem areas mentioned earlier. Shallow understanding of the text, excess tension (or its opposite—the so-called "realistic" flat delivery) and lack of appreciation for vocal dynamics are handicapping our young actors. The following section will attempt to detail those three areas in the hope of offering a methodology for establishing a powerful and uniquely American identity for heightened language:

Objective and Text

We do a great job of helping our young actors break down the text. They understand the scansion. They know what the words mean. But most often the words don't come out of their mouths as living, breathing moments in time. Our students have to be taught to go beyond simply knowing what the words mean. They must know *why* they have chosen those *specific* words! When a character feels the need to communicate passion and depth of feeling, the *way* in which the words are found in the moment tends to endow a very particular color and value to those words. The tried and true method for getting students to be specific with the text is to have them paraphrase. While this is definitely a useful and successful technique, it too often gets short shrift. The student is inclined to be much too general, failing to appreciate how dense the text can be and how unique much of the language is. In order to be truly spontaneous in discovering language in the moment, the actor has to be intimately familiar with not

only meaning, but also the nuance and shading of virtually every word. This kind of specificity takes the actor to new levels of spontaneity, not only enhancing meaning but making it possible to refine and strengthen the character's choice of action and objective. And, of course, the audience will be far more inclined to suspend their disbelief when they see the actor organically living the process of finding language in the moment.

What is your objective? This question is the fundamental pillar of the Stanislavsky Method. Most actors recognize its importance and even if their training tends to de-emphasize its value, they usually will find an "action" through reaction to either a character or situation. Generally the student is taught that "acting is doing" or some variation on that theme. This works well with the writing found in a lot of contemporary plays and works especially well in film and TV. However, with heightened language, negotiating the text adds a unique challenge for today's young actors. The character is expressing ideas and feelings in a way that goes beyond mere physical reality—it has been abstracted into verbal images as well. This is where the conventional approach to finding an action/objective falls short. **The actor has to choose an action to win the objective that involves or incorporates the use of extraordinary language to impact the receiver of the action.** Using the highly charged emotional state of the character to fuel an "action" to find words in the moment that are capable of vividly communicating the size and power of that emotional state, is the only way to achieve the desired objective. In other words, **the language is the tool**—not emoting, not being believable, but actually making the receiver of the objective **understand** what you're saying. This is the first step in elevating heightened text to a plane where it is immediate and compelling. When this happens, the audience will be held captive by the language regardless of whether it's another character on the stage or themselves that is the receiver of the actor's action/objective.

Emotional Honesty & Relaxation

The undeniable fact is that the emotional size of great poetic drama places huge demands on the technique of the actor. What happens to the student who is cast as Cleopatra, Juliet and Viola, or Othello, Mercutio and Oberon? In the great characters of dramatic literature from Lysistrata to Roy Cohn, in *Angels in America*, the actor is faced with crises that are extraordinary. The writers have dealt with the immensity of these events and emotions through brilliant poetic images. But the American acting student's distrust of language and fear of being phony forces them to shift these overwhelming events onto an experiential plane. The result falls into one of two areas—either the actors "push" for the emotional obligation, or they subvert the material into a pseudo-contemporaneous style. In the first case they become so bound up by physical tension that they are reduced to quivering masses of flesh incapable of making themselves understood and in the latter they will indulge in pauses and mannerisms and flatten out the emotional arc in an attempt to make it appear "natural."

Most young actors tend to move and gesture more than is necessary. This is often referred to as "bleeding dramatic tension." As the actor focuses on the receiver of the objective and as the language accumulates in intensity, the inexperienced actor doesn't know what to do with this accumulation of tension. They will "bleed" the moment of its tension with movement because it "seems right." The compulsion to move "feels" motivated. The problem is that not only are they bleeding tension, they're letting the audience off the hook. They're saying, "I'm bailing out, so it's okay for you to bail out too." In other words, they're releasing the audience from the obligation to follow the character's train of thought. With language that is as dense and complex as Shakespeare the actor simply cannot afford to allow the audience to check out. The student must be taught to refocus the inclination to move into a greater commitment to the objective, using it to make the meaning and impact of what they're saying more vivid. The exciting thing is that great writing, whether it is verse or prose, has the innate ability to trigger powerful emotional responses in the audience as well as the actor—but for this to happen the actor must be able to carry the receiver of the objective through the arc of the poetic passage to its ultimate conclusion. The more the actor uses an action that incorporates language to sustain meaning and focus the more the extraneous movement falls away and the more powerful the performance becomes.

Text and Technique

The cadence and melody of American English is dominated by the downward inflection. In part, this is due to the influence of our puritan heritage that stresses plainness and simplicity of expression. Our fascination with film and TV and its emphasis on honesty and brevity are also a contributing factor. And perhaps another reason is that as a society we no longer appreciate a good vocabulary and articulate expression the way we have in the past. The result is that today's young actors no longer *feel* honest unless they remain in a very narrow range of vocal expression. The result of this syndrome is that when faced with "heightened language," the average actor will opt for the "believable" choice rather than risk the failure of seeming phony. In fact, the phrase "word decoration" has been coined to describe the work of anyone who would travel down the forbidden path of rhetorical technique. In our mania for truth, plainness and the American Way, we've thrown the baby out with the bathwater! In an attempt to

divorce ourselves from "hokey" old-time Shakespearean acting we've limited ourselves to a verbal toolkit that is missing most of its arsenal!

Repetition or reiteration is a common device used in heightened language. In some of the most complex instances the sentences can be ten to fifteen lines long or more. The responsibility of keeping the point and focus of multiple examples and images clear is generally viewed as a burden and many good actors will look to the director longingly for a "cut," doubting the audience's ability to follow the thread. All too often cutting is a quick fix for a lack of skill or confidence. There's no question it is possible to put a quasi-realistic spin on a shortened line. The meaning will be clear, but the passion of the character and excitement of the writing is often lost. It takes great courage and skill to sustain a complex build in Shakespeare, but very often the rewards are equally great! **The audience loves to be taken through the arc of an exciting build and the effect can actually enhance both the literal and emotional meaning for them.** As with a powerful musical passage, the dramatic effect on the audience is actually amplified. In addition to reliving the process of finding words in the moment, we must help our students to appreciate the value and rewards of using vocal dynamics to assemble complex thought progressions. This is the bane of American actors young and old! They lock on to a certain pitch, rate of speech or volume level and just sit there. The whole thing becomes a boring chain of repetitive sounds. Rather than facilitating meaning, they are obviating it. The audience is lulled into boredom! With their limited pitch range and distrust or lack of skill in the use of rate, volume and inflection, the average American actor is incapable of finding the fluidity, movement and passion Shakespeare actually built into his writing.

Practical Application

For the past ten years, I've been a teacher of acting and period style on both the graduate and undergraduate level—first at California State University, Fullerton and more recently at Temple University in Philadelphia. Both schools feature well developed actor training programs that have provided me with the opportunity to combine the training I received at ACT with my own personal experience as an actor and director to evolve an effective methodology that fuses intuitive acting with vocal dynamics. This work is not intended for beginning actors. Technical skills are being introduced and they have a very steep learning curve. It is essential that the students have a sound foundation in the fundamentals of acting so that they are able to incorporate the material into an established organic process.

The first step is to develop the student's appreciation for rhetorical technique. The cornerstone of this approach is based on the conviction that **pitch, rate of speech, volume, inflection and architecture are an organic part of the way we as Americans make ourselves understood**. The principal challenge is to help the student recognize when and how they use rhetorical tools in their everyday lives and then find ways to get them to relate that to dramatic text.

Energy

Begin by having the students memorize selections from writing rich with poetic images such as *Spoon River Anthology, Under Milk Wood* or maybe some of the shorter pieces from Frost, Cummings, etc. They like the material and it gets them used to using vowel and consonant sounds to endow the material with meaning. The most difficult thing to overcome in the beginning is to get them to appreciate how much energy is required to really make the poetry come alive. The universal tendency is to underestimate the passions that are motivating the writer and as a consequence they come in underneath. By getting the students to hear how much more effective they can be when they energize is the first major hurdle. It's not simply a matter of telling them to "pump up the energy." Instead, we start to look at the meaning of the text. What is the writer trying to say? Why is she or he compelled to speak? By delving into the psychological forces that are working on the writer (character), the student is forced to raise the stakes. The more passionate the experience, the more driven the speaker, the stronger the objective, with the result that the actor feels honest energizing the text. Fuller commitment to a powerful, actable action sets the imagination free and this is when the actor's intuitive, organic rhetorical techniques begin to emerge.

Objective and Text

The next step is to introduce the notion that **the objective really has to do with making the listener understand the images!** The student begins by tackling more complex text. Shakespeare's sonnets are good for this because the language is dense and the use of imagery similar to that found in his plays. If the students haven't had an effective introduction to scansion, then it's important to spend at least a week going over the fundamentals. Scansion fits in well with the sonnets and is an integral part of text analysis for Shakespeare.

Most students view "objective" as "what I want in the scene." When applied to a piece of heightened text this usually equates to "I want him to love me—I want them to fight for England—I want to know what to do" or "I want them to know how I feel." In general these choices are right. However, even when asked to refine their choice by picking a stronger, actable verb and a more specific goal, most students will still choose a physical action to get the desired result. The

breakthrough comes when you can get them to realize that **the language is the tool** and that the action has to somehow involve effectively using that tool to get the objective.

Emotional Honesty and Relaxation

Once the student is comfortable energizing the language and committing to the objective, give them their first scenes, selecting material from relatively straightforward plays that can be rehearsed without much difficulty. Plays like *Twelfth Night, Romeo and Juliet, Comedy of Errors, Richard III,* etc. all have great material for students to sink their teeth into. Until now the work has been principally monologs and tension hasn't been an overriding issue since the emotional stakes have been relatively low. With higher stakes comes a much stronger need to move and for tension to begin to creep into the work. Generally this is the result of a physical habit being associated with a specific emotional feeling. This might result in tension in the lips, forehead, eyes, or a compulsion to pace or gesture in a repetitive way. As this happens, try not to put the student's focus on the external, but rather work with them in committing more fully to the objective and to really listening and reacting. Most of the time with positive reinforcement this is enough to get rid of the problem. Some students however are working with a greater deal of tension than others. The habit is so firmly entrenched that the more organic approach simply isn't enough to break through the habit. At this point it becomes necessary to actually make the student aware of the connection between the emotion and the habit. Even though you run the risk of affecting spontaneity by "putting the actor in her/his head", it is at times the only way to eliminate the relationship between an emotional response and the physical feeling of the problem with which it is associated.

Final Project

The last step is to introduce the final scenes and monologs. The scenes should provide each student with the opportunity to work through an emotional progression concluding in some kind of climactic moment. It should also include a monolog of at least 14 lines. In addition to their scene each student is assigned what I call a "power monolog." These monologs are *not* the usual Shakespearean audition material. They are a selection of some of the most vocally demanding pieces of text in dramatic literature. They represent the culmination of the work over the course of the semester. Using an organic, truth based analysis of the text, sound acting fundamentals and positive reinforcement, you can then encourage the students to expand their horizons and explore the outer limits of pitch, rate and volume.

The performance of the final Scenes and Monologs is the culmination of a semester's worth of study. The students leave the class with a renewed sense of excitement about where they'd like to go with their classical acting. Perhaps the most difficult thing is to get the students to understand it takes many years and much practice to become really good at this kind of work. But it's no greater challenge than the learning curve for Speech, Movement, or Voice training. All are technical and all require much practice. It's important that they understand that in the beginning, conscious effort must be applied to any skill whether its pottery, painting, singing or dancing. But that with dedication and discipline, those skills will become second nature. As that happens, the fun begins!

Conclusion

The excitement and fascination of theatre is based on the power of the spoken word. The greatest writers the world has known have been playwrights. They are masters of language and language is what great theatre celebrates. The techniques I've been discussing are not just limited to Shakespeare and the few other dusty classics that are occasionally trotted out in regional theatres. The American tradition of O'Neill, Miller, Williams and Albee is still very much alive in writers like Kushner, Wilson and Orlandersmith. The actor that possesses the skills to serve these masters of language is needed more than ever and not just on the stage. Film and TV are tremendously powerful media and the very fact that there are fewer words makes it all the more important that within that genre and style, the language is brought to life in the most powerful way. Great stage actors can and do make great film actors!

I think it's fair to say that the American Theatre has suffered from a sense of inferiority to the British when it comes to Style and the Classics. Of course, many will insist that those days are past and that we're producing students that are the equal of the best that London has to offer. I'm not sure that I would agree. There's no doubt that we have phenomenally talented young people entering the profession. But as I watch the work I feel that I'm seeing more potential than actual accomplishment.

We have outstanding acting programs and the work our students do in Contemporary Realism is unequalled. **But we must integrate the success we've had in this arena with the challenges of heightened language.** Then we'll be poised for opening a new page in the history of Modern theatre. If our goal is to establish a truly "American Voice" for the classics, then our young actors must have command of the skills needed to bring true meaning and life to the greatest writing in English literature.

Essay *by Lyn Darnley*

Flying Like Ferlinghetti or Voice and the Aerialists

Lyn Darnley is the Senior Voice Coach with the Royal Shakespeare Company where she has worked since 1992. Formerly Head of Voice at the Rose Bruford College of Speech and Drama in London, she has an MPhil from the University of Birmingham's Shakespeare Institute. With Stephanie Martin she is co-author of *The Teaching Voice* (Whurr, 1996); and *The Voice Source Book* (Winslow Press, 1992). She has been an external examiner on many courses including the Voice Course MA at Central School of Speech and Drama. Her work has taken her to the USA, the Far East, France and Africa.

Walking along the Royal Mile at the Edinburgh Festival I watched the jugglers, fire-eaters, acrobats and a variety of dance troops perform on the wide street teaming with tourists and costumed actors handing out fliers advertising their shows. Above the hubbub I occasionally heard the hoarse and painful sounding barks of street performers but was unable to decipher any meaning from their words. Suddenly my attention was caught by a performer who was "walking" across the cobbles balanced on a vertical aluminium ladder while juggling with swords. This performer was conspicuous by the fact that he was producing a naturally projected sound that carried and communicated with the audience. Fascinated, I stopped and watched him with interest. What was he doing that allowed him to use the body so extremely yet keep the voice free when those around him failed abysmally?

I have often watched the street performers at Covent Garden and other venues and been puzzled by the fact that physical performers do not extend their physical accomplishments to the voice and language. Although the role of the body in voice work is well known and understood, we seem to separate the training of the physical aspects of performance into "body" and "voice" when surely one should facilitate the other. In British theatre the forms have traditionally remained apart with little integration. We teachers tend to work with one group or another because training institutes are separate but the connections between voice and movement have been understood for many years. Elsie Fogerty identified this link in her writings:

> In the art of making or speaking poetry the first place must therefore be given to a sense of the essential meaning of rhythm as a law of audible movement. Every movement must pass through some portion of space, must occupy some interval of time, must be accomplished by some degree of force. The right measure of these things depends entirely on the intention of the movement. When space, time and force are all rightly measured under the exact guidance of intention the action which results is said to be rhythmical.[1]

So the forms of textual performance and physical theatre share common ground but are the *skills* of the verbal actor irreconcilable with the *skills* of the physical performer? I recently was able to consider this question more fully when working on three late Shakespeare plays performed in the Roundhouse in London, a circular theatre space with a high domed roof which lent itself to the use of aerialist performers, and later transferred to the Royal Shakespeare Theatre in Stratford-Upon-Avon. The RSC is not the only company to employ aerialists. The Royal National Theatre, London has performed *The Birds* using aerialists. The Royal Opera House, London has also included acrobats and aerialists among its cast recently.

For me, working from a vocal perspective on Shakespeare with aerial performers is a new challenge—it is also an intriguing one because these actors have never fully focused on the speaking of any text, let alone the speaking of classic text. As members of the acting ensemble they were offered both voice and verse work as part of the rehearsal process. A piece of verse which sprang to mind because it draws comparisons with the work of the poet and that of the acrobat, was *Constantly Risking Absurdity* by Ferlinghetti. I introduced it when working with the actors and it opened up a lexicon and a wealth of mutually understood images.

> Constantly risking absurdity
> > And death
> whenever he performs
> > above the heads
> > > of his audience
> the poet like an acrobat
> > climbs on rime
> > > to a high wire of his own making[2]

The aerialists

The aerialists had been cast in *The Tempest, The Winters Tale* and *Pericles.* The plays were directed by Michael Boyd, Matthew Warchus and Adrian Noble respectively. As members of the ensemble the aerialists worked primarily as actors applying their physical skills where necessary. In *The Tempest* they performed in the air, in the masque, and on ladders and ropes as sailors and spirits of the island; in *Pericles* they performed fights and worked on ladders as sailors and dancers. The role of Dian was performed suspended high above the audience while the aerialist spoke and performed intricate moves simultaneously. These actors also played speaking "earthbound" roles in all the productions.

Over and above their principal roles and their aerial work there was an enormous understudy demand. The need to develop their voices was largely in order to facilitate the performance of these understudy roles. The lack of women in the cast meant that the female aerialists were required to understudy roles as demanding as Miranda and Ariel in *The Tempest* and Marina and Thaisa in *Pericles.*

The need to work on voice and text was constantly frustrated by the other demands made upon the actors. These demands included heavy understudy commitments which were unrelated to their aerial work (at times they were understudying three or four speaking characters in a production) and the essential time needed to work on their aerial routines. These routines were often dangerous and time had to be made for proper warming up, building of muscle and practising of routines. It was also necessary to spend time developing the artistic interpretation. There was a wide range of vocal experience among the aerialists and three of them had had no formal verse or voice training. Others had explored voice work as part of short courses and workshops. In contrast to this, the level of their physical skills was exceptional. Without exception they were all eager to develop their skills with classic text.

Time was at a premium because the shows were rehearsed twice as the plays were staged first at the Roundhouse and then at the Royal Shakespeare Theatre. Unfortunately the project did not allow the usual amount of time for work on the understudy roles as the transfers meant the company was permanently in production from January until the middle of September so there was a sense of the understudy work being pressured. It was difficult enough for them to find time to work on their physical work so what little time there was for working on the voice and text needed to be maximised.

I remember while working in a drama school the criticisms often expressed about actors from a strong physical or dance background:

> They can't breath— they won't breathe—they hold the chest—the lower back is arched—they don't release the abdominal muscles—they have no weight, their shoulders are over-built.

What I don't remember is hearing anyone talk about the remarkable way in which they *think physically* or of the joys of working with actors with highly developed kinaesthetic intelligence.

As voice teachers we work for more physical and muscular engagement in language so it seems to follow that those who are physically able should be able to transfer their skills to the word. Although this seems likely, there are difficulties which result in a different use of breath and effort and these differences have to be negotiated and overcome. What I have learned from this experience is that by working from the skills these actors *know* rather than from what they *do not know* they quickly assimilate the new knowledge and develop their skills. It was exciting to work with physical actors of this calibre who understand *impulse, rhythm and expression* not cerebrally but in every bone and sinew of the body, and so it is very possible to help them to learn new voice and language skills through active physical engagement.

Pluses and Minuses

We are familiar with the neurological connections between physical and verbal skills and actors who are able to perform to the physical extremes that these actors do must trust their bodies, their timing and their physical communication skills. I found it unusual therefore that they often mistrusted their voices. This was often related to the fact that they held the breath. They were very ready to acknowledge this and to identify tensions in the shoulder and neck area. They were acutely aware of locking the occipital joint without always linking this lock to the need for concentration or the "startle effect". While some knew of the "fight or flight" syndrome, others did not but quickly related not only their reaction to the fear of speaking but also to negative "fixing" in their own work. The common ground was enormous. When we spoke of efficiency and specificity in terms of voice and verse – something we did frequently—the actors would say—"it's the same for aerial work".

As well as mutual benefits there were contradictions. The greatest seeming conflict lies in the area of the shoulders. While the opening and elasticity of the upper body produced by advanced physical abilities is beneficial, the strength that has been built in the shoulders has often lead to rigidity in the shoulder and neck area and an inability to release this area. It was important to find the time to work on this area and to encourage stretching for release. This locking of the upper body tended to restrict chest resonance. The point of most tension for almost everyone was the occipital joint at the top of the spine. When considering the need for alert and concentrated work this is understandable. Most of the aerial actors were previously not aware of the connections and similarities between their discipline and voice work. They were however totally open to the notion that they could apply their strengths to the new challenge.

The pluses were considerable. These actors were by their very nature both superb athletes and kinaesthetic thinkers—they were able to make connections between their skills and the necessary skills for voice and the delivery of the text. They were quick to understand the anatomical need and function and had an ability to respond to both "information" based work and image based exercises. I found that when working with each individual it was necessary to access the right approach and to judge whether to use anatomical and/or image based exercises and in what proportion when using both.

When looking at articulation and muscularity I found that working with the images of fluidity or explosion alongside the physical perception of the muscular action was useful. The actor/aerialists had some difficulties around the creation of volume for all the well known causes of breath holding and upper body tension. It was possible to find exercises that were helpful for the voice as well as for their own physical work and they pointed out that the tension that inhibited the voice was a tension that was not helpful in physical performance either. Their instinctive understanding of the dynamic of the space and the movement of the body through it, could be related to the way in which language and sound moves through space, passing through vowels and being interrupted by consonant clusters before finally impacting upon a listener.

The acrobat is a physical poet communicating in space and producing dynamic and sensual shapes and patterns that tell a heightened story. Working on the text offered opportunities to make further connections. The questions that all actors ask about the delivery of the verse and particularly the "correct" way to speak the line came up frequently. The discussion produced the comparison between the delivery of the verse line and the swing, trajectory and momentum of the trapeze. The completion of thoughts and words related to execution and completion of the move or the "swing".

While exploring the *energy of ideas* when related to raising the stakes of a textual situation it was easy to draw physical comparisons. In some instances we made use of the ladders in the rehearsal room and physically climbed from rung to rung while speaking the text. Use was also made of the ropes in the exploration of the length of the line or the thought. It was possible to explore the swing of the rope and the apex of the swing and to relate this to the extension of the line and the thought. We spent time comparing the *exchange* of language to the acrobat *catching and receiving,* then passing the idea on or changing the idea and moving it on. The acrobat in the air is so dependent on his or her fellow actor that they "read" each other and the moment superbly. For them timing is everything and the stakes are always high.

The actors all knew how to juggle and when we were looking for physical analogies for textual jargon one of the actors compared the vocal "poise" to the "dead point" which is the highest reach of the ball on its journey upwards and the point at which it appears to hover before its descent.

The beat of the verse was something they were able to grasp quickly as all of them had a feel for the pulse and the rhythm. In their work as dancers and aerialists they are ready to repeat floor and air patterns. In text and in movement and music the interest and the drama often come from the breaking of the pattern, leading to the creation of the unexpected. Raising awareness of these similarities and of the value of these skills is often enough to facilitate their transference from one art form to another.

They also had an intuitive understanding of the delicate balance of skill and art and of the way in which technique supports interpretation by freeing it from physical restriction. I suspect this is because without technique their work is dangerous so the stakes are always high.

Many young actors who have spent three years at drama school, still feel that their techniques is lacking. What do they do when they have a bad day and cannot reproduce the feeling they rely on? Because so much of the training they receive is behavioural, they are often let down by their lack of technique. Technique depends on patterning muscle memory, so that the action occurs unconsciously. The aerialists found voice technique foreign to them but they absolutely understood the need for it. They always prepared both mentally and physically before a performance—many actors do not, nor do actors always consider the need for muscular maintenance.

They knew their bodies' strengths and weaknesses and worked on them. As physical performers they are used to using the body as a vehicle of expression.

Their facility with the word and communication through language was less exercised than conventionally trained actors. The work on words was the same as I would do with text trained actors. We explored the physical dynamics of the language rather than the "well made sound" and worked to keep the language active and engaged. To begin with they tended to use stress as their prime mode of emphasis but quickly related to inflection as the *movement in the word* and intonation as the *movement of the thought*. As well as movement in words and in the impulse of an idea, they also quickly understood and used momentum.

With practice they soon began to gain confidence and their creativity was freed.

> and balancing on eyebeams
> > above the sea of faces
> paces his way
> > to the other side of day
> performing entrechats
> > and slight-of-foot tricks
> and other high theatrics
> > and all without mistaking
> any thing
> > for what it may not be[3]

Working with one of the physical actors, on his understudy in *The Winters Tale* (Antigonus), we explored finding the length of the line and then the weight of the momentum into the first stressed syllable of the next line—so as to connect ideas and making sense of the text, by harnessing the form.

> I have heard, but not believed, the spirits o'th'dead
> May walk again: if such thing be, thy mother
> Appeared to me last night; for ne'er was dream
> So like a waking.

> *The Winters Tale* Act III.3

Finding this momentum reveals the sense by helping the actor feel the impetus of the thinking. This approach is that of the director Declan Donnellan who calls this momentum "acceleration". I believe it answers the question most frequently asked by actors, "What do I do with the end of the verse line?"

> This acceleration between the last word [of the line] and the following first stressed syllable is the major means by which the line ending makes itself felt. The actor may go with the acceleration, may deny it, may obey it, may disobey it, but the actor cannot simply ignore it.[4]

Working with these actors reinforced the fact that all performance whether physical or textual is based on the rhythm, direction, focus, impulse and momentum and a clear idea of what you are doing and want to achieve with the language or the pattern.

The skills of the two disciplines are not irreconcilable but must be positively applied to the current focus and activity. My regrets about the work on the late plays was that the period was so busy for the actors that time had to be snatched to do the work and that this was usually a matter of problem solving rather than relaxed exploration. I found that if I could phrase the suggestions in terms that related directly to a shared vocabulary and a physical sensation they understood immediately.

As part of the problem solving I had worked with the female aerialist on her understudy of Miranda. Her interpretative skills were very good and she used the language with great intelligence, but her tone was thin and she was unable to release volume. In an attempt to create volume she was pushing the language. Her posture was very upright with extreme tension in the shoulder girdle, which was problematic in her physical work. We had worked on breathing and opening the chest through various exercises and stretches which released her sound while she was prone or standing on her hands, but in an upright position the voice reverted to its habitual sound. Once *Pericles* opened, she was performing the role of Dian and performed suspended in 'tissue' while speaking. She spoke as she "unwound" and her head and arms were below her torso so that the whole chest area was open. The voice that emanated from her was full and resonant and had volume. The freedom this offered meant she did not have to 'push' and subsequently the language was not pushed either. Because of the regularity of the performance this quality was then assimilated into the muscle memory and became one part of her performance vocabulary. She was able to transfer this freedom into her performance of Miranda.

Throughout the process we spoke of the connections which revealed themselves, and a short while after the final performances Dan Crute, one of the aerialists, reflected on the experience. I asked him if the connections between physical and vocal performance had become clear.

It's a huge subject—and it's complex but movement is a strong metaphor in voice work. Some things stand out—filling space for instance. Projection is not a matter of pushing but is akin to the swing of the trapeze—the actor initiates the idea and then takes the thought to its completion. Filling the spaces depends on preparation of the breath before speech just as the acrobat 'takes the moment' before launching into the swing. When breath and release are synchronised the effort is minimised. I am used to working in a small space where small movements suffice as well as in large spaces and I understand the physical changes that need to be made. I am going to India soon and will be performing out of doors. I will have to suit the scale of the movement to the space. The amount of 'air time' will increase.

Most of the work we did and the work in the rehearsal room was about the language of the texts, while their ability with the language improved, they had always displayed a natural sense of the dynamics and music of the verse.

Although I am a physically trained actor, I always loved the words, the poetry, but about halfway through the process I began to hear—really hear the language, and to understand it in a deeper way. I also began to feel the iambic pentameter rather than seeing it as 'a rule'. The opportunity to work with experienced classical actors like Malcolm Storry was invaluable, his investment in the words was amazing. His ability to be heard in a vast space depended on textual precision and he was able to engage the audience emotionally through his vocal delivery.

I asked Dan if he thought that a lot of physical actors had a natural feeling for language.

Some are natural communicators, but the creative verbal skills of some very strong physical performers are not as dynamic as their strength and physical skills. I thought the language was fantastic but classic text isn't to everybody's taste and some of my friends who are physical actors saw the shows and didn't *hear* the verse in the same the way that I did. To me the language was stunning.

It is very likely that those physical actors, given the opportunity to work on text in a similar way would also be able to develop their facility for language—both as actors and audience. After all if those of us who work with the expressive voice began to work seriously on the expressive body we too would both perform better physically and develop a critical eye.

When I asked Dan if his experience had altered his perception of himself as a physical actor he said "Yes, people compartmentalise themselves too much. I'm an actor, I'm not going to define myself anymore. I am going to work in a wider theatrical field now."

To return to the Edinburgh Fringe Festival—The ladder walker had to find a low centre of gravity. He had to stay flexible and unlocked in order to continually adjust his weight in order to maintain his balance. His shoulders were relaxed, spine was long and his head and neck were unlocked and free. His chest was open and he breathed rather than holding his breath. His eye-line was outward and his peripheral vision was wide. He spoke to his audience and gave them attention rather than competing with the noise around him and yelling at them. These are the simple and basic qualities of an integrated actor: balance between mind, voice and body. Qualities all actors aspire to—whether their medium is text based or physical theatre.

Notes

1 Elsie Fogerty, *The Speaking of Verse*, published by J.M.Dent, New York (undated) p5.

2 From: *Constantly Risking Absurdity* by Lawrence Ferlinghetti.

3 Ibid.

4 Declan Donnellan, *The Actor and The Target*, published by Nick Hern Books, London, 2002, p260.

Essay *by Kevin Crawford*

Tangents and Parables:
alternative pathways into exploring Heightened Text

Introduction

Heightened Text is a term that we use to designate texts that occupy a linguistic territory that is not part of an everyday idiom. Heightened Text presupposes a refining and concentration of verbal energy. It conjures up the notion of a "poetic", dense stratum of text that demands an actor's full powers of intellectual and emotional comprehension. This kind of text requires reserves of verbal and vocal robustness to do it justice. If ordinary speech is like walking, then the performer of Heightened Text is an acrobat of the word, juggling many balls or leaping through fiery hoops, taming several hungry lions…

My background is primarily that of a performer and teacher working with Roy Hart and Roy Hart Theatre over a twenty-five year period from the late sixties on. During this period I started to engage with the field of Professional Actor Training and moved to Ireland in 1993 where I worked initially with a wide variety of theatre companies before being a full-time member of staff at the School of Drama in Trinity College, Dublin. My experience with Extended Vocal Techniques led me quite naturally to grapple with texts from Greek and Shakespearian Tragedy that express extreme emotional areas in extreme or heightened language. Through working on student and professional productions as well as on student scene study of five of the most linguistically vibrant plays by Shakespeare—*The Tempest, Midsummer Night's Dream, Coriolanus, Troilus and Cressida,* and *Macbeth*—I have endeavoured to find alternative pathways to textual exploration. My tenet has been that these texts can be approached tangentially, not directly, and that the student and potential performer can achieve great insight into the text, the character and the story in this way.

In this article I'll be looking at Heightened Text in Shakespeare and in particular in *Macbeth*. There is no sense in which I believe that this approach can replace a full understanding of the text and an appreciation of its linguistic and rhythmic structure and cultural background. What I propose is to let the actor in training fill out the full spectrum of responses, vocal, corporeal and imaginative, to the text and scene in question. My premise is that the actor can benefit from exercises that require them to put aside for a moment their intellectual and verbal grasp of the text. The hoped-for result is that they rediscover this text on a "deeper" level, meeting it with their full intuitive and visceral functions.

I do this in a number of ways, depending on the experience of the student actors and the stage that they are at in rehearsal or scene study.

One of my favourite tangents is to develop a series of movements that have their own choreographic value outside and apparently uninfluenced by the character or play. Such a slice of choreography can vary from the simple basis of a sculpture with one's own body on three levels (low, medium and high) to an evolved duo form, which can develop through 6 or more moves. The important elements being that the students know their choreography, that they design it themselves and that they do this without reference to the text. A second phase is to introduce sound into this choreographic landscape. And then to drop one word from the text into it and see how that word places itself in that new context.

Kevin Crawford is a founder member of the Roy Hart Theatre Company, whose groundbreaking influence on contemporary Voicework for theatre is internationally recognised. Resident at the Roy Hart Centre in France he toured extensively with the company for over twenty years, during which time the company received several prestigious prizes including an OBIE award in New York and the Prix Jean Vilar at The Printemps des Comédiens. In 1993 he moved to Ireland, where he was a full-time member of faculty at The School of Drama, Trinity College on the Professional Actor Training program. Kevin is now based in the Paris region and is a Visiting Lecturer at the Université d'Artois at Arras in the north of France. His current research focuses on the use of voice in the Greek and Shakespearean canon as well as on texts from the French classical tradition. He is also studying interdisciplinary links between Voicework and the Feldenkrais Technique.

In a sense I try to replace the notion of "contextualizing" with the idea of "incorporation", creating a new "context" for the word. We tear it out of its "home" in the written Shakespearian canon and give it a new if somewhat alien home, framed by the unrelenting choreography. And, surprise, the word attracts new substance to it because of being pressured through this "false" context. Building on from the word, we can introduce a whole phrase, and if we have evolved an appropriate choreographic structure we can play a whole scene using a series of tight telegrams from the written text. This way the student experiences the text/scene quite differently. They cannot rely on their usual points of reference or context for what happens. They have to fall back on their intuition to distil meaning and create another logic out of what might appear at first sight to be senseless, chaotic. More often than not I've found that the student actor is not "repressed" by submitting the text to this kind of choreographic inhibition; rather the opposite, they are stimulated to find new solutions to the problems the text poses and this may provide sudden insight into how they (not one, in general) will interpret the role.

Introducing tangents like this actually demands an even greater discipline and engagement from the performer. They cannot rely on their knowledge of the text nor the part but must submit to the sometimes apparently arbitrary nature of the choreographic process. The "actions" they play have a real physical root and this influences profoundly how they grapple with word, meaning and character. The tight structure of a Heightened Text finds its corollary in the tight choreographic structure. The two forms sometimes oppose and sometimes combine to produce startling, surprising or even shocking interpretations.

Collaboration on Scene Study : (1) The Training
A recent illustration of this approach is my collaboration in 1998 with Peter McAllister, at that time the Coordinator for the Professional Actor-Training Program at The School of Drama, Trinity College, Dublin, who was directing *Macbeth* as a scene study (in fact the student actors performed a good two hours worth from the play!) for the second year students. My task was to research the relevance of an indirect approach to language and character. This project was thoroughly documented and formed the basis for the "practitioner" aspect of my research for an MA in Voice Studies at Central School of Speech and Drama. For this collaboration I was to lead a series of nine workshops of a three-hour duration.

In the training strategies I employed in approaching character building for *Macbeth* I concentrated on two powerful matrices of expression, the vocal (from breath to free sound to text) and

the physical (including the facial). Concomitantly I invited the students to explore emotional, imaginative and inner sense impressions. This two-stranded process engendered a dialogue from outer to inner and from inner to outer that informed much of the work. After a thorough warm-up, which prepared both voice and body for the sometimes extreme and strenuous demands of the structured improvisation and studies, we concentrated on elaborating and defining a range of techniques. These were principally: 1. Isolation—the ability to disassociate face, body and voice 2. Visualization—the development of emotional depth and sense-perception through imagination 3. Dynamic Variations—the capacity to vary the dynamics in space, time and quality of any of the expressive pathways (vocal, physical and facial). We could further subdivide or segment these expressive pathways into mouth, hands, breath, and eyes only, and so forth, and then play on any combinations of these segments. At the same time, exercises were devised to develop the students' capacity to translate mental images and sense perceptions into concrete vocal and physical actions. They were encouraged to make decisions in a fast intuitive way that broke down barriers, and enabled them to experience events in the class afresh.

During the first three sessions we explored the nature of breath in relation to character and emotion, and investigated a continuum of expression around single words or emotions that stretched from the most infinitely small, barely perceptible, to the most expansive and dynamic. In parallel we made a series of animal studies based on references to Lady Macbeth and Macbeth in the text (Macbeth as beetle, bear, wolf...) This led in the next few sessions to a series of studies based on translating the events of Act 2 Scene 2 of *Macbeth* into a series of spatial moves. This took the form of dividing the space up into boxes or circles, each of which enfolded a different beat of the scene (sometimes including what happens off-stage). The students explored this by alternating between being the physical or the vocal embodiment of one of the characters, and using only their voice or body to drive the character forward. They also worked as pairs sharing the character and the spatial journey between them. These studies developed the students' capacity to "translate" from one expressive form to another: to "convert" a word into a breath, to "subvert" a verbal response into a physical action, to speak words through the eyes, and to deviate from a word to a gesture and back again.

All these studies enabled us to build up a vocabulary of references and an ease in the ability to isolate body, breath, voice, face and text, as well as to define parameters of rhythm, pace, intensity and quality that control dynamics. The visualisation work also deepened the students' capacity for subtle inner changes and transformations. This web of references and techniques served as a context where character could be apprehended on a pluri-dimensional level, words being only one of several sources of information and expression.

(2) "*Warrior-Lady*": a strategy for approaching language

We then brought these different strands together in a more complex structure that I call "Warrior-Lady" based on Act 2 Scene 2 of *Macbeth*. In this scene, which occurs simultaneously to and just after Duncan's murder, Lady Macbeth and Macbeth confront each other in an atmosphere fraught with excitement and overwhelming emotion. As there were several "pairs" of Macbeths sharing the role for the scene study it seemed appropriate that all ten students should explore this seminal scene even if they would not all ultimately perform it.

By this point the students knew the text quite well, they had a grasp of some basic elements for the characters and they were well used to working with contact improvisation and isolating body movement and vocal expression. They were also trained to be able to vary the dynamics of a movement phrase once a basic choreography was constructed and they could approach a verbal text in an abstract way, isolating the basic vocal constituents of pitch, colour, rhythm and volume. My brief was to see if the different "techniques" they had mastered could really be useful for delving deep into the scene.

First the pairs experimented with different qualities of pushing and pulling. This was always communicated by a hand-to-hand contact where grasping or pressing movements expressed the tone and movement quality. Once they had explored a wide variety of dynamics, making full use of the floor level and developing this through the space, the students began to play with movement fundamentals of acceleration and deceleration. On top of this they began to search out "stops" in the movement and moments when only one partner might move, or one limb (i.e. face or hands) might move. Once this "vocabulary" was established I asked them to construct a series of 6 moves with "holds" to punctuate them. Each partner was asked to imagine that 3 moves corresponded to them as "Warrior" and 3 as "Lady". I didn't explain at length what I meant by these descriptions but left it up to them to find their own interpretation; the important point being that there should be a wide variety in the form and quality of the six moves. Basing their approach on the kinds of moves they had already established, the students built up the choreography till they could repeat it and play with it in terms of timing, force and breath.

Once the sequence was established I asked them to play vocally in the moves before the "hold" moments. Then this was inversed so the vocal expression only came in the moments when the bodies were frozen. The next stage was to introduce some textual elements from the scene.

I broke the scene down into a series of six mini-scenes or beats for each character. This included events both on and offstage. This meant that Macbeth's beats would begin with his vision of the dagger in Act 2 Scene 1, include the murder that happens offstage and would terminate with him hearing the knocking at the door at the end of Act 2 Scene 2. Lady Macbeth's story would begin with her entry in Act 2 Scene 2, continue with her soliloquy and greeting of her husband and finish with her closing words to Macbeth. To coincide roughly with each beat of the scene I asked the students to use one key word (or phrase) that I had selected from the text. Thus each student had only six "words" (Macbeth had five words and a free vocal moment) to make the transitions and changes that happen so dramatically in the space of that short scene. I assembled this breakdown of the scene into the table below. For each move of the choreography there is a corresponding beat for each character and one key word or phrase.

First we thoroughly investigated these six "words", experiencing and speaking them without the choreographic structure, evolving an intense inner resonance of these words and filling in imaginatively the gaps between them.

Move	Macbeth's Beat	Macbeth Text	Lady Macbeth's Beat	Lady Macbeth Text
1	Vision of Dagger	"Bloody"	Entry II.2	"Bold"
2	The murder offstage	Free vocal	Hears the owl	"Hark!"
3	Return and frenzy	"Hark"	Fears deed not done	"Hark"
4	Remorse	"Amen"	Greets Macbeth	"My Husband"
5	Horror	"Wash"	Rebukes Macbeth	"Infirm of purpose"
6	Hears knocking	"Knocking"	Calms Macbeth	"Clears"

Having thoroughly rooted these words in an emotional and imaginative way we returned to the choreography of "Warrior-Lady" to see how they would sit in this new situation. The students were not obliged to speak the words in the order above but they were limited to one per move. This meant that it took some time before there was a synchronicity between the two partners in terms of the events in the scene. However, this disparity was not disturbing but sometimes quite refreshing to them as it meant they could experience the events in a non-linear way and they could make imaginative jumps from one beat to another, sometimes with surprising effect. They were forced to really discover the scene as they moved through their choreographic and verbal world. A richly layered physical expression with a tightly concentrated verbal one gave plenty of time for the students to magnify the emotional and mental pathway of their character. Subsequently they used longer phrases from the text based on these single words, so they could begin to make the transition to the full text.

Responses from Students and Director

Responses to the sessions were varied but on the whole positive. Some responded very well to the tighter organization of "Warrior-Lady" and maintained that this clear structure actually liberated them vocally and imaginatively. Others, though, preferred some looser forms that we had developed previously and found that the complexity of the choreography sometimes got in the way. One student in particular felt that the exercise really honed his sensitivity to each word and to the partner but questioned initially whether it was really helping him in the scene in question. However, when he came to review the whole process he was very clear that in fact this had had a very beneficial effect on this scene and the following ones, although he would have liked to continue further in this exploration (time certainly was a limiting factor!). Another student underlined the importance for him of non-verbal sound and the "translation" of a character into two contrasting presences, one vocal, and one physical. In some strange way his imaginative world was augmented by the non-verbal nature of the exploration. Yet another student intimated that the use of breath, through this series of workshops, had been exposed to him as a very powerful tool or lever into character.

What these comments don't tell us is how the students' relationship to the language was affected by their research in class. Were they, as I hoped, influenced on a deep level, where language meets consciousness? Did the sense of emotional connection with the situation, with the journey, with one word spread into the wider flow of the full text? Was there a possibility of a leap from this concentration on the "underbelly" of the scene to its realisation within a defined *mise en scène* with a full textual manifestation? I would have to wait longer for some more clarity in this respect. In an interview with Peter McAllister, the director, a short time after the presentation of the Scene Study he articulated the following in relation to the pertinence of the Workshop sessions to the final "performance":

> I felt they had an opportunity outside of the rehearsal process to explore something which I didn't have time with them, in the very limited time that I had… for them to free themselves physically, emotionally, imaginatively, and vocally of course: and I felt that in addressing all those kind of areas, they came to it with a greater fullness that I don't think they could have had if they had followed the

traditional kind of analytical text-based work that most directors including myself would do in rehearsal, where you would be trying to deconstruct the scene and work from moment to moment sort of exploration … I thought you gave them plenty of room to take some of the mythical kind of conceptions of character by sometimes taking the animal imagery or taking some of the changes from location to location or the journey through the play—I felt they were able to confront some of the bigger issues in a much freer way than if they had had to do that just through the text—I felt that sometimes they were liberated by not having the text, by leading them to make, say, a sound journey or a physical journey.

However, these responses don't fully address the question of the text for me, although they throw light on the approach to character: because the difficult transition or transposition is from the structured improvisation to the tight web of words that bind the play together. An exploration of character and the dynamics of a scene through "parables" or "similes" (i.e. in movement only, or in gibberish or in "splitting" a character up into a physical and a vocal manifestation, or in breath only) is very useful. But how can this feed into the main arteries of the play, the text? "Warrior-Lady" is a strategy to bridge that gap, by introducing first one word, then a phrase, leading into the possibility of performing the scene as written. And this did have some success but, as one student pointed out, it needed to go one step further.

My vision of this "one step further" includes the partners gradually relinquishing their physical contact but maintaining the "actions" of pushing, pulling, stopping and so forth in their inner imagination. Finally this "crutch" too is withdrawn until the words and their physical and vocal "foundation" are experienced as one "action".

Further thoughts and tangents

The relationship between words, thoughts, emotions and neuro-linguistic processes is a complex one with which I am not sufficiently conversant to make clear assertions in this paper. However, I am struck by the statements of eminent scientists, mathematicians and artists who describe their experiences in this domain. Albert Einstein asserts:

> The words or the language, as they are written or spoken, do not seem to play any role in my mechanism of thought. The psychical entities which seem to serve as elements of thought are certain signs, and more or less clear images…of visual and some muscular type. Conventional words or other signs have to be sought for laboriously only in a second stage (quoted by Oliver Sachs in *Seeing Voices* p. 41/42).

Similarly Sachs, speaking of Sign, the sign language of the deaf, notes:

> We see, then, in Sign, at every level - lexical, grammatical, syntactic—a *linguistic* (*sic*) use of space: a use that is amazingly complex, for much of what occurs linearly, sequentially, temporally in speech, becomes simultaneous, concurrent, multileveled in Sign (*Seeing Voices* p. 88).

The notion that sign language is cinematic with the capacity for close-ups, panning and jumps from past to present to future is contrasted with the linear march of narrative language.

My intuition is that the approach to words, language and character that unfurled over the nine sessions was an attempt to open up a linguistic territory that was a complex of verbal, gestural and spatial signs enabling the student to invest deeper mental and emotional layers in the act of speech. It seems to me, too, that heightened language such as we find it in Shakespeare is precisely a language that defies simple narrative reading or expression and yearns for a more complete grasp of the wonderful chemistry of image, sign, word and sound. This kind of Heightened Text reaches out to the richly textured landscape of Sign where the word is visible, and time and space concur to render it palpable. Heightened language demands an equally ferocious attachment to the invisible, the unthinkable, and the unimaginable, to translate its full force.

The experience that I've outlined above has not been an isolated one for me. I have tried out these and many other strategies with both students and professional actors. For them to be effective we need time—time outside a normal rehearsal structure—and participants who are already at ease with vocal and movement work, capable of structuring and defining their improvisations. I would say that such an approach could enable the participant to overcome natural resistance, fear or awe of the text/character. This allows them to really tap into the wellspring of energy in the words and situations. This doesn't take away the need for as full as possible an understanding of the text and the overall world it takes place in but it does allow the performer to reach out to it from within; to tackle these big moments or speeches from a less refined place, enabling them to lean into it with the full weight of their own emotional and imaginative world.

It clearly is a great challenge to find the key to unlocking the potential for emotion in such a text. The whole body, breath and voice galvanised can help the actor to bypass a purely cerebral, deductive approach. Psychology here is not a question simply of understanding the character. Rather the aim is to undercut a purely psychological approach, by not deciding motivation in advance. Often this is achieved by letting the words themselves give clues to the actor. In my case I prefer

not to even rely on them but to place the performer in an artificial context of heightened sensitivity and awareness. This in turn creates its own field of force and attracts the words into it. When they fall into this orbit they can re-emerge, slightly tattered, but shredded of unnecessary cladding, and are ready to be reawakened without assumptions. The memory of the force of these words, their verisimilitude to genuinely experienced physical, vocal and emotional states can be very telling.

A parallel that comes to mind in relation to the tangential nature of the work I propose is research modern astronomy makes whereby the presence of a "dwarf star" or an hitherto unknown part of the galaxy is apprehended through an absence of radio waves emitting from that source. It is deduced by its absence, its silence. Perhaps that is what I hope for too: that the "unknown planet" of a text will be thrown into relief by tuning in to the cosmic buzz that surrounds it.

Bibliography

Sachs, Oliver *Seeing Voices* (1989) University of California Press

Crawford, Kevin *An Interdisciplinary Approach to Character Building in Macbeth* (2001) Unpublished Dissertation for Masters In Voice Studies at Central School of Speech and Drama

Interviews with Patsy Rodenburg and Cicely Berry

Interview with Patsy Rodenburg

Patsy Rodenburg is one of the world's foremost voice and acting coaches. She heads the Voice Departments at Britain's Royal National Theatre and London's Guildhall School of Speech and Drama. Patsy has worked with and trained some of Britain's best actors including Judi Dench, Ian McKellen, Ralph Fiennes, Martine McCutcheon, and recently, Jude Law. She has been involved, among others, with the Royal Shakespeare Company, Cheek by Jowl, Shared Experience and the Michael Howard Studio for Actors in New York. She is the author of *Speaking Shakespeare* (2002) *The Actor Speaks* (1997), *The Need for Words* (1993) and *The Right to Speak* (1992). Patsy Rodenburg lives in London.

DC: We're talking on the eve of publication of *Speaking Shakespeare*, your latest book, and because it's obviously going to be in the forefront of your mind, I just wanted to start with what you think are the important issues that young actors—modern actors—face when dealing with Shakespeare?
PR: Well, *Speaking Shakespeare* actually was born in the rehearsal room at the National Theatre. I was attending a workshop given by a very great Shakespearean director...

DC: Would you like to...
PR: ...no, I'm not going to name this director, but about forty actors were in the room, and he was being absolutely brilliant. But it became apparent as I was attending this session that a lot of the younger actors were falling asleep and getting extremely restless, which I found rather graceless. So I talked to a lot of them afterwards, and they just all said the same thing, that they didn't understand what he was talking about. They didn't understand what an iambic was—they didn't understand that there was a difference between a line and a thought—and so he was talking beyond their knowledge. So the book is a very, very simple manual. It's a body of work which is about looking at how to start working on Shakespeare. Now, you know a lot about this because you were at the Royal Shakespeare Company at the time I'm going to talk about, but I think actors under the age of forty haven't been taught a lot of the very basic knowledge. I mean as basic as this, that if you don't speak every syllable, you cannot speak an iambic.

DC: Right, yes.
PR: Now that sounds very rigid but it's like -

DC: Or if you put in modern contractions, then it just doesn't work...
PR: ...it's not going to work. So what I think happened was, that there was a break from traditional ways of working on text—which happened really in the late sixties, early seventies—and that was a very important break, because being too formal with the text can make Shakespeare very dull and frigid really. Cicely Berry did a very important thing of breaking from that way of speaking, but the actors that were there at the RSC—in the sixties, seventies and to a certain extent into the eighties—had all the formats imbedded in them, so that there could then be a marriage. And I started to feel, and I've felt it for many years, that there's just basic knowledge, which I call the givens—you know, rhythm is a given; energy of thought line; prose into verse is a given. So the book initially just tackles what's there [in the text]. You've got to look and see—the clues are there. You must have had the same experience. I mean I regularly have the experience of actors saying, 'What's the difference between verse and prose?'

David Carey is Principal Lecturer in Voice Studies at the Central School of Speech and Drama, London, and Course Leader for the School's MA/Postgraduate Diploma in Voice Studies. He trained in Speech and Drama at the Royal Scottish Academy of Music and Drama in Glasgow, and has been awarded degrees in English Language and Linguistics from both Edinburgh University and Reading University. A voice teacher for over 25 years, David has worked extensively at both undergraduate and postgraduate level. His work in the professional theatre includes 4 years as assistant to Cicely Berry at the Royal Shakespeare Company during the 1980s.

DC: Yes. 'Is it just the way it's arranged on the page?'

PR: Well, that's a start, isn't it? But some of them don't even know that. They can't identify it. So the book is a response to that experience, and it's also a response to actors saying, 'Well, if I do all the givens, do I lose my imagination, my connection?' So part of the book is about how the imagination can be used to release the language, the imagery. You can make connections to the language imaginatively, so that the givens are a frame, a scaffolding in which you can actually give life and force with your imagination to the language. So it's not one road, there are two roads

Patsy Rodenburg

there. And the book is also a response to the fact that you have to be fit to do classical heightened text. So there's a regime in the book, which is about working out in order to do Shakespeare, because I think a lot of actors use the rehearsal to get fit and therefore don't rehearse properly. It sounds very tough, but unless we speak Shakespeare fully we're going to lose the plays.

DC: We'll lose the connection with the language.

PR: Yes, we will lose the heart of the play, which is experience through language, and forms, and structure. So that's how it came about.

DC: And why do you think we've lost that...

PR: It's so complicated, isn't it...

DC: ...or young actors under forty have, in this country...

PR: ...It's partly education isn't it, it's partly...

DC: ...general education?

PR: ...general education. I mean you must have noticed, as I have, that in the last fifteen years, the number of young students coming in to train don't have basic knowledge of certain things.

DC: Grammatical structures...

PR: I mean, what a full stop means. That's partly it. It's also partly that theatre has deconstructed itself away from the ensemble. You used to learn from other actors or you used to do it enough so you could find out how to speak Shakespeare by just doing it every night, eight times a week...

DC: And being with other actors who were doing it every night...

PR: I mean, old actors will talk about being in rep in bed sits together. And over breakfast the older actors would teach the younger actors and say, 'Well, last night that didn't work because of this, but if you try that...' And most actors around the age of sixty have that as a memory actually. And now, theatre is based around stars and a lot of the stars know much less than the other actors, so there's a feeling that you can't share information in that way. So I think it's very complex, but the main thing is the play. You're trying to give oxygen and life to the play, and it seems that most of the structures around are stifling the ability to give life and oxygen to the play.

DC: Would you relate it to the notion of heightened text? When people say that term to me I think 'Okay, well, Shakespeare's an obvious example of heightened text,' but then I think 'Well, okay, Pinter and Beckett are examples of heightened text in their own way.'

PR: I often say this—because I'm lucky enough to have worked with most leading American and British playwrights—but I have never had a playwright say to me make them more naturalistic. They've all said to me, 'Heighten it.' And what I mean by heightened—maybe in Shakespeare you're using language to probe and to survive, but it can be equally heightened if you are trying to hide. It's about precision isn't it, that something is so important that you can't be casual. That doesn't mean to say that you have to use your voice in a silly way—it means it's the precision of language...

DC: And that precision could be manipulative as well as revealing.

PR: Absolutely. And I talk a great deal, at this moment in my work, about a state of readiness, about heightened being a moment when a click happens in you. Be it that you're walking down the street and somebody's following you—you go heightened—click! And that's where great plays start and that's the state you have to be in. There's nothing casual about a great play, and that's what I think heightened text is. And people misunderstand this word. I don't want them to misunderstand it. It's formal, it's not informal. I was very intrigued on September 11th, for all sorts of reasons, but everyone interviewed in the street was heightened...

DC: they were heightened, yes.

PR: ...they were very clear, they wanted to cry, their voices might have broken but they were clear—because the precision of language is essential at that moment. So it starts and it ends with the word.

DC: And the word is all one has, to express how one's feeling.

PR: Yes. So as I get older, I think—and I've explored this through *Speaking Shakespeare*—that everything that you have to do to speak Shakespeare, everybody knows. Because the greatness of Shakespeare is his humanity. I've invented nothing in my life. As you get older you realise that. You've invented nothing...

DC: ...you inherit a lot...

PR: You've inherited a lot. And all it is, is about how humans work and that we need structure. As Wallace Shawn says in one of his wonderful plays—we all need stories. We need stories and we need structure in order to tell those stories safely. And that is Shakespeare's brilliance. So in order to speak Shakespeare—it's not that some people can and some people can't—it's just that we have to tap into what we already know. Do you know, those people being interviewed on September the 11th knew that they had to explain this very clearly. And so they did.

I've been doing this BBC programme—*Walking with Cavemen*. I've been training all the actors. I've been meeting all the leading anthropologists in the world...

DC: ...fascinating...

PR: ...and it got very relevant to Shakespeare, because the moment we moved into our full power, was when we realised that thought could be sequential. So that's what Shakespeare is asking us to do. I'm not asking anybody to do anything that they can't do.

DC: But to be fully human...

PR: Fully human, and not to be frightened of going up to something. The fear is that you've got to go up to these plays—and he's asking you to fully engage in your body, he's asking you to fully engage in your breath and your voice and your imagination and the speech muscles. And you've got to go up. And talking about September the 11th, I've been pondering a great deal why, why would the Taliban ban balloons and kites? And I suddenly thought, well of course, because you have to look up, and that's all Shakespeare is asking you to do, look up.

DC: Look up, yes.

Patsy And go up. So, that's the spirit of the book.

DC: You've done a lot of work with both American and British actors and, I know, international actors of all sorts. Do you see any difference in...

PR: Good actors are good actors. Maybe they go through different doors to the same place. I think, still, British actors tend to have more connection to language, but not always...

DC: No.

PR: American actors do have much more courage, in a way. They dive in, they have a lot more energy...

DC: ...they embrace it...

PR: ...and they just dive, which is fantastic. But all great actors are the same all over the planet, because it's about being an interested, curious human being that wants to work. It doesn't help when you go into acting studios in America—and you have to teach Shakespeare—and on the wall there is a saying, 'The word comes last', because a certain form of subtext is taught which is about denying the word. And all the work that we do in this country is to access the word, not to deny it and then paraphrase it. So that's a problem. But as I said, great artists are great artists.

DC: And to come back to what we were saying about being fully human, actors the world over have that capacity.

PR: And to go into Shakespeare you're going into very difficult, rugged landscapes. So you need courage, and you have to acknowledge you're fear. But the thing that we have to cherish in this country—and it's very important to talk about it at this moment, isn't it—is the great companies, like the National Theatre or the Royal Shakespeare. Companies that young actors can go in and play—and fail to a certain extent—and find their way, and have a structure that they can move in. And that's why we have to defend it at this moment—the Royal Shakespeare Company being in a very difficult period of its history. So we do have those structures. We have grants. I mean, it breaks my heart in New York, some of the finest actors in the world you meet, and they never go on stage to play Shakespeare and be paid. You know, they have to have another job...

DC: ...so there isn't the subsidised theatre...

PR: ...and it's heartbreaking, because they're some of the finest Shakespearean actors in the world in New York. And the only way they can do Shakespeare—because they're not a big enough star, they haven't got the box office appeal—is to do it in the evenings.

DC: In a loft.

PR: In a loft. And on one level Shakespeare is the easiest person to speak, because he does help the actor enormously; and on another level it's demanding. So there's a paradox there. But you definitely need help in a sense. And the more you do it, the more he'll help you. So that, I think, is why we've got to fight for that in this country. And I still think the good training's in this country. Shakespeare is at the heart of the training, which is not necessarily true in America. Does that answer the question?

DC: Yes, I think it does. I'm interested in exploring the training issue a little bit more—just in the British context—and just thinking about the role of voice, speech, text work in our training at the moment.

PR: Well, we have to just keep on demanding that it is the centre of training. I mean movement and voice work, you know, if the body isn't engaged, if the breath isn't engaged, if the voice isn't engaged, it is a very hard job to speak Shakespeare. I mean, the guy that played Frasier...

DC: yes, Kelsey Grammer...

PR: I saw that production of *Macbeth* and thought it was cruel to him because he had a very good go at it. The one thing the critics couldn't bear was his walk. Now that says a lot, because when we train somebody, we train them to be centred and free and open so that they can then transform in any direction through their body, through their voice. So, if you walk on stage as Romeo, you should look—long before you open your mouth—you should look as though you can be Romeo. Now that takes a huge amount of work and that takes twenty, thirty hours of technical training in body work and voice work a week for at least a year to clean that out. Now that's a huge investment of craft work and that is being eroded constantly. Now if you don't do that work, then you will only play to your habits; and Shakespeare, as I said earlier is asking you to go somewhere further.

DC: To go beyond that.

PR: To go beyond yourself. You know, you use yourself but you go beyond yourself. So we have to defend this in Britain now. If you're realistic, it's very hard to train a voice classically in under eight or nine hours a week of voice work. Now that is extremely expensive. Now from what I understand in

America—the correspondence I have with American teachers and professors—sometimes they get only a few hours a week. So it's hard, and you're then having to ask the student to do a lot of work on their own—which they can do, but by nature actors, unlike musicians, are very social, they're social animals, they work together. It's a social art form...

DC: They like the community of work.

PR: Yes, so it's very hard to say to a young person, 'You've got to put in an hour every day.'

DC: By yourself.

PR: By yourself.

DC: And be disciplined about it.

PR: So those are big issues I think. My American friends that come to London are amazed at the level of debate about how we feel that we're dumbing down on television and radio, but at least you can hear a debate going on. A recent visitor staying with me—and he was listening to BBC Radio Four in the morning—and he said, 'My god, they're attacking these politicians, and they're being expected to answer backwards and forwards!' You know...

DC: ...spontaneously...

PR: ...it's quite Shakespearean isn't it? That's Shakespearean. So you've got to hear this, you've got to know that it exists, and that language is an active tool. And debate is not about reinforcing something but, as Shakespeare asks us to do, any great debate moves you forward as you speak. In Shakespeare you transform, you move forward, but if you watch the majority of really bad shows—like *The Jerry Springer Show*—no debate is happening, it's just stuck like a needle, so...

DC: it's conflict...

PR: ...it's conflict and it's not debate and there is no movement of the idea, or shift. So we have to hold on to that, we've got to cherish those things.

DC: So where do you see modern theatre in this? We've been speaking a lot about Shakespeare—and obviously Shakespeare we still feel is a contemporary of ours—but just in terms of modern texts...

PR: Well, I think great young writers are very heightened. I mean people like Sarah Kane. I've worked on all her plays, and this is very heightened poetic text that has to be precisely spoken. *The Weir*, Conor McPherson's play, this is very heightened writing. It's about need, the greater the need. I am going to be very interested to see the plays that come out of America after 11th September because I think you might find that people will reach into themselves again to say something very important, very precisely. Imprecision doesn't move you. What breaks your heart in life is the detail of things, but when argument is important you want precision. How many of my

American friends were very bowled over by Tony Blair responding because, you know, he's alright isn't he as a speaker, he's not great, but he's alright...

DC: ...yes, he's fine...

PR: ...but he did respond much more precisely than George Bush could. And at that moment you, as a leader, to be able to speak, eloquently...

DC: ...on your behalf...

PR: ...on your behalf, you didn't want the man to say 'folks' about the people who had killed—the hijackers—and then 'folks', the firemen. You wanted somebody who could respond. And so when Blair did, they thought it was wonderful. So there is a yearning. I'm optimistic. I think there's a yearning.

DC: Yes, so you're not pessimistic about the future of theatre or the future of language?

PR: I'm not pessimistic at all. I think that it will change.

DC: Inevitably.

PR: I mean, Shakespeare was writing on the cutting edge and we have to risk cutting edge writing. If a young playwright is trying to work in that way, we must support them.

DC: Do you think theatre enables us to be more dangerous, to take more risks than film and television and radio?

PR: We have to *be* there, and we have to be engaged and we have to be human, don't we? I mean, we make a decision to go to the theatre, which is active. And if we don't like it, there is a decision to leave as opposed to a sort of television channel hop. So we have to be engaged, it makes us engaged. I mean, storytelling is needed. I don't see how it can be old fashioned, it's hardly started.

DC: It's sort of hardwired into us, isn't it?

PR: Yes, absolutely.

DC: The need for stories.

PR: Absolutely.

DC: To tell them and to receive them.

PR: And to use our voice. You know, the moment when the larynx dropped was a very dangerous moment, two million years ago. Why would it drop, when we are much more prone to choking? Well, there is a body of belief that it was because we needed to use our voices more—more specifically. So that's two million years ago.

DC: Yes, it's fascinating that moment—something happened in humanity's development, which required the larynx and facilitated speech, language...

PR: and to pass on knowledge, to educate, which is what great theatre does as well. Shakespeare educates us. Be better, he says to us.

DC: Be better.

PR: Be better—see clearer, be better.

DC: Thank you.

Interview with Cicely Berry

Cicely Berry has been Voice Director of the Royal Shakespeare Company since she joined in 1969. In addition to working artistically with the Company, she has been deeply involved with its education work, working extensively in schools to develop ways of working on classical text. She is also very involved in work in prisons. She has worked with theatre companies around the world, and for the last four years she has been working regularly in Brazil with 'Nos de Morro', a youth theatre company based in Vidigal—one of Rio's favelas. She is also an Artistic Associate of the New York-based company—Theatre for a New Audience. She is the author of four influential books: *Voice and the Actor* (1973); *Your Voice and How To Use It* (1975, revised 1994); *The Actor and the Text* (1987, revised 1993); and *Text in Action* (2001). Her directing work includes productions of *Hamlet* for the National Theatre Education Unit, and *King Lear* for the RSC at The Other Place. She was awarded an OBE in 1985 and has received honorary doctorates from the Bulgarian National Academy of Film and Theatre Arts, and from both Birmingham University and the Open University in Britain.

DC: We're talking in Stratford at a time when the Royal Shakespeare Company is going through some changes.

CB: Yes.

DC: So I just thought that this might be an appropriate time to ask you what you see as being the changes and the challenges facing modern actors and voice teachers in the coming years.

CB: I think that we are basically at a crossroads, and I think this is a time of great challenge for actors—for several reasons. First I think that internet technology, and all that has to do with it in the way of business jargon etc, has so taken over our lives that we are in danger of losing the imaginative essence of our language. From a world perspective, what concerns me very much is the number of languages that are lost every year: now, of course, we will not lose English because it is the basic language for commercial and exchange purposes—it is a world currency at the moment. However, just for that very reason, the spoken language has lost some of its power and we do not use it in an imaginative or creative way—we are not a storytelling culture any more. So the actor has to work very hard to keep that imaginative link.

Secondly, obviously television and film have made a huge difference: actors going to drama school for instance have to do a lot of work regarding training for television and for film because that is where a lot of their work will come from—and where they're going to earn their living. But they will have to work on dialogue which is so often downbeat and minimal, quite opposite to theatre where the word is living at the moment of speaking. Also actors are having to compete in a different way—because theatre is so often wanting people with "names," actors who have become popular in the media and are a recognisable type—a "product" if you like, and so actors are so often chosen for their persona, and not necessarily for their ability as actors to inhabit a part and transform into that other character.

So the answer to your question is that the actor in theatre today has quite a tricky job I think. For he/she has to be able to move delicately between the heightened language of Shakespeare and the classics, and the much more naturalistic sound of modern text. And for all these same reasons I think the voice teacher today in theatre has a difficult job in finding how to help the actor honour that heightened poetic expression yet make it sound as if it is being spoken for now—not easy. I have written very fully about this in *Text in Action*: a book which I wrote primarily to aid the directorial process, and in which I set down all the physical exercises that I have found particularly useful in bringing together these two areas of heightened language and naturalism.

DC: What you're describing seems very much the case in this country, in Britain, do you see a similar...
CB: ...in America? I think it happens just as much in America as it does in England—could be even more so.

The RSC at the moment, I think, is at a very interesting crossroads. For a number of years I think we have been taken over by the business ethic of expansion and popularism—this out of necessity to keep healthy financially; also in the last two years Adrian Noble [former RSC Artistic Director] began to rethink and revise our scheduling in a very radical way. He felt that our work was being dictated over much by the spaces that we work in, so we have left the London base at the Barbican and have started to do more touring in order that the scheduling can be more flexible. Touring has in fact become a major product, which is good both financially and can be very stimulating from an artistic viewpoint. However, although this has been very fruitful in many ways, particularly financially, it does mean that the Company has become over-expanded I think, and I am certainly one of those who believe that we have got to pull the Company back and get in touch with our core values in Stratford—that is, get a really good core company together who work on their craft and explore Shakespeare and other classical work as well as modern plays. That is how we built up our work in the past—and I think made our name—and how so many actors bore fruit and became famous—actors like Ian Richardson, Judi Dench, Ian McKellen, Ralph Fiennes—they began with the RSC and with Shakespeare—all made their name that way. And the good news is that our new Artistic Director, Michael Boyd, wants to

do just this. He is planning a core company here in Stratford, which will have long rehearsal periods, daily classes in movement and text, and will interact with other disciplines, and other areas of work which will be going on in the Swan and The Other Place. I think his plans are great and it is going to be very exciting. For we surely have to keep asking—why is Shakespeare important to us today—and why is he relevant.

DC: "How does he speak to us today?"
CB: Absolutely.

DC: And what do you think is Shakespeare's importance?
CB: Well, I think one of the important things is the fact that he is nearly always dealing with very strong political issues—issues so often part of today's world. The dilemmas posed in *Romeo and Juliet*, for instance, could be centred in the Palestine/Israel conflict—or even with the Protestant/Catholic issue in Northern Ireland. I think in all his plays there is a basic political issue which is informing the story. So I think we will always respond to his work in that way. I also believe there is something in the language which catches our feelings in a very deep way. I was in Cardiff prison last week, for instance, working on *Julius Caesar*—and they got very moved by Brutus' soliloquy debating to himself whether Caesar should die. And as in so much prison work that I have done they found it difficult to read the text at first—maybe they can't read, maybe they're dyslexic, as 69% of people in prisons *are* dyslexic—but once they got over their initial shyness, the joy they got out of speaking that language was just wonderful. Somehow the fact that they are able to put these feelings into that elegant and heightened language gave them an extraordinary pleasure. Somehow Shakespeare catches peoples' inner need to speak—it is magic!

DC: Do you think that's true of any kind of poetic heightened language or does Shakespeare have something particular to offer?
CB: I think it is true of all good poetry. I think there is something about Shakespeare though that is particular—unique I would say—he wrote the spoken word—that is the only way I can put it. However heightened the language it is accessible to everyone. Somehow the language is speech in action. And until you speak Shakespeare out loud, you can never totally understand all the implications of it, because the sounds of the language and the rhythms of it give you a bottom line—they underscore it in a way. And I do think that academics have actually hijacked him and have made it so dry and literary. Because school kids now, or students, have to study it and find out all the meanings and look up the glossary, and 'is this the right punctuation?', and they have to look at all sorts of academic issues like that and I think then that's...

DC: ...they lose the experience of the actual language...

CB: ...yes, what the language actually tells us, and the underscoring of it, how the rhythm itself is its dynamic. When you are reading something off the page, you are engaging the left side of your brain as opposed to, when you're speaking it, you're imagination can be let free by the very sound of it. You can talk about the images

Cicely Berry

by reading it, but you're only talking about them and you're not finding them in your own imagination as you do when you speak the text aloud.

DC: Yes, and you said something just there about the rhythm having its own dynamic, and there's a physicality about that as well, isn't there?

CB: Yes, amazing. And, as Edward Bond says, the language should go through your body. You feel it in your body not just in your mind. I mean, I think actors have a difficult job because they have to learn text by reading it and learning it, but then somehow they've got to let it go free and allow it to inhabit themselves and their bodies. I've gone off the point a bit there.

DC: No, not at all. But given the cultural context of the devaluation of language by financial concerns and television and everything that you've described, what do you feel we as voice teachers need to do to address the needs of young actors? Yes, maybe a lot of their work is going to be in film and television but nonetheless a lot of them will want to work with Shakespeare which requires this kind of...

CB: It's what we have to live with of course, this two-way thing that young actors need to be able to work in television and need to have television presence. But what is interesting in the RSC, certainly, is that young actors are really avid, are really greedy to work on the language and to work on the verse of it, and literally enjoy it and make it their own. And I think they get a great satisfaction out of it and a feeling of excitement. And I think that that's what the actor's job now is in the theatre, to excite people with language. But we have a difficulty there, because people are so used to going to the theatre to see musicals, etc., that they often go to the theatre to be entertained and to be passive. And if you go into other

countries—like Brazil, where I do a lot of work—you witness a totally different kind of reaction from audiences.

DC: Where audiences engage.
CB: Absolutely, and get angry and...

DC: ...passionate...
CB: ...and I think that's incredibly important. Theatre has become, in the west, a thing for the middle and upper classes. I mean, there are lots of groups that go round and work in inner cities, etc., but that is somehow not the answer to the whole of it. People go to the theatre to be entertained—and I believe theatre should provoke and stimulate.

DC: Well, I know that you do a lot of work with Theatre for a New Audience in New York, and I'm just wondering how you find that that feeds into the theatre culture, certainly in New York, or the States in general?
CB: I am very keen on doing the work in America, simply because their root is in method acting whereas our root is much more in language.

DC: What do you see as the kind of essential difference or focus...
CB: I think that there is a wonderful mix. What is interesting in America—because, you know, my husband was American and trained in method acting—I think the focus there is in what you feel and how you react to the situation; whereas in Shakespeare, I believe, the whole thing is about survival, and that the characters/actors have to think through the situation—debate it if you like—in order to survive. So it's a lovely mix between the English way of working out what everything means and bringing that together with how that then makes you feel...

DC: ...something more visceral...
CB: Yes. But for the Americans, I am always getting them to think and experience the physicality of the language before they feel the emotion of it, to try and make them *think* it through how the character's mind ticks. And perhaps with the English actors, through exercises on restraining people and restricting people, you get them to *feel* it more physically.

Cicely Berry at work

DC: How far do you think form and structure within the verse, in Shakespeare, contributes to that kind of balance between feeling, physicality and mentality?

CB: I think it is very important actually. Take Brutus' soliloquy [in *Julius Caesar*]—'It must be by his death'—and the central question of when do we say "no" to tyranny—the way he has to think that through himself—that Caesar must be killed. Does he come to the conclusion at the beginning of the speech and then justify it, or does he [argue it through to that conclusion]? How it's structured tells us so much about how Brutus thinks. And how in Brutus' case he goes from what is happening in the present to his own internal philosophising about everything. And it's the structure of how he debates his problem through for himself that tells us so much about how we ourselves think. The structure of his argument is so like how we think ourselves. You think, 'Oh, I must do this' and then you think, 'Or should I?' or whatever. And it's the fact that you have to think it through that matters. It is how you think in order to survive your best that then informs your decision and maybe your feelings.

DC: I'm interested in the fact that you referred to Shakespeare and the situations in Shakespeare as being about survival and how vital the language is in that context. It strikes me that when we are facing situations where survival is important, then we use all our faculties. It's an emotional situation—we are heightened emotionally. We feel something physically as well, but also our brains are working much more actively.

CB: Absolutely, much more actively in order to find out what is important to us and how we can survive and keep surviving. One of my favourite quotes is that by Thomas Kyd [from *The Revenger's Tragedy*], 'When words prevail not, violence prevails.' I think the wonderful thing about Shakespeare, and possibly why he is so universally accepted, is that he is able to catch how people think and how people think in order to lead them through situations. You know, you think of the Hostess describing the death of Falstaff [in *Henry V*, Act II.3], and the precision with which she describes it—'up'ard and up'ard, and all was as cold as any stone'—and how we in real life, when something tragic happens, have to find each of those particular precise moments—and that releases her and makes her able to go on instead of keeping it all...

DC: ...so the expression of it in the right way...
CB: ...is a positive thing.

DC: Can I change the subject slightly? We've spoken a little bit about the differences between American actors and British actors, but what similarities do you see? Do you feel that English-speaking actors, as a whole—whether it's British, American or Australian, wherever—are we facing similar challenges with Shakespeare and heightened text of any kind?

CB: I think so most definitely. I was working in Australia last year in October, and our whole way of expressing ourselves in this modern age is to underplay what we are feeling or what we are thinking, we do it through a laid back way of communication and...

DC: ...so we don't reveal?

CB: No, and we don't allow ourselves to think right the way through things. But I think all actors—whether they're American, English, Canadian or Australian, whatever—realise that. And they can hear it in the language, but they need confidence. I mean, it's basic confidence to actually fill the language without feeling they're being a bit false or a bit classical or whatever. That's why I do a lot of exercises which are physically strong. Even if you set up an exercise where people hold somebody back, physically—now the actors know that that is an exercise and not to be taken seriously, but at the same time they still get upset at the fact that they have to get away from each other. And that gives the language an extraordinary power. And you find them opening up the vowels, lengthening out the vowels, being much more poetic. And it's simply, really, that we have lost that way of speaking and therefore we feel—and that's not quite true—but we feel a little false by doing that.

DC: ...or we don't feel allowed to do that....

CB: ...yes, but when you are really angry you do come out with something which is much fuller and more expressive than normal. And I think actors realise this. I think all intelligent young actors realise this, but they find it difficult to do, because they don't want to look as though they're putting something on. And you're *not* [putting it on], providing you can tap into that centre—and the violence and the passion that everybody has inside—and allow the actual physicality of the language to do it. I do think that Received Pronunciation in Britain and the American equivalent, Standard Stage American, actually stop actors. I mean, it's an inhibiting force and I think we should be much more open to dialects or variants. Unfortunately, some accents go with Shakespeare very well. I've heard wonderful Shakespeare in the Blue Ridge Mountains of Virginia, wonderful *Macbeth*, or Northumberland [in England] is wonderful.

DC: So what contribution do you feel that drama schools have to make to developing this kind of culture?

CB: I just feel that I learnt so much. I mean, I was always as a child absolutely obsessed by poetry. I learnt to read so that I could read it. But I never forget the work we did at Central School when I went there, back in '43 I suppose it was, and Gwynneth Thurburn was then Head. There was so much emphasis put on verse speaking. And I think the more actors are asked to just read verse out to the rest of their group—not in a formal way—the more they will tune in to the richness of our language and its possibilities. I think that is one of the best ways of doing it, and I don't think nearly enough is done on that.

DC: Do you think people have a fear of poetry and so doing regular reading of verse would enable them to get through that? Or is it more to do with that familiarity with the heightened...

CB: ...I think it's to do with familiarity, and one day suddenly hearing 'Oh, that is exciting to hear.' I don't think people are frightened of poetry for I think so much poetry is written—you see it on the underground, you see it everywhere—by not necessarily educated people. Poetry, people love it. But I think that work has to be done in drama schools—you know it has to be put into the curriculum—so that people start to listen to it, and listen in an organised way so that they can hear what is going on and then respond to it. I mean, they don't have to like it or whatever, that's up to them. But I think if you don't have that experience over a period of time, a regular experience, then that is a great shame.

DC: It is interesting to think that in effect maybe our first, but sometimes our only experience of verse is as children, as quite young children...

CB: ...and they love it. If you think of reading to your kids when they're young—and I just used to adore it—you get into the rhythms of it, then you make up silly lines and play with the words, and they love it. It is something very, very innate in us, which I think we educate out of people because I think we...

DC: ...it becomes something we study ...

CB: ...or a religious, formal thing—which grew up from, in very primitive times, rhythms and things. It's there in us.

DC: That's great. Can we leave it there? It feels like a very good place to finish—it's there in us!

CB: It is!

Voice and Speech Science *Ronald C. Scherer, Associate Editor*

LABORATORY RULES

The lab is a sanctuary of thought and activity.

Study important questions only.

Respect every one, disrespect no one.

Be honest always.

Be helpful always.

Never panic in the lab. Move slowly. Be patient.

Always ask "What's wrong now?"

Know today's calibrations for sure.

Fix problems now.

If you can't figure it out, ask for help.

Keep organized and detailed notebooks.

Keep the lab orderly.

If we need to buy it, put it on the list.

The computers and printers are not for personal use.

Humming and singing in the lab, yes.

Gum chewing and radios, only if you are really alone.

REMEMBER:

Your research is wrong until you prove it right.

Persistence is rewarded.

We are spending someone else's money.

Quality is remembered long after the pain is forgotten.

Ronald C. Scherer, PhD, is a Professor in the Department of Communication Disorders at Bowling Green State University, Bowling Green, Ohio. His prior position was Senior Scientist in the Wilbur James Gould Voice Research Center at The Denver Center for the Performing Arts, where he also taught Voice Science in the Theatre Voice Coaches and Trainers Program at the National Theatre Conservatory (DCPA). He is strongly interested in the science and pedagogy of performance voice and speech, as well as in models of voice production.

Editorial Column *by Ronald C. Scherer*

Laboratory Rules and the Humanity of Research

Many of us have not worked in a research laboratory where data on voice and speech production are obtained. Successful research activities require expertise, planning, dedication, financial backing, and encouragement, not unlike successful theatrical productions. Understanding how research is performed in voice and speech laboratories lends an appreciation to the significance and artistry of such endeavors. More important yet is to understand the *behavioral and attitudinal orientations* that are necessary in the *doing* of successful research. The focus of this essay is on the "humanity" of doing research, the vehicle being an explanation of "rules" to live by when conducting research.

In our Laryngeal Physiology Laboratory at Bowling Green State University, we have posted a framed list of "Laboratory Rules". These rules help to set the tone of our attitudes and behaviors, encourage cautious success in our work, and establish professionalism in our students. These rules are shown in the accompanying figure, and each one is discussed below.

Rule 1: The lab is a sanctuary of thought and activity.

The lab is a place of exploration and testing of ideas, and the aura of sanctity of this concept must prevail as soon as one steps into the room. It is like entering a different world where there is a special mission. When this sanctity is accepted, students and colleagues feel safe. They feel free to think creatively, speak without inhibition, and participate in joint decision making.

Rule 2: Study important questions only.

Every day we must ask what the worthy questions are. Why waste time, energy, and money studying an idea with no real payoff? To know what ideas are actually worthy of study in voice and speech production, one needs a strong understanding of (a) how we make sounds, (b) what basic notions need clarification, and (c) what the various voice professions need to know. A broad perspective with adequate research training is necessary. The guiding thought should always be, "What is the important question for us to tackle?", not, for example, "What can we do with this piece of equipment?". Questions (the answers to which would improve our theories and models of voice and speech) are always important. They are not always practical in the short run, however, to the dismay of practitioners. What is the easiest way to find out what the important *practical* issues are to research? Ask any voice professional who works with students, clients, or patients most of the time. They can tell you what new information would help him or her the most. An important lesson, then, is not to waste time with relatively meaningless questions, and once the questions are posed, figure out a way to answer them satisfactorily.

Rule 3: Respect every one, disrespect no one.

People in voice and speech, no matter what profession, do not succeed without effort and dedication. This observation alone would be sufficient to garner our respect. Students need to adopt a respectful attitude, and witness it first-hand from the faculty associated with the lab. Respect must be *practiced* pervasively, at school (that is, in the lab, department, college, and university) and when away at conferences and meetings. Respect must be shown to everyone. Disparaging words about others only have negative outcomes. Critical statements must be about ideas, not about people. Showing disrespect is the classic "four fingers pointing at oneself while only one points at the criticized person." Showing disrespect is the quickest way to professional isolation. Showing respect for everyone else is the best way to gain it for yourself.

Rule 4: Be honest always.

The heart of research is the honest search for better understanding. Issues about honesty in science usually concern making heavily biased decisions when obtaining data, analyzing the data, or expressing the data, with self-enhancement (money, prestige, employment) as the goal. People who intentionally change data run a high risk of being caught and heavily punished by the scientific community. There is a more subtle, lower level of dishonesty, however, that can be a constant challenge to the researcher. What does one do when inconvenienced by minor mistakes or slightly inaccurate measures, estimates, or calculations? Minor mistakes easily can be made. A classic example is incorrectly recording a datum point, which then is seen as an inappropriate "outlier" when viewing a figure of the data (that is, the incorrect point is graphed away from the other data as if it were an outcast of the clan of data). If the erroneous point were not too far from the other points, the researcher may think that the datum was wrong, but not *too* wrong, and therefore might leave it be, thinking it probably would not affect the trend and interpretation of the data. This would constitute a minor dishonesty for convenience, and may indeed not affect the outcome; but it *should* weigh on the conscience of the researcher, because it would be an unnecessary and intentional inaccuracy of data representation.

The student must learn to avoid such minor dishonesty. How do we encourage students to acknowledge and change minor errors that might occur? We declare that we are permitted to fail. If a mistake is made, it is declared immediately and fixed without penalty. Mistakes are part of the learning process, and the truth of human imperfection. Both the student and seasoned researcher may be embarrassed when making minor mistakes, and feel somewhat guilty or hesitant to acknowledge the problem. Frankly, we can not wait around for guilt and confessions, but must move forward with improved practices. Actually, I laugh when noninjurious mistakes are made in the lab, because I think they are funny, especially when I make them (they produce unexpected variations, and challenge me to find out what is wrong "now", see Rule 7 below). But then there must be an immediate correction, otherwise it no longer is humorous, educational, or efficient. Furthermore, a central realization is declared in the lab that data we gather are never about us, but about the question being asked and the methods used to answer it, and therefore must be valid. Indeed, we might go months, even years, until certain raw data are sufficiently valid and defendable. This objectivity about the data allow graphs of the data to speak for themselves, and we are disinclined to force them to fit some bias of how they should look. Then there is no question of dishonesty; there is only impartial reporting. Despite the high-pressure expectations imposed by employers and funding agencies for successful research, scientists care first about honestly answering meaningful questions with valid data.

Rule 5: Be helpful always.

This is straightforward. We need to help each other out since there are many aspects of laboratory activity that are learned only by doing, and require constant cross-help by both students and faculty. Technology changes, a second pair of hands or eyes are frequently needed, activities accelerate before conventions, and so forth. Each person tends to know more about something than everyone else, and sharing when needed brings efficiency to the entire enterprise. We all must be committed to each other's success.

Rule 6: Never panic in the lab. Move slowly. Be patient.

This rule is more important than it at first appears. The issue of safety is obvious. If one moves relatively slowly and deliberately in the lab space, there is less danger of tripping over a cable, walking into the edge of a table, cutting oneself, spilling something, and so forth. For example, just recently I moved too quickly getting up from a chair, bumping a notebook that pushed a bottle of soda pop onto the floor. A corollary to the rule is "If you have a bottle of soda pop in the lab, keep the cap on tight!" (which, by the way, was the case). Another important point of view of this rule is that minimizing the speed of physical movement promotes calm thinking and more complete conceptualization, as well as consistent carefulness in keeping organized records and maintaining the correct sequencing of tasks. Time must seem to stand still, so to speak, so that there is full commitment to the task at hand. Moving fast is the quickest way to destroy equipment, cause bodily injury, make mental mistakes, and produce incomplete work. Slow is careful, and slow is efficient.

Rule 7: Always ask "What's wrong now?"

This rule is perhaps the most important rule of the lab. It is a negative question with a most positive outcome. It is the critical question that saves the researcher time after time. When we are performing research, like recording a person speaking some text, we have set up the lab for the occasion, making sure that all the equipment is working correctly, the transducers are calibrated, the procedures with the subject are well known and tested, everyone has a specific job to do, and redundancy in monitoring signals is established. During such a procedure, each of the experimenters and assistants must keep repeating *consciously* in his or her mind "What is wrong now? What is happening that is not right or correct? What seems to be inconsistent with expectations?" We must assume that right now there is something that *is* wrong. If we do not find out what is wrong right now, our recordings and data may be compromised and the whole recording session wasted.

The bottom line with this concept is that all activities are "guilty" until proven "innocent". We have to constantly prove to ourselves that the subjects are performing as requested, that signals appear right, that the equipment is working correctly, that we have written down the correct numbers and statements. We have to have built-in redundancy of information, two simultaneous recordings of some signals, and that if possible, two people monitoring the same signals or procedures. We have to have more completeness in the written notebooks than seems reasonable, because later we will need the extra information to solve problems that inevitably come up. Note that this orientation of asking "What's wrong now?" takes place all the time, even when we are trying to analyze the data (Is this analysis correct? Is it reasonable that the data look like this when graphed? Did I make a mistake in these calculations or equations?), when we are writing reports (Am I expressing this clearly?), and even when we are reading other peoples' papers (How do I know that their data are valid? Are they representing their findings in a reasonable way or are they oversimplifying, over generalizing, or missing the point?). Critical thinking of other peoples' research is only good when you first are your own worst critic, and an important role of a research critic is to continually ask "What's wrong now?"

Rule 8: Know today's calibrations for sure.

When we are measuring air pressure, air flows, sound pressure level, torso extension, or any other aspect that deals with dimensions, we will use instruments that must be calibrated. Calibration means that we have obtained the relation between the input levels to a device and the output levels of the device. For example, air pressure is put into a pressure transducer whose output is a voltage level, the magnitude of which is proportional to the actual air pressure. The calibration of the instrument is a graph and an equation relating the amount of

Pressure In versus the amount of Voltage Out. One of the worst frustrations in research is to painstakingly obtain great data after careful planning and execution of a research project, only to discover that the transducers were not calibrated well enough, making the data useless because their real values are unknown. The calibration of equipment should be checked just before an experiment is performed, and then rechecked after the experiment is over to make sure no changes have taken place. The researcher must know the calibration for sure; otherwise the data may be no good.

Rule 9: Fix problems now.
The issues here are the size and solution of problems, disruption of organization, and departure from expectation. To delay the correction of a problem in the lab is to delay progress. Large problems (for example, fixing or replacing an important piece of equipment we all use) are sometimes easier to deal with than other problems (for example, finding the minor error in some measurement, determining the source of noise on a signal, replacing a specialized and difficult-to-find item, or finding the right person to perform a minor repair). If something needs to be fixed, organization of the lab can be disrupted, and the normal expectation of availability, completeness, efficiency, and timing of activities may be disrupted, leading to frustration and loss of time (and money). These disruptions are minimized by rectifying problems quickly.

Rule 10: If you can't figure it out, ask for help.
This concept is not as straightforward as it might appear. In an educational setting like ours, students are instructed in concepts and methodologies as well as encouraged to learn on their own, the latter to develop more independent skills. Students therefore are trying to figure things out, often on their own. There is a point when it is best to ask for help, however, and that point is certainly reached when *not* asking for help creates risks for others in the completion of the group's research tasks or puts projects behind schedule.

Rule 11: Keep organized and detailed notebooks.
We know for sure that (a) we never know when we will need certain information, (b) we must not rely on memory for anything important, and (c) we must always be ready for a science audit of our research program. This means that the research notebooks must be nearly immaculate. These notebooks contain our experimental designs, set ups, calibrations, theories, difficulties and solutions, results, and conclusions. They tell the real story, and must be elegant and complete. They must include redundant and overlapping information so that checks of information and details about how we got some result or solved certain problems are clear, and not just clear to us, but would be clear to an outside reader. Not only must the notebooks be written with the intent to include all information that might be important in worst case scenarios (like lost data files), but also written with a keen aesthetic in mind. That is, the notebooks must have a visual balance and organization that is beautiful to the eye, an attraction that says research is a beloved practice. The notebooks are the heart and soul of the research endeavor, that which lasts forever after the experiment is done, and that which is the source of life for any publication and presentation on the project. They epitomize human creativity, and physically embrace new truths.

Rule 12: Keep the lab orderly.
Visual organization helps one think with order and with care. It also allows one to move easily in the lab, find objects quickly, and be ready for the occasional visitor. However, orderliness is not always a virtue, and can often work against one. When we are in the middle of a project, for example, papers may accumulate, cables might be plentiful, and other signs of important activity may prevail. When this happens, the disorder must have an intended familiarity and function. It is important, however, to regain order and clean surfaces when the flurry of the project comes to an end, because reliable order does invite further research activity. Also, consistent order avoids the problem of individualistic differences in favorite expressions of disorder.

Rule 13: If we need to buy it, put it on the list.
This list is the supplies list, not the big ticket item list. We recently needed nine-volt batteries. This object was on the "list" for over a month. When we finally needed one for sure, I had failed to purchase the batteries, and we did not have one. Little things like this can become huge problems at the wrong time. A good example, again relative to batteries, concerns the sound level meter with which we measure sound pressure level. We routinely change its batteries just before an experiment so that we are sure to have no failure of that instrument (relative to power, anyway). Once we did not change them, and we lost important data due to old batteries failing. We failed first by not keeping sufficient supplies.

Rule 14: The computers and printers are not for personal use.
It is important to separate personal from non-personal use of lab resources. This is not easy to do, and full restriction would defeat our purpose because many personal uses teach new awareness that eventually contributes to our success (like learning web skills). However, class reports and the like constitute a misuse that we could not defend relative to the federal dollar purchase of lab resources. We forbid personal email use of the research computers, and warn against other uses that

also may provide "viruses" and "worms". Also, personal use might occur at a time when others may need to use the computers for research purposes.

Rule 15: Humming and singing in the lab, yes.
Rule 16: Gum chewing and radios, only if you are really alone.

It is a voice lab, so humming and singing (and whistling) are typically encouraged, unless they are potentially distracting to anyone nearby. Too many voice people don't sing, but singing and humming give important insights. On the other hand, we discourage gum chewing because of the possible trouble the substance can cause once it leaves the mouth (and partly because some people have not learned to chew gum with grace), while knowing full well that gum chewing can have the positive effect of vocal tract lubrication. Radios are a problem when they distract others, which can be most of the time. We do not want to get into the social quandary of asking others to alter their listening habits, even if they might be called work habits.

The Rules list also includes a few important reminders that shape our attitudes and sense of responsibility.

Reminder 1: Your research is wrong until you prove it right.

Even though there are no real "wrongs" and "rights", the intent of this reminder is that we have to be our worst critics. We have to make sure that our data are valid and that our ideas are as solid as possible. We must be able to show, beyond any doubt, that our studies are trustworthy. If the studies are trustworthy, so shall we be perceived.

Reminder 2: Persistence is rewarded.

We all feel some resistance to our work, be it insufficient time or support. However, the mission of helping the world through our work must drive us forward, to persist until we are proud of the results. The reward is feeling good about reaching the first goal, which usually is the submission of a research paper for publication, and then feeling even better when the paper is published.

Reminder 3: We are spending someone else's money.

This reminder is sobering, and immediately suggests that we can not *waste* the resources we have, that our work is *for* the taxpayers of this country (since most of our work is through tax dollars, state or federal, in one way or another). This is a good pressure to have, and for the student a maturing experience, because it might be the first time he or she realizes that the work being done is not only paid for by the public, but is ultimately for the benefit of the public. It then has the feel of a real job, and a heavy responsibility, and this is good.

Reminder 4: Quality is remembered long after the pain is forgotten.

This must be a guiding principle when the going gets tough, and when sacrifices of time, family, health, money, and social activities occur because of the research. There are moments of varying types of pain, and the researcher must not be overly discouraged. It is better to seek perfection and be known for excellent and meaningful research, than to seek, attain, and be known for mediocrity. I do not know any excellent researcher who has not learned this lesson. You have to live with your product and the impression others (and you) have of your product long after the efforts have passed. Always seek the highest quality of work that you can imagine, and never feel satisfied unless you get reasonably close. It is far better to know the highest level of excellence and strive for it, even if you miss it, than to knowingly accept lower quality, because the latter will not last long, may not be very helpful to others, and may leave a bad taste in your mouth.

Final Remarks

Research is a culture of creativity with discipline. It is obligatory for civilization's advancement and stability. Research skill does not come easily nor quickly. Training with those who are good researchers is imperative.. The discipline, the critical sense, the desire to contribute to society, are purely human and humanistic aspects. Passions run high for the serious scientist; he or she attempts to move mountains to find what might lie on the other side. The "rules" and "reminders" discussed above help to teach the student about the world of research, the requirements of dedication, discipline, respect, honesty, organization, clarity of thought and writing, and the connection to the outside world.

Essay *by Joanna Cazden*

Dionysus, Demi Moore, and the Cult of the Distresssed Voice

Joanna Cazden, MFA, MS-CCC is a voice therapist at Cedars-Sinai Medical Center in Beverly Hills, CA. She lectures widely to speech pathology and arts groups, including presentations at the Voice Foundation Symposium, Philadelphia, and at ATHE. Her performance credits include 20 years as a touring singer-songwriter. A recent CD collaboration with Ronnie Gilbert, Pete Seeger and others, was featured at the Library of Congress in 2001. She holds a BA in Drama from the University of Washington; an MFA in Acting, from CalArts; and a Master of Science from California State University, Northridge. She writes on vocal health and technique for several musicians' magazines.

The Sorrow and the Pity

As a voice therapist, singing teacher, and former touring musician, I've heard my share of Voices in Trouble (VITs). (This catch-all term for raggedy, rough, husky sounds that are probably related to overuse/misuse has a few advantages. It is descriptive rather than diagnostic, and avoids the implication of intentional vocal abuse. Offering clients and friends a presumption of innocence or ignorance, along with honest concern, can lead to a constructive conversation, a blame-free educational opportunity.)

At any rate, voices in public media these days often sound very much "In Trouble." Like wardrobe fashions these public voices inevitably influence private expression; as the VIT becomes more common, it becomes more tolerated. The aesthetic of the clear, pleasant, melodious voice sometimes seems as outdated as the social requirement that ladies wear hats and gloves.

But is this really just ignorance, carelessness? Is the VIT just one more sign of humans coping their best in a chaotic, loud, polluted, and dangerous world? Or are there more specific, voice-damaging forces at work? Does a VIT represent more definable stresses or social pressures acting on a performer's body, breath, and speech?

What about the perceived *advantage* of a VIT? Vocal damage is now so common, it's cool. How long before it's required? What VASTA member has not heard a rough-voiced female student say, "My boyfriend/manager/director likes me to sound like this. He says it's sexy"? Actress Shannon Doherty has been quoted as saying that she took up cigarette smoking in order to get a better voice.

Compare the problems of vocal artists to those of athletes or dancers, who are at constant risk of musculo-skeletal injuries. These performers may opt to play through the pain or take time off to recover, depending on their schedule, career level, and financial circumstances. They are never chosen specifically *because* they're injured.

Imagine if a stage director announced, "We're only casting dancers with broken ankles today. We want a really angular, unstable look for this show." There would be lawsuits, picketing, allegations of sadism! Although oppressive working conditions and financial pressures remain, deliberate injury in dance or sport remains generally taboo. But a voiceover actor or studio singer who refuses to sound hoarse may be replaced by a hungrier one.

An actress I know went to an audition while very ill with bronchitis and barely able to speak. She knew the casting director, and suggested that she visually fit the role and would be happy to read in a few days. "Oh no," she was told. "You should read right now! This is the sound we love." She politely refused and went home to bed. Not all artists are as wise.

Self-Sacrifice

The first voiceover actor I treated—I'll call him A—felt his injury come on suddenly during a commercial session. As A told me, he'd gotten booked for a car ad that used "hot!" as the repeated hook. The client and director insisted that A emphasize the word using a very low pitch.

Physiologically, producing a loud, emphatic voice at the very bottom of the pitch range is difficult and risky, especially over time. A hook written with a weak initial consonant made matters worse. After two and a half hours, A felt something snap, like a pulled muscle. The client wanted more takes, and rather than lose the gig or be tagged "unreliable" by his agent, A complied.

He saw a doctor, who told him that his larynx looked fine except for some mild acid reflux. Months later, his voice remained weak, easily fatigued. He was very afraid that it was "broken for good."

I treated A's complaint as a muscle injury, with rest and gradual retraining. At first he resisted turning down work and limiting the hours of his day job (teaching comedy traffic school). This was 1993, before most ENTs understood and prescribed anti-reflux medications, but A did change his worst habits such as lying on the couch with a TV snack until late in the evening. He learned some stretching and breathing warm-ups, and we negotiated how to rest his voice with minimal loss of income.

Within a few weeks, A accepted that protectiveness in the short term would save his career in the long term. He adjusted his schedule and became diligent with both non-vocal and vocal warm-ups. Despite bouts of anxiety that he'd never recover, he gradually regained his former power and range. I even recognized the "hot" commercial when it ran and wished him many happy residuals.

A and I also talked about the callousness and ignorance in his industry, the lack of concern he'd been shown when he'd tried to perform in a way that didn't hurt. I thought back to the myth of Dionysus, whose free expression and painful sacrifice seem to underlie common beliefs about art.

The archetypal Dionysus, of course, is not just an uninhibited, handsome wino having a good time. He is ritually killed by observer/participants in the party, a death that echoes the yearly pruning of grape vines and other agricultural rituals such as the English John Barleycorn. At the moment of his greatest, frenzied freedom, Dionysus is expendable. Like "talent," as performing artists are derisively called, his destiny is to be replaced.

The typical commercial actor carries the Dionysian role lightly, compared to rock musicians who ritually scream their throats out and destroy their own gear. Many artists fall somewhere in between.

A few years ago, singer Michael Bolton performed in a televised concert special—a formerly rich-voiced blues artist now turned pop-star screamer. The mostly female audience played the Dionysian Furies, going wild every time Bolton's voice approached and then passed the outer edge of endurance. Each long, distorted, throat-bulging, high note seemed to prove that his emotions were real, his devotion to them complete. Each was answered by an approving roar.

It is not hard to spin out this story: the crowd wants satisfaction, and the singer-as-high-priest agrees to martyrdom. The more spectacular the catharsis, the higher the artist's fee. The producer promises a wealthy retirement, overlooks or enables ameliorating drugs, and quietly auditions the next godlings in line.

After treating A, I suggested the Dionysus theory to a few other clients, but they appeared more puzzled than impressed by my insight. Maybe artists' victimization goes so deep that few can look it in the face for very long. Like dedicated warriors, they don't have time for philosophy. They need an immediate patch-up job so that they can return to battle.

Demi Moore and Dietrich

Client A's muscle pull was an acute strain. Chronic, repetitive strain is more common, and is sometimes brought on for semi-conscious reasons. Simply put, a husky sound signals sexuality. Laryngologist James Kaufman termed this "The Bogart-Bacall Syndrome."

Some female clients who cling to their huskiness cite Demi Moore as a role model. This actress is known for devotion to physical training, not vocal. Perhaps women who can't imagine looking like her imagine that they can at least sound like her.

One more insightful stage actor explained that to him, a low, rough female voice is like Marlene Dietrich: smoky, sexy, and comfortable in a bar. Taking this vocal persona to an extreme, a girl with a wrecked voice will also gladly wreck her reputation.

For men, a rough sound is less strongly associated with sex appeal but nevertheless signals masculinity, physical courage, and abandonment of personal safety. At least that is what advertisers seem to believe. This casting note for a steak-house ad was shown to me by a voiceover actor:

Male, mid-40s to early 50s. Gruff. A man's man, rough around the edges. ...And every time he says the word "steak," his voice gets a little extra gruffness.

Time to Cry "Enough"

If roughness has a career benefit for both men and women, no wonder that few non-singers seek vocal help simply because they sound hoarse. The threshold for seeking care, however, does seem to vary by gender. In my experience, men go to the doctor and then come to my clinic with sensory complaints: pain, tickling, throat-clearing, or other discomfort. Women often don't come in until they lose their voices completely, repeatedly, over weeks or even months.

My caseload this year included a character actress, a location photographer and overworked mom, and two female theater students, all of whom put off voice care until they could barely talk. In contrast, male clients seem to have more self-esteem, fewer demands on their time and money, or both.

Recently, young woman came to my clinic, and stated "I know I've had nodules since I was a kid. I just love to talk, and no matter how I sound, I'm the best sales girl at my store. I just don't like losing my voice totally, which is happening, like, every day. Can you give me a few pointers or something before I leave for college next month?"

That same night, actress Lorraine Bracco of *The Sopranos* chatted with a TV host, her Voice In Serious Trouble. In the video clip she'd brought to promote her show's new season, she sounded no different. Nothing was said about an injury or a vocal-recovery plan. Not knowing her or her history, I had to assume that the hoarse voice was normal for her and an acceptable, possibly sex-appealing, part of her image. College girls have another, unfortunate model for sounding cool.

A different attitude was shown by a man I'll call B, a radio sportscaster. He'd worked steadily into his mid-30s without vocal problems. Then he took an off-season job coaching a minor-league baseball team. The added demand—hours of outdoor shouting—was too much, and his voice started to give out.

Acoustic testing showed that he was using too low a pitch even for his large, gangly frame. Subtly pulling his larynx down to accomplish this, he was straining the muscles below it and on the sides of his neck. As a sports reporter B was familiar with muscle retraining, and he engaged in therapy with enthusiasm.

Treatment started with exercises to tighten the thyro-hyoid area and counteract the pull-down habit. He also rested his voice whenever possible for the first few weeks, and adjusted his fitness routine to soften and stretch his over-contracted abs for better breath support.

Diaphragmatic-abdominal breathing was a revelation that B enjoyed, and once his colleagues assured him that a slightly higher pitch sounded fine on the radio, he accepted that change too. He returned to coaching at the training camp before being fully recovered, but took with him a long list of vocal strategies and a referral to a speech pathologist in the area. I expect that he is doing well.

Foolishness and Wisdom

Not all VITs reflect destructive social forces or inappropriate models. Country singer Emmylou Harris was first known for pristine, clear singing that fit her straightforward image. Now silver-haired but better-known than ever, she told the *Los Angeles Times* last year that she doesn't mind the increased huskiness in her voice, because it has come with maturity. Just as some older actresses affirm that wrinkles accompany wisdom, she implied that a roughed-up voice can fit a performer whose persona has aged well.

At best, hoarseness like this can represent honesty, an integrity shown through imperfection. Like distressed furniture and faded blue jeans, the world-worn voice seems reassuringly real. Unfortunately, it also reinforces public denial of the serious penalty for ignoring vocal problems, including missed medical diagnoses.

Finding the most charitable social meaning of hoarseness helps me overcome private anger at clients who resist change. A last example is client C, a producer for a raucous beach-babe TV show, diagnosed with vocal polyps and scheduled for surgery.

Although C hated and feared the idea of going under the knife, he said that he hated his "wet voice" more. He wanted therapy to be sure there would be no recurrence and said he would do his best. While preparing for his post-surgery vocal rest ("Don't call my cell phone! Use the Blackberry!"), C discovered that several coworkers had gone through the same ordeal. This diminished his fear.

Vocal surgery began to sound as commonplace in his world as cosmetic surgery. He dropped out of therapy after two post-op sessions, did not return phone calls, and returned to location with the same risk factors as before. There is no way to know with such clients exactly why rehabilitation fails. A social environment of carelessness and short-term production pressure must bear some of the blame.

We who love the human voice know that this instrument can reveal deep truths about internal health, stamina, and mind-body integrity. Some VITs reveal cultural self-destruction. Others may symbolize inauthentic, objectified sexuality or a premature patina enjoyed by producers as "novelty." We can speculate forever; our job is still to heal, educate, and guide the willing toward voices of health and energy, voices that reveal human glory.

Resurrection

Laryngologist Steven Zeitels, MD, of Harvard University speaks of "redefining socially acceptable hoarseness." To him, only improved treatment, widely available, will counter the popular belief that vocal destruction—like faded fabric—is inevitable and unchangeable. He looks toward molecular compounds that will return stiff vocal fibers to elasticity and an era when wear-and-tear injuries or surgical scarring are fixed by a quick injection.

Other voice scientists seek to define precisely how vocal folds respond to various degrees and durations of collision stress. This could lead to occupational safety guidelines like those for noise exposure or heavy lifting. While awaiting these and other scientific breakthroughs, prevention of misuse-based voice problems must be part of VASTA's mission.

The world of sports understands its injuries; the music business has begun to overcome significant denial about hearing loss. In the 1990s, the fashion industry approached, then backed away from, a look known as "heroin chic." Redefining socially acceptable hoarseness and weakening the cult of vocal distress is a long overdue public health campaign for the occupations we serve.

Prevention efforts must reach not only voice users, but also producers, agents, directors, and casting directors. Artists carry personal responsibility for their health choices, but their occupational environment shares the burden. It is time for those who profit from vocal art to respect the functional limits of the larynx, so that performers are not encouraged or required to hurt their voices on the job.

All such cultural changes require prolonged effort and advocates committed to human wellness and effective communication. Simply telling people that they're hurting themselves or others is unlikely to work, even if we could grab headlines with our concern. Understanding the conscious and unconscious forces at work will help us make our case.

My speculation about these forces is not empirical research, but will, I hope, spark discussion and change. May this cause inspire our own strong voices.

❧

References

Cazden, J: "Say What? New tech tools can protect your hearing, but it's up to you to practice safe sound." *Onstage* magazine, June 2001.

Gunter, HE: "A mechanical model of vocal-fold collision with high spatial and temporal resolution." *Journal of the Acoustical Society of America 113*(2), Feb. 2003.

Hilburn, R: "Listening Only To Herself: Emmylou Harris." *Los Angeles Times*, Calendar section, July 22, 2001.

Kaufman, J.A., and Blalock, P.D.: "Vocal Fatigue and Dysphonia in the Professional Voice User; Bogart-Bacall Syndrome." *Laryngoscope* 98: 493-498, 1988.

Marge M: "Disability prevention. Are we ready for the challenge?" *ASHA 35* (11). Nov. 1993.

Otto, W.M. Palmer, R.B.: *Dionysus, Myth and Cult.* Indiana University Press, 1995.

Rosenthal, Phil, "90210 star's stupidity knows no ifs ands or butts," *Los Angeles Daily News*, Wednesday, October 27, 1993.

www.cnn.com/ALLPOLITICS: "Clinton decries 'Heroin Chic' Fashion Look." May 21, 1997.

Zeitels, Steven: "Advances in Laryngoscopy and Phonosurgery." Lecture, Cedars-Sinai Medical Center, Los Angeles, CA. July 2, 2002.

Peer Reviewed Article *by Rita Bailey and Linda Bowman*

Securing Treatment for Voice Problems:
What Professional Voice and Speech Trainers Need to Know

Introduction

In the wake of the many changes in healthcare funding over the past decade, it has become more complicated to secure insurance funding for the treatment of voice problems (1). However, it may be possible for speech-language pathologists (SLPs) providing therapy for voice disorders to provide documentation and other support that can help with this issue. Lack of insurance funding may prevent some patients from seeking help. Neglecting to treat a problematic voice for lack of insurance coverage (or any other reason) can have harmful ramifications, both personally and professionally. Voice and speech trainers and their students should have a basic familiarity regarding insurance coverage and related issues and the limitations of individual insurance plans. Speech-language pathologists need a heightened awareness of documentation protocols and methods for helping their patients secure payment for voice evaluation and therapy services.

Think about these far too common scenarios. A famous actor in a popular Broadway play develops voice problems and his performance is in jeopardy. News of this man's personal and professional catastrophe captures national media headlines. This problem must be resolved. In another part of the same city, a sixth grade teacher develops voice problems in early fall. By November, she is unable to sustain her teaching voice for a 50-minute class period. The result for this teacher is devastating, both personally and professionally. This problem must be resolved. Both the famous actor and the not-so-famous teacher will likely seek treatment for their voice problems from a medical professional. After receiving any necessary treatment for medical conditions affecting the voice (i.e., acid reflux, allergy, asthma), they may be evaluated by a voice-qualified speech-language pathologist.

Voice Treatment and the Speech-Language Pathologist

SLPs provide treatment for vocal disorders caused by vocal abuse, misuse, and overuse. Sometimes, the vocal trauma has occurred with enough force and duration to have caused a pathologic response, such as vocal nodules or epidermoid cysts. When no organic pathology is present, voice problems are no less problematic, and failure to begin treatment could lead to the development of vocal fold pathologies. Treatment for voice problems caused by phonotrauma involves the use of techniques designed to reduce vocal fold hyperfunction, reduce muscle tension in the laryngeal and pharyngeal regions, and restore normal tone to affected speech muscles (2). Generally, voice therapy with a SLP requires several sessions. However, the duration of treatment varies according to the individual voice problem and the needs of the client.

Common therapeutic techniques for a variety of voice disorders involve breathing exercises, phonatory exercises, and movement exercises (3,4). Additional treatment possibilities include the use of resonant voice therapy (5), confidential voice therapy (6), vocal rest (7), and any one of a number of well-proven facilitating techniques (8).

When extensive and lengthy voice therapy by an SLP is required, the cost of treatment may be significant. While the cost of treatment may or may

Rita L. Bailey received her EdD in Special Education, and her BS and MS degrees in Speech Pathology at Illinois State University where she is currently an Assistant Professor in the Department of Speech Pathology and Audiology. She has practiced as a speech-language pathologist in both educational and medical settings. Her teaching and research areas include swallowing and voice disorders, augmentative/alternative communication, and communication and swallowing issues related to tracheostomy and ventilator dependency.

Linda S. Bowman received her BS and MS degrees in Speech Pathology at Illinois State University. She has been an adviser and instructor in the Department of Speech Pathology & Audiology at ISU since 1986. Linda's professional experience includes higher education and public school practice. Her clinical interests lie in the areas of articulation, phonology and fluency. Teaching and research areas include correction of articulation disorders and professional issues.

not be an issue for the affluent Broadway actor, it is most likely an issue for the sixth grade teacher. Unfortunately, speech-language pathologists have not had a good history of gaining reimbursement from many health insurance companies (1). Although individual experiences have varied, the recent tightening of our nation's healthcare belt and the nation-wide shift from indemnity plans to managed care has made reimbursement for services more difficult for many SLPs. For example, a spokesperson for ASHA's Private Health Plans Advocacy Division recently observed, "…reimbursement in general has become more difficult, with voice treatment also facing that problem" (McCarty, J., Personal communication, November 7, 2001). However, there is reason for hope. According to the Code of Federal Regulations (CFR), recent changes in legislation require that federally qualified Health Maintenance Organizations (HMOs) provide or arrange for "outpatient services and inpatient hospital services (which) shall include short-term rehabilitation and physical therapy, the provision of which the HMO determines can be expected to result in the significant improvement of a member's condition within a period of two months" (42 CFR 110.102). McCarty's comments are in agreement: "…if voice treatment can be shown to be effective and likely to prevent future surgery or need for voice treatment, most payers will listen and pay" (McCarty, J. Personal communication, November 7, 2001). Reimbursement provisos may differ across geographic regions and even within the same provider company, so terms must often be negotiated on an individual basis.

Evidence of the efficacy of voice therapy (8,9,10) demonstrates to insurance companies a reduction in cost by eliminating the need for vocal surgeries and other medical treatments. Use of efficacy research to document the medical necessity of voice therapy prior to treatment greatly increases one's chances of gaining reimbursement (1). Delays in the submission of documentation may delay the authorization of treatment. Delays in beginning treatment may allow the voice problem to worsen, and may necessitate more extensive treatment over a longer period. The potential increase in costs for insurance companies should be stated in the initial request for reimbursement in order to expedite the authorization of services.

What the Client Can Do to Facilitate Reimbursement

Several additional recommendations have been made regarding documentation issues that may facilitate reimbursement for voice therapy (11). Prior to seeking the services of a speech-language pathologist, the client should review his/her policy to insure that the services are covered. Next, s/he should determine whether or not referral from a licensed physician is necessary. Finally, s/he should contact potential service-providers to locate an SLP with both a clinical interest and experience in the evaluation and treatment of vocal problems.

What the SLP Can Do to Facilitate Reimbursement

When filing claims, the SLP should be familiar with and use the diagnostic codes and/or categories used by the insurance carrier. For managed care, these are most often the ICD-9-CM and CPT Codes. When using these codes, practitioners should select categories with an easily identifiable organic basis. Finally, SLPs must determine the professional qualifications that the service provider requires for eligibility (i.e., SLP licensure, ASHA certification) and document appropriately. Following these guidelines makes possible the prompt processing of claims.

Once treatment has been authorized, SLPs must submit documentation of functional improvement on a consistent basis throughout the treatment period. Clear and concise language and objective data must support the continuation of speech pathology services, or claims will likely be denied. If a claim is denied, the SLP can resubmit the claim with a letter of explanation for why treatment should continue. Sample letters to insurance carriers to assist clinicians with writing these letters are available through ASHA, and other healthcare advocacy groups.

Recommendations for the Voice and Speech Trainer

The Voice and Speech Trainer can facilitate the therapeutic process in several ways. If the client is in agreement, s/he can offer to provide personal insights to the SLP regarding the client's vocal problem, its progression, and speaking and singing situations that have been observed to exacerbate the client's vocal condition. These perceptions can serve to enhance the clinical picture and facilitate the development of an effective therapeutic program. Secondly, when given information regarding the therapeutic plan by the client, s/he can provide verbal reinforcement for the client's use of therapeutic strategies during voice and speech training sessions and use a finely-tuned ear to note subtle improvements, which may serve to motivate the client. Individual supports will vary; however, it may also be helpful to adjust the length and intensity of training sessions until vocal improvements are noted.

Case Example

Consider the following story: Henry was a caseworker for a social service agency in a Midwestern state. He used his voice in nearly every facet of his job, in home visits, meetings, phone conversations, case presentations, and counseling. One winter, Henry developed laryngitis following a severe upper respiratory infection. When the acute illness ended, Henry's vocal problems remained. His vocal quality improved for a while, but he never regained his former voice. He experienced pitch and phonation breaks, and complained that his voice "wore out" by the end of each workweek. At first, Henry's voice was stronger on Mondays, but soon he experienced a consistent hoarse voice quality all of the time. This interfered greatly with his ability to carry out his job responsibilities and caused him much distress.

Henry sought help from his physician, a general practitioner, who referred him to a specialist. The specialist diagnosed him with bilateral vocal nodules and recommended that he receive voice therapy. Henry made an appointment with a speech-language pathologist and had a voice evaluation. His insurance company was contacted following the evaluation, to determine what coverage his policy offered. The insurance company paid for the voice evaluation, but denied him the opportunity to receive voice therapy. Their rationale for the denial was that the voice problem "wasn't work related". Henry didn't know what to do. He finally changed careers altogether, choosing a position that didn't require consistent voice use. Unfortunately, the social service agency lost a needed and respected employee.

Stories like Henry's are all too common. Voice problems shouldn't have to result in a career change. This situation might have turned out much differently if the voice therapist had become involved at the pre-approval level and if proper documentation had been resubmitted in response to the denial. Henry's boss might have been asked to send documentation of the high level of vocal use required for his job. The specialist might have been asked to write a note documenting the need for voice therapy, and suggesting that therapy might allow Henry to avoid surgery, a more costly alternative for the insurance company. Henry might not have had to accept chronic voice problems and an unplanned career change.

Summary and Conclusions
The voice portrays the personality, mood, meaning, and convictions of every speaker. It is used to entertain, to educate, and to relate. For professional voice users, the necessity of projecting the voice at higher intensity levels and with exaggerated prosody for long periods of time places them at high risk for developing voice problems. Teachers, actors, and singers often experience unwanted and potentially devastating interruptions of their careers due to vocal problems. Many professional voice users work closely with voice and speech trainers to enhance their vocal performance.

For this reason, professional voice and speech trainers are often among the first to notice voice changes in the clients with whom they work. It would be advantageous to establish and/or tighten referral links with speech pathologist/ENT teams that specialize in the treatment of voice problems, especially those who advocate for patients in the reimbursement process. Individuals who are aware of the extent and

limitations of their insurance coverage, paired with professionals who are knowledgeable regarding reimbursement policies and practices, can preserve those preventative and therapeutic methods that work to overcome vocal problems. The play will go on, and the wisdom of a teacher will be passed on to tomorrow's adults.

Endnotes
1. Uffen, E. Clinicians take on insurance companies. *The ASHA Leader, 5,* 1-10, 2000.
2. Deem, J F, Miller, L. *Manual of voice therapy* (2nd ed.), Chapter V, pp. 103-138. 1999, Austin: Pro-ed.
3. Kotby, N. *The accent method of voice therapy.* 1995. San Diego: Singular.
4. Stemple, C. Management of functional voice disorders in the adult population. Presented at the Kentucky Conference on Communication Disorders, 1997, Lexington.
5. Verdolini-Marston, K, Burke, M, Lessac, A, Glaze, L, Caldwell, E. Preliminary study of two methods of treatment for laryngeal nodules. *Journal of Voice, 9,* 74-85, 1995.
6. Colton, R, Casper, JC. *Understanding voice problems: A physiological perspective from diagnosis to treatment.* 1996. Baltimore: Williams & Wilkins.
7. Sataloff, RT. *Professional voice: The science and art of clinical care.* 1997. San Diego: Singular.
8. Boone, DR, McFarlane, S. *The voice and voice therapy* (5th ed.), 1997, Englewood Cliffs, NJ: Prentice-Hall.
9. Roy N, Gray SD, Simon M, Dove H, Corbin-Lewis K, & Stemple, J. An evaluation of the effects of two treatment approaches for teachers with voice disorders: A prospective randomized clinical trial. *Journal of Speech, Language, and Hearing Research, 44,* 286-296, 2001.
10. Stemple, C. *Voice therapy clinical studies.* 1993. St. Louis: Mosby.
11. Chwat SE, Gurland, GB. National trends in third party reimbursement in speech-language pathology and audiology: Our professional crisis. *ASHA, 26,* 27-32, 1984.

Vocal Production,
Voice Related Movement Studies *Marth Munro, Associate Editor*
Ursula Meyer, Assistant Editor

Vocal Production, Voice Related Movement Studies *Marth Munro, Associate Editor*

The third edition of our Journal! A silent testimony to some of the work that goes into a not so silent discipline. This time the focus is on a topic that provides core entertainment and escape(ism) to most humans. This section does not add directly to nor reflect on the main focus of this edition. Indirectly, this section deals with the core elements, voice quality and breathing.

As voice teachers we want to improve the voice quality of our students, yet at the same time we want to do good, and consequently all the exercises and explorations that we teach are geared towards vocal health, improving voice quality and enhancing functionality of the performer's voice. This is a relatively old *profession*, which has led, because of its vibrancy, to a relatively new *science*. We are always questioning the exercises and explorations that we teach, always sharing and learning from each other. As such this section is making a contribution to the main focus:

Anne-Maria Laukkanen from the University of Tampere in Finland shares with us scientific justifications for voice exercises. As such, she provides that invaluable contribution of vocology to the development of exercises that we know work, but now we have physiological and acoustic discourses to assist us in our arguments.

The theme of the 2002 VASTA Conference was "breathing" and as such "breath" was in the air! Ruth Rootberg reflects on a study done by her in 2002 in an article in this section. Most of the VASTA members are aware of this study, as Ruth published a book with the results from a questionnaire that she asked 13 voice teachers to answer. What makes this work important is that it reflects the points of view of voice teachers currently active in the field. Here Ruth has extracted some pedagogical principles held by these teachers, from this study. Ruth follows this up with a round table discussion about clavicular breathing.

In the column "Voices around the World" the spotlight falls on two women, living and teaching on two continents, coming from two different voice and body backgrounds, both believing in body/voice integration: Lesley Ann Timlick from the United States of America, and Tiina Syrja from Finland..

A rather small contribution in size and numbers this time, but in my view a vitally important one. Science and Practice fit so comfortably together.

Marth Munro (Associate Editor) specializes in performance voice building, body/voice integration and vocal pedagogy. She holds a PhD in which she investigated the acoustic properties of Lessac's Tonal NRG and the "Actor's formant" in the female voice. She has completed a team research project on computer-aided training of the singing voice. She is a Certified Laban/Bartenieff Movement Analyst and a Certified Lessac Teacher. She teaches at the Departments of Drama and Vocal Art at the Pretoria Technikon, South Africa. Munro is a member of VASTA and chair of SAPVAME (South African Performers Voice and Movement Educators). She frequently teaches workshops for actors, singers and musicians. She directs for musical theatre and does voice and movement coaching.

Voices Around the World

We are certainly living in interesting times, and being involved in an association like VASTA always makes life exciting. "Why?" I hear you ask. Well, because we are always learning from each other, sharing with each other. It is through VASTA that I realized that so many of us/you are pushing the envelope of experience and teaching. But what I also realised was that what you stand for is simply also a reflection of the current zeitgeist. For me what this current zeitgeist is suggesting, is a move towards body/voice integration, no matter what specific system or methodology we choose to specialize in. Stalwart colleagues like Tom Casciero, Ruth Rootberg, Barbara Adrian, Diane Gaary, Kevin Crawford, to name but a few on the cusp of the wave—all have qualifications in both voice and movement disciplines. Many VASTA members are qualified in various voice systems, such as the Lessac or Linklater Approaches, for example; both of these approaches include an awareness of the necessity of body integration as do so many other systems. Other members have studied yoga and added that to their teachings.

VASTA member Lesley Ann Timlick is a voice teacher at the Florida International University in Miami. She is a qualified Feldenkrais teacher and uses the combination of voice and movement work within her teaching brief. What makes her work so interesting is the fact that she has to wrestle continually with her multi-cultural environment.

Lesley Ann explains, from the Feldenkrais perspective, that:
> the human voice is a very complex overlaid function, involving the whole body, and is influenced by the environment. It is produced by reflexive muscular actions that take place inside the body. When any physical tensions and/or habits form in the body, the voice suffers adverse effects. To understand, develop and improve the voice, the actor must gain a greater knowledge of the body and it's best possible usage in relationship to the voice.

She further argues:
> in order to meet the broad spectrum of production styles required by the modern theatre and media, the actor's vocal instrument must be flexible, strong, specific and truthful. The actor's voice and physical body are part of the whole self and therefore must simultaneously develop the capability to serve organic acting impulses, individual characterization and clear articulation of the story to the audience.

Lesley Ann moves closer to the problem of multiculturalism as she notes:
> Our sensory-motor organizations respond to the stresses and *cultural movement patterns we are exposed to on a daily basis* (Editor's emphasis), with muscular reflexive actions. If these movement patterns and stresses are activated often enough they create habitual patterns and contractions which become hard to release voluntarily. Therefore, *our life histories are disclosed by the way we move our bodies* (Editor's emphasis). These movement patterns and emotional pains from life, which become housed in our bodies, can limit functional movement, body mind connection, sensory awareness, kinesthetic awareness and alignment of the body. In turn, these physical and mental restrictions directly affect the voice that is produced by a functional movement of the body. Please note that I am not stating that cultural movement patterns are bad or wrong, but that they can limit the choices we have available to us if they are so ingrained inside us that we are unable to move outside them.

Given this insight into the potential limitations that such habitual patterning may have on optimal voice, Lesley Ann challenges all students:
> Regardless of cultural heritage, students all have the capacity to learn to change so that they can reach their goals. However, if they do not know how they are enacting, it becomes impossible to reach their goals and make the changes they would like. Moshe Feldenkrais believed that real learning was the ability to have several ways of doing the same thing. His Method allows the student to learn to do the things they know how to do in different ways so they have more choices available to them. They find these new pathways of action by using less effort, increasing awareness, learning to detect small differences and most importantly paying attention to how they do as opposed to what they are doing.

She notes the very real danger that "when we cannot move beyond our habits and patterns we often become neurotic because we do not have a balanced expression of the whole self." Nevertheless, for her the way out is a realisation that "if we have access to more than one choice we expand our self-image and are not bound by one mode or action, behaviour or cultural pattern. We begin to operate from our individual self rather than what society and the family has thrust upon us."

Lesley Ann ultimately challenges "the actor who wishes to be more transformational vocally." Such an actor:
> must embrace his/her own cultural patterns but must also have the ability to convert in and out of them with ease. The Feldenkrais Method, integrated with vocal practice is, in my opinion, a very effective way to help the acting student, who has to operate in a multicultural environment, to discover new vocal possibilities, making

them more adaptive actors who can better meet the professional vocal needs of their industry.

From another continent we hear from another voice teacher who has specialized in another body integration system. Here we find the same awareness, the same urgency to combine voice and body work in the training of performers. Allow me to introduce to you Tiina Syrja.

Tiina is a qualified speech therapist and Alexander teacher lecturing at the Department of Acting of the University of Tampere, Finland. Other studies preparing her for her career included performer's voice, dance, acting, music and various bodywork methods such as body mind centering. Nowadays she performs mainly as an actor in Playback theatre (a form of improvisation theatre developed by Jonathan Fox) and as a singer. Previously she also worked as a semi-professional dancer.

Tiina believes that voice and movement cannot and should not be separated. What is particularly interesting here is the interweave of the so-called hard-sciences (the speech therapist training) with the integrated body (the Alexander), the ancillary and diverse experience, the acknowledgement of the demands of the performer, and then the teacher. According to her it is the lecturer's duty to use whatever methodology is needed for the profile of the specific student, and as such she uses an eclectic approach in her teaching. To her advantage the department where she is teaching is small and there is plenty of time for individual contact with students.

The programme is a four year course leading to possible entrance into a Masters programme and then a Doctorate should the student so wish. The student intake happens only every second year and they accept 12-14 students. As many as 800 or more potential students audition for the course. The department stresses the importance of movement and voice. Lecturers do solo as well as team-teaching classes. Tiina mentions that she works specifically in close relation with the singing, acting and movement lecturers.

One of those zeitgeist moments that link the work of Lesley Ann with Tiina is the fact that a focal point of the training is the chance that each student gets to perform in a foreign language during his/her course. These students cannot speak these foreign languages and this approach thus raises the awareness of the importance of the envoicing of subtext. The department has done some plays in Spanish whilst the foreign language play in 2003 is in Italian and done in co-operation with the Teatro Emilia Romagna.

Another special attribute of this department if the fact that they work closely with the Department of Speech

Tiina Syrja

Communication and Voice Research of the University of Tampere. The development of each student's voice is monitored by the use of phonetograms, long-term average spectra and the like. Studies on the use of bio-feedback mechanisms in teaching performer's voice have also been done. An article written by Anne-Maria Laukkanen, head of the Department of Speech Communication and Voice Research, can be read elsewhere in this Journal.

Like all voice teachers Tiina likes being closely involved with all the productions done in the department and she frequently acts as co-director, as she sees it as a way of making sure that voice coaching is an organic part of the rehearsal process.

Responding to a question about voice for film and television, Tiina informs us that a lot of work in this genre is done during the student's training. She is of the opinion that, although the scale of voice work for film and television is different when comparing it to stage work, the basic requirements of healthy voice usage are the same. In a really fascinating turn (which will endear her to many a technician!) she also makes the point that the use of optimal voice for the specific genre will make the work of the technical sound recording crew easier!

Tiina is available for workshops.

So what does the zeitgeist entail? Well, body-voice integration is taking off around the world; the demands of multiculturalism (and multilingualism), which will eventually need to address the problems of accent acquisition vs. accent reduction is beginning to rear its head; the use of technology to assist in training the performer is being used more and more—we are indeed living in interesting times!

Peer Reviewed Article *by Anne-Maria Laukkanen*

On the Goals and Bases of Vocal Exercises

Anne-Maria Laukkanen is Professor of Speech Technique and Vocology in the University of Tampere, Finland since 2001. The post is the first one in Europe. Dr Laukkanen is the head of the Department of Speech Communication and Voice Research at the University of Tampere. Dr Laukkanen's background is in Phonetics. She got her Masters Degree in 1990 and her Licentiate Degree in 1993, both in the University of Helsinki. She defended her doctoral Thesis in the University of Tampere in 1995. Her interest in voice stems from studies in singing in the 1980s. Her primary research interests concern the effects and basis of vocal exercises and the communicative role of voice quality. She has served as a visiting scientist in the world's leading voice laboratories at the University of Iowa, in the Denver Center for the Performing Arts and in the Royal University of Technology in Stockholm.

Introduction

Vocal training has long traditions. Vocal exercises are mainly based on experience, and the vocal training process traditionally relies on sensory information—mainly auditory, tactile and proprioceptive sensations of the trainee and auditory and visual perceptions of the teacher. The process takes advantage of imitation and imagination. This is all natural and, to a large extent, inevitable. Voice is the product of a delicate co-operation of many muscles (including respiratory, laryngeal and vocal tract muscles) and we do not have direct conscious control over these muscles. The goals of voice training are thus usually achieved mainly through imitation and imagination. But what are these goals? And how do various vocal exercises help to achieve them? This paper is intended to give the voice practitioner ideas about how to take advantage of voice science and acoustic voice analysis methods in voice training.

Good Voice

Most of us would probably agree that the goal of voice training is a good voice. However, to find an objective definition to "good voice" may seem an impossible task, since there are naturally lots of cultural and individual differences in our opinions of various matters—including the voice. On the other hand, the task may be easier if we make a distinction between "good" and other adjectives like "beautiful", "pleasant" etc. To define "good" through "adequacy" can bring objectivity and generality to the discussion about the goals of voice training. The descriptions given for these goals in voice training literature seem to support this definition. "Optimal vocal function" with "adequate loudness", "effective pitch level", "flexibility" and "ease" in production is searched for, "maximum output" is aimed at with "minimum effort" (Anderson, 1961; Proctor, 1968; Perkins, 1971; Cooper, 1973; Bauer, 1973; Aronson, 1985; etc.). In other words, we could define good voice as being acoustically, communicatively and physiologically adequate. Acoustical adequacy means that the voice is easily heard—and when it comes to the linguistic content of speech or song: the words can be perceived clearly. In addition to all of this, communicative adequacy requires sufficient alterations of voice in time (variation in pitch, loudness, timbre) to convey e.g. emotions. Finally, physiological adequacy refers to economy in voice production. Good voice production preposes as little as possible mechanical and physiological loading to the vocal organ. This ensures the best possible endurance in vocal performance and helps to avoid vocal fatigue and other vocal problems related to voice misuse.

Acoustic Correlates of Good Voice

In order to be loud and well projecting, a voice needs to meet certain criteria: It must have a sufficient sound level and an adequate frequency distribution of sound energy. The latter is also important from the voice hygienic point of view since it is related to resonances of the vocal tract and thus to our possibilities to improve projection without increasing effort.

Figure 1 illustrates the glottal sound spectrum and the effects of the vocal tract on it. A sound produced by vocal fold vibration consists of a series of harmonics, the lowest of which is called the fundamental. Its frequency mainly corresponds to the perception of pitch. The other harmonics (overtones) are multiples of the fundamental, and their relative level (amplitude, loudness) affects the quality of the voice. In a hypofunctional, soft, weak voice the overtones are relatively weak and the spectrum tilts strongly. In contrast, in hyperfunctional voice the overtones are quite strong but the fundamental is relatively weaker (Gauffin et Sundberg, 1989). A voice that combines the best characteristics of these two opposite voice qualities may be seen as optimal: It has relatively strong overtones which make it sound rich and helps projecting, and it also has a relatively strong fundamental, which is needed for a voice to sound free and effortless.

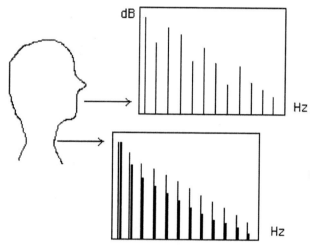

Figure 1. Schematized spectrum of human voice. Frequency at horizontal axis, amplitude at vertical axis. The spectrum shows that the human voice consists of a series of partials. The lowest one, called fundamental, corresponds to the frequency of vocal fold vibration and that, in turn, mainly explains the perception of pitch (e.g. 100 Hz = 100 vibrations per second = ca. G/GIS). The other partials, also called 'overtones', are multiples of the fundamental. The strength of the overtones in relation to the lowest and thus strongest ones (i.e. how steeply the spectrum tilts toward higher frequencies) depends on the type of phonation. Weak and hypofunctional voice has a steeper slope (= relatively weaker overtones, see thick bars in figure) than normal or pressed voice. The outcoming voice has peaks (stronger partials than their neighbours) caused by vocal tract resonances that strengthen certain partials.

As the voice propagates through the vocal tract (the combination of the laryngeal tube, pharynx, mouth and the nasal cavity) it is filtered by the resonance properties of the tract. Those harmonics that are close to the resonance frequencies of the vocal tract get stronger and others will be damped. Therefore the spectrum of the outcoming sound typically has peaks and valleys. The peaks are frequently referred to as formants (although this is somewhat inaccurate: the resonances of the vocal tract are formants and the peaks are the results of the formants). Theoretically a resonator—like the vocal tract—has a countless number of resonances, but in practice mainly the

lowest four or five (traditionally numbered from the lowest one up and marked F_1, F_2 etc.) can be seen in a spectrum—at least when the voice is sufficiently loud and the pitch is not very high. A high-pitched voice may pose the problem that since the harmonics are distributed wide apart, the formants may fall in between them without affecting the amplitude of them (i.e. without forming a peak in the spectrum). (This is why it may be hard to perceive words in high-pitched singing.) The location of the formants is related to the dimensions of the vocal tract. These can be altered through articulation. For example, the frequency of F_2 can be raised by moving the tongue forward in the mouth, while retracting the tongue causes opposite changes. Lowering the lower jaw/opening the mouth wider raises F_1. Protrusion of the lips and lowering of the vertical position of the larynx (as in yawning) lower all formant frequencies. In contrast, all formant frequencies tend to rise when the lips are retracted as in smiling or when the larynx is raised. Figure 2 illustrates that each speech sound has a different spectrum. (Figures showing the results of acoustic analyses have been made with a speech analysis system called Intelligent Speech Analyser, ISA, developed by Raimo Toivonen, M.Sc.)

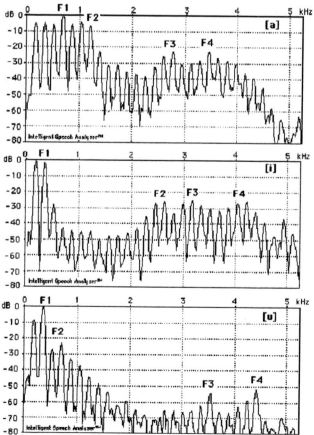

Figure 2. Spectra of the vowels [a, i, u]. Female speaker. F_1-F_4 = peaks resulting from the lowest four vocal tract formants.

A Finnish voice trainer and voice scientist, the father of Finnish Vocology (science and practice of voice habilitation) Timo Leino searched for objective basis for speech training and posed the question: What does a good voice look like? He recorded text reading from a group of voice professionals, actors, who are supposed to need a good voice and thus to possess it. Leino made a long-term-average spectrum (LTAS) analysis of the voices. LTAS is an average of various individual spectra taken, for example, every 40 ms in a speech (or singing) sample of e.g. one minute duration. Thus, LTAS is no longer affected by the individual speech sounds but illustrates the average voice quality. Leino had the reading samples evaluated by a listening panel, which consisted of voice and theatre professionals, voice scientists and naive subjects. Based on this evaluation, Leino was able to find some acoustic correlates of a good speaking voice (Leino 1976, 1994). Figure 3 illustrates these correlates by comparing one good and one poor male speaking voice.

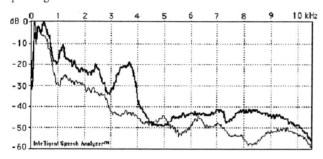

Figure 3. Long-term average spectra (LTAS) of a one-minute text reading sample from two male actors. Thick curve: good voice, thin curve: poor voice. The strong peak between 3 and 4 kHz is called an actor's formant.

We can see in Figure 3 that in the good voice the spectrum tilt is more gentle, which means stronger overtones, and there is a clear peak at about 3500 Hz. (In good female voices it is typically located about 1000 Hz higher in frequency). This peak Leino called an actor's formant. It is formed by a cluster of adjacent formants (mainly F_4 and F_5 or F_3 and F_4). This peak does not seem to be related to Finnish language but it has also been found in good voices of South-African, American, German and Norwegian speakers (Munro et al, 1996; Nawka et al, 1997; Bele, 2002). The actor's formant resembles the singer's formant found in classically trained (especially male) singers' voices in that it makes the voice project better and gives it a ringing quality that is typically regarded as esthetically eligible. Both the actor's and the singer's formant are present more or less regardless of loudness level and vowel. However, the actor's formant is about one thousand Hz higher in

frequency and clearly weaker than the singer's formant (see Fig. 4). Both the singer's formant and the actor's formant increase the perceived loudness since our hearing threshold is lower at the frequency range of about 2-5 kHz. The singer's formant is the characteristic that makes the (male) voice carry through the orchestra (Sundberg, 1974). In normal speech so great a carrying power is not needed. The fact that the singer's formant is lower in frequency than the actor's formant is related to laryngeal lowering used by the singers. The strength of the actor's and singer's formant is based on how strong the overtones are and how close the adjacent formants come to each other in forming a cluster. The singer's formant is stronger than the actor's formant for various reasons. One reason is that since the singer's formant is located at a lower frequency range than the actor's formant, the overtones that form it are stronger to start with. Furthermore, singers typically use higher sound levels and consequently the overtones are stronger. Lowering of the larynx may also lead to a closer clustering of the upper formants.

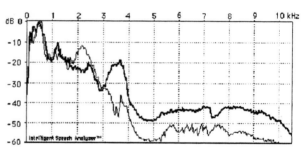

Figure 4. LTAS of speaking (thick curve) and singing voice (thin curve). One-minute text reading sample from a male actor is compared to a one-minute singing sample (without accompaniment) from an operatic baritone. The peak between 2 and 3 kHz in singing sample is called a singer's formant. It is located more or less 1 kHz lower in frequency than the actor's formant and it is also typically stronger in amplitude.

The origin of the actor's or singer's formant seems to lie in the dimensional relations between the laryngeal tube (epilaryngeal region) and the pharynx. When the pharynx is sufficiently wide the laryngeal tube starts acting as an independent resonator. This leads to the clustering of upper formants (Sundberg, 1974; Titze & Story, 1997). Sufficiently strong overtones are needed, though, in order to establish a singer's or an actor's formant, since the resonances cannot strengthen very weak overtones. In order to get strong overtones the vocal folds need to get into contact sufficiently fast and tight during vibration. This requires sufficiently strong adduction and adequate subglottic air pressure.

Female singers do not seem to have as clear a singer's formant as the males. The female singer's projection mainly results from a technique called "formant tuning" (Sundberg, 1975). In speech and in singing at low pitches the frequency of the fundamental is always lower than the frequency of the first formant, F_1. However, in singing the frequency of the fundamental can well exceed that of F_1 (this occurs at different frequencies depending on the vowel; for instance in [i] F_1 lies at about 350-450 Hz but in [ɑ] it is about 600-700 Hz.) When singing at pitches that are higher than F_1, the female singers open the mouth sufficiently wide and thus raise F_1 to the same frequency as the fundamental. This may increase the sound level up to 30 dB (Sundberg, 1986). It also improves intelligibility of the vowels.

Physiological Correlates of Good Voice

Loud and effortlessly produced voice requires a wide and free movement of the vocal folds during vibration. The vocal folds need to get together fast in order to produce strong overtones. The vocal folds need to move wide apart in the opening phase of the glottis to make the fundamental strong (Gauffin et Sundberg, 1989). As a consequence of this wide movement of the vocal folds the air flow is typically higher in trained versus untrained singers (Sundberg et al., 1990; Titze & Sundberg, 1992) (AC flow—i.e. pulsating air flow coming through the glottis during vocal fold vibration; the opposite is DC flow resulting from a permanent leakage of air due to incomplete closure of the glottis. That in turn can be higher in untrained hypofunctional voices.) Trained singers also seem to be able to preserve a reasonably constant AC flow regardless of variation in sound level—in contrast to untrained singers whose air flow tends to diminish at high sound levels. This is a sign of a change towards hyperfunctional voice production.

Figure 5 illustrates different voice types from the point of view of (AC) air flow through the glottis during vocal fold vibration. Pulsating glottal airflow, the so-called voice source, can be estimated with a method called inverse filtering. It is based on cancellation of the effects of vocal tract resonances on the signal (Rothenberg, 1973; Alku, 1992). In Figure 5 we can see that pressed voice is characterized by a low air flow and a long closed phase of the glottis. These characteristics result from an inadequately strong adduction in relation to subglottic pressure. In hypofunctional voice the total DC flow is high but AC flow can be low; closed phase is short or lacking. Obviously, the adductory force is insufficient in this voice type. Characteristics of normal and optimal voice lie in between these two opposite non-optimal voice qualities.

An other method for an indirect study of the vocal fold vibration is electroglottography (EGG) (See Titze, 1990; Baken, 1992). Two (or more) small metal electrodes are placed on both sides of the larynx. A weak high frequency current is fed through the larynx. During vocal fold vibration the electric

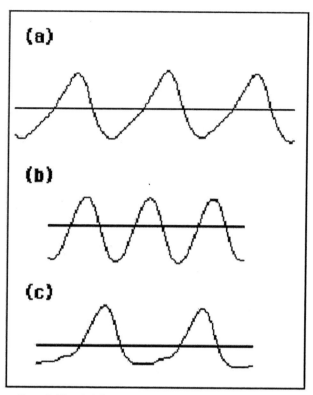

Figure 5. Glottal air flow derived with inverse filtering (IAIF method developed by Alku). Time on horizontal axis, air flow (arbitrary scale) on vertical axis. (a) Normal voice, (b) hypofunctional voice and (c) hyperfunctional voice. (Material: Long vowel from the word 'paappa').

impedance of the larynx changes. When the vocal folds are together (glottis is closed) the current passes easily through the larynx and, consequently, the impedance is low. The air, in turn, is a poor conductor of current and therefore when the vocal folds are apart (and the glottis is open) the electric impedance of the larynx is high. Thus, electroglottigraphic signal illustrates the varying contact between the vocal folds through varying electric impedance. Figure 6 shows examples of EGG waveform in various voice types. In pressed phonation the contact between the vocal folds is strong and therefore the closed phase of the glottis is long. In hypofunctional or falsetto voice the contact between the vocal folds is weaker and thus the open phase is long and the amplitude of the EGG signal is also low.

In singing training the goals of vocal exercising naturally differ somewhat from those in speech training. A singer needs the capacity for a wider and predetermined pitch range variation, a higher sound level and more efficient projectability and longer phrases. The main difference between a classical singer and a speaker is related to the register, i.e. the mode of vibration of the vocal folds. A speaker mainly uses chest register characterized by a relatively large activity of the thyroarytenoid

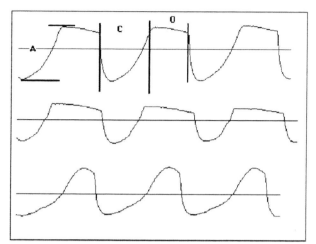

Figure 6. EGG signal. Time on horizontal axis, electric impedance (representing the amount of contact between the vocal folds) on vertical axis. C = closed time of the glottis, O = open time, A = amplitude of the signal. Top: normal voice, middle: hypofunctional voice, bottom: hyperfunctional voice.

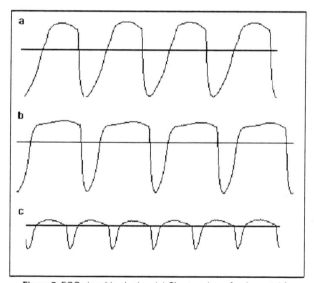

Figure 7. EGG signal in singing. (a) Chest register, fundamental frequency 275 Hz, (b) "mixed" register, fundamental frequency 275 Hz, (c) falsetto, fundamental frequency 418 Hz. Trained female singer, vowel [a].

(TA) muscle (Hirano et al., 1970; Hirano, 1988). The vocal fold mucosa is loose and makes a rolling vertical movement during voice production. The closed phase of the glottis is relatively long. The resulting sound has strong overtones and a rich timbre. An untrained singer may either sing in chest register and thus the song resembles speech or he/she may use falsetto: Then the TA muscle is relaxed, the activity of the cricothyroid (CT) muscle dominates, and the vocal fold mucosa is stiff. No rolling movement of the mucosa can be seen and the glottis

closes either for a short time or stays open during voice production. The resulting sound has weak overtones and the timbre is pale. In classical singing an intermediate alternative has been developed, the so-called "mixed register" (or "mid" and "head"). There the activity of the TA is higher than in falsetto but lower than in chest register (see Hirano, 1988). It enables, for example, a more marked mucosal movement (mucosal wave) even at high pitches—and, consequently, the sound is richer in overtones than a natural falsetto voice. On the other hand, since TA activity is lower in mixed than in chest register, it is possible to raise pitch with less effort in mixed register. The X-ray studies by Aatto Sonninen, the Grand Old Man of Finnish Phoniatrics, suggest that when a singer raises pitch in the so-called "open mode"—i.e. in an untrained singer's speech-like style, more extralaryngeal muscle activity is needed to stretch the vocal folds to overcome the shortening effect of inadequately high TA activity (Sonninen et al., 1999). This should be stressful for the vocal fold tissue and there lies a risk for vocal fold nodules and other trauma. Recent observations made by using electromyography, a method to register muscle activity, seem to suggest that a certain TA/CT activity relation is aimed at in classical singing (Laukkanen et al., 2002). An optimal TA/CT activity relation might also be important to establish a wide movement of the vocal folds needed for the production of loud and effortless sound (Titze & Talkin, 1979). Figure 7 compares the EGG signals of a female singer's chest, falsetto and mixed register phonation. In chest register the signal resembles that typically observed in speech (see Fig. 6). In falsetto the pulse form is rounded and the amplitude of it is low, suggesting a very slight contact between the vocal folds. Mixed register phonation has an EGG waveform which is a mixture of the characteristics found in chest and falsetto.

Voice Training Methods

As a comparison between trained and untrained speakers and singers and subjects with good and less good voices has made the goals of voice training clearer it is easier to see rationale behind various traditional vocal exercises and instructions given by voice trainers. Instructions like: "Relax the pharynx" or "Think of yawning" may be used in order to teach the trainee to widen the pharynx, which in turn would help in establishing the singer's or the actor's formant and also in avoiding hyperfunctional voice production, which is characterized by hyperadduction and typically also raised larynx and contraction of the pharyngeal muscles. Furthermore, it is known on the basis of voice physiological research that when the distance between the thyroid cartilage and the hyoid bone decreases the intralaryngeal tissue gets folded. This, in turn, hinders free vocal fold movement, deteriorates voice quality and increases mechanical load preposed on vocal fold tissue.

This folding occurs either when the larynx is raised or when the tongue is retracted (see Zenker & Glaninger, 1959; Zenker & Zenker, 1960; Vilkman & Karma, 1989). This knowledge gives rationality to voice trainers' traditional instructions according to which the tongue should be kept in a frontal position and the larynx should not rise.

The so-called diaphragmatic breathing, i.e. breathing which allows the diaphragm to go down thereby bulging the abdomen out, also tends to pull the larynx down (Zenker & Glaninger, 1959; Zenker & Zenker, 1960). In this way a certain type of breathing assists the free movement of the vocal folds (Sundberg et al., 1986; Leanderson et al., 1987). The widely used term "breath support" seems to refer to a delicate control of the air pressure and flow conducted by the respiratory muscles during voice production. This control requires the participation of both inspiratory and expiratory muscles. It enables an adequate subglottal air pressure needed for loud and well-projected voice as well as for rapid and controlled changes in loudness and for long phrases. It also implies that the responsibility of adequate subglottal air pressure is carried by respiratory muscles, not adductory muscles. Breath support is thus prone to help in avoiding hyperfunctional voice production.

Phonation into tubes and on voiced fricatives like [z:, β:, v:] has been widely used in vocal exercising (tubes: see e.g. Gundermann, 1970; Habermann, 1980; Sovijärvi, 1965; fricatives: Berry, 1975; Linklater, 1976; Carroll & Sataloff, 1991). One possible reason may be that they help in finding an adequate adduction. During these exercises the supraglottal airflow diminishes and the air pressure above the vocal folds increases. In a condition like that, a hypofunctional voice production gets impossible and it is also very strenuous to use hyperfunctional voice production. Furthermore, these exercises require more activity of the respiratory muscles so they can also give training in breath control. These exercises also allow the use of high air pressures and high pitches without preposing much stress on the vocal folds since the intraglottal air pressure is high during the production of them and tends to hinder a forceful collision between the vocal folds (Titze et al., 2002). Phonation into tubes and on voiced fricatives as well as on nasals give the trainee a good idea of the goal of vocal training, i.e. "maximum output with minimum effort": during exercises that raise the supraglottal air pressure one gets strong vibratory sensations in the vocal tract and the adjacent tissues (facial bones) and at the same time vocal fold vibration is characterized by a gentle collision (Titze, 2001).

Recent research has also shown that nasalization may raise the level of the singer's formant (Birch et al, 2002). This would offer one explanation why nasals are so widely used in vocal exercises (e.g. Anderson, 1961; Machlin, 1966; Pahn, 1968;

Berry, 1975; Fisher, 1975; Linklater, 1976 etc.). This may not be the only explanation, though. There is evidence of a co-operation tendency between the laryngeal and velopharyngeal muscles (obviously related to respiration): as the velum lowers, the adductory activity tends to cease (Fritzell & Kotby, 1976; Kogo et al., 1987). Exercising on nasals would thus assist in avoiding hyperfunctional phonation.

Teachers of singing often say that the secret of fortissimo lies in pianissimo. In soft phonation the TA muscle is relaxed (Hirano et al., 1970; Hirano, 1988). Therefore, it seems plausible that the use of pianissimo and messa di voce exercises (a change of loudness from pianissimo to fortissimo and back on the same note) train the control over the TA activity, which is needed in order to find mixed register.

There are still lots of questions waiting for answers in voice science and many of the above mentioned explanations to various vocal training principles and vocal exercises are just tentative hypotheses needing to be tested. However, the rapid development of research methodology has already made it possible to obtain lots of new information of the manifold and fascinating human voice. The prospects of future voice science are interesting. One of the newest traits in voice research exploits molecular biology (see e.g. Gray et al., 1999). It is known that gene expression changes according to the outer forces applied to a cell. This results in changes in the protein production of the cell. There are lots of different types of proteins in a cell and the amount of various proteins has an impact on the properties of the cell itself. This concerns the cells of the human vocal folds as well. We may, for example, pose the following types of questions: do certain type of voice use result in excessive production of collagen in the vocal fold mucosa making it too stiff and thereby deteriorating the voice quality—or could an optimal voice training increase the amount of elastin in the vocal fold mucosa making it more pliable for vibration thus also improving the voice quality?

Practical Applications of Voice Science to Voice Training
In a way, Voice Science always lags behind Voice Pedagogy, trying to find explanations for different phenomena in voice training tradition. We might say that science tries to prove what has been known already by intuition. On the other hand, intuition is not always right. Sometimes science may be able to help, for example, in distinguishing between adequate and inadequate voice use (inadequate = acoustically inefficient and/or possibly physiologically traumatizing). Furthermore, science may help in establishing a more general language to be used between all those who are interested in voice: voice scientists and pedagogues, singers, actors and various other voice professionals.

Voice research methodology not only gives information to be used in explaining things but it also offers a way of visualizing voice and voice production—in many cases in real time. This in turn makes it possible to take advantage of these methods in voice training. Biofeedback has been applied with success, for example, in actors' training in the University of Tampere already in the 1970s. The student actors used real time spectrum analysis during exercising. The aim was to get strong overtones in the region of the actor's formant (3-5 kHz). The training period lasted for eight months. The goal was achieved, the voices were evaluated better after training and still after one year the actor's formant was present although somewhat weaker than right after the training period (Leino & Kärkkäinen, 1995). A similar experiment was carried out in 2000 in a co-operative project between the Department of Acting and the Department of Speech Communication and Voice Research at the University of Tampere (Laukkanen et al., 2002). This time a control group was used. The students in the control group were trained traditionally, relying on auditory perception and imitation. The biofeedback group was able to see the spectrum of their voices in real time. According to the results the positive changes in the students' voices (less steep spectral slope, development of an actor's formant, better perceptual voice quality) were more marked in the biofeedback group. The students also found the visual feedback motivating. It made them understand better the goal of training. On the other hand there is a danger of changing towards hyperfunctional phonation if strong overtones are aimed at and too much attention is paid to the visual representation of voice. No biofeedback method can ever replace the role of human ear in the evaluation of voice. Visual feedback can only be an extra aid. Learning can be made easier, faster and more motivating if an extra sensory channel is included in the process. One problem related to imagination-based training is the fact that we may understand the same instruction in different ways—and one expression may result in wonderful results in one trainee but make no sense to another. Biofeedback can offer help in establishing a common language between the teacher and the trainee.

Conclusions

Vocal training is traditionally based on sensory information and experiences. Development of voice science and various acoustic analysis methods have provided us with plenty of tools that could also be applied in voice training practice. The use of analysis methods could help in setting objective goals for training and in evaluating the results of it. Furthermore, for example, real-time spectrum analysis could be used during training sessions to make the goals of voice training and the relation between phonation and the acoustic results more concrete. This could facilitate training and help in building a

261

common language for the trainer and the trainee when talking about voice.

❧

References

Alku P (1992). Glottal wave analysis with pitch synchronous iterative adaptive inverse filtering. *Speech Communication* 1992, 11, 109-118.

Anderson V (1961). *Training the Speaking Voice.* Oxford University press, New York, 2nd edition (1.st 1942)

Aronson AE (1985). *Clinical Voice Disorders. An Interdisciplinary Approach.* 2nd edition. Thieme Inc. New York.

Baken RJ (1992). "Special article: Electroglottography". *Journal of Voice* 6(2), 98-110.

Bauer H (1973). Klinik der Stimmstörungen. In *Phoniatrie und Pädoaudiologie*, eds. P. Biesalski, G. Böhme, F. Frank & R. Luchsinger. Georg Thieme Verlag, Stuttgart.

Bele IV (2002). *Professional Speaking Voice. A perceptual and acoustic study of male actors' and teachers' voices.* Dissertation. University of Oslo, Norway.

Berry C (1975). *Your Voice and How to Use It Successfully.* Harrap, London.

Linklater K (1976). *Freeing the Natural Voice.* Drama Book Specialists, New York.

Birch P, Gumoes B, Karle A, PrytzS, Stavad H, Sundberg J (2002). Effects of velopharyngeal opening on the sound transfer characteristics of the vowels [a, u, i]. Paper presented in the Voice Foundation's 31st Annual Symposium: Care of the Professional Voice, June 5-June 9, 2002, Philadelphia.

Carroll LM, Sataloff RT (1991). The singing voice. In *Professional Voice: The Science and Art of Clinical Care*, ed. RT Sataloff. Raven Press Ltd, New York.

Cooper M (1973). *Modern Techniques of Vocal Rehabilitation.* Springfield: Charles C. Thomas.

Fisher HB (1975). *Improving Voice and Articulation.* Houghton Mifflin Company, Boston, second edition (1.st 1966).

Fritzell B & Kotby MN (1976). Observation on thyroarytenoid and palatal levator activation for speech. *Folia Phoniatrica* 28,1.

Gauffin J, Sundberg J (1989). Spectral correlates of glottal voice source waveform characteristics. JSHR 32, 556-565.

Gray SD, Titze IR, Chan R et al (1999). Vocal fold proteoglycans and their influence on biomechanics. *Laryngoscope*, 109(6), 845-854.

Hirano M (1988). Vocal mechanisms in singing: Laryngological and phoniatric aspects. *Journal of Voice* 2(1), 51-69.

Gundermann H (1977). *Die Behandlung der gestörten Sprechstimme.* Fischer, Stuttgart.

Habermann G (1980). Funktionelle Stimmstörungen und ihre Behandlung. Arch. *Otorhinolaryngol.* 227, 171-345.

Hirano M, Vennard W, Ohala J (1970). Regulation of register, pitch and intensity of voice. *Folia Phoniatrica* 22, 1-19.

Kogo M, Nishio J, Matsuya T, Hamamura Y., Miyazaki T (1987). "Coordination of the Levator Veli Palatini and Intrinsic Laryngeal Muscles: An Evoked Electromyographic Study in the Dog. *Cleft Palate Journal*, 24, 2, 119-125.

Laukkanen A-M, Syrjä T, Laitala M, Leino T (2001). Effects of two-month vocal exercising with and without spectral biofeedback on student actors' speaking voice. Paper presented at Pan-European Voice Congress in Stockholm, 2001. Submitted for publication.

Laukkanen A-M, Titze I, Finnegan E, Hoffman H (2002). Laryngeal muscle activity in a tonal scale: Comparing speech-like to song-like productions in a mezzo-soprano subject. *Journal of Singing* 2002, vol. 59(1):49-56.

Leanderson R, Sundberg J, von Euler C (1987). "Role of Diaphragmatic Activity During Singing: a Study of Transdiaphragmatic Pressures. *Journal of Applied Physiology* 62(1), 259-270.

Leino T (1976). [*The spectral characteristics of good voice.*] In Finnish. Licentiate Thesis in Logopedics. Helsinki: University of Helsinki, Finland.

Leino T (1994). Long-term average spectrum study one speaking voice quality in male actors. In *Proceedings of the Stockholm Music Acoustics Conference* July 28-August 1, 1993. A. Friberg, J. Iwarsson, E. Jansson, J. Sundberg, eds. Publication issued by the Royal Swedish Academy of Music, no 79. Taberg 1994, pp 206-210.

Leino T, Kärkkäinen P (1995). On the effects of vocal training on the speaking voice quality of male student actors. In: K. Elenius & P. Branderud, eds. *Proceedings of the XIIIth International Congress of Phonetic Sciences,* Stockholm, Sweden 13-19 August, 1995. Stockholm: Department of Speech Communication and Music Acoustics, Royal Institute of Technology and the Department of Linguistics, Stockholm University,Vol. 3 of 4, 1995:496-499.

Machlin E (1966). *Speech for the Stage.* Theatre Art Books, New York.

Munro M, Leino T, Wissing D (1996). "Lessac's Y-buzz as a Pedagogical Tool in the Teaching of the Projection of an Actor's Voice." *South African Journal of Linguistics,* suppl. 34, Dec. 1996.

Nawka T, Anders LC, Cebulla M, Zurakowski D (1997). "The Speaker's Formant in Male Voices." *Journal of Voice,* 11(4), 422-428.

Pahn J (1968). Stimmübungen für Sprechen und Singen. VEB Verlag Volk und Gesundheit, Berlin.

Perkins WH (1971). *Speech Pathology. An Applied Behavioral Science.* The C.V. Mosby Company, Saint Louis.

Proctor DF (1968). The physiologic basis of voice training. *Annals New York Academy of Sciences,* vol 155, 208-228.

Rothenberg M (1973). A new inverse filtering technique for deriving the glottal air flow waveform during voicing. *JASA* 53(6), 1632-1645.

Sonninen A, Hurme P, Laukkanen A-M (1999). "The External Frame Function in the Control of Pitch, Register and Singing Mode: Radiographic Observations of a Female Singer." *Journal of Voice* 13(3), 319-340.

Sovijärvi A (1965). Die Bestimmung der Stimmkategorien mittels Resonanzröhren. Verh. 5. int Kongr Phon Wiss, Münster 1964. Basel/New York, S. Karger.

Sundberg J (1974). "Articulatory Interpretation of the Singing Formant. *JASA* 55, 838-844.

Sundberg J (1975). "Formant Technique in Professional Female Singer." *Acustica* 32, 89-96.

Sundberg J (1987). *The Science of the Singing Voice.* Illinois: Northern Illinois University Press.

Sundberg J, Leanderson R, von Euler C (1986). "Voice Source Effects of Diaphragmatic Activity in Singing." *Journal of Phonetics* 14, 351-357.

Sundberg J, Scherer R, Titze I (1990). Phonatory control in male singing. A study of the effects of subglottal pressure, fundamental frequency and mode of phonation on the voice source. *STL-QPSR* 4, 59-79.

Titze IR (1990). "Interpretation of the Electroglottographic Signal." *Journal of Voice* 4(1), 1-9.

Titze IR (2001). "Acoustic Interpretation of Resonant Voice." *Journal of Voice* 15(4), 519-528.

Titze IR, Finnegan EM, Laukkanen A-M, Jaiswal S (2002). "Voice Research: Raising Lung Pressure and Pitch in Vocal Warm-ups: The Use of Flow-Resistant Straws." *Journal of Singing* , Vol 58 (4), 329-338.

Titze IR, Story BH (1997). "Acoustic Interactions of the Voice Source with the Lower Vocal Tract." *J Acoust Soc Am* 101(4), 2234-2243.

Titze IR & Sundberg J (1992). Vocal Intensity in Speakers and Singers. *JASA* 91(5) 2936-2946.

Titze IR, Talkin DT (1979). A Theoretical Study of the Effects of Various Laryngeal Configurations on the Acoustics of Phonation." *JASA* 66(1), 60-74.

Vilkman E, Karma P (1989). Vertical hyoid bone displacement and fundamental frequency of phonation. *Acta Otolaryngologica* 108,142-151.

Zenker W, Glaninger J (1959). Die Stärke des Trachealzuges beim lebenden Menschen und seine Bedeutung für die Kehlkopfmechanik. Z. Biol. 111, 154-166.

Zenker W, Zenker A (1960). Über die Regelung der Stimmlippenspannung durch von aussen eingreifende Mechanismen. Folia phoniatrica 12, 1-36.

Peer Reviewed Article *by Ruth Rootberg*

Principles of Breathing, Pedagogy and Language

Derived from
PRACTICES OF THIRTEEN VOICE TEACHERS
(Christine Adaire; Barbara Adrian; Eric Armstrong; Michael Barnes; Marina Gilman; Jane Heirich; Mary Howland; Ellen Margolis; Marth Munro; Lise Olson; Natalie Stewart; Phil Timberlake; Lynn Watson)

About the Editor
Ruth Rootberg is a designated Linklater voice teacher, Alexander Teacher, and Certified Laban/Bartenieff Movement Analyst (CMA). Performance credits include Zurich Opera and St. Gallen Opera, The American Medieval Players, Court Theatre, Drury Lane South, and the New Haven Film Festival. Ms. Rootberg toured as a puppeteer and has clowned in the streets. She was voice teacher and coach at the Yale School of Drama/Yale Repertory Theatre, Northern Illinois University, The Theatre School, DePaul University, and Shakespeare & Company. She has presented workshops in Chicago, New Haven, and South Africa and has written for *The Voice and Speech Review* and *The Complete Voice & Speech Workout*.

We have intuitive knowledge that teaching breathing needs to be part of a voice curriculum. There are several pedagogical approaches to teaching voice that are currently in vogue. Breathing is always a component. Despite real and perceived differences among pedagogical styles, one can find **principles of breathing pedagogy** that are universal, whether one subscribes to one specific pedagogy or draws eclectically from a range. These principles inform one of the components to be addressed for optimal breathing coordination, what basic strategies are involved in teaching the principles, and how language choices affect learning outcomes.

Contextualization

I have derived these principles by analyzing the original source material, responses to a questionnaire, and the published version of an in-depth study reflected in the Monograph, *Teaching Breathing: Results of a Survey.*[1]

The purpose of the questionnaire originated from my personal journey to understand the relation among several approaches to breathing I have encountered, and to broaden my theoretical knowledge of those I have not experienced first-hand.

The names of the participants are placed as part of the title. They are primarily voice teachers for actors, educated and/or having posts in the United States, England, South Africa, Canada and France. The group's training and approach represent a well-distributed range of currently popular or historically esteemed vocal pedagogy and complimentary movement practices.[2] Their specialties are reflected in the forthcoming table:

Alexander [1] (10)	Herbert-Caesari	Smukler
Allen	Knight	Speech/Language
Bel canto/classical song	Laban/Bartenieff [2] (5)	Pathology [1]
Berry (6)	Lessac [1] (7)	Suzuki
Estill [1]	Linklater [1] (11)	T'ai Chi
Feldenkrais [1] (9)	McCallion	Turner
Fitzmaurice [2]	Newham	Wade
Grotowski	Qi Qong	Yoga (9)
Hart/Wolfsohn	Rodenburg (8)	

Numbers in square brackets e.g., [1] indicate how many people have certification/designation in this specialty.
Numbers in parentheses, e.g. (3) are used if a person or style was mentioned three times or more, and includes the person with certification.

The years of teaching experience range from two to thirty-four. The average number of years teaching is fourteen and the median is ten. No contributor is the originator of currently reigning pedagogies. Their responses are representative of the sum total of their experience and values, rather than any one pedagogical style, unless they refer specifically to another authority.

Between August 2001 and the following July, I reviewed, analyzed, conducted on-line discussions with the participants, and edited their generous and detailed responses.[3] During my analysis of the data, I broadened my intention to include the dissemination of the data in detail. The *Monograph* was published to provide the vocal pedagogue with varied points of view, allowing the reader to resonate, respond and draw individual conclusions.

This article presents trends of the universal components that must be addressed to provide a comprehensive breathing curriculum. Because the number of questions addresses so many different aspects of breathing, and because the contributors represent a wide range of pedagogical backgrounds, I believe the principles put forth, although they may not be the only principles that govern teaching breathing, set a standard for pedagogy in the vocal community.

This article is thus not argumentative in nature, but presents and then reflects on the three universal components: principles of breathing, principles of pedagogy, and the principles of language choices in the classroom as posited by the thirteen voice teachers. Each set of principles is first presented, and then discussed separately with pertinent examples derived from the *Monograph*.[4]

Principles of breathing

- Teaching breathing is an essential, if not fundamental part of a voice curriculum.
- The teaching of breathing to an actor or singer must have expression as its ultimate goal.
- The organization of the whole (i.e. "posture") is related to the coordination of the breath.
- Although the entire coordination of the individual during static and dynamic movement must be considered, in particular there must be some torso movement for optimal breathing to occur.
- The breathing cycle during quiet respiration has three parts; the "space" between inhale and exhale can be described many ways.
- Breath should be very quiet or silent if phonation is not intended.
- The inhale and the exhale involve separate muscular coordination; teaching how to do either may be emphasized separately.
- Choosing where the breath enters and exits (nose and/or mouth) affects the breath, the voice, and the actor.
- Inspiration can happen with or without consciousness, and as such, students will derive different benefits from learning to breathe in reflexively or with control.
- It is useful to have transitional stages from breath work to fully articulated text.
- In order to maintain optimal vocal health throughout the various demands of performance, one must learn to a) coordinate the breath and b) expand the capacity for situations beyond the tidal breath of quiet respiration.

Discussion of principles of breathing

Teaching breathing is an essential, if not fundamental part of a voice curriculum.

Breathing is either the first or close to the first thing taught in every

About the Contributors

Christine Adaire is a Master Linklater Voice teacher, trained by Kristin Linklater. She is also an actor and director in professional as well as educational venues. Regional theatre work includes: Shakespeare & Company, Milwaukee Repertory Theatre, Chicago Shakespeare, The Court Theatre, Theatre for a New Audience, and American Shakespeare Theatre. She has taught at The Theatre School, DePaul University, University of Massachusetts-Amherst, Ithaca College, Escuéla Eòlia in Barcelona, and the Shanghai Theater Academy in China. Currently she is Head of Acting at the University of Wisconsin-Milwaukee.

Barbara Adrian is presently an Assistant Professor of Theatre at Marymount Manhattan College teaching voice, speech, and movement for the actor in the BFA and BA theatre program. She also coaches professional actors for television, film and stage as well as free lances as a movement and voice/speech/dialect coach for productions throughout the New York tri-state area working with such notable directors as Robert Brustein, Elizabeth Swados, Tina Landau and playwright/director David Rabe. Ms. Adrian holds an MFA in Acting from Brooklyn College and is a Certified Laban/Bartenieff Movement Analyst (CMA).

Eric Armstrong taught an eclectic approach to voice, speech and dialects at Roosevelt University and has just recently joined the faculty at York University in Toronto. His training includes an MFA with David Smukler and work with Andrew Wade. Past teaching includes Canada's National Voice Intensive, Brandeis University and The University of Windsor. Eric dialect coaches in Chicago, including HBO's upcoming *Normal* (Tom Wilkinson).[6] He's been involved with VASTA as a Director of Internet Technology, Director of Conferences (2001-2002), and has recently been elected to the Board. He has written on Technology for the VASTA Newsletter, and his interview with Andrew Wade was published in the *Voice and Speech Review*.

Michael J. Barnes is voice, speech and dialect specialist for the University of Miami Acting Conservatory. He has coached regionally and off-Broadway at theatres which include: Shakespeare Santa Cruz, Arena Stage, Wilma Theatre, Studio Theatre, Rep Stage Company, Pearl Theatre, People's Light and Theatre, Venture Theatre, Denver Center Theatre Company, and Colorado Shakespeare Festival. He also coaches for broadcast professionals and acts professionally in regional theatre. He is a Certified Associate Teacher of Fitzmaurice Voicework and assists with training new Fitzmaurice teachers. He holds an MFA from The National Theatre Conservatory and a BFA from the University of Oklahoma.

Marina Gilman, BS Indiana University, MM Ithaca College, MA Northwestern University. Ms. Gilman is a licensed speech/language pathologist, voice teacher and certified Feldenkrais Practitioner. Ms. Gilman maintains a private voice/movement integration studio teaching singing, voice, and Feldenkrais. In Chicago, she has taught voice at the Steppenwolf Theater School, and served as an adjunct faculty member at The Theatre School, DePaul University. She has also taught voice at Syracuse University and Cornell University in New York State. Ms. Gilman currently serves as speech language pathologist with a voice specialization at the Loyola University Medical Center Voice Institute and as voice consultant to the University of Chicago Voice Center.

Jane Heirich, after graduate school at Harvard, worked as a choral conductor, which led to private study of vocal pedagogy, which in turn led to further study of vocal anatomy, physiology, and acoustics. These studies eventually led to a professional focus on the mind-body system and its effect on the voice. Ms. Heirich holds STAT (UK) and AmSAT (US) certification in the Alexander Technique, having completed her training with Joan and Alex Murray in Urbana, Illinois in 1987. Since 1972 she has taught at the Residential College of the University of Michigan, Ann Arbor, where she offers a basic voice technique class for actors and singers that includes Alexander work as its foundation. She also maintains a private studio for voice study and/or the Alexander Technique.

Mary Howland is currently Head of Voice at the Birmingham School of Speech and Drama. After leaving University with a Degree in English and Drama, she worked in a variety of capacities at Birmingham Repertory Theatre before gaining her Equity card and pursuing a career as an actress. She studied at the Central School of Speech and Drama on the MA Voice Studies course, where her specialist research was vocal characterization.

Ellen Margolis works as an actor, director, teacher, and voice and dialect coach. She received an MFA in Acting from the University of California at Davis. Currently she teaches at the University of Wisconsin-Stevens Point, where she is an Assistant Professor and Coordinator of the BA/BS Program in the Department of Theatre & Dance. Her areas of special interest include Shakespeare, dialects, new play development, and a physical approach to actor training.

Marth Munro specializes in performance voice building, body/voice integration and vocal pedagogy. She holds a PhD in which she investigated the acoustic properties of Lessac's Tonal NRG and the "Actor's formant" in the female voice. She has completed a team research project on computer-aided training of the singing voice. She is a Certified Laban/Bartenieff Movement Analyst and a Certified Lessac Teacher. She teaches at the Departments of Drama and Vocal Art at the Pretoria Technikon, South Africa. Munro is a member of VASTA and chair of SAP-VAME (South African Performers Voice and Movement Educators). She frequently teaches workshops for actors, singers and musicians. She directs for musical theatre and does voice and movement coaching.

classroom. Many teachers are passionate about the overall importance of breath to the whole scheme of voice and performance. In addition to agreeing that it is the central focus or one of a few central foci (others including physical awareness, intention and vibration), they describe it as the *centerpiece, foundation,* or *cornerstone* of the curriculum. It is *life itself* and *related to total somatic organization.*

The teaching of breathing to an actor or singer must have expression as its ultimate goal.

The writers are very committed to the vital importance of making connections. A few find value in working on breath alone in some exercises. When asking for a connection from their students, the reasons to do so vary, from getting the proper amount of breath without tension (function) to stimulating imagination and spontaneity (expression). Marina Gilman talks about the organism's ability to regulate airflow when there is connection.

> Speech or song must be connected to meaning. The breath must be part of that meaning. The body self-regulates how much breath to have depending on the task. If I say 'no,' I need much less breath than if I say 'I saw a great big, giant, red and green lizard on the street in front of John's house today as I was walking past.' If I plan to *take a big breath* and parcel it out, I will be introducing excess tension. However, if I begin my thought of this sentence including the breath, my body will automatically regulate the airflow. (MG, p. 10)

The connection of breath to text works in two directions. When the actor frees the breath, it is usually easier to make the necessary connections. Most teachers will also agree that a deep connection to text and dramatic situation will change breathing patterns according to the emotional content. Some will use the breathing patterns associated with certain affects to help generate that affect; others avoid such techniques. Mary Howland explains how she puts changing patterns to use in the classroom.

> Breath patterns change observably under emotional states, and according to personal/character rhythms. At a later stage in their training, students will be asked to breathe with different parts of the body—clavicular, belly, ribs—and at different rates or patterns, and to comment on the emotional or mental sensations that these patterns produce. By using the breath as the origin of any sound, you are making sure that the whole body is involved. (MH, p. 11)

Furthermore, changes in breath, body and level of connection may trigger somatic or emotional reactions, including yawning, nausea, and laughter. These occurrences are respectfully handled in the classroom, and, in the case of yawning, encouraged. When they occur during performance, teachers may support their inclusion if they work aesthetically, or coach students to shed them if it disrupts the performance. Phil Timberlake talks about yawning; Christine Adaire about nausea; Eric Armstrong about laughter.

> I try not to interpret a yawn. It could mean many things, including (Great Scot!) boredom. I do not, however, stifle yawning; I encourage it. It is such a great way to feel the soft palate stretch open, stretch the

jaw, stretch the tongue, etc. Also, it seems that once a student stifles a yawn, they start to shut down physically in class. They become embarrassed and limit their vocal and physical freedom. I find that if I allow spontaneous yawning and stretching, the students are physically and vocally freer in class. (PT, p. 151)

I've had students become nauseous. I ask them to try and stay with the exercise. I have found that many times when a student is on the verge of a break-through, they will get nauseous or dizzy. Certainly if someone is feeling very ill, I would give them permission to leave the room. If it's a milder case, I might ask them to sit down, or move a waste basket near them, but to continue working. (CA, p. 154)

I do have students begin to laugh, sometimes out of joy, sometimes out of a giddiness that comes with the exercises, sometimes out of self-consciousness. I love laughter—I think it breaks down much of the armoring that people experience, and in some ways, I think of it as a great antidote to the 'I have to cry' feeling some students bring to their training. Emotion is a good thing in class—I do take time at the end of the experience to talk a bit about it when it arises for the first time, so that people who weren't laughing (often because they are self-conscious or afraid that would be 'doing it wrong') are given permission to go where their impulse leads, without a feeling that one *must* be in an exaggerated emotional state all the time. That's as big a distortion as avoiding emotion completely. (EA, p. 164)

I usually drop the story that Dale Genge[5] tells at the Canadian Voice Intensive into the mix too—that Buddhists say that, in the theory of non-attachment, an emotion only lasts 20 breaths, and then it can change (note: it can get worse!) If you go longer than that, you're making an attachment to the emotion, and then an emotion can last years. (EA, p. 164)

The organization of the whole (i.e. "posture") is related to the coordination of the breath.

All the respondents agree that there is a relation between good posture and good breathing, although the word *posture* is sometimes avoided, for fear it might be associated with holding a particular position. Barbara Adrian uses "dynamic alignment;" Marth Munro uses "optimal body integration." Some teachers avoid calling it by a nominative, preferring to describe the movement and or dynamic direction of the interior. Principles of the Alexander Technique that aim for three-dimensional expansion, rather than contraction, are inferred from discussion of balance, lengthening and widening. Feldenkrais practice as a means to improve alignment is also mentioned.

Teachers generally agree that the head must balance on top of the spine, and that there is a vertical relationship to bony landmarks. Some discuss the natural curves of the spine, while others, not denying the curves, see the spine as a vertical core that encourages a flow of the breath. Metaphors mentioned for this internal integrity are *string* and *hose*.

Some teachers will describe the visual look of the "ideal" when the body is static in vertical alignment, a neutral stance, so to speak. Others remind us

Lise Olson is an ex-pat American who has lived/worked in the UK for over a decade. Lise is currently at the Liverpool Institute for Performing Arts. West End credits include *Witches of Eastwick* and *View from the Bridge*. Her work has been seen at the Birmingham Rep, Bristol Old Vic, Central, Welsh College of Music & Drama, Rose Bruford, East 15, Purdue, Duke, NCSA and others. A busy director/teacher with specializations in acting, voice, Shakespeare and musical theatre, Lise is a consultant for Digitalbrain, pioneering a test project for online voice training...and she's a BBC Masterchef.

Natalie Stewart is an Assistant Professor of Voice and Speech at East Carolina University. She received her MFA degree in the Theatre Voice Coaches and Trainers Program at the National Theatre Conservatory in Denver, Colorado. She has taught voice and speech at the University of Texas at Austin, Brandeis University, and the American Conservatory Theater. Some of Natalie's roles have included Eliza in *My Fair Lady*, Rita in *Educating Rita*, and Cherie in *Bus Stop*.

Phil Timberlake recently received his MFA in Voice and Speech Pedagogy from Virginia Commonwealth University where he taught Voice, Speech, Dialects, and Acting. Phil was the 1996 Annette Kade Fulbright Fellow to France (studying voice at the Roy Hart International Arts Centre) and VASTA's 1999 Clyde Vinson Memorial Scholarship recipient. He appeared in numerous Off-Loop theatres in Chicago where he lived for 10 years. Phil was an Adjunct Professor of Voice and Speech at The Theatre School, DePaul University, and led "extended voice" workshops with Lookingglass Theatre, Roosevelt University, and Purdue University. Phil is an Associate Teacher of Fitzmaurice Voicework.

Lynn Watson currently teaches voice and speech at the University of Maryland, Baltimore County and vocal coaches for Arena Stage in Washington, DC. Other coaching includes four seasons at South Coast Repertory, ACT. San Francisco, Mark Taper Forum, Maryland Stage Company, and private consultation for stage, film and television. She has coached world premieres of plays by Richard Greenberg, Howard Korder, and Zora Neale Hurston. She has also taught voice for the University of California, Irvine MFA program. She has acted off-Broadway and in leading classical and Shakespearean roles regionally. She is certified as an Associate Teacher of Fitzmaurice Voicework.

that the body is in constant motion, and the actor/speaker must discover how to maintain good breathing and vocal use whether embodying a character with "ideal" or "less than ideal" postural and movement habits. Therefore they focus on the necessity of free breathing, i.e., the ability of the diaphragm and ribs to move freely whether the silhouette looks "right" or not.

Teachers also remind one that whatever the goal, it will take time for the student to make adjustments. Some of the more detailed "ideal" postures are listed as follows:

Feet under the hip sockets, knees soft (not locked), pelvis and belly muscles released, a sense of the spine rising from the tail-bone through the lower back, mid-back, between the shoulder blades, through the neck, the skull resting on the top vertebra, with the crown of the skull as the top of the body. The arms should hang easily in the shoulder sockets, jaw released with lips closed. (PT, p. 21)

The pelvis is free allowing the diaphragm to freely descend on inhalation and lift under the ribs on exhalation and throughout voicing. (MG, p. 21)

Soft feet sensing plenty of contact with the ground, and the skeleton rising up out of those big feet; knees dropped; legs energized; tail-bone dropped, which is to say it's neither extended behind nor tucked forward; spine floating out of the hips, with the head as an extension of the spine that would float away if it were not attached. (EM, p.21)

Weight evenly distributed on the feet; ankle, knee, hip alignment; awareness of the flexion of ankle, knee, hip for rising or lowering; awareness of the curves of the spine; and finding length through the lower back and neck spine; head balanced on the spine. (EA, pp. 21-22)

The aligned body balances openness in the small of the back with appropriate tension in the abdomen, with open shoulders, chest and back of neck to encourage low, easy breathing and resonance. A vertical line through the crown of the head, the hole in the ear, the highest point of the bone of the shoulder, the highest point of the bone of the pelvis, the knee joint and the highest point of the instep provide a balanced efficiency. (MH, p. 22)

Maintaining the two natural inward curves in your back, which are in your neck and in the small of your back. The head should be directly over the torso and not hunched forward in front of the torso. The intercostal muscles and diaphragm can freely contract. (NS, p. 22)

Knees over feet, shoulders relaxed, an upright chest and ribcage that is not collapsed, nor pushed out, head floating on top of the neck (or the old string through the top of the skull image). (LO, p. 22)

The principle of body organization presumes then that movement must be part of a vocal curriculum. Many aspects of movement are included in a breathing curriculum, some with formal disciplines such as yoga, Suzuki, massage, Alexander, Laban or Feldenkrais as their source. Integrating movement becomes part of the teaching principles, and is discussed in depth in the *Monograph* (pp. 102-146).

Although the entire coordination of the individual during static and dynamic movement must be considered, in particular there must be some torso movement for optimal breathing to occur.
During inhalation pedagogues look for forward movement in the abdomen, either in the whole area, or more specifically above, at, or below the navel. The thorax is seen as relatively quiet, although sometimes rib movement is mentioned, and for some is dependent on the demands of the text and environment, (e.g., in a larger space more rib movement is needed). The terms most often used to describe optimal breathing for speaking are *abdominal, belly,* and *coordinated.*

Jane Heirich gives a detailed description of how the abdomen and the ribs of the thorax each can move when things are working well. Phil Timberlake points out how an ideal may need to be approached in stages.

Thoracic breathing needs elastic ribcage muscles (the intercostals) which work the bellows, and this activity is naturally a part of healthy breathing—less for quiet breath, more for running the 100 meter dash or singing Wagner. If we are not corseted by constricted intercostal muscles, the entire ribcage coordinates with the diaphragm on every breath. Before intake—the diaphragm contracts and descends, and the ribcage springs up and out. During exhale—the diaphragm returns to its domed position, and the ribcage/bellows returns back home (inwards). Meanwhile, the abdomen moves slightly outwards at the point of the diaphragm's contraction/descent, and this abdominal movement is necessary to accommodate the displaced viscera that need to go somewhere. The healthy tonus of the abdominal muscles will return back to 'normal' as the viscera follow the diaphragm back up into its domed position. The flexible elastic toned-up abdominals thus move in and out (back to front) in coordination with the diaphragm's descent and rising. If the abdominal group of muscles is held too tightly, the intake of breath will be limited because the diaphragm cannot descend very far because the viscera aren't willing to move out of the way because they have no place to go. The abdominals need to be left alone rather than manipulated in order for the natural breath to be re-learned, should such re-education be needed. (JH, p. 52)

My goal is for coordinated breathing, but it isn't a term I use as frequently as belly breathing. I would define coordinated breathing as breathing in which there is full and free expansion in the belly (below and above the navel), the ribs, and the chest. The image I use is that of an umbrella or bellows, in which the greatest expansion is in the belly below the ribs, tapering to a slight expansion below the collar-bone. In my teaching, however, I find the greatest challenge is helping the student create a habit of belly breathing. So what I often end up doing is focusing on belly breathing and rib expansion, and then encouraging the students to allow chest/sternum area to be free to move in response to the breath. I will sometimes talk about diaphragmatic breathing as a good use of the breathing apparatus. So although my goal is coordinated breathing, I don't often use the term in my classes. (PT, p. 52)

The breathing cycle during quiet respiration has three parts; the "space" between inhale and exhale can be described many ways.
There is total consensus that, during quiet breathing, a third part of the cycle exists between exhale and inhale where nothing seems to be happening. But *holding* is seen as an inappropriate word to use with normal breathing. Many writers offer substitute words such as: *pause, suspension, stillness,* and *waiting to replace.*

As a side note, it should be mentioned that, although the breath is never held during a normal cycle of breathing, holding the breath as an exercise may or may not be useful. It is used to find the impulse to breathe, relax, strengthen, or lengthen the outgoing breath.

Breath should be very quiet or silent if phonation is not intended.
The pedagogues are united; they expect the breath to be silent during quiet respiration. Lynn Watson makes slight exception to this, suggesting there will be something heard, but that it should not be loud or constricted.

Many teachers use words based on auditory representations that describe what they don't want to hear. The breath should *not* have

noise	*rasp*	*rattle*	*snore*
stridor	*vocalization*	*wheeze*	*whistle*

There are also static kinesthetic representations. The breath should *not* be

bound	*constricted*	*pushed*	*strained*

Some teachers talk about the ideal that is not happening when unnecessary sound occurs: the vocal folds are not abducted enough; the passage of air is obstructed; they are thinking or working too hard. *Ragged*, from our visual context, is also used.

The problem of audibility of an incoming or outgoing breath is perceived as initiating in the larynx (stridor), the mouth (position of soft palate and tongue), or nose, with a held rib position being a fourth possibility. Depending on what is perceived as the problem, the solutions lie within the interrelated areas of building awareness, releasing tension, and allowing full function. Teachers will refer to other professionals when the solution lies beyond the classroom.

The inhale and the exhale involve separate muscular coordination; teaching how to do either may be emphasized separately.
Breathe in to speak; breathe out to breathe in. Is there something that changes in the quality of breathing when deliberate focus is put on one part of the cycle rather than the other? The writers have good reasons to put emphasis on one or the other parts of the cycle.

Reasons to emphasize the inhale:
• To set the groundwork for determining the quality and type of exhale.
• To discover the seeds of and to diffuse holding or tension patterns, which are observed more often during the inhale than the exhale.
• To learn how the three-dimensional space grows.
• To develop a larger capacity, more flexibility and spontaneity.
• To learn how to more rapidly get more air.
• To learn how to get the right amount of air to fit the thought.

Reasons to emphasize the exhale:
• To learn to exhale efficiently to set the groundwork for an inhale that will just happen.
• To learn to manage and support various needs of duration and power while using text; i.e., to learn to control the subglottic pressure.
• To learn how the three-dimensional space shrinks.
• To learn to get out of the way.

Reasons for equal emphasis:
• To learn to release.
• To learn to be present at every moment.
• To learn effective communication of text.

Choosing where the breath enters and exits (nose and/or mouth) affects the breath, the voice, and the actor.
Some teachers will present a range of possibilities, i.e. in and out through the nose, in and out through the mouth, in through the nose, out through the mouth, then leave the choice to the student. Nose breathing is favored for moistening, filtering, and warming the air. It is also used as a way to slow down the rate at which the breath comes in, so as to train students not to gasp or gulp the air. It is also possible that breathing in through the mouth promotes gum disease, and thus should be avoided.

Some teachers perceive breathing through the mouth as a way to access feeling more directly and assist in releasing jaw muscles. Those that favor nose and mouth simultaneously want the best from both worlds. Some feel one should not make a conscious choice to open or close the mouth in order to breathe, but rather breathe through whichever aperture is available.

Even if mouth breathing is seen as the favored practice for performance, teachers have observed or will guide students to character choices using nose breathing:

> If a character is angry and trying to control herself, she might breathe through the nose before speaking. Or if she is gathering herself up for a verbal assault, that gathering might manifest itself as a strong inhale through the nose. One actor who played a very 'put-upon' browbeaten character frequently expressed his barely concealed frustration with loud nose-breaths before speaking. (LW, p. 32)

Marth Munro, teaching in South Africa where there are several first-languages represented in the classroom, raises awareness that questions a basic assumption:

> Since most vocal sounds in the eleven languages used in South Africa are being made on the egressive sound, as opposed to the ingressive, the tendency will be there to breathe out through the mouth while voicing. (MM, p. 33)

Inspiration can happen with or without consciousness, and as such, students will derive different benefits from learning to breathe in reflexively or with control.
When teaching breathing, the issue of how much the student must learn or re-learn natural processes comes up against how much the student must learn skills specific to performance. Debate arises around the issue of using a "reflexive" or "controlled" inhalation. Even then, dialogue ensues as to whether "controlled" refers to a conscious process where the rate of the breath is somehow volitionally altered, or any occurrence of breathing during which the person is aware. We do not actually learn what a controlled breath looks or sounds like in

269

comparison to a reflexive breath, but we do learn the different functions they carry.

A controlled inhalation is associated with:
- Slowing the rate of the breath.
- Dramatic effect, such as a non-naturalistic style.
- Observing the process of breathing to gather personal information.
- Expanding the breath into other areas of the body.
- Moments of vocal violence.
- Strengthening and training muscles.
- Planning.

A reflexive inhale is associated with:
- Involuntary action.
- Efficiency, freedom and spontaneity needed in performance.
- Connecting to thought, image, and/or impulse.
- The volume of a tidal breath.

It is useful to have transitional stages from breath work to fully articulated text.
Whispering, mouthing, single or double phonemes, a short "Touch of Sound" and the sigh are commonly used as transitions to text.

Whispering and mouthing offer these options:
- Create a strong thought-breath connection for text work.
- Deepen connection to imagery.
- Strengthen character objectives.
- Find optimal tones/pitches.
- Improve focus and intention.
- Prevent the actor from listening to himself.
- Increase amplitude.
- Improve diction.
- Practice a stage whisper.

Single phonemes, particularly unvoiced fricatives, but also voiced fricatives, affricates, lip flutters, some vowels and consonant-vowel combinations like Linklater's "Touch of Sound" are useful because they serve as a bridge from inner work to communication outward, from simple breathing to active, from unvoiced to voiced sound.

Phonemes, particularly the fricatives and vowels, restrict the flow of breath. Teachers talk about how this restriction helps slow the breath, develops even control, and assists the student because it's audible. Following is a table of phonemes commonly used.

Phonemes for transition from breath to sound:
/s:/   /z:/   /ʃ:/   /ʒ:/   /f:/   /v:/   /ɸ:/

/ʙ̥ː/　　/ʙː/　　/tʃː/　　/ŋː/　　/rː/　　/g/　　/k/
/h/　　/hɑ/　　/ɑ/⁺　　(YEE)*　　(huh)**　　(hu-u-u-uh)**

⁺　Alexander's "whispered ah"
*　Lessac transliteration
**　Linklater transliteration

When it comes to initial sighs in the classroom, usually on /ɑ/ or Linklater's (huh), every possibility of duration is represented among the group: short first, long first, and "it depends." It moves through the range and registers or not. It is gentle and releasing, pleasurable, relaxing, freeing and more. It is not used for projection or placing the voice. Ellen Margolis and Eric Armstrong use it to create only one expressive quality of voice among many.

In order to maintain optimal vocal health throughout the various demands of performance, one must learn to a) coordinate the breath and b) expand the capacity for situations beyond the tidal breath of quiet respiration.
Most participants agree that during quiet respiration, because of the natural recoil force, the less active work, the better. However, as soon as even a silent breath is used in the context of training, many teachers encourage activity in the ribs and abdomen. Sometimes the word *support* is used to describe the activity, but there is division over the usefulness of the term. The following describes the pros and cons associated with the word and/or activity. It is followed by substitute terminology.

Benefits of breath "support":
• Finding enough breath for the thought without tension.
• Finding strength and freedom.
• Connecting to the need to communicate and express.
• Getting the appropriate subglottal pressure.
• Creating the appropriate quality of sound including volume, dynamics, energy, and flow.
• Getting the appropriate balance of muscular use needed in the outgoing breath.
• Using the need to communicate as well as muscle to create support.
• Avoiding sound that is squeezed out of the chest or throat.
• Coordinating use of breath and muscle.

Negative associations with breath "support":
• Holding, pushing, sucking, pushing the epigastrium out.
• Thinking about particular muscles rather than the whole, organic system.
• The meaning is vague or taken for granted.

Other terms and phrases used instead of *breath support*:
• Supported tone/voice.
• Structuring (Fitzmaurice term).
• Take time to breathe/a breath to fit the thought/a breath when you need one.

• Have enough air for the task.
• Whole-system support.
• Breath management.

Teaching capacity does not carry the same pedagogical disagreements. However, teachers have different ideas as to when such training belongs in a curriculum.

> It seems to me to be a fundamental part of acting—speaking a long thought. Also, it's relatively simple to lengthen the exhale in small increments and the student is therefore able to 'succeed' quickly. (PT, p. 82)

> I believe that, by increasing the amount of time the student performs exercises returning to an autonomic breath, the breath capacity increases. It is important to show them how it can be focused in usable fashion. Thus, once I take the students onto tone, we begin working with counting out longer phrases. (MB, p. 82)

> The potential for developing more tensions rather than less is a definite downside to starting work on increasing the length of the exhale too soon. (BA, p. 82)

> I think the focus needs to be on developing the spontaneity, sensitivity and depth of breathing before beginning to place any sort of restriction on it. (LW, p. 82)

We now turn to principles of pedagogy. Following are basic tenets of a curriculum. They are applied to teaching breathing, but would form the foundation for teaching other aspects of voice as well.

Principles of pedagogy
Teachers may find themselves shifting between offering principles of breathing as new information, and seeking strategies of intervention to change behavior according to their understanding of basic principles. These principles reflect both aspects of a curriculum:
• Students need to be motivated and inspired.
• A change in the classroom atmosphere can promote learning.
• Some learning takes place when receiving information.
• Learning to breathe includes developing awareness through visual, auditory and/or sensory feedback.
• Students learn when the teacher models for them.
• It is useful to prepare or cue the student to help change habits.
• Altering the belief system of what has to happen can foster new learning experience.
• Some problems can be solved through analyzing and offering a solution based on principles.
• Some problems can be solved when the task is simplified or taken out of its original structure.

- Sometimes the learning occurs when the focus is on change through the breath.
- Sometimes the learning occurs when the focus is on change in the mouth/throat.
- Sometimes the learning occurs when the focus is on change through sound.
- Sometimes the learning occurs when the focus is on change through touch.
- Sometimes the learning occurs when one approaches the problem as an acting issue.
- Sometimes the learning occurs when there is a change of imagery.
- A variety of goals can be met by using movement.
- Homework reinforces learning and creates a sense of independence.
- Preparation for performance sometimes includes expedient, short-term solutions.
- The health and well-being of the student should always be addressed by an offer of immediate assistance or triaging the need for medical attention.
- When the needs of the student exceed the experience of the teacher, the teacher should confer and/or refer.

Discussion of pedagogical principles

Students need to be motivated and inspired.
It is not much of an intuitive leap to say that all teachers are objects of inspiration, and that students become motivated when they are inspired. Teachers counsel students to become active listeners, to work for themselves. Sometimes the first kinesthetic taste of less tension will be a good incentive for a student to continue with the work. However, Jane Heirich reminds us that the true willingness to change must come from within the student.

> We can't change this habit for them, because we are not always with them. Only they can do so if they are sufficiently motivated. (JH, p. 99)

A change in the classroom atmosphere can promote learning.
Teachers often speak about creating or recreating a safe environment in which to work. The content of the image, the use of their voice, the establishment of the student in control of his/her learning, attention to group dynamics and a willingness to slow down the pace are some of the valuable tools available. Teachers will also use humor to dispel tensions, or perhaps a group song to settle students down. It is one of the first steps needed to set the tone for a single period, or a semester.

I offer full, descriptive scenarios that take students on a

journey to a place that feels safe for them (especially in the first few weeks of their training). (LO, p.15)

I do think that once a safe space is provided and the students know that they are still in control and only allowing to happen that which they feel comfortable with, any fear that may initially exist will vanish. (MM, p. 159)

As for how I deal with the defensive reactions: usually as holistically as possible, which is to say I take a step or two back with that student (or even with the whole class), so as to create an even safer environment and encourage more complete whole-body relaxation. (EM, p. 162)

I support the student with my voice by reassuring the student that he/she is safe and that tears are often a natural response to releasing. (BA, p. 157)

I will always make sure that no one leaves the class in a bad mood—either sad or angry. I may take time at the end of the class to do some kind of silly group song or an energetic game to diffuse the atmosphere, and where necessary, speak to the student before the class leaves the room and find out if they want to talk—either to me, or to another member of staff. (MH, p. 161)

Some learning takes place when receiving information.
One of the primary goals of a teacher is to give new information. It is one of the distinguishing factors that differentiates a learning environment from a therapeutic one, although there are some crossovers.

> They need to know that when the glottis closes, using the muscles within and/or outside the larynx, it causes a noisy intake. (JH, p. 100)

> When the soft palate lifts gently, like in the beginning of a yawn, the back of the tongue reacts by relaxing down low in the mouth, giving sufficient space between the two for a relaxed outgoing breath. (BA, p. 102)

Learning to breathe includes developing awareness through visual, auditory and/or sensory feedback.
Simple techniques are often effective. Slowing down processes helps one observe. If a teacher calls attention to a problem, the student can begin to change. Teachers will rely on observation of self and others:
- Visually, with or without a mirror.
- Aurally, using a tape recorder or listening for aural feedback.
- Tactilely, with one's own hand, a teacher's, or another student's.
- Kinesthetically, recognizing and/or comparing feelings.

Students learn when the teacher models for them.

Teachers will do an activity for or with their students, or assume that their own coordination is observed consciously or unconsciously. Modeling develops awareness, but also facilitates learning through imitation.

It is useful to prepare or cue the student to help change habits.

Teachers give specific directions to encourage or avoid behaviors. They might instruct the student to consciously take in more air, take a quick, pick-up breath or to breathe silently, depending on the task at hand. They might remind the student to continue breathing while listening to the instructions. Some teachers continue to feed in reminders during class. However, Phil Timberlake makes a good point that the instruction "breathe" itself may be shorthand, which may not adequately inspire the students to drop the old habits in favor of newer skills.

> Often, when given the instruction, 'Breathe,' a beginning student will resort to habituated means of breathing, rather than a free breath that we've been exploring in class. I'm trying to give instructions to a group of people in as concise a way as possible, and sometimes it doesn't turn out the way I would like. If I'm working with a student one-on-one, I will usually take time to say, 'Let the breath fall down to your belly'. (PT, p. 93)

Jane Heirich goes a step further, discounting the value of cueing in reminders and seeing breath holding as a more pervasive problem.

> The problem is not really addressed by the constant reminders (phrased in a variety of ways) to BREATHE. If a student holds her breath while listening for directions or for a cue, it is most often a habit that permeates her life—tying shoelaces, putting in contacts, fastening earrings, turning a doorknob, doing math, shifting gears in the car, getting something off the bottom shelf, etc. The issue at its most basic level is to unlearn the breath-holding habit, so that the natural phenomenon will be able to do its stuff. Repeat: reminders to breathe are working at a more superficial level than learning to STOP holding the breath, in all daily waking moments. (JH, p. 95)

Altering the belief system of what has to happen can foster new learning.

Sometimes students get caught up in their belief that there is only one way to accomplish a task, and they don't know how to do it. When it comes to managing long phrases in particular, teachers may work with the student on finding new strategies. For instance, if a student is perturbed because s/he can't say a phrase without breathing in the middle, the teacher may analyze the text with the student and show how catch breaths may not break up the thought or momentum.

Some problems can be solved through analyzing and offering a solution based on principles.

Again, using phrasing as the topic, teachers examine what specifically is preventing the student from accomplishing the task, and then prescribe remedies.

> Examine whether it is the vowels or consonants that are making it more difficult. If it is the vowels, then they sing or intone the phrase. If it is the consonants, they breathe-- through (whisper) it for more efficient consonant action. (BA, p. 92)

Some problems can be solved when the task is simplified or taken out of its original structure.

Teachers will also deconstruct and reconstruct, building phrases backwards and forwards, suggest doing a phrase on one vowel sound, etc.

Of course there are times when specific exercises are given to learn a skill, increase strength or coordination, or break a habit. These exercises might focus specifically on the breath, the mouth and throat, vocalization, or on the entire body. The voice teacher is well aware of the numerous exercises available. As this article is not intended to provide specific exercises, these following items are summarized briefly.

Sometimes the learning occurs when the focus is on change through the breath.

Attention may go to breathing principles, such as offering exercises that deter gasping, that slow down the inhale or exhale, that allow the breath to drop deeper into the body, that encourage a reflexive inhale.

Sometimes the learning occurs when the focus is on change in the mouth/throat.

Attention is put on releasing holding or tension in the extrinsic or intrinsic muscles of the throat, finding more space in the mouth by relaxing the jaw and tongue or toning the soft palate.

Sometimes the learning occurs when the focus is on change through sound.

Teachers will use humming and buzzing, fricatives, and shaking out of sound to foster change. Some of the same phonemes may be used to explore resonance, but in other exercises they are intended to teach a breathing skill.

Sometimes the learning occurs when the focus is on change through touch.

Teachers raise awareness, diagnose and encourage release

through touch. They are sensitive to gender and harassment issues, making sure the student feels safe and in charge.

Sometimes the learning occurs when one approaches the problem as an acting issue.

Sometimes if the student puts attention on the overall goal, breathing happens organically.

> Breathe where they feel the impulse and it will usually be the right place if the thought/intention of the acting is clear. (LW, p. 92)

> If the actor understands that the character is always reacting to an impulse—from his/her fellow characters and from the things that he/she does/says him/herself, then it is usual that he/she permits him/herself to be in a constant process of change—and this leads to breathing. (MM, p. 95)

Sometimes the learning occurs when there is a change of imagery.

The teaching strategy of using imagery is considered in depth under Principles of language.

A variety of goals can be met by using movement.

It was mentioned earlier that, because "posture" is related to breathing, movement is integrated into the curriculum. This subject is vast and deserves separate analysis. Below is a list of ways that briefly characterizes how movement supports teaching breathing:
- Awareness of self, space and/or environment.
- Relax, release, strengthen, condition, improve coordination.
- Diagnostic tool.
- Recuperation/transition.
- Experience full range of motion.
- Take the body into fight/flight mode to induce more oxygen.
- Learn to stop interference with natural processes.
- Tool to connect voice and imagery by integrating the whole body in the acting process.
- Explore interpersonal relations.
- Externalize what is happening inside.
- Add a difficult physical task to what they're doing to challenge the breath further.

Homework reinforces learning and creates a sense of independence.

Some teachers believe that the real learning happens outside the classroom. They will suggest students build their awareness of their habits, or assign particular routines and exercises to be practiced at home. (See "Clavicular Breathing" article pp. 278-295 for more detail).

Preparation for performance sometimes includes expedient, short-term solutions.

The actor will not always be able to use new skills by the time a production is ready to go up. At that point, a voice teacher/coach can assist by suggesting expedient solutions.

The health and well-being of the student should always be addressed by an offer of immediate assistance or triaging the need for medical attention.

Changes in breathing, release in tensions and misunderstanding of instructions can engender somatic reactions including hyperventilation, nausea, panic, and asthmatic reactions. Teachers should be prepared to assist students in getting appropriate medical attention. The following is suggested:
- Know some medical history beforehand in regard to any breathing disorders.
- Distract the student if they are panicked.
- Offer water.
- If the student becomes dizzy, s/he should focus on either a hand or other object.
- Breathe with them.
- Ask them if they are all right or if there is a need for assistance with medication, or in an extreme case, a call to 911.

When the needs of the student exceed the experience of the teacher, the teacher should confer and/or refer.

Some students enter a course with vocal or breathing problems that require attention of other professionals. Some habits don't change after work in the classroom. The teacher must know his/her limitations and get outside help as needed, referring students to an ENT, SLP, etc.

Principles of language choices

We now turn to the use of language in the classroom. Because most teaching moments involve language, this is an underlying principle of all pedagogy. We use language to transmit information, give instructions, and create imagery through which we may then represent any one of our senses. We use language to analyze vocal needs and reflect on new experiences. It is, of course, the basis of text.

Language can serve to shift a person in and among cognitive, associate and creative thinking processes. It can imbue movement experiences with meaning. It is, for many reasons, a primary coin of exchange in communication. The principles are:
- The language choices in the classroom are vital to the learning outcome.
- Imagery is a highly effective tool when teaching breathing.
- Selecting active or passive voice may determine outcome.

• Language represents visual, aural, kinesthetic and tactile experience; varying the representational value of imagery is useful to expand the possibilities of learning.
• Offering technical terminology is useful.

Discussion of principles of language choices

The language choices in the classroom are vital to the learning outcome.
The way language is chosen reflects a variety of values that emphasize:
• Learning modalities.
• Ease.
• Kinesthetic, somatic and whole body connections.
• Balance between work and ease.
• Clarity and specificity.
• Link to later character work.
• Freshness.

Imagery is a highly effective tool when teaching breathing.
Some teachers use imagery so pervasively in their classroom, they can't possibly remember everything they say. For some, the images change and shift in the moment as they speak. Two teachers expressed the effectiveness of using imagery this way:

Many of the sensations that we are trying to get a better handle on can be explored effectively with imagery, especially the image that movement in the belly is caused by the air that is entering the body in a direct manner, rather than an indirect one, e.g., 'fill the bowl of the pelvis with air.' Alignment issues are also very effectively addressed with imagery, e.g., 'head floats up like a helium balloon', and 'your spine is the string'. (EA, p. 14)

Imagery provides an indirect and therefore a safe way of getting the voice to do what we want it to. We cannot work directly and manipulate the vocal cords to do our bidding. (JH, p. 14)

Following are examples of imagery used to gain various objectives.

Imagery to promote relaxation:
Imagery is often selected to reduce tension and/or promote relaxation or postural adjustments that will in turn affect the quality of the breath. Note how many use derivatives from words like: *warm* and *melt*, or others that evoke a sense of softness.

'Notice the golden air falling in, filling your body and warming you. And notice that, as it falls out, it takes with you anything you don't need for today's work.' (EM, p. 14)

'Feel the muscles of your body melting off the bones, and the bones dropping into the floor.' (EA, p. 15)

'Feel like you're a melting ice-cream cone.' (NS, p. 15)

Imagery that suggests whole environments or scenarios:
To encourage an open throat, I use a highly imagistic exercise, in which the students consider the description of Aslan the Lion in C.S. Lewis' stories [*The Chronicles of Narnia*] when he breathes on the stone animals in the witch's palace, asking them to think of the breath as being powerful and warm. (MH, p. 15)

'Imagine you're lying on a warm sandy beach, feeling the warmth of the sand underneath and the heat of the sun on the top of your body'. (CA, p. 15)

Imagery to awaken the imagination:
Notice how Lise Olson's description of "fire in the belly" creates a whole environment using color, light, heat, speed, and force.

The fire in the belly image is from the miner's cry 'fire in the hole:'
'Imagine that your abdominal area is a beautiful fireplace, laid with aromatic branches and twigs. Someone has lit the kindling, and as you breathe in, the fire grows in strength and intensity. As you breathe out, the fire burns down to the embers. With each inward breath, the fire's flames lick higher until light and warmth fill your insides. On the release of breath, the fire lessens. You can feel the fire from the top of your pelvis to the clavicle.' (Some people actually feel warmth up through the pharynx into the head, but concentrate on the lower abdominal area and let it grow from there—that's where the fire is laid.)
This fire can either be gentle or rage, depending upon the quality and duration of the inhalation and the exhalation. It can be slow or fast, building easily or enveloping swiftly. Because we take it gently for the first few times, students don't feel threatened or afraid of fire in this exercise, but come to view it as light and warmth, without being uncomfortable. (LO, p. 16)

Imagery developed by the student:
There can be a difference in effectiveness depending on whether the teacher or the student creates the image. Christine Adaire and Eric Armstrong report how they elicit images from students:

If a student feels like their breath is blocked somewhere in their body, I will ask them to describe it in metaphor. The image that they come up with gives me a lot of psychological insight into their holding patterns. For instance, if a student is holding in the solar plexus area, they might describe it as a 'steel wall in the middle of their chest.' I would work with that image to transform it into something soft and permeable. (CA, pp. 16-17)

After I've led a visualization, often I get students to come up with their own visualization trip through the body that they lead a partner through—it might be a 'light in the joints', or a 'desert wind racing through from the soles of the feet to the top of the head', or what have you—the idea is to get students to apply their imagination to a positive experience of awareness and relaxation for their partner. (EA, p. 17)

Marth Munro poignantly reminds us that the efficacy of imagery is dependent in part on the language and/or cultural orientation of the students:

When working in a multi-lingual situation, teachers have to be careful not to indulge in the use of too many metaphors. These metaphors will be understood by people from one language group or one culture but may be interpreted differently within the paradigms of another culture. For instance, you can't let your body give over to gravity as an ice-cream melting on a hot tar road if you are mostly accustomed to dirt roads and can't afford ice-cream. Balloons cannot become a metaphor for the lungs if a student never had the chance to play with a balloon! When I use a metaphor I clearly state that it is a metaphor and will rather encourage students to choose their own according to their subjective experiences. (MM, p. 17)

The process then, is 1) explore the organic process, proceeding from work already established; 2) describe the process in physiological terms; 3) provide my own metaphor; 4) encourage the student to find his/her own, culturally specific metaphor; and 5) explain to me why that metaphor is effective to him/her. (MM, p. 17)

Language represents visual, aural, kinesthetic and tactile experience; varying the representational value of imagery is useful to expand the possibilities of learning.

Breathing is a physical activity, and thus one might first assume that kinesthetic learners would have the easiest time of learning optimal breathing skills. We cannot assume this is so. Visual, tactile, auditory as well as kinesthetic representations can assist students. It may be that a combination of modalities aids the learning process. The representation of the various modalities through language may not be the same as learning in the modality itself. In other words, a teacher may use a visual image of the vocal folds being as wide apart as two goal posts. The student may either see or feel that width, or perhaps hear the difference in the sound of the breath as the goal posts move closer or further apart. One must also consider

that in the classroom students will present a variety of learning modalities, and in order for all to learn, teachers should vary the modality not only of instructive activity, but also of language representation.

Jane Heirich's example speaks to several representative experiences:

As much as possible, we use imagery based on anatomy, physiology & acoustics rather than poetry. For instance, to quieten down a noisy breath intake, we persuade the throat area generally to expand horizontally—or at least, to become less constricted. The information given to a student or class: 'Looking at this drawing/picture of the glottis, we can see that the air passageway lies between the vocal folds. Noisy intake of breath often comes from excess constriction at that vocal-fold level, although the whole throat pipe can be overly constricted. Gently touch your throat at the laryngeal level, persuading the external muscles to soften. Now use your hands to represent this throat pipe, or to think about expanding (not constricting) the glottal airway. Now let the air come in silently through a relaxed throat/larynx, rather than through a drinking straw. Allow it to come in without trying to get as much air in as possible. Give it time.'

Kinds of imagery used in the example above: tactile (touching throat); kinesthetic (sensing hands moving away from each other horizontally to invite less laryngeal constriction); visual (watching hands); auditory (listening for the silent breath); visual/conceptual/verbal (the idea of the glottal opening/throat pipe being as small as a drinking straw). (JH, pp. 15-16)

Visual representations:

'Imagine your breath is the color....' I use combinations of bright, pale, warm, cool colors. I find this allows the student to imagine sending the breath out, a transition toward projection. (PT, p. 15)

'Begin in your center, a light filling you and growing within until it encompasses and is a bubble all around you and then encompasses others.' (I call this one 'angel light'). (LO, p. 15)

Kinesthetic representation:

The breath shoots up like a fountain, arching upward and forward. (MB, p. 15)

'Picture the spine as the rod of an umbrella. The umbrella begins to open on the inhale, with the belly and ribs opening the farthest, tapering toward the collar-bone.' I believe this image encourages the feeling that breathing is an act of movement, not of holding. (PT, p. 15)

Offering technical terminology is useful.
Most of the discussion of language to effect change has shown how teachers favor imagery. The other side of the coin would be to offer vocabulary that more specifically, perhaps scientifically, represents things.

This group uses technical/medical/anatomical terms, often in conjunction with more common terms. Some prefer to use as many common terms as possible, unless there are none to be found. Many discuss the need for the more technical words so the students, should they have vocal problems, can converse intelligently with health professionals. Others consider introducing a scientific vocabulary as a good educational opportunity. Some need to give the students an experience in the body before naming the body part. Some abbreviate this part of the curriculum so as not to burden the students in a way that might impair their creativity. Others will use the scientific terms, but not without also relating it to a more image-based vocabulary. The list predictably names bone, muscle, and general areas most specifically related to breath, phonation, resonance and speech (e.g., *lungs, ribs, abdomen, pelvis, glottis, false cords, pharynx, uvula, teeth, mandible, masseter, tongue*). Terms relating to physiological function are also used (e.g. *recoil force, resting expiratory level*). Some teachers are selective in what they would use; some choose to refer to muscle groups rather than individual muscles. Words that some prefer to use without referring to anatomical cognates are: *belly, gut,* and *tummy.*

Selecting active or passive voice may determine outcome.
Another point to be made is that the decision to use active or passive voice can also affect outcome. Mary Howland explains the value of passive voice.

> Usually I will use passive terminology—things happen to the breath, rather than the students doing it to themselves. Part of this is encouraging the students to lose their own habits, especially if those habits involve tension or inappropriate effort. (MH, p. 16)

Conclusion
This article has given an overview of three sets of principles related to teaching breathing: principles of breathing, principles of pedagogy, and principles of language choices used to create teaching experiences.

The principles can form the foundation of any voice teacher's curriculum. The principles of breathing are based on physiological and functional realities. Where there is more than one possibility for an aspect of breathing, there is choice.

For instance, air can move through the mouth or the nose. Thus the principle, "entry and/or exit location of the breath will affect outcome," is derived from this fact; teachers can

choose what to teach, but all need to address this aspect of breathing.

A teacher who addresses breathing without phonation will have many avenues to choose from if he or she applies the principle "It is useful to have transitional stages from breath work to fully articulated text." Single phonemes can be varied to elicit affective changes inherent in their sounds, to avoid repetition or monotony, or as a choice based on the effectiveness the pedagogue perceives and intends.

When a teacher has included teaching material that covers each principle and has made the necessary choices, the basic aspects of teaching breathing will have been covered, and a teacher will have determined the values on which his or her pedagogy is based. The teacher can then make informed assessments as to why a popular pedagogy is effective, or can include aspects that address each principle while selecting eclectically from a range of styles.

The pedagogical principles included provide the teacher with a checklist. If all students have not yet learned to perform a certain task, the teacher may refer to the list to see whether there is another strategy based on a principle that has not yet been used. For instance, additional motivation, more information, or a more immediate connection to an acting issue might open the student to a deeper learning. By keeping the checklist in mind, a broader range of learning styles may be met, and more students will experience/learn what the teacher intends.

This research has shown that the third principle underlies all others: the language used in the classroom affects every aspect of teaching. Whether an exercise is based on a totally verbal routine involving imagery, or consists only of movement where the language is merely used to provide step-by-step directions, the choices the teacher makes will affect the outcome. Teachers may notice their own language preferences are useful for certain learning situations and certain students. By expanding their language choices, they may again, as with principles of teaching, provide more learning links for their students. For instance, a pedagogue who feels too much information crowds out creativity may find that some students need to satisfy themselves intellectually with detailed anatomical information before they can enter a more creative mode. This pedagogue may need to depart from his or her own comfort zone of generalization and metaphor in order to bring the student along. One can easily imagine the opposite scenario to also hold true, where the detail-oriented student may need to accept a more simple or imagistic approach in order to access a fundamental point in the curriculum.

By following principles and making the necessary decisions, teachers can choose from a seemingly endless number of exercises already in vogue, or develop new ones. For instance, if one wants a student to understand a basic principle of breathing that the unvoiced breath should be silent, one might want to use the teaching principle: "Some learning takes place when receiving information." In this case one can draw from many possibilities. One might give a verbal lecture, refer to 2-D pictures and 3-D models, show a video, go on-line to a Web Site, or offer selected reading material that will support your point. Using another teaching principle, "Learning to breathe includes developing awareness through visual, auditory and/or sensory feedback" might follow the earlier principle by offering any number of sensory experiences to raise the awareness of what occurs when the throat is open, and for comparison, when it is not open enough. The teacher may continue by addressing other principles. He or she may choose anatomical language plus imagery to support the learning. The imagery might be varied so as to appeal to visual, auditory and kinesthetic learners. The teacher may need to motivate the student by explaining the health benefits of a silent breath, and refer the student to a doctor or speech pathologist if sufficient change doesn't occur in the classroom.

Breath is such a fundamental and vital part of vocal life that it deserves every possible inroad of attention, skill, experience and inspiration we can bring to bear on it. Study of these principles benefits the uninitiated and veteran pedagogue alike. When all three sets of principles—breathing, pedagogy, and language—are operating at once, there will be a well-rounded curriculum of Teaching Breathing that offers room for variety based on the values and aesthetics of each pedagogue, while serving students of many diverse learning modalities.

❦

Endnotes:
1. Ruth Rootberg, Editor, Marth Munro, Asst. Editor (Amherst: privately printed, 2002). Referred to subsequently as *Monograph*. All quotations come from the *Monograph* and are followed by the page number and initials of the contributor.
2. This data is drawn from responses asking about primary influence as well as questions about what movement disciplines teachers draw from. See *Monograph*, pp. 3-4 and p. 177.
3. The contributors spent an average of twelve hours answering the original questions, and several more responding to further editorial questions and notes.
4. See also "Clavicular breathing, held shoulders, and related issues" page 278 in this volume. It comes from an additional electronic round table discussion conducted as the *Monograph* was being edited.
5. Dale Genge is Head of Voice at Studio 58, Langara College, Vancouver. She is a certified Laban/Bartenieff Movement Analyst (CMA).
6. See "This is Normal?—A Theatre Coach Works in Film" page 33 in this volume.

The Monograph, *Teaching Breathing: Results of a Survey*, is available for purchase by contacting Ms. Rootberg at RRootberg@attbi.com.

Round Table Discussion *by Ruth Rootberg, Moderator*

Clavicular Breathing, Held Shoulders and Related Issues

Contributors:

Christine Adaire; Barbara Adrian; Eric Armstrong; Michael Barnes; Marina Gilman; Jane Heirich; Mary Howland; Ellen Margolis; Marth Munro; Lise Olson; Phil Timberlake; Lynn Watson

Contextualization

The contributors listed above participated in an extensive project that culminated in the Monograph *Teaching Breathing: Results of a Survey.*[1] As the *Monograph* proceeded towards completion, these twelve of the original thirteen voice teachers[2] pursued the topic of Clavicular Breathing further, agreeing to look at that subject in more depth as well as to explore related issues as they arose. Thus whereas the *Monograph* presents, for the most part, collated responses to many questions that were asked and answered independently and in one phase, this article began with material from the *Monograph*[3] and then was built through several stages of distributing questions, collating responses and distributing more questions based on the responses. The intention of this procedure was to use Internet Technology to simulate a panel discussion, thereby bringing together a formidable range of expertise[4] in a timely and cost-effective manner. An advantage of this process over a live discussion is that each writer had time to articulate and revise responses.[5]

The responses of the writers are listed in a consistent and randomly selected order. There are instances where a writer chose not to engage in a particular question.

RR: Would you agree that if the shoulder girdle moves up and down during the breath cycle, or if the shoulders are in a constantly raised position, that it will impede optimal voice production?

MH: Yes, I do. Breathing patterns are likely to be shorter, less full, and the voice less resonant. On a more psychophysical level, the kind of tension/effort required to lift the amount of bone and muscle in the shoulders, chest and arms interferes with the free flow of thought, either of the character or the actor.

PT: Yes, excessive movement in the shoulder girdle during breathing will impede vocal production. It is an indication of a tension pattern that is limiting the breath. Shoulders in a constantly raised position would also impede vocal/breathing function, but may indicate a pattern of holding that goes 'deeper' (psychophysically) than raising the shoulder girdle, which may be simply a learned behavior.

EA: Sure. Though, I must say, one works with what one gets... both as a performer and as a teacher. Personally, my joints

aren't very flexible, yet I make the most of what I've got. Similarly, if someone has kept their shoulders near their ears for the last ten years, one hopes that together we can find a way to allow those shoulders to drop. But even a small change in this area can increase the ease in the throat, neck and shoulder area, which will lead to improved vocal use.

JH: Yes, if the shoulder girdle *significantly* moves up and down during the breath cycle, it will impede optimal voice production. And if the shoulders are in a constantly raised position, that too will impede optimal voice production. However, I see these as two related but quite different issues or problems for human beings in general, not just for actors and singers, with the latter situation causing more interference than the first one.

The first problem indicates that the student is breathing 'shallowly,' i.e., that the rest of the rib cage is probably constricted and hardly moving, if at all. The abdominal muscles may be overly developed in the interest of having a 'flat' tummy, and this impedes the diaphragm's descent. Hence the only area that is available to move is the upper part of the thorax/chest, and we may call it *clavicular breathing*.

The second problem—constantly raised shoulders—is much more difficult to change. My students have called it 'coathanger shoulders' (as if the person is hung up on a coat hanger), and there is little movement anywhere in the thorax. Usually the person also has a very stiff neck.

BA: There is some vertical movement of the shoulder girdle during the breathing cycle that is acceptable. In fact, to try to inhibit it entirely would result in excessive tension as well. I think, in this instance, we must think about degrees of movement. In other words, if the shoulder girdle moves up and down in a visible or exaggerated way during the breathing cycle, then I agree this would impede optimal voice production. This remark is predicated on the assumption that the shoulders would stay raised during the phonation, only lowering after that last sound or when out of breath. As to the statement, 'if the shoulders are in a constantly raised position...,' I agree that this would also inhibit the voice. Whether the breathing cycle exaggerates a lifting of the shoulder girdle or if the shoulder girdle is 'stuck' in the raised position, the results will be that the space for the larynx to function freely is severely reduced.

MG: If the shoulder girdle moves up and down during the breath cycle, the breathing pattern is generally what I call 'down and out'. By that I mean on the exhale the lower abdomen moves down and out. When the shoulder girdle is lifted on the inhalation, the shoulders must come down to some extent through the exhalation usually collapsing the ribs and resulting in the chest sinking, with increased downward pressure on the sternum and lower ribs. While some schools of singing teach a version of that—not usually with clavicular involvement—advocating a downward and outward pressure against the lower ribs, the result in terms of sound is often more strident, with increased laryngeal compression of the vocal folds. However, the lyric coloratura Kathleen Battle[6] uses a lot of clavicular breathing during performance and one can hardly say she does not have optimal voice production, nor is the sound strident! So I would amend the statement to say that moving the shoulder girdle up and down during the breath cycle *may* impede optimal voice production.

If the shoulders are in constantly raised position optimal voice production *is* impeded. Shoulders that are constantly raised are tense. The ribs are lifted but held in the lifted position, impeding the ability of the rib cage and the lower abdominal muscles to move appropriately. In addition the extrinsic strap muscles that support the larynx are all attached to the 1st rib, clavicle or sternum. Tension in the shoulder girdle which is also attached to the 1st rib and sternum will impact on the larynx, preventing the free movement of the laryngeal cartilage and the vocal folds.

LO: I find that increased movement in the shoulder girdle tends to increase the instances of 'shallow breathing'—referred to by many other terms as well—and continued usage does indeed take the student away from optimal voice usage. I also find that shoulders 'locked' in a high position tend to cause tension in the body that transmits itself to the voice. However, I think in terms of being prescriptive about certain body positions, we are in danger of setting very rigid rules for our students. So, in the classroom I would teach that shoulders down and released would be an optimal position, but if an occasional shoulder were raised, I might address the issue and then let it alone once the student had awareness of when h/she was raising the shoulder girdle.

LW: It's a matter of degree. The shoulders may move up and down slightly, but a large degree of movement indicates unnecessary tensions and holding patterns that may, to varying degrees, inhibit all aspects of performance, not just voice.

MM: Richard Miller[7] mentions that clavicular breathing may give the impression to the voice user that a deep inhalation has been taken, as muscle tension in the pectoral area is experienced. This must not be confused with lung expansion. When the shoulder girdle is raised, it may thus feel as if I have taken in a deep breath but this is not the case. A raised shoulder girdle, secondly (in my experience) very often leads to a larynx

that is held relatively high due to the involvement of the muscles in the neck in the raising and fixing of the shoulder girdle. So, we have possibly two things at play here that will impede voice production: shallow breathing and a high larynx. Having said this, I again need to stress that fixing the shoulders in a low position and stopping all organic free flow movement of the shoulder girdle during breathing will just lead to another set of tension patterns which will also impede the quality of the voice. I guess that I am trying to say that fixing the shoulder girdle in any position, but yes, in this case, too high, will impede voice production. The shoulders 'pumping' up and down will also impede voice production, but the shadow movements which are always happening everywhere in the body and here especially in the shoulders must not be stopped.

EM: Yes, I agree. The shoulders are not involved in a natural or coordinated breath cycle. Constantly raised shoulders would certainly be a symptom and cause of tension that would impede vocal production as well as physical and emotional availability.

MB: I do feel that there is an impediment to optimal voice production if there is substantial movement from using muscles to raise the shoulders. This is also true if the shoulders are in a constantly raised position. These tensions will also affect the ribs and shoulder girdle as well. I do not want the student to push the shoulders down, however. It is common and normal that there be some secondary movement of the shoulder girdle and clavicle from the ribcage swinging outward and up. Since this is not due to a muscular lifting of the shoulder girdle, it is not going to impede the voice.

CA: Yes. If the shoulders are active, or held, it indicates to me that the breath is shallow. It is an inefficient way of breathing that involves effort and tension. This increase of effort might transfer to tension in the neck, that might affect the voice.

RR: I am going to call the kind of breathing we have been discussing, where the shoulder girdle moves up and down during the breath cycle, or the shoulders are in a constantly raised position, *clavicular breathing*. Would you please describe the quality of sound you associate with clavicular breathing?

MH: Sound-wise, there is very often breathiness, hard glottal attack, slightly raised pitch, loss of lower resonant formants in the voice—I identify it as a 'metallic' sound. It can also sound 'unconfident.' Breath patterns are usually snappy/choppy, unsmooth or 'surgy'. My students and I have also recently started to recognize that clavicular breathing often brings with it rushed and sloppy articulation, stumbling over words.

PT: Interestingly, I don't directly equate clavicular breathing with a particular sound—I tend to make the connection to limited breathing which will limit the voice in many ways. In my experience, one who habitually uses clavicular breathing will tend towards breathiness and be limited to speaking short phrases.

EA: I must say this is a great question. I don't think that there is an easy answer here. I believe that tension in the shoulder girdle increases the tension in the entire system of the voice. This tension acts like a chain, linking one tense muscle to the next, along the lines of the ideas of Françoise Mézières and Thérèse Bertherat.[8] This, in turn, leads to pressed phonation. On the other hand, it can also be associated, in my experience, with a thin tone—often somewhat breathy.

To be honest, I often don't try to associate the sound I hear with the issue of clavicular breathing! I know it is an issue that may affect vocal performance, and so I try to reduce any tension in this area that I observe. I think the important words are 'may affect performance' because I have certainly had students who were riddled with tension who miraculously had wonderful voices. I've also had students who seemed close to limp rags, who were strongly affected by tiny tensions.

I think that character work will obviously involve tension in a variety of body areas, including the shoulder girdle, and they, the students, need an awareness so that they don't carry chronic tension, and so that they can use tension areas for performance which they then take off as they step off-stage.

JH: The quality of sound in the first instance (shoulders moving up and down during the breath cycle) is likely to be thin, 'breathy,' and of short duration. Often we would hear a gasping sound on the inhale, as the singer/actor tries to gulp in enough air for the task.

The quality of sound in the 2nd instance (constantly raised shoulders) is going to be like a young child's voice, perhaps breathy, certainly pinched or shrill in quality. The excess tension in the shoulder girdle feeds into the neck/throat, hence into the larynx. Tension is directly related to the pitch of the voice, and too much tension makes it too high a pitch, even when not intending to do so.

BA: Depending on the degree of constriction on the movement of the larynx, I would expect some of the qualities evident in the sound to be high, strained, narrow, or inflexible. Over the long haul, I believe hoarseness and early vocal fatigue could also become factors.

MG: The tone quality I associate with clavicular breathing is often shallow, weak, lacks resonance or is harsh. It is often 'too presentational', that is, it lacks depth of tone, or warmth, and does not generally project well.

LO: The quality of sound that I often associate with someone who consistently uses clavicular breathing varies depending upon the type of voice production that is required. In everyday situations, the voice quality tends to be thin and lacking depth or support. It is often breathy. In an extraordinary use of the voice (shouting, etc) it tends to constrict due to lack of support.

LW: I don't particularly make a direct correlation between what is being defined as *clavicular breathing* and specific qualities of sound in the voice. I want students to have access to the entire range of sounds that can come from the human voice, and that includes sounds that might be considered less than optimal or ugly. Ugly can be desirable; an ugly situation might call for an ugly sound. For me the question is one of appropriateness and vocal health—is a sound appropriate given the theatrical context? Can the sound be produced in a way that will not damage or place undue strain on the voice. I also try to avoid making students self-conscious about their sound. I may notice sounds that I feel are unhealthy or are not contributing fully to a theatrical situation, but I generally keep those observations to myself. That said, my personal observations of less than optimal sound might include: pushed, strained, tense, forced, strangled, weak, thin, lacking in resonance, restricted, clamped, overly controlled, calculated (lacking in spontaneity).

MM: This is a difficult question as generalization is a dangerous thing when dealing with body integration and voice production. However, having said that, one can probably, with safety, indicate that breath management will be impeded and so a phrase may lack duration, not have an even tone quality and show a lack of consistent volume. Seeing that the raised shoulder girdle possibly leads to a high larynx, the tone will lack the energy of the lower formants, sound sharp and the possibility may be there that projection may be impeded.

EM: Typically a breathy quality, as one might associate with a very timid, ineffectual speaker; a quality that lacks power and clarity. The voice also tends to fall into the chest and throat, as the breath lacks the energy required to resonate higher in the body.

MB: If a person is breathing clavicularly, there tends to be less chest resonance. The voice has a thinner quality. Because the sternocleidomastoid muscles are usually helping to raise the shoulders, there is often a pressed, tight sound as well.

Normally, because there is not enough breath to get through longer phrases, students will also tend to go off voice at the end of phrases.

CA: Because the shoulders are tense, that tension can very easily travel up to the neck, larynx and jaw. The quality of sound might be thinner, or have an 'edge.' However, many asthmatics use clavicular breathing because it is difficult for them to drop the breath deeper in their bodies. I work with them to release the neck and jaw, therefore helping to free their voices.

RR: One might then think that a remedy for habitually raised shoulders, or shoulders that rise with every breath in, should be for them to be pushed down. How do you respond to that?

MH: No. If they are pushed down, they are unlikely to stay down without tension.

PT: I wouldn't say 'pushed down,' I prefer to say 'released'.

EA: I don't believe in pushing anything down. What's going to push them down? Pushing them down isn't going to release the tension that is holding them up or lengthen those muscles that are holding them up—work should be done to lengthen/release those muscles over time.

JH: One cannot push anyone else's shoulders around and accomplish anything. We can ask a student to release or let go or allow the shoulders to drop, but it must come from within them. And if they try too hard to drop their shoulders, they can create other kinds of problems for themselves. Honest change can only come from self-observation (realizing that their shoulders are held high or going up and down), thinking about not doing the habit—over and over and over again, and learning to re-educate the whole breathing mechanism. It is not just a matter of inappropriately behaving shoulders, but a matter of the whole-system patterns, and that takes time and guidance for genuine change.

BA: I believe giving the student something to do to replace the behavior they are trying to change is very useful, but instructing him/her to 'push' the shoulders down is too violent and will not yield the desired result of released shoulders. In fact, pushing will most likely create additional vocal constriction.

MG: Perhaps and then they will only raise again. The elevation of the shoulders is usually a sign that the breath is really thoracic and not abdominal, or there is increased upper body tension relative to posture.

LO: I wouldn't say 'pushed' down, but students should find a way to relax the shoulders so the tension of keeping them raised does not spread to the larynx.

LW: Generally agree, but would use different terms. If they are habitually raised, one should be reminded to let them drop or 'soften' in that area.

MM: No—the shoulders should rather be released towards optimal integration—no pushing should take place, as this will only lead to the creation of another holding pattern. If one part of the body is not optimally integrated this will affect the whole body. The guiding towards an optimal body integration should take this into account—small adjustments have to be made on a level where the student is ready to 'make things happen' in his/her own body.

EM: I would not say 'pushed,' which implies muscular force.

MB: This is partly true. The shoulders should drop down naturally. If they are 'pushed' down, the student is using other muscles to hold them down and will be creating another form of tension. They should be encouraged to release so that there is no lifting of the shoulder girdle.

CA: I disagree. I would want to encourage the shoulders to do less. To push them down sounds like it involves a lot of tension.

RR: So 'pushed' is not an appropriate word or action. What then, do you do when you see that a student's shoulders move up and down? Please include what you like of verbal instruction, touch, or movement.

MH: Either another student or I will stand behind them, applying a little weight with the hands on the shoulders to monitor movement. The type of pressure applied when hands are placed on the shoulders to encourage them to lower is with a feeling of weight, rather than resistance. The movement is more outwards than down, following the direction of the muscle fibers in the deltoids, based on a general principal that massage should encourage muscles to lengthen. I may also ask a couple of partners to shake the arms while the student speaks, to encourage relaxation in the shoulders, or ask the student to shimmy and twist him or herself. Also again, I may place a hand at the back of the neck to encourage length.

Some of what I teach includes rolling the shoulders or an exercise borrowed from physiotherapy where the head is rolled to the left, looking forward, and the weight of the left hand placed onto the right ear. The student gives a few moments to allow the weight (*not* a pull) to encourage the scalenes and sternocleidomastoids to relax. If necessary, the right arm can be pulled straight down, as if being pestered by a small child, to add extra stretch. The same process is repeated on the right. I will also make use of a lot of exercises to encourage a more open posture generally, and to ask them to think about opening both the voice and the heart to the audience. This may involve speaking text as if it were opera, with appropriate arm movements, as if conducting themselves, or trying out a space by walking round, humming down on a pitch glide, opening the sound out to 'ah' while the arms and hands open out in an expansive gesture, palms facing up, to encourage the shoulders to open back and the chest to expand.

PT: The first step is to bring awareness to the issue. I think that self-awareness is very empowering for the student. Then the student is in control of his or her destiny, so to speak. I begin with a verbal prompt, 'remember to release your shoulders,' or, 'see if you can inhale without moving your shoulders.' I may also use a gentle touch to help this process. I will also remind the student to 'allow the breath to fall into the belly.' It seems that sometimes the student has simply reverted to the stereotypical 'take a deep breath' that many of us grew up with. Micro-movements of the shoulder blades (as taught by David Smukler[9] at the VASTA 1999 conference) can help create that awareness. I also teach shoulder rolls, stretching/massaging work in partners, and have students lie on tennis balls, slowly moving the balls up along the spine.

EA: Shoulder awareness exercises are an important starting place when the shoulders are held, like the one I learned from Judith Koltai,[10] where one merely places the palms of the hands on your partner's shoulder blades (scapulae) so that they begin to notice them, and then gently slides the palms down the shoulder blades with the image of them melting down the back. Then with melted shoulder blades we go for a walk around the classroom, the student trying to be present—in their experience, in the space, and in relationship to their classmates. It is a great way to introduce touch, and it also begins to suggest the idea of undoing that tension. I suppose that's an Alexander concept.

When the shoulders are seen to be moving up and down, usually they are riding on the upper ribcage action, so that they, the students, aren't lifting the shoulders, they are lifting the upper ribs and sternum. Here I might get them to lie on a ball to relax the muscles around the sternum, focus directly on greater range of movement in the side/back ribs and in the abdomen. Once they can get enough air in these other areas, the habit of shoulder rising tends to drop away.

Beginning to feel the weight of the shoulder falling off the ribcase is explored with a series of exercises that I learned from

Bob Chapline[11] (so perhaps they're in the Linklater Canon?). Instead of just circling the arms windmill fashion, we start by shaking all the blood out of the hand and then letting the arm drop toward the back, letting it swing by its own momentum until it stops. Using as little energy as possible, the arm is brought back up to vertical, and the dropping is repeated. Then we add just enough momentum to get up to the top without waiting for the arm to hang. Eventually we speed up to the old windmill-style arm circles. Then I do the Qi Qong style arm swinging, where one rotates the torso and the arms swing around and smack the shoulder. I always refer to *Karate Kid III*—those with a good pop-culture base will immediately know what I mean!

Increased flexibility is definitely needed here, so on top of a series of neck/trapezius stretches that most people know, I do shoulder stretches I learned when I was doing Pilates. However, I don't think that they are Pilates based, actually. They are similar to the stretches that one sees football players doing, where you push against a partner, and then on the release you can stretch even more. I do this with the arms, to stretch the pectoralis muscles. A variation of this exercise can be done one arm at a time against a wall—place the arm, with the palm flat, up against a wall at shoulder height, then rotate the torso away from the wall, until you feel a stretch. Press the palm of the hand into the wall as hard as you can for 10 seconds. Then see if you can increase the rotation of the torso away from the wall.

JH: Although your question asks only about shoulders moving up and down, I continue to separate the two problem patterns, because I think they are both challenging but need different approaches. The clavicular breathing situation would be easier to address. If the problem is one of shoulders moving up and down during the breath cycle (and not one of constantly held up shoulders), I work one on one both as an Alexander and as a voice teacher. Through speaking and/or singing, we would eventually wake up the rib cage muscles, and if necessary, undo overly constricted abdominals. As the thorax becomes more elastic, then the diaphragm will be able to do its job with greater freedom—assuming that the abdominals are not too tightly held. Only then might it be appropriate to gently place my hands on the tops of the shoulders and invite a release, but that won't happen until and unless other parts of the system are working freely. If all the parts of the breathing mechanism are working with freedom and elasticity, i.e., when the old breathing patterns are no longer useful/needed, there will be no need for the shoulders to heave up and down. The shoulders will be quieter because the rib cage and the diaphragm are free to do their stuff. These changes will take time but can be addressed in a 4-month term.

In my experience 'coat-hanger shoulders' are much more difficult to undo, and I've worked with several such students, although more in my private teaching than in the university voice/AT class. This problem is not simply a breathing issue but a systemic one because the high-held shoulders are deeply embedded in a whole-body pattern that is often fraught with emotional issues. The shoulder girdle will hang appropriately only when the whole torso/neck/head organization is addressed, and that takes individual work and time and patience, and above all, the interest of the student in making such basic changes. The daily homework of awareness and Alexander Lying-Down would be the same as for 'clavicular' breathing, but the time frame would be much longer. The situation is not just a matter of re-educating the breathing mechanism for more normal/natural operation, but it involves the person's entire being and necessitates greater introspection on the student's part—and sometimes they are not ready to do so. So the shoulders stay high until the person is ready to change.

There are two movement activities that I often use in class to help loosen up the whole torso, particularly stuck shoulder girdles. These can be done one by one, with others observing, or can be done all together but with each person working in their own timing: 1) walking while singing a vocalise or a song, taking time between phrases for the breath to return, consciously letting the arms swing as naturally as possible with the walk; 2) spiraling around while singing a vocalise or song, flinging the arms around the torso, with ankles/knees/hip joints free to bend slightly with the spiral/swing. This sort of movement can break out into moving through space while continuing the spiraling arms.

I would add that there is a danger of bringing too much attention to either of these patterns of shoulder girdle organization, because the singer/actor may go to the opposite extreme and try to *hold* or *fix* the shoulders in a downward direction.

BA: I believe exercises that deepen the students' core support for the breath will begin to unravel some of their inefficient or tense body reactions to breathing, such as hiking the shoulders up. Some of the same activities I use to combat holding the breath or depressing the chest, such as lying over a physioball or using the yoga strap across the back and over the shoulders[12] would be useful for this problem. I use mostly Bartenieff Fundamentals[13] to promote this connectedness. To be more specific, I teach 'arm-circles' and 'arm swings' (as in a skiing motion) to help develop hand to scapula connection; 'head rolls' to help the body understand head/scapula connection. I also address the lower body by teaching them 'pelvic rocks' which promote heel to tail connection. I find 'heel rocks' to be

an efficient way to develop head to heel connection. 'Thigh rotations' help the student feel how the legs connect into the pelvic bowl. The more grounded the lower body becomes, the better the chance that the student will relax the shoulders. There are variations on these and other exercises too numerous to describe for this article that I like to draw upon as well. I will also use touch to facilitate the learning process.

I have occasionally had a student (usually male) who was extremely tall and whose shoulders were in a permanently raised position. This student's scapulae tended to wing out away from his back and his profile was always hunched. It seems this type of student grew so quickly that the muscles that surround the bony structure were unable to keep up with the demands of his new body. While these students make some progress with me, I typically recommend that they see someone, such as Irene Dowd[14] or Lynn Martin[15], who is likely to more efficiently guide them towards a result than I can. I also recommend weekly yoga or ballet classes to strengthen and align the muscles closest to the bony structure. These strategies have been successful in overcoming excessive shoulder tension and clavicular breathing when the student was patient with himself and uncommonly highly motivated to change.

MG: Building awareness of the pattern to be changed is as important as changing the pattern itself. Something needs to replace the pattern; so just saying 'don't do' is not enough. With students who use clavicular breathing or some other less efficient way of breathing, I will have them scan to see if they are locking the knees, holding the buttocks or shoulders tight, or ask where their feet are. I will ask them to increase their pattern, asking them to lift the shoulders more, exaggerating the movement to really feel what they are doing while singing or speaking. I ask them to feel the movement of the shoulders, the ribs and notice where their weight is on the feet.

Next I may ask them to stand or sit leaning over (hands resting on the thigh in standing or forearm resting on the thigh in sitting). From this position, I will ask them to feel the lower belly release towards the floor on the inhalation. On the exhalation—on a sustained /s/ (only short exhalations) feel the movement of the belly in and up towards the shoulder blades or back towards the spine. They are to repeat /s/ /s/ /s/ feeling a full release of the lower belly each time. I may then ask them in the same position to lift the shoulders on the inhalation and exhale on the /s/ noticing which direction the belly moves (generally it will go out and down). This is repeated with voiced sounds beginning with /z/, then /v/, /m/ and /n/, gradually adding vowels.

Once they have a sense of this new way to breathe, I ask them to stand comfortably (habitually) and speak or continue with the voiced sounds. If the breathing shifts back to the old habit, then I will ask them to bend over again, renew the sensation of releasing the belly on the inhalation and in stages come to standing. At the point in coming to standing at which the belly does not fully release, I ask the student to sense what is interfering with the ability of the abdomen to let go, where is the weight, is the pelvis free, etc. There may not be total success on the 1st pass, but the student begins to feel within his or her own system what they are doing to interfere with the target movement.

LO: I ask them if they feel their shoulders moving, then ask if they can keep them still without tensing them, often asking them to pull them down and up so they feel the difference—shoulder shrugs. Then I have them sigh out on breath while moving the shoulders, then whilst keeping them still.

LW: I coach them to release at the shoulders. Sometimes I will lightly touch the shoulder area and ask them to soften there. Fitzmaurice destructuring addresses tension patterns, not only in the shoulders but also in the entire body, and the structuring helps students focus the movement for breath/text into the lower rib and abdominal areas. Currently my students have Alexander as part of their movement training, so I remind them to consider their 'use.' They also learn the usual head rolls, shoulder rolls and shimmies, and gentle neck stretches.

MM: I work on relaxation. This problem usually happens due to tension. I focus on the relationship between breath and body integration. In the class situation I use a combination of different movement systems and/or approaches, as I believe that a teacher should have several different ways of addressing the same problem/issue, because different students may connect to different approaches (maybe this refers to a Neuro Linguistic Programming—NLP—influence?). Anyway, I draw, primarily, from Alexander principles, Feldenkrais, Laban/Bartenieff and Lessac when dealing with optimal body integration for voice.

As clavicular breathing affects and is affected by the whole body, I address body integration as a whole and specifically weight release, spinal integration and contra-lateral movement patterns—all eventually whilst voicing. When addressing the shoulders specifically, I explore (also whilst voicing) the freedom of the shoulder girdle and specifically the movement of the rotator cuff, as well as shaping in the thoracic cavity. We'll explore positions where the arms act as stabilizers during exploration of inner space changes during breathing. Directing movement of the arms into space whilst allowing shaping of the thoracic cavity to take place provides the student with the

familiar event of an integrated body alignment where the torso is free and open and the shoulders hanging 'down and out.' I do expect the students to take these explorations outside the classroom and explore more during their own time.

EM: I usually do the following things to remind the student that shoulder involvement is not needed: 1) have the student place her hands on my lower back and watch my shoulders while I breathe and speak a long line; 2) have the student speak with her hands on her own abdomen while speaking the line (at the same time, I may place my hands on her lower back); 3) if those steps don't lead to improvement, I will have her work with my hands moving down along her shoulders—this is not a strong pressure, more like an easy wiping-off motion. More often, though, we are able to focus the student's breath lower in the body through coaching and touch, and the shoulder thing usually takes care of itself.

This is definitely an area where my approach is to substitute a desirable habit for a less useful one. My attention goes into grounding the body, deepening the relationship of the hips and legs to the earth, and sensing a downward dynamic of the breath. That is to say that the focus is on the kind of effort and location of effort that I want to see, and much less on what I don't want to see (shoulder holding, etc.) So, other than some touch reminders, I don't do much to work on the shoulder/clavicular breathing issue directly.

MB: I will verbally remind them to relax the shoulders and avoid letting them lift. If that does not seem successful, there are two things I do: 1) gently lay my hands on the top of the shoulders and ask them to allow the shoulders to release so that they do not rise; 2) apply pressure to the acupressure points at the base of the neck and just inside the shoulder joint. This will help to release the scalene muscles, which are primary muscles in raising the shoulders.

In class I use a combination of exercises that are made up of gentle neck stretches where one uses the weight of one's arms and head to stretch the scalene, sternocleidomastoid, trapezius, and splenius muscles. I also have the students working through the Fitzmaurice exercises, which helps to not only release these areas, but also move the breath into the lower thoracic region. I will also have the students perform movement exercises that shake out and flick the arms, thus encouraging the shoulder girdle to release.

CA: I encourage them to bring their attention to their belly. The more the belly can take over, the more the shoulders and upper chest can let go. I will give them images and instructions to let the breath drop to the belly. I will also, sometimes, put my hand on their belly so they get a kinesthetic anchor. I might put a light hand on their shoulders to encourage them to let go, or give them images to soften the shoulder muscles.

I use several exercises that help the shoulders let go: the diagonal stretch for dropping the breath to the belly and moving it down from the shoulders and the chest; raising the shoulders and then letting them go; circling the shoulders to the front and then to the back; arm swings. Also, I think it's crucial to loosen the neck: letting the head drop over to one shoulder and breathing into that stretch, adding an arm on top of the head for weight, to heighten the stretch. I also use partner work to release the neck and heighten awareness of the relationship between the head and the neck. One person lies on the floor on their back, knees up, feet on the floor (semi-supine). The other partner sits near the head and holds it in their hands. The person on the floor gives up the weight of the head while the partner gently rolls the head from side to side.

I learned this next exercise from 'Body Dynamics,' developed by Carol Reynolds. When the head is over to one side, you try to lift your ear to the ceiling. This action articulates the sternocleidomastoid. The partner then gently grabs that muscle and traces its path, from the sternum to behind the ear. 'Body Dynamics' also works on the spine with two rubber balls (tennis ball size). You place the two balls on either side of the spine at the shoulder blade level, and then lie on them. You can then move up the spine by rolling on them, adding more weight by lifting the pelvis slightly. This is a terrific exercise for opening up the ribcage and releasing the shoulder girdle. I also use the instruction I learned from a yoga class: 'feel your shoulders going down your back.'

RR: Some of you have mentioned it takes time for these habits to unravel, particularly if the shoulders are constantly held in the 'coat hanger' fashion, as Jane calls it. I was wondering what, if anything, you might recommend or assign the student to think about or do when outside of class to help with the process. Please consider this question two-fold: first, would you focus on what the student can do on his or her own; then if you also recommend other expert assistance as Barbara has mentioned, would you discuss that.

MH: Most of what I do is geared towards making the student self-aware and self-responsible; after all, we can't go on stage and do the speaking for them! Students exhibiting a lot of shoulder tension will be advised to do a lot of work on the Qi Qong exercises, used by both the voice and movement departments in our school, so that they come to associate voice work with relaxation. They are also advised to do a short voice warm-up; using exercises I described above.

PT: I encourage students to practice the same exercises we do in class as their out-of-class work. One key is to help the student determine what their strengths and weaknesses are so they know what to practice. In terms of expert assistance, I recommend a local Alexander Technique teacher. But as she is not on staff at the university, I do not know of any student who has paid out of their own pocket to study with that teacher.

EA: First I would like to say that the shoulders look like an *inverted* coat hanger—they are flat, rather than sloping gently down from the neck.

I spend considerable time working with the shoulder and neck area in my classes. Many of the effective exercises they do are with a partner, and they're not easily replicated alone. But I suggest that they might trade off with a partner, 'you stretch my shoulders, I'll give you a neck massage,' so that they can get what they need.

I would generally start by suggesting the student investigate some massage therapy for the upper shoulder area, so they can begin to know what that area might feel like without so much tension. For those people who insist on lifting very heavy weights, I send them to our exercise guru at the student center, who is a genius with shoulders. He won't let someone lift heavy weights until their shoulders are more open, and works to stretch and balance those muscles with simple but challenging exercises first.

JH: The student would need to become more self-observant (that's the daily homework), and learn to use the Alexander Lying-Down exercise to good advantage in exploring their habitual breathing patterns (that's more daily homework). Sometimes I suggest other routes to unlocking the whole system, e.g., working with a particular Hatha Yoga teacher, or working with a particular cranial-sacral therapist. These modalities complement what we do together in the Alexander and voice work and give the student another set of tools for self-awareness.

BA: I have already written about recommendations I would make in special cases for expert assistance outside of class. Additionally, since I only get to train them for one school year, I give them a list of teachers and classes outside of the college to continue their training. But the bottom line is I expect my students to practice the exercises on their own. Otherwise it is like buying a new dress and then never taking it out of the bag. The students must quickly shed the notion that showing up for class twice a week means that they are making changes on a body level. Class time is a guidepost; the real learning goes on between the classes if the student attends to the work. The only prop they may not be able to recreate outside of class is the physioball and even then, after discovering the benefit, I have had a fair amount of students purchase one. So to answer the question, once an exercise has been introduced it becomes their assignment to 'take it out of the bag' several times a week. Until a student makes this commitment, it is hard to make other recommendations to support their learning.

MG: During class/studio time, alternatives will have been presented. The student is asked to *do* the new exercises or think about the *new* way of breathing. If the *new*, in this case low abdominal breathing, is understood, then the old, clavicular breathing becomes another choice to make where appropriate for expression or character, rather than the only game in town.

There are certain specific physiological/anatomical constraints that relate to any function. Some means of organizing the body for action are more efficient than others. In addition there are individual constraints, ways in which we as individuals inhibit movement, generally unconsciously, which need to be brought into the somatic picture. I can only move from my internal sense of myself. If I have no internal awareness of my pelvis and where it is in space and how it relates to my ribcage and shoulders, *not doing* clavicular breathing is almost impossible. If I am not able to differentiate the movement of my ribs one from the other but rather my internal picture is of a rigid cage, my movement will reflect that. Turning twisting, bending and certainly breathing will all be impacted, as I will be turning, twisting and breathing with the cage, not with the subtlety of movement possible when the ribs are differentiated in the internal image.

The movement explorations during class time are designed to effect the internal organization that will make it possible for the student to personally discover the correct way to breathe. It is my job as a teacher to set up circumstances in which the student can discover for him/herself what works. Even so, it takes time to change the internal image. Therefore the student needs to continue working with the images and lessons given in class to expand on his/her image of self in movement. If the student is continuing to have difficulty, I will suggest some Feldenkrais lessons for them to do, or suggest they take a Feldenkrais, Alexander or yoga class, to help the student become more aware of their own somatic patterns of moving, standing, etc.

LO: As our teaching time is so limited, I always try to find ways that a student can take work out of the classroom and personalize it. In fact, private study is actually built into the module handbooks for every course that we teach at Liverpool Institute for Performing Arts (LIPA), letting students know that substantial rehearsal work is required before coming into class. As odd as it may sound, for students whose shoulders are constantly held, I recommend they take hot baths—the shoulders often release in the water. I then ask the student to recognize the release and try to establish the released feeling outside of the bath, first on breath, then on tone, then on text. When I suggest this to students they have a good old laugh, then try it and are amazed that it works. A simplistic strategy, I know. I would also recommend doing body-release work that has been discussed in the *Monograph*[16] and put them in touch with the appropriate practitioner.

LW: One of the requirements for my voice classes is that students do practice sessions on their own at least 3-4 times each week, during which they destructure and work on exercises from class. If they need to focus attention on particular areas of tension, I remind them that they can focus the tremoring, breath and/or stretch of the destructuring into an area to help release it.

MM: I do make it clear in all my classes that this is process-orientated and that we dare not have short-term goals when dealing with re-patterning habitual holding patterns that influence voice production. Other than verbal guiding and explorations during the actual class time, I may ask the student whether we could have a hands-on session. I will also ask the student to explore some Feldenkrais movements (e.g., the 'washing of the hands') and do body halves and arm circles (or arm circle variations) from Bartenieff. Depending on the profile of the student, I may advise him/her to schedule a private class with an Alexander teacher or go to a Feldenkrais workshop (if I know of one happening during that time span dealing specifically with the shoulder girdle). Lastly I will send the student to a bio-kineticist for a program to enhance core stability and flexibility in the shoulder girdle. Very important is the fact that I will make the initial observation in the class and refer the student as I see fit, but I will never alone make a final prognosis. If the run-of-the-mill class work still does not address an obstacle, I find it vital to refer and work in a team to benefit the development of the student.

EM: I understand shoulder tension as a problem that has to be addressed holistically. Like several other issues, I recommend out-of-class work for it that is very simple—a few minutes of finding the neutral stance in the morning after stretching, a few minutes of awareness of the shoulders, letting them drop and release downward in bed at night before falling asleep. Otherwise, again like most of the habits I try to re-enforce, it's mostly a matter of repetitive work in class—the body getting the same message over and over again and yielding into the new habit.

The other thing I do is to recommend our excellent and affordable on-campus massage therapists. I talk them up in a general way once or twice during a semester and occasionally talk to a specific student about the option of getting some massage or bodywork.

MB: I insist that the students must work outside of class in order to progress, and encourage them to take the exercises that we are doing in the classroom into their daily practices. The destructuring exercises will normally do a great deal toward releasing all of the tensions that develop through the shoulder girdle and the neck muscles used to hold it up. Also, the students in our program are doing Alexander work in their movement class. First and foremost, I encourage them to work on these lessons at home. Most often, this will take care of the problem. However, there have been times that a student may have an incredible amount of tension that simply does not seem to be releasing. My colleague, who teaches movement, and I often talk with one another to recommend a course of action for these students. We sometimes recommend the student work with a Rolfing practitioner.

CA: I encourage my students to practice the exercises we use in class, every day. It's only through that constant practice that a new pattern of behavior can replace the habit. If they carry heavy tote bags that have shoulder straps, I recommend that they switch to a backpack where the weight is more evenly distributed, and also to carry lighter loads! In addition to the practice, I think it's important to have patience. It does take time to change, and 'beating oneself up' is not going to make the change happen any faster; in fact, it adds to the tension. I certainly would recommend Alexander and/or Feldenkrais work. I think that both of those techniques are excellent for releasing places that are held in the body and also to integrate the whole. If there is habitual tension in one part of the body, very often it is compensating for another part. In all of this work, one needs to consider the whole.

RR: In an earlier response Christine Adaire relates clavicular breathing to asthmatics. I wonder whether this is universal. If you have taught asthmatics, would you say they tend to use clavicular breathing? Do you need to teach them any differently than other students? Have any of you noticed (or has the student reported) a reduction in symptoms that seems to be related to a change in their usual breathing habits?

MH: We get a medical list at the beginning of each year that tells us in confidence about issues like asthma. It is something I am becoming more aware of—if I see a student using clavicular breathing, I will ask if they have asthma first before addressing any other issues. When working with individuals, I will work on what ever *they* need, so the issue of treating anyone differently does not really arise. I will often ask them to work more on lower rib breathing, but to develop what they can rather than completely change their breathing pattern. I am also lucky enough to have two colleagues with asthma, who I will suggest students go to for additional advice. In my group work, I use a lot of breathing exercises intended to slow down the rate of breathing—Qi Qong and yoga. Part of the reason for using this, besides developing breath capacity and encouraging full-body use in vocalizing, is to encourage focus and calmness in the actor, which may have an impact on asthmatics, giving them a technique to control the panic that goes with the condition. I am not aware of any of the asthmatics finding any of these breathing exercises unusually difficult.

So far, no one has reported any changes in symptoms, per se, though I have had a student who has found herself less 'wheezy' and presents with less husk, though that is more through vowel placement and resonance than from changing breathing itself.

PT: I have not had a great deal of experience with asthmatic students, but I do notice clavicular breathing in asthmatics. I wouldn't say I teach them differently than other students, although when they are having particularly asthmatic problems, I give them freedom to work at their own pace. I will often tell them to focus on quiet breathing to allow their bodies to focus on getting oxygen.

EA: The asthmatics I have taught (who are having a 'bad asthma' day) are using everything they've got to get breath in and out. So I see shoulder and neck muscles involved that, ideally, we don't want to see. I think that they come to realize that they can get more air into other parts of their torsos, so they don't rely so heavily on the upper chest, but when they're really stressed, it's a big issue. Trying to manage their stress level and their medication is an important task for them. I have had a student say that they've felt better, but I'm worried about taking credit for that. It could be that the things that induce asthma for that person have been reduced, rather than my exercises have made a huge difference.

JH: Yes, I've taught many asthmatics and students with allergies in my 3-decades-plus of teaching—although, there seem to be more asthmatics now in the campus voice class every Fall than there used to be. In my experience, asthmatics do not necessarily use clavicular breathing at all. They often have frozen the whole torso and nothing moves much in any dimension. I would work with both asthmatics and students with allergies on a one on one basis, although the work would be similar to that with any other student whose rib cage was too constricted. The asthmatics have the biggest challenge, because panic sets in from some trigger, and seizure of the rib cage muscles happens habitually as part of that panic reaction. Alexander Technique lessons are usually quite effective to help asthmatics unlock this behavior. Asthmatics in particular report dramatic changes in the course of a 4-month term: song phrases last longer, the breath comes back in more quickly, they swim faster, and can run farther without getting winded.

BA: Yes, I have taught asthmatic students and they do tend towards clavicular breathing. I think it is important to know a student's medical history in regards to breathing disorders like asthma or past trauma, such as almost drowning. If there is a history of gasping based on specific medical issues or life experience, then I try to influence the student towards trusting that a little bit of easy air can go a long way and that the act of gasping makes one panic and feel out of breath. Since most of what I do in class would not promote an asthma attack, the panic the asthmatics feel is related to anticipating not being able to breathe. I say this because I have never had a student actually have an asthma attack in class, but I have witnessed plenty of high quick breathing during classes in this population. I have found that giving a count to breathing in and out and gradually increasing the count on the exhale often helps to slow down the impulse to grab more and more air. Distractions, such as instructing the student to observe his rib cage and abdomen as he counts, help the student to slow down the heart rate and decrease the feeling of panic.

MG: Asthmatics tend to have a shorter inhalation phase than exhalation phase. With severe asthmatics, breathing tends to be shallow, and often clavicular, high thoracic, or compressed where the thoracic area does not move much at all. Teaching them is different from other students in that they are initially *not able* to get a low abdominal breath. The lower ribs are often not very mobile, and their system is set for sucking in the air quickly. They need to learn first that the middle and lower ribs *can* move, that the breath will be there as they gradually learn to release and let it in. I teach the students with asthma to breath deeper in a graduated release—asking them to first breathe high (clavicular), then imagine the breath gradually dropping to the upper chest, then mid-chest then gradually below the level of the diaphragm, thus giving them a strategy for calming the breath. Gradually releasing the ribs so the breath can be a little deeper has helped several students. They reported improved voice use as well as more manageable symptoms.

LO: I find more and more that many incoming students arrive at drama school equipped with an inhaler. The rate of

students with asthma has increased substantially since I have been teaching in the UK. I don't know if it is particular to geographical settings or the time in which we live, but I don't ever remember so many students with asthma coming for training in the past. Clavicular breathing is the norm with these students. I advise them to keep their inhalers when they are doing breathing work, so they don't panic, and to use them when they need to. Most students find that they are able to do the deep (belly) breathing work and that with repetition, it becomes easier for them. Many stop using their inhalers altogether and are able to connect with the breathing work. They have reported a decrease in their symptoms and a new feeling of openness with regard to their breathing. This usually occurs at the end of the second or third term of work, so it tends to be a slow process. I find that when they are away from training (and not doing their breathing work), they tend to place increased importance on their inhalers, so it is easy for them to correlate the breathing study/ease with their decreased dependence on the inhaler. Some asthmatic students don't feel comfortable doing breathing work in semi-supine, so I suggest they use a chair, either sitting normally or straddling the chair, leaning forward resting their arms on the top. This seems to work for the initial stages; many of them join the class on the floor in a few weeks' time.

LW: I have worked with asthmatics on a couple of occasions that I am aware of, and there did seem to be a tendency to clavicular breathing in the beginning. I let everyone in class know from the start that they should feel free to make adjustments for their own particular physical needs or situations, which may include dropping out and stopping to rest to take care of themselves, so in that way I suppose everybody is taught 'differently,' including asthmatics. Breath work can be intimidating for anyone who has spent years controlling and restricting their breathing, not to mention coping with asthma. I always let students know that the breath work can be gradual and that little by little it will become easier—I think asthmatics may need some extra reassurance and confidence-boosting on this, and on feeling free to stop and rest if they need to. Yes, students have reported improvement in symptoms that they attributed to a change in breathing habits, one student saying that instances of asthma attacks had become quite rare.

MM: Asthma is a chronic submucosal airway inflammatory disease and although we may be confronted with it in the classroom set-up, I feel very strongly that I have to make it very clear, in the beginning of working with a new group of students, that the asthmatic student and his/her pulmonologist are in control of the situation. The student is always in charge of his/her own class work—I will not force *any* student, but even more so, the asthmatic, to participate in any exercise should he/she feel that it will not have a positive influence. Having said this, I will then encourage the student to have a good relationship with a pulmonologist and depending on the severity of the case, to use a peak flow meter daily—self-medication or irregular use of medication does not keep asthma under control.

During my class I will pay attention to whether the asthmatic student starts coughing, wheezing, or complains of a tight chest. I agree with Christine Adaire in the sense that a 'tight chest' can lead to clavicular breathing as the student alters breathing patterns in order to get enough air into the lungs. (I have, outside the class, experienced cases where the neck muscles of the asthmatic go into a spasm due to the altering breathing pattern, or even when the asthmatic complains of a burning sensation under the tongue. All of these are tell-tale signs that the asthma is not under control; in such cases a visit to the pulmonologist will be the advised thing to do.) Chest tightness can lead to panic and although emotions cannot *lead* to asthma, the students with asthma can actually *increase* an asthma attack when experiencing severe emotions—a chicken and egg situation. If the student can thus be guided to persist with three-dimensional breathing, especially with the use of a bronchi-dilator, the attack may subside

As a whole, I think that it is important for the asthmatic to always use optimal three-dimensional breathing; it is in the times when it is going well with the asthmatic that three-dimensional breathing should be learned. I would speculate (and I have no hard evidence) that a combination of optimal breathing and controlled management of the asthma, which would initially include medication, can eventually lead to an improved profile of the asthmatic to a point where the use of medication can be terminated—just think of how many good swimmers started swimming because they were asthmatic. The key in living with asthma is taking charge of the situation; the key to teaching students with asthma is encouraging them to take charge and guiding them, through sensory awareness explorations, to note when the situation is changing and then to react accordingly through release, three-dimensional breathing and the use of medication when required.

EM: My comments reflect work with a limited number of asthmatic students rather than a systematic approach. I have found that such students tend to come in with clavicular breathing unless they have had singing training (as half or more of my students have had). I don't have any different way of working with asthmatic students as opposed to others; I don't have the background to do so. I have had one or two students report a lessening of symptoms over time in voice class—again, this is anecdotal.

MB: As asthmatic students have a shorter inhalation, I have found that their breath tends to be a higher breath—as if it is moving from top to bottom. I do not teach asthmatics any differently than my other students. I always tell my students that they must work all exercises at their own pace. As asthmatics are less comfortable with a full breath (and can often become frightened by deep breathing), I support them in their need to take more breaks from the exercises. The asthmatic students I have taught do begin feeling more and more comfortable with the exercises and do have improvement in their comfort, capacity, and usage of the breath. Interestingly, after studying and teaching breathing for quite some time, I was diagnosed with allergic asthma. My pulmonologist could notice slight changes to my breathing when allergies were worse, but I never felt any deficiency in my usage of breathing for vocalization. I do attribute this to continually working with the Fitzmaurice destructuring/restructuring exercises.

CA: I've been severely asthmatic most of my life, so I know first-hand about that breathing pattern. During an asthma episode, the bronchial tubes constrict, so it's very difficult for much breath to come in, or to go out. It's almost impossible for the breath to drop in very deeply. The upper chest works very hard. I can usually tell if someone has had severe asthma from childhood, because they will be 'barrel-chested.' Panic at not having enough breath can be held as tension in the upper chest and shoulder area, so I spend a lot of time with asthmatics releasing shoulder and neck tension. Also, if a student is having a difficult time breathing, they might not be able to work on the floor. It will be easier for them to breathe if they're sitting up. I myself, and many of my students, have noticed a reduction of symptoms as a result of practicing breath awareness.

RR: Here is a similar question. What about students with allergies? Do you notice whether they tend to have more clavicular breathing than others? Can you talk about how you teach them, if it is different from what you said in regard to asthmatics?

MH: I am not aware of having dealt with anyone so far who has had an allergic reaction that has affected their breathing—other than asthma—so there is nothing that I do differently for them.

PT: I treat students who have asthmatic symptoms from allergies pretty much the same as other asthmatics.

EA: I don't believe that it is similar. Apart from allergen-induced asthma (which *is* asthma), I treat them differently. Upper airway response (nose, pharynx) doesn't constrict the breathing the way asthma does, and so people with allergies have it far easier than those with asthma. Not to belittle severe allergies, but I haven't encountered allergies that affect breathing similarly to asthma. Maybe I'm just lucky! Since I tend to advocate mouth breathing for speaking, constriction of flow due to plugged noses isn't so much an issue, though when they're just standing around, nose breathing is likely to help, as it is a filter.

JH: Respiratory allergies are so closely linked to asthma that I would not do much that was different with those students. In fact, working with asthmatics and those with respiratory allergies is not really very different from working with the ordinary student. Freeing up the breathing mechanism is a useful process for all of us.

Some other symptoms that are often manifest with respiratory allergies, e.g., stuffy or drippy nose, sinuses, excess mucous, etc., need basic vocal health care education. This means adequate hydration with non-chlorinated water, adequate rest, healthy diet to boost the immune system, flushing out the crud with extra fluid if using decongestants, and vocalizing on the [ŋ] (open-mouth hum), which shakes things loose up in the head and relieves congestion. This information would accompany anything we would do in the area of breathing education.

BA: Allergies are certainly more commonplace than asthma. It is rare when I don't have at least one student per class who reports discomfort from allergies. The symptoms of allergies, as far as I can surmise, are not like the symptoms of asthma. The allergic person does not seem to have the fear the asthmatic has about being cut off from their life support of air. I can't say that I treat the allergic person any differently from the non-allergic student except I ask the same questions that I do of the asthmatic regarding any medications that may make them sleepy, dizzy, or extremely dry-mouthed.

MG: There are allergies and there are allergies. If the allergy symptoms trigger asthma-like symptoms, then I do work with the students in the same way. Most of the students I see with allergies have upper respiratory symptoms—stuffy nose, sinus, postnasal drip, etc. These generally do not affect breathing in the same way as does asthmatic breathing. They often cannot breathe efficiently through the nose, are distracted by the postnasal drip and complain about sounding too nasal. However, there is no reason why they cannot learn low abdominal breathing. I counsel them on allergy management—take meds that are not too drying, avoid allergens if possible, and see a singer-sensitive allergist if allergies get out of control.

LO: Other than hay fever, which I suffer from as well (blocked nasal passages), I tend to not deal specifically with allergies in the teaching. If students cannot breathe through the nose,

they need to use the mouth. I will use Shiatsu Massage to teach them to clear their nasal passages.

LW: I have allergies, so I sympathize, and might informally ask if they have investigated treatment options. Other than that, my response above regarding 'physical needs' covers this.

MM: When dealing with the allergic student in connection to breathing, the allergies are usually due to seasonal allergens or house mite and dust. As these allergic reactions lead to allergic rhinitis, a direct link to asthma can be traced as this can in turn lead to an asthma attack when the asthma is of an extrinsic nature. The profile is thus the same as that of the asthmatic student. Precautions that have to be taken are to keep the classroom/studio clean and to use an air filter—neither of these is always practical or economical. I advise the students to bring their own yoga mat for floor work (as they have some kind of control then over how clean the mat is); I ask for the studio to be cleaned every morning; I advise students to take good care of themselves and if that means having to use a humidifier or nebulizer, I will encourage them to do so without becoming a hypochondriac.

EM: A lot of students I've worked with—and a lot of people I know—seem to have some mild allergies, maybe just hay fever and so on. I don't think students with allergies tend more toward clavicular breathing than others. Again, I don't work with allergic students any differently than others. When students ask me for advice about how to compensate for or live with their allergies, I reiterate the general voice care information that I'm always promoting anyway (including consulting health professionals as needed).

MB: As I stated earlier, I have suffered from allergies my entire life. I have not noticed any correlation between clavicular breathing and allergies—unless asthma accompanies the allergies. Thus, I don't teach breathing any differently. As South Florida is especially bad for people with allergies, I do speak of the importance of keeping good vocal hygiene as well as maintaining an environment that will be the least irritating. I also encourage people who suffer with allergies to maintain a good relationship with his/her allergist and ENT.

CA: Many times severe allergies will trigger asthma, in which case I would teach them in the way I work with asthmatics. However, many allergies tend to clog the nasal passages, which makes breathing through the nose difficult. Since most of the Linklater voice work uses breathing through an open mouth, this usually is not a problem. However, some capacity breathing exercises, which are designed to open up the ribcage, rely on the breath coming in through the nose. If someone is really clogged up, I will have them hold their nostrils open with their fingertips.

RR: I have noticed that film and TV performers may use less optimal breathing patterns, including clavicular and 'coat-hanger.' We have the advantage of seeing their work close up; they have the advantage of the microphone—there is much they can do without depending on the best of breathing circumstances. Do you have any opinions on this matter? In other words, do you think it is as important to re-train the on-camera actor (or singer) as it is the voice user who depends entirely upon his or her own power?

MH: I think my main concern with clavicular breathing is the thin vocal sound that tends to be associated with it—either the loss of lower resonances, or going off support completely, resulting in creak or breathiness; and what then happens when the actor returns to theatre, or even interviews when they have to send the voice a little further than to a very sensitive microphone. We all know of TV actors who have had to cut short a theatre run because of voice issues. I do work with my students on microphone technique, with the idea of dropping volume/'projection' while staying 'on support'—i.e., maintaining a level of breath flow to keep the folds adducted and vibrating evenly—which is usually found more easily when using abdominal breathing. They all love playing the 'sexy' characters, and have commented that low-pitched, resonant voices sound sexier than creak or breathiness.

I suppose it is also worth pointing out that in the stillness required for a close-up, movement of the shoulders/upper chest will be seen.

PT: It is true that less vocal power and stamina is required for on-camera work. But I don't think that it requires any less connection to one's inner life, and deep breathing helps to create that connectedness. But is it 'important to re-train the on-camera actor or singer?' That entirely depends on if the on-camera actor or singer wants to work on their voice. If the individual doesn't think s/he needs work, then forcing her/him to do it probably won't yield much in the way of results.

EA: If I'm training an actor to 'do it all,' then I want them to be able to do all the breathing techniques I teach. However, if I'm coaching on a film set, I never try to change the actor's breathing patterns. It isn't appropriate in that time. Film is going for a form of realism that we cannot afford on the stage—real people breathe clavicularly, so it is okay that they do so on film. However, if you have to play to a large house, or outdoors, or scream in a production eight shows a week, you can't afford that kind of realism. Technique is about finding another choice that is still realistic, but is more effective and safer. I don't believe that clavicular breathing is less truthful or emotional. Nor do I think it is more so. It's just less efficient.

JH: Voice use is far more than breath, but the film and TV performers do set an example or a standard for those who are studying to be actors, etc. Gasping of breath, lifted-up shoulders, newscasters leaning forward for intimacy while hunkering down into themselves ('turtling') are all negative examples.

BA: I think it is important that the on-camera spokesperson gives the impression of being in charge of the material. The speaker must seem credible to the public whether reading the news or acting in a film. Release and stillness in the upper chest can give that impression more readily than a heaving clavicle or hunched shoulders. A head balanced easily on top of the spine and a relaxed neck and jaw are also beneficial to this end. A newscaster has the advantage of usually being seated. I say this because being seated relieves the body of the burden of supporting its full weight on the legs. Being seated can promote ease and stillness in the upper chest and connected breathing, if the speaker can feel the sit-bones firmly grounded into the chair and the underside of the feet on the floor with the spine lengthening up through the skull.

The TV or film actor, on the other hand, is often portraying a character who is not necessarily using optimal dynamic alignment to portray a character. Still, I believe the audience intuits when an actor is using tensions not related to the character (i.e., working from habits rather than choices) and this hurts the actor's believability. A well-trained actor finds the releases within the parameters of the character, ensuring that even a 'character voice' will sound connected and honest. Consequently, while projection is not a goal of training these performers, reduction of tensions and habits that inhibit a connected voice is, because the camera is so unforgiving. The camera magnifies every extraneous tension the speaker carries. An audience is subliminally affected by these tensions and will believe or disbelieve the spokesperson or actor in part because of these tensions. Excessive physical and vocal tension can be the culprits undermining the performer's goal. Acquiring an understanding of breathing that is suited to the task they are called on to do helps the spokesperson and actor to be credible to the listener.

MG: The voice is a very flexible organ. It can be used in many different ways, producing many different kinds of sounds. Clavicular breathing does work. It is not pretty to look at; it can limit expression, but, in my opinion, it is functional. Ideal or optimal vocal production is not necessary 100% of the time. However, when performers get 'lazy' with voice production, there is no vocal reserve for them to fall back on should they become ill or stressed, etc.

In my role as speech pathologist I see many patients with benign voice disorders (vocal fold swellings, nodules or polyps) as a result of vocal overuse and misuse. Many of these patients are performers who work with mics either speaking or singing. Since the microphone does the work of amplifying the voice, they do not feel that it is necessary to utilize the same techniques as they would onstage. As a result they tend to under-support the voice, resulting in cases of vocal problems.

Actors whether on camera or on stage need to project energy, both vocally and physically. However, the fashion in TV and film is towards 'natural' or 'man on the street,' 'person next door' feel. It may have a de-energized look or feel, but it actually takes energy to be convincing. When actors or singers are poorly trained in voice use, it is easier for them to fall into bad habits, confusing the 'casual' look with the 'casual' voice.

LO: I deal primarily with training students for the theatre, but in the UK there is much crossover work into TV and radio. Unlike the USA, we rarely train people specifically for TV, film and radio—I would hope that the good practice they learn would be transferable to the other mediums. For the most part, the close work that these mediums encourage doesn't put the dependence upon deep, diaphragmatic breathing. 'Coat-hanger' shoulders don't look good, regardless of the medium, and I would always advise actors to rid themselves of tension that affects their breathing.

LW: In my opinion, any 're-training' would depend entirely on the wants and needs of the actor/performer in question. I would consider teaching a different approach to breath if I felt it would contribute to what I had been hired to assist the actor/performer in doing *and* if I felt I had sufficient time to teach it. When I was coaching in California, I had the sense that even actors with substantial theatre careers had spent so much time doing film and television that they weren't as strong vocally as they once had been, and were happy to spend some time reviewing and practicing vocal technique, including breathing. Actors who had come from highly regarded training programs would say, 'Oh, yes! I remember doing this sort of thing at (fill in the name of the program),' but often they had forgotten about the work and how useful it was until putting it into practice again. Of course, being an advocate of the importance of breath to all aspects of performance, I think breath work is useful for all performers, but I do think it is more critical for stage than for film/TV.

MM: There should be no difference in the basic training—they still need optimal vocal health and that includes three-dimensional optimal breathing. The on-camera actor or singer may be able to get by with less but the price that they will eventually pay will be just as high as that of the insufficiently

trained stage actor or singer. Voice problems are a common occurrence amongst this population and as such they need the same solid training. I am very much in favor of Lessac's concept of 'diluting the sound' when dealing with these artists. This concept implies that there is a solid foundation with good projection capabilities and healthy vocal fold function to work from, thus protecting their vocal instruments whilst performing.

EM: If the performer wants to work in a way that is alive, responsive, colorful, powerful, and fully expressive, then yes, I absolutely think they need to train thoroughly. And to me, this means training from the ground up, even though a camera/microphone may not rely on the potential power of their breath as fully as a stage performer does.

MB: I serve as a consultant for the news department of our local ABC affiliate. Most every time a client is referred to me for some type of quality that is deemed less than pleasant (e.g. 'whiny sounding,' 'too-high pitch,' or 'twangy'), there is less than ideal breathing. I also find that very often these clients are unable to make it through a thought phrase without breathing in the middle of it. Thus, I always end up doing some type of breathing exercise with them.

If the on-camera actor has no desire to work in a forum without a microphone and s/he is operating the voice in a healthy manner, then there really is no need to re-train his or her breathing habits. I would tell these performers that I could make things easier and more efficient, as well as give them the ability to speak longer phrases. It is ultimately a choice of the actor and whether s/he is happy with his or her abilities. Thus I would suggest further training is essential only if he/she wants to be able to do theatre, or if there are already vocal problems occurring within the on-camera context.

RR: We have covered a lot of territory, most of it having to do with two faulty patterns, clavicular breathing and 'coat-hanger' shoulders that ultimately prevent optimal voice production. I would like to turn towards the connection between the technical production aspects and the student's ability to connect to the more imaginative, character-based, performance values. Some of you have touched on the need for self-introspection, motivation, and increasing self-awareness to overcome clavicular and held-shoulder breathing. Marina Gilman made a distinction earlier when she mentioned Kathleen Battle's clavicular breathing: 'One can hardly say she does not have optimal voice production nor is the sound strident.' How and when do you motivate the student who, like Kathleen Battle, has enough talent to provide a good 'product,' despite such breathing problems?

MH: I encourage my students to try everything, and find what works. When working through the elements of Laver's Vocal Profile Analysis,[17] I ask them to experiment with clavicular and other foci of breathing, along with rhythms, pace and depth of breath, and to find out what it does to them, and to a character. By doing so, each finds out their own habit and finds what a change of habit can do to their sound. Whatever pattern they find produces the best sound—for their purpose—is the one they aim for.

I have found that a lot of voice work requires the ability to trick the student into optimum voice use—getting them to stop controlling their sound and try something new. Once they have found a voice they like for themselves, developing this voice gives them the impetus to continue working on the breath pattern that produces it.

PT: Doing the least amount of work to 'get by' is a constant temptation for an actor—myself included. This laziness is hardly limited to voice work. I encourage my students (and myself!) to think of themselves as artists striving for perfection and beauty. With that as a goal, the actor is thinking beyond 'product' towards art.

As to Kathleen Battle's breathing, I have not studied it. But I am willing to bet that her breathing is not *limited* to clavicular breathing. I expect that her entire ribcage is moving with the breath.

EA: I think that it is great that someone who has non-ideal breathing patterns can be as successful as Kathleen Battle. It is quite possible, obviously, to breathe clavicularly and not injure oneself. But my students can't be sure that, when things start to go wrong (illness, an accident, etc.), that they will be so fortunate. These skills are there to save you in that case. Often at the beginning of their career, it is the most difficult to deal with the issues that might stress the voice. One needs to reduce the stresses you can reduce, and something like clavicular breathing is, at very least, changeable, whereas some things (like allergies) are beyond your control. Whether or not someone with those great innate talents will believe me, and commit to preparing for that possibility is not within my control. I think that clavicular breathing is something that is worth working to solve. However, there are people with hugely successful careers who still breathe in that manner. Do I believe that the battle is worth fighting? Absolutely.

JH: Even when a student sounds 'good' to the trained ear, she/he may respond to useful changes if such changes will help preserve the voice for life-long professional or semi-professional use. There will frequently be a student for whom everything has come easily—and he/she has gotten by without having to work very hard and with no attention to how she/he does what she/he does. Only if the student recognizes this as a

habit will he/she be motivated to learn available technical skills for better life-long vocal and whole-system function. It is always exciting to work with such a self-aware student, and the sky's the limit here.

BA: This really underlines the importance of the individual. The strength and stamina of any one individual's voice will determine how much abuse it can take. Some individuals would be fried after one performance during which they misused their voice, while others may hang in there not knowing they are chipping away at their vocal health until after many years, or they may never suffer ill effects at all. With my students, I use the analogy of cigarette smoking. We all know smoking causes cancer. Why then are some individuals able to smoke their whole lives without ill effects? Are they willing to play roulette with which individual they are?

MG: If the student is producing voice well and the breathing pattern is not interfering, I would focus on musical and other issues and not make a big deal out of the less than ideal pattern. However, I would continue to work indirectly to bring the student to a point of body use in which that pattern begins to disappear. In the case of Kathleen Battle, I have heard several people comment that they find it difficult to watch her sing, because of the physical mannerisms. We are not doing our students a service by not addressing these physical 'ticks'.

LO: This is a tricky one that comes up in all areas of teaching, not just in the area of breath. A student may be successful at many things without good technique, but this is what it boils down to, really, isn't it? There are many people who have great product without technique in voice, acting and breath work. When the great product that comes from 'inspiration' or 'chance' ails, without technique of some kind, the actor will have nowhere to go. Whether this puts me on the side of the angels or the devil, I would always advocate technique and explain it to my students in exactly this way. You cannot force someone to develop techniques to deal with all circumstances, but by teaching students a range of technical work, they will be prepared. One of my very favorite Olivier quotes refers to those perfect performance nights when 'God sits on my shoulder'—I want my students to be prepared for the nights when He is busy with someone else.

LW: Motivation? There are hordes of 'good' actors out there. If you're 'good' now, it means you have the potential to be *great*. Also, I think Kathleen Battle is not a good example to use in talking about actors' vocal use. Although great singing includes spontaneity, the degree is much less than for the actor. A classical singer is expected to adhere quite closely to tempo, note length, volume, rhythm, pitch, etc. A script rarely includes specific, detailed dynamics, so actors have much more flexibility in terms of how they 'play' a script; usually scripted text is intended to sound as if it were thought up and spoken in the heat of the moment. I don't believe I have ever seen a student with a 'good' voice who I didn't think had the potential to be exceptional if they worked on their technique, range, and sensitivity.

MM: Can I be naughty and ask you to consider what she would have been like if she did use optimal breathing? In all seriousness, this is something to consider as it is not only the aesthetic sound quality that must be taken into account, but also the question of whether a singer or speaker is producing the sound in such a way that he/she will have a long and fruitful career. This is usually the angle I will take…Anyway, the amount of performers (singers or actors) who can get away with this kind of 'seemingly less than optimal' voice production (and specifically here breathing) is so few and far between that they should not be used to set the standards. As an aside, I need to mention that a teacher should be very careful to not oversimplify the visual profile of optimal three-dimensional breathing, as it will be embodied differently in each person's body due to build, physical and emotional history and cultural body patterns—but now I am off on something else again!

EM: I think this may correspond to students I have encountered on occasion who are having a degree of success in the musical theatre, but whose voices to me do not seem organic or connected. In these cases, I try to mirror what I hear and to help the students understand that they are working with a kind of limitation, albeit one that hasn't been standing in their way in practical terms. After that, I consider it their business how they want to work with their instrument. I am more assertive in a case where I believe someone may be harming the voice, but even there I believe I can only show options and let the student know I will help when ready. We are all here for different reasons and all have different things to explore through our work.

MB: I think everyone has worked with someone at some point in time that has horrible technique yet still has an exceptionally fine product. I do not think this always has to do with an exceptional ability in connecting with imaginative character-based values either. It may or it may not. I have met people who just seem to have 'cords of steel.' When I work with a student that consistently has a good product or has had a product which has received a great deal of praise, I usually say something along the lines of 'Just imagine how good it could be if you used better technique,' or 'It frightens me to think how good you would sound if you could release those tensions'.

RR: Thus ends a Round Table discussion of clavicular breathing, 'coat hanger' shoulders and related issues. It is also the end of a year's in-depth look at many topics related to breathing and breathing pedagogy.

In addition to the many voicings of appreciation for the learning opportunity these two projects, the *Monograph*, and this discussion, have afforded them, a few offer these final statements:

EA: Today I watched auditions for my returning students, and since I had been writing on clavicular breathing, I observed their clavicles quite a lot. Those who still breathe in that manner even after two years of training, continue to struggle to support their voices, tend to have issues with stridor and tend to hang on to the exhalation (that is they don't let the air come back in until just before the next thought). The clavicular breathing seems to be connected to this gasping for the thought, and hanging on to the moment before for too long causes that gasp. Then they must rush to draw the breath in. When this happens, they resort to all their 'bad habits' that push the pattern up into their upper torso. To fix their habit, were they truly willing to change, they would have to change their acting. And to change that, they need to address the thinking that engenders the breath pattern.

It is always more than just 'technique.' Finding the root of the issue is harder, and just getting the shoulders to come down is like trying to cure a disease by treating its symptoms. It is important for me to remember that clavicular breathing is a symptom more often than not, and not the core issue.

JH: As I commented earlier, good voice use is so much more than breath. However, if we use ourselves well in our daily life-with the child's 'natural' non-interfered-with breathing function—we will do okay for singing, speaking, and acting in performance.

MG: Breathing and changing breathing patterns is not just about posture and movement of specific parts of the body. We need to keep in mind that we are dealing with the whole body—body/mind/voice/psyche when teaching. Shoulders back, belly down, head up do not make for good vocalizing although they may 'appear' to promote optimal voice work. As teachers we need to look at what is there and just as often what is not apparent to the eye in problem solving. How does poor breathing relate to a vocal self-image? Is poor breath management reflected in the speaking voice as well as in singing? Are the habits I see and hear in singing reflected in other aspects of the student's demeanor and speech? What is happening with balance and the feet is just as important to singing and breath control as what is happening in the larynx.

LW: There is only breath.[18]

Endnotes

1. Ruth Rootberg, Editor, Marth Munro, Asst. Editor (Amherst: privately printed, 2002). Referred to subsequently as *Monograph*. See also "Principles of breathing, pedagogy, and language derived from practices of thirteen voice teachers" in this Journal.

2. Natalie Stewart wrote for the *Monograph*, but is not represented in this article.

3. Responses to Questions three and four have some revisions in this article, but are based on pp. 144-145 of the *Monograph*.

4. See the "Principles of breathing..." article for a summary of pedagogical experience and approach, and for other biographical information.

5. One to two weeks was the standard turn around time.

6. Kathleen Battle, (b. 1948) is a world-renown operatic, concert and five-time Grammy Award winning lyric coloratura soprano.

7. Miller, Richard, *The Structure of Singing: System and Art in Vocal Technique* (New York: Schirmer Books, 1996).

8. Bertherat, Thérèse, *The Body Has its Reasons* (Rochester: Inner Traditions Intl. Ltd, 1989).

9. David Smukler, voice teacher at York University, Toronto, Canada, is Director of Canada's National Voice Intensive.

10. Judith Koltai, MA, ADTR, studied under Thérèse Bertherat, a long-time associate of Françoise Mézières. Ms. Koltai teaches Syntonic Exercise, a body awareness and postural alignment technique.

11. Robert Chapline, Linklater teacher formerly with Boston University.

12. For continued explanation of this strap exercise, see *Monograph*, p. 141).

13. Irmgard Bartenieff (1900-1981), was a student of Rudolf Laban and developed a series of movements now known as the Bartenieff Fundamentals (BF). For details, see her book written with Dori Lewis: *Body Movement: Coping with the Environment* (Amsterdam: Gordon and Breach, 1980).

14. Irene Dowd, neuromuscular specialist, teaches in the dance program at Julliard and is author of *Taking Root to Fly* (New York: Irene Dowd, 1995).

15. Lynn Martin, Carl Stough Breathing Coordination, body alignment and movement re-education specialist.

16. See pp. 107 ff.

17. John Laver, author of *The Phonetic Description of Voice Quality* (Cambridge: Cambridge University Press, 1980), and creator of the Laver Vocal Profile Analysis, examines separate components of voice, e.g., lip use, position of larynx, breathing patterns, in order to clearly identify voice quality.

18. Cicely Berry attributes this quote, found in her book, *Text in Action*, to her teacher, Gwynneth Thurburn, of the Central School of Speech Training and Dramatic Art (London: Virgin Pub., 2001), p. 82.

Reviews and Sources *Mandy Rees, Associate Editor*

In a world where communication is increasingly the moving of fingertips over a keyboard or the listening to a voice on a cellular phone, our experience of human expression is becoming more and more limited. Our most time consuming relationships are often with machines rather than with human beings. I find my university students' ability to listen and to focus attention on vocal nuance is waning. In light of this, the training of young voices and bodies to communicate is crucial. And for all of us, it is important to spend time in the theatre—listening.

One of the unique aspects of this publication is the inclusion of "vocal reviews", reviews of theatrical productions from a vocal perspective. It is our chance to listen, to write about what we hear, to document vocal choices and to celebrate the art of the human voice. Writing about what we hear is vital, and is part of how we preserve and advance vocal expression. In this issue we have a chance to "listen" to productions from three countries, and to hear from key vocal coaches about their work. Judylee Vivier writes about two British productions of *Hamlet*, one directed by Peter Brook, and the other by John Caird of the Royal National Theatre. This is a chance to compare and contrast how two companies grapple with one of the most challenging texts in the English Language. Kate Foy treats us with a look at a new work, *Cloudstreet*, a play with a distinctly Australian flair based on one of her favorite novels. Claudia Anderson visits two Chicago companies producing classic work, the Chicago Shakespeare Company and the Court Theatre, both of whom employ vocal coaches. She shares with us part of her conversations with these coaches—Linda Gates and Eric Armstrong—and their impressions of working on the productions.

Happily, there are many people writing new books about or relating to voice and speech. In the following pages we review ten new publications. Shakespeare is the clear winner in this round, with six books relating to how we speak his language. Other publications cover topics on accent reduction, movement studies, and the actor's speaking and singing voice. Pamela Prather provides a thorough overview of books on the art of voice-over, the featured topic of this issue of the Voice and Speech Review.

And perhaps most impressive, and most reaffirming, are the large batch of thesis abstracts we have to share with you. There are many new voices out there ready to write about what we do, to contribute to our field, and to help us listen.

Mandy Rees teaches acting, voice and movement at California State University, Bakersfield and regularly directs in their theatre season. Her book, *Between Director and Actor: Strategies for Effective Performance*, co-written with John Staniunas, was published in 2002. She has worked with Cornerstone Theater Company, CSU Summer Arts, Madison Repertory Theatre, and the Los Angeles Actors Theatre. She is a former board member of VASTA, and is also active in the Association of Theatre Movement Educators and has served as editor of their Movement Bibliography.

Selected Resources on Voice-Overs

Pamela Prather teaches speech at Yale School of Drama and Vocal Production for Actors at New York University in the Playwright's Horizons BFA program. She earned her MFA in Acting from UCLA. She has taught Voice and Speech at The Academy of Music and Dramatic Arts, The School for Film and Television and Marymount Manhattan College. She recently coached *A Winter's Tale* for the Hampton's Shakespeare Festival and the U.S. premiere of *Fighting Words* at the Yale Rep. Pamela worked as an "on-air talent" in England, Florida, New Mexico and Tokyo and has recorded numerous voice-overs. She enjoys studying Japanese performing arts—including Kyogen, Noh and Butoh.

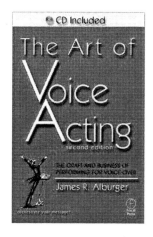

Alburger, James R. *The Art of Voice Acting*. Second Edition. Massachusetts: Focal Press, 2002. 278 pages + CD. This book and CD cover just about everything an actor needs to get started in voice-over work. The author offers basic warm-up exercises, a variety of scripts, and techniques for creating characters. The CD provides a variety of voice-over samples. This book is a really thorough and up-to-date place to start digging into the voice-over profession.

Apple, Terri. *Making Money in Voice-Overs: Winning Strategies to a Successful Career in TV, Commercials, Radio and Animation*. Los Angeles: Lone Eagle Publishing Company, 1999. 233 pages.

I found Terri Apple's book to be clear, concise and laid out in a logical fashion. The first four chapters deal with fact gathering—defining voice-over, developing technique, and looking at voice-over options including animation, looping, dubbing and audio-books. She includes short three-page interviews with working professionals in their areas of specialty. Chapters 5-9 are focused on getting the agent and the gig. Some of the chapters are laid out in a Q/A format which is helpful for beginners. The remainder of the book looks at auditioning, marketing yourself, stereotypes and trends. Nine pieces of sample copy offer a few basic ideas of what an actor will find at an audition. Specific phone numbers and agent information are geared for the Los Angeles actor.

Berland, Terry et al. *Breaking into Commercials: The Complete Guide to Marketing Yourself, Auditioning to Win, and Getting the Job*. New York: Penguin, A Plume Book, 1997. 352 pages. This book looks at all mediums of commercial work, however, Chapter 15 spends 20 pages looking at voice-over work as it relates to commercials. This chapter moves through: What are Voice-overs and Who Does Them?, Voice-over markets, Types of Opportunities in Voice-over, What It Takes to Succeed, How to Get Started Doing Voice-overs, Marketing and Packaging Yourself as a Talent, Tapping the Regional Markets,

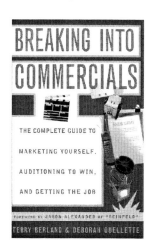

The Taping Session, Interview with Barbara Goldman, and Animation. These topics are skimmed.

Blu, Susan and Molly Ann Mullin. *Word of Mouth: A Guide to Commercial Voice-Over Excellence*. Second Edition. Beverly Hills: Pomegranate Press, Ltd., 1996. 182 pages. This book was originally published in the late 1980s and though this is the second edition, some of the information and copy feels dated. The basic info is there with chapters like: How to Begin, Animation, Tags and Doubles, The Demo Tape, The Agent, The Audition, Your First Job. Much of the book is laid out in Q/A format.

Clark, Elaine A. *There's Money Where Your Mouth Is: An Insider's Guide to a Career in Voice-Overs*. New York: Back Stage Books, 2000. 232 pages.

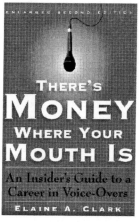

Clark's book covers all of voice-over bases. The first half of the book looks at the basic of getting started and preparing for a variety of voice-over gigs. The second half of the book deals with specific voice-over skills: announcer, spokesperson, real-person and characters. She includes chapters on industrial narrations and multimedia and audio books. She doesn't waste space with addresses and phone numbers, but rather gives practical information and provides clear examples of resumes, sample cover letters and marketing ideas.

Cronauer, Adrian. *How to Read Copy: Professionals' Guide to Delivering Voice-Overs and Broadcast Commercials*. Chicago: Bonus Books, 1990. 208 pages + companion cassette.
Though this book is more than ten years old, the basic information is still very useful. The companion cassette helps illustrate the author's points, although it is difficult to use the cuts with the textbook,

unless reading straight through. Some information is outdated, such as the Demo Reel section. It talks about LPs, speeds of tape for recording—no mention of CDs, minidisks and current technology.

Douthitt, Chris and Tom Wiecks. *Voiceover: Putting Your Mouth Where The Money Is*. Grey Heron Books. 1997. 229 pages.
A relatively comprehensive and clear introduction to the voice-over market geared for beginners. This book covers the basics (getting an agent, demo tape, auditioning) and provides sample scripts as well as specific guidelines for narration and animation voice-overs. There is a chapter that looks at the basics of recording in a studio as well as the information about unions. A clear read.

Fraley, Patrick. *Creating Character Voices*. California: The Audio Partners Publishing Corp. 1993. 2 cassettes.

Enjoyable and full of information. Fraley says, "The right stroke of the vocal brush brings a character to life." This LA based voice-talent offers extremely useful advice and helpful exercises. He really packs a lot into two hours. He provides clear advice for creating and cataloguing your own characters. Animation voice-over and commercial character voice demos are included. He calls one clever exercise "character husbandry", in which the actor carefully combines specific elements of characters he/she has created to form personal hybrids.

Hogan, Harlan. *VO: Tales and Techniques of Voice-Over Actor*. New York: Allworth Press, 2002. 249 pages.
Hot off the presses, this book is a combination of biography and how-to. The advantage of a book like this is a very personal approach combined with detailed practical information. The

resources section includes "Books on Voice-Over", "Books on Acting in Commercials", Other Books, Periodicals.

Kozloff, Sarah. *Invisible Storytellers: Voice-over Narration in American Fiction Film.* Los Angeles: University of California Press, 1988. 167 pages.
Kozloff looks at the history of voice-over narration in American fiction films. This is pure history rather than "how-to". This book is more appropriate to a film history class rather than vocal performance.

McCoy, Michell et al. *Sound and*

Look Professional on Television and the Internet: How to Improve Your On-Camera Presence. Chicago: Bonus Books Inc. 2000. 203 pages.
This book is a survey course for anyone who will ever be on television. Chapters include specific assistance for news anchors and reporters, talk show hosts and guests as well as on-camera commercials and industrial videos. Ten pages are dedicated to film and TV acting, while over 40 pages focus on make-up, cosmetic surgery, hair and wardrobe for TV. Twenty pages give the basics on broadcast voice work.

Thomas, Sandy. *So You Want To Be A Voice-Over Star.* New York: In the Clubhouse Publishing, 1999. 142 pages.
This book is extremely basic and reads like a scrapbook of Sandy Thomas' career. The last page of the book has a black and white photo of a golf course where Santo Castellano a.k.a. Sandy Thomas hit a ball into the water. Hmmm. There are 30 pages of sample scripts—which is helpful. There are a lot of photos of Sandy Thomas throughout his career.

Utterback, Ann S. *Broadcast Voice Handbook: How to Polish Your On-Air Delivery.* Third Edition. Chicago: Bonus Books Inc, 2000. 348 pages.
This book is quite thorough and geared for broadcast journalists. It includes a 1999 survey of News Directors and the importance of voice, diction and clear communication. The chapters include Breathing, Phonation, Resonance, Articulation, Stress and Intonation, Sounding Conversational, Going Live/ Live Experiences and Coping with Stress. There are some good black and white photos of the vocal folds including smoker's vocal folds.

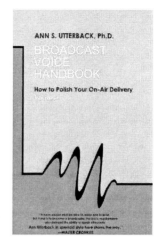

Whitfield, Alice. *Take it From the Top! How to Earn Your Living In Radio & TV Voiceovers.* New York: Ring-U-Turkey Press, 1992. 209 pages.
The first six chapters focus on the very basics of voice-over auditioning—including information such as signing in at the door, picking up the script and reading the copy. Advice like "if you are good enough and lucky enough to make it, you will have more longevity in voice-overs than in on camera" is practical if not rather simplistic. Whitfield brings in the jargon and defines it clearly. Eight pages on the demo reel—useful, clear. The second half of the book is called "From The Horse's Mouth" and include Q/A format with agents, and actors. The final chapters give phone numbers and contact information for agents and useful resources.

"How Are We Saying This?"—
Three Books on Pronouncing Shakespeare

"How are we saying this?"

For years I've depended upon my dog-eared, tea-stained, xeroxed copy of Helge Kokeritz' 1959 book *Shakespeare's Names: A Pronouncing Dictionary* to answer that inevitable question at the first rehearsal of a Shakespearean play. Though Kokeritz gives British pronunciations, not American, what choice was there? No other comprehensive guide existed.

But now, after a scholarly fast of more than forty years, three new pronunciation dictionaries for Shakespeare's plays serve up a banquet of choice. Best of all, the three dictionaries have been assembled by American authors, all of whom resist the tyranny of British pronunciation in Shakespeare on American stages.

As rehearsals began for *Titus Andronicus* at the Oregon Shakespeare Festival, I kept all three references at my table, ready to put them to the test.

Louis Colaianni's book, *Shakespeare's Names*, was reviewed in the last VASTA journal, but for the sake of comparison, I'll give a quick overview here. As the title suggests, Colaianni focuses only on proper names. He arranges his book play by play, and lists the names within each play from A to Z. He gives pronunciations in IPA, as well as his own system of simplified phonics. He also includes RP pronunciations indicated with little diamond symbols. The book is published by Drama Publishers and costs about $22.50.

The newest book on the scene is Louis Scheeder and Shane Ann Younts' *All the Words on Stage: A Complete Pronunciation Dictionary for the Plays of William Shakespeare*. It goes well beyond proper names, giving pronunciations for an extensive list of Shakespearean vocabulary words, taking scansion into account where it affects pronunciation. Rather than play by play, the book is arranged like a standard dictionary, word by word in alphabetical order. Pronunciations are given both in simplified phonetics, and IPA. No RP pronunciations are given. It's published by Smith and Kraus and priced at about $25.

Dale F. Coye's book, *Pronouncing Shakespeare's Words: A Guide from A to Zounds* has been around for several years now, but has been much overlooked. The reason? The book was published by Greenwood Press, and sold only as a hardcover for the outrageous price of $120. Routledge has recently reprinted it in paper though, and it's now available for about $20. But *caveat emptor*! While the hardcover includes all 38 plays, plus *Edward the Third*, plus the poems and sonnets, the paperback eviscerates this body of material to less than half of the original, leaving only "the twenty-one best known plays." And one of the plays cut away was—you guessed it—*Titus Andronicus*. (Good thing I spent like a king, and bought the hardcover when it first came out.)

Coye's guide is arranged play by play, like Colaianni's, but goes one step further, adopting the scene and line numbers from G. Blakemore Evans' 1974 *Riverside Shakespeare* for easy reference. Like Scheeder and Younts, Coye gives pronunciations for every challenging word from Shakespeare's vocabulary, but again, Coye goes one step further, offering concise definitions for each word as well. One drawback for voice and speech professionals: Coye uses a system of dictionary symbols only, shunning IPA as "unfamiliar to many potential users."

Scott Kaiser is the Head of Voice and Text at the Oregon Shakespeare Festival in Ashland, where he has served as Voice and Text Director on 65 productions. His new book, *Mastering Shakespeare: An Acting Class in Seven Scenes*, published by Allworth Press, will be released in October of 2003. His new adaptations of Shakespeare's three *Henry the Sixth* plays will be produced at OSF in the 2004 season. Scott will co-direct with Artistic Director Libby Appel.

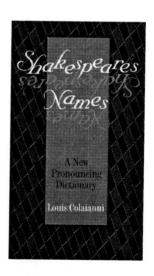

The fun of having three references on hand, as we hacked our way through the Titus text, was not in observing how often they agreed, (which was most of the time), but in discovering where they *disagreed*. The dilemma: how to select the best of the variant choices?

"Then, Aaron, arm thy heart..."
Take the name Aaron, for example: is it AIR-un or AAR-un or EH-run? Checking all three guides did not resolve the conflict, as they all give more than one possible pronunciation. Which is best? After hearing the candidates, the director made his election: AIR-un.

"What news with thee, Aemilius?"
Aemilius! Here's a name that caused endless confusion, because of the horrific spelling and the fact that it scans with both three and four syllables. Scheeder and Younts, as well as Coye, give ee-MIL-yuhs or ee-MIL-ee-uhs. Colaianni recommends i-MEEL-yus or i-MEE-lee-yus. How to choose? The director had no problem, decreeing that Colaianni was correct. (It was the pronunciation he'd been using.)

"So Bassianus, you have play'd your prize."
The British pronunciation given in Kokeritz of this name, and inexplicably adopted by all three of the newest guides, BAA-see-AY-nuhs, gave our all-American cast a bad case of adolescent giggles. *Bassy anus?* The director quickly suggested his own version of the name, "bah-see-AH-nis," and we moved on, (before we lost our heads).

"'Tis well, Lavinia, that thou hast no hands."
Coye says Lavinia can have "3 or 4 syllables depending on meter." Scheeder and Younts concur. Colaianni, surprisingly, while taking care to show how other names, like Lucius and Mutius, expand and contract, gives only a four syllable pronunciation of Lavinia. Was the cast able to pronounce the proper number of syllables in each instance in the text? Well, let's just say I had to give them a hand.

"Not far one Muliteus my countryman..."
An off-stage character mentioned only once in the text wins the "Most-Gnarly-Name-in-the-Play Award." Muliteus. Go ahead, try to say it aloud. Muliteus. Don't worry, there's violent disagreement among the guides on this one. Most scholars feel the line has been hopelessly mutilated anyway.

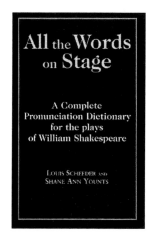

All the Words on Stage

A Complete Pronunciation Dictionary for the plays of William Shakespeare

LOUIS SCHEEDER AND SHANE ANN YOUNTS

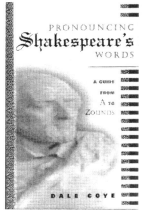

PRONOUNCING **Shakespeare's** WORDS

A GUIDE FROM A TO ZOUNDS

DALE COYE

Eventually the director lopped off the name, and rewrote it to read: "Not far there lives a countryman of mine..." (Sorry, Muli.)

"Was never Scythia half so barbarous."
Is that "th" in Scythia voiced or not? Colaianni says the "th" should be voiced. Scheeder and Younts say it's unvoiced. Coye gives both. When there's no superior choice, it's sometimes best to go with the pronunciation that first came out of the actor's mouth. In this case, the actor used an unvoiced "th" as in SI-thyuh. So I held my tongue.

"Terras Astraea reliquit."
Titus is stuffed with Latin words and phrases like this one, which our director said he wanted to keep. On the subject of Latin, Colaianni is silent. Scheeder & Younts serve up a very good list of Latin words and phrases in the back of their book, but for some reason abandon IPA just where it would have been extremely helpful. Coye once again goes beyond the call of duty, giving both Anglican and Classical Latin pronunciations, as well as clear and concise translations underneath. But alas, he doesn't use IPA either.

Eventually, for the sake of clarity, instead of spouting Latin in this moment, the director ruled that Titus should say: "Astraea, Goddess of Justice, has left the earth." By opening night the rest of the Latin had been butchered off the bones of the text as well.

"Till all the Andronici be made away."
All three dictionaries agree that the family name "Andronici" ends with a *sigh*, as in "an-DRAHN-ih-seye." Even so, the director dictated that we should use his own pronunciation, which ends in a *key*, as in "an-DRAHN-ih-kee." Why? Because it "felt right." (How can you argue with that?)

At the end of the day, I found all three books to be very useful and authoritative resources. Why choose between them? Own them all, and keep them close at hand for that first rehearsal, and the inevitable question– *"How are we saying this?"*

But remember, in the realm of the rehearsal room, the absolute authority on pronouncing Shakespeare is neither the voice coach, nor Scheeder, nor Younts, nor Colaianni, nor Coye, nor Kokeritz. In the era of the auteur, the final word on how to say the words belongs to the director.

Book Review *by Rena Cook*

How to Speak Shakespeare by Cal Pritner and Louis Colaianni

How to Speak Shakespeare is a quick overview of the basic skills needed for acting Shakespeare. The book addresses the major questions that are asked by young actors and demystifies the areas of Shakespeare that they find the most daunting. This user-friendly volume is clearly divided into three sections: word meanings and paraphrasing as part 1, stress and verse rhythm as part 2, and identifying and using the poetry as part 3. This book is a practical, accessible tool for the student working on his own. It could also be used to kick-start an interest in Shakespeare in an introductory course as it effectively outlines some skills that will lead to performance success. It is also useful in conjunction with traditional texts such as *Freeing Shakespeare's Voice* by Kristin Linklater or *The Actor and the Text* by Cicely Berry.

The book is laid out in workbook form which is especially helpful for the self-directed student. The information is structured to present a concept, give examples, provide an exercise, and then summarize what has been learned.

The idea of "Syncopate for Meaning" is unique to this book and is a fresh approach to the often daunting subject of rhythm and scansion. The concept of "stress tied to meaning" is introduced, and actors are guided to stress the nouns and verbs with extra emphasis, helping them to avoid the mind-numbing effect of unbroken iambic pentameter and to highlight the key words.

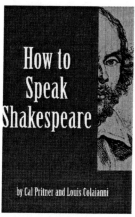

Two other strong sections of the book cover how to use punctuation as a road map for structure and clarity of meaning, and how to identify and use repeated sounds.

The book directs students to three useful resources: the *Oxford English Dictionary*, the *First Folio*, and a helpful bibliography, each pointing the students to worlds of information they will need for further study in Shakespeare performance.

In conclusion, *How to Speak Shakespeare* is a highly recommended new book in the field of Shakespeare performance studies. It simplifies and demystifies the subject, something numerous books attempt, but few succeed as well.

Rena Cook is on the faculty at University of Oklahoma where she teaches Voice and Acting. She has served as vocal coach for the Illinois Shakespeare Festival on *The Merry Wives of Windsor*, *Richard III*, and *Wild Oats*. She has directed *Dancing at Lughnasa*, *The Prime of Miss Jean Brodie* and *Medea*. Rena holds an MA in Voice Studies from the Central School of Speech and Drama. Her theatrical reviews have appeared in *The Journal of Dramatic Theory and Criticism* and *Theatre Journal*.

Kevin Otos is an Assistant Professor of Theatre at Oklahoma State University where he teaches Acting, Movement, Text, and recently directed Measure for Measure. His MFA in Acting is from the Florida State University Asolo Conservatory for Actor Training where he was privileged to work with the late Jose Quintero.

Clues to Acting Shakespeare by Wesley Van Tassel

Clues to Acting Shakespeare by Wesley Van Tassel aims to instruct the actor already familiar with a contemporary acting process in the speaking skills necessary to begin understanding and acting Shakespeare's language. Nearly identical information is presented three times in three formats: one for the actor in training (most applicable to undergraduate students), one for secondary education, and one for the working professional with little experience acting Shakespeare. The success and beauty of this book is in its simplicity, clarity, and focus on the fundamentals. It provides a useful foundation from which to begin more thorough language investigation.

Van Tassel begins by stating common mistakes made by actors acting Shakespeare. He then tells the reader how to avoid these pit-falls by applying four fundamental skills: end-line support, scansion, breathing, and phrasing. Antithesis and imagery are also introduced, though with less emphasis than the aforementioned skills.

Van Tassel offers clear explanation of these skills illuminated with numerous examples. He also includes several unique and very applicable exercises that reinforce these lessons physically. These exercises put these fundamentals into the actor's muscle memory so that s/he can then "forget" the skills while performing and concentrate on the moment. The exercises ultimately help the actor live truthfully in the imaginary circumstances rather than focusing on speaking technique.

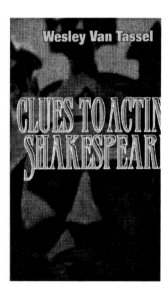

There are some minor problems in the book. One is the overuse of Shakespearean quotes that, while sometimes interesting, make the book choppy and difficult to read. Another occasional problem is that a term, such as *caesura*, will be used and not adequately defined until later. Also, Van Tassel's passion for the material can sometimes come off as heavy-handed. These are comparatively minor concerns relative to the book's success.

Van Tassel has succeeded in making the daunting world of acting Shakespeare accessible to undergraduate students and complete with useful exercises. He takes care in reminding students to integrate these new skills into a more Stanislavski-based contemporary acting process. The book is useful for both beginning students of Shakespeare and for those seeking to strengthen their fundamentals. *Clues to Acting Shakespeare* also contains a very useful bibliography on the ever-increasing number of films based on Shakespeare's plays. A more detailed explanation of Van Tassel's pedagogy is available in the peer-reviewed article by Van Tassel, "Teaching Shakespeare's Language Skills" in the *The Voice and Violence* VASTA 2001 publication.

Book Review *by Mandy Rees*

The Applause First Folio of Shakespeare in Modern Type
Prepared & Annotated by Neil Freeman
Supervised and Produced for Applause by Paul Sugarman

The First Folio of Shakespeare is widely recognized as an important resource for scholars and performers, but due to its original hard-to-read typeface and a number of printing mistakes, this valuable document was often difficult to use. An ambitious new version, prepared by Neil Freeman, presents the Folio in modern fonts and with extensive annotations making it readable and accessible.

Freeman provides a great deal of introductory material to educate readers in the history, qualities and benefits of the *First Folio*. Divided into six parts, and embedded with numerous headings to make information easier to browse, this text provides an expert commentary of the available scholarly research. By perusing this material, the reader learns about the genesis of the *First Folio*, its sources and its amazingly jumbled printing history. Freeman aptly recounts the convoluted journey the plays took from the author's original manuscripts to the first published versions, and on to the edited versions we now rely upon. He also furnishes a theatrical history of Shakespeare in order to provide a context for understanding the world of the plays.

Of most interest to voice and speech experts is the section entitled "Modern Interventions Changing the Nature of the Plays". Here is explained how modern editors have handled the many irregularities contained within the Folio—Freeman calls them the "warts"—including irregularities in line length, scansion, punctuation, and ambiguous lines (those lines that could be verse or prose). Referring to numerous examples, Freeman discusses how what are often judged to be mistakes in the text, are actually fascinating clues into the emotional lives of the characters.

The text of the Applause Folio, according to Freeman, is 99% intact, with the remaining 1% reflecting changes made for increased clarity. These alterations include correcting obvious mistakes, eliminating some italicized fonts, and changing confusing spelling conventions (such as using "u" for "v" making the word "avoid" appear as "auoid"). These simple changes immediately make the text more "reader friendly", especially for students encountering the *Folio* for the first time.

Alongside each page of the *Folio* are a number of extras to help the reader navigate through the text. Additional stage directions are printed in the margins, often drawn from a quarto version of the play, to help make the action easier to follow. Modern act and scene breaks are included at the foot of each page, as are consecutive page numbers, and as anyone who has used a facsimile of the *Folio* would agree, these are valued improvements.

Shaded text indicates where modern texts have altered the *Folio's* original line structure or have switched from verse to prose or vice versa. Thus, a performer can quickly identify these passages to see what acting clues may be offered—an extremely helpful feature. Endnote markers are placed throughout the text, leading the reader to the extensive endnote section. Here, matters of stage directions, line structure, punctuation, and changes to words and phrases are addressed, each note coded to indicate its topic. Colons and semicolons appear in bold, and when they occur mid-sentence, they are followed by an extra blank space to highlight their importance in sentence structure and to suggest a momentary pause in a character's delivery. The

Mandy Rees teaches acting, voice and movement at California State University, Bakersfield and regularly directs in their theatre season. Her book, *Between Director and Actor: Strategies for Effective Performance*, co-written with John Staniunas, was published in 2002. She has worked with Cornerstone Theater Company, CSU Summer Arts, Madison Repertory Theatre, and the Los Angeles Actors Theatre. She is a former board member of VASTA, and is also active in the Association of Theatre Movement Educators and has served as editor of their Movement Bibliography.

aforementioned tools are the most immediately relevant for students of voice and speech. In addition, Freeman places symbols to note alterations in prefixes and proper names, and significant omissions from the Folio as compared to a quarto. To determine what all these symbols mean takes a little bit of patience and a lot of flipping back and forth between the text and the introduction. A sample page of the *Applause Folio*, with symbols marked and a clear legend, would

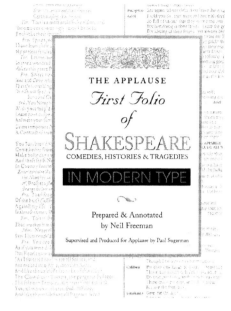

have been helpful. Such a sample page of the *Folio* in its original type is included, illuminating the problems of using that text.

At the back of the book, preceding the endnotes, Freeman includes an introduction to each of the thirty-six plays. Each consists of a brief introduction to the history of the play; a "scholars" assessment of its source manuscript; an account of the compositors who set the *Folio* version; a discussion of issues in "stage management" including errors in act and scene divisions, asides, character prefixes and stage directions; a brief look at inconsistencies of character or plot; a section covering modern "interventions", including the reasoning behind why modern texts have made changes to the *Folio*; and a list of suggested modern texts specific to the play.

This publication represents an enormous amount of effort, care and extreme detail. The readability of the Folio text, combined with the wealth of information available in the margins, the endnotes, and in the introductions to the plays, makes it a significant new resource for both theatre practitioners and scholars.

Book Review *by Cynthia Blaise*
Accent Reduction Workshop for Professional American Speech
by Ginny Kopf

This book, with its three CDs, is designed to help people who wish to change and/or improve the way they speak English. It teaches professional sounding American speech that is devoid of any distinctive regionalism. Individuals who speak English as a second language can find guidance in improving their understanding of the nuances of our difficult and confusing language. English speaking Americans who choose to alter their speech ("upscale" is the expression used by Kopf) or dissipate an existing dialect for professional or personal reasons will also find this book beneficial. The author's overall goal is to help people communicate with greater clarity and, when necessary, lessen a region specific distinction/identification.

Kopf has conducted extensive research regarding the most common and difficult challenges faced by individuals who strive to expand their speaking skills. For instance, ESL speakers struggle with cognate exchanges, identifying stressed syllables, pronunciation rules and learning to acquire entirely new sounds. All of these challenges are addressed in this text. In addition, the book discusses the most common mistakes made by weak public speakers, including volume control, falling inflections, pitch variety, word emphasis, articulatory energy and overall specificity. Exercises designed to dissipate these tendencies are also provided.

Since the way one speaks is intricately entwined with one's identity, changing one's speech patterns may be perceived as diminishing one's culture. The author is sensitive to this potential stigma in speech work, and describes the text's goal as simply to enhance communication. The guide begins with several general and useful tips, such as, "Talk louder!" "Move your mouth more," and my favorite, "Find a skilled and empathetic diction or dialect coach." Excellent advice!

The CD begins with basic warm ups including exercises which address the flexibility of the tongue and releasing the jaw. Listeners are reminded to keep the tone "forward," though unfortunately this term is not defined.

Kopf has divided the workshop into three sections. The first section of the book/CD mainly covers the consonant sounds of spoken English. After warming up the voice and articulators, Kopf continues with exercises for word emphasis that demonstrate a variety of inflection choices. The varying inflections change the meanings of the phrases, demonstrating the value of emphasis as it pertains to interpretation and definition. Kopf discourages "even" rhythm within a phrase as well as in a multi-syllabic word, "…because it is difficult to understand a sentence's meaning if every syllable is stressed equally."

Part One continues with a review of consonant sounds regarded as "major trouble spots" in spoken English. These drills stress medial and final consonants as well as consonant clusters. One of the text's approaches is to demonstrate the difference between sounds by comparing similar and frequently confused sounds.

For example, listeners are taught to make a distinction between the voiced affricates found in the word *judge* and the consonants found in the initial positions of *cheese* and *genre*. Additional cognates are drilled in a similar

Cynthia Blaise is an Associate Professor at University of Illinois at Chicago. She is an actor and director as well as a voice and dialect coach, having coached over a hundred plays in regional theatre and the actor training programs at Temple and Wayne State University. Cynthia is a certified Associate Fitzmaurice voice instructor, an associate editor for IDEA, and she conducts voice workshops for performers at Second City. In film and television, some of her clients include: Hilary Swank, Frances O'Connor, Julia Ormond, Jeremy Northam, Lena Olin, Gabriel Byrne, Ellen Burstyn, Simon Baker, Adrian Brody, Mekhi Phifer, and David Morse.

Accent Reduction Workshop

for Professional American Speech

by
Ginny Kopf

~~~**2nd edition**~~~
2002

Voiceprint Publishing
3639 South Semoran Blvd. PMB 243
Orlando, FL 32822
(407)381-5275

fashion. ESL speakers will find exercises that are ideally suited for their respective challenges. A number of these exercises will serve the needs of many American speakers as well.

Part Two of the book/CD begins by introducing the vowel and diphthong sounds of spoken English as well as what Kopf describes as, "…the neutral American 'r'." Additional drills for vowels are cleverly combined with choosing word emphasis. As demonstrated with the consonants, Kopf compares similar vowel sounds as well as comparing their relative length. The end of Part Two looks at pronunciation as it pertains to syllabic stress. This section includes words that are frequently mispronounced, as well as those words considered particularly challenging.

Part Three addresses common American slang. Kopf discourages and corrects such vernacular as *gonna*, *gimme*, *lemme*, *gotta*, *lotta* and *coupla*. These expressions are placed in the column labeled, "too casual" and the listener is encouraged to try the, "more professional" pronunciation. There is a lesson in the use of secondary stress as well as one comparing the pronunciation of identically spelled nouns and verbs, as in, *present* and *present*. Kopf clearly explains the rules of pronunciation regarding tense as it pertains to "ed" endings, and the distinction between the *S* and *Z* sounds, as they relate to plural and possessive nouns, pronouns and verbs. Also, there are examples of words where no rules apply. Finally, participants are cautioned about the difference between the pronunciation of a final *S* or a *Z* sound, and how it can change the meaning of the word, as in *hers* and *hearse*, *face* and *faze*, and *loose* and *lose*.

Perhaps the most useful and unique contribution made by this author is found on page five and begins with, "If you are originally from:" This section addresses specific speech exercises, in descending order of importance, for people from various cultures. Included are instructions and suggestions for people from seventeen different regions, from Asia to the Middle East to Africa.

Though individual tapes that offer similar guidelines are available, a voice coach will appreciate the convenience of being able to work from one text. Despite the fact that I disagree with the pronunciation of a few words, I feel that this text could save a teacher considerable time researching, analyzing and preparing practice material. For the student, Kopf possesses a soothing tone, her instruction is uncomplicated and her delivery is natural. She is enthusiastic and offers supportive encouragement. The phonetic symbols are simple to identify and the CDs are easy to follow. The consumer receives a great deal of valuable material for the price. It is ideal for students, professionals and anyone else who has a desire to address the way in which they communicate.

Book Review *by Michael J. Barnes*

Voice for Performance
by Linda Gates

As I picked up *Voice for Performance*, I realized that a book of its size (219 pages) would aim to give a condensed overview of voice and speech training–not an entire voice training curriculum. I expected a book that I could easily use with my BA voice and speech class. The back cover explains that Ms. Gates offers a foundation of respiration, vibration, resonation, and articulation with additional information about anatomy, relaxation and alignment, vocal health, and approaching text. This is a book that reaches out to people with no previous background in voice training who want to improve their voices.

Gates begins her book with an examination of relaxation and alignment and offers six basic steps of body alignment which are incredibly clear and very good advice to the reader. She presents several exercises for general relaxation of the body as a whole as well as relaxation and coordination exercises for the lips, tongue, and jaw—incorporating them into a warm-up for relaxation and flexibility. Many of these exercises are good basic practices, though some of the descriptions are slightly confusing. Thus, I fear that untrained readers might miss their benefits due to confusion.

Following the natural progression of vocalization, the book moves into teaching the breathing process and offers good encouragement to the reader for obtaining good breath control. Gates begins by giving descriptions of the various types of breathing and breath support training. Interestingly, she spends more time describing the methods that do not work well for actors (chest breathing and rib breathing) than the methods that do work well for actors (diaphragmatic and composite breathing). As one would expect, this chapter includes exercises for improving breath control. These are easy to follow and should help a person begin developing better breathing skills. Even though Gates stresses in her summary the importance of avoiding over-breathing (p. 38), it seemed her instruction, "Whenever you pause, no matter how short the pause, you should replace the amount of air you just used" (p. 37) could lead an untrained reader to do exactly what she cautions against. Also, sometimes, I think that the reader might better understand the goal of the exercises if their reasoning was given. In an attempt to simplify for the layperson, many times Gates oversimplifies the anatomy and physiology of the respiratory system and muscles so that the anatomical descriptions are not entirely accurate. An example of this is her description of the lungs pushing the diaphragm downward on inhalation, rather than indicating that the diaphragm's musculature contracts to expand the lungs. (p. 6)

Gates uses a simplified version of Edith Skinner's pedagogy for speech training. As this methodology is known by many voice and speech trainers, it is a good foundation upon which teachers can assist students in understanding the process of shaping the voice. I was happy to note that Gates loses much of the prescriptive nature that is found in *Speak With Distinction*. Gates uses jaw opening for teaching the delineation of vowel sounds rather than tongue positioning. This technique will be easier for the untrained actor in learning the vowel sounds. It is also nice to see that Gates explains that the rules for lengthening vowels and diphthongs are helpful for the speakers of English as a second language and not something on which native speakers need to concentrate. All of this is complimented nicely by a plethora of examples for studying the sounds. The highlight of the chapter, by far, is the literary and

Michael J. Barnes is Head of Voice and Speech for the University of Miami BFA Acting Conservatory. Theatres at which he has coached include Shakespeare Santa Cruz, Arena Stage, Denver Center Theatre Company, Wilma Theatre, Pearl Theatre, and Colorado Shakespeare Festival. He coaches for television and has acted professionally in regional theatre. He has an MFA from The National Theatre Conservatory, BFA from the University of Oklahoma, and is a Certified Associate Teacher of Fitzmaurice Voicework. He has taught at Temple University, the University of Delaware and the University of Central Oklahoma. He assists with the instruction of Fitzmaurice Voicework National Training Workshops.

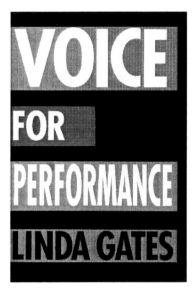

VOICE FOR PERFORMANCE

LINDA GATES

poetry selections for practice. Because of the foundation in Skinner's work, I found several points where the teaching of sound production and transcription do not accurately reflect the current *Handbook of the International Phonetic Association.* Examples of these include the lack of rhoticity on the R-colored diphthongs and the mid vowels /ə/ and /ɜ/, as well as the classification of the consonant /r/ (/ɹ/) as a fricative rather than an approximant. Gates does speak of R-coloring and gives examples of the /ə/ and /ɜ/ symbols; it is also referred to for diphthongs and triphthongs but no rhoticity is indicated on the glyphs. Overall, the descriptions and examples do not aid in understanding any differentiation. This was further confused when speaking of the ability to "color" a consonant /r/ when it comes at the end of a word or it is followed by a consonant.

Gates also offers a chapter for assisting readers with special speech problems. I appreciated her opinions and advice to actors trying to cope with their regionalisms. There are also some nice highlights of the sounds present in regionalisms from the South, New York, the Midwest, and California. Problems that plague many actors are also covered, such as nasality, denasality, a whistling /s/ and a lisp. The exercises for conquering nasality and denasality are particularly helpful, though I found that the exercises to reduce a whistling quality in the /s/ seemed to increase it.

I was particularly taken with the chapter on the usage of microphones in contemporary theatre and its relationship to voice and speech training. This chapter should be required reading for every actor that insists on being miked for productions or feels that problems will be taken care of once s/he is fitted with a microphone. I would love to see this chapter expanded and turned into a full-length article.

As one would expect, this book concludes with a focus on approaching text and shows that Gates has some insightful ideas on the subject. It is unfortunate that she did not go further in demonstrating them. It has a very good breakdown of how stress affects meaning using all of the components of grammar and has some great exercises for understanding the phrasing of subordinate phrases. The discussion of phrasing ends with a list of weak and short forms of words. Unfortunately, many of these are transcribed with pronunciation errors.

Overall, this book could be good for a course dealing with fresh students with no voice training. There are numerous helpful exercises. I would like for Ms. Gates to have spent more time with clarification. This would ensure that the beneficial points of this book reached all its readers. ❧

Making Connections:
Total Body Integration Through Bartinieff Fundamentals
by Peggy Hackney

Peggy Hackney's book, *Making Connections*, is informed by years of experience in movement education including Bartenieff Fundamentals and Laban Movement Analysis. Although her primary audience is dancers, Hackney's approach to the body, stressing a "feeling connection between thoughts" and "moving with intention is the key", is a very useful reference for voice and movement teachers. It would not, however, be an adequate text for a course focusing on movement for actors.

The strength of the book is its concentration on helping the reader achieve higher states of integration through explorations that build kinesthetic bridges across common body polarities (core-distal, head-tail, upper-lower, body-half and cross-lateral). Bartenieff concepts provide the fundamental basis for the explorations, and include focus on breath support, grounding, developmental progression, phrasing, personal uniqueness and expression. Hackney also builds upon Bartenieff's ideas of finding stability within mobility, using clear intent, embodying multifaceted complexity, and studying the relationships of inner vs. outer and exertion vs. recuperation. Thus, with the goal of total body integration, the book moves from fundamentals to explorations of the body's polarities in a series of thoughtfully graduated exercises.

Barbara Sellers-Young is a professor in the Department of Theatre and Dance at the University of California/Davis. Her articles have appeared in *Theatre Topics, Theatre Research International* and elsewhere. Her book *Breath, Exploration, Movement* was published by Applause Press in 2001.

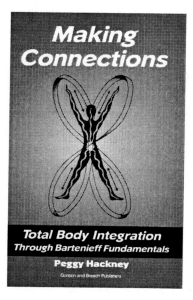

Despite the fact that this text was written more for the movement specialist than the general public, it is highly readable, and within the explanations of the explorations manages to avoid dance related jargon. In fact, the text has moments of true inspiration in relating movement awareness to knowledge. This is particularly true in the initial chapter in which Hackney referencing Bartenieff notes, "Moving and willingness to perceive the movement, brings access to bodily knowledge—particularly the feeling connection between thoughts. Frequently, moving reveals the nature of the relationship between ideas—the pattern of the contexture, or the interweaving of parts." (3) Regardless of the popular position of somatic therapies, the conception of knowledge as residing in the body as well as the mind is still a revolutionary concept. Besides providing some useful approaches to training for performers, Hackney presents us with a challenge to further our understanding of the relationship between movement, consciousness, and the arts.

Singing and the Actor
by Gillyanne Kayes

John Staniunas is an Associate Professor at the University of Kansas and the Artistic Director for the University Theatre in the Department of Theatre and Film. He is a professional director, choreographer and actor and has worked from coast to coast in regional and university theatres. He is the co-author of Between Director and Actor: Strategies for Effective Performance and the associate editor for The Encyclopedia of Stage Plays into Film. His expertise is in Musical Theatre production and scholarship.

Although the cover art for this book is unfortunate, the content is outstanding. The title may also be a bit deceiving as I believe this book is useful for singers as well as actors. I had the distinct pleasure of working with Gillyanne Kayes over a two-day period when she visited the University of Kansas to conduct master classes with our musical theatre students. After her visit, I reread her text and found it to be even more illuminating.

The book attempts to put down in words for the first time the vocal pedagogy of the great Jo Estill. But make no mistake, this work belongs to Kayes. Her writing style is both friendly and straightforward with an occasional touch of humor. She minces no words, speaking her mind about what she believes to be the truth about singing. She dispels the notion that the larynx is a mystical piece of bone that one can only imagine. Instead she has you actually feel it moving up and down in order for you to learn to maneuver it at your own will. This is the first book I know that openly discusses the joy of belting a song and offers clear techniques on how to sing belt both healthfully and properly. The text is broken into three parts, covering first how the voice works, then how actors should train as singers, and finally how actors should work on the text of a song for clarity and emotional content. Each chapter has introductory remarks, awareness exercises, practical exercises and concluding lists.

Kayes hits almost every relevant problem that actors and singers face in audition, rehearsal and performance situations for musical theatre, including projection problems, diction problems, why actors tighten up at auditions, and posture and support problems. The last chapter deals with the actual requirements for performance, and the section on "Creating voice qualities" (speech, falsetto, cry, twang, opera and belt) is especially valuable. If you have a basic understanding of how the singing

Singing
and
The Actor

Gillyanne Kayes

voice works you will find the content easy to follow. Kayes' work is both exciting and rewarding. Having seen her teach her magic, I can guarantee you that her techniques, when done properly, reap amazing results. If your knowledge of singing and voice science is limited, it will take you longer to master the techniques. But this book is worth your time and patience. So go ahead, touch your larynx!

Play Review *by Kate Foy*

Cloudstreet by Nick Enright and Justin Monjo
Directed by Neil Armfield, a Company B, Belvoir Street Production

By any standards, *Cloudstreet* is a play of epic proportions. Based as it is on the celebrated 1991 novel by Tim Winton, playwrights Justin Monjo and the late Nick Enright and their collaborator in the process, director Neil Armfield, wrestled a captivating theatrical work from its 436 pages that has gone on to delight audiences first at home in Australia and, more recently, away. The production, like the novel before it, has won awards at home and abroad for its portrayal of two dysfunctional families thrust together over several decades in a rambling home in suburban Perth, Western Australia. Out of its apparently homely narrative emerges a contemporary myth of national identity and a captivating vehicle for its artists.

The novel has long been a favourite of mine. I've read it conventionally, cover to cover. I rediscover it frequently in the many passages I've lifted for my acting students as class performance pieces—vocal "life" projects—that require brave, passionate characterization and detailed study of nuance in Australian language and dialect. Winton writes rich narrative and intersperses it constantly with dialogue. Some chapters are in fact little "scenes". Small wonder really that I pounced on it when I realized its dramatic potential for my acting students.

I'd always thought that, despite its length, it would make a great full-length play, so when I heard Nick Enright had adapted it for Company B, Belvoir, (one of Sydney's best theatre companies), I was thrilled. Nick was a prolific playwright, acting teacher, and no slouch as an actor himself. The name may be more familiar to you as an Academy Award nominee (with George Miller) for best original screenplay for *Lorenzo's Oil* in 1992.[1]

Company B is under the artistic leadership of Neil Armfield, a director held here in high esteem and with much affection. His original *Cloudstreet* production broke records in Sydney in 1998, playing to more than 15,000. It ended up touring Europe in 2000 winning the Best International Production Award at the Dublin Festival that year. I tried then to get the rights for a production here at University of Southern Queensland, but I knew even before I wrote to Nick that my chances were slim. I didn't really mind when his gracious refusal on the grounds that it would tour nationally and then again internationally this time to the US in 2001 came through.[2]

I caught the Company B production at the final dress rehearsal in Brisbane at the end of July 2001. I was flying out next day to the VASTA conference in Chicago. The Sydney production was being hosted by Queensland Theatre Company shortly before it was to tour to London, Washington and New York. I recall thinking that night what a superb piece of theatre this was and of how colleagues in the US were in for a treat in September. Despite the five hours (with meal break), I didn't want that night to end. It did at 11:35 pm to a standing ovation.

When I first read the novel, I remember that it captured for me the "voice" of Australia through the many, individualised voices of its characters. The Australian voice in the book is that of another time, with its vernacular capturing the spirit of another age. The novel's themes range over identity; it is in large measure about leaving home and finding it. The house that holds both families in Cloud Street is a metaphor for modern Australia. It comes

Kate Foy (stage name Kate Wilson) has been working in professional theatre for 30 years as actor and director with some of Australia's leading performance organizations, including Queensland Theatre Company, New England Theatre Company and the ABC; in the US with Kennedy Theatre in Honolulu. PhD from University of Hawaii: doctoral dissertation researched developments in contemporary Australian theatre. Since 1987, Head of Department of Theatre and head of voice and speech program at the conservatory actor-training program, University of Southern Queensland, Toowoomba. Continues to work as a voice-over artist and has supplied the voice for many corporate and educational videos.

1. Nick succumbed to skin cancer on March 30, 2003, at the age of 52. He is deeply missed by the arts community in Australia.

2. *Cloudstreet* played at BAM Harvey Theatre, New York October 2nd to 7th 2001 and at the Eisenhower Theatre in Washington October 12th through 14th 2001.

"Simply awesome. Cloudstreet is a winner from beginning to end...something native, new, vast and unforgettable." **Sydney Morning Herald, January 1998**

"The audience is hooked into a dialogue that often touches the soul." **The Age, January 1998**

"I don't think I've seen a more enthralling epic since the RSC's Nicholas Nickleby 20 years ago". **The Times, (London), September 1999**

"Cloudstreet is the kind of show that comes along about once a decade to remind us why we keep going to the theatre in the expectation of plenty." **International Herald Tribune, September 1999**

complete with the ghosts of past wrongs done in the house—expressed in shadows on the wall that haunt the children living there. The narrative charts the comings and goings into the world outside the house, noting the couplings, the petty hatreds and loves that bind together the Lambs and the Pickles. On one epic level, it speaks of Australians as a nation. It is also a superb, intimate family history in its own right.

Wyllie (Fish Lamb) and Claire Jones (Rose Pickles). Photo by Heidrun Lohr.

with integrity and credibility. Wyllie's vocal work was quite extraordinary in its range, close observation and consistency. His speech patterns changed across the play, beginning with the quickness and sureness of the clever child. After his return from drowning, the actor's speech was crafted to catch the rhythms and sounds of an intellectually impaired boy. Vocal sound effects by the company of actors joined in with the musical score for cello and piano (performed by Matthew Hoy). One reviewer noted the extraordinary effectiveness in the play's soundscape of the cello in providing a range of sounds from "seagulls to engine revving sounds."[3]

In tone the language of *Cloudstreet* is recognisably Australian. It is ironic, laid back, sparse, and lyrical. Enright and Monjo's adaptation results in dialogue that is as richly sensual as that in the novel. The book tells a great "yarn" along the way using speech registers and dialogue that not only accurately individualise characters, but also set them in another time. The vernacular that peppers the dialogue is the sort of now old-fashioned language that is so resonant of the past—think of the "cobbers" and "crikeys" of the iconic bushmen characters of Australian culture. In the stage version, Enright and Monjo also capture the peculiarly Australian "larrikin" quality (mischievous energy) of the characters in the dialogue. Under Armfield's direction, the staging captured the epic-lyricism and free-flowing structure of the novel via simple, open staging, audience incorporation into action, multiple casting using the 15 actor ensemble, and dream-scapes embodied by the actors and enhanced by sound and light. It is a superb play—hard to imagine its being done better in another production.

The narrator and central figure is a boy-man Fish Lamb (played by Dan Wyllie)—brought back forever altered from drowning as a child, and drawn to water ever since. The land of the living is figured as hot, harsh and dry—like Australia itself, and Fish, our moral touchstone observes and inhabits this world with affection and tolerance, but he is always drawn away to the cool, wet world he knew so briefly. He is reconciled to it at the end of the novel/play in the midst of a joyous family reunion.

Wyllie's performance was a standout in a production where every performance—often of multiple characters—in the 15-person ensemble was signal. In playing Fish the actor needed to meet the challenge of playing a brain-damaged boy-man

Like all great theatre experiences, *Cloudstreet* touches individuals on several levels. On the one hand there is the exhilaration of a five-hour theatrical tour de force sweeping everyone along—on the other, a profound engagement with the play's themes of home and belonging. Its collective impact on the audience was exponential, and we left the theatre entranced on that and on successive nights. The Brisbane season went on to be a sell-out for Queensland Theatre Company, and the production went on its planned tour to the UK and US shortly afterwards. That touring production was playing in London on September 11, and director Neil Armfield assured audiences that the events of that day would not prevent Company B Belvoir's taking the play to BAM in New York and the Kennedy Center in DC. He expressed the belief that the play's "life-giving quality and themes of togetherness and sense of place and belonging would resonate more strongly than ever with American audiences."[4]

Later amongst the many terrible television images out of New York city, the optimism and love that marks the production spilled out into a simple, silent gathering of the *Cloudstreet* company in a sidewalk memorial to the September 11 victims.
❧

3. William Hatherall. "Cloudstreet: A Certified National Treasure" M/C *Reviews* 6 Aug. 2001. (22.10.02)
http://www.,media-culture.org.au/reviews/events/cloudstreet.html

4. Elyse Sommer review *Curtain Up* October 7, 2001
http://www.curtainup.com/cloudstreet.html

Two Play Reviews and Interviews with the Vocal Coaches *by Claudia Anderson*
***Love's Labors Lost* by William Shakespeare, coached by Linda Gates**
***Phaedra,* by Jean Racine, coached by Eric Armstrong**

Love's Labor's Lost
Chicago Shakespeare Company
Director, Barbara Gaines
Vocal Coach, Linda Gates
First preview, Sept. 6, 2002

Claudia Anderson is on the voice and speech faculty at DePaul University's Theatre School. She coaches dialects professionally in the Chicago theatre community. This year, she coached *The Dead* for the Court Theatre and *Entertaining Mr. Sloane* for Next Theatre. This winter, she's directing *Book of Days* at the Theatre School.

I came to Chicago Shakespeare Company's production of *Love's Labors Lost* with two objectives. The first was to enjoy it on its own merits. This proved an easy task since the casting, production values, and director Barbara Gaines' approach were all of high quality. My second objective was to identify those issues I that captured my interest as a vocal coach and a trainer of actors' voices.

The verbal action in the play was very clear. The audience was caught up, engaged in the action and also following very closely the arguments and the comic wordplay. I was able to easily hear and understand almost every line. The actors spoke the text at a good pace—they neither seemed to be rushing or plodding. Almost every actor seemed to be confident in the use of him or herself, using the text rather than departing from it. Vocal coach Linda Gates had told me that Gaines was very good about getting the actors to bring themselves to their roles, and I could hear evidence of that in the vocal confidence and freedom in the actors, particularly the men. The text was very easy to hear, except in those few instances when an actor turned his back on the audience. The audience seemed to be fully engaged and appreciative of the wordplay, even in complex scenes. Occasionally it seemed that the audience would be searching for the punch line so that they could respond, and so they may have missed a deeper or subtler point, but they clearly wanted to stay with the actors.

The quartet of young men—Navarre (Timothy Edward Kane,) Longsville (Jay Whittaker,) Dumaine (Krishna La Fan) and Berowne (Timothy Gregory)—seemed to be cast partially for their differing and complementary vocal qualities. They sounded almost like a singing quartet of tenors and baritones. Their qualities seemed genuine and truthful, and served to make each character distinctive. From the perspective of this vocal coach, all four of them could release the backs of their tongues more, for the tension affected their delivery of the text. In Navarre, the tension in his jaw and tongue seemed to limit his range of expression including his pitch range. Berowne sometimes lifted his shoulders for breath, then held his breath, then spoke. Longsville and Dumaine had an overbalance of nasal resonance in the vowels.

Berowne was very much in the moment in his monologues, working through the text by living through each word. When speaking of love, he often became breathy, or went "off his voice" rather than becoming more released or more connected to his voice in those moments. Emotion seemed to take him into himself rather than making him more expressive.

The four young women—Princess of France (Karen Aldridge,) Maria (Hollis McCarthy,) Katharine (Michele Graff) and Rosaline (Kate Fry)—were not as well matched as the men. The Princess spoke without much vocal confidence, although she had fine physical presence. She didn't carry energy through to the ends of her lines, and lacked energy in her consonants. Rosaline enjoyed

Love's Labor's Lost: Tim Gregory (Berowne) and Kate Fry (Rosaline). Photo by Liz Lauren

or relished the language much more, and in contrast seemed to be self-conscious in her speaking in comparison to others. The other two women, Maria and Katharine, were not as well differentiated in their approach and seemed to fade into the background.

Costard (Ross Lehman) spoke with the most ease and vocal color, and every word was clear. He used his body to point up the language, fully embodying the text. Moth (Chris Herzberger) used mask resonance to reinforce his voice, and although his tongue tension colored his vowels, his voice was clear. Constable Dull (Bradley Mott) spoke within a small pitch range—almost in a monotone—a distinctive character choice.

In general, there seemed to be some distinction among accents, without drawing attention to accent in the production. The higher-class characters used more open vowels, and generally fewer "flat" Chicago vowels. The lower class comic characters seemed to use the flat sounding vowels for comic effect. An example was Constable Dull's flattening the vowel in "not" to a vowel closer to that in "cat." Don Adriano (Scott Jaeck) used an accent that reminded me of Saturday Night Live's "wild and crazy guys" accent and he seemed to be playing the part of a foreigner speaking a language not his own. The audience appreciated his choices, his timing and the way he handled the language. Old Nathaniel (Bernie Landis) was hard to understand because his voice was not released forward, so his articulators didn't shape it. Jaquennetta (Luisa Strus) spoke with a very husky voice, sounding like someone who had trashed her voice with smoking and drinking. It added to her characterization as a loose, appealing woman suited to Don Adriano. Her voice sounded to me like an actor with an abused voice, but the audience seemed to appreciate her vocal characterization.

Two Play Reviews and Interviews with the Vocal Coaches by Claudia Anderson
Love's Labors Lost *by William Shakespeare, coached by Linda Gates*
Phaedra, *by Jean Racine, coached by Eric Armstrong* (continued)

This production was the first of *Love's Labors Lost* by the Chicago Shakespeare Theatre and drew a lot of attention. It was a wonderful banquet of sight and sound for me to observe from the perspective of the vocal coach.

Interview with Vocal Coach Linda Gates

Linda and I talked in the Chicago Shakespeare Theatre lobby an hour and a half before the first preview. As I began the interview, an actor came up to us and talked to Linda. I incorporated him into the interview.

Chris Herzberger (Moth): I missed the voice class…
LG: Voice warm-ups are not a substitute for actual vocal technique. A lot of people don't know the difference or it's not ever been connected to their acting. But you had a real good session last class and you're amazing. You picked that up right away.

CA: What did you pick up right away?
Chris: I was taking all the ends of my lines down, which just makes it boring, I guess. And I wasn't doing anything with the antithesis; I didn't even know what the word meant. But immediately in rehearsal, the first time we were going to run it, Barbara said, "What happened? That's amazing." And I said, " I worked with Linda and she just helped me take the lines all up and make them sound more interesting."
LG: What we really worked on was lifting the stressed syllable in pitch. It's a big problem with actors, and not just with American actors. All my notes fly away if you do that. It seems like a huge leap to get it up, but you did it; I was really pleased.
Chris: It felt much better too. I'm still in high school and I've never done Shakespeare before, so I didn't know anything about how you're supposed to talk. I expected actually, when they said you're having voice class, I expected you were coming in and we'd be working on the songs in the show. I was shocked to find out what it really was.

CA: (to Linda) How did you approach this project?
LG: I've known Barbara Gaines for years, since when I first came to Chicago as an actor. Barbara had started Chicago Shakespeare and I took one of her workshops. I had previously studied with Edith Skinner, actually more with Margaret Pendergast McClean. She was a marvelous teacher and had more influence on me certainly than Edith. I was not one of Edith's favorites. We didn't have difficulty really; I just never quite understood what her approach was all about. Whereas with Margaret Pendergast McClean, I really did. Do you know who she was? She was Edith's teacher. Her book *Good American Speech* is a wonderful book. I had worked with many different approaches to Shakespeare. Most of the emphasis was on iambic pentameter and all of that. And it seemed to me there was always too much emphasis on the endless counting

of iambic pentameter. I think that's ridiculous. It was made so complicated. But in Barbara's workshop she used the Folio, which I had never worked with. It was for me a kind of revelation. Not so much the Folio. I personally don't use the Folio because there are so many errors in it, and I like to take advantage of the editors. But she made a very good argument for using the Folio. What she emphasized to us was to use the antithesis, the operative words, and the alliteration—all of the elements that were a part of the Folio and I thought that made great sense. I saw that her productions were very clear, very well spoken because the actors really paid attention to the text. And since then I followed her work; she is also an adjunct faculty member at Northwestern. So we've known each other but we've never worked together until this show. Kristine Thatcher was Chicago Shakespeare's vocal coach before this, and Kate Buckley was usually their verse coach, and neither of them were here. So what happened was, the week I was leaving for Europe, Barbara asked me to coach *Love's Labors Lost*. And I said I'd love to, but I wasn't getting back until after rehearsals had started and she said she didn't feel that was a problem. Usually the way I work is that I'm part of the whole team, and that first week is so crucial. So I came in and did voice classes.

CA: About how many voice classes did you do?
LG: I did about eight. But again, they don't know me. So it's new. And a lot of what I do is different from—

CA: —from what they're used to.
LG: There are used to a Linklater approach. And I have worked with Kristin Linklater and I know her work really well. I think there's a point you have to get up off the floor. And this is one of them. I don't think that's very productive after a while. I like to work with the piano. The actors' breathing—I thought that they hadn't really connected to their breath. They were exhaling on the line. We worked with that and they were really responsive. I think this is the first time Barbara's directed *Love's Labors Lost* and we've never worked together, and she is used to have Kate Buckley as text coach, so I feel that we've all been flying by the seat of our pants to see how this works. I think Barbara relies on Kate and has not had Kate, and then I stepped in and did what I could. I feel like I've helped here and there and I think they trust me.

CA: You're starting to build a relationship.
LG: That's it, so in the process I didn't want to say anything that would make them feel like I'm critical or that I'm not supportive.

CA: I'm hearing you and I think it's clear where Barbara and you are with this. It's interesting for me to hear this, and then go on to see the show.
LG: You need to build a working relationship. I feel that I have been very influenced by Barbara and it's interesting to

now be able to see how she really works. I hope it's an ongoing relationship. I would like to feel a company aesthetic.

CA: That's so rewarding, isn't it? To have a company that you're working with, like you are with Remy Bumpo Theatre Company.
LG: I think James Bowman is such a gifted director. He's the kind of director I think I am, in a way. He is so text-based. You take a play like *Secret Rapture.* It's very interesting working on this play with James, because the table work goes on for maybe ten days. He takes every line and asks, "What does he mean by that?" And we all are part of the discussion and part of the team. I really have a close relationship with him and with the company.

CA: Wouldn't that be great if you started to have that kind of relationship with Chicago Shakespeare, because a Shakespeare company needs someone like you.
LG: Yes, it will be interesting.

Phaedre
Court Theatre
Joanne Akalitis, director
Eric Armstrong, vocal coach
September 22, 2002

I was interested in comparing two Chicago productions of classic plays, so Court Theatre's production of *Phaedre* was a natural choice. And like the Chicago Shakespeare Company, the Court Theatre is one of few companies in the area to employ a vocal coach.

The play was clearly a tour de force for Jenny Bacon as Phaedre. She is an actor of tremendous physical and vocal skill and imagination. Her Phaedre was insanely obsessed with her love for Hippolytus, and it was clear from the moment she appeared that the single focus would be her tragic undoing. Jenny Bacon used screams, throaty gasps, whines, moans, whispers, shouts—usually abruptly shifting moment to moment, thought to thought. At times the abruptness was frightening, sometimes humorous in its honesty. She almost appeared to have multiple personalities.

All of the other characters were very controlled by contrast. There were only seven actors in the cast, and yet the play had size physically and vocally. The staging placed actors at a distance, even in intimate moments, and the actors filled the space emotionally, physically and vocally.

Every word of the play was crystal-clear and ringing, except for one moment when Jenny intended to speak at breakneck tempo. All of the speaking seemed very deliberate with much consonant energy and clear vowel definition, and the speaking seemed to call attention to itself when occasionally paired with an unvarying tempo or pitch. I had the sense that the "sane" actors were meant to contrast Phaedre in their speech by being more contained than she. Theseus (Jim Krag) seemed to be forcing his voice low, pushing for a large-sounding voice. The choice made him appear smaller rather than larger.

"Mudras" were used by all of the actors onstage to emphasize key words. The theatrical convention of stopping the action for these gestures was riveting, and gave weight to specific moments.

Theseus and Phaedre spoke French in emotional moments. Clearly there was a deeper dimension conveyed in those moments—an insight inside the characters. Phaedre's French-speaking reminded me of a person for whom French was her first language or a childhood language, which she retreated to when deeply affected.

Photo of Jenny Bacon as Phaedre by Michael Brosilow

Two Play Reviews and Interviews with the Vocal Coaches by Claudia Anderson
Love's Labors Lost *by William Shakespeare, coached by Linda Gates*
Phaedra, *by Jean Racine, coached by Eric Armstrong* (continued)

The play was only 85 minutes long; the deaths occurred so quickly and all of the messages of death were conveyed clearly and simply. I was struck with how well the production was shaped and the strength of the director's choices.

Interview with Vocal Coach Eric Armstrong
Eric and I talked about his work in *Phaedre* a few days after I saw the show. I met him at his office at Roosevelt University and we went for coffee.

CA: What did you get to do for *Phaedre*?
EA: They called me up because I had done dialect and vocal coaching and led some warm-ups for *Mary Stuart*, and Joanne Akalitis, who had directed that—she said she wanted me back to do warm-ups. In the process of the conversation they said do you happen to speak French, and it just happens that I did half of my schooling in French, in Ottawa in Canada. I had always had an ear for French language as a result of that. So they brought me on board to do the French language coaching primarily, and the warm-ups. I think I ended up doing five warm-ups, so not a lot of vocal work.

CA: With the whole cast?
EA: The whole cast. Some of who were extremely excited to be doing it. I think they felt it was a luxury that they got to have class, and Joanne Akalitis really doesn't like to rehearse very much. About halfway through the rehearsal process she said, "Well, I'm not really too sure what we're going to do for the remaining two weeks." I mean the play is short—85 minutes or something like that—and she has this method where she doesn't block until really late, and until then the actors wander around onstage. It's mostly about shaping the script.

CA: Table work kinds of things?
EA: No, they do it on their feet. She expects a lot of actors in terms of memory work, because she needs them to be off-book very early, and then she cuts half their lines after they've memorized them. And not in one go. One day she'll say, "That line's gone," and then the next day, "This line's gone." And it's not just cutting; she puts stuff back in. And rewrites stuff. Hugely challenging for the actors. So I have huge respect for those actors' skill level in terms of memory work.

CA: Did you coach the speech of the entire production?
EA: Well, I gave some notes on audibility in speech to the actors, the whole company, at the end, when we were at the run stage. Most of them were intelligibility notes about tempo, and the scale at which they were playing things. I often was giving Jenny notes about screaming and going so fast that people couldn't understand. And sometimes she'd give me a look that said, "that's an artistic choice, shut your mouth."

CA: I remember at least one moment, where that was an artistic choice, where as I was listening I was thinking, she does not intend me to get this.
Eric There's a passage that she played at a hundred miles an hour. She's a very aware, very skilled actor. She loves the emotional extremes, so this show was perfect for her. She took it further than I could have imagined it. She played it constantly on the edge and had great delight in flipping back and forward. But I had to give her notes on occasion, that "you're distorting that line so much I cannot understand it, and I think your goal is to be understood there." Jenny was very good about taking those notes but you could tell it was a battle for her. She would then work it to find how far she could go without it being lost.

CA: It was a very small-cast show, with a Greek largeness. It seemed like the space was supposed to be defining some of the size. People were not three feet from each other having speeches. They were almost always in some kind of diagonal, as far as possible from one another.
EA: I really liked that about Joanne's blocking; she forces the actors to reach each other with their voices and fill the space. And there is size for those big emotions. And when Jenny was flipping out and throwing herself around the stage, she's not in everybody's lap, there's space around her. The most intimate scene is where she's asking him to kill her, and Jenny played that at full stretch. She was in a lunge—imagine somebody doing a fencing lunge, the greatest fencing lunge you could do—to reach Theseus, because that's how far away he was from her, and he'd step back so he was right on the edge of the platform. And he was hugely expanded and yet it seemed like they were in each other's laps because that's how they played it, like we were right in each other's laps. That's something I wish my students would take in—that you can find intimacy within a large space.

CA: One of the things in relationship to the space and the intention that the director had, it seemed to me that what I'm calling that deliberateness of speech, it seemed like that was related to that. That gave it size.
EA: Absolutely. And it also relates to the physical mudras that she used. It comes from south Asian. I think it's like Balinese dance. On key words they do these physical actions.

CA: Who decided what those were?
EA: She did. Sometimes the company did. She'd say, "Well what's the mudra for that?" And the actors would come up with one. One time the actor was going, "If I have to think of another mudra, I'm going to shoot myself in the head, and she had her finger to her temple. And Joanne went, "That's it, perfect." I don't know if there was some, whether Joanne was being funny about that or if she was just clueless, but we'll never know with Joanne because she has the world's driest sense of humor, you'd never know she was making a joke, she's so serious about everything.

CA: The mudras were so deliberate and they slowed everything down for a moment, so it made sense that then words had weight, and the only time words had lighter weight was when someone chose to do so. But mostly the tempo was set and even; maybe this was to contrast Jenny Bacon. If everybody is fixed, she seems more crazy within that. Can you talk about the use of French in the production?

EA: The idea was that the French would pop out at the introspective moments, that the characters would drop back to their core French. Jenny had spoken some French in high school. Jim Krag never had spoken a word of French in his life. We had to do it syllable by syllable with every single word. I recorded it for Jim several times and we would go through it. When we first worked, I got a desperate call from Joanne, "This isn't going to work, he can't do it." And I said, "You know you can't expect him to learn how to speak French overnight. I don't know how good his ear is, but I suspect it's not perfect. But I think he deserves at least a weekend to rehearse." So I felt really good being an advocate for actors, which I think so often is what our job is, to give them a little bit of backing so they can do their work. I said, "There may be things we need to cut because it's too hard to say," and she said, "Well that's good to know." I said, "If he doesn't get it, feel free to cut it. I don't think he'll take it personally, but he will take it personally if you cut it before he has a chance to fix it." So she warned him of that, and that was the biggest kick in the pants. "Fix it or I'm going to cut it." That meant he worked his ass off to get it. So the next time I saw him, he had worked very hard on it. We found the phrase "au jour d'hui" was impossible for him. Too many sounds lined up in a row. So that line was cut and replaced with a shorter expression. And it was interesting because having spoken French since I was four years old, I don't realize how my mouth goes to all those sounds so easily, and having to teach someone to make those vowels is more challenging than I thought it was. The only way I could actually figure out some of the words was to say them and find out what my mouth was doing.

CA: So when you say the words "au jour d'hui" the middle thing there...

EA: There's a trilled r, that's not fully realized. Luckily he could do a uvular trill, but the problem is, like in English, there are chronological things happening. Yes there is a trill there, but because of the context, because it's going into a voiceless consonant afterwards, it's voiceless. You have to find a way to silently roll your r. And most French speakers wouldn't even know they were doing that. I didn't even know I was doing that, except my ear is tuned to hear it, and because it's a foreign language to me even, I had a little more distance from it. I could notice. With "au jour d'hui" we cut it into ten phonemes and that's why he couldn't get it. We had to break every word down to its smallest possible unit, and then reassemble those into packages. He was just getting the pronunciation, and I was saying, "You have to use the words, you have to stretch them out—you have to act them." And ultimately the artistic director came to me and said, "I don't know if you're responsible for this, but he's actually more emotionally connected during the French than he is on English." And I had said to Jenny and Jim, and I think this was the best part of my whole job, this is where they earned my money for me, I said, "You have to switch into French and then back into English, and there has to be something that the audience sees that says you're about to change and you're about to change back. It's an internalization of—I need to speak French, I need to speak English. It's like a code shift, and you have to internalize that to the extent that the audience can see that." And both actors, it was like a huge light bulb went over their heads when I told them that.

CA: You gave them permission to make something clear.
EA: I think that's what I enjoy most about my job, is finding ways to help actors act a dialect or act French language, rather than "here are the rules, follow them."

CA: Did you talk anything about where to find it in their bodies? Did you talk about it physically?
EA: I didn't. Maybe because I don't work that way personally. I don't know where French lives in my body. And maybe I'm just not that kind of kinesthetic person.

CA: But somehow you stimulated them to find it.
EA: Yeah. And I got the sense that they were physical actors. The way they were working with me just sitting around with the tape recorder was physical. And when I was teaching them the sounds it was always about physically what was happening in the mouth. I never just do, "Make this sound, copy me." It's, "Open your mouth more, pull your tongue back more." It's always very kinesthetic. We did talk a little bit about placement. Jenny already has placement, so I didn't have to worry about that, but for Jim we had say, "This is going to live further back and there's more awareness of your lips."

❦

Two Play Reviews *by Judylee Vivier*

Comparison Review of Two Productions of Hamlet produced by the Brooklyn Academy of Music

The Tragedy of Hamlet, written by William Shakespeare
Adapted and Directed by Peter Brook
BAM—The Harvey Theater
April 26, 2001
The Royal National Theatre production of *Hamlet*, by William Shakespeare
Directed by John Caird
Vocal Coach, Patsy Rodenburg
BAM—The Gilman Opera House
June 2, 2001

Theater artists, generation after generation, keep returning to the mystery of Shakespeare's *Hamlet*, "to hold, as t'were, the mirror up to nature," seeking a truth and reflection of their own age. It is not surprising then, that the new millennium has witnessed a whole spate of *Hamlet* productions on both the stage and film. Within a month, two important productions of *Hamlet* were seen at The Brooklyn Academy of Music in New York: one adapted and directed by Peter Brook, and the other from London's Royal National Theatre, directed by John Caird.

Judylee Vivier, assistant professor and director of the MFA acting program at Brooklyn College, CUNY, is a former Fulbright Scholar who came to the US from South Africa to pursue an MFA at New York University, Tisch School of the Arts. She also holds an MA from the University of Natal, Durban, South Africa. Vivier specializes in teaching acting and voice production for actors. Her acting credits include Lydia in the film *Fugard's People,* a collaborative effort with Athol Fugard, and she is currently working on a solo performance piece, based on her experiences growing up in South Africa. She is also Conference Director for VASTA.

Originally performed in English for a French audience, the text of Brook's production of *Hamlet* was condensed and rearranged with the intent to transcend cultural barriers. The adaptation runs approximately two and a half hours without interruption. True to Brook's notion of stripping theater to its barest essentials, this production bears many of Brook's classic features: an essentially empty stage (save a bright orange carpet, smaller rugs with cushion, ottomans and shawls that are reassembled into different scene-setting configurations), Eastern music that accentuates mood, a multinational ensemble of eight actors who play thirteen characters, and an emphasis on the lively inventiveness and flexibility of actors who bring the text alive by means of their bodies and voices. Brook says his goal in adapting this text is to challenge the tendency to make a false god of the text, and "to penetrate what is behind the text, what the author ...[is] truly trying to say ...to make something from the past live in the present—*representing...*" the play to make audiences see a new play: essentially the personal tragedy of a boy forced to grow up too quickly, to take revenge, and learn to kill or be killed.

It is a vigorous, highly dramatic, accessible, entertaining, but not very illuminating or surprising piece. The environment in which these characters find themselves, i.e., the Peter Brook vision, dominates. It is as if the idea or concept of the production is larger than the story, the thoughts or the discoveries of the characters—making the performers appear immaterial, incorporeal, inconsequential, in comparison and not very sympathetic. The sense is certainly there, but not the sensibility. Ultimately Brook's stylistic elements cause the piece to become mythic and ceremonial, distancing the audience rather than compelling them.

The ethnically mixed ensemble provides a universal quality to the production. Natasha Parry (Gertrude), Adrian Lester (Hamlet), Scott Handy (Horatio) are English actors. The other five performers hail from various parts of Asia; they speak the Received Pronunciation with hints of their native Eastern sounds, which serve to emphasize the mood-defining Eastern score composed and performed by Toshi Tsuchitori. Adrian Lester, who was last seen in New York playing Rosalind in The Cheek by Jowl Company's production of *As You Like It* some years ago, plays Hamlet with intense energy, intelligence and self-assured arrogance; he is a mischievous, dreadlocked, adolescent Hamlet who needs to be brought down a peg or two. When he counterfeits madness, he speaks in the voice of the "nerd" and the demon, he barks like a dog, and his soliloquies overflow with literal gestures, which are superficially amusing but impose on the text. He is enchanting but seldom emotionally gripping.

The story is largely told through gesture and wildly expressive and inventive physicality rather than through the sounds, textures and meanings of the words in the text. The performers literally scamper around the stage, which is interesting to watch but distracts from the listening to, and hearing of the text. Perhaps this is a consequence of performing in a different language from that of the original audience; when the performers are speaking the language of the audience, the text becomes too literal, superficial and indicative of being "acted out."

Although the RNT production of *Hamlet* is trimmed and also focuses on the domestic tragedy of Hamlet (Fortinbras has been cut in both these productions), it is a more traditional and fully realized interpretation of the play and runs approximately three and a half hours. Simon Russell Beale, who plays Hamlet, is conceived as the student prince who yearns to return to his natural environment, the university. However, Beale does not embody the conventional idea of Hamlet—he is short, stocky and forty—but his performance is unique and memorable. His journey (and the set designed by Tim Hartley, is literally comprised of luggage that is assembled and broken apart to create various scene-settings) is one that takes him into the reality of loss, which he has previously encountered only in abstraction.

The Tragedy of Hamlet by William Shakespeare. Adapted and directed by Peter Brook. Adrian Lester (Hamlet). Photo: P. Victor. With permission from BAM Communications.

This production is deeply affecting emotionally. For John Caird, the director, the play is about love

destroyed but he places the characters above the concept at all times. The actors are not contorted into unnatural poses for thematic purposes, and the characters have been allowed the time to discover and establish their motives through the text, through the words, the thoughts behind the words, and the structure of the thoughts, language and verse. Consequently the play unfolds with the experience of each word that contributes to a whole thought in the text, and never does the play appear sluggish. I think much

The Tragedy of Hamlet by William Shakespeare. Adapted and directed by Peter Brook. Adrian Lester (Hamlet); Natasha Parry (Gertrude). Photo: P. Victor. With permission from BAM Communications.

credit for this feat needs to go to Patsy Rodenburg, who is responsible for the voice work of the company. Peter Brook's Hamlet seems constantly trying to catch his breath as the action hurtles forward. Hamlet's vulnerability in the RNT production is emphasized constantly by his "in the moment" discovery of his relationship to himself, to the people around him, and to the harsh world in which he finds himself. There is no resorting to vocal tricks that impose on and distort the text in favor of a directorial concept or a specific acting choice. Hamlet is grief-stricken, overcome by his loss and sudden intimate exposure to death, and therefore he is vulnerable, open, and present in the text. The soliloquies never separate from the action, but flow with the action, and are moments of immediate and intense discovery for both Hamlet and the audience. This Hamlet is fascinated with "words, words, words"; they are all he has left. This Hamlet delights and finds comfort in an elegant phrase, writing in the journal he keeps in his pocket, until the metaphor behind the words jerk him into painful awareness of the truth as he moves towards reality. He registers every moment of that pain, because his Hamlet remains open to hope. His interactions with both Gertrude and Ophelia are tender as he reaches out and attempts to connect with kindred spirits. It is when he realizes that he has been betrayed, that this sweet prince retreats into imposed madness with a new viciousness as he is forced to learn to take revenge.

Two Play Reviews by Judylee Vivier
Comparison Reviews of Two Productions of Hamlet
Produced by the Brooklyn Academy of Music (continued)

Hamlet (Royal National Theatre) by William Shakespeare Directed by John Caird. Denis Quillery (Gravedigger); Simon Russell Beale (Hamlet). Photo: Catherine Ashmore

The Gilman Opera House did not successfully support the vocal production of this company. The acoustics were poor and the actors' voices, with subtle emotional nuances and tremendous dynamic range and resonance, were lost in the huge space. At intermission, I heard audience members complaining about the actors' lack of projection, which really annoyed me. Although I am disdainful of the use of microphones for trained stage actors, it is sometimes a necessary evil when auditoriums used for huge operas and spectacles, are technically ill-equipped to deal with the spoken human voice. I believe the rhythm of the quick, articulated, crisp Received Pronunciation added to the confusion of the predominantly New York audience.

In contrast, the Harvey Theater where the Brook *Hamlet* played was an acoustic marvel; the wood, soft plaster and steep circular shape of the auditorium nurtured the human voices; quiet whispers resonated easily in the "gods."

It was a truly inspiring and stimulating experience to see each of these productions, which offer so much richness from very different perspectives. In terms of dramatic structure both of these approaches chose to eliminate Fortinbras completely, forsaking the political for the metaphysical world of Hamlet. Neither of the plays adopted the Oedipal interpretation popular in the past century; neither of these Hamlets is mad. Lester may be literal and unpredictable, Beale may be figurative and ironic, but both are clear-headed, charismatic, capable of action, hampered by grief, despair, but never by inertia.

Selected Thesis and Dissertation Abstracts

Edited by Mandy Rees, Associate Editor

Editor's Note:
The following abstracts are provided as a service to help researchers and interested readers stay abreast of current thesis and dissertation work in the field of voice and speech. The papers themselves have not been read or vetted by the Journal editors. Material submitted to this department may be edited for space and style.

Title: **A small-scale study of the teaching and learning issues involved in coaching an accent, using the Belfast accent as an example.**
Author: Peter Ballance
Type: MA Voice Studies
Year: 2001
Institution: Central School of Speech and Drama
Faculty advisor: David Carey

This project is a sequence of my discoveries. It is a reflection of the processes and difficulties that I encountered when teaching the Belfast accent to students of acting and to professional actors. I have in no way attempted to derive a definitive approach to accent coaching. What I have attempted to cover is a method of teaching myself about what it means to be an accent coach, in the hope that it might allow me to experiment with, and, sometimes fail to grasp my ideas of what a 'good' (Belfast) accent is.

The core of the project is my assumption, *that knowing how to do an accent and what it sounds like as opposed to teaching that accent are two completely different things.*

We learn on many different levels: visually, aurally and for some, through pure effort and determination. I wanted to meet as many different types of learners as I could in the time available. It was and is a journey. There is not a lot available for the accent coach (ironically, there is a wealth of information for the student) to use and so, this is a process of trial and error.

I thought that it would be appropriate to evaluate the two most common methods of teaching an accent, i.e. phonetic transcription versus listen and repeat and measure my success at both. I discovered that success as an accent coach is interminably difficult to measure. The stakes for both parties vary from project to project.

This project therefore falls into a no-mans land of accent coaching. There is not a narrow transcription of the Belfast accent (the accent is irrelevant) nor a path of successful steps that will make an actor absorb an accent simply through repetition alone.

My conclusions deduct five major areas in which I will construct my teaching strategies from now on and I hope to further refine those issues in the future.

Title: **Searching for a More Holistic Approach to Accent Learning**
Author: Jane Beckmann
Type: MA Voice Studies
Year: November 2001
Institution: Central School of Speech and Drama
Faculty advisor: David Carey

My original aim was to find a system for teaching accents that used as many teaching modalities as possible and would make the process more holistic. I wanted to make accent learning more accessible to those students who were not natural mimics and who had difficulty relating to the IPA phonetic changes.

During my action research I found that I was being too ambitious for this length of study. I then focused my work down to searching for a way of teaching accents that included movement in the same way as all other aspects of voice work.

I felt the nature of accent learning was too academic and that the use of movement might free up the process and make it more accessible. I have researched the methods used for teaching accents and the benefits of using movement in all aspects of learning.

I experimented with other titles such as "searching for a psycho-physical approach to accent learning" but decided that "Holistic" was indeed the word that best described what I am searching for in this study.

Title: **Voice and Anxiety: The Importance of Anxiety Management in a Theatrical Voice Classroom**
Author: Rebecca Bossen
Type: MA Thesis
Year: December 2002
Institution: Northwestern University
Faculty Advisor: Linda Gates

Anxiety has a profound negative effect on the voice. Performance, both onstage and in the classroom, inherently contains an element of anxiety-provoking stress. Because anxiety inhibits both vocal production and learning ability, voice teachers must find ways to help students manage anxiety in the classroom. The concept of hardiness, a term used in psychology to denote the quality of being able to cope with stress without falling ill, can be applied to the construction of an anxiety-managed environment. The main principles are a commitment to self and community, a sense of an internal locus of control, and a perception of change as challenge rather than threat. A classroom with these principles at its foundation will be more likely to produce proficient, self-reliant voice users.

Title: **Voice Qualities in Women's Voices Today: 1. What qualities are considered "desirable" in contemporary women's voices working in theatre and the media? 2. How can the voice practitioner help achieve these safely?**
Author: Mel Churcher
Type: MA Voice Studies
Year: October 2000
Institution: Central School of Speech and Drama
Faculty advisor: David Carey
This dissertation investigates what spoken voice qualities are demanded of women working in theatre and the media today —both by the performers themselves, their directors and the dictates of the wider social environment. It then attempts, by means of literature research, interviews, questionnaires and working sessions to identify key exercises that might help to achieve those needs in a healthful manner and to find ways to benefit the voice practitioner's practice. Action research is chosen as the most appropriate way to conduct the study.

The concept of voice quality is explored and put into a historical and gender framework. Definitions of voice quality are discussed and an attempt is made to reach a shared terminology. The role of the voice teacher, both past and present, is looked at and how being a reflective practitioner can help with the work.

Extensive literary searches are made into key areas of voice: vocal fold function, pitch, resonance, posture, the breathing mechanism, onset of tone, "support" and "centre", the link between thought, breath and voice and text work.

Four female actors took part in the study that involved a semi-structured interview and a questionnaire. Four directors were also interviewed—two men and two women—about their needs and views on voice qualities. The four participants of the action research project were then given three working sessions with feedback documented throughout. At the end of the sessions they were interviewed again to see if they felt there had been any changes and which exercises they felt had helped. Finally, four voice practitioners were sent extracts from these sessions and asked to record their instinctive reactions. Participants and practitioners noted some progress in key areas such as confidence, pitch and resonance.

Title: **Speaking Shakespeare's Late Plays**
Author: Rebecca Clark

Type: MA Voice Studies
Year: October 2001
Institution: Central School of Speech and Drama
Faculty advisor: David Carey
This dissertation, *Speaking Shakespeare's Late Plays*, asks how the voice and text coach can help actors meet the challenges posed by the language of Shakespeare's late plays. Specifically it investigates three Romance plays: *Cymbeline, The Winter's Tale,* and *The Tempest.* The author has identified five characterizing aspects of the language of these plays that might prove difficult for the actor: enjambment, when thoughts do not end with the verse line; irregular metre, which appears in the earlier plays, but is more prevalent in the later; dense images and convoluted syntax; magical and mythical characters; and the close blending of tragedy and comedy.

In the literature review, the author presents the thoughts of both scholars and theatre practitioners regarding these traits of the late plays. She also gives an overview of three leading voice teachers' approaches to speaking Shakespeare's language. As a practical investigation into the topic, the author conducted a series of five workshops with student actors, each focusing on one of the potential challenges. In the chapter treating this reflective practitioner research project, she discusses the outcomes of a few representative exercises from each workshop. To further explore her research question, she conducted interviews with professional voice and text coaches. A chapter devoted to those interviews chronicles their thoughts on the late plays and the specific work that the language demands.

In conclusion, the author postulates that when text is irregular or heightened, as it so often is in Shakespeare's late plays, the actor can benefit from work designed to help him or her intellectually and experientially understand the specific mechanics of the language. The actor will then be able to use that understanding to more effectively communicate the thoughts, feelings, and intentions of the character.

Title: **Vocal Coaching: Current Methods, Practices, and Strategies**
Author: Rena Cook
Type: MA Voice Studies
Year: July 2000
Institution: Central School of Speech and Drama
Faculty advisor: David Carey
This dissertation presents a study of vocal coaching in the professional theatre, its role and functions. Specific questions are explored: how to establish a collaborative relationship with the director, what is the extent of text preparation undertaken, which rehearsals should the vocal coach attend, when and how should the vocal coach give actor notes, and what is the extent and nature of respect and credit afforded the vocal coach within the professional theatre community.

Seven vocal coaches employed in the London theatre were interviewed. Four vocal coaches from North America responded to a series of questions. Their responses were collated around the above topics of inquiry.

A series of four practical projects were undertaken to explore methodologies and practices described by the vocal coaches interviewed. The organization and procedures of these projects, conclusions and lessons learned are chronicled.

Title: **Theatre Voice Training in Speech Pathology**
Author: Lucy Alexandra Cornell MAppSc, BABed, LTCL
Type: MAppSc
Year: 2001
Institution: The University of Sydney, Australia
Faculty Advisors: Isobel Kirk, Karin Isman, Assoc. Prof. Pamela Davis
Voice specialisation encompasses a number of voice disciplines. The methodologies, training and philosophies for each discipline differ, but the medium in which they practice is the same: voice. This study aims to provide information about the outcomes of integrating two of these disciplines, spoken voice for the actor and voice specialisation in speech pathology. It examines the effect of voice techniques as used in theatre voice training on a group of speech pathologists. It explores the effect of experiential voice training (learning by doing) as opposed to theoretical voice training (learning by talking about). Its aim is to reveal how some techniques and methodologies in a theatre voice approach might enhance the conceptual skills and clinical approaches of a voice specialist in speech pathology.

Qualitative and quantitative research methodologies were used in this study, which involved a group of six practicing female speech pathologists. They underwent a training weekend of theatre voice techniques examining voice from physical, perceptual and sensory levels as well as considering the effect of language choice on vocal outcomes. In addition, a more intensive theatre voice training course, over a four month period, was taken by two speech pathologists from the initial group.

Data was collected from the six subjects over three periods; pre-training, one week and four months after the initial training weekend. At each of these intervals there was a questionnaire, which required participants to answer questions based on their subjective observations of their voices, describing their approaches to voice and perceptions about voice. Additionally, they were asked to describe shifts in clinical practice, resulting from the training. At one week and at four months, the subjects were also interviewed regarding their perception of their voice.

The results show that the theatre voice training significantly shifted the speech pathologists' concept of voice and that there was significant carry over from their own experience into clinical practice.

These results have direct implications on speech pathology training and clinical practice. They also offer valuable information for the voice community, supporting current interest in cross-fertilization of knowledge between vocal disciplines.

Title: **An exploration of the potential role and contribution of a vocal coach working within a collaborative group devised process**
Author: Juliet Craig
Type: MA Voice Studies
Year: October 2001
Institution: Central School of Speech and Drama
Faculty advisor: David Carey
This dissertation explores the possible ways in which the skills of a vocal coach can be utilized within the organic development of a devised theatre production, as opposed to a text-based play. The study focuses on the potential role of the vocal coach throughout a devising process, the type of vocal work that can be offered, both practically and creatively to aid the development of the production, and the ways in which the coach can become a collaborative member of the company.

After initial consideration of the available literature on both vocal coaching and devised theatre, research was carried out through reflective practice; the vocal coaching role being undertaken with a professional Theatre in Education Company. The role was explored further on two productions with the MA Advanced Theatre Practice students at Central School of Speech and Drama.

To add further perspective to the inquiry, the opinions and views of both vocal coaches and devised theatre practitioners were gathered through interviews and questionnaires.

Descriptions and analysis of this research are chronicled within this document.

Title: **The Power of Voice: An Investigation of Voice Skills Training for Female Welfare-to-Work Job Trainees**
Author: Jacqueline Farrington
Type: MA Voice Studies
Year: November 2000
Institution: Central School of Speech and Drama
Faculty advisor: David Carey
This study investigates the need for and benefits of voice skills training for female welfare recipients about to enter the job

market for the first time. The study examines as a case study one particular group, a job training class for women in a Welfare-to-Work education training programme in New York City, NY. The researcher developed a two-day workshop teaching voice and self-presentation skills to fourteen women in this programme. The study also considers the perceptions and opinions of current voice/presentation skills training practitioners and potential corporate employers on the need for and benefits of this work. Is there a specific and imperative need for voice skills training for this audience? What potential does this training offer to enhance personal confidence and self-worth in these individuals? Can this training help to increase job success and employability for entry-level women? The study attempts to raise awareness of the need for this training for this particular audience.

Chapter 1 gives a rationale and historical background to the study, as well as an outline of the study's objectives, methodologies and limitations. Chapter 2 offers a definition of voice skills and examines the relevant literature written on voice and presentation skills training as pertinent to women. Chapter 2 also examines current literature on interview skills and the extent to which this literature addresses the importance of voice skills in a successful interview. Chapter 3 summarises the research component of the study: the interviews and questionnaires conducted with current voice/presentation skills training practitioners and business executives. Chapter 4 details the practical component of the study, the case study of the workshop developed and conducted by the researcher for clients of a Welfare-to-Work programme. Finally, Chapter 5 presents a study review and conclusion and investigates professional and personal learning outcomes as well as possibilities for future research.

Title: **Can methods in experimental theatre companies be incorporated into vocal training for the actor?**
Author: Anna Ferris
Type: MA Voice Studies
Year: February 2001
Institution: Central School of Speech and Drama
Faculty advisor: David Carey
The purpose of the dissertation is to explore the question "Can methods in experimental theatre companies be incorporated into vocal training for the actor?" Given the practical realities of conventional acting courses, the dissertation asks whether there is the possibility of bringing the same intensity of focus into prevailing vocal training without losing the integrity of the original work.

The research model is qualitative and the research design is an action research project, focusing on the notion of reflective practice. Answers to the research question are sought by

researching a selection of the vocal techniques, exploring this further in a practical project, and by studying the working environment of five experimental theatre companies and their associated practitioners. These are chosen because of the critical recognition of their avant-garde work. They are: the Moscow Art Theatre, and Constantin Stanislavski; the Roy Hart Theatre, and Alfred Wolfsohn, Roy Hart and Noah Pikes; the Teatr Laboratorium, and Jerzy Grotowski; the Odin Teatret, and Eugenio Barba; the Centre International de Recherches Théâtrales, and Peter Brook and Yoshi Oida.

The main findings of the dissertation are that the stability of the experimental companies, in terms of the familiarity of the "home" theatre and the continuity of the company members, provide the key to opening up vocal creativity. Within this "safe" environment the actors can be given autonomy for artistic exploration. These would be very positive aspects to transpose to other training environments. With regard to specific techniques, many of the vocal exercises that the experimental practitioners evolved employ the extensive use of imagery and it is suggested that this is the most fruitful area to incorporate into mainstream vocal training.

Title: **What is the current position of RP within actor training and what are the implications for future training needs?**
Author: John Finn
Type: MA Voice Studies
Year: July 2000
Institution: Central School of Speech and Drama
Faculty advisor: David Carey
This thesis examines the current position of RP within actor training, to see what lessons can be learned, and what recommendations can be made for future training.

There is a look at the evolution and development of RP, and its establishment as the prestige accent of Britain. To understand the historical development of RP was considered crucial in attempting to understand its present standing and what the future might hold. The teaching of RP and the changing climates in which it has been taught is looked at. The leading practitioners and their writings are used to examine the key pedagogical issues that need addressing for the teacher of RP. There is also a look at RP in a broader perspective with educational and social and political considerations.

An attempt is made to give a representative picture of how RP fits into the syllabus of a three year actor training programme at some of Britain's leading drama schools. Heads of voice and accent coaches were interviewed to examine how much RP is appropriate in training, how the subject should be approached, and any key considerations or tips to take into the classroom. From these interviews and the information gained from the literature search, it was possible to formulate conclusions from the observations made, and draw up a set of recommendations.

Title: **Voicing Archetypes**
Author: Wendy Lee Hagenow
Type: MFA in Theatre Pedagogy
Year: 2001
Institution: Virginia Commonwealth University
Faculty Advisor: Janet B. Rodgers
The purpose of this thesis was to use Archetypes as a vehicle to explore the dynamics of the voice. This paper documents the planning and executing of the Voicing Archetype class. Using Frankie Armstrong's Archetype work as the basis for the five-week one credit course, the students were challenged to work in an experiential environment. The course began with breath work and the Devil archetype and traveled through to vocal extremes and the Oracle. Each session consisted of a series of acting, movement and vocal work. The end result was a greater understanding of vocal dynamics of the voice and the application of this information to acting work.

Title: **What Value Does a Choral Approach to Voice Training Have for the Actor-in-Training?**
Author: J. A. Harley
Type: MA Voice Studies
Year: July 2000
Institution: Central School of Speech and Drama
Faculty advisor: David Carey
This dissertation sets out to establish the *value* of choral voice work for actors-in training and in doing so explores the particular vocal demands that make it an essential addition to solo voice work.

The following enquiry can be described as a multi-perspective, multiple data source study following a qualitative model of research. My data is drawn from a variety of sources including: the literature on choral speaking; interviews and correspondence with current practitioners in theatre and education; visits to recent productions using the form; four Greek Chorus workshops I taught at Rose Bruford College; a small-scale, single site case study carried out at Guildford School of Acting.

The dissertation begins with a discussion of previous research and practice which "grounded" my proposal for the value of choral speaking. Chapter 1 presents a comparative analysis of the available literature on the subject charting its roots in the early years of the twentieth century to the start of World War II. In Chapter 2, I look at the development of different styles of approach to choral work in the theatre up to the present

day, and set this in the context of current practice in education. In Chapter 3, I record and analyse the data collected as a 'reflective practitioner' at Rose Bruford and data collected as an observer of a choral voice project at Guildford School of Action. My data is placed in the context of two other perspectives at Guildford—a small sample of students, and their voice tutor. I do not claim generalizability for my findings here, but rather use the perspectives to interrogate and corroborate each other.

This study concludes that, based on the multiplicity of perspectives gathered, choral voice and speech has much to offer the student in terms of their development as voice 'technicians' and vocal 'artists'.

Title: **Toward Vocal Presence: Assessing the Step from Technical Acuity to Expression and Communication**
Author: Catherine L. (Kate) Hennig
Type: MA Voice Studies
Year: October 2001
Institution: Central School of Speech and Drama
Faculty advisor: David Carey
This dissertation describes a qualitative enquiry into the step from technical acuity to expression and communication required in the vocal process of the actor.

The step from vocal acuity to expression and communication is often left in the hands of directors and acting teachers, leaving the voice dangling between vocal skill and its integration into the product of acting. This dissertation proposes a definition of the attributes of *the step*, so that they can be engaged fully by the actor. These attributes are facilitated by vocal study inspired and fueled by vocal exercise in an intercultural context, and seated in the deepest roots of vocal expression: the body and the psyche. Breath, sound and word become unified with acting technique in the body and mind of the actor, and the actor expresses fully from an integrated source.

In Chapter One *the step* is defined and discussed in reference to relevant literature. In Chapter Two the research design is detailed and discussed. In Chapter Three, support and discussion of claims are made from analysis of the information gathered. In Chapter Four conclusions and implications are reached from the research process and the dissertation question.

The enquiry concludes that current voice study for the actor can benefit from a psycho-physical study of voice work in an intercultural context, and that this context facilitates the experience of the attributes of *the step* from technical acuity to expression and communication.

Title: **What are the processes by which the voice for a character role is created, and what can the voice coach contribute to those processes?**
Author: Mary Howland
Type: MA Voice Studies
Year: September 2000
Institution: Central School of Speech and Drama
Faculty advisor: David Carey
The aim of this investigation was to discover what methods can be identified by which an actor can be encouraged to find a vocal sound—a "voice"—for a character he is playing which requires the development of a heightened persona.

Background research was conducted into texts on voice, dealing with non-standard voice use, the processes of those performers who are noted for their unusual voice use in character as described in their biographies, into the psychological and physiological links between voice, the mind and the body, and into other performance-based texts dealing with processes of characterisation.

Interviews were conducted with a selection of performers, movement, acting and voice coaches and directors. Using information and suggestions from the above sources, practical research was conducted, using both group and individual sessions, exploring a variety of approaches to vocal charaterisation —anatomical, physical, intellectual and instinctual—ending with individual work on a named role from the canon of English Drama, locating a voice for the character while maintaining concerns for safe and sustainable voice use.

Title: **How can I apply western voice technique to Japanese actors?**
Author: Minako B. Ikeuchi
Type: MA Voice Studies
Year: November 2000
Institution: Central School of Speech and Drama
Faculty advisor: David Carey
This dissertation examines the possibility of applying western voice technique to Japanese actors. Following the author's belief that "voice work is for everybody" (Rodenburg 1994: ix), current problems that Japanese actors have with their voices are detailed along with areas where western techniques can help.

Interviews are conducted to see how English voice practitioners have worked with Japanese actors and what they have discovered. Characteristics of Japanese actors are described with a historical background to a unique culture with its own aesthetics.

The characteristics: the incredibly strong self-discipline, the eagerness of receiving information, a history of imitating a

"master" actor, the lack of auditory theatre, non-linear progression of thought process are discussed. It is shown how these can be both an advantage and disadvantage in learning this particular skill towards "freeing the voice".

These issues are addressed by drawing a model workshop with a particular emphasis on the needs of the contemporary Japanese actor. The need which is identified centres on freeing the mind by freeing the voice.

Title: **The Sound of Meaning: Theories of Voice in Twentieth-Century Thought and Performance**
Author: Andrew M. Kimbrough
Type: PhD Dissertation
Year: May 2002
Institution: Louisiana State University
Faculty Advisor: Les Wade
This dissertation addresses the problem of the denigration of the voice in poststructural theory and contemporary performance criticism. The problem has antecedents in twentieth-century language philosophy. Saussure defines language as a compendium of arbitrary words recognized according to the degrees of phonetic difference between them. Since for Saussure the arbitrary words of language also designate arbitrary concepts, he concludes that the sounds of words cannot be thought constituent of their sense. After Saussure, structuralism dislodges the voice from its privileged position in the phonologic discourses of Western thought. Poststructuralism views meaning as a product of socially constructed language systems, and it argues that neither the voice nor the speaking subject can be afforded linguistic agency. A strain of contemporary theatre criticism, premised upon poststructuralism, interprets the postmodern stage as a site in which the voice, language, and the speaking subject come under critique and suspicion, stripped of agency and communicative efficacy.

This dissertation investigates twentieth-century theories of voice, language, and speech in order to define the status of the voice in various disciplines ranging from paleoanthropology, phenomenology, structuralism, speech act theory, theatre semiotics, the philosophies of technology, and media studies. By comparing the status of the voice in other disciplines, this dissertation argues for a recuperation of the voice against the denigration evident in poststructural theory and performance criticism. Relying on Heidegger's phenomenal view of language, the autonomy of the voice in speech act theory and theatre semiotics, the centrality of vocalized language in human evolution, and the resurgence of orality in electronic media, this dissertation argues that the voice continues to act as an important and primary signifying agent on the postmodern stage, regardless of poststructural arguments to the contrary.

Title: **The Optimum Use and Perception of Voice for the Trained Singer. A Teaching Study.**

Author: Annemette Kristensen
Type: MA Voice Studies
Year: March 2000
Institution: Central School of Speech and Drama
Faculty Advisor: David Carey

The thesis defines the distinctiveness of the singing voice and examines trained singers' use and understanding of their voice. The characteristics specifically related to the singing voice are described in the areas of breath, vocal quality, resonance, articulation, body use, emotion and expression.

This thesis builds on the hypothesis that a certain vocal behavior is related to trained singers in singing as well as other voice modes. In order to pitch, to sustain notes and create specific voice qualities the singer has a heightened technical ability. An understanding of the whole voice is essential for the singer. However, it is the author's experience from her own singing as well as teaching singers that there are vocal tasks that the trained singer manages less successfully in spite of that heightened capability. The aim of this thesis is therefore to examine the behavior of trained singers when they are working with other aspects of voice, for instance spoken text, and to enable the subjects to expand their use and perception of voice.

Practitioners from the areas of voice teaching and singing teaching were interviewed about the existence and handling of this issue and a teaching philosophy with definite aims was set up and tried out with four singers from various professional backgrounds. The outcome of the research showed that in these four cases the author's assumption was confirmed. It is likely that the behavior of these four case studies is representative, hence the results useful for a broader application.

Title: **Phonetics in Actor Training: Serving the Needs of the Professional Actor**

Author: Richard Lipton
Type: MA Voice Studies
Year: October 2000
Institution: Central School of Speech and Drama
Faculty advisor: David Carey

This is a case study designed to explore the research question: does the study of phonetics in actor training serve the needs of a professional actor? The survey of literature includes a comprehensive look at the place of phonetics in the context of acting and actor training. Phonetics is defined, including historical developments contributing to the phonetics used today. Various means of phonetic representations from accent, voice, and phonetic literature are compared. The intersections of accent, speech codes and character are discussed. The

application of phonetics to text is also considered. And finally the learning of phonetics is explored. A semi-structured interview was conducted with twelve acting students, five professional voice coaches, and six professional actors to investigate how phonetics relates to the actor's process. The results confirm that phonetics in actor training serves the needs of the professional actor by giving the students tools, a process, and the awareness to investigate the specifics of voice portrayal. They suggest that phonetics may be disconcerting to an actor that does not work with phonetic symbols in their process. To best serve an actor, phonetics must be used in conjunction with other modalities of learning. Ultimately, phonetics has proved to be of the most value to the teacher or coach.

Title: **The Accommodation of the Ulster Accent to Shakespeare Texts: An examination of the accentual options available to Ulster actors when engaging with Shakespeare's texts and the role of the voice coach in facilitation learning in this area.**

Author: Patricia Logue
Type: MA Voice Studies
Year: October 2001
Institution: Central School of Speech and Drama
Faculty advisor: David Carey

This dissertation is a piece of work investigating the question of accent for the Ulster actor in the performance of Shakespeare's texts. It highlights the accentual choices open for consideration for the actor, and identifies problems the performer might encounter in each of these. The choices identified are an RP accent, an Ulster accent and an RP influenced accent. The role of the voice teacher within this particular culture is also examined, as I question how we can facilitate learning in each of the available choices so that the actor can gain ownership of the work while increasing his/her range of performance skills.

Title: **Lessac's Tonal Action in Women's Voices and the "Actor's Formant": A Comparative Study.**

Author: Marth Munro
Type: PhD Dissertation
Year: 2003
Institution: Potchefstroom University for Christian Higher Education, South Africa
Faculty Advisor: Prof. D.P Wissing
Assistant Advisors: Prof. K. Verdolini (USA); Prof. A. Laukkanen (Finland)

The purpose of this study is to investigate the Tonal NRG (previously known as the Tonal Action) of the Lessac Approach as a voice-building tool for the female voice in theatre. It provides an overview of existing scholarly writings on the pedagogical, physiological and acoustical qualities of the Lessac Approach. It reflects on current literature about the characteristics of good voice quality and especially the actor's formant. The empirical research on voice building in this study demonstrates that a randomised pre/post test/control group quasi-experimental design was used and is fourfold in dimension: it deals with a control group, a test group with 14 contact hours, a test group with 28 contact hours and a test group who had an extensive six-week workshop. Other variables that are reflected on are culture, language, teacher and training methodology specificity. Investigative procedures include a questionnaire, various means of acoustic analysis and a perception panel. Where applicable, inferential statistics were done on the data. Results of the investigation are compared with existing, parallel research outputs.

Title: **An enquiry into the use of actor-voice training in developing presentation and public-speaking skills.**
Author: Carol Noakes
Type: MA Voice Studies
Year: October 2001
Institution: Central School of Speech and Drama
Faculty advisor: David Carey
This study attempts to assess the use of actor-based voice training in the development of presentation and public speaking skills. It examines the requirements of these disciplines—for the purpose of which "presentations" and "public speaking" are treated as synonymous—to consider which transferable skills would serve the non-actor. The focus is on the business client, but there is an assumption that these questions are relevant to speakers in any environment.

The Introduction explains the writer's practical and philosophical interest in applying actor-voice techniques in a corporate context. Chapter Two examines the vocal requirements of each discipline, within the context of their historical development, to see where they interface. It then extracts elements on which to build a practical workshop programme, while recognising the potentially differing objectives of the business client from the actor. Chapter Three looks at current practice as it is presented in literature on the subject, with reference to the workshop elements chosen. Chapter Four describes the methodology, process and observations of the practical workshop project that developed from the preceding research. Chapter Five reflects on interviews with five practitioners. Chapter Six contains the overall conclusions and recommendations resulting from research, observation, practice and subsequent experience.

Title: **What Teaching and Learning Methods in Voice are Effective in Enabling BA Acting Students to Access Classical Text?—this study makes specific reference to British comedies written between 1660 and 1778**

Author: Catherine Owen
Type: MA Voice Studies
Year: October 2000
Institution: Central School of Speech and Drama
Faculty advisor: David Carey
This report describes a piece of Action Research carried out in an attempt to identify effective teaching and learning strategies to enable second year Acting students to deliver classical text for performance purposes. It analyses a series of strategies, designed to enable student actors to draw on their existing knowledge and resources pertaining to the actor's vocal technique.

Exercises are presented in a series of innovative combinations designed to inspire vocal confidence and relish of Restoration and post-Restoration comedy of manners texts. The report outlines the research methods and explains the delivery of the teaching of two workshops. It summarises data gathered from detailed video tape analysis and analysis of questionnaires. It discusses learning gained. In the cyclical nature of Action Research it makes recommendations for the next series of workshops. It identifies the teaching units which are most successful in achieving their aims and recommends a different approach for the least effective. It raises issues of time management and a stronger adherence to procedures for more reliability and validity of data.

It concludes that establishing a positive learning environment is a necessary pre-requisite for maximum learning. It notes the times that teaching has been more effectual as a result of greater efficiency in organisation. It concludes that the value of the workshops can only be realised fully when the workshops are followed up with practical acting work on Restoration and post-Restoration comedy of manners texts.

The report suggests that this learning could be adapted to guide trainee voice teachers in work of this era. As we begin a new century where classical text will be even more of an alien concept than it was in the twentieth century, it presents a modus operandi for working with students from an increasingly tele-visual age.

Title: **Play as an Effective Teaching and Learning Tool for Good Voice Use in Adults**
Author: Suzanne Park
Type: MA Voice Studies
Year: 2000
Institution: Central School of Speech and Drama
Faculty advisor: David Carey
This dissertation is an exploration into the use of play in the voice class environment. Stemming from the researcher's original interest in the creative freedom of childhood, this study set

off to determine how effective play is as a teaching and learning tool for adult voice students. Underlying the research is the assumption that the personal nature of voice work and the classroom environment can sometimes cause self-conscious tensions that inhibit good voice use. It is proposed that play has inherent qualities that help bypass self-consciousness and aid in the effective teaching and learning of voice in adults.

To research this thesis the author undertook a review of the academic literature concerning play, effective teaching and learning, and good voice use. She also interviewed five currently practising voice teachers to hear their views on play. And finally, she carried out a single case study at the Guildford School of Acting where a group of voice students participated in three vocal workshops that focused on the use of play.

The information, insights and results from the literature review, interviews and case study has led the researcher to believe that there are many aspects of play that make it a very effective teaching and learning tool for good voice use in adults. The most prominent being its ability to create a separate space in which students can explore, experiment with and discover new aspects of their voice. The play space can be safe and supportive, free from feelings of self-consciousness and the fear of failure. But ironically the study also shows that play can have the opposite effect. Depending on the individual students' learning style and how play is used in the class, play can be the cause of self-conscious tensions that inhibit good voice use. The researcher concludes that play is an effective teaching and learning tool when it supports the learning styles and the desired learning outcomes of the voice class in which it is used.

Title: Evaluation of Voice Skills
Author: Joanne Parton
Type: MA Voice Studies
Year: November 2001
Institution: Central School of Speech and Drama
Faculty advisor: David Carey
This study is concerned with the evaluation of voice skills. It includes an examination and discussion of the reasons and the criteria for evaluation in related fields of education and health, and identifies common conceptual factors, including objectivity, measurability, validity, relevance, clarity and functionality.

The most significant voice parameters were identified by voice teachers as alignment, body tension, larynx tension, breathing, pitch range, projection and articulation. The comparative ease with which various voice parameters can be evaluated was examined.

Students' voice skills were evaluated in an experimental workshop setting. There were three methods of evaluation: student self-questionnaires, perceptual evaluation by a panel of three speech and language therapists, and objective measurement of pitch by Speech Studio. Pitch and octave range were seen to change significantly in response to workshops on "love" and "fear", with good correlation using all methods of evaluation.

Methods of evaluation are discussed, and it is concluded that a perceptual voice profile by a trained assessor could provide an appropriate means of evaluating voice skills in drama schools.

Title: Vocal Pedagogy: What are the teaching issues when working on Voice and Text with Dyslexic actors in training?
Author: Anna Polydorou
Type: MA Voice Studies
Year: April 2001
Institution: Central School of Speech and Drama
Faculty advisor: David Carey
This dissertation is the study of the teaching issues, which can occur when working on voice and text with dyslexic actors in training. To this end, it examines the nature of dyslexia and its potential impact upon a student within a vocal-learning environment, the assumption being that dyslexia does affect a students ability to engage effectively in voice and text work. Chapter One seeks to provide a background and rationale for the basis of this study.

Chapter Two explores the nature of dyslexia through a literature review looking at the potential impact upon a student within a learning environment and within the teacher/pupil dynamic. Areas of concern focus on the primary symptoms of dyslexia such as literacy, information processing and social interaction, and secondary symptoms such as anxiety, low self esteem, and lack of confidence. In Chapter Three these headings are explored further through a specialist practitioner interview, aimed at eliciting practical strategies and impressions about dyslexia and the needs of students who are dyslexic. Chapter Four outlines the aims and objectives of my practical component and Chapter Five charts the process and findings of that component. Chapter Six concludes this research through summarising my overall findings and making practical recommendations when working on voice and text with dyslexic actors in training. An appendix and bibliography include all the relevant information pertinent to this study.

Title: **For an actor trained primarily for performance in theatre, what—if any—modification of vocal technique or quality is necessary to be an effective performer on camera?**
Author: Emma Rosalind Rogers
Type: MA Voice Studies
Year: October 2001
Institution: Central School of Speech and Drama
Faculty advisor: David Carey
This dissertation explores the way in which an actor might need to modify a vocal technique learned primarily for use in theatre to make it appropriate for use on camera. Providing a context for this exploration is a review of available literature by voice teaching practitioners, television/film directors, and actors.

At the core of the inquiry is a research project undertaken to explore how the use of voice differs moving from stage to camera. The project consisted of two one-day workshops, working with actors approaching the second year of their professional careers.

Subsequent to the research project, several expert practitioners in varying areas of the film and television industry were interviewed to add clarity to findings, expand overall knowledge, and provide different perspectives to the subject.

Each of the above phases of inquiry is detailed in the document.

Title: **Why the vocal coach is particularly useful in supporting the Beckett actor**
Author: Gerard Slamon
Type: MA Voice Studies
Year: November 2001
Institution: Central School of Speech and Drama
Faculty advisor: David Carey
This dissertation seeks to show that the vocal coach is particularly suited to the job of supporting the Beckett actor, through highlighting a close correspondence between:

A. The nature of the physical and vocal challenges which
    Beckett's theatre poses for the actor —and—
B. Ways of working used by the vocal coach

A qualitative research model is used in which Beckett's challenges are explored through a consideration of the scripts, the history of the productions, and accounts and interviews given by actors and directors. Ways of working used by the voice coach are examined through a review of manuals written by the leading practitioners. A case study is used to test out the efficacy of adopting voicework solutions as a response to the problems which Beckett poses.

The study concludes that Beckett's own way of working has a great deal in common with that used by the vocal coach and that the needs of his theatre are particularly well served by some of the most fundamental approaches and methods used in contemporary voicework. Recommendations are offered as to how the vocal coach can best serve the Beckett actor within the rehearsal process.

Title: **Is it possible to transfer esoteric vocal exercises into voicework within a drama training? A Case Study**
Author: Harriet Whitbread
Type: MA Voice Studies
Year: October 2000
Institution: Central School of Speech and Drama
Faculty advisor: David Carey
"Esoteric vocal exercises" are exercises that use the inherent power contained within sound, devoid of any semantic meaning, to effect physiological and emotional changes.

This study looks at the experience of using esoteric vocal exercises with drama students in their first year of training at the Poor School. The study will then investigate how "possible" the experience was. The term "possible" encompasses the following issues:

i)   Do the exercises improve the students' voices and
     connection with text?
ii) What safety issues arise?
iii) Are the effects of the exercises within the boundaries of a
     drama school training?

The conclusion is that the exercises were effective in connecting actors to their text but this result is not necessarily transferable to different students at another drama school.